History of Bartow County, Georgia

Formerly Cass

By:

Lucy Josephine Cunyus

This volume was reproduced from
An 1933 edition located in the
Publisher's private library,
Greenville, South Carolina

All rights reserved. No part of this publication
may be reproduced, stored in a retrieval system,
transmitted in any form, posted on to the web
in any form or by any means without the
prior written permission of the publisher.

Please direct all correspondence and orders to:

www.southernhistoricalpress.com
or
**SOUTHERN HISTORICAL PRESS, Inc.
PO BOX 1267
375 West Broad Street
Greenville, SC   29601
southernhistoricalpress@gmail.com**

Originally published: Georgia 1933
Reprinted with New material by:
Southern Historical Press, Inc.
Greenville, SC
New Material Copyright 1983 by:
Southern Historical Press, Inc.
ISBN #0-89308-005-5
All rights Reserved.
Printed in the United States of America

Gen. Francis S. Bartow, for whom the county was last named (from an oil painting in the library of the Georgia Historical Society, Savannah).

Dedicated

To Those Who

Love, Honor and Cherish

Their Nativity

In This County

1. George H. Aubrey. 2. Lucy J. Cunyus. 3. Arthur V. Neal.
4. Claude C. Pittman.

INTRODUCTION

At its regular session in the year 1929 the General Assembly of the State of Georgia passed the following resolution:

No. 36

"Resolved, by the General Assembly of Georgia, both Houses thereof concurring therein, that the judges of the superior courts of the State are hereby earnestly requested to give in charge to the grand jury of each county in their several circuits, at the next term of the court therein, the urgent request of this General Assembly that they will secure the consent of some competent person in their county to prepare between now and February 13, 1933, being Georgia Day, as nearly a complete history of the formation, development, and progress of said county from its creation up to that date, together with accounts of such persons, families, and public events as have given character and fame to the county, the State, and the Nation. And that said county histories be deposited on Georgia Day in 1933 in the State's Department of Archives and History—there to be preserved for the information of future citizens of the State and prospective biographers and historians. And this action is recommended to the judges, grand juries, and the people of all the counties of the State, for early procedure, because delay will leave action in this behalf too short a time for the necessary research and accumulation of data to make the county histories as full and accurate as they should be for full historic value."

In the grand jury presentments of the July term, 1930, Judge C. C. Pittman, Judge G. H. Aubrey, and Commissioner A. V. Neal, were appointed as a committee to employ an historian to write the history of Bartow.

Miss Lucy J. Cunyus was selected in June, 1931 for this purpose.

FOREWORD

This history—with apologies to John Galsworthy—is but the story of people who took things into their own hands and made themselves accountable or of no account.

As we write this foreword in 1933 many changes are taking place. This history closed with the year 1932 and we cannot mention those changes.

Facts and not flowers have been diligently sought; common sense in subject matter and possible information for the future historian and genealogist has been kept in mind. The plan to sketch the type of pioneer men and women, from 1830 to 1860, who made this county what it is today, has been a difficult task. Time permits no further research, though lack of family data and interest make the record incomplete. Financial conditions make it impossible to include as many illustrations as we wanted.

Grateful acknowledgments are made to:

The earlier historians—White, Stevens, McCall, C. C. Jones, G. G. Smith, Northen, Evans, Knight, Howell, etc., and the Civil War autobiographies;

Miss Leila Darden of Kingston who so generously shared all the data she had collected during her residence here;

Miss Callie Jackson, the only official appointed by a woman's club, named to assist from the Stilesboro community;

Mrs. A. R. Davis who collected data from Taylorsville;

Willis M. Boyd, Dr. Joe Bowdoin, Mr. B. E. Lewis, Mrs. W. P. Whitworth of Adairsville;

Dr. Warren K. Moorehead for his interest and generous permission to use his data on the Etowah Mounds;

Wilbur G. Kurtz, artist and writer, who ably and

generously assisted with valuable data on the "Atlanta Campaign";

Mrs. Hallie Alexander Rounsaville of Rome, Mrs. Louise Best Cline of Washington, D. C., Mr. James A. LeConte of Atlanta, who through their interest gave much valuable local color;

Mr. C. M. Brown of Marietta for the loan of valuable histories;

The State Library, the Mary Munford Library, and the private libraries of W. T. Townsend, George S. Cobb, John T. Norris, C. M. Milam, and Fred Neel.

The county newspapers for their valuable printed matter;

Judge G. H. Aubrey for the use of his office and unlimited cooperation and interest;

Judge C. C. Pittman, Commissioner A. V. Neal, W. C. Walton, Sr., W. C. Walton, Jr., Murray Upshaw, C. M. Milam, Paul Akin, M. L. Fleetwood, W. C. Henson, Ben C. Gilreath, Mrs. O. T. Peeples, Roy A. Flynt, Mrs. Lily Bradley, Mrs. R. E. Adair, Mrs. Kate Candler, Mrs. H. B. Robertson, Miss Jessie Wikle, P. A. Bray, W. W. Daves, Connor Pittard, all of Cartersville, Mrs. Lucy Hicks Rucker of Elberton, Mrs. Bethel Quillian of Cass Station, Miss Ada Beck of Kingston, J. L. Milhollin of Cassville, Mrs. Alice M. Gibson and Miss Virginia Hardin of Atlanta, E. M. Vary of Atlanta, W. P. Griggs, Sr., of Emerson, for courtesies and help in compilation;

Miss Ruth Blair, State historian, an ever-ready source of inspiration and information.

LIST OF ILLUSTRATIONS

Gen. Francis S. Bartow	Frontispiece
Author, Historical Committee	VIII
Cherokee County Map	12
Original Land Grant	15
Different Types of Homes	50
Judge J. W. Hooper	66
Madison Milam	82
Group of Settlers	94
Rev. G. W. Tumlin	98
Sam Jones Tabernacle	136
Churches and Schools	124
Monuments	138
City Officials, 1933	160
Mining Scenes	198
Maps of Cassville Battlefield	232
Dr. and Mrs. W. H. Felton	282
Charles H. Smith and Sam P. Jones	290
Mr. and Mrs. W. J. Neel, Mark Cooper, Gen. Young, Col. Boyd	298
County Officers	302

CONTENTS

Introduction
Foreword

Chapters
I	Indian Occupation	1
II	How the County Was Formed	10
III	Land Grants	12
IV	The "Empire County" of the State	17
V	Pioneer Settlers, 1830-1860	42
VI	Militia	107
VII	Judiciary	110
VIII	Early Churches	124
IX	Schools	139
X	Newspapers	155
XI	Politics	161
XII	Railroads	167
XIII	The Topography of the County	174
XIV	Agriculture	180
XV	Minerals	187
XVI	Etowah Mounds	206
XVII	Civil War	209
XVIII	Organizations	252
XIX	Manufactures	264
XX	Banks	269
XXI	Negroes	272
XXII	Bartow's Distinguished Characters	277
XXIII	Registers:	
	Justices of the Inferior Court	303
	County Officers	304
	Officers in C. S. A.	308
	Spanish-American War Veterans	314
	World War Veterans	315
	Doctors and Lawyers	322
	Members of the General Assembly	325
	Census of 1840	329

CHAPTER I

INDIAN OCCUPATION

The northwestern part of the chartered limits of this State, north of the Chattahoochee river, prior to and in 1827, was occupied by the Cherokee Indians.

Their government was republican and their capital was at New Echota, near Calhoun, Georgia. Besides their own form of government, the United States Government claimed the right of enforcing intercourse laws for the government of the Indian tribes, and Georgia had extended her criminal laws over the portion where the Cherokees were located. This same year, 1827, the resolution was introduced in the 20th U. S. Congress to provide for their removal west of the Mississippi river.

At this time the Cherokees in Northwest Georgia were the most intellectual and best educated tribe of Indians. They had their written constitution and code of laws by which they declared themselves to be a free and independent state and people. They had their own newspapers, the "Cherokee Phoenix", 1828-34, edited by Elias Boudinott; the Cherokee alphabet by Sequoya was known and taught; and their children had had missionary training.

Sherwood's Gazetteer of 1827 cites a Brainerd Mission on the Etowah river, then called Hightower, "80 S. S. E.". Robert Sparks Walker in his recent book, "Torchlights to the Cherokees",* gives some interesting facts about the Brainerd Missions. Some of the following statements are gleaned from the book.

Cyrus Kingsbery was sent out in 1816 by the American Board of Commissioners of Foreign Missions in Massachusetts to investigate the possibility of opening a school and mission among the Cherokees, and in 1817 the school at Brainerd began. In 1818 Chickamauga

*Macmillan, N. Y., 1931.

was changed to Brainerd, honoring a northern missionary, to prevent any confusion with the Indian village called Chickamauga. Brainerd was 2 miles north of the Georgia-Tennessee line, near what is now Chattanooga. With Brainerd as a central station, other missions were opened and their locations were on an encircling route that made it possible for a missionary to lodge at a mission school every night when traveling.

Mr. Walker's statement that the Hightower mission was 80 miles south of southeast of Brainerd and founded in 1823 agrees with Sherwood's citation. Its actual location was about a mile and a half from Salt Petre Cave, in the 17th district.

On March 25, 1822 (or 1823), Isaac Proctor opened a new mission and school at Hightower, serving until March 1826. In 1823 Elizabeth Proctor came to Hightower and in 1827 married Daniel Sabin Butrick who, also, served at Hightower. In September, 1830 the Rev. John Thompson was stationed at Hightower and, also, Miss Catherine Fuller who was at the Hightower Mission when the Georgia Guard came to occupy the house. Miss Fuller sent word to Rev. Thompson, who was away at the moment, and after his refusal to allow their occupancy of the mission house, the Guard re-arrested Rev. Thompson and cruelly treated him until Camp Gilmer was reached. This was during the excitement of the arrest of Dr. Elizur Butler and Rev. Samuel Worcester by the Georgia Guard. The third arrest of Rev. Thompson in July, 1831, soon closed the Hightower mission.

The Moravians already had missions among the Cherokees, at Spring Place and "Oochgelogy". What denomination the Brainerd Missions claimed is immaterial, they and the Moravians worked together. Records show that the Hightower mission was among the mission churches received into the Union Presbytery of East Tennessee in 1824. In the Brainerd Journal of 1822 there is mention of the establishment of a mission at "Yookalooga", which might have been Oothcalooga.

It has been said there was a mission station in the Oothcalooga valley in this section of the present county.

The Rev. Elias Cornelius visited the Brainerd Missions in 1817 and in October a joint council of the Creek and Cherokee Indians was held at the "Etowee" river which he attended. It was during this visit that he saw the great mounds which he reported in Silliman's Journal in 1818.

In Cherokee Georgia on the Etowah river lived the Cherokee chief, Yonaguski, who ruled from 1796 to 1828. A daughter married an Irishman who gave his name as John Smith. Their grandson, Nimrod Smith, was chief from 1872 to 1893, and at this time a tribe of Cherokees were located in the North Carolina Indian Reservation. His son, Sibbald Smith, is an independent Baptist preacher in western North Carolina and to him have been handed down the legends of his tribe, and from him comes this information.

In October, 1831, Wilson Lumpkin was elected governor of Georgia. Seeing the Indians as a handicap to the progress of the State, he ordered an immediate survey and occupancy of the Cherokee territory. In December, by an act of the legislature, all territory west of the Chattahoochee river, north of the Carroll county line, with parts of Carroll, DeKalb, Gwinnett, Hall and Habersham added, formed a new county called Cherokee.* This part of the country was known as Cherokee Georgia for many years.

In 1831 William Hardin was appointed by Lewis Cass[†], secretary of war, to negotiate with the Cherokees in signing a treaty to relinquish their holdings. In 1833 he was appointed an enrolling agent and had to sign such notices as can be found in the Executive Minutes of the State: "To his Excellency Wilson Lumpkin. I certify that William Hicks, a Cherokee occupant of lot No. 182 (now in Floyd county) in the 15th district, and third section of the Cherokee Territory, has enrolled

---
*Acts of 1831, p. 47.
†Original order of appointment in possession of Miss Virginia Hardin of Atlanta.

for the Arkansas, and agreeable to the late enrollment, he is bound to give possession after the early part of the winter ensuing. I, however, anticipate no difficulty in the Grants issuing instanter. Given under my hand this 17th of October, 1833. Wm. Hardin, one of the Enrolling Agents for Emigration."

In June, 1833, Cornelius D. Terhune was appointed Indian agent to provide for the government and protection of the Cherokees and their property in the county of Cass, and later was made one of the enrolling agents.

The two chieftains, John Ridge and John Ross, were the influential causes of their lingering in the homes they rightfully claimed as the domain of their forefathers, and where they had lived peaceably for generations. John Ross did not want to leave Georgia and appealed to the supreme court of the United States. In some Cherokee histories it is found that Ross was betrayed by the missionary Schermerhorn and sold his people. John Ridge favored their removal.*

Governor Lumpkin charged that one cause of delay in the removal of the Indians was that the lawyers were holding the Indians by making civil cases in the courts through them. As long as Ross could employ lawyers to fight for their rights, he was hopeful that Washington authorities would listen to their entreaties.

For 18 months, 1837-38, Wilson Lumpkin was in this section executing their removal. He reported that in the county of Cass and the adjoining county of Cherokee, September, 1837, that there were 8,000 Indians among a very sparse white population†.

By the Treaty of 1835‡, made by a committee of 20 prominent Indians with the U. S. Commissioners, the Cherokees relinquished and conveyed to the United States all their land east of the Mississippi river for 5 million dollars, with an additional sum for spoliation of every kind, for a perpetual reservation in Arkansas.

---
*One is referred to the State Library for the history and customs of the Cherokee Indians.
†Lumpkin's, Removal of the Cherokee Indians, Vol. II, p-145.
‡See Lumpkin's, Vol. II, pp-15-28.

This treaty was signed by Stand Watie who became a Confederate general in the Civil War, and John Ridge, who with his son, was murdered by Ross conspirators after their removal West.

In the treaty it was agreed that the Cherokees would remove within 2 years after the ratification of the treaty, and according to Cherokee Indian history, the official removal was from 1835 to 1837.

By a legislative act in December, 1837, the white citizens of the Cherokee country were protected by the organization of a company of 60 mounted men in each county, the officers of the companies were elected at the court houses, and it was the duty of each commander to cooperate with the United States troops in removing the Indians after the 24th of May, 1838. On this date the regiments collected the remaining Indians in stockades and began the tragic exit of the red race from the hills coveted by the white man. The company organized from Cass county that assisted in the removal follows:

Payroll of Captain Berry W. Gideon's Company of Mounted Volunteers of Cass county, organized under an Act of the General Assembly of the State of Georgia, assented to 26th December, 1837, for the protection of the Cherokee and Creek Indians from the 15th January, 1838, to June, 1838, and ordered into service of the State by Colonel Samuel Stewart by order of the Governor of the State of Georgia.

Captain, Berry W. Gideon; 1st Lieut, James M. Hamilton; 2nd Lieut., William Pearson; 1st Sergt., John H. Miller; 2nd Sergt., Joseph T. Hamilton; 3rd Sergt., William B. Lowry; 4th Sergt., Jonathan Long; 1st Corpl., Lemuel Howard; 2nd Corpl., Lorenzo D. Jones; 3rd Corpl., M. F. Gathright; 4th Corpl., Patrick Moore; Ensign, W. Terry.

Privates: Reuben M. Pogue, James Lowry, John Watson, Joseph Wood, H. Gillis, Leander Nicholds, Leander Morrow, Samuel I. Ray, William Simpson, William D. Hassell, William Turner, William Dunaway, William H. Willson, William I. Cantrell, William Bolt, William Terry, William Dunagan, Isaac Tate, Christopher Dodd, Anderson Massey, Anderson Owens, Bailus Person, Bainbridge Casey, Carter Lowry, David Quarles, Daniel Barton, Duncan Murkerson, Elijah Perkins, Elijah Pinson, Franklin A. Dunagan, Gideon Y. Youngblood, Green Lowry, Hiram Dunagan, Isaac Pinson, John H. Huchison, James N. Watson, James F. Jones, John McElroy, Joseph Wilson,

Jackson Nicholds, John Wilson, Joseph H. Stokes, John Ponder, Joseph H. Dodd, Jackson Ruff, Jackson C. Hatly, Jeremiah Green, Daniel Furr, Ranson Owens.

(These soldiers served anywhere from 30 days to 2 months; those serving 2 months received $56.00.)

"Auditor's Office of Cherokee Claims,
"Milledgeville, May 28th, 1858."

"I hereby certify that the amount respectively attached to each of the names on this Roll was audited and allowed to the claimants in accordance with the Acts of the Legislature relating thereto amounting in the aggregate to one thousand two hundred and twenty two 58/100 dollars.

"T. M. Bradford,
"Auditor of Cherokee Claims."*

Though the Creeks had inhabited parts of this county, there is more evidence of the occupancy of the Cherokees in this county.

Pine Log mountain, called "Notsensa" by the Indians because the course of the mountain resembles a huge pine log, and Pine Log creeks were named for the traditional chief, "Pine Log", who lived in that section. Two Run creek was named for another chief, and Connesena creek, meaning "winding serpent", for another. Traditionally, Salt Petre Cave was a meeting place for Indian pastimes and festivities; and in the springtime of the year, the Indians visited what is now known as Rowland Springs for the healing qualities in the waters. On the old Alabama road, south of Cartersville, was one of the oldest ball grounds. In the present home of Mrs. Corra Harris, near Pine Log village, when the carpenters were rebuilding, they found in the floor centers evidences of Indian fire places.

Remains of Cherokee Indian villages can be found along both sides of the Etowah river. Pottery and implements are found after inundations, but time will soon obliterate all traces before many more years. Unexplored villages may be found in the Oothcalooga valley and in and near Pine Log.

Locations for villages are known to be on the site of the Etowah mounds; at the mouth of Pumpkinvine

---
*Original in Georgia Department of Archives and History.

creek; on the present Leake property on the Stilesboro road where mounds are yet visible; on the site of the W. H. Stiles home; on the Hawkins property on Raccoon creek was a village called "Cherokee"; on the Jones-Puckett property along Pumpkinvine creek; on the R. S. Munford property on Two Run creek where there are mounds, also; near Hardin's bridge; on the east side of the Etowah river going up to the Iron Works. Unexplored mounds and caves are scattered and not confined to any one location. There is an Indian fort on Quarry mountain. The Indians mined magnetic manganese for ornamental purposes and they used native graphite for designing. Their gold and silver mining is discussed in another chapter.

The Cherokees were the most friendly of all the tribes. Only a few cases have been found in this county of spoliation and murder. The re-told story of the conflict between a white man and an Indian follows:

During the early settlement of this portion of Georgia by pioneers, John Seaborn, a North Carolinian, camped with a party of surveyors on the banks of the Etowah river, in the 17th district, a mile and a half from Salt Petre Cave.

He was in the prime of young manhood at the time of this story. Having no family and a roving disposition, he traveled the new country with a huge brindle dog for his companion. By a peculiar whistle between his fingers, he could call the dog from a good distance.

Near the camp of the surveyors was a missionary station, sent out by New England churches, and on this morning John Seaborn had planned to visit them. He had gone about a half of a mile, when the sound of voices attracted his attention. With caution acquired by long residence in the woods, he stepped behind a bush and listened attentively. Two figures came into view—one an Indian of gigantic size, and the other the most beautiful white girl he had ever seen! She was seated on a jet black pony and the savage held the bridle with one hand while in the other could be seen a tomahawk. Suspecting that she was not a voluntary companion, his opinion of the situation was confirmed, when by a sudden and ineffectual effort on the part of the fair rider to extricate herself from his grasp by a jerk of the bridle, the Indian raised his tomahawk and exclaimed, "Hold, white fawn, or by the Great Spirit, my tomahawk shall drink of your blood! Me, the son of a chief, must have pretty white squaw for his wigwam."

Here the motion of his uplifted weapon caused such a violent start of the pony, that she was thrown, but was instantly grasped again by the savage. With an impulse of rage and a heart throbbing with excitement, Seaborn sprang from his hiding place with a yell which so startled the Indian that he instantly released the girl and started toward the woods.

Seeing him, the girl exclaimed, "Oh! Sir, Save me! Save Me"!

The savage now turned and stood at bay. The pony was near the girl.

"Mount quick and fly!" exclaimed Seaborn, lifting her in the saddle.

As she moved off, Seaborn faced the Indian and recognized him as the famous and blood-thirsty George Took, known among the Cherokee Indians as "Unakayah-wah", white man killer. He stood, of tremendous size and strength, with hatred and revenge in his eyes, and as Seaborn looked he realized for the first time his immense disadvantage. He had left his camp with no weapon except a short hunting knife which hung at his side.

With a step backward, his plan to induce pursuit toward the direction of the camp was at once divined by the savage. The Indian sprang forward with a yell and Seaborn turned to run, giving as he started a long keen whistle through his fingers. Following with a velocity equal to his own, and fearing that he might draw him into ambush, the Indian threw at Seaborn his tomahawk which, knocking his cap off and passing him, buried itself in a tree some feet beyond.

Suddenly Seaborn turned on his foe and coming together aimed a blow at his head with his fist. Evading with a side motion and stepping back, the Indian rushed him, attempting to throw him over his head. Seaborn understood the move and avoided it by causing the Indian to strike his knee, though it knocked his own feet backward and staggered him. Recovering, Seaborn dealt another blow and threw himself on the Indian's back, pressing him to the ground, his face downward. The Indian rose on his hands, but Seaborn jerked his hands from under him. While trying to seize his knife unsuccessfully, because it had caught under his waistband, the savage seized one of his thumbs in his mouth and bit it to the bone. With rage he beat the Indian's head and neck until he let go of the thumb and with superhuman effort he sprang from beneath Seaborn. Then a fisticuff ensued. Being a practiced boxer, Seaborn soon had the Indian's nose bleeding. As a last resort, after trying to upset him by running through his legs, the Indian rushed toward the tree where the tomahawk was sticking. Within three feet of it Seaborn clinched him and then began a desperate wrestle with the one aim of both—to secure the tomahawk. In one of these struggles, Seaborn's foot became entangled in a vine and he fell, the Indian upon him. Grappling now with each other's throats, and each panting with rage and exhaustion, Seaborn determined to secure his knife at all hazards. With a mighty effort he grasped the handle of the knife, which seeing the Indian clasped him with all his strength and tried to bite his face.

While in this position, "Bruno", Seaborn's dog, appeared and with a fierce growl fastened his teeth in the shoulder of the savage. This caused him to loose his hold on Seaborn and in an instant Seaborn raised his knife, aimed at his throat but his arm received the knife blow instead. As he raised his arm to repeat the blow, the Indian exclaimed, "Enough! Enough!" in the Indian tongue and in broken English added, "Take dog off quick, brave white man, no kill chief! Me give up!"

With reluctant admiration, Seaborn accepted his surrender and, taking off his buckskin suspenders, bound him tightly around the wrists. Noticing his bleeding arm, he bound that and received a grunt of satisfaction and thanks from the Indian. Stepping to the tree and withdrawing the tomahawk, he pointed the direction in which to go.

At this moment the girl, accompanied by men from the missionary station, where she lived, and the surveyor's camp, returned to aid the white man. Seeing the bloody and bruised appearance of both men, they all gave vent to expressions of congratulations that the desperate struggle had ended in the capture of the Indian.

George Took was hanged in Cassville, Georgia, in 1835, under the judgeship of John W. Hooper. He had murdered a white family for revenge, set fire to their home, and when the little girl of the family recognized him and ran to him for rescue, he picked her up and threw her into the flames. He was pursued and captured by the sheriff, Lewis Tumlin. In the desperate resistance, Took had been shot in the shoulder and in consequence his arm was amputated before his trial. John Seaborn and the fair young lady fell in love after the exciting rescue, and married in three months' time.

CHAPTER II

HOW THE COUNTY WAS FORMED

In 1832 with added parts of Habersham and Hall the county of Cherokee was divided into 10 counties: Cass, Cherokee, Cobb, Forsyth, Gilmer, Lumpkin, Murray, Paulding, Walker and Floyd.

By a legislative act in 1832*, assented to December 3, Cass county was formed from parts of the 21st, 22nd, and 23rd districts of the second section; the 4th, 5th, 6th, 15th, 16th, and 17th districts of the third section*.

Cass was named for General Lewis Cass, born in Exter, New Hampshire. He was admitted to the bar in 1802; in 1831 was made secretary of war by President Jackson, a commissioner to Paris; in 1845 was elected to U. S. senate; in 1848 nominated for presidency but was defeated.

In 1834 part of Murray along the Oostanaula river in the 24th district was added to Cass. (Acts of 1834, p. 71-72.)

In 1843 lot No. 210 in the 16th district of Cass was added to Floyd. (Acts of 1843, p. 26.)

In 1845 lot No. 80, and lots owned by certain persons on the county lines of Floyd and Cass, in the 15th and 16th districts, were added to Floyd. (Acts of 1845, p. 73.)

In 1850 a residence lot owned in Cass by Thomas O. Christian became a part of Murray. (Acts of 1849-50, p. 129.)

In 1850 a new county, called Gordon, was formed from parts of the 24th, 7th and 14th districts of Cass. (Acts of 1849-50, p. 124.)

In 1852 lots Nos. 181, 183, 150, 151, 120, 121, 90, 91, 60, 61, 30, 31 and 1, in the 16th district, between the county lines of Cass and Floyd were added to Floyd.

*Acts of 1832, pp-57-8.

(Acts of 1851-52, p. 65.)

In 1852 two lots, Nos. 35 and 36, in the 18th district of Paulding, were added to Cass. (Acts of 1851-52, p. 69.)

In 1852 lots Nos. 27 and 28, along the county line of Cass and Polk, in the 18th district, were added to Cass. (Acts of 1851-52, p. 75.)

In 1852 a lot, No. 136, in the 23rd district, on county lines of Cass and Gordon, was added to Gordon. (Acts of 1851-52, p. 69.)

In 1854 on the county lines of Cass and Gordon residence lots and a lot, No. 21, in the 15th district, were added to Gordon. (Acts of 1853-4, p. 312.)

In 1854 lots Nos. 33, 34, and 40, on county line of Cass and Paulding, in the 18th district, were added to Cass. (Acts of 1853-54, p. 321.)

In 1855 lots Nos. 22 and 39, in the 15th district of Floyd and Nos. 130 in the 15th district of Cass, were added to Gordon. (Acts of 1855-6, p. 125.)

In 1856 a lot, No. 81, on county line of Cass and Gordon in 15th district, was included in Gordon. (Acts of 1855-6, p. 131.)

In 1856 lot No. 298, in 23rd district of Cherokee on line between Cass and Cherokee, was added to Cass. (Acts of 1855-6, p. 134.)

In 1860 lot No. 1282, in the 17th district of Cass, was added to Polk. (Acts of 1860, p. 143.)

In 1869 lot No. 111, in the 15th district of Bartow on a line dividing the counties of Bartow and Gordon, was included in Gordon. (Acts of 1869, p. 173.)

Bartow is now bounded on the north by Gordon, on the east by Cherokee, on the south by small portions of Cobb, Paulding and Polk, on the west by Floyd.

CHAPTER III

LAND GRANTS

The accompanying map was drawn by Capt. Henry J. McCormick, one of the county surveyors, and is known as the Cherokee Purchase. Originally Cherokee county, it is now Bartow, Catoosa, Chattooga, Cherokee, Cobb, Dade, Dawson, Fannin, Floyd, Forsyth, Gilmer, Gordon, Haralson, Lumpkin, Milton, Murray, Paulding, Pickens, Polk, Towns, Union, Walker and Whitfield counties.

In 1831 Cherokee Georgia was surveyed by order of the governor into four sections, and these sections were laid off into land districts nine miles square. Thirty-three districts, in the 1st, 2nd, 3rd, and 4th sections, were laid off into 40-acre lots, called "Gold Lots" because of the possibility of their containing gold. Sixty districts were laid off into 160-acre lots, called "Land Lots" to distinguish from the "Gold Lots".

These lots totaled fifty-four thousand. Due to errors in the original surveys, there were fractional lots, and because it was difficult to survey accurately the 40-acre and 160-acre lots, the grant was always printed, "more or less". Some of the lots were never applied for and became known as "Wild Land".

The State issued a plat and grant to the drawee, with the great seal of the State attached to it, for a fee ranging from $3 to $18. In S. G. McLendon's "History of the Public Domain of Georgia"* is this statement: "Grants for Cherokee lands under the Land Lottery of 1830 and its amendments, and the Gold Lottery of 1831, and the subsequent Fraction Lottery, paid $18 for whole or fractional lots; and $10 for gold lots or fractions, to be taken out within five years from the drawing. The Land and Gold Lotteries were drawn in the winter of 1832-3, and the fractions in the ensuing December. A resolution of December 1823 (Vol. IV, p. 35 of Recs.) prescribed the fees ($4.50) on fractions sold by the State. —Prince's Digest, p. 568."

By an act of the legislature in 1831, persons qualified to one draw in the Gold Land Lottery were: white males above 18 years of age having been within the organized limits of the State 3 years, preceding January 1st, 1832; all widows with like residence; all families of orphans under 18 years of age of like residence, except those that drew whose fathers were dead (an act had provided that a family of more than 2 orphans should have 2 draws); all heads of families one additional draw in consideration of the number in the family; all widows of like residence whose husbands were killed or died in service of their country, or on their return march from wars with Great Britain or the Indians; all orphans of soldiers; and every deaf, dumb, and blind person of 3 years residence.

By acts of the legislature time was extended for the

---
*p. 129.

fortunate drawees to take out their grants. In 1843 it was provided that grants had to be taken before October, 1844, or they were forfeited and reverted to the State. Many of the grants were sold and re-sold.

Bartow county, or Cass, was made up of the 17th, 4th, and one-half of the 21st districts, containing 40-acre lots, "more or less", and the 16th, 5th, one-half of the 22nd, lower half of the 15th, 6th, and one-half of the 23rd districts, containing 160-acre lots, "more or less". The lots were distributed by the lottery system.

Many people in the county have preserved the original land grants that came into their hands through transactions of real estate. The following case is an example:

In Smith's "Cherokee Land Lottery" of 1838, page 197, is found in the 5th district, 3rd section:

"195, Zachariah Hopson, sol., Marsh's, Thomas."

"195" is the lot number; "sol." is soldier; "Marsh's" is the captain's district; "Thomas" is the county of his residence in Georgia.

An uninterrupted chain of title of this lot No. 195 from the above grantee is as follows: A deed from Zachariah Hopson of Leon county, Fla., Sept. 25, 1833, to James J. Blackshear and Donald McClain of Thomas county, Ga., is recorded in the Cass county office of the clerk of the superior court in Book A of Deeds, page 304, March 5, 1835. On May 10, 1849, Donald McLean—spelled thusly in this deed—"bargained and quit-claimed" for the sum of one dollar this lot to Harriet Blackshear, Thomas E. Blackshear, and Mitchell B. Jones, administrators of the estate of James J. Blackshear, deceased, of Thomas county. This was recorded in the county clerk's office in Book K, page 598, on September 1, 1852. On September 2, 1857, the administrators of the estate of James J. Blackshear of Thomas county having advertised this lot for sale, Lewis M. Munford, of Cass county, bought it for $601. This deed was recorded in the clerk's office in Book N, page 584, October 7th, 1857.

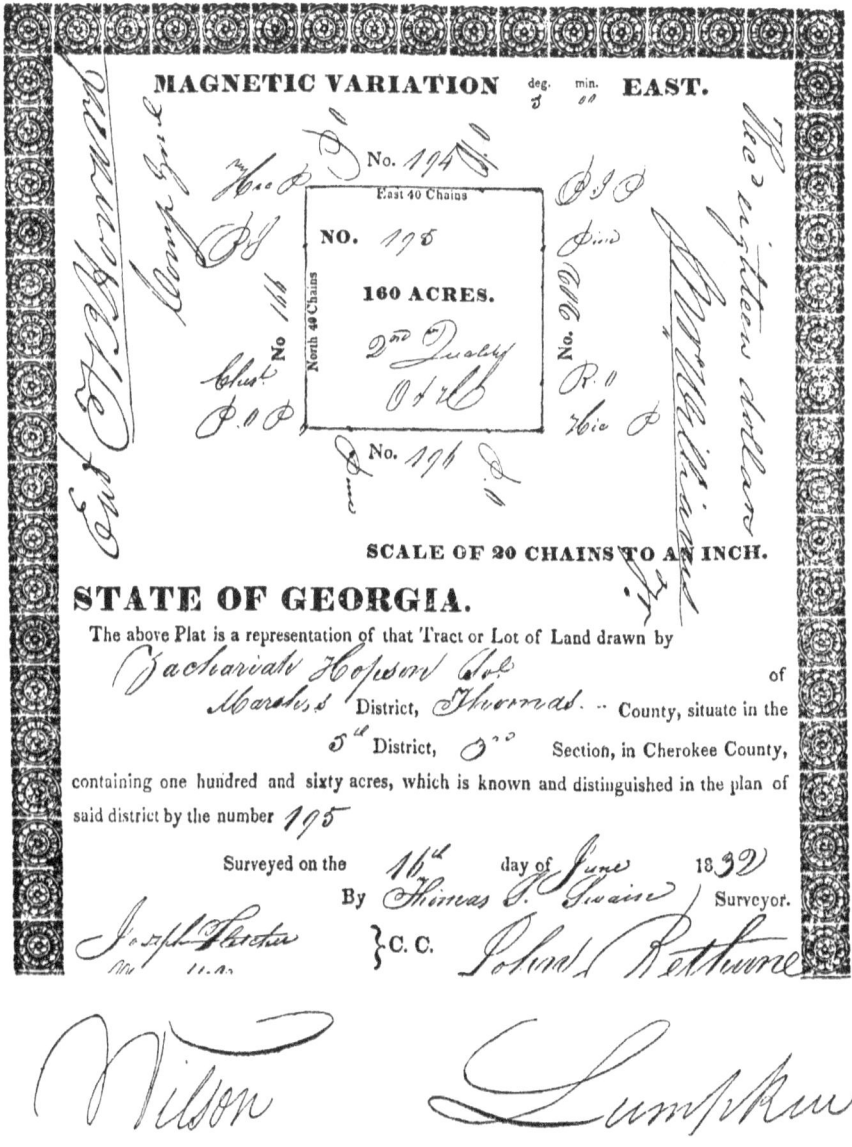

On the lot was erected the Munford home and in the course of years, this lot, among others in the estate, has come from Lewis Martin Munford to his son, Lewis

Sims Munford; and from L. S. Munford to a daughter, Mrs. Louis Munford Peeples; and from Mrs. Peeples to her children, Lewis Munford Peeples and Mary Peeples Daves.

CHAPTER IV

THE "EMPIRE COUNTY" OF THE STATE

(So-called by the editors of the old newspapers.)

While the Cherokees were yet lingering about the scenes that for generations had made the local attachments of their tribe so strong, the sturdy emigrant from the Carolinas and eastern Georgia came into their midst with the axe, the rifle, and the plow. By the majority in numbers the Indians called the new settlers "the Carolinas".

The early settler was not a man of means. Some came in search of gold and not finding it re-sold it cheaply. Some came because they drew land in the lotteries of 1832-3. Some came from the sea coast to spend their summers in a higher and healthier climate. After 1840 an influx of wealthy men came from South Carolina, attracted by the fertility of soil and the salubrious climate.

The panic of 1837 retarded progress for 10 years, but during that time cotton grew in importance; the question of transportation came up the prospective railroad joining the Tennessee river with the Atlantic ocean, and river traffic on the Coosa river with railroad connections, drew men here to purchase property where there seemed a future.

The pioneers who came to Cass not only established log cabin homes, but soon a camp-ground, a log church, or a log school was built in a neighborhood.

Roads were impassable in the winter. These "first families" sent teams to Augusta once a year for household effects, a long and arduous journey. The poorer class raised their necessities on their newly bought plots of ground, or traded with the Indians.

HOW THE PIONEER CAME

Alabama was admitted to the Union in 1819 and the

Alabama road, crossing the State of Georgia, was the main artery for emigrants into this section. This road came through what is now Allatoona, first following the south side of the Etowah river, then going by way of what is now Stilesboro and Taylorsville into Floyd county. It is said to be the only road originally deeded 100 feet wide by the State. Many settlers remained on this road, others left leaving no sign, while others crossed the river to the northern part of the county.

The Jackson military road, now the Tennessee road, was opened about 1825 and entered the northeastern part of the county to cross its length.

Above what is now Adairsville, there was a mail route from New Orleans to Washington city. It came by the old Cato farm, now known as the George Ellis farm, and horses were changed at the Milwee farm west of Adairsville. The road continued by way of Spring Place in Murray county*.

It is said that an Indian trail from Wilmington, N. C. to Mobile, Ala., or the path between Coosa and Tugatoo, crossed the south side of Kingston and that there was a trading post near Two Run creek. This may have been a branch of the Hightower Trail.

New Town road is shown on the Cherokee Lottery maps and traversed the center of the county. The Federal road, made in Jefferson's administration, went west and east, but all traces are now lost.

Sir Godfrey Barnsley was given instructions how to come from Savannah to Cass county in the late 30's as follows:

    One route was "From Hardwicks—122 miles station—
    To Sparta, 31 miles, viz—
    From Hardwicks to Fenns, 8 miles—tolerable house.
    From Fenns to Cummings, 7 miles—tolerable house.
    From Cummings to Sparta, 15 miles—tolerable house.
    Sparta to Parks Bridge on the Oconee, 28 miles and at Parks Bridge, a good house.
    From Parks Bridge to Madison, 11 miles.
    From Madison to Covington, 26 miles—excellent houses along

---

*Information handed down to Bayless E. Lewis.

that road, one of the very best 6 or 5½ miles from Madison, a good house (cheap as to charges) to rest for a day with a fine lawn and shade trees in front.

From Covington to Decatur, 30 miles, viz—

From Covington to Lattimer's*, 20 miles, a good house.

From Lattimer's to Decatur, 10 miles—Thomson's.

From Decatur to Marietta, 23 miles—no good house on the road.

From Marietta to Cassville, 30 miles, only decent house on the road—Dawson's."

Rev. John Crawford opened a road from Cassville to Adairsville when he first came to the county. Just which route he took is uncertain.

Transportation in and out of the county was done by stage coaches. Cassville was a terminus between there and Morganton, via Ellijay.

White in his "Historical Collections of Georgia" gave the early settlers as: Colonel Hardin, Z. B. Hargrove, John Dawson, D. Irwin, T. G. Barron, Robert Patton, L. Tumlin, the Johnsons, the Wyleys, Dr. Hamilton and others. In his "Statistics", White gives Mr. McAdams, Mr. Lowrie, Capt. Tumblin, and Mr. Johnson.

INCORPORATED TOWNS
CASSVILLE

"Old Cassville, in thy early days, the Indian of the wood,
Amid thy tall and stately oaks, in buckskin garments stood;
By nature, they were savages, but 'twas not by their hands—
Dear Cassville stands a monument of far more savage hands!"
    Mrs. J. D. Carpenter, in The Standard, 1867.

When the county was created in 1832, Cassville was the name given to the county seat and the town was laid out in July, 1833. As the seat of justice and the home of prominent lawyers in the Cherokee circuit, it soon became populous. A brick court house and jail were erected by 1837 or before 1849, and the town was built around the court house square as are so many of our southern towns.

It was incorporated by an act of the legislature in December, 1843, with Samuel Morgan, William Latimer,

---
*Home of Mrs. Rebecca Lattimer Felton.

Thomas A. Sullivan, George B. Russell and Julius M. Patton appointed as town commissioners*.

By 1849 Cassville was the largest and most prosperous town in Cherokee Georgia. Letters addressed to Rome, Ga., were directed "via Cassville". There were 4 hotels: Brown & Dyer, kept by Higgs; Cassville Hotel, kept by John Terrell; Eagle Hotel, kept by Aaron Burris; and the Latimer Hotel, kept by William Latimer. Leading merchants were George S. Black, T. A. Sullivan & John A. Erwin, J. D. Carpenter†, Fain & Fain, Sam Levy, John W. Burke, insurance and bookstore, Patton & Chunn, Humphrey W. Cobb, and George Upshaw. There was a Baptist, a Methodist, a Presbyterian and an Episcopal church.

During the construction of the State Railroad, tradition has it that the Cassville citizens did not want their town demoralized—nor their horses frightened—by having a railroad through the town. The colleges were advertised with that as a crowning merit. Later they mooted the idea of a branch going through Cassville via Fairmount and Gainesville. J. H. Johnston in his history of the "Western and Atlantic Railroad", 1932‡, states that, "The original surveys of the Western and Atlantic Railroad developed the fact that it was practicable to build the line through Cassville, then one of the most flourishing towns in Northern Georgia. The citizens of Cassville finally succeeded in getting the legislature to pass an act§ providing for an alternate route via the town, leaving the Western and Atlantic above Cartersville and again intersecting it at some point south of Kingston; and also requiring the citizens of Cassville to bear all expense connected with the surveys and cost of constructing the new route. There is nothing in the records to show what was done in the matter, but evidently the people of Cassville found that the cost of the

---
*Acts of 1843, p. 94.
†W. W. Carpenter, of Dalton, is the only survival of this large family.
‡pp. 44-5.
§Acts of 1851-2, p. 117.

project would be far greater than they would be justified in assuming."*

When the name of the county was changed by an act of legislature in 1861, Cassville was changed to Manassas in honor of the victory gained there. In the December session, recorded in the journal of the house, there is the resolution of Mr. Sheats to change the name and for the postmaster general of the Confederate States to be notified of the change, and the governor was requested to forward the resolution to the postmaster general of the Confederate States. Naturally, the Federal postal authorities never recognized the name of Manassas and the name of Cassville was retained.

This change in name is said to have been the reason for the utter destruction of Cassville in 1864. Another reason was that Federal prisoners saw some young ladies wave a black flag as they passed through the town. The official reason was to eradicate the giving of enemy information in the home of rebels. On the day of the entry of the Federals, May 19th, the home of Col. Warren Akin was burned. On October 12th, the Male and Female Colleges and the homes of President Rambaut and Judge Nathan Land were burned. On the 5th of November, the 5th Ohio Regiment with 300 cavalrymen set fire to the remainder of Cassville, leaving the churches and a few homes that were used as hospitals.

After the war it never regained its population nor prominence. When the court house was moved to Cartersville, many of the citizens removed to Cartersville. Cassville has been romantically described in poems and speeches, as: "Though the old town is but a memory, it is like the shattered vase in which the bouquet of roses has been garnered, there is a faint but lingering sweetness of the good old times."†

When the colleges were incorporated in 1853, Cassville restricted the sale of intoxicants; and again by an

---
*See Railroad History in this edition.
†The Courant-American, 1889.

act of legislature in 1875 had the sale of liquor restricted, thus becoming one of the first towns in Georgia to adopt such measures.

The city and Confederate cemetery is at Cassville.

ADAIRSVILLE

About 5 miles north of the present Adairsville site was Oothcalooga village. The name was taken from the Indian name of the stream that runs through the valley*.

Here lived the petty chiefs of the village. White in his "Historical Collections"† states, "Oothcaloga was the residence of the Adairs. It was sparsely inhabited but the Indians here lived better than in any other part of the nation." The Adairs were the descendents of some Scotch adventurers who settled among the Cherokees, married into their families, and by the time the Cherokee country was ceded to the U. S., they were prominent representatives of the nation. They went by the name of Red Watt and Black Watt to distinguish from each other. Oothcalooga valley was called the "garden spot of the Cherokee country" by the pioneers who settled in it.

After the Indians left, a little settlement, with a store or two about 2 miles north of the present town, was called Adairsville in compliment to the Scotch Cherokee chiefs who had been friendly to the whites. Hodge & Bailey had a store there in 1837 and it fronted a large section of cleared land. A ledger, kept by the young bookkeeper, Augustus C. Trimble, is still in the possession of the Trimble family—whites and Indians are listed on the credit side of the ledger.

During the building of the State Railroad, Governor Towns intended Adairsville to be the terminus of the road and had built large machine shops on the site where the present town grew and absorbed the name and function of the above village. Adairsville was then ex-

---
*Octhcalooga mean "beaver".
†p. 476.

actly half-way between what is now Atlanta and Chattanooga. It was incorporated in February, 1854*, with D. A. Crawford, Joseph L. Neel, H. G. Lawrence, A. C. Trimble and John W. Parrott appointed as town commissioners. There were amendments to the town charters in August, 1872; October, 1887; December, 1901, and August, 1907. The public school system was established in 1909†.

The town was not totally destroyed during the Civil War. Skirmishes were frequent on the roadway. In 1864, when the Federals were known to be approaching, a gun factory in the town was removed to Cuthbert, Ga.

CARTERSVILLE

A little hamlet grew up where the railroad underpass is now below Cartersville, and was called "Birmingham" by the Englishmen who came through this section in 1832. Only one Englishman and his son remained to see this hamlet grow—David Lewis, who fought in the War of 1812 and is buried in the old Friendship cemetery, and one of his sons, Nathaniel Deery Lewis, b. in 1818 in Hereford, England. He was only 14 years of age then and later he returned to England to see the coronation of Queen Victoria. On his return to Birmingham, he established a blacksmith's shop, being a wheelwright by trade, and ran a stage route between Rome and "Marthasville". He died in Sandersville, Miss. Of his 5 children, Mary, who married Seab Hicks of Cartersville, is the only living child in the county.

One day Col. Farish Carter, who lived at Carter's Quarters on the Tennessee road and traveled from there to Milledgeville frequently, stopped to see Mr. Lewis and jestingly suggested that he change the name of Birmingham to Cartersville for him. Mr. Lewis told Col. Carter he thought the town would grow further up the road and told him to tell the few settlers that were there

---
*Acts of 1853-4, p. 227.
†See the Acts of Incorporation and Ordinances and By-Laws of the Town of Adairsville, 1910.

about it. Col. Carter, still jesting, did so, and Cartersville became the name of the town which later was to become the county site and the largest town in the county. Much of the property upon which the city grew was owned by Joseph J. Hamilton, whose family is identified with Floyd county.

It was incorporated in February 1850*, with R. H. Cannon, W. W. Leak, Wm. H. Puckett, J. F. Sproull and Coleman Pitts appointed as town commissioners. Its population in 1849 was 150. Four or five stores and one hotel.

In 1864 the town was almost completely demolished by fire of the Federal soldiers. Only 2 business houses survived. The present homes of Mrs. Lydia Tumlin and Mrs. Samuel F. Milam were among the few houses left standing. The former home was used as a post office and Federal headquarters, and officers occupied the Milam home. By 1866, 20 new business houses were built and though natural fires have wrecked property, a steady but slow growth has been evident year by year. Before the war the main part and majority of business houses were on the east side of the railroad.

In August, 1872, it was incorporated as a city with a mayor and aldermen to constitute a quorum. A bill to change the name to "Etowah City" was protested by Mark A. Cooper, who claimed that there was already a renowned town by the name of Etowah and it had been a post office for 20 years.

Paving of the city streets in 1925 has changed the appearance from a town to a city. Its population in 1920 was 4,350. In 1930 it was 5,250.

EMERSON

This was called Stegall's Station until in 1889† it was incorporated with the name of Emerson, in honor of Ex-Governor Joseph Emerson Brown. It was a mining

---
*Acts of 1849-50, p. 103.
†Acts of 1889, p. 976.

center for many years and boasted a three-story frame hotel. It was a station on the railroad. There are Methodist and Baptist churches, consolidated school, and cemetery. In 1889 the city of Emerson was surveyed, by H. J. McCormick, with the street names of Minnesota, Tennessee, Kentucky, Ohio, Indiana, Michigan, Wisconsin, Georgia, Florida and Vermont running east and west; First, Second and Third streets running north and south.

EUHARLEE

This little village was first called Burge's Mills. Several grain mills had been built on the creek on the south of the village as early as 1844. Because of the fertility of the soil, many farmers settled in and around Euharlee.

In 1852 it was incorporated as Euharleyville with Thomas W. Brandon, E. B. Presley, Leonard Morgan, Allen Dykes and B. D. Dykes as town commissioners.

In 1870* it was incorporated with the name of Euharlee, the academy being in the center, and with Dr. Franklin R. Calhoun, Elihu G. Nelson and Thomas Tumlin as commissioners. The town has never grown to any size. Most of the community life revolves around the school and church activities. There are Presbyterian and Baptist churches.

KINGSTON

(Compiled by Miss Leila Darden)

Before vandalism destroyed its forest, Kingston was beautifully situated with dense forests forming a background and two streams—Two Run and Connesena—named in honor of Indian chiefs, marking its distant boundaries.

It was named in honor of Judge John Pendleton King, of Augusta, a noted lawyer, a personal friend of LaFayette, U. S. senator and Georgia senator, and a

*Acts of 1870, p. 188.

railroad financier.

It had a reputation of being very wicked, but by 1852 was reported as "improving in morals".

Prior to the building of the railroad, the stage coach route passed through the town and the hotels and the spring there were well patronized.

In December, 1849, the Memphis Branch railroad from Kingston to Rome, Ga., was opened for business, and this made Kingston an important point as distributor on the W. & A. and in connection with transportation on the Coosa river. There was a large stone depot on the railroad.

Kingston was also a cotton market and summer resort. There were 40 business houses—and most of them were on the west side of the railroad; four churches; four hotels—one was owned and managed by the widow of Dr. Mark Johnston (b. May 4, 1801, d. Dec. 11, 1851); one by Thomas R. Couche (b. Mar. 31, 1827, d. Aug. 19, 1873); one by Mrs. Millie Huson and one by a Mr. McCrary. The site of the Johnston hotel is the present home of Irby Sheats and on the adjoining lot was the Wayside Home during the Civil War. The population in 1849 was 100.

During the Civil War, Kingston was a supply and hospital center, due to its location on the railroad, and was headquarters for the Federal army from May to November, 1864. Most of the houses were destroyed during this time.

In 1866 Kingston was offered by a committee, with Mark A. Hardin as chairman, as an eligible site for the Georgia Orphans Home.

It was incorporated in 1869*, with a town council composed of L. M. Gillam, T. F. Towers, C. N. Mayson, T. R. Couche, and M. McMurry.

Though it has been a place "where you change cars", Kingston has honored the past and can proudly

---
*Acts of 1869, p. 81.

claim over 250 unknown soldiers buried in the town cemetery.

STILESBORO

A community grew along the Alabama road which became a settlement of prominent farmers who believed in schools and churches.

The community life finally grew around an academy that was the center of a thriving interest. The village proper has always been scattered.

It was called "Stilesborough" in honor of one of its prominent neighbors, William H. Stiles, and was incorporated by the name of Stilesboro in March, 1866*, with John T. Sproull, Larkin Floyd, W. O. Bowler, as "a body corporate and politic and the name and style of the Town Council of Stilesboro." The corporate limits extended one mile in every direction from the Stilesboro Academy, and the commissioners had power and authority to grant licenses to retail spiritous liquors under such rules as were incident to incorporated towns and cities. In 1870 a road was surveyed from the academy to the depot and later opened on property belonging to Dr. S. F. Stephens, and E. T. and J. R. Henderson.

The town proper is on the branch of the Seaboard Air Line. It has never grown to any size. It was a cotton market at one time, but now there are only one or two stores.

Sherman's route from Kingston to Dallas followed through Stilesboro. Many homes were saved, it is said, on account of the Masonic emblem attached to doorways. The academy was used by the Federal soldiers and property damage was done by the usage of desks and benches as feed troughs.

TAYLORSVILLE

After the Civil War the community which grew into the town of Taylorsville developed, but was not

---
*Acts of 1866, p. 293.

officially incorporated until 1916*. J. W. Kennedy was mayor, W. M. Dorsey and W. D. Trippe were aldermen.

The town was surveyed by a Mr. Taylor and named for him about 1869, or 1870, on property belonging to Thomas Ausley and Israel P. Davis of Polk county. Mr. Ausley came here from Dallas and was probably the first mayor. No record can be found of the date of incorporation. The first house was built by John Loudermilk, east of the present town. Some of the first merchants were J. M. Smith, Sr., and Rowan Hanie.

As a lumber and agricultural center it attracted many settlers. When a narrow gauge railroad was built from Cedartown by A. G. West, a turning table was erected near the center of the business section. As the old Cartersville and Van Wert railroad grew into the present Seaboard, Taylorsville has had railroad connections with the outside world. The town cemetery lies partly in Polk county and Israel P. Davis was the first to be buried in that portion, as he gave the land for it. The town has never grown to any size. There are Methodist and Baptist churches, a bank, a brick school house, post office, and stores.

WHITE

This was a small community on the L. & N. railroad and the Tennessee road, and was not incorporated until August, 1919. Dr. W. B. Vaughan was appointed mayor with J. W. Tierce, J. T. Peace, L. G. Hughes, W. R. White, aldermen.

UNINCORPORATED TOWNS AND VILLAGES

Allatoona: a station on the W. & A. railroad, takes its name from the creek, which runs near the village, the Indians named in their day of occupation. Gold has been mined here since the 30's. Here was fought a sanguinary battle on October 5th, 1864, and

---

*Acts of 1916, p. 972.

the house used as a hospital is yet standing with marks of bullet holes still visible.

Atco: derived from the name of the American Textile Company, is one of the most modern mill towns in the South. It is a flag station on the W. & A. railroad and has a post office. It is now under the management of the Goodyear Company.

Bartow: a small mining settlement below Emerson on the W. & A. railroad.

Bolivar: a flag station on the L. & N. railroad.

Cass Station: once considered a site for the county seat, is now a flag station on the W. & A. railroad. Bethel Quillian and Tom McKelvey operate the only large store. There is a post office.

Corbin: is named for John Corbin* who came from North Carolina to this county in 1849 and settled on Stamp creek. A school house is the most important structure now.

Cave: a flag station on the W. & A. railroad south of Kingston.

Cement: an abandoned site.

Flexatile: a mining settlement on the Tennessee road.

Folsom: a small village of stores and houses in the 6th district.

Five Forks: is in the 5th district and has a grist mill, filling station and houses.

Grassdale: in the 5th district, was an old community of pioneer families. Some parts of this section are called Sophia and Little Prairie. Nothing left of any settlement now, except scattered farms and houses.

Halls Station: a station on the W. & A. railroad;

---
*Will Kay (dec.) of Cartersville was a grandson.

it is called Linwood as a post office.

Ladds: a shipping station on the Seaboard for the Ladd Lime and Stone Company.

Ligon: a small community on the old Chulio road to Rome, takes its name from "Red" Ligon, who lived there in the 17th district.

Pine Log: near Rydal, takes its name from the Pine Log mountain and is the largest village community in the county.

Rydal: a station on the L. & N. railroad and a post office.

Iron Hill:

OFFICIAL CENSUS OF THE COUNTY

(From the Department of Commerce, Washington, D. C.)

Bartow County, Ga.

Census	Population
1840	9,390
1850	13,300
1860	15,724
1870	16,566
1880	18,690
1890	20,616
1900	20,823
1910	25,388
1920	24,527
1930	25,364
1960	*28,267*

Extract from the census of 1850 from White's "Historical Collections of Georgia": "Dwellings, 1,712, families, 1,750; white males, 5,333; white females, 4,938; free colored males, 11; free colored females, 10; total free population, 10,292; slaves, 3,008; farms, 601; manufacturing establishments, 8; value of real estate, $1,773,689; value of personal estate, $1,942,121."

In The Cassville Standard of September, 1852, is a complete census of the county as follows:

	Militia Districts	Heads of families	Number of persons	Free white persons	Free persons of color	Slaves	Lunatics	White male children between 6 and 15	White female children between 6 and 15
Cartersville	822nd	268	2487	1146	2	1039	2	201	227
Cassville	828th	212	1794	1178	1	615	1	183	152
Sixth	936th	111	737	621	2	114	3	96	73
Adairsville	856th	233	1565	1326	0	239	2	219	178
Kingston	952nd	144	1169	876	9	281	1	131	133
Euharlee	851st	279	2228	1649	2	577	7	261	198
Allatcona	819th	145	873	320	0	53	3	120	115
Stamp Creek	963rd	148	959	797	0	162	2	125	112
Pine Log	827th	120	944	665	1	278	0	99	100
Wolf Pen	1041st	159	808	765	1	42	2	152	114
TOTAL		1819	13564	9343	18	3400	23	1587	1402

The wealth of the county is seen on the tax receiver's book for 1857:

261,600 acres of land, valued at _____ $2,687,079.00
City and town property, valued at _____ 226,918.00
4,040 slaves, valued at _____ 2,369,918.00
Money and solvent debts _____ 1,203,178.00
Merchandise, valued at _____ 151,313.00
Capital employed in Banks _____ 154,585.85
Capital invested in stock, manufacturing,
 etc. _____ 171,700.00
Household and kitchen furniture, valued at 30,530.00
All other property not before enumerated,
 valued at _____ 467,298.00

Grand Total _____ $7,460,028.85

Polls returned, 1,375; professions, 39; dentists, 3; daguerrean artist, 1; free persons of color, 6. Out of about 2,000 tax payers, only the names of 1,604 were known.

Prominent men in the county are shown as they were delegates appointed by the town councils to the Southern Commercial Convention in Knoxville, Tenn.. July, 1857. From Cassville: Maj. Abda Johnson, Col. Warren Akin, Capt. W. T. Wofford, Geo. L. Upshaw Gen. John H. Rice, Joseph Bogle, R. F. Wyley, Arthur Haire, Col. H. F. Price, Madison McMurry, Hon. John W. Hooper, Col. George W. Brown, Wm. T. Trammell, H. W. Cobb. From Cartersville: Hon. Mark A. Cooper, Col. James C. Sproul, Maj. John S. Rowland, Dr. William Anderson, Col. James C. Young, B. H. Conyers, J. C. Jones, T. H. Goldsmith,*D. B. Cunyus, T. S. Miller, Dr. Samuel F. Stevens, Col. Lewis Tumlin, James A. Maddox, Col. H. P. Farrow, C. T. Shelman, J. R. Parrott, Col. James Milner, J. J. Howard, John A. Irwin, Dr. R. M. Young, W. C. Barber, Col. J. R. Fullmore, U. Stephens, Dr. J. W. Lewis, Dr. William Benham, William Milam, Col. Mark Johnston, William T. Burge, Maj. Willis Benham, Col. R. H. Cannon, Dr. N. Hart, Col. James G. Ryals, Col. J. W. Watts, Dr. William Felton, Maj. William Milner, Thomas Wofford, W. P. Hammond, Silas Bell, Dr. W. W. Leake, Dr. D. Hamiter, J. A. Howard, D. W. K. Peacock, Maj. N. Nickolson, Thomas Kennedy, Col. John L. Rowland, Capt. E. D. Puckett, J. R. Wikle, Capt. William Rich, Dr. William Kirkpatrick, David Quarles. From Kingston: William Solomon, William Tumlin, F. J. Sullivan, Mark A. Hardin, W. W. Long, Samuel Sheats, Cristopher Dodd, F. A. Huson.

*MY GRANDFATHER

CASS COUNTY TAX RETURNS IN 1860, JUST BEFORE THE WAR

Number of polls	1,834
Professions	53
Dentists	2
Free persons of color	22
No. acres first quality land	14,964

No. acres second quality land	117,159
No. acres third quality land	137,122
No. acres pine	44,660
Total No. of acres of land	313,905
Aggregate value of city or town property	$ 272,935
Aggregate value of land	3,435,559
Number of slaves	4,813
Aggregate value of slaves	$3,445,924
Amount of money and solvent debts	1,675,556
Capital invested in manufactures, stocks, etc.	133,302
Value of household and kitchen furniture	35,050
Merchandise	167,236
Value of all other property not mentioned except plantation and mechanical tools, crops, etc.	568,421
Value of whole property	9,739,820

John F. Milhollin, Clerk, Inf. Court,
A. F. Morrison, Tax Receiver.

In the November session of the house of representatives, Samuel Sheats, who with Warren Akin, was representing this county, introduced a bill to change the name of the county.

"Whereas, the county of Cass . . . in its organization was named in memory of Lewis Cass of Michigan; and the said Lewis Cass having recently shown himself inimical to the South by voluntary donations of his private property to sustain a wicked war upon her people, and by utterance of sentiments such as the South must be subjugated, the Union must be preserved; and has thereby become unworthy of the honor conferred by the name of said county; and Whereas, deeming it the duty, it is always the pleasure of a brave and free people to perpetuate the memory of those who have fallen upon the field of battle in defense of the honor, rights, and liberties of our common country, and by their noble deeds and self-sacrificing devotion, have endeared their names in the hearts of the present generation. We should in some measure hand down their names and cause their memory to live ever green in the hearts of succeeding generations, therefore,

Sec. 1. Be it enacted, That from and after the passage of this Act, the name of the county of Cass be, and the same is hereby changed to the name of Bartow, in honor of the late Colonel Francis S. Bartow, of Chatham county of this State, who fell at the battle of Manassas Plains, gallantly leading his men, on the 21st day of July, 1861.

Sec. II. That the name of Cassville, the present county site of the county of Cass, be and the same is hereby changed to the name of Manassas.

Sec. III. That no writ or process of any kind, deed, contract or agreement in said county, shall be vitiated by being entitled Cass county; but the same may be amended upon motion when necessary, without any delay or cost.

Joseph E. Brown, Gov.

Assented to December 6, 1861"*.

Of the ten counties in the United States named for General Cass, Cass county, Georgia, was the only one to change. The others are in Illinois, Iowa, Indiana, Michigan, Minnesota, Missouri, Nebraska, North Dakota and Texas.

In the house of representatives in 1866, a member from Bartow proposed to change the name back to Cass. It caused much discussion, although it was known not to be favored by the county as a whole. Mr. J. W. Tench from Coweta county made his debut against this bill.

Francis S. Bartow, born in Savannah on September 6, 1816, graduated from Franklin College in 1835 with high honors. He was a law student in the office of Hon. John M. Berrien and married his daughter, Louisa G. Berrien; he attended the Yale law school and was admitted to the Bryan superior court, in Savannah, in 1837. He had a lucrative and popular practice. He was a member of the general assembly from Chatham county from 1841, and in 1861 was a member of the

---

*Acts of 1861, p. 101.

Confederate Congress in which he served as chairman of the military committee. He was an instructor and captain of the Oglethorpe Light Infantry, which was organized in 1856 and which participated in the seizure of Fort Pulaski on January 3, 1861. With this company he proceeded to Virginia, where he was promoted colonel of the 8th Georgia Regiment and later brevetted a brigadier-general of the 17th and 8th Georgia Regiments. When Bartow and his gallant company went to Virginia, after the refusal of Governor Brown to allow their services there, they were equipped with guns which Governor Brown claimed belonged to the State of Georgia. In an exchange of letters between Governor Brown and Captain Bartow over this matter, Bartow wrote in one of these letters the famous line, "I go to illustrate Georgia."

During the battle of First Manassas, General Bartow, commanding the brigade consisting of the 7th, 8th, 9th Georgia, and the 1st Kentucky Regiments, dashed up to General Beauregard, the commanding officer and asked, "General, what can my brigade do now, and if mortal effort can accomplish it, we will."

General Beauregard, pointing to a stone wall from which cannon was pouring on the Confederates, said, "That battery should be silenced."

General Bartow waving his hat, cried, "Boys, follow me!" While leading this charge his horse was shot from under him, and, mounting another, continued his charge. It was after a few minutes when he seized the colors of his regiment from a falling wounded bearer, that a Federal bullet pierced his heart and he was caught in the arms of Col. Lucius J. Gartrell. He lived long enough to say, "Boys, they have killed me, but never give up the field!"

General Bartow was buried in Laurel Grove cemetery in Savannah and a granite memorial marks his grave.

His mother, Mrs. Frances L. Bartow, had a home at Cave Springs, Floyd county, Georgia, and after her son's death, she came back to her Floyd county home*.

OFFICIAL CENSUS OF BARTOW

The official census of Bartow in 1880 was 18,690. The following is a more complete census of 1880:

	Citizens
Allatoona	778
Cartersville district	5,650
(Town of Cartersville)	2,037
Pine Log	1,120
Euharlee district	3,425
(Town of Euharlee)	24
Cassville district	1,943
Town of Taylorsville	95
Adairsville district	1,559
(Town of Adairsville)	391
Little Prairie	884
Kingston district	1,908
(Town of Kingston)	483
Stamp Creek	522
Wolf Pen	901

Whites, 12,419; colored, 6,271.

Foreigners: 6 British-Americans; 8 English-Welchmen; 14 Irishmen; 7 Scotchmen; 13 Germans; 1 Frenchman; 2 Swedes.

Of the natives: 1,907 born in South Carolina; 575 born in North Carolina; 355 born in Alabama; 266 born in Virginia; 378 born in Tennessee.

Bartow had 63 manufacturing establishments with a capital of $400,780, employing 285 males, 25 females, 27 children; a pay roll of $57,872; 25 breweries and malsters were listed, the smallest number in any occupation in the State.

BARTOW'S WEALTH IN 1881
Real and Personal Estate

Cartersville district	$1,471,414
Allatoona district	79,800
Stamp Creek district	30,506

*See "The Mothers of Some Distinguished Georgians," p. 36.

Wolf Pen district	84,981
Pine Log district	130,544
Sixth district	105,876
Cassville district	307,858
Adairsville district	346,401
Kingston district	229,692
Euharlee district	503,625
Value of property of white	3,290,697
Value of property of colored	56,816
Value of wild lands	11,718
Default property, white and colored	9,100
Total grand aggregate for 1881	3,368,331
For 1880	3,251,223

POLLS, PROFESSIONS, ETC.

White polls _____ 2,033
Colored _____ 868

Total _____ 2,901

Lawyers _____ 25
Doctors _____ 28
Dentists _____ 2
Photographers _____ 1

No. of hired hands in the county are returned at 770.
W. W. Ginn, Tax Receiver.

TAX RETURNS FOR 1932

District—	White	Colored
Adairsville	$ 489,400	$ 20,715
Allatoona	85,815	200
Cartersville	3,570,363	128,628
Cassville	236,909	8,321
Emerson	133,144	7,690
Euharlee	284,216	818
Iron Hill	56,210	2,603
Kingston	294,725	11,646
Pine Log	249,296	-------
Sixth	120,120	-------
Stamp Creek	2,905	-------
Taylorsville	213,497	935
Wolf Pen	307,187	151
Total	$6,043,787	$181,707

The following is a table showing returns for the past thirty years:

1903	$3,900,000	1924	7,055,285
1908	5,926,781	1925	7,088,518
1915	6,991,671	1926	6,930,495
1917	7,115,078	1927	6,953,782
1918	7,602,406	1928	7,140,799
1919	8,043,699	1929	7,059,350
1920	8,936,036	1930	7,022,735
1921	8,453,530	1931	6,749,282
1922	7,505,757	1932	6,225,494
1923	7,226,286		

COUNTY HIGHWAYS

From minutes of the Court of Ordinary, for county purposes, recorded in February, 1871*, the public roads of the county are listed as follows:

"Ordered by the Court with the concurrence of a majority of the Commissioners of Roads in and for said county, that the following public roads in and for said county be classed and designated as follows, to-wit:

ADAIRSVILLE DISTRICT, 856th District, G. M.

The road known as the Cassville and Calhoun road, first class, 30 feet wide.

The Rome and Canton road, via Adairsville, first class, 30 feet wide.

The Kingston and Adairsville road, second class, 30 feet wide.

The Early Ferry road, second class, 30 feet wide.

The road via A. C. Trimble's, second class, 30 feet wide.

The road via John Riddy's, second class, 30 feet wide.

The road via James Venable's, second class, 30 feet wide.

KINGSTON DISTRICT, 952nd District, G. M.

The road from Kingston to Floyd line, first class, 30 feet wide.

The Kingston and Adairsville road, second class, 20 feet wide.

The Kingston and Cartersville road, via Oglesby's Mills, first class, 30 feet wide.

The Kingston and Cartersville road, via Rodger's Mills, second

---

*p. 83.

class, 20 feet wide.

The Kingston and Euharlee road, via Gillam's, first class, 30 feet wide.

The Connesena Creek road, via Roper's, second class, 20 feet wide.

The Kingston to Adairsville, Mountain road, second class, 20 feet wide.

The road from J. S. Harris' to district line, via Barnsley's, second class, 20 feet wide.

The road from Kingston, via Howard's Mills, second class, 20 feet wide.

SIXTH DISTRICT, 936th, G. M.

The Canton road from Adairsville, first class, 30 feet wide.
The Cassville and Spring Place road, second class, 20 feet wide.
The road from Mosteller's, via A. M. Linn, second class, 20 feet wide.

The Calhoun road, via Mosteller's, second class, 20 feet wide.
The Fairmount road, via L. Beamon's, second class, 20 feet wide.
The Fairmount road, via R. Floyd, second class, 20 feet wide.
The Pine Log road, via Mrs. Richie, second class, 20 feet wide.

CASSVILLE DISTRICT, 828th Dist., G. M.

The Cassville and Adairsville road, first class, 30 feet wide.
The Cassville and Cartersville road, first class, 30 feet wide.
The Cassville and Kingston road, first class, 30 feet wide.
The Cassville and Pine Log road, first class, 30 feet wide.
The Spring Place road, via A. M. Linn, second class, 20 feet wide.
The Canton road from Cass Station, east, second class, 20 feet wide.

The Canton road, via J. Bogle's, second class, 20 feet wide.

The Spring Place road, Ashworth's, north, second class, 20 feet wide.

The Burnt Hickory road from Cass Station, south, second class, 20 feet wide.

The Kingston and Cartersville road, via Cass Station, second class, 20 feet wide.

The Maj. Benham's road, via Col. Saxon, second class, 20 feet wide.

The Kingston and Cartersville road, via Station, first class, 30 feet wide.

CARTERSVILLE DISTRICT, 822nd District, G. M.

The road from Cartersville to Burnt Hickory, via Rowland's Ferry to Alabama road, first class, 30 feet wide, and then to county line, second class, 20 feet wide.

The road from Cartersville to Burnt Hickory, via Douthit's Ferry, first class to Alabama road, 30 feet wide, and then to county line, second class, 20 feet wide.

The Alabama road, first class, 30 feet wide.
The Cassville road, first class, 30 feet wide.
The Allatoona road, via Puckett's Ferry, first class, 30 feet wide.
The Tennessee road, first class, 30 feet wide.
The Puckett's Ferry road, first class, 30 feet wide.
The Rowland Springs road, first class, 30 feet wide.
The Jim Young road, first class, 30 feet wide.
The Burnt Hickory road, from Cass Station, first class, 20 feet wide.
The Cartersville and Euharlee road, down river, first class, 30 feet wide.
The Newton Dobb's road, first class, 30 feet wide.
The Canton road, via N. F. Guyton, Kirkpatrick place, second class, 20 feet wide.
The Cartersville and Canton road, up river, first class, 30 feet wide.
The Kingston road from Cassville road to Mrs. Johnson, first class, 30 feet wide.
The Maj. Benham's road, first class, 30 feet wide.

WOLF PEN DISTRICT, 1041st District, G. M.

The Tennessee road, first class, 30 feet wide.
The Canton road, via J. Wofford's place, second class, 20 feet wide.
The Belle's Ferry road, via George Erwin place, second class, 20 feet wide.
The Calhoun road, via Bostwick, first class, 30 feet wide.

STAMP CREEK, 963rd District, G. M.

The Alabama road, county line to Kirkpatrick place, first class, 30 feet wide.
The Cartersville road, down the river, first class, 30 feet wide.

ALLATOONA DISTRICT, 819th District, G. M.

Allatoona and Marietta road, first class, 30 feet wide.
Alabama road, Cherokee line, first class, 30 feet wide.
Sand Town road, via Elliott Moore's, second class, 20 feet wide.
Canton road, via Fred Ross, second class, 20 feet wide.
Pumpkinvine road, second class, 20 feet wide.

Tennessee road, first class, 30 feet wide.
Cassville road, via Weem's, first class, 30 feet wide.
Mountain road, second class, 20 feet wide.
McCanless Mill road, second class, 20 feet wide.
All other roads, second class, 20 feet wide.

Road Commissioners at this date were H. W. Fite, W. W. Cotton, Wm. Chitwood, W. L. Rowland, W. A. Chunn, John P. Lewis, Wm. Sheelar, J. K. Gilreath, P. Yarborough, G. B. Loveless, Wesley Pearson, Wm. Rodgers, M. Anderson, M. T. Hays, John J. Jones, A. Willis, I. O. McDaniel, Jr., A. F. Woolley, J. S. Harris."

The Dixie Highway, U. S. No. 41, which traverses the county through its center, has been paved since 1927, and the No. 41 west, which goes by Rome, is paved. The Tennessee road is now under construction for paving by the State Highway Department.

Congressional District, 7th
Senatorial District, 42nd, 51st

CHAPTER V

PIONEER SETTLERS, 1830-1860

ADAIR, John R.: b. Oct. 16, 1824, in Henry county, Ga., came with his wife, Sarah F. Paul of Abbeville, S. C., who died in Feb. 1906, about 1849 to Cass county and settled in the Pine Log district where he lived until his death on Jan. 4, 1896. Both are buried in the Pine Log cemetery. Mr. Adair was active in the political and educational affairs of this community. Their children were : (1) S. Cornelia, m. in 1874 T. E. Arnold by whom there were Sallie, Joe and Agnes. (2) Elizabeth, m. in 1875 Elbert M. Upshaw. (3) William J., graduate of Atlanta Medical College, practiced medicine in this county until his removal to Rockmart where he practiced until his death on Feb. 3, 1930, m. Emma McBride. (4) Agnes E., m. in 1885 Ausley E. Vincent by whom there was one child, Lillian m. Virgil Bradford. (5) John P., b. Aug. 18, 1864, m. Stella Vincent by whom there were Ernest, Myrtice (Boyd), and Ethel (Evans) and after her decease he married Annie Hall; N.P.&J.P., in Cartersville district. (6) Robert Edgar, b. May 6, 1866; in 1890 graduated from Southern Medical College; has practiced medicine in this county, and when a young man taught school; m. Lula Mahan by whom there is one daughter, Frances. (7) T. Marcellus, a twin, (dec.); m. Tommie Maxwell by whom there were Candler and John, who live in the old Adair home.

AKIN. Warren: b. Oct. 9, 1811, in Elbert county, of Virginian parents. Youngest of 10 children, farmed with his father in early youth. A visit to an Elberton court scene decided his profession and at the age of 10 made his vow "to be a lawyer." At his father's death when he was 18, he took his share of the small estate to acquire seven months of schooling in Walton county. While clerking in a store in Monroe, the excitement over the Dahlonega gold mines reached Warren, and with a knap-sack on his shoulder, he walked to the new Eldorado. While working there he studied law and was admitted to the bar in Cherokee superior court, March 15, 1836 and immediately moved to Cassville. Without friends, poor, this boy began his career amid the foremost lawyers of north Georgia. He soon earned enough money to buy lot No. 44 in the town of Cassville in 1838 for $20, upon which he erected an office made of logs cut by himself and hauled by a team loaned by a neighbor. His first law partner was the Hon. A. R. Wright. By 1845 he had made $7,000 and in this same year married Eliza Hooper, daughter of Judge John W. Hooper. (One daughter Eliza Akin Baxter from this marriage.) He was appointed colonel of a militia company by Gov. Crawford. Col. Akin argued the first four cases decided by the first supreme court of Georgia in 1846. His first wife having died in 1848 he married Mary F. de Verdery, b. July 6, 1830, daughter of A. N. de Verdery of Floyd county. He became a licensed Methodist preacher in 1853. In 1859 he was nominated, against his wishes, by the opposition party to run against Gov. Brown. His campaign was noted for its professional and political purity. In 1861 he was chosen, without candidacy, to the Georgia House of Representatives and on the first ballot elected speaker of the house. In 1863 he was elected to the Confederate congress and was a warm friend of President Davis. While at the Confederate capitol, Col. Akin helped the soldiers with his influence and ministerial services. His family found refuge in Oxford and Elberton, during the war, and all returned to war-swept Cassville in October 1865. In 1870 they moved to Cartersville where he devoted his time to his profession. In 1874 he refused nomination for Congress from the 7th district and in 1877 his name became associated with Robert Toombs on the important question of calling a Constitutional convention. Twelve days before he died his ideas were incorporated into the Constitution and adopted. He was on the board of trustees of Emory College; an old time Whig, after the Clay school; considered by the Cartersville bar "as the first man in his profession in north Georgia." He died Dec. 17, 1877, and is buried on the family lot in Cassville cemetery. Of the 10 children of Warren (Bishop Warren A. Candler is a namesake) and Mary Akin, the following are identified with this county: (1) T. Warren, b. August 10, 1851; admitted to the bar in 1874 and practiced with his father and brother until he became identified in Governmental service in Washington, D. C.; married Libbie Shelman, (dec.) daughter of T. P. Shelman. He died in Macon on Jan. 10, 1930. (2) John W., b. June 10, 1859; graduate of Emory; admitted to the bar in 1878; judge of city court; member of house of representatives; president of Georgia Senate; served as secretary and president of the Georgia Bar Association and his speech, while president, on "The Aggressions of the Federal Court" was commented upon editorially by every leading newspaper in the State and a legislature of Kansas passed a resolution endorsing it; Methodist; author of "Akin's Lodge, Manual and Masonic Law Digest"; president of local city school board; married Frances Trippe Johnson by whom there were Verdery, Lillian (dec.) and Frances. (See war records.) Judge Akin died October 18, 1907 and is buried in Cartersville. (3) Sallie May, librarian in the Washington Memorial Library at Macon, Ga. (4) Paul F., b. Feb. 23, 1877; graduate of University of Georgia; admitted to the Cartersville bar in 1896; filled unexpired term of his brother in State senate; Mason; Methodist; Rotarian; married Katherine Lovejoy by whom there are Katherine and Warren. (5) William Akin.

BAKER, Jesse: b. in 1800 in Pendleton district, S. C., went from there to Habersham county in the early 20's, married Parthenia Moss of that county and in 1834 they removed to Cass county where he acquired a number of large estates and slaves. He was a Whig and a personal friend of Gen. Scott and Franklin Pierce. In 1870 his horse threw him and killed him instantly. He is buried near Pine Log. His wife died in 1894. Of 12 children only the following were identified with this county. (1) Thomas Hudson Baker*, b. Apr. 28, 1839, received his early education in Pine Log and at the age of 18 he entered the University at Washington and later the University of Maryland where he graduated in medicine in 1860. At the beginning of the Civil War he served as assistant surgeon in Wofford's Brigade and commanded Co. K in a Georgia regiment. At the battle of Sharpsburg he received a wound while bearing a message from Gen. Wofford to Col. Darrot. In October, 1865 he began his life as a county physician in Bartow and he probably covered more miles on his horse or in his buggy attending his patients than any doctor in north Georgia at that time. From 1873 to 1876 he represented this county in the legislature. This was during a strenuous period and Dr. Baker helped in clearing the condition of the illegal railroad bonds. He served as senator from this county from 1889 to 1901 and introduced a bill providing for the teaching of hygiene and toxicology in the public schools. He owned more than 5,000 acres in the Pine Log and Etowah river districts. He was a Royal Arch Mason; weighed 240 lbs. and never married. He died June 9, 1920 and is buried in Pine Log cemetery. He was an eccentric old man and until his death could be seen riding in his buggy with a little Negro boy attendant. (2) W. C. Baker m. Carrie Gower formerly of S. C., was a merchant and banker in Cartersville before going to Oklahoma City. A daughter, Mrs. Ella Baker Smith, lives near Cartersville. (3) J. A. Baker, lawyer, later moved to Oklahoma. (4) Mary Jane m. T. N. Stanford; of 7 children, J. W. Stanford, lives in Cartersville, Viola (dec.) taught for many years in the city schools. A son of J .W., Dr. James W. Stanford, is a practicing physician. (5) Elenor E. Baker m. William K. Brawner.

BARNSLEY, Godfrey: b. in Black Forest, England, came to the coast of Georgia and became an important citizen of Savannah and New Orleans. While at Savannah was appointed by Andrew Jackson on May 29, 1829, vice consul of the Netherlands for the Port of Savannah and on July 28, 1829, vice consul of the Two Sicilies. He was a past president of the Savannah Chamber of Commerce and officially resigned on December 1, 1845, but became an honorary member for life†. Francis S. Bartow for whom this county was named was Mr. Barnsley's attorney in Savannah. Mr. Barnsley was a cotton buyer in Savannah and New Orleans and the first bales of cotton shipped to Europe were shipped on his own vessels to Norway and he received

---

*From Knight's "Georgia and Georgians", p-2177.
†These commissions are in the possession of Mrs. A. B. Saylor.

iron chairs as a token of respect from the Norwegian king. Rev. C. W. Howard, W. H. Stiles and Mr. Barnsley were friends and encouraged each other to buy in upper North Georgia. In the late 30's or early 40's, Mr. Barnsley came to Cass county and selected a site in the 16th district for his home that was to become famous in North Georgia. Buying hundreds of acres of land near a spring and branch, hiring slaves by the year from other owners, he began building a brick home from native material that was to have the appearance of an English castle. The house plan was for a central section of 2 stories, topped with a tower, and with a right and left wing. Imported shrubs and trees from all over the world were planted and the formal gardens of boxwood from England laid out by Mr. Burkman, of Augusta, gave the place its name, "Barnsley's Garden." Modern plumbing was another feature of the plans. When the Federals under McPherson came to Barnsley's, in May 1864, led there by an enemy who told of Mr. Barnsley's wealth, as a British subject he requested protection. He had remained at home while his family refugeed. Being a connoisseur, the home contained many objets d'art and handsome furniture. These and the house were damaged when the Federals occupied the home, using it as a fortress. War, cyclones, time, and financial changes wrecked a dream mansion and a great estate. Only the left wing is now livable. The house was nearly completed except for the hand-carved stairway that was captured by Union soldiers in Nashville at the time of the Civil War. Mr. Barnsley married Julia Scarborough of Wilmington, N. C., by whom there were Anna G. Gilmour of London, England; Dr. George S. Barnsley who served in the Confederate army and later went with his brother, Lucian Barnsley, to Sao Paulo, Brazil, where they lived and died; Adelaide married a Mr. Reed of Glasgow, Scotland and died at Barnsley's; Julia Bernard married Capt. James P. Baltzelle who was a provost marshall in the Confederate army, and was killed after the war at Halls Station at a lumber mill; a daughter of their's, Mrs. Addie B. Saylor and her sons, Preston and Harry, live at the old home. Mr. Barnsley died in New Orleans on June 6, 1872 and is buried at Barnsley's.

BARRON, Thomas Green: b. July 28, 1807 in Hancock county, died May 24, 1872. Admitted to the bar in 1830 in the county of Bibb, Flint Circuit, after graduating from the State University. He first practiced in Jones county and married Nancy B. Jones of this county in 1836. Deed records show that he bought lots in the 5th district in 1836. He was a law partner of David Irwin in Cassville during the removal of the Indians. Ill health forced him to give up his practice and he gave all his time to his farm on the present Rome road, where Major Barron was considered a rich landowner. No descendants in the county.

BENHAM, Maj. Willis: b. Dec. 12, 1795 near Bristol, Conn.,

of well-to-do parents; in 1818 located in Laurens district, S. C., and in 1820 married Elizabeth Irby, a sister of Dr. William Irby, of Laurens, S. C. Following the Howards to Georgia, the Benhams, Youngs, and Milams came to Cass county from Laurens. In 1850 Maj. Benham purchased a plantation from Col. Irwin, an erratic old bachelor who raced horses, which was 3½ miles north of Cartersville. Col. Irwin had erected a brick home with an unusual flat roof; after this home was destroyed by the Federals in 1864, Maj. Benham rebuilt it as it stands today. Being a northern man he had to swear amnesty to President Johnson in 1865 as he had acquired a large estate of land and slaves.* He was a Methodist and a beloved character to friends and family; died Sept. 25, 1875, a year after his wife and both are buried in the Benham family cemetery near the old home. Their children were: (1) Dr. William Irby Benham, b. Aug. 6, 1822, d. Jan. 21, 1904, was a graduate of a medical school in Charleston, S. C., served as 2nd Lt. in the 16th Ga. Battalion during the Civil War, was a physician and farmer near Euharlee at what is now known as the Nick Adams place and at the old Benham home, m. Louisa Schulte of Charleston, S. C., by whom there were: (a) Louise, m. William Henry Lumpkin (b. Feb. 22, 1852, d. Mar. 10, 1913) who served the county as senator in 1894-95, and their son, W .H., Jr., served as representative in 1925, and as 2nd Lt., 326th Inf. 82nd Div., in World War, and m. Margaretta Womelsdorf of Cartersville. Their daughter, Bessie (d. June, 1932) m. W. H. Howard, Jr., of Cartersville and Wilmington, N. C. (b) Elizabeth, m. Thomas Lumpkin who died in 1930 and who with his brother, W. H., established the Lumpkin Hardware Company which is now the Gilreath Hardware Co. Their children were: Henry, lives in Fla.; Christine, who served in World War, m. Felix Jackson; Benham, who served as 1st Lt. and Capt. of Infantry in World War; Loulie m. Ed Strickland of Cartersville; Stuart, lives in Va.; Roslyn of Cartersville. (c) Kate, m. Albert Strickland (died 1926). She and her son, Sidney, live at the old Benham home. Willis and Herman Benham died when young men. (2) Lois, in 1845 m. J. J. Howard† in S. C., and soon came to this county. (3) Frances, m. Capt. John D. Wright of Laurens, S. C. Their daughter, Frances E. Wright, was reared by her grandfather, Maj. Benham, and she married in 1866, Rev. J. Joe Jones, a brother of Rev. Sam P. Jones. He was a private in Co. G, 22nd Ga. Inf., 1861 and a 2nd Lt., Co. H, 4th Ga. Res. C. S. A. in 1864, later 1st Lt.There were 8 children who were reared and married in this county: Lois m. Lee Simpson of Laurens, S. C., (both dec.); Annie Laurie m. A. B. Cunyus of this county; Lucy m. J. G. Simpson of Pendleton, S. C.; Evelyn m. B. L. Sims (dec.) of Shelbyville, Tenn.; W. Benham Jones, b. 1879, d. July 22, 1907; Hattie m. Dr. H. C. Hend-

---

*The names and values of these slaves are in the possession of the family.
†See Howard sketch.

erson of Charlotte, N. C.; Mrs. Frances W. Jones died in 1887 and in 1888 Rev. Jones m. Bossie Farrow of Spartanburg, S. C., by whom there was one child, Helen (Winslow). Rev. Jones and his first wife and children are buried in the Benham cemetery.

BEST, Rev. Hezekiah: b. April 15, 1801, Hagerstown, Md.; d. Jan. 12, 1878, buried at Cassville; in 1826 joined Baltimore conference in which he served 30 years; biographical sketch in "The Old Baltimore Conference"; served Rockingham and Greenbrier circuits in Virginia; instrumental in founding Seamen's Bethel in Baltimore where he also served as pastor of M. E. Church on Broadway and Old Foundry church in Washington; m. on Jan. 29, 1833, Adeline Ball of Prince William county, Va.; in Nov. 1857 moved to Cass, settled on a large estate, paying $30,000 in gold, on Two Run creek, called "Forest Home" a home noted for its hospitality; a Whig; never joined the southern conference, but built churches and preached without pay; Best's Chapel was named for him; erected grist mill, gin and saw mill on Two Run creek. Children of H. and Adeline Best, d. May 8, 1880 were: (1) Louisa A., b. Dec. 1833, m. S. K. Phillips; buried at Cassville. (2) Alfred Ball, b. Mar. 23, 1835 in Va., m. Isabella Saxon; major in Confederate army; removed to Md. (3) John W. F., b. 1837, m. Sarah V. H. Harris. (4) Hezekiah S., b. Oct. 10, 1838 in Hereford, Md., sergeant in Cobb's Legion, later in 23rd Regt.; m. Julia Clayton Trippe, daughter of Turner H. Trippe.* (5) Emory F., m. Mrs. Mary Hill. (6) Robert Newton, b. Oct. 28, 1841 in Heathsville, Va.; a scout during war; m. Oriana L. Saxon; children born in the county: Waring and Hugh, identified with Rome history; Robert of Camden, N. J.; Aileen m. Dr. Will Battle, a physician in Cassville who died on Nov. 12, 1925; Orie m. Dr. Clark Griffin, a dentist in Cartersville.

BRANDON, Thomas Wiley: b. May 16, 1803, in Halifax county, Va., a 4th son of William and Mary Langley Brandon; was reared and received what little schooling he had in Gwinnett county where the family moved in 1806 or 1807. On Jan. 7, 1830, he married Louisa Avery Green, daughter of Joseph and Bellariah Green of North Carolina. In 1835 Thomas W. Brandon came to Cass county with his brothers, Moses A., who died in Floyd county; Frances Lawson whose grandsons, John L. Burnett served 20 years as congressman from Alabama until his death in 1919, and W. W. Brandon served as governor of Alabama 1923 to 1926; and Leroy J. Brandon. Thomas W. settled on the Etowah river in the 17th district which at the time was a wilderness, and where there were only 10 voters in the district, and but two of those could read and write. At the age of 17 he joined the Methodist church and as soon as his home of logs was erected, he started a Sunday school class that was the beginning of Brandon's chapel.†

---

*Information from a daughter, Louise Best Cline of Washington, D. C.
†See history of early churches.

He was one of the early justices of the peace in his district and held the office for many years. Acquiring a large plantation he became one of the leading farmers, and this property was divided among his sons at his death. Inflexible in his principles, he was called "uncle Tommy" by those who knew him. An "old-time" Whig, he later became a Democrat. He died at his home, near Euharlee, June 11, 1874, and was buried in the family cemetery on the place. The children of T. W. and Louisa Brandon were: (1) Mary Anne m. W. J. Byers (both dec). (2) Elizabeth B., m. John S. Leake.* (3) William J., b. Jan. 4, 1835, served in Co. "F", 18th Ga. Inf., C. M. S., was taken prisoner until close of war, m. Martha S. Kirkham by whom there were: Annie m. Lee Jolly of Taylorsville and their sons, Oscar served in Co. B. 102nd Regt., 26th Div., and Walter served in 136th Co. 30th Div. in World War. Blanch m. Clarence A. Dodd of this county and Menlo, Ga., and 4 of their sons, Harold, Glover, Paul and Jerry served in the World War. Walter lives in Norman Park, Fla. Jeff m. Jack Beazley, son of Dr. J. S. Beazley (b. Aug. 12, 1832, d. May 25, 1907) and Sarah E. Asbury. Dr. Beazley was born in Fredericksburg, Va., served as surgeon in the 7th Ga. Cav. and came to Georgia, settled at Stilesboro where he practiced medicine after the Civil War. There were 2 other sons, Reuben, and Ned m. Hessie Baker. Jeff and Jack Beazley have one son, Frank. Maude† m. Jim White of Kingston. Frank† lives at the William Brandon home. W. J. Brandon was one of the founders of the Oak Grove Methodist church. (4) Parthenia A., m. W. A. Templeton who died in Confederate service and by whom there were: Clio m. Frank Colbert (dec.), lives at Stilesboro; Mary L. m. Pendleton Gaines (both dec.); Willie m. N. M. Adams (dec.). (5) Jefferson R., b. May 9, 1839, served in Co. F, 18th Ga. Regt., until rank of lieutenant in 1863, later captured prisoner and held until close of war, served as county commissioner in 1877-8-9, m. Kate Sumner by whom there were: Paul H., Will D., Moses T., Claude S. who live in the county, Hugh R. lives in Rome. (6) David P., b. Oct. 13, 1842, served in Co. F, 18th Ga. Regt. C. M. S.; m. Bettie Ida Hay (both dec.), a daughter of W. Pinckney Hay who refugeed to this county during the Civil War and settled at Taylorsville, and by whom there were: Tom W., Mary m. Abel Skannal, John R., David U., and Charles who live in Louisiana where they reared families. Joseph G., m. Martha Cole and lives on the David Brandon place. Virginia m. Marcellus Conyers. Betty m. Lawson Jackson of Cartersville. Two grandsons, D. F. Brandon and R. B. Skannal served in World War. (7) Virginia, (dec.). (8) Florence, m. W. E. Puckett (both dec.) of this county, formerly of S. C., lived at Taylorsville. Served in Co. "I", 1st. Ga. Cav., C. M. S. Their children were: Thomas B. Puckett of Valdosta, Ga., and Lois m. T. I. Charles

---

*See Leake sketch.
†Brandon.

of Conestee, S. C. (9) Avarilla, m. Henry H. Milam (both dec.) by whom there were Louisa and Henry H. Milam, Jr. Always lived near Euharlee. (10) Susan, m. John Henry Walker (both dec.) who served in Co. F, 1st Ga. Regt., Confederate service and whose father and mother were pioneer settlers, coming to this county from S. C., in 1835. Of 8 children Ethel is the only living one in the county. Thomas B. served in the 11th Bakery Co. in the World War and is now at Kelly Field, Texas. A Negro, Noah Brandon, saw Civil War service with the Brandon boys.

BOSTON, Frederick Anton: b. Feb. 5, 1809, in Rowan county, N. C.; married Fanny Houser who was born in 1815 on the 6th of January, 1833 in York district, S. C. He died March 7, 1902; was buried at Stamp Creek. Of 14 children the first one born after their removal to Cass county was Nancy Jane Boston in 1843. Other children identified with the county were: (1) Katherine Elizabeth Boston, b. in 1845 and died May 17, 1932, married J. P. Alexander and lived in the county all her life. (2) Henry F. Boston, b. 1839 in Lincoln county, m. Cora Dyar, lived in the county until their decease. (3) Jefferson Johnson Boston, b. Jan 21, 1862, lived and reared a family in the house where he was born near the Cherokee line in the Stamp Creek district. He married Zonie Matthews, daughter of Mr. and Mrs. J. A. Matthews, by whom there are 8 living children. He died April 20, 1932.

BOWDOIN, Joshua: b. Nov. 2, 1803, in Edgefield district, S. C.; came to Cass in 1835 and was one of the early Baptist preachers in the county. He was ordained at Oothcalooga church in 1837. In 1820 he married Bethsheba Fails. Justice of the inferior court in 1845-49. Their children were: (1) Frances M., b. June 2, 1822. (2) John W., b. Sept. 29, 1825 in Putnam county, graduated from University of Ga., Medical Dept. in 1852 and registered as a Bartow county physician as late as 1881. (3) Elisha F., b. Jan. 17, 1828. (4) Josephus Daniel, b. April 17, 1829 in Putnam county, member 66th Ga. Inf. in Confederate service; and later pharmacist in Kingston Hospital; J. P. for many years, m. Elizabeth Patman; died Dec. 20, 1882 at his home in Adairsville. Their son Joe P. Bowdoin, M. D., b. May 7, 1866, graduated from Atlanta Medical College in 1889, and began his practice in Adairsville, is at present Deputy Commissioner of Health for the State of Ga.;* m. Mary E. Bibb in 1889 by whom there were: Hypatia m. T. N. Ray, Joe Bibb, Max M., Mary Bess, Charles Daniel, Esther m. W. J. Crouch. Dr. Bowdoin's residence is in Adairsville, where he has been active in all the affairs of his city. (5) Joshua W., b. Nov. 2, 1834.

BURGE, Nathaniel: b. January 8, 1790 in Virginia, a son of Woody and Judy Burge who moved from Virginia to Rutherford county, N. C., where he was reared. On November 18, 1815 married Nancy

---

*See Georgia O. & S. Register, 1929, p-23-24).

Green, daughter of Joseph and Bellariah Green and they settled in 1824 on Sweet Water creek in Gwinnett county until in 1837 they removed to Cass county where he purchased 800 acres on the Etowah river in one of the "horseshoe bends." He and his wife were among the founders of the Raccoon Creek Baptist Church where he served as deacon and gave the land for the present church and cemetery. A prosperous farmer, public-spirited, Democrat; he died Dec. 18, 18⎵ at his home near Euharlee and is buried in the Burge family cemetery. Children of "Natty" and Nancy Burge were: (1) Joseph G., b. Dec. 1, 1815, (dec.). (2) William Twitty, b. Jan. 20, 1820 in North Carolina. After coming to Cass, was engaged in sawmill business, in 1845 purchased a farm in the Stilesboro community, during Civil War was a quartermaster of the State troops; was in 1862-65 justice of the inferior court, a Whig, then Democrat, was active in organization of Populist party, represented the county in the general assembly, 1890-91, on Feb. 3, 1845, married Melissa Smith, daughter of Samuel Smith by whom there were 10 children: Nancy, lives in Atlanta, m. John Munford of Polk county; Texanna, m. John T. Wofford, has children in Fla.; Susan, living near Rockmart, m. J. S. Davitt of Polk county; Dora, m. A. S. McGregor of Cedartown (both dec.); Ida, m. Samuel E. Smith, who served in Confederacy, his wife and children live in Rockmart; James W., b. Dec. 3, 1857, d. Dec. 28, 1928, m. Etta Hines, lived at home place, a daughter, Idora, is only survival in the county. (3) Adolphus Green, b. Oct. 5, 1823, d. May 22, 1854, is buried at Euharlee. (4) Mary Elizabeth, b. June 2, 1826, m. Daniel Brunson Cunyus of Houston county who came to this county in 1843 and became a large and prosperous land owner near Stilesboro. He died May 12, 1889, and he and his wife are buried in the Burge cemetery on the Etowah river. The old home is yet standing. Of 10 children these reached maturity: (a) Dr. Henry D., b. April 1, 1848, m. twice, lives in Rome. (b) Nannie J., m. Elias Skannal and has descendents in La., d. Dec. 1887. (c) M. Frances m. J. T. Conyers, d. Dec. 16, 1928. (d) Robert N., b. Oct. 23, 1851, d. Sept. 14, 1929, unmarried. (e) John William, b. Dec. 1, 1853, m. Cora Whaley by whom there are Susie, May Belle, and John who served in the World War, lives in Decatur. (f) M. E. (Ella), m. Charles Jones (both dec.) by whom there were 3 children, buried in Cartersville. (g) Adolphus Burge, b. July 17, 1860, d. April 1937, m. Annie Laurie Jones, d. Dec. 5, 1953, by whom there were Dorothy m. the Rev. B. F. Pim, and Lucy, the historian of Bartow county. The half brother of D. B. Cunyus, Rev. William Cunyus, was a teacher and preacher in Stilesboro and Taylorsville and reared a large family. Of his children, Sallie, m. J. K. Rowan; Creed, m. Villa Leake of this county (both dec.), Charlie, Fort, and Homer removed to Texas, Daniel, m. Alice Hawkins of this county (both dec.), Mittie, m. E. H. Janes (dec.), Ida and Maude Jessie never married. (5.) Eliza Anne, m. Russel H. Cannon, b. Feb. 24, 1815, d. May 5, 1890, represented

1. The A. W. Buford home. 2. The rock house built by I. O. McDaniel. 3. The Shelman home before it was burned. 4. The W. H. Stiles home. 5. The home of Mrs. Corra Harris.

the county two terms in the senate, active in the political and educational affairs of the Stilesboro community and Cartersville. Their children were: (a) Henry (dec.). (b) Fanny, m. Jim Colbert (both dec.), children live in Fla. (c) Nathaniel B., died in 1931, has a son, Roy, who lives at Stilesboro. (d) John, (dec.). (e) Joseph B., m. Mattie Sproull by whom there were Willie Belle, m. C. B. Hawkins, Charlie, m. Allie Tinsley, Flossie m. Dr. M. F. Haygood, Fanny (dec.) m. Roy Harris. (6) Jane m. John F. Sproull. (7) Joseph P., died in 1861, 1st Lt. Co. K, 19th Ga. Regt. (8) Robert M. (dec.).

BUFORD, Rev. Alfred Welsh: b. in 1809 in Garrard county, Ky.; educated at Center College, Danville, in the graduating class with John C. Breckenridge; desired to enter the Presbyterian ministry, but took up study of law. Not feeling inspired by law, he came to Georgia in 1832 with a letter of recommendation from Gov. Letcher of Ky. to Gov. Lumpkin, upon which he was placed in charge of Prospect Academy in Oglethorpe county, beginning an active life in educational affairs; in 1838 married Sarah Emolyn, daughter of Andrew Woody Jackson, a rich land owner of Gwinnett county who had bought the same year (October) from an Indian, Johnson Thompson, 8 160-acre lots for $12,000 in the 5th district of this county, which later became their home; ordained for the Baptist ministry in 1840 and spent the remainder of his life preaching and organizing Baptist churches; a trustee of Cherokee Baptist College; trustee of Mercer, traveled in interest of it; children of A. W. and S. E. Buford were: (1) Cyrena, m. Albert Eakin of Shelbyville, Tenn. (2) Sarah E., m. in 1866 Dr. Joel G. Greene, b. Jan. 15, 1842 in Troup county, served as captain in the regiment of his brother, Col. Alec Greene, all four years of the war and was wounded in battle of Peachtree creek, after war studied medicine, graduated from Atlanta Medical College 1886 and came to Cartersville in 1888 where he was identified with the professional, religious and civic life of the community until his death, Oct. 2, 1906. Children: Lillian; Dr. Alfred B. Greene, graduate of Atlanta College of Physicians and Surgeons 1900, d. in March, 1924, a prominent and popular physician in the county, m. Ida Vernon; Mary H. (dec.), m. C. N. Waits of Rockmart; J. Garnett, Jr. (dec.) m. Geneva, daughter of Wm. S. Attaway, their daughter, Marion, m. Lewis Peeples. (3) Alfred Jackson, m. Ella Kinabrew, children in county: Alberta L. m. W. D. Rowland; Andrew William m. Grace Gilreath; Louis J. m. Ida Vernon Greene, now living on original Buford home place; Cyrena E. m. T. W. Simpson, two children, Eleanor and T. W., Jr. (4) Martha Eliza, m. James C. Milam (both dec.). (5) Marion, in 1891 m. Dr. Joel G. Greene, d. Jan. 20, 1930. (6) Oliver H., b. in this county, graduate of University of Georgia in 1889, surgeon in Spanish-American War, in charge of Ft. St. Phillips in La., practiced medicine with his brother-in-law, Dr. J. G. Greene, in Cartersville, owned Buford Drug Co., active in church and social life, batchelor, died 1909. The Bufords are buried in Cartersville. (7 and 8) Andrew Marshall and Edward Franklin Buford died young.

CHUNN, Samuel Love: b. Oct., 1806 in Buncombe county, N. C., d. Sept. 8, 1863. He came to Cassville when a young man, courted and married in 1838 Elizabeth Word, a daughter of James and Elizabeth Vance Word, while visiting the Hooper's. They bought property in 1837 from Z. Hargrove on which he built a store with one of the Patton relatives and a home place which yet belongs to the Chunns. They removed to Asheville, N. C., for a number of years where Mr. Chunn's father owned much of what is now the city of Asheville, later returning to Cassville where they lived until they both died and were buried in the Cassville cemetery. Mr. Chunn was a retiring, stern man; an elder in the Presbyterian church—he always wrote out his prayers. Their only child, William Augustus, was born near the French Broad river in Tenn. He lived and died in Cassville. He married Lila Land by whom there were: Helen m. W. A. Gilbert (dec.), lives near Cassville; Jennie (dec.) m. Robert Garwood; Gertrude and Eugene live at the old home place; Mona m. A. J. Conyers (dec.), lives in Athens; Freeman L. lives in Cincinatti; William S. m. Fannie Sue McTier, lives in Cassville.

COBB, Humphrey W.: b. in Greenville district, July 16, 1816. In 1837 married Mary Grace Black, sister of Gen. George S. Black, and they came to Cass in 1840 and first settled near Stilesboro. He and Gen. Black had a mercantile store in Cassville and were later in the same business in Rome, Ga. Mr. Cobb was elected clerk of the superior court in 1852 and served as county treasurer from 1875 until his death on June 12, 1894. Children of H. W. and M. G. Cobb were: (1) Mary J., b. Aug. 1838, m. T. G. Wilkes, d. 1900. (2) John H. Cobb, b. Dec. 25, 1840, married Ida Douglas of Va., d. Dec. 19, 1921. Children: Mary m. W. C. Satterfield and L. J. Backus, lives in Cartersville; Lizabel m. Bob Gilreath, lives in Cartersville; Harry m. Dot Bilbro, lives in Cartersville. (3) George Seaborn Cobb, b. March 10, 1842, d. Feb. 5, 1909, m. Buena Vista Cooper, of Franklin Co. who died in May 1932. Children: George S., b. 1874, d. April 4, 1932; Jessie m. J. T. Dixon. (4) Sarah E., b. Jan. 25, 1845, d. July 24, 1899.

CONYERS, Bennett Hill: b. March 22, 1800, in Franklin county, N. C., was the 6th son of Ross and Betty Denson Conyers, descendents of a long English and French line. In 1804 Ross Conyers and his family moved to Greene county, Ga., and he and his son, Bennett, were surveyors. Having surveyed in this section, Bennett Conyers bought a number of acres on the Etowah river and moved his family here in 1835. He became a large slave owner, hired them out, and was a neighbor of the Tumlins, Sproulls, Fouches, Stiles and Shelmans. He died

Nov. 6, 1865 at his plantation home and is buried in Cartersville. In 1830 he married Elizabeth Bowen in Carroll county by whom there were the following children: (1) Christopher B., b. in Coweta county, m. Frances H. Bullock by whom there were 6 sons and one daughter; served in the Confederate army as a private; was sheriff of this county in 1873. A son, Christopher B., is a prominent jurist in Brunswick, Ga. (2) William J., b. Sept. 12, 1835, graduate of Emory College, m. Virginia, daughter of Col. Lindsay Johnson, by whom there were Flora m. A. W. Fite, and Arnold lives in Florida; served in Confederate army, solicitor for county court at the time of his death on Sept. 6, 1866. (3) Sarah, m. Marcellus Pritchett (both dec.) by whom there were 7 children born in Cartersville who are now identified with other states. (4) James Bennett, b. Nov. 22, 1846 in Cass County, served in the Confederate army under Col. Robert C. Saxon and Lieut.-Col. Allen D. Candler in Co. H., 4th Ga. Regt., was paroled May, 1865 at Montgomery, Ala.; in 1866 married Maria H. Field, daughter of E. Field, who died one year later, in 1874 entered the University of Georgia, in 1876 married Eliza B. Newton of Athens, a Baptist, practiced law in Cartersville until he died June 6, 1909. The children of J .B. and E. B. Conyers are Kittie m. Frank Matthews (dec.), Elizabeth B. m. W. T. Townsend, James Bennett, lives in Ft. Myers, Fla., William N., John L. and C. T. were born and educated in Cartersville, University of Georgia, served in the World War and are now identified with Atlanta. (5) Rebecca, m. Miller Gilreath by whom there were 5 children who are identified with Atlanta. (6) Joel T., b. Oct. 31, 1850, d. Jan. 31, 1915, m. Mary Fannie Cunyus, daughter of Daniel B. Cunyus, was a farmer, acquiring the Cunyus plantation near Stilesboro. Their children were: Mary m. Rev. J. J. Bennett, Claude (dec.) m. Minnie Leake, J. Marcellus m. Virginia Brandon.

CRAWFORD, John: b. May 11, 1789 in Greenville district, S. C., of poor Virginia parents. In 1814 he served 6 months in the Creek war under Gen. Jackson. He returned to farming in Laurens district and married Martha Clore, b. Mar. 21, 1801, d. July 4, 1875. He joined the Rocky Mountain Baptist church, S. C., in 1819 and was soon ordained to preach. About 1838 he came to this part of the State on horseback looking for a place on which to settle, carrying money with which to purchase. He located on a tract of land of 400 acres just west of Cassville on which was the Peggamore spring, named for an Indian family that lived near it. In January 1836 he moved his wife and 6 children to this home among the Indians and the few white settlers. His brother-in-law, Mason Clore, came with him from S .C., and they, with their Negro slaves, drove the first wagon from Cassville to Adairsville. John Crawford ministered to the pioneers amid the roughness of frontier life and organized and served Baptist churches in Cherokee Georgia at a time when there was a great need for the Word of God.

He served the Cassville Baptist church 21 consecutive years; a prime mover in the organization of the Middle Cherokee Association, serving as moderator for a number of years. He gave the land for the Cherokee Baptist College, was a large contributor and was the first president of the board of trustees; a progressive farmer; an ardent Democrat; active in all matters affecting the welfare of the people; died on Aug. 3, 1873. and was survived by his wife and all his children; buried in the Cassville cemetery. The children were: (1) Eliza, m. D. H. Hodge (both dec.) and there were 7 children. (2) Harvey S., m. 1st Lydia McElvane, 2nd to Mrs. Martha Cobb. (3) John Aaron, b. July 4, 1824, d. May 20, 1876 from a bee sting, was a lawyer and represented this county in the legislature of 1853-4, a captain of Co. K, 18th Ga. Regt., serving until Dec. 1864, was wounded at Sharpsburg and Gettysburg, never married. (4) Belton O., b. Jan. 11, 1827, d. Sept. 3, 1903, went to school to Rev. "Jimmie" George near Kingston, read law and was admitted to the bar in 1851, locating at Adairsville until 1858. He returned to his father's farm and became a progressive planter, he was a justice of the inferior court from 1861-65, in 1863 he was commissioned captain of Co. E, Price's Battalion; a trustee of the Cherokee Baptist College and later of Ryal's high school in Gordon county. In 1852 he married Biddie Fullilove, b. July 29, 1834—d. Aug. 1, 1868, by whom there was Sally W., m. John C. McTier, and James B. (dec.) m. 1st Della Griffin by whom there were: Tom, Paul and Corinne, 2nd Louodire Redwine by whom there are Bessie m. David Bishop and Lucy (Harris). Belton O. m. a 2nd time, Sarah F. Fullilove, a sister-in-law, by whom there were: Johnnie, m. Joe Gordon (dec.) by whom there are Robert C., lives in Cartersville, O'Neil, Joseph and Sarah; Michael lives in Decatur. (5) Michael J., b. Aug. 27, 1829, (dec.) never married 1st Lieut. Co. E, 18th Ga. Regt. in Confederate service, wounded in 1861. He was elected to the legislature in 1868 but could not qualify because he had held public office before the war. (6) Mary S., b. April 24, 1832, m. John C. Farris (dec). A daughter, Mrs. Lyda Tribble Smith, lives at Cassville. Her sons are Farris, Harold and J. C. Tribble.

DODD, William: b. 1792 in Union district, S. C.; married Nancy Griswold by whom he had 15 children. With his family he came to Cass in 1831, settling where Cass Station now is. His wife died there. While living there he gave the right of way for the W. & A. R.R. through his property. He removed to Spartanburg, S. C., after his wife's death and while there married Judith Rhodes by whom he had 3 sons. He returned to Cass county in 1845 and settled near Fairmount where he died in 1872. He and his wife are buried at Ryo. Two of these sons are yet living, T. J., 90 years of age, lives at Fairmount and Alec Dodd. The children of William Dodd identified with county history are: (1) Christopher Dodd, b. in 1818, helped to remove the Indians from the county in 1838, m. Sarah Lowry, daughter of David

Lowry, lived and reared a large family near Euharlee and died there in 1894. Their children were: Thomas W., was admitted to the Cartersville bar in Sept. '66, died in Loredo, Tex.; Serena, a graduate of Cassville Female College, m. C. V. Gemes of Kingston by whom there were T. V., Christopher of Kingston, Viola m. Frank Stephens, Fanny lives in Kingston; Warren A., m. Emma, daughter of the Rev. Edmond Harling, represented the county in the legislature in 1913-14, farmer, Baptist, of 8 children Mamie, m. W. M. Dorsey, lives in Cartersville. (2) James H., has three daughters living in the Iron Hill district, Mattie, Etta, Willie, a son, J. H., lives at Halls Station. A nephew of William Dodd, R. Hayne Dodd, a son of Jesse Dodd, was a rominent farmer on the Etowah river, near Kingston after the Civil War. He married Fannie Gore, who was a graduate of Cassville Female College, and they reared a family of boys prominently connected with the State.

DOUTHIT, James: b. in 1800 in Rowan county, N. C., came to Cass county in 1833. He was followed in 1838 by his father and mother, William (b. 1776—d. 1859) and Lovey Cooper (of Maryland) Douthit. James Douthit, a bachelor, and his father operated a chartered ferry on the Etowah river and acquired a plantation on the old Dallas and Alabama roads. The original home was burned. James, who died in 1881, and the older Douthits are buried on the home place. Besides James the children were: Frances, Pauline, William, Annie, Sarah (b. 1816-d. 1884) m. James Cleghorn (1811-1889), a brother of Charles Cleghorn who was identified with Cassville until his removal to Columbus, and N. Charles W. Douthit. A daughter of Sarah and James Cleghorn, Mary, married W. S. Hills and was a member of the Etowah Chapter D. A. R. before her decease. A son of Sarah and James Cleghorn, William Douthit, served in the Confederate army and is buried in Cartersville. N. C. W. Douthit m. Nancy Hutchins (both dec.) and their daughter, Mrs. Emma D. Stephens of Cartersville, owns the old home place.

ERWIN, John Askew: b. Nov. 13, 1824, in Habersham county, Ga., came with his father to Cassville in 1834. He first clerked in the store of Sullivan & Black and in 1848 started in the mercantile business for himself. On December 13, 1848 married Jane E., daughter of Judge J. W. Hooper, by whom there were: Ella m. O. E. Mitchell (dec.) of Cartersville, now lives in Calif.; Hugh died in Cartersville in 1868; Harry died in Athens in 1930; Hattie m. L. L. Peak and lives in Chattanooga, Tenn. Mr. Erwin moved to Cartersville in 1854 where he engaged in the mercantile business before and after the Civil War, the first firm being known as Erwin, Stokely & Williams; then later the firm name was Erwin & Howard and last, Erwin & Ramsauer. He was active in educational and civic affairs of the city; Erwin street was named for him. During the war he served in the Confederate army, ranking as major. He was a member and steward in the Methodist church and superintendent of the Sunday school for years. Mrs. Erwin died Sept. 16, 1859, and he afterwards married Isa Beall by whom there were: (1) Grace m. John C. Henderson (dec.) lives in Athens, Ga. (2) Sam m. Annie McConnell, lives in Chattanooga, their son, McConnell Erwin, is a graduate of the Tennessee School for the Blind, Cincinnati Conservatory, Fontainebleau and a pupil of Philipp and Dupre, and at present is city organist of Chattanooga. (3) Justine m. C. A. Talmadge (dec.) lives in Athens, Ga. (4) Allie m. Charles Aull (dec.) lives in Chattanooga. Major Erwin left Cartersville in August, 1879 and moved his family to Tennessee where he had bought a farm. He died in 1883 and he and his family are buried in Cartersville.

FIELD, Elijah Murphy: and his twin brother Elias E. Field were born Jan. 3, 1819 in Pickens district, S. C.; settled in Canton, Cherokee county, in 1843. In 1845 he represented Cherokee county in the legislature. In 1854 he bought a large plantation from Pumpkinvine creek to the Etowah and property in Cartersville. He was appointed assistant commissary general of the State of Georgia on Nov. 16, 1861. During this service while with his family, who refugeed to Bethany, now Wadley, Ga., he died on Oct. 9, 1864 and is buried there. Col. Field, as he was called, was related to the Lewises and Earles, and on May 10, 1849, at "Earle's Furnace" in Cass county, he married Cornelia Maxey Harrison, who was born in 1820 in Greenville, S. C., while on a visit in this county. Of 9 children these were reared and married in this county: (1) Mariah H. m. J. B. Conyers, died Jan. 17, 1869. (2) Richard H., b. Dec. 27, 1853, near Canton was admitted to the Cartersville bar, later removing to Kansas City where he died in 1930, m. Annie Camp of Marietta. (3) Jeremiah Elijah, b. Jan. 14, 1856, m. May Hampton of Kentucky, was a cotton merchant in Cartersville until his death in 1916. There were two children: Cornelia m. Harris Cope (dec.) by whom there is one son, Harris, Jr.; Hampton (dec.) m. Irene Walker, daughter of the late B. S. Walker of Monroe, and there are two children. (4) James Madison, b. Oct. 21, 1857, m. Loula Shepherd, a daughter of John W. Shepherd and Mary Skinner who owned the Smith plantation before the Civil War where the J. H. Gilreath farm now is. Other children of J. W. and M. S. Shepherd were: Georgia m. Samuel Wilkins of Atlanta; Dr. J. Thomas who practiced medicine in the county, and was born in Troup county and a graduate of Univ. of Maryland in 1874, married Emily Shulte; Virginia m. J. H. Wikle; Alice m. A. J. Shropshire; Fannie m. Dr. Henry C. Ramsauer, and Estelle lives in Atlanta. Mr. Field lived in Cartersville until his death on September 2nd, 1929. Their children were: J. M., Jr., Margaret (White), Carolyn (Crane) and Alice. (5) Eliza Earle, b. May 23, 1860, in Cartersville, m. James S. Tumlin, (dec.) son of Thomas Tumlin by whom there were 4 children, Sarah (Connor), Bernice and Clarence live in Cartersville. (6) Caroline S., m. J.W.L. Brown, (both dec.) by whom there was one son. (7) Cornelia Maxcy, b. Feb. 28, 1865, m. Herbert A. Camp (dec.) and lives in Hattiesburg, Miss.

FITE, Henderson Wesley: b. Nov. 27, 1824 in McMinn county, Tenn., came to what is now a part of Gordon county in 1844. He was a descendant of Johannes Vogt or Fogt in Saxony who migrated to Pennsylvania, and thence to North Carolina. A graduate of the Nashville Medical College, he served as surgeon of the 40th Ga. Regt. until its surrender in April, 1865. After the war he practiced medicine in the Pine Log district where he was a member of the county board, a Mason and member of Presbyterian church until his death on Oct. 30, 1911. He married in 1850 Sarah Denman, daughter of Felix G. Denman who, also, came to this county and was a land and slave owner. Of 7 children Augustus Warren Fite and Dr. Richard L. Fite, who was licenced to practice in 1881, are identified with this county. A. W. was born on his father's farm in Gordon county, June 15, 1852. He was educated in the common schools of Gordon and later attended the Pine Log Masonic Institute, where he later taught. He read law in the office of Col. Abda Johnson in Cartersville and was admitted to the Cartersville bar in 1874 where he began an active practice. He opposed Dr. Felton in the Felton-Clements race for Congress, and continued active in Democratic politics all his life. He served as a member of the State executive committee and was delegate to various State conventions; represented Bartow in the legislature in 1882-4 and advocated the bill that made Bartow a "dry" territory in 1884; served as solicitor general of the Cherokee circuit from 1888 to 1892; was elected judge of the circuit in 1896 and served 20 consecutive years. He was considered one of the ablest prosecuting officers in the State, and as judge he administered the law without fear or favor. He was active in all Masonic circles and was an elder in the Cumberland Presbyterian church near Pine Log. He married on Dec. 22, 1880, Florida Lillian Conyers, daughter of Col. William J. and Virginia Johnson Conyers, and of 10 children 6 were reared in Cartersville: William Conyers Fite, a graduate of Emory and Annapolis, was assitsant pay master in the U. S. navy with the rank of lieutenant-commander,m. Rosebud Johnson, daughter of Dr. Lindsay and Mary Curry Johnson; Augustus W. Jr., (dec.); Flora (dec.); Lindsay Johnson, lives in Oklahoma; Sarah, lives in Cartersville; Joel A., lives in Florida. Judge Fite died at his home in Cartersville on Dec. 25, 1919, and is buried in the city cemetery.

FORD, Francis Marion: b. 1832 in Dickson county, Tenn., came to Cass county with his family in 1850 and immediately engaged in the iron business. He and D. S. Ford, a brother, ran a furnace on Stamp creek until the war. In 1861 he raised a company for infantry service and was made captain of Co. H., in the 18th Ga. Regt. After the battle of Fredericksburg he was promoted to lieut.-col. of the regiment until its surrender in 1865. After the war he was in the mercantile business in Cartersville; in 1868 he was elected to the State legislature from the county; he was serving his 2nd term as mayor of Cartersville when he died September 21, 1903. He was a member of the school board. He married Fanny Barber and their children were: Frank, lives in Baltimore, Md.; Lena was a teacher in the Cartersville schools for years, now lives in Miami; James lives in Maryland; Lizzie lives in Memphis; Hugh F. lives in Miami, Fla. Henry P. Ford, a brother of Col. Ford, m. Hamiter Poole, a daughter of Benjamin J. Poole who had a furnace on upper Stamp creek in the 50's. H. P. Ford died in 1890, leaving Harry D. Ford and Bessie m. Tom Foster, the only children in Cartersville. Lou, a sister of Col. Ford, m. Reuben Satterfield. A son, Frank Satterfield, lives in Cartersville.

FOUCHE, Col. Simpson: educator and farmer in the county, built homes and schools near Cartersville and Rowland Springs. His son, R. T. Fouche, b. in 1836, Hancock county, d. in 1908, was a lawyer in Rome, m. Rebecca Sproull, daughter of Col. and Mrs. J. C. Sproull; represented this county in the State senate in 1880-81 and 1898-99. Col. Sproull built a home on the Etowah river, about 1836, called "Valley View", which is one of the few remaining southern mansions in the county. It is now the home of Sproull Fouche, son of R. T. Fouche, b. in 1871 at the old home, a former president of the Citizens Bank in Rome, Ga., married Edith Carver of Chattooga county; was appointed to consular service in Roumania in 1920, later studied the economic and cotton situation by traveling in India, China, and Japan; in 1924 appointed commercial attache by the secretary of commerce to the American Legation at Bucharest, Roumania, in which he is yet serving.

GAINES, James: b. 1791 in Laurens district, S. C., was a son of Richard Gaines, "the Minute Man"—so called in a "History of the Gaines Family"*. He was a soldier in the War of 1812 and fought the Indians in South Ga., and Fla. He married Margaret Clore about 1812 and selling his farm in Laurens at a loss in the 30's, he with his family and slaves removed to Georgia, working on rented lands near Adairsville on the old Hamilton-Fitten place. He was one of the charter members of the Oothcalooga Baptist church. Later he bought land near Cassville and by hard work he left his children an estate; died Oct. 1856 at Adairsville. The children identified with this county were: (1) Ava, b. 1814, m. Mansfield Simmons about 1835 in Laurens county, S. C., and moved in 1837, near the McDow-Stoner place at Adairsville. He was a tax receiver for Cass county. There were 3 children. (2) Reuben, b. 1815 in Laurens district, went to school in that district, m. Elizabeth Walker in Jan. 1836 and moved near Adairsville and lived 19

*In possession of Mrs. Jno. C. McTier.

years at the Tillman Leake place, then in 1856 he moved to Texas and during the Civil War served in the Texas state troops. They returned to Gordon county in 1871 and she died in 1886. He m. Alice Sanders of Rome, and he died in 1899 and is buried at Oothcalooga. Most of the children are identified with Texas in Navarro county, except the following: James M., oldest son of Reuben, b. Mar. 15, 1841, in Adairsville, d. Dec. 19, 1916, buried at Adairsville, served in 22nd Tex. Reg., Walker's Div., his wife and children are identified with Anderson county, Tex. Henry W. Gaines was born in 1852 in Adairsville and is identified with Calhoun. Lewis Pendleton (dec.), b. Mar. 24, 1849 at Adairsville, m. 1st Mahala Barrett by whom there were these children identified with Bartow, James Pendleton, b. 1878, m. Lillie Graves of Halls Station; Bessie L. m. J. M. Lang, attorney in Calhoun; Ethel Lee m. O. B. Bishop of Adairsville; Milton P., a son by a 2nd marriage, m. Susie Veach of Adairsville; Hallie m. M. Jolly of Rome, Sarah Frances m. Max Bowdoin; and Claud Gaines of Atlanta. Lewis Pendleton Gaines ran a mill in partnership with L. P. Lewis at Cave, near Kingston but later he removed to Adairsville; he, like all the Gaines, loved singing and family ties; is author of the "History of the Gaines Family". (3) Frances, b. 1816, m. Bayless W. Lewis in 1841 and lived in Adairsville, their children were Jesse, Bayless, Maggie, Fannie, John Prince, m. Ada Galt and lived in Cartersville. (4) Enoch, in 1873 m. Delia Wright and was a merchant in Adairsville, died at the age of 49 and is buried at Oothcalooga cemetery. (5) Amelia, m. O. D. Anderson in 1845 and lived in Adairsville. Before the war he served as railroad agent and postmaster there. Their children were: Laura m. A. M. Foute of Cartersville; Ella m. Z. A. Reynolds, of Tex.; Anna and Julia m. J. M. Neel of Adairsville and Cartersville. (6) Susan, b. 1826, d. 1912, m. O. D. Anderson after the death of her sister Amelia. Another Gaines connection was the family of James H. Gaines, b. Oct. 1856, a son of Richard and Mary Daniel Gaines, who lived at Cass Station all his life. He traveled only in his latter life. He said at one time, "I have traveled 40 miles north to Shumake in Murray county where I attended one of Showalter's normal singing schools; and I have traveled south 40 miles to Smyrna where I taught a singing school myself; and I have traveled east 20 miles to Waleska where I carried some of my children to attend a better school; and I have traveled 40 miles west to Gadsden, Ala., to marry Miss Susie Kelly, the best woman in the world." There were 10 children; the youngest daughters, Bessie, Katie, Mattie and Maggie, before they married traveled this section as the Gaines Quartet. All this family were singers. Mr. and Mrs. Gaines are still living at the old home and a son, Albert, lives with them. Another son of Richard and Mary Daniel Gaines was: William P. Gaines, b. in Cassville, Jan. 11, 1846, enlisted in Co. I, 1st Ga. Regt. in 1863 and served until he surrendered with Gen. Wheeler at Greensboro, N. C. In 1868 he was converted under the preaching of Gen. Clement A.

Evans, who was preaching in the Cassville circuit at that time, and for 25 years Mr. Lewis served as superintendent of Best's Chapel Sunday school. On Dec. 23, 1875, he married Sarah E. Linn, who died April 17, 1886 leaving a son, Orr (dec.), and Mary F., who married Rev. T. L. Rutland, and Ida. On Dec. 29, 1897, he married Mary Carlisle near Folsom by whom there was one son, W. Paul Gaines. "Billie" Gaines lived near Cassville all his life and is buried in the Cassville cemetery. He died Sept. 19, 1913.

GILREATH, Nelson: b. 1812 in Scotland, came with his brothers, George H., Caleb, William, Wesley, and Perry from South Carolina to Cass county in 1837. Nelson was an Indian trader between Cassville and Augusta, Ga., and settled at one time at Cass Station. In 1852 he was appointed agent of W. & A. R.R., at Cass Station in place of T. G. Dunlap. George H. was a farmer all his life and a local Methodist preacher around Cassville and was interested in the agricultural and religious life of his community. His sons in the county were Jabez and Patrick and Dr. Geo. H., and Spartan A. Gilreath, who lives in the county, are grandsons. Dr. Geo. H. Gilreath moved to middle Georgia after 1881. Caleb left no heirs. Nelson Gilreath married three times. His first wife was a Gibson and their eldest son, James H. Gilreath, b. in 1839 in this county served as 1st lieutenant of Co. I, 1st Ga. Regt., in Confederate army, was the son in the Nelson Gilreath & Son firm that was successful in Cartersville in the 70's, a progressive farmer near Cartersville, represented the county in the legislature 2 terms, member and deacon of the Baptist church, married twice, 1st to Bettie Munford on Oct. 30, 1866, 2nd to Kate Tomlinson who died April 12, 1931. He died Dec. 18, 1931. The following children are living in Cartersville: Louie, Serena, J. Hugh, Ben C., Grace, m. A. W. Buford. Nelson Gilreath's 2nd wife was Martha Hardin, daughter of James H. Hardin, by whom there were Miller H., and Elliott m. W. Ferguson of Rockmart. Martha Gilreath died Jan. 9, 1852. His 3rd wife was Elizabeth Hargis by whom there were 14 children. Paul Gilreath is the only one living in the county at present. He has been mayor of the city of Cartersville several terms, m. Marilu Wofford by whom there were W. H. (dec.), Pauline, Paul Jr., Henrietta, "Jeffie," Susie, and Nelson. Lem Gilreath, another son of Nelson and Elizabeth Hargis, was an evangelistic singer and reared a family of 4 boys Reid, Samuel, Robin & Morgan Gilreath in the country near Cartersville. He died in 1910. Nelson Gilreath died Dec. 9, 1889 and is buried in the city cemetery. Mrs. Nelson Gilreath married W. A. Pepper and removed to South Carolina.

GOLDSMITH, Major Turner: came to Cass county with his wife, Maria L., and children from Charleston, S. C., in 1848. They first located on Pumpkinvine creek. He was a farmer; a Baptist. All of the children reached maturity in the county: Dr. William T. Goldsmith, Lucie Elizabeth m. Col. Lewis Tumlin, Maria L. m. Geo. J. Howard of

Cartersville, John H., Washington L., attended Cherokee Baptist College and was comptroller general of the State 1872-79, James M. attended Cherokee Baptist College, left Cartersville a member of the Etowah Guards which later formed the 1st Ga. Battalion and is yet living, Jere W., and Paul T. All six of the sons saw Confederate service and their descendants are identified with Atlanta and other cities in Georgia.

GRAY, James H.: came with his wife, Jemima Reynolds, and their two children from near Augusta, Ga., to Cass in 1832 where he had drawn land, and built in what is now Adairsville the second house of a white settler among the Indians. Their son, John W. Gray, b. June 5, 1829 in Columbia county, grew up in Oothcalooga valley, went to Calif. during the gold rush of '49, returned to Adairsville and became a merchant, married Sarah Venable, daughter of James L. Venable, organized the 8th Ga. Battl. and became colonel of the 42nd, in 1871-72 represented the county in the legislature, erected a cotton mill in Adairsville, died Nov. 11, 1911. Children of John W. and Sarah Gray: (1) Lucinda J. m. W. W. Trimble, lives near Adairsville. (2) Franklin Pierce, died in 1886, was a lawyer in Cartersville and Atlanta, editor of Cartersville Express in 1878, m. Cora Tumlin, daughter of Lewis Tumlin. (3) Ella, died young. (4) Josephine, b. Nov. 17, 1857, postmistress under Pres. Cleveland's administration, d. Oct. 13, 1932. (5) James Richard, b. Sept. 30, 1859, educated at Annianna Institute, graduated in 1878 from Dahlonega, studied law with Abda Johnson in Cartersville, was admitted to the bar in January, 1879, and soon located in Atlanta where he was successful in the profession. In 1881 he married May Inman, daughter of W. P. Inman of Atlanta by whom there were 5 children. In December, 1901, he began editorial and business management of The Atlanta Journal, and in 1905, by purchasing interest of Morris Brandon and H. M. Atkinson, became controlling owner of the Journal until his death in 1917. Mr. Gray is further identified with Fulton county history.

HARDIN, William: b. in 1798 in Washington county, a son of Valentine and Margaret Castelberry Hardin; served for a very short time in forts during the War of 1812; in September, 1821 m. Nancy Cloud, a daughter of a Revolutionary soldier, Ezekiel Cloud, who is buried near McDonough, and Elizabeth Harman. He built the first house in McDonough and was elected first clerk of Henry county superior court. In 1831 he received a commission from Lewis Cass, then secretary of war, to go to New Echota in Murray county to persuade the Cherokees to sign the treaty to exchange lands. He was appointed colonel of the 7th Div. Ga. Militia on Jan. 3, 1833, by Gov. Lumpkin. Col. Hardin lived at New Echota, in a house formerly occupied by Moravian missionaries, when in 1833 he was appointed one of the enrolling agents. In 1835 he represented Cass county in the senate and at this time his family lived in Cassville. He brought into North Ga. the first mahogany furniture. The furniture was bought by Gov. Geo. R. Gilmer, ordered made by him in England, and by the time it reached Charleston he was out of office. John Howard Payne,* author of "Home Sweet Home", was a visitor in the Hardin home after his release in 1835 from arrest by the State troops. Col. Hardin hurried from Milledgeville to help prove his innocence. Col. Hardin was president, 1837-45, of the Western Bank of Georgia in Rome. He had plantations in Randolph county, but in 1837 sold it to his son-in-law, Dr. Burdett, and the Armuchee mill plantation in Floyd county. After a short residence in Rome he settled in Cass in 1847 in the 17th district, near what is yet known as Hardin's ferry and bridge on the Etowah river. He died there on Aug. 7, 1854 and is buried in Rome. There were 9 children: (1) Martha, m. Dr. S. P. Burnett, a physician who settled in Cassville for a time and represented the county one term in the legislature, removed to Randolph county where his wife died and is buried. (2) Mary m. William Johnson. She was a pupil in the Howard school near Kingston. (3) Elizabeth, m. James H. Spullock and they are identified with Rome, Ga. (4) Mark Anthony, b. in 1831 in McDonough, was educated at the Rev. "Jimmie" George's school and attended West Point in 1848-50. At 19 years of age he became senate clerk and was deskmate of Alfred H. Colquitt; in 1851 he married Emma A. Sullivan of Greenville county, S. C., by whom there were 7 children; represented Cass in the legislature of 1859-60; operated Salt Petre Cave with the aid of 400 slaves until it was seized by the Federal Government; served as a colonel in Confederate service and was imprisoned at Fort Warren, Mass., 27 months. He was secretary of the first Southern Commercial Congress which met after the war in Louisville; was clerk of the house of representatives for 30 years; secretary of the constitutional convention in 1877; secretary of every congressional 7th district meeting while in the county. He was a prominent citizen of Atlanta until his death on May 19, 1924†. (5) Josephine Hortense, b. Feb. 21, 1839, graduated with 2nd honor at the Cassville Female College, m. John H. Beck, of Griffin, by whom there are Ada and Harry who live south of Kingston. Mrs. Beck died in 1903 and has left her descendants valuable recollections in her own hand writing. (6) John Forsyth, b. Oct. 9, 1842, in Floyd county, entered Confederate service as 2nd Lt. of the Davis Guards in Phillip's Legion, was elected in 1863 captain of Co. "F". 18th Ga. Regt., and while serving in this company captured the flag of the Zouave Regiment which was afterwards presented to the State by Gov. Brown. He married Mary R., daughter of J. C. Roper of Kingston, by whom there were:

---

*Lumpkin's "Removal of the Cherokee Indians," Vol. I, p-234.
†Information from his daughter, Miss Virginia Hardin of Atlanta.

Lucile m. J. D. Evans of Washington, D. C., William who now owns the old Woolley home near Kingston, John, Augusta W. m. Ralph Smith, writer of "Crackerland" in The Atlanta Journal, and Mark. Capt. Hardin died in Atlanta, Aug. 3, 1887, and is buried at Kingston.

HARGIS, Milton: b. 1809 in Person county, N. C., came with his wife, Lucy Long from Bushy Fork, N. C., to Cass in 1838. They settled on a farm near Cass Station where Mr. Hargis farmed and lived a quiet life until his death in 1857. He and his wife, who died in 1887, are buried in the family cemetery near the old home. Their children were: (1) Catherine, b. 1835, m. 1st John R. Banton who was killed during the Civil War, a son, John R. Banton m. (2) Madeline Walker, daughter of F. M. Walker, a shoemaker at Cassville and a sister of Robert B. Walker who was a newspaper man in Ga. and his wife, Belle Long Walker, lives in Cartersville. Catherine married the 2nd time William Magee Loveless, a son of Nathaniel and Rachel Deweese Loveless, by whom there was Felton of Atlanta. (2) Thomas Van Buren, b. 1836, m. Eliza Jack Fuller, who attended Cassville Female College. Their children were: Katie m. John McKelvey of Kingston, Mattie (dec.) m. James D. Rogers, Charlie, Frank lives in Ala., Hattie Lee lives at Kingston. (3) Elizabeth, b. 1838, m. Nelson Gilreath by whom there were 14 children.* (4) Richard Reuben, b. Sept. 9, 1842, was a member of Stuart's Cav. in Phillip's Legion, m. Cornelia Loughmiller of Spring Place by whom there were Harry Warren (dec) m. Edna, daughter of F. P. Sewell of this county, Wm. Richard m. Eloise Robinson of Atlanta, Dixie Lee m. I. Q. Richardson and lives at the old home place, Robt. Banton m. Mary Phillips, lives in Marietta, Ruby m. Glenn Giles and lives in Marietta. Mr. Hargis died Mar. 26, 1916 and before his death family reunions were held at the home place. For a long term of service he was a popular conductor on the W. & A. railroad. (5) William Henry, b Mar. 4, 1844, served in Co. B, Phillip's legion, d. June 20, 1909. (6) Othinel Pope, b. 1846, served in 1st Ga. Cav. He wrote his "Thrilling Experience of a 1st Georgia Cavalryman in the Civil War"†, before his death he was a guide at the Cyclorama in Grant Park, Atlanta. (7) James Francis ("Fant"), b. May 26, 1847, m. Fanny McKelvey. Of 7 children there are living in the county, Lucy m. Clifford Johnson at Kingston and Frank N. m. Susie McDonald at Kingston. He died Jan. 14, 1925.

HARRIS, Col. James Watkins, Sr.: b. April 26, 1812, in Putnam county; was a son of Judge Stephen Willis Harris; graduated from the University of Georgia when it was Franklin with first honor. He married Eliza Anne, daughter of Thomas Napier and Mrs. Hamilton of Athens, by whom he had 4 children. He was a lawyer by profession, solicitor

---
*See Gilreath sketch.
†Possession of Richard Hargis, Gainesville, Ga.

general of the Western circuit; ran for Congress on the Whig ticket against Howell Cobb and was defeated. He moved to Cass county in 1852 and resided on a large plantation on the Etowah river called "Thistledole", but removed to Cartersville after the Civil War. His first wife died in the fall of 1857 and he later married Florence Candler, sister of Milton, Warren, Asa, and John Candler. Col. Harris was a local minister of the Methodist denomination, and though he did not belong to the conference, he received appointments to preach. He was instrumental in rebuilding the Methodist church in Cartersville. He died Nov. 19, 1896. The children were: (1) J. Watt. Jr., admitted to the bar and practiced in Cartersville, once with W. T. Wofford until 1876, m. 1st Eva Lowe by whom there were Watt III, lives in Fla., Anise m. Henry Allen, lives in New Orleans, Clarence lives in Atlanta. He married the 2nd time, Annie de Rousette by whom there were Willis, Armond (dec.) and Hamilton. He died in 1904. (2) T. W. Hamilton, m. Ethel Hillyer of Rome by whom there was one daughter, Maude m. Benjamin Yancey of Rome. (3) Sarah, m. Dr. W. H. Best by whom there was one son, Harris, m. May Johnson, sister of M. L. Johnson. (4) Anne Eliza, b. April 6, 1851, m. T. W. Milner*, d. Mar. 15, 1921.

HEADDEN, William: b. Feb. 16, 1813, in Chelsea, England; came to the United States with his parents in 1818, landing at Charleston, S. C., and first settled in Greenville, S. C. He came to Cass county in 1837, settling at Cassville where he made warm friends with the Indians. In 1837 he married Amanda Johnston, of Ala., by whom he had ten children. Owning and operating a large carriage and wagon shop in Cassville, he made beautiful carriages that brought a fancy price until the shop was destroyed by the Federals in 1864. He was a Baptist and a large contributor to the Baptist College where he educated his children until it was burned. After his first wife's death he married Caroline Alexander of Boston, in 1872. He died December 6, 1884. His children identified with this county were: (1) Robert Benjamin, b. Dec. 25, 1838 in Cassville, was educated and was a graduate in the last class of the Cherokee Baptist College. During the Civil War he was a member of Co. B, Phillip's Legion and at the battle of Gettysburg was terribly wounded in the hip, but he reentered and became a sergeant. After the war he returned to his native county and began teaching and while in Campbell county was baptized at Ramah church and was ordained to preach in 1868. He began preaching at Cassville, where he served as pastor until 1870 when he was called to the Cartersville Baptist church, serving until 1883 when he went to Rome and served there until his death. On April 22, 1869, he married Mary E. Dyar by whom there were 5 children. The 3 surviving him at his death were: Mamie m. R. S. Kennard, Lois m. Francis S. Key Smith, Nancy m. S. M. Prince. Rev. Headden was a man beloved by

---

*See Milner Sketch.

all classes of people; he had a delightful personality, spotless character and consecrated zeal. He was a Mason and a member of the Rome Knights Templar and was general prelate of the Grand Commandery of Georgia in 1897 and 1898; a trustee of the Theological Seminary in Louisville and of Mercer University; a member and at one time president of the State Board of Missions of the Baptist denomination. He died in Rome on Aug. 14th, 1913. (2) Joseph W., b. Feb. 19, 1843, d. Feb. 7, 1870, m. Rachel Neville, daughter of James B. Neville, by whom there is one surviving son, J. W. Headden of Atlanta and who owns his mother's home place above Kingston. (3) George Heine, b. July 26, 1849, d. Nov. 6, 1919, farmer and resident of Cassville all his life, m. Lollie Haynes (dec.) by whom there were: L. Delle, Robert F., John K., L. Marie, all of whom are living in Cassville. The old Headden home is yet standing at the south end of the town of Cassville.

HENDERSON, Ortney E.: b. 1798, d. Oct. 12, 1868; was a grandson of Robert Henderson, b. 1751, a resident of Augusta county, Va. Revolutionary soldier, who served with the Va. troops under Capt. William Robinson and Capt. Henry Waterson, migrated to South Carolina and in 1796 removed to Jackson county, Ga., where he drew a lot of land in the 13th district, 2nd section according to the Cherokee Land Lottery of 1838. He died in Jackson county in 1839 leaving a large estate and his wife, Mary Carroll. His father was Robert Henderson, Jr., who served as a major in the War of 1812 and married Abigail Ratchford of S. C., by whom there were 6 children. Besides O. E., Leanna who married Vinson Brown, and Robert Franklin, b. 1812, d. 1873, and married a daughter of Martin and Hanah Stidham, lived in this county. Major Robert Henderson died in 1847 at the age of 78 years and is buried in the Cassville cemetery. His son, Robert F., was appointed administrator of his estate and he sold the Hall county property to O. E. Henderson and the Cass county property to Nathaniel Burge and W. H. Stiles in 1848. In 1829 Ortney E. Henderson came to Cass county and settled on the present Henderson estate on the old Alabama road; on Jan. 1st, 1831 he married Elizabeth Van Winkle in Jackson county and returned with his bride and his father and family to his new home, where he was a prominent planter prior to the Civil War and active in the affairs of the county. They are buried in the family cemetery on the estate. Elizabeth V. W. Henderson died Dec. 12, 1890 at the age of 90. Their 6 children were: (1) Robert Henderson, b. 1831 in this county. (2) Mary who married John King and moved to Texas. (3) Rufus who moved to Mississippi. (4) John Ratia, b. April 19, 1836, d. Dec. 24, 1895, served as courier in Phillip's Legion, Co. B, Cav. during Civil War; managed his father's ruined property after the war; in 1867 married Jennie Everidge in Surry county, N. C., by whom there were 3 children. (a) William Ortney, b. Oct. 27, 1867, d. March 21, 1918; a graduate of Univ. of Ga., married 1st Minnie Stegall, daughter of John P. Stegall, by whom there was one son, J. Ratia; married the 2nd time Annie Leake, daughter of Thomas Leake, by whom there was Thomas. Ratia and Tom live on the original plantation. (b) Bernia Henderson, b. Nov. 2, 1870, d. April 18, 1909, m. Wallace Emsley Stegall, son of John P. Stegall, lived and died in Chattanooga, leaving W. E. Jr., who died in 1930, Daisy, and Jo who is a dentist at Lindale, Ga. (c) Daisy Henderson, b. July 7, 1874, m. in 1896 William Herschel Griffin, son of Ransom L. Griffin of Cartersville, by whom there were William Herschel, b. Apr. 19, 1898, Carl H., Ralph LaFayette who practiced law in Rome, and Howard Preston. They lived in Kingston where Mr. Griffin was a merchant until his death in 1912. During the World War, John Ratia Henderson had 3 grandsons in service; Wallace E. Stegall, Jr., U. S. N., J. Ratia Henderson and W. Herschel Griffin. (5) Thomas Henderson, removed to Tenn., after service in Civil War. (6) Jane Elizabeth who married W. S. Attaway of Cartersville.*

HENDERSON, William B.: lived and died in Laurens, S. C., but bought property before the Civil War just above Kingston and erected a home place called "Glenmore". During the war his overseer, a Mr. McMicken, looked after this property. After his death and the Civil War, his wife, Frances Irby, a daughter of Dr. William Irby and Mary Eichelberger, of Laurens, S. C., with her 8 children came and lived at "Glenmore." The children were: (1) Louisa m. James Oliver ("Red") Ligon who came from Meriweather county before the war, and entered Confederate service from this county. Lived in the 17th district. (Both dec.) .(2) Mary Frances m. Bias Beazley. (3) Katherine m. James K. Rabb and their daughter, Nan m. G. C. Phillips of Rome and Birmingham. (4) William Irby m. Alice Everidge and their son, William I. Jr., m. Grace Rabb and lives in Kingston. (5) James Albert m. Ada Wingold (dec.) and lives in Rome. (6) Lois (or Lucy) Howard m. Luther Peek Colbert and lived in Cedartown. (7) Elizabeth (Jacobs) lived in West Point.

HENDRICKS, George Washington: b. March 25, 1848, on the farm of his father, Lindsay Hendricks a native of Franklin county, 15 miles north of Cartersville. His father died while in a Federal prison at Chattanooga in Nov. 1864. His mother was Anna Louise Vincent of Ala. He received his early education in Bartow county and Cumming, Ga. For 12 years he taught in public schools in Georgia and Texas. In January 1889 he was made ordinary of Bartow county and served in that office until his death on Dec. 7, 1928, at his home in Cartersville. With poise and gentleness he was a type of judge the word implies. On Nov. 22, 1876, he married Anna Virginia Carson, daughter of Maj.

*This sketch was compiled by Mrs. Grace Gillam Davidson of Quitman, Georgia.

Judge J. W. Hooper, first judge of the Cherokee circuit (donated by Mrs. Hallie Alexander Rounsaville).

James M. Carson who served in the South Carolina militia and came with his family to this county in 1854 and settled at Pine Log where he lived and died. The children of Judge and Mrs. Hendricks are: Gideon W. who is the present county coroner, Alma m. Dr. D. H. Monroe, (dec.) who was born at Pine Log and graduate of Univ. of Ga. 1900, and by whom there is one son, Bonnie m. J. L. Padgett, Effie m. W. D. Trippe (dec.), Gabe m. P. C. Franklin by whom there are 2 children, Blanche m. L. C. Hannon by whom there are 2 boys, Bossie m. Dr. H. P. McElreath by whom there is one son, Sam T., who served in World War, Annie, Lucy m. J. L. Layton (dec.), Robert A. All live in Cartersville except Effie and Sam. Judge Hendricks was a member and steward of the Sam Jones Memorial Church; a Macon; a member of Ga. Asso. of Ordinaries. A brother of Judge Hendricks, W. A. Hendricks, m. Rosa, daughter of Rev. Elija M. Harris who taught and was a Christian preacher in this county until he was killed in the Battle of Atlanta in '64. Their children are Fannie (Smith,) Walker, the Rev. Lindsay, Myrtle, the Rev. Lucilus, Olin, Frank, Fred, and Addie Hendricks.

HOOPER,* Judge John Word: a second son of Matthew Brooks Hooper and Elizabeth Adams Word Hooper, was born Dec. 23, 1797 in Pendleton district, S. C. On Jan. 18, 1827 he married his second cousin, Sarah Joyce Allen Word, b. July 17, 1803, in Laurens district, S. C. Mr. and Mrs. Hooper were both descendants of Charles Word. She was a granddaughter of Thomas Word. "Early in the 18th century Charles Word I, the progenitor of an extensive family, come from Llandaff, Glamorganshire, Wales and settled in Va. His five sons, Charles II, Thomas, John, Peter and Cuthbert, were all soldiers in the Revolutionary War . . . Charles Word II was born 1738 in Virginia. While a mere youth of seventeen he volunteered, and went out with "the Virginia Blues", under command of Col. George Washington, to guard the frontier against the French. Taking part soon after in the battle near Fort Duquesne where Gen. Braddock was defeated, he was one of that gallant band of colonials who, under Washington, covered the retreat of Braddock and his Regulars, thus saving them from complete destruction. He was one of the 30 "Virginia Blues" to escape alive. Later, Charles Word II married Elizabeth Adams, a relative of John and Samuel Adams, and about the time the Revolutionary War began, moved to North Carolina, settling in Surry county, near a place now called Mt. Airy. When his youngest child, Elizabeth Adams Word, was one year old, he was killed in the battle of Kings Mountain, October, 1780. This daughter married Matthew Brooks Hooper, of the Virginia family a young kinsman of William Hooper, Representative of North Carolina in the Colonial Congress and signer of the Declaration of the Independence. Both came originally from the New England Hoopers

---

*Information from Mrs. Hallie Alexander Rounsaville of Rome, Ga.

and by family tradition were descendants of Bishop John Hooper, of England—who, rather than recant, was burned at the stake, in 1555, by 'Bloody Queen Mary'."* John Word Hooper enjoyed exceptional educational advantages followed by a course in law at Columbia, S. C. With his family he came to Franklin county, Ga.; returned to S. C. for his wife and prior to 1829 he began the practice of law in Decatur, Ga. While living there he was elected solicitor general of the Chattahoochee circuit, Dec. 15, 1829, serving until Nov. 1832. When he received the appointment, Dec. 8, 1832, as the first judge of the Cherokee circuit, he with his family removed to Cassville where they made their home until sometime in the 50's. Their home was several miles west of the town. At the time of the removal of the Cherokee Indians, Judge Hooper tried to protect them in their rights, a course which greatly antagonized the speculators and politicians. When reading the columns by Wilson Lumpkin of this era, a different conception is given of Judge Hooper's actions. But from the Executive Minutes of Dec. 1834, the Investigating Committee appointed at Judge Hooper's request to investigate his official conduct served a notice on Gov. Lumpkin to appear before the committee and he refused. A letter as follows, written to Federal Officials in Washington on Jan. 14, 1838, signed by John Ross and 4 other prominent Indians, indicates his square and fair dealings: "The Cherokees were proud to find a Georgia judge who possessed sufficient virtue and honesty to stay the hand of unprovoked injustice, by granting bills of injunction to insure them the peaceable and quiet possession of the houses and farms which they occupied, and they themselves had made on their own land, until the question of right could be fairly tried. These proceedings, however, afforded the Cherokees but a momentary relief. The sequel will be found in the subsequent proceedings of the legislative and executive departments of Georgia of which the inclosed is one of their fruits. Suffice to say that whilst the honorable judge has been made to feel the wrath of the most vindicative policy of his own government, the unoffending Cherokees are made victims of the insatiable propensities of tyranny and cupidity. The property, the peace, and the existence of the Cherokee people are in jeopardy, and nothing but the timely interposition of the General Government can save them; and to it, with intense anxiety, they now appeal."† Judge Hooper bought property in Texas and after the Civil War, he became interested in the Dade county coal mines and died at Trenton in that county on July 15, 1868. Sisters of Judge Hooper, Amelia M. Hooper, was the mother of Mrs. H. V. M. Miller, and Justiana Dickerson Hooper married Noble P. Beall and was the mother of Martha Beall who married Samuel C. Candler. The

---
*From Bullock's "History of the Habersham Family."
†This extract is from a letter preserved in the Federal Archives in Washington.

children of Judge and Mrs. Hooper were: (1) Eliza E., b. May 30, 1828, on May 5, 1845 married Warren Akin in Cassville by whom there was one daughter, Eliza, who died in July 1876. She m. Thomas W. Baxter by whom there were Andrew and Alice (died 1932). Andrew Baxter worked with Mark A. Cooper for many years at the Iron Works. Mrs. Akin died in 1846. (2) Jane Elizabeth, b. Sept. 22, 1829, d. in 1859, was the first wife of John A. Erwin of Cassville. (3) John W. Jr., b. Oct 13, 1833, m. Frances Stuart. He was one of the first to go in a company from this county into Confederate service and served as captain and major, represented this county in the legislature of 1863-64-65 and at this time lived at Kingston. He died July 31, 1886 at Clarendon, Ark. (4) Sarah Joyce, b. June 6, 1836, in Cassville. When very young her mother died and she was placed under the care and teaching of Rev. and Mrs. C. W. Howard at Spring Bank, later making her home with Judge Hooper's niece, Mrs. H. V. M. Miller and Dr. Miller, by whom she was beloved as an own child, and married from their home, "Coligni", near Rome. She was the first graduate of the Cassville Female College in 1855; in Nov. 1857 she married Col. Thomas Williamson Alexander of Rome. Their children were Mrs. Martha A. Pegues, (Judge) Hooper Alexander of Atlanta, Mrs. Hallie Miller (J. A.) Rounsaville, and Mrs. Sarah Joyce (C. W.) King of Rome. (5) William Thomas, b. Jan. 7, 1840, d. 1886, resigned from the Navy to become a colonel in the Confederate service, m. Martha Trippe, daughter of T. H. Trippe of Cassville and their children are identified with Oklahoma. Mrs. Sarah Joyce Word Hooper, wife of Judge Hooper, died March 26, 1840 at Pontotoc, Miss., while on a visit there to Mrs. Noble Beall. On September 13, 1852, Judge Hooper married the 2nd time, Mrs. Martha Lamar Force, daughter of John Lamar, in Griffin. Judge Hooper is buried in the Myrtle Hill cemetery in Rome, Ga.

HOWARD, John J.: b. April 8, 1816 in Spartanburg district, S. C.; attended old field schools during intervals of farm work. At 19 years of age, located at Hamburg across from Augusta with a merchant, Mr. Sullivan, and at the end of four years organized the firm of Howard and Garmany which grew to success. On July 18, 1845, he married Lois Hall Benham of Laurens, S. C., b. March 2, 1824—d. Nov. 4, 1890, and before 1850 they moved to Cass county and erected a home on the Cassville road, Howard's Hill, which later burned. He was an active Baptist and for many years a banker in Cartersville. He died March 29, 1891, and he and his family are buried in Cartersville cemetery. Of six children these left descendants: (1) William H., b. Dec. 9, 1847—d. June 15, 1911, m. Hattie Leake by whom there were, Bradley (dec.) m. Octavia Aubrey by whom there were Jack, Harriet, Octavia, Rosa and Willis; William H. Jr. m. Bessie Lumpkin (dec.) by whom there were Louisa, Elizabeth and William; Horace m. Mary Barton by whom there were Clara (Humphries) and Sarah, and Mrs.

Ora Burton by whom there is one son; Albert, unmarried. Horace is the only son in the county at present. (2) Fannie, b. May 22, 1850—d. May 23, 1915, m. Richard A. Clayton, b. June 29, 1841—d. May 13, 1907, by whom there were Julian, Harry and Lorrimer who live in Florida and Atlanta. (3) Mary, m. T. B. Cabaniss (both dec.) of Forsyth by whom there are 2 living children, May and Lois (Peeples). (4) Constance, b. Aug. 16, 1854—d. Sept. 12, 1880, m. Herman M. Clayton, brother of R. A., by whom there were Willie, George and Connie who are living in Florida.

IRWIN, David: b. Jan. 8, 1807 in Wilkes county; married Sarah Royston of Athens; first senator from Cass county, lived at Cassville and was one of the lawyers during the removal of the Indians. While at Cassville two daughters were born to David and Sarah Irwin; Margaret, married George N. Lester, Julia, married Greenlee Butler. Judge Irwin moved to Cobb county and died Nov. 26, 1885 at his home on the Powder Springs road.

HUSON, Francis: with his wife, Amelia Cloud Huson, settled on the Terhune place on the Etowah river near Kingston before the Civil War and were land and slave owners. They kept the Huson house in Kingston on the stage and rail route. During the war they returned to Milledgeville where they owned and operated the Mark Huson's hotel in which the Georgia solons stayed and where Gen. Sherman, or his staff, later had headquarters in 1864. Mark Huson's hotel was advertised in a copy of the "Federal Union" published in Milledgeville in Oct. 1830. They returned to Kingston after the war where they lived until their death. They are buried in Griffin. Mrs. Huson, "Aunt Mille" to those who knew her, was of Revolutionary ancestry and was herself a Nancy Hart type and an early believer in woman's rights. There were two children: Frances Woodruff and Mark A. Huson who served on Gen. Cobb's staff during the *Civil War.

JACKSON, Mark: and his wife, Bashaby Hargis, came from Green county, N. C., to Cass county in 1838 or 1839 and became one of the early settlers in the Stilesboro community. Of their ten children two left descendents in this county: Rebecca Shaw, and William Jackson, b. in 1800, m. Suan Martindale in 1823, by whom there were 12 children. Of these Lucy, who married John Hilton, James, who m. Celia Hollin, and Levi, who married Mary McFadden, left descendants. W. I. Jackson is a son of James. J. W. Jackson (died 1932), R. L., Lula, Della and Callie of Stilesboro are children of Levi Jackson and Mary McFadden, whose mother was a daughter of Joseph and Bellariah Green.

JACKSON, Zimri W.: b. Jan. 26, 1824; came with his wife,

---

*Information from a daughter of M.A. Huson, Mrs. Stella Huson Swann.

Eliza A. Hill, from N. C. to Cass in 1846. His brother, Milton C. Jackson, came with him and they established themselves as building contractors at Cassville. During the Civil War, Zimri Jackson served in Co. I, 40th Ga. Vols. After the war they came to Cartersville in the same business. Zimri died May 20, 1892 and is buried at Cassville. Of 5 sons the following lived in Cartersville all their lives: (1) William A. b. May 25, 1852, m. in 1881 Cornelia Fricks of Walker county by whom there were R. W., A. F., Sallie Maude m. Prince Lewis (dec.), Ralph O., Annie Lee (Brumby). "Billy" Jackson received his education in the county and has lived and become a large property owner on Pettit's creek. (2) George M., b. Nov. 4, 1854, m. in 1882 Florence Dickerson of LaFayette county by whom there were Zim (dec.), m. Annie Jackson, and R. D. (twins), Lydia (David), Walter G., Lawson E., Frank T. m. Guill Monfort, Aileen, and Dickson. (3) Arthur lives in LaFayette, Ga. (4) E. L. now lives at Calhoun, Ga. Milton C. Jackson m. Emily Millican by whom there were two sons, Allison, and Felix P. Jackson who married the 2nd time Christine Lumpkin.

JOHNSON, Erastus V.: b. July 13, 1827 in Lincoln county, N. C., d. Oct. 1892; came from Alabama to Georgia and at 21 years of age served as conductor on the railroad between Rome and Kingston; was the first conductor to take the train into Rome. He later became connected with the Georgia Railroad, until his appointment as agent by Gov. Johnson at Kingston. Before 1860 Mr. Johnson erected a merchant mill, a general merchandise store, a branch of the "Exchange Bank", and was a cotton merchant. For the purpose of buying wheat he issued script, as money was scarce, which passed as a medium of barter in several counties and was known as "Rat" Johnson's "shin plasters." The mill was used during the war until the Federals occupied Kingston. The machinery was shipped to Barnesville where it was later captured and destroyed. Mrs. Osborne Shaw retarded its destruction while it was in Kingston. It is said that in the home of Mr. Johnson Gen. Wofford had his headquarters in 1865. Mr. Johnson married Anne Elizabeth Smith (d. in 1911) by whom there were Ella (dec.), and Wade C. Johnson, who lives in Kingston.

JOHNSON, John J.: b. Oct. 14, 1826 Laurens district, S. C., d. in 1901, was a son of William C. and Cassandra Lindsey Johnson. He came with his father from S. C. to Cass county in 1845, settled at Poplar Springs and lived there until the father died in 1866. Before the Civil War, J. J. bought a farm near Adairsville where he lived and farmed all his life. He was one of the 6 children reared to maturity. He served in Co. I, 1st Ga. Regt., during the Civil War. He married Mary E. Barton, daughter of W. T. Barton of this county formerly of Franklin county, by whom there were 12 children. Those living in the county at present are: Inez, Louella m. S. Davis, Bertie m. A. W. Dodd, all of

Adairsville. One son, Henry W. (dec.) m. Lillian Woodberry, a sister of the late Rosa Woodberry of Atlanta; Lowell W. Johnson lives in Fla.

JOHNSON, Lindsay: b. Mar. 28, 1797 in Amhurst county, Va., a son of Thomas and Mary Christian Johnson; came to Elbert county, Ga., in early youth. He came to Cass in 1830 prospecting for copper and very soon established a home which is yet standing in the Pine Log district where in the course of years he owned an almost baronial estate. Generous to his friends and neighbors, liberal in all things but his political opinions, he entertained with open-handed, southern hospitality; but the day of an important election found him occupying the position of a feudal lord. In his opinion the old Whig party was the only organization fit to govern the country and he wanted voters in his district to vote like he did. The numerous drivers from Kentucky and Tennessee who made their annual trips to the cotton states enjoyed the hospitality of his home on the old Tennessee road. He was a colonel by right of militia service or in respect. He served in the Seminole War in 1836; died June 8, 1863 and is buried at Cassville. He married 3 times. By Miss Wood of Elbert county he had: (1) John, m. Miss Seabrook, a son, Smiley S. Johnson, lives in Rome, Ga. By Miss Sallie Oglesby he had: (1) Mary, m. Dr. Walton Wyly who died and is buried at Cassville. (2) Abda, b. Oct. 8, 1826, in Elbert county, came to Cass with his father when a lad, attended common schools until he prepared himself for college. In 1844 he entered the Junior class of Franklin College and graduated in 1846 with 2nd honor. He later became a trustee of the University, serving until his death; was a trustee of Wesleyan College until 1880. He read law with Col. Murphy in Decatur and was admitted to the superior court at Lawrenceville. During the March term, 1848, he was admitted to the supreme court at Cassville. He settled at Cassville, soon winning the reputation of a sound and able lawyer. Having an analytical mind, he was distinguished for the accuracy of his legal information. Judge Erskine of the U.S. Court said that he regarded Col. Johnson as the most sensible lawyer who ever practiced in his court, "he knows how to talk, when to talk and exactly the time to stop talking." On March 30, 1852, he married Frances E. Trippe who died Jan. 23, 1907. In 1855-56 he was a member of the general assembly and declined re-election. Although a Union man in sentiment and opposing secession, he followed the policy of his State when war was declared. Early in 1862 he raised a company of infantry from Georgia volunteers at Big Shanty and was elected colonel of the 40th Ga. Regt., which saw action in the battles of Chickasaw, Bayou, Baker's creek, seige of Vicksburg, Missionary Ridge, Resacca, and New Hope church, etc. During the battle of Atlanta, Col. Johnson commanded Stovall's Brigade on the 22nd of July. Some one remarked to him that day that a certain Alabama regiment was falling back; he replied, "It makes no difference, ours is forward." He was with the operations of Gen. Hood until the surrender in North Carolina in 1865. After the war he resumed his law practice, moving to Cartersville when the county seat was removed. He was a member of the Constitutional Convention of 1877 where his legal acumen was of service in framing the fundamental laws of our State. He was a Methodist, a Royal Arch Mason. He died at his residence in Cartersville, July 10, 1881, and is buried in the city cemetery. The Cartersville bar wrote in their memorial, "The bar has lost its leader and its abliest ornament." The children of Col. Abda and Frances Johnson were: (a) Lily Gatewood m. William Albert Bradley of South Carolina (dec.); (b) Frances Trippe m. John W. Akin.*; (c) Stovall m. Nellie Norris of La., a lawyer in Cartersville and Texas where he died in October 1916; (d) Albert Sidney, b. 1862, admitted to the bar when 20 years old; lieut. col. on Gov. Gordon's staff, 1886-90, in 1900 delegate to National Democratic convention in Kansas, unmarried, died while on a case in Cartersville June 8, 1903; (e) Julia Trippe m. M. L. Johnson, d. Mar. 15, 1920. (3) Jefferson, served as major in the Confederate Army, m. Miss Price of Chattanooga. (4) William, (dec.) m. Jane McConnell of Fairfield county, S. C., by whom there were: (a) McConnell Lindsay, b. Oct. 22, 1850 at Pine Log, mayor of Cartersville in 1884, Cleveland elector, 7th Congressional district in 1888, member of State Democratic Executive committee for the State at Large in 1896-98, inspector of fertilizers under administration of Commissioner Nesbit in 1892-98, Democrat, represented the county in the house of representatives in 1898-99, 1900-01-09-10-11-12, 1917-18-19-20-21-22, in the senate, 1931-32, m. Julia T. Johnson, farmer in the 5th district. (b) Mary, m. W. Harris Best (dec). By his 3rd wife, Mrs. Mary Word Powell, Col. Lindsay Johnson had: (1) Dr. Lindsay, b. Aug. 1851, died May 11, 1910, was a graduate of the Southern Medical College of Louisville in 1874, a popular physician in the county and had many namesakes. In 1876 he married Mary, who died in 1885, daughter of Dr. and Mrs. J. W. Curry, by whom there were 3 children. Yandel, Rosebud m. Conyers Fite of Cartersville, and Will Henry (dec). In 1886 Dr. Johnson married the 2nd time Valentine Goulong of New Orleans, who lives in Rome now Mrs. R. V. Allen. (2) Virginia, m. 1st William J. Conyers,† 2nd, W. W. McDaniel of Pine Log. (3) Lou and Flora died young.

JOLLY, Joseph: b. 1785 in South Carolina of Irish ancestors who settled in Virginia; married Zilla Dickerson and came to Cass in 1837, purchased 160 acres near Stilesboro. They were among the original members and founders of the Raccoon Creek Baptist church. He died in Nov. 1861, leaving his wife and 10 children. The following have lived and reared families in the county: (1) Elizabeth, m. John B. Kennedy (both dec..), one grandson, R. Ed Kennedy, lives near Car-

---
*See Akin sketch.
†See Conyers sketch.

tersville. (2) Henry, died while in Confederate service in Virginia. (3) Rachel, m. 1st Archie McDaniel, 2nd Elbert Shaw, a son of William and Rebeccah Shaw who came to the county in 1837 and were among the founders of the Raccoon Baptist church. "Uncle Billie" Shaw was a deacon and janitor for many years. (4) Levi, b. July 5, 1827 in Anderson district. S. C., was a farmer near Stilesboro and Euharlee, an original member and founder of Oak Grove church, in 1851 married Hannah, daughter of Rev. Thomas Carpenter, by whom he had: R. Frank (dec.), Joseph Tom (dec.) whose 2 sons, A. C., lives in Cartersville and J. Mark lives at Kingston, Elizabeth m. Dr. I. N. Van Meter (dec.), James C., lives near Kingston, W. Alfred lives at Halls Station, Lee W. lives at Taylorsville, John Henry lives at Taylorsville, H. J. lives at Marietta. (5) James, m. Mary Baker, one daughter, Sally, m. David Taff of Stilesboro. Of 5 sons, John lives at Taylorsville. (6) Sarah, m. 1st Mr. McKelvey, 2nd, Thomas Booker, a son, Lee McKelvey lives at Taylorsville. (7) Maria, m. Elbert Shaw by whom there were: James (dec.) who has a son, Robert A., living in Cartersville; Levi F. has always lived in the county and reared a large family in Cartersville. (8) Mary, b. in 1838 in this county, m. the Rev. Edmund Harling of Edgefield, S. C., by whom there were 14 children. The mother lived to see 12 of these children grown and married—9 of them daughters. Rev. Harling lived near Euharlee, farmed and did evangelistic work in the county Baptist churches. Their children born in the county were: Zilla (dec.), m. S. C. Etheridge who taught school at Oak Grove and did much for the education of youths in that community; Ada m. C. J. Dodd; Emma m. W. A. Dodd*; Willie m. Robert Clayton, a resident of Cartersville and later removed to Alabama; Fanny m. S. L. Yarbrough and removed to Edison, Ga.; Mary Lou m. Walter Kennedy and now lives in Plains, Ga.; E. L. lives in Atlanta; James R. m. 1st Birdie Griffin, 2nd Lutie Abbott, lives at Taylorsville; Joseph D., Baptist preacher, (dec.) lived in Sherman, Tex.; Jessie m. T. V. Gemes, lives in Cartersville; Bessie m. R. T. Eberhardt, lives at Comer, Ga.; Ola (dec.) m. E. O. Davis of Taylorsville.

JONES, Robert Harris: b. Sept. 1828 in Elbert county, a son of the Rev. Samuel G. and Elizabeth Anne Edwards Jones; came to Cartersville in 1853 where he established a carriage factory that acquired a reputation in North Georgia. He was admitted to the Methodist conference in 1849. In 1859 he and John Greenwood were partners in the carriage business. On August 3, 1861, at the organization of the 22nd Ga. Regt., at Silver creek, near Rome, Ga., he was elected colonel of the company and distinguished himself on Virginia soil. When his superior officers were killed, or disabled, at Sharpsburg, he commanded the R. H. Anderson division. He never fully recovered from a severe wound in the lung that he received at the time, and had to resign in

---

*See Dodd sketch.

1863, just before being made a brigadier general. Dr. D. Hamiter rescued him on the field of battle. His company had an annual reunion where a monument was erected to Col. Jones at Silver Creek until about 1928. In 1866 he returned to Cartersville and reorganized his business under the name of R. H. Jones and Son. He served many of the county churches and was active in the religious and civic affairs of the city; was a Knight of Honor, Mason, I.O.O.F. He died Sept. 1, 1897 and is buried in Cartersville. In 1851 he married Lucintha Elizabeth Cotton of Troup county by whom there were these children: (1) Emma, m. W. B. Sadler, lives in Cartersville, one daughter Ethel E. Bass and her daughter live in Cartersville. (2) Lula, m. C. R. Bilbro, one daughter, Dot, m. Harry Cobb, lives in Cartersville. (3) L. Glenn, m. Charlotte, daughter of Dr. W. L. Kirkpatrick, lives in Anniston, Ala. (4) John William, m. Sallie Quillian by whom there were Vail (Weems), Dr. H. Q. Jones, Dr. J. W. Jones and Sarah (Pollock) now living in Fla., carried on father's business and undertaker in Cartersville. (5) Frances B., m. A. S. Quillian (dec.), lives in Anniston. (6) Felton Howard Erwin (dec.) m. Caroline Louise Garner of Chattanooga and lived in Cartersville until his death in 1915.

JOHNSTON, Mark: b. in 1818, in Hancock county; was a son of Rev. Malcolm Johnston and brother of Richard Malcolm Johnston, the author of "Dukesboro Tales", "Life of Alexander Stephens", "Mister Billy Downs; His Like and Dislikes", and other stories about Georgia.* Rev. Malcolm Johnston gave the lot for the old 1st Baptist church in Cartersville and was buried in the cemetery back of the church. His body was later removed to the city cemetery by citizens of the town. He was a trustee of Mercer University from 1838 to 1842. Mark Johnston was educated at old Penfield and was a graduate of the University of Virginia. Just before the Civil War he purchased a farm in Cass county and soon became a law partner with Col. Abda Johnson. He was elected to the State senate from this county in 1859. He was a teacher. He died in Atlanta in 1884.

KEY, John J.: b. in 1835 was the son of Moses Key, b. Nov. 26, 1797, d. June 15, 1845, from the effects of a fall while working on the first railroad bridge over the Chattahooche. The wife of J. J. Keys, Sarah J. Marshall, bought a 40 acre lot for $100.00 in Cass county in 1853, near Emerson and in the course of years added more to her estate. This property now belongs to the granddaughter, Georgia Keys who married W. M. McCrary and lives at Emerson. The deceased members of the family are buried in the Key cemetery north of Emerson.

KINABREW, Dr. Jordan W.: b. 1819, was a son of a Frenchman, William J. Kinabrew who settled in La., after finishing his medical

---
*See "Men of Mark in Georgia."

education, he married in 1846 Louisa Jane Steed of Augusta. He came to Cassville where he practiced his profession and taught in the Cassville Female College until the Civil War; enlisted in Co. I, 1st Ga. Cav., where he served as company surgeon. After the war Dr. and Mrs. Kinabrew settled at Kingston where they lived until ill health forced him to give up his practice and they removed to Piedmont, Ala., where they both died in 1890 and 1889 respectively. Their children were: (1) Ella m. Alfred J. Buford.* (2) Alberta, died Aug. 31, 1877, aged 24 years, buried at Kingston, m. the Rev. George Dent Harris who was born Jan. 29, 1850, and served as pastor of the Connesena Baptist church for many years and other pastorates in Ga. and Ala., died and is buried at Piedmont; their children were Frank (dec.), William (dec.), Ella L. (dec.) who married Walter Hawkins by whom there are Walter, Harris, Frank, and George who live in Cartersville. (3) William H. m. Elizabeth Harris, daughter of J. K. Harris of Kingston (both dec.).

KING, William Henry : b. Oct. 8, 1817; came to Cass county in 1838 from South Carolina with his wife, Clarky Carolina Holland, b. 1822. They settled at Pine Log and lived there until their deaths. He died April 22, 1888. Of 8 girls and 3 boys these lived and reared families in the county: (1) Abbie m. C. P. Anthony by whom there were 10 children. Those living in the county now are: Clara m. W. W. Daniel, lives in Cartersville; Emma and Lennie live at the old Anthony home near Rydal. (2) Ella m. S. W. Bradford and with their children Frank, Talmadge, and Rosebud (Strickland), live near Pine Log. A daughter, Alma m. H. R. Maxwell, lives in Cartersville. (3) Eliza m. Bailey Barton, tax collector, 1881-85. (4) Betty m. Tom Higgins (both dec.) and have one daughter, Mamie, m. George W. Gaddis, living in Cartersville. Several of the children live in Gordon county and Florida. The King, Upshaw, Vincent, Barton, Adair and Jackson families lived in the same community at Pine Log and their offsprings ran mostly to daughters. When calico was in fashion as a material, their numerous daughters, bedecked in their calico frocks, gave this community the name of "Calico Valley".

LAND, Nathan: b. May 11, 1812 in Twiggs county; came to Cass county in 1848 and lived in Cassville until he died on August 3, 1880. He was admitted to the bar and practiced law for 10 years in his native county at Marion. After removal to this county he was elected, in 1850, to judgeship of the inferior court and was elected later to the office of ordinary, which office he held during the Civil War until the family refugeed to Brooks county. His home, called "Cassville Heights", a 3 story brick building, on College Hill, was burned by the Federals. Judge Land gave the land on which was erected the Cassville Female College and was prominently connected with its activities. Many students

---

*See Buford sketch.

boarded with Judge and Mrs. Land, and their home was noted for its hospitality. His daughter, Temperance, was a graduate of the college in 1858. He was a man of wide influence and was known for his integrity and love of justice. On Dec. 2, 1838, he married Mona Ricks Arrington of Twiggs county, formerly of N. C., by whom there were 9 children: (1) Harriet Ione, died in Cassville. (2) Elizabeth Temperance, lived and died in Cassville. (3) Mona Arrington m. Henry F. Land, their son, Judge Max E. Land of Atlanta is State Commissioner of Commerce and Labor. (4) John T., James Henry, Nathan Freeman, Robert A. were the sons. (5) Susan Louise m. C. F. Price, lives in Atlanta. Judge and Mrs. Land (d.Jan 17, 1897) are buried in Cassville cemetery.

LEAKE, John: came from South Carolina with his wife, Sally Holland, to Cass in the early 40's and acquired much of the property upon which the city of Cartersville developed. Their children were: (1) Dr. William Wesley Leake, b. in Laurens, S. C., was a practicing physician in Cartersville, gave property for the present Presbyterian church, m. Rachel Leake of S. C. by whom there were Ollin (dec.), Bascom, John (dec.), Bartow (dec.), Harry, Julia (dec.). (2) Thomas Holland m. Nancy Leake. (3) Sallie m. 1st Samuel H. Smith, editor of The Cartersville Express, 2nd to the Rev. Tom Gibson, member of the North Georgia Conference. Thomas Simmons Leake, who married Charlotte Dilliard, Sallie Leake (Carlyle) and Armsted Leake followed their brother John Leake to Cass county. Armsted Leake: b. 1788 in S. C.; came to Cass in Dec. 1846 with his wife, Mary Hanna, and 7 children, all of whom were born in Laurens district, S. C. They first settled on Pettit's creek, then later just outside the city limits of Cartersville where they lived until his death on Apr. 28, 1860. The Leakes are buried in the family cemetery on the Stilesboro-Euharlee road. The children were: (1) William B., m. Margaret E. Campbell, was killed at Sharpsburg, Md., while in Confederate service in 1863. (2) Moses A. m. Katherine Scott—Mrs. Mattie Lydie of Cartersville is only living child; m. Charlotte Wofford the 2nd time. (3) Thomas W., served 3 years in Co. B, Phillip's Cav., lived on one of the original Rowland farms where he spent remainder of his life as a farmer, Methodist, died Dec. 13, 1909, married Mary A. Furr of Habersham county by whom there were: Walter T. m. Sadie Gillam, Annie m. W. O. Henderson, Herman W., Romie m. Henry H. Milam, Jr., Elizabeth m. Ratia Henderson of Tenn., Mary, Martha, William A. m. Eliza Knight, daughter of A. Knight. (4) John Simmons, b. Nov. 27, 1837, educated in county schools, served 3 years in Co. B, Phillip's Cav. After the war devoted his time to his farms until at the time of his death he was recognized as one of the largest land owners in the county and a leading, successful farmer. On Feb. 18, 1869 he married Elizabeth, daughter of Thomas W. and Louisa G. Brandon, by whom there was only one child, Minnie, m. Claude B. Conyers (dec.), by whom there is one son, Claude B., who m. Rachel Stephens. In 1870 became steward in the Methodist church, a Mason, president of the Bank of Cartersville, died July 25, 1917 and is buried at Cartersville. Thomas and John Leake were life partners in business and for years had only one bank account. It was a partnership of mutual devotion and constant companionship. They were just plain "Tom" and "John" Leake to their friends over the county. (5) Martha Ann m. Jere A. Howard, ordinary of the county for a number of years. George H. Howard of Atlanta, and Mrs. Nannie E. McQuire of Oklahoma, are children. (6) Nancy E. m. Thomas Holland Leake. A son, Mark A. Leake, lives near Cartersville.

LEWIS, Baylis Washington: b. 1806 in North Carolina; in passing through this country going to Alabama, bought before 1836 land on the Oothcalooga creek, near Adairsville, where the Lewis family farmed, lived and died. He and his sister, Thomasin who married Ezekial Graham, both settled in Adairsville and were children of Maj. John Lewis and Ann Berry Earle, who was a daughter of John and Thomasin Berry Earle. Maj. Lewis was born in 1757 in Albermarle county, Va., volunteered under Capt. John Mark in Revolutionary service and at one time belonged to a regiment that served as a bodyguard to Gen. LaFayette. He was in the battles of Monmouth, Princeton, Brandywine, Stony Point, Germantown and at Yorktown. From Virginia he migrated to North Carolina and in 1786 married Miss Earle. In 1836 he and his wife followed their son to Cass county where he died on Nov. 4, 1840. His grave in Oothcalooga cemetery is marked: "A Soldier of the Revolution", and this inscription, "How sleep the brave who sink to rest, with all their country's wishes blest." Baylis W. Lewis married in 1841 Frances Gaines, b. 1820 in Laurens, S. C., and d. in 1889, by whom there were: (1) John Prince Lewis, b. 1842, served in the 8th Ga. Battalion, C. M. S., and afterwards became interested in a milling business with Lewis P. Gaines, establishing the Gaines-Lewis mill south of Kingston; in 1889 he moved to Cartersville where he erected the Cartersville Milling Company, and was a director in the Bank of Cartersville, property owner, member of the Baptist church, a Mason, died on September 6, 1917; married Ada Galt of Canton who died in 1904 and by whom there were: Prince L. who died June 1932, m. Sallie M. Jackson by whom there are Leon, Cornelia and Earle; Frances m. J. J. Hill by whom are Frances and Jack; Mildred m. R. C. May; John B. m. Pearl McClain; and Evelyn, all of whom live in Cartersville. (2) Jesse Caleb, d. in 1925. (3) Margaret A. (4) Baylis Earle, lives in Adairsville with Margaret. (5) Fannie M., d. in 1928.

LEWIS, Dr. John W.: b. Feb. 1, 1801, Spartanburg, S. C.; after medical education practiced in Spartanburg; member of S. C. state legislature in 1830-31; ordained for Baptist ministry in 1832 and preached in S. C. before he came to Ga; in 1835 married Maria Earle of Pendleton, S. C.; in 1839, or 40, he moved to Canton and while there assisted in organizing Baptist churches in Cherokee Georgia, at one time serving as pastor of Pettit's creek church when it was one of the largest in north Georgia; built roads in this and other counties along with agricultural interests; in 1847 erected an iron furnace on Stamp creek; in 1845 represented 41st district in the senate, securing by his vote the establishment of the supreme court of Georgia; name was thrown in for governor in 1857; member of Confederate Congress; on Jan. 1, 1858 he was appointed superintendent of the W. & A. R.R. In The Cassville Standard, of Jan. 1858, is an order from his young friend, Gov. Joseph E. Brown, "to cut off every expense which is not in your judgment necessary to safety and success"—Dr. Lewis' policy requested that the engineers blow their whistles only when necessary. He resigned in Sept. 1861 and was succeeded by his brother-in-law, John S. Rowland. He lived in the red brick house on what is now the Rowland Springs road; died at his home in Canton, July 11, 1865; of 7 children the following lived in this county: John Wood; Pickens, b. 1838, lived at Cass Station; Mary W., b. 1840, m. John D. Thomas and lived at Cass Station.

LEWIS, Harleston D.: About the middle of the 17th century two brothers, John and Robert Lewis, emigrated from Wales to the United States, settling in South Carolina. To John Lewis, a son named John was born and to John Jr., a son named David was born in 1730. To David were born two sons, Isaiah and Tarleton. To Tarleton was born James W. Harleston D. Lewis, b. March 19, 1837, in Pickens county, S. C., came to Cass county when a lad with his father, James W. Lewis, and his grandfather, Tarleton, who was one of the early settlers and is buried near Flexatile. On April 27, 1858, he married Janie A. Walker of near Cassville by whom there were: Will, James Wallace, Mrs. Alice Bibb, Mrs. Agnes Denman (dec.) and Mrs. Janie Luther (dec.). After Mrs. Lewis' death in July 1867, on Dec. 29, 1868, he married Martha A. Linn, daughter of Maj. A. M. Linn of near Cassville, by whom there were: Ora m. Dr. R. S. Bradley whose daughter Dicksie m. B. J. Bandy and are makers of candlewick bed-spreads and bath mats at Dalton, Ga., and Lurlyne m. Ernest Clark and lives in Cartersville; Lalla m. R. J. Raiden, lives in Rome; Ethel m. H. L. Jolly of Taylorsville; M. Frank is the miller of Mosteller Mills; Harleston Jr. (dec.); and Alfred Lewis of Texas. Mr. Lewis enlisted in March 1862 at Big Shanty for Confederate service and was a member of Co. "I", 40th Ga. Regt. In 1864 he re-enlisted in Co. "A", 8th Ga. Batt., and became a lieutenant, serving under Gen. N. B. Forrest until his surrender in 1865. In 1873 he became a member of the Cassville lodge No. 136, and in 1883 joined the Cedar Creek Baptist church; a member of the board of county commissioners from Jan. 1891 to Jan. 1893. He died Sept. 13, 1913 and is buried in the Lewis cemetery beyond Folsom.

LOCKRIDGE, James: a son of Maj. Andrew Lockridge who was commissioned major in 1778, saw service in Virginia in the Augusta county regiment, died in 1790 and his wife was Jane Graham; came to Georgia with his wife, Jane Gay, from S. C., in 1830. Their son, James Lockridge, Jr., married Dec. 3, 1835, Nancy Tumlin, a sister of Lewis Tumlin and came to this county to live. Of 10 children, only Lewis N. Lockridge is living in Texas, but two great grandsons, Randolph and Clarence, children of James and Nancy Lockridge live in this county. Little James Lockridge, son of Randolph, is of the 10th generation. The James Lockridge family is buried in the Tumlin cemetery on the Cassville Road.

LOWE, Isaac: came from Newberry, S. C., with his sons-in-law Bradford and Bill to Cass county about 1850 and settled at Pine Log. Those of his children to rear families in this county were: (1) Nancy m. Samuel M. Bradford. (2) Jane E. m. James R. Bell, and their daughter, Minnie, m. Oliver Bradford by whom there were the following children who live in the county, in the Pine Log community: Sam m. Jessie Roberts; Bertie m. Jim Dorrah; Dr. Harry B. Bradford, practicing physician at Pine Log, m. LaNelle Moon; Trammel m. Miss Roper and lives at home place. Mrs. Bell married A. A. Vincent the 2nd time. (3) Mary m. Thomas S. Upshaw.

LUCAS, Maj. William H.; b. in Hancock Co. in 1814, came to Cass in 1858 and settled at "Clarendon". He was a student in the Univ. of Ala., and a graduate of Va.; was associated with the Alabama Journal in Montgomery; a Whig and very active in politics. He was a member of the "Silver Greys" during the Civil War. Maj. Lucas first married Mrs. Maria Champ Bradfute, of Va., then to Mrs. Frances L. Martin of Augusta. He died at his home on May 24, 1880. At his father's house in Sparta was held the first conference that ever assembled in the history of Methodism in Ga., when Bishop Asbury presided, and Dr. Lovic Pierce was ordained for the ministry. There are no descendants in the county.

MAXWELL, Martin: b. Dec. 17, 1805; married Juliann Upshaw in Jan. 1835 and came to Cass county in March 1836 from Elbert county. They settled in the Pine Log district where he farmed until his death on Oct. 12, 1886. Their children were: (1) James William, b. Feb. 1836, m. 1st Miss Teazley, 2nd Flora Pierce; children identified with Andrews, S. C. (2) Thomas Benjamin, b. July 11, 1838, m. Phoebe Barton, daughter of another old settler. Of 7 children these lived in the county: Irene (dec.), m. M. L. Upshaw; Martin m. Mary Lou Richards by whom there were Ben, J. M., and Louise, live at home place; Julia m. A. Johnson and 2nd time to Linton C. Crow; Izetta m. Mark Bolding and lives at White. (3) John Upshaw, b. July, 1840, m. Sarah Carson by whom there were: Tommie m. Marcellus Adair; May m. Will Henson; Ruby m. Willie Roberts; Ab. J. m. Mattie Goode and died at Adairsville in 1932. (4) McCarter Oliver, b. Sept. 1849, m. Maggie Roberts, no children. (5) George Middleton, b. Dec. 3, 1851, never married. (6) Henry Robert, b. Dec. 1854, m. Alma Bradford, died in Cartersville, Aug. 27, 1924. (7) Walter Chrisler, b. Aug. 19, 1859, m. Spicie Reynolds by whom there are Cleo, Chester, Teazley m. Mattie Boston, Verda, and Warren. (8) Curren M., b. Oct. 27, 1861, never married. M. O., George M., H. R., and Curren formed the company, "Maxwell Bros." in 1874.

MAYSON, Charles Newton: b. March 14, 1823 in Edgefield, S. C., a son of Archibald and Elizabeth Lowe Mayson; graduate of medical college in Augusta, began practice at Edgefield; came to Cass in the fall of 1846. In 1844 he married Frances E. Roper of Edgefield who died in 1863. During the war Dr. Mayson gave his services to the hospitals located at Kingston until he refugeed to Boston, Ga. In September, 1866, he married Mrs. Addie Davis of Atlanta and they lived in Kingston where he practiced and served as a life member of the Baptist church. He died there February 6, 1906 and was survived by his wife and Ella who married J. C. Rollins, J. F. Mayson, Susie Mayson, children of the first wife, and Mary who m. J. H. Hall.

McTIER, Henry Furgeson: with his sister, Nancy, came to Cass county from Maryville, Blount county, Tenn., in 1838. They came of sturdy pioneer stock and were "blue stocking" Presbyterians. Their mother, Martha Furgeson McTier, had many experiences with the Indians. She saw her younger brother scalped and another brother vowed vengeance on the chief, "Slim Tom", and in later years killed him. Henry and Nancy came to Cass on horseback, bringing their worldly possessions in an ox-wagon. In 1840 Henry McTier married Amanda Ivey of Gwinnett county and to them were born: (1) Nancy Ann m. Frank Verner (both dec.), a son, Sam Verner, lives in Cartersville. (2) Martha F., died young. (3) Rachel m. H. H. Holmes of Cassville (both dec.). (4) John Calvin m. Sallie Crawford, is a farmer at Cassville and a prominent citizen of the county. A daughter, Fanny Sue, m. W. S. Chunn. (5) Sallie Louise, m. Ed Bruce (both dec.); a son, Bertie, lives at Cassville. (6) Eliza Jane and Mary Priscilla never married and live in Cassville. During the Civil War Mr. McTier was too old for service, but when he died on' Feb. 22, 1864, his only request was to be buried in a casket like the Confederate soldiers. He is buried at Cassville.

MILAM, Mrs. Mary*: widow of William Milam, was a daughter of Robert and Sarah Pasley; born June 15, 1786; died Feb. 15, 1855; buried at Euharlee, Ga., in the Presbyterian graveyard. Her husband,

---

*This sketch was written by Herbert M. Milam of Atlanta.

William Milam, was a son of Bartlett and Elizabeth Milam; he was born in Halifax county, Va., Dec. 25, 1777; moved with his parents to Laurens district, S. C., in 1796; died Feb. 5, 1844. They had eight children, six sons and two daughters. Mrs. Milam moved from Laurens county, S. C., to Cass county in 1850, during that year and the two years following five of her sons, Thomas, William P., Madison, Riley, and Turner R., moved from Laurens county, S. C., to Cass. A short account of each of them follows: (1) Thomas Milam, b. April 4, 1807, d. Dec. 31, 1874, came to Cass about 1850-52, and settled on the Etowah river about one mile below Madison Milam's. He was a physician. He married Judy F. Ewing (his cousin), they had six children. One of his grandsons, T. Warren Tinsley, is now mayor of Cartersville. (2) William P. Milam, b. Sept. 7, 1809; d. Feb. 8, 1890, came to Cass in 1850, and settled on a place on the Etowah river about four miles west of Cartersville and on the north side of the river. He married first Charlotte Cothran; married second Sallie Newell; had three children by first marriage, and four children by second marriage. (3) Madison Milam, b. Feb. 4, 1812; d. Feb. 4, 1890, came from Laurens county, S. C., to Cass in 1850. He first rented the McLean farm on the Etowah river near Douthit's ferry, and was there about two years; he then bought a farm on the Etowah river about opposite where the Euharlee creek empties into the river, and seven and one-half miles from Cartersville. This was his home until his death in 1890. The ferry known afterwards as Milam's ferry was being operated when the property was acquired by him. The first bridge at this place was built in 1859, and it was destroyed by the soldiers about 2 P. M. May 21st, 1864. The present bridge was built about 1887. He married first Mary Ann Adams; married second Dorothy Ann Cothran; married third Susan Kirkpatrick. Had children: one by first wife; seven by second wife; six by third wife. One of his grandsons, Charles Madison Milam, is now president of the First National Bank at Cartersville. (4) Riley Milam, b. Feb. 9, 1818; d. Oct. 30, 1894. He came to Cass about 1852 and settled just across the Etowah river from Madison Milam, and near Stilesboro; for a good many years he was railroad agent and postmaster at Stilesboro station, and ran a general store there. He married Martha Kirkpatrick, and they had nine children, one of whom, Fred A. Milam, is now living in Cartersville. (5) Turner R. Milam, b. Feb. 9, 1820; d. May 27, 1872; came to Cass about 1852, and settled near the town of Stilesboro. He married first Barbara H. Kirkpatrick; married second Mary Day; there were four children by first marriage, and seven children by the second marriage. One of his sons, Benjamin F. Milam, now lives at Euharlee.

MILHOLLIN, John F.: b. in 1832 in Iredell, N. C.; removed with his family to Tennessee, then to Calhoun, Ga. When a young man he started teaching at Allatoona and married while there, Lucinda E. Dodgen who was born in DeKalb county. They removed to Cassville

Madison Milam (donated by Herbert M. Milam).

and he was elected clerk of the inferior court in 1855, serving until he enlisted in Confederate service. He became 2nd lieutenant of the Cherokee Cavalry organized at the Cassville Armory in January 1861 which company later became Co. B, Phillips' Legion. He died from wounds received in Virginia while attached to Gen. Stuart's brigade in 1863. On Sept. 29, 1863, May. Gen. J. E. Stuart wrote on a 4 days' leave permit that, "Captain Milhollin is regarded as a highly honorable man and one of the best officers in the service." Mrs. Milhollin with her 6 small children did not refugee in 1864 and at the time Cassville was burned found refuge at the fresh grave of her husband. Three of these children are yet living: John L., Mrs. Corra King lives in Gadsden, Ala., William Tatum Milhollin lives in S. C. John L. Milhollin, b. 1851, m. Carrie Elliott (dec.), daughter of Chappel Elliott who was a prominent citizen of Kingston, and their children are: Gertrude m. J. J. Barge, Clara m. H. W. Henderson, Mary Lee m. B. L. Pettit of Cartersville, Arthur m. Annie Morris, lives in Rome, Lindsay m. Lydia Adams lives in Cartersville, Willie May lives with her father at Cassville.

MILLER, Dr. Homer Milton Virgil: b. April 29, 1814 in Pendleton district, S. C., was the son of Gen. Andrew Miller who helped in the preservation of order during the removal of the Indians from North Georgia. By Gen. Miller's friendship with Judge J. W. Hooper, Dr. Miller came to Cassville, met the niece of Judge Hooper, Harriet P. Clark, a daughter of Amelia Hooper and John Clark, and married her on Oct. 22, 1835. After his marriage and wishing to complete his medical course in Paris, France, he left his wife with the Hoopers in Cassville. Dr. Miller started his practice of medicine at Cassville; later going to live at his home "Coligni" at Rome. He taught in medical colleges in Memphis, Augusta, and Atlanta. Dr. Miller died in Atlanta May 31, 1896. A sketch of Dr. Miller may be found in "Men of Mark in Georgia", Vol. III, and "Members of Georgia," p. 865. He was familiarly called "The Demosthenes of the Mountains", famed for his oratory and statesmanship.

MILNER, Arnold: b. in Laurens district, S. C., May 8, 1786 of English parents. In mercantile and farming business in South Carolina until he came to Georgia in search of health; he purchased land at Sallie Hughes' ford on the Etowah river; removing his family there in December 1834. After a year's residence, because of the Indians and scarcity of Anglo-Saxon families, he removed to Cassville to secure church and school privileges for his children. He was proprietor of the States Rights hotel there; in the meantime acquiring more land near the Pitner ferry. After removal of the Indians he returned to his fertile farm on the Etowah (near the present railroad bridge) and remained there until his death in 1869. In 1835 Mr. Milner experimented with cotton, planting two acres on an Indian field; finding no yield, he confined his crop to grain. He drove hogs for several years to lower Georgia and he invested in land and Negroes, accumulating an estate valued at $130,000 at his death on April 24, 1857. He was a Democrat;: with a few neighbors' help built and organized the Presbyterian church which was later moved to town. Judge A. R. Wright said of him, "No man stood higher in North Georgia than he, in every element of a true Christian manhood." He was married twice. First to Miss Lucy Neity Rodgers by whom he had one daughter and five sons. Second to Mrs. Isabella Saxon, mother of R. C. Saxon. Children of Arnold and Lucy Milner were: (1) Richard Andrew, b. Oct. 29, 1816, d. Nov. 13, 1855. Married Lucinda Brogdon, b. Jan. 9, 1828 in Gwinnett county, daughter of Wiley Brogdon of Oothcalooga valley on Dec. 12, 1843. Practiced law with his brother, James, in Cherokee circuit; spent last twelve years of his life as the first pastor of the Presbyterian church in Cartersville. Of their 6 children these are identified with the county: Thomas W. Milner, b. Sept. 1, 1846, d. Jan. 3, 1915, was admitted to the Cartersville bar in 1866, member of house of representatives, judge of the Cherokee circuit, in the impeachment of J. W. Renfroe, state treasurer, in 1879, he was elected one of the impeachment managers, Democrat, Methodist, m. Annie (dec.), daughter of Col. J. W. Harris by whom there were: Watt, b. Dec. 10, 1872, d. March 27, 1920, lawyer, city solicitor; Florence; T. W., Jr.; Eva (Trippe); Marilu (O'Rourk). Ida, b. Feb. 9, 1850, m. Sam F. Milam (dec.) who served in Co. H, 4th Ga. Res. C. M. S., and by whom there were: Idalu, William, Madison, James C., and Edwin, all of Cartersville. Lucy, b. May 22, 1853 (dec.) m. Charles M. McEwen (dec.), by whom there were ten children: William of N. Y., Alice of Nashville, Tenn., Ida m. C. G. Hern, Eloise, Annie m. D. E. John, Matthew, Lucy m. M. Dodd of Savannah. (2) James, was appointed aid-de-camp with rank of colonel by Gov. Cobb in March 1852, ranked at head of the Cherokee bar in his day, judge of the Cherokee circuit, died in 1869. He married twice and had many children but none are identified with this county at present. (3) Henry, farmer, manager of the Cartersville cold blast furnace up to 1852, married 3 times, is buried in Leeds, Ala. (4) William, farmer and manufacturer, m. Sally Borker of S. C. by whom there were: T. C. m. Ella Ingram, and their son, J. C. Milner lives in Cartersville; C. A.; W. Henry m. Grace Stephens; Richard Andrew, b. Oct. 2, 1857, d. Feb. 25, 1932, m. Leila Weems, daughter of Andrew Jefferson Weems formerly of S. C., who was an early settler in the Grassdale community; the children are: Beatrice, T. C., Joe, Charlotte (Beam), Mary (Keys), and Leila Milner.

MUNFORD, Lewis Martin: b. May 7, 1814; d. July 10, 1870; came to Cass county in the late 30's. In 1839 he married Serena Dillard, daughter of John Dillard who was born in 1785 and came to Cass with his wife, Elizabeth, from South Carolina before 1839. (She died in 1841 and is buried at Cassville.) L. M. Munford bought land in the 5th /district in 1840 and from then acquired a large plantation which has remained in the family to date. Their children were: (1) John m. Nancy Burge, served in the Civil War. (2) Nancy m. Patrick Gilreath. (3) Elizabeth m. James H. Gilreath (both dec.) by whom there were Annie (dec.) m. Harris Hall, Serena, and Louie, who live near Cartersville. (4) Lewis Sims, b. 1850, in 1874 m. Emma Jones (dec.) of Chattooga county, Ga., was a pioneer in developing the mineral resources in the county, at the time of his death, Oct. 12, 1916 at his home in Cartersville, he was recognized as one of the largest property owners in the county. Their children were Louis m. O. T. Peeples and lives at old home place, Mary died in 1902, Robert S. m. first Katherine Aubrey (dec.) by whom there are Sims, George and Dillard, and m. second Marilu Young, lives in Cartersville. (5) Serena m. George H. Gilreath (dec.) of S. C., by whom there were: Frank m. Gordon Cassels of Savannah, Robert G. m. Lizabel Cobb, Marie m. first E. D. Cole (dec.) and second Madison Bell, and Emory Gilreath. (6) Lemuel D. (dec.) m. Kathleen Saxon by whom there were Emmett, D. D., and Emogene m. Sam Q. Roberts of Cartersville. Maj. Lemuel Dillard, b. Dec. 25, 1801 in Laurens district, S. C., was a son of John Dillard and a sister of Serena D. Munford. He lived in the Grassdale community until his death on Dec. 12, 1883. He married 4 times. One wife, Martha, d. Feb. 3, 1869, aged 65, is buried at the old Mt. Zion cemetery. He is buried at Cassville.

NEEL, Joseph L.: b. in 1826 on a farm near the city of Birmingham, Ala., was a son of James H. Neel of Jasper county and of Irish descent; came to North Georgia in early manhood and began as a merchant in Adairsville. In 1848 m. Mary Ann Swain, of Adairsville. At the outbreak of the Civil War he enlisted in Company H, 40th Regt. Inf., and was made captain of the company. He served in several important campaigns; was taken a prisoner at Vicksburg; was wounded while with Gen. Johnston in battle of Atlanta and again at Bentonville. After the war he returned to Adairsville and engaged in farming and the mercantile business with his brother-in-law, W. Jesse Swain, where they were outstanding merchants. He was active in educational, civic and political affairs locally and in the State, and represented the county in the house of representatives in 1857-58 and again in 1875-76. In the year 1882 he removed to Cartersville where he lived until his death in March 1909. He was a Mason, a member of the Cumberland Presbyterian church. The children of Capt. Joseph L. and Mary A. Swain Neel were: James Monroe, whose sketch is found elsewhere; Nora, unmarried; Joe N., m. Blanch Hall, a prominent citizen of Macon, Ga.; William J., whose sketch is found elsewhere.

NEVILLE, James B.: a son of Jesse Neville, a Revolutionary

soldier; came from Rabun county with Duncan Murchison in 1834 to Cass and in 1836 he settled on 10 acres bought from a Mr. Ransom above Kingston at what is now McGuire's crossing. Tradition has it that Duncan Murchison bought his land on the Etowah from an Indian for a hound dog and a shot gun. The children of J. B. Neville were: (1) Adeline, never married. (2) Minerva m. a Mr. Burns and lived in Gordon county. (3) Margaret m. Terrance McGuire, an Irishman who came to this county and built the rock wall in 1836 or 1838 around Rev. Howard's place at Spring Bank; during Mexican War he was a volunteer in the 1st Ga. "Irish Greys". During the Civil War his wife Margaret, carried $4,500 in gold around her waist, ably guarded by a dirk in her bosom. This money was a godsend to neighbors around in the lean years following. Their son, John McGuire, b. on Jan. 4, 1851, was 14 years old when the Federal and Confederate armies passed his home and he remembers many stirring instances around this one-time cabin home. He has two sons in the county, Henry T and George McGuire. (4) John m. Nancy Murchison, daughter of Duncan Murchison. (5) Rachel m. on Dec. 22, 1870, Joe Headden by whom there is one son, J. W., who still owns his mother's share of the estate.

PARROTT, Josiah R.: b. in Cook county, Tenn., Feb. 1826; came to Georgia in 1848 and in 1852 settled in Cartersville where he practiced law. He was an elector on the Fillmore, Bell and Everett ticket in 1860; in 1862, quarter master with rank of major in Gen. Wofford's Brigade; in 1863 appointed solicitor general of the Cherokee circuit, reappointed in 1865; a delegate to the Constitutional convention of 1865; delegate to the Constitutional convention in 1868 and was elected president of the body; he was considered at this time for the governorship; in July, 1868, he was appointed judge of the Cherokee circuit which he served until he died in office, June 10, 1872. Judge Parrott was a Republican and presided in a circuit having a large Democratic majority; he possessed unequaled administrative ability, commanded the respect and confidence of the entire circuit and was prominent in the affairs of the city and county. The children of Judge and Mrs. Parrott were Lula, Sallie (Pillow), Flonnie, Mary (Hollingshed), Charles, and Julia (Hollingsworth).

PITTARD, William: b. 1764, d. Nov. 4, 1870; married twice; came to Cass with his first wife, Curacy Meadows, and four children from Oglethorpe county in 1841, first settling in the 5th district near the Buford place. The children were: (1) Thomas N. m. Annie Holcomb and their son, W. T. Pittard served two terms as tax receiver; served in Wheeler's Cavalry during Civil War, and lives in Atlanta. (2) Samuel L., b. Dec. 11, 1833, d. May 23, 1900, m. Margaret J., daughter of Lemuel Dillard and Martha Lofton, served in Wheeler's Cavalry, lived at Grassdale and had the following children: William Davis, b. Dec. 20, 1861, m. Cynthia Myers by whom there were Lois (died

1932), Sam and Paul who live at Cassville; James D., b. Feb. 25, 1867, served as tax collector, m. Ovie Layton and Ollie Strozier; Betty m. G. M. Serett and lives in Chicago; Carrie S. m. Dr. R. E. Wilson, graduate of Atlanta School of Medicine, a prominent physician in Cartersville, and by whom there are three children; Connor H., b. Oct. 29, 1879, m. Mamie Smith and lives in Cartersville. (3) Elizabeth, b. 1831, m. Henry Lumpkin who served in Co. A, 8th Ga. Batt., C. M. S., by whom there were W. H.*; Thomas; Fannie m. Thomas Hicks (both dec.) by whom there was a large family born and reared near Cartersville—only one son, W. L. Hicks, lives in the county; Ida m. a Mr. Osment by whom there was Harry; Elizabeth m. J. E. Scott, and lives in Adairsville; Dell (dec.). (4) Eliza, b. Aug. 20, 1835, d. June 22, 1892, m. in 1854 Robert L. Rogers, b. Aug. 1, 1826, d. Sept. 9, 1906. who came to Cass from Spartanburg, S. C., in 1848, settled at what became known as Roger's Station on the W. & A. railroad where he engaged in mining and farming. His brothers, Tom and Minus Rogers, lived and reared families near Rogers. The station has been discarded.

PRICE, Hawkins F.: b. 1822 near Raleigh, N. C.; came to Cass county when a young man and settled in Cassville where he lived until his death on December 8, 1874. He was prominent in the patriotic and political affairs of the State. He represented Cass in the State senate in 1857-58-63-64-65 Ex. He was one of the nine men on the ticket that nominated Jefferson Davis president of the Confederacy and was one of three delegates from Cass to the Secession convention in 1861; a member and steward in the Methodist church; married Louise Elizabeth Upshaw of Elbert county by whom there were: C. F. Price m. Susie Land; Ida m. Alfred Truitt of Atlanta. Col. Price and his wife are buried in the Cassville cemetery. His home was one of the landmarks during the campaigns around Cassville in 1864.

PUCKETT, Edmund Douglas: b. in 1806; came to Cass county with Lewis Tumlin from Gwinnett county, bringing his wife, Nancy Lane Pullium of Franklin county, and two children. They settled among the Cherokee Indians and found them friendly. Mr. Puckett acquired a plantation of 1700 acres south of Cartersville on the Etowah river and his first home was a house near what was known as Puckett's crossing. It was destroyed by the Federals in 1864 while the family were refugeeing. He died in 1876 and is buried in Cartersville. Of eight children there were these in Cartersville: (1) Ab married and had three sons. (2) William served as sheriff of the county, died in March, 1884. (3) Richard went west during California gold rush and never returned. (4) Tom m. Carrie Hendricks (dec.). (5) Douglas never married (dec.). (6) Kittie, b. in 1843, m. on May 12, 1868, William A. Deweese, who was a son of Cornelius Deweese

*See Benham sketch.

and a brother of Rachel Deweese Loveless, and Ruth Shockley, of S. C. He served in Confederate army. Their children were: Pearl (Jones), Daisy m. the 2nd time Dr. H. L. Irvin of Dalton, Nelle m. Jack Bishop. In the 70's Mr. Deweese ran the ferry below Cartersville. In 1869 Kittie m. Maj. P. H. Larey who organized the first company from this county as captain, died and is buried in Rockmart, Georgia.

QUARLES, David: b. Sept. 11, 1812; d. 1878; came to this county from one of the Carolinas. Deed records show that he was buying and selling lands in the county in 1837-38. He bought and traded property in Paulding, Floyd and as far away as Chatham. He and Lewis Tumlin were rivals in getting possession of property. Settling on the Alabama road, David Quarles was a friend to the Indians: an early member of the Raccoon Creek Baptist church. In 1839 he married Catherine Shaw, daughter of William W. Shaw, by whom there were ten children: Drusilla F. m. John F. Edward; Louisa P. m. a Mr. Morris; Mariah W. m. a Mr. Sims; Armanda S. m. W. B. House by whom there are George, Sam, Lena m. Davis Shaw and lives in Cartersville, and Newton m. Floyd Boston, lives on the old Alabama road.

REED, Joseph: moved to Adairsville several years prior to the Civil War from Pennsylvania and died there in 1877. His son, George Oliver Reed m. Mrs. Nancy Gholston Lovelace by whom there were: Oliver; Alice m. Edward L. Payne of Cartersville, by whom there are Wallace, Grace m. C. S. Cassels, Jack and Warren Payne. Ellen Reed 1st married Martin H. Butler, son of Maj. H. A. Butler of Kennesaw and to them were born: Ruth (dec.) m. Joe Bibb Bowdoin by whom there are Joseph Martin, George Reed and Warren Daniel Bowdoin; Alice m. George Harold Howard by whom there was Patricia Howard. Ellen Reed Butler, after the death of Martin H. Butler, m. Warren P. Whitworth of Adairsville. George Oliver Reed was a well known merchant in Adairsville after the Civil War. Although he was blind, he went back and forth to his store alone and looked after the business himself, except for the help of his small daughter.

REYNOLDS, Benjamin J.: b. in 1792 in Fredericksburg, Va., oldest son of Larben and Elizabeth Arnold Reynolds. He later went to Habersham county where he owned a gold mine, and in 1846 he came with his wife, Didama Proctor, to Cass county where he bought 4000 acres of land along the Etowah river near Kingston. He built a 12-room brick home which was completed in 1850. He died at this home on Feb. 6, 1855 and is buried in the Reynolds family cemetery on the place. The children buried there are: (1) Benjamin F., b. 1837, was killed in Confederate service. (2) P. H.: b. 1840, m. Mollie **Maynor.** (3) J. C., b. 1841, died from injuries received in 1863. (4)

Elizabeth M., b. 1846 in Habersham county, in April 1862 m. John Calvin Branson, oldest son of Levi Branson and Jane Willson, who was of Irish descent and a descendant of Lord Antrim. John C. Branson, b. March 27, 1839, at Due West, S. C., served in the Civil War, was judge of the county court, represented Bartow county in the legislature, 1880-81, and died at the Reynolds home on March 28, 1888. Their son, Bertram Bismark, was born here and died at this home on March 27, 1931. At the time of his death he was married to Orie Vincent who lives in the old home. Elizabeth Reynolds married the 2nd time, Capt. Charles R. Stone who died in 1918. She died Nov. 8, 1926. (5) Mary, b. 1849, m. J. S. Moore. (6) H. P., b. 1852. (7) Martha, b. 1853, m. Alex Wright of Rome.

ROWLAND, John Sharpe: b. 1795, Rutherford county, N. C., son of a Revolutionary soldier, Thomas Rowland, was a merchant in Spartanburg, S. C., and for a number of years tax collector before he came to Cass in 1839. Married in 1816 Frances Machen Lewis, b. 1799, sister of Dr. John W. Lewis. "Major" was attached to his name either from respect or militia service. He acquired extensive holdings in this county and others, in slaves, in railroad stock and was owner of the ante-bellum resort, "Rowland Springs", which he bought in 1843. He raised sheep on this Rowland Springs property. The original homestead was called "Etowah Valley" (now the home of the Leakes) and Maj. Rowland gave and settled a home for each of his sons. During the war he gave corn to the families of Confederate soldiers. He succeeded his brother-in-law, Dr. J. W. Lewis, as superintendent of the W. & A. railroad, serving until his death on Sept. 18, 1863. He and his wife are buried on the old home place. His biography is in "Lives of Eminent Americans, Now Living". Speaking of Mrs. Frances Rowland, who was an active member of the Raccoon Creek Baptist church, a brother-in-law remarked, "When John's wife got to heaven, should there be any spinning and weaving going on there, she would be placed at the head of that department."* She died Dec. 6, 1869. Of the 11 children of J. S. and F. M. Rowland the following lived and married in this county: (1) Mary, m. in 1851 the 2nd time, Dr. S. C. Edgeworth, one of the pioneer doctors of this county. (2) Eliza Frances never married. (3) J. Thomas, b. 1827, m. in 1852 Louisa Keith of Sweetwater, Tenn. Lived at "Music Hall", had two sons, John died young, a promising violinist; Charles K. is yet living in Cartersville. (4) John L., b. 1830, m. Ida Walker, Madison, Ga., lived at "Richlands". (5) William Lewis, b. 1833, m. Serena J. Dillard in 1855; settled in Cass, became a prominent farmer and land owner. Lived at "Forrest Hills", now the home of Julian Emerson Brown. Children: Fannie m. Charles Sproull; William m. E. Mayson, and 2nd Alberta Buford; John B.; Mamie m. B. V. Henry; Lydie m.

---

*From Genealogy of the Lewis Family, p. 248.

Charles Rudicil (dec.). (6) Robert H. (dec.) m. Cornelia Hollingshead, of Fort Valley. Inherited the old home place.

RUSSELL*, George Bell: b. Feb. 1, 1810 in Maryville, Tenn., a son of Robert Russell who is buried at Cassville; came with his wife, Jane Alexander Bell from Tennessee to Cassville where he was an early settler. He died in Atlanta June 17, 1892. The children were: (1) Elizabeth McReynolds, b. in Cassville Aug. 8, 1835, d. July 26, 1910; m. in 1859 Judge Samuel B. Hoyt of Atlanta by whom there were William R. Hoyt and Corrie Hoyt, who married G. M. Brown. Both live in Atlanta. (2) Mary V., b. Jan. 9, 1845, d. in Atlanta. A son, John J. Eagan, Jr. (dec.), m. Susan Young and have children in Atlanta. (3) Tennessee, m. John Berry of Rome, and they had one son, George B. Russell Berry. (4) Georgia m. Robert W. Murphy, a former lawyer of Cartersville. The Russells are buried at Cassville and Atlanta. John Russell, Sr., another citizen of Cassville, d. Dec. 22, 1857, aged 67 years, is buried at Cassville.

RYALS, The Rev. James G.: b. in 1824 in South Georgia, a grandson of Rev. Wilson Connor of pioneer Baptist ministry; graduated from Mercer in 1851; in 1852 married Mary E. Janes, daughter of Col. Absalom Janes of Penfield. He taught school in Columbus and studied law under Judge Francis Cone. He removed to and settled in Cass county in 1853, practicing law in Cassville and Cartersville, and built a home south of the Etowah river, on the old Alabama road, which is yet standing. After the war he entered the Baptist ministry and began teaching in the Stilesboro Academy, educating his own daughter and four sons in the meantime. He served the Raccoon Creek Baptist church from 1864 to 1883, and the Cartersville church for many years; a trustee of Mercer from 1872 until in 1883 he was elected to the chair of Theology at Mercer University, which position he filled until his death in September 1892. The children were: (1) Lucy m. Col. James J. Connor. She died in 1921†. (2) James G., a graduate of Mercer, died in 1885 while president of the State Normal College in Jacksonville, Ala. (3) Walter Mell, a graduate of Mercer, practiced law with A. M. Foute in 1884 and was in newspaper work in Cartersville and Anniston, Ala., died in 1886 in Birmingham, Ala. (4) Thomas Edward, a graduate of Mercer in 1885, has been a trustee and large donor for many years, is a lawyer in Macon, Ga. (5) Robert Lee, a graduate of Mercer, professor of mathematics at Mercer in 1892, died in Denver, Colo., in 1920.

SAXON, Robert C.: b. Aug. 10, 1821 in Laurens county, S. C.; d. June 1908; son of Mrs. Isabella Saxon Milner; moved to Gordon county in 1850; removed to Cassville in 1859; served in Confederate army as captain of a company of Georgia Reserves, adjutant of 55th

---

*Information from Miss Margaret Hoyt of Atlanta.
†See Connor sketch.

Ga. Regt.; quartermaster in Gen. Lucius Gartrell's Brigade; county school commissioner from 1881-97; married Elizabeth Croker by whom he had these children: (1) Isabella m. Alfred B. Best (both dec.), son of Rev. H. Best. (2) Orianna L. m. Robert N. Best, son of Rev. H. Best (both dec.). (3) Clara m. R. L. Saxon (dec.), farmer; children born in the county: Lizzabel, Bonnie Kate (Platt), Harold, Eva. (4) Kathleen m. Lem Munford (dec.). (5) Anna m. William King (dec.), lives in Calhoun. (6) Manie, taught in county schools for 30 years, lives in Calhoun. (7) Lydie, a beloved trained nurse. (8, 9) Charles and Henry, bachelors (both dec.). Mr. Saxon married in 1892 Mrs. Georgia Whitaker of Eatonton, Ga. The Saxon home was in Grassdale after the Civil War.

SHEATS, A. Y.: b. Dec. 9, 1830 at Villa Rica, Ga.; came to Kingston in the early 50's where he was a prominent merchant until war began. He enlisted in Confederate service, but soon organized a company of his own. After the war he returned to Kingston where he lived until his death in 1909. In 1864 he married Mrs. Louisa Irby Watts of S. C., a daughter of Dr. William Irby and great-granddaughter of Joseph Irby, a Revolutionary soldier. Captain and Mrs. Sheats are buried in the Kingston cemetery and only one son survives them, Samuel Irby Sheats who m. Emma Hill by whom there are two children. They make their home on the site of the old Johnston Hotel in Kingston.

SHELMAN, Charles T.: b. 1824 at Eden, Ga.; came to this county in 1848; bought land on the Etowah river and built a home called "The Glen", where later all his children were born. A brother, Pleasant Stovall Shelman, b. 1828, came to the county and lived near Raccoon creek church, married Caroline Hoxey, in 1865, by whom he had nine children, all of whom left the county when grown; he died in Polk county in 1886. In 1848 Charles T. married Cecilia Stovall of Augusta, the heroine of "Etowah Heights" which is included elsewhere. Her father was Pleasant Stovall, a wealthy cotton merchant who lived near the old U. S. Arsenal. Her brothers were General Marcelus A. Stovall, Bolling Anthony and the two who lived at one time in this county: Thomas Pleasant Stovall, married Volumnia Cooper, eldest daughter of Mark A. Cooper and from 1878 to 1885 they lived in London, Eng., where he was foreign agent for American grain; was captain of the Richmond Hussars, Co. A, later given rank of colonel; his second wife was Genl Orchard of S. C., a writer and painter; he tried to introduce foreign immigration to the farms in Georgia and was appointed commissioner for the State; died at Etowah Heights in 1895. John Stovall, married Eloise Edwards, by whom he had several children; after the war lived and farmed at "The Glen". In 1861 Mr. Shelman erected the southern mansion which, after being saved by Gen. Sherman, burned in 1911 from a defective chimney. Members of the family who were living there at the time saved a few valuable possessions. The children of Charles T. and Cecilia Shelman were: Cleo (dec.), Pleasant (dec.), b. 1851, was proprietor of the Shelman Hotel in Cartersville, m. Lelia Dallas; Robert (dec.), Charles T. Jr., Cecilia (dec.), Margaret (dec.). Mr. Shelman died at his home in November 1886. Mrs. Shelman, considered one of the brightest women of her day, died at her home in 1904. The only surviving member of this family, Charles T. Jr., built a home, called "Waverly Oaks", in 1897, near the old mansion. This home of Mr. and Mrs. Shelman stands sentinel over the historical spot which is a strand woven in the romance of Georgia history.

SMITH, Samuel: Came to Cassville with his brothers and sisters from Anderson, S. C., at the same time Lewis Tumlin and James Lockridge came. He had married Melissa Grey, and with him came 100 slaves who were superintended by a Mr. Layton. They settled on what is now known as the Shepherd-Gilreath farm in the 5th district. He represented this county in the house of representatives in 1845-47; his daughter, Melissa, m. William T. Burge. His brothers and sisters who settled here were: (1) John Lewis Smith b. Nov. 15, 1808, d. Jan. 21, 1872 and is buried at Cassville m. the 1st time in 1837. a cousin of Dr. W. H. Felton's, Rebecca Felton by whom there were: Susan, b. 1838, m. Capt. John Loudermilk who went from this county in Confederate service and was killed at the Battle of Gettysburg, leaving three children; Robert B. and Richard, twins; Samuel E., b. 1844, m. Ida Burge; John L., called "Sugar John", b. 1846, had a store for years in Cartersville, and his twin, William (both dec.); Mildred m. Robert Burford and their daughter, Alie, m. J. W. Jackson (dec.). The 2nd wife of John L. Smith was Nancy Elizabeth Loveless, daughter of Nathaniel Loveless, b. 1798, d. 1848, and Rachel DeWeese who died in 1857 and they are buried at Cassville. Her brothers, Wm. M. Loveless m. Mrs. Kate Hargis Banton, and Harrison Abner m. Mrs. Mary Lockridge Johnson. A cousin, Milton Loveless, b. 1818, d. in Cartersville in 1886, leaving his wife and daughters, Mrs. Jennie Rich, Evelyn, and Cora. The Loveless families lived between Adairsville and Kingston. The children of J. L. and Nancy Loveless Smith were: Nancy Elizabeth, b. 1853, d. 1924, m. in 1871 Samuel C. Smith—Mrs. Connor Pittard and Mrs. Creighton are daughters; Dora Jane, b. 1855, m. Thomas J. Lockridge and their daughter, Gertrude L. Kibler of Atlanta, gave this family data; James Nathan, b. 1859, m. Jane Taff and still owns the Smith farm three miles from Cassville and lives in Decatur; F. V., b. 1861, m. Fannie Layton by whom there is a large family who live in Cartersville; Martha A., b. 1864 (dec.) m. Burton Morgan; Abner Lee, b. 1866, m. Maime Merchison (both dec.); Lula M., b. 1870, m. R. H. Ferguson and lives in Atlanta. J. L. Smith had five sons in the Confederacy (2) Elija Smith m. in 1850 Mary E. Gaines, daughter of William and

Nancy Gaines and lived at Cassville. (3) Rebecca m. Ned Burford. (4) Nancy m. Jesse Jones. (5) Polly never married.

SPROULL, Charles: b. July 16, 1787; came with his wife, Fanny Sproull, from S. C. to Cass county about 1852. They settled in the Stilesboro community and reared a large family which annually celebrates a reunion known as the "Sproull Clan." Charles Sproull died Sept. 27, 1867, and he and his wife are buried in the Sproull family cemetery on the Taylorsville road. Of 10 children these have left descendants in the county: (1) John m. Jane Burge (both dec.) by whom there were eight children; a son, James W., lived in Polk county and has one daughter, Fanny, m. W. I. Jackson, who lives in Stilesboro. (2) Malinda S. m. Isaiah McCormick who died Dec. 2, 1870 and by whom there were: (a) Henry J. McCormick, taught in the Stilesboro academy, was captain in the Confederate army, served as county surveyor, m. Josephine Hawkins by whom there were: Clara m. Irving Wilson (both dec.) and they have a daughter, Mrs. May Ragsdale living near Cartersville, Bob (dec.), Charles, Grace, John m. Ida Munford and they live on the old Sproull place, and Jessie (dec.). Capt. McCormick died Nov. 17, 1929. (b) Frances m. Tomps McGinnis (both dec.), one daughter lives in the county, Rebecca C. m. Park Lanier. (c) Martha m. Van B. McGinnis (both dec.), a farmer in the 17th district and served as J. P. His father was a commissioned officer from Gwinnett county to remove the Cherokees. The children were: Bob H. m. Roberta Duke, and Mallie m. A. G. White (dec.), lives in Cartersville. (d) Sue Taylor m. Thad S. Hawkins whose parents came from S. C. to Cass county in 1848 and settled in the Stilesboro community where Mr. and Mrs. Hawkins, their daughters, Bessie and Campie, yet live. Annie Hawkins m. R. L. Jackson, of Stilesboro, Leona m. A. R. Davis of Taylorsville. (e) Charles m. Sarah Stephens (both dec.). (f) Anne Hunter (dec.). (g) Tom m. Lula Cason and lives at Stilesboro. (h) John, a twin of Tom's, m. Lula Baker (both dec.). (3) Elihu m. Mary Dowden by whom there were 10 children, no descendants in the county. (4) Thomas K., served as captain of Co. O, Phillip's Legion in Confederate service, m. Willie Thurman by whom there were: (a) Mattie m. Joe G. Cannon (dec.). (b) Charles William m. Mary Forrester, lives in Cartersville. (c) Octavia m. J. Y. Baker (dec.), lives in Stilesboro. (d) Moss lives at Etowah. (e) Kary m. O. M. Miller, lives in Stilesboro and Florida. (f) James m. Mary Baker, live at Stilesboro. (5) Emily m. John Auchmutey by whom there were three children. Sons of J. A. Auchmutey are: Ed, who lives in Cartersville and Charlie Bob, who lives at Euharlee. (6) McDuffy m. Lou Stedham by whom there were three children. (7) Robert died in Confederate service.

STEGALL, Emsley: b. Jan. 6, 1812 in Pickens county, S. C.;

came with his parents, Blackwell and Sarah Stegall, before 1840 to Cass county where he had drawn a 40 acre lot; in 1841 he married Sarah Lackey, of S. C. They settled where a station was named for him after the railroad was constructed, and Mr. Stegall was the first agent. Stegall's Station later became Emerson. By hard work Mr. and Mrs. Stegall acquired a large farm and in the late 50's erected a log church in which Dr. Felton, Rev. R. H. Jones and Sam H. Smith served as pastors. He died at Emerson Nov. 25, 1888. R. B. Stegall*, the eldest son, lives at Rossville, Ga., was retired in 1925 after 47 years of service with the Southern Railway. He married Carrie Murphy, Mary J. Jefferson and Bessie Lowry. The other son, John P., was reared at Emerson and was agent of the W. & A. railroad for 25 years. He married Justina Williams of Tenn., by whom there were: Minnie m. W. O. Henderson (both dec.); Wallace Emsley m. Bernia Henderson (both dec.); Sallie (dec.) m. in 1895 A. Abramson who came to this county in 1888; Paul, D. D. of Atlanta.

STILES, William Henry: b. Jan. 1, 1810 in Savannah, Chatham county, Ga., was the fourth son of Joseph and Catherine Clay Stiles; after preparatory studies, studied law at Yale and was admitted to the bar in 1831, beginning practice in Savannah. In 1832 he married Eliza Mackay in Savannah. He was solicitor general for the Eastern circuit of Georgia, 1833-36; received honorary degree from Yale in 1837, and about this time was appointed by Andrew Jackson district attorney for Georgia†. In 1838 he was selected by the Federal Government to pay off the Cherokee Indians in gold. He, riding horseback to North Georgia and being attracted by the beauty and climate, purchased land for "Etowah Cliffs", and built a wooden house to which a brick part was added in 1850. He was elected as a Democrat to the 28th U. S. Congress, serving from 1843 to 1845; on April 19, 1845, was appointed by Pres. Polk, charge d'affaires to Austria and lived in Vienna with his family until October 1849, when he returned to Georgia and divided his time practicing law in Savannah and living at Etowah Cliffs. While at his home here he wrote and published in 1852, two volumes, "Austria, 1848-49", which includes the full account of the revolution in Austria and Hungary, and historical sketches of the Austrian Government. In the State convention of 1857 his name, among others, was mentioned for governor, but was later withdrawn. He was a member of the house of representatives and served as speaker in 1858; a delegate from the State at Large to the Commercial Congress in Montgomery, Ala., in 1858, and to the Baltimore Democratic National Convention in 1860. He served in the Civil War as colonel of the 60th Ga. Regt., which he organized, serving until his health failed in 1863. He died in Savannah Dec. 20, 1865, and is buried in Laurel Grove cemetery. Col. Stiles was famous as a "silver-

---

*90 on June 15, 1932.
†Commission in possession of John C. Stiles of Brunswick.

1. Godfrey Barnsley. 2. Mrs. Julia Henrietta Barnsley (from a miniature taken in 1829). 3. John L. Smith (donated by Mrs. Forrest Kibler). 4. William Henry Stiles (donated by his descendants). 5. Mr. and Mrs. O. E. Henderson (from a daguerreotype given by Herschel and Carl Griffin).

tongued orator" and was popular as a public speaker in conventions and college commencements on account of his good looks and splendid oratory. He was active in the affairs of this county and his home on the Etowah river, on lot No. 721 in the 4th district, is now owned by a grandson, William Henry Stiles. At one time the grandsons owned and operated a race track, in the 80's and 90's, which made a profitable and attractive sporting feature for the county. The tracks were on the estate of W. H. Stiles. The children of W. H. and Eliza Mackay Stiles were: (1) Mary Cowper, 1833-1863, m. Andrew Lowe of England by whom there were: Katherine M. (dec,); Mary m. Charlie Guthrie, a member of Parliament, died July 1932; William M. (dec.) m. Juliette Gordon, daughter of Gen. W. W. Gordon of Savannah, and she was the founder of the Girl Scout movement in America and died in January 1927; Jessie m. Hugh Graham of Warwickshire, England. (2) William Henry, 1834-1878, lived most of his life in this county at Etowah Cliffs; m. Eliza Clifford Gordon of Savannah who died in 1926 and by whom there were: (a) William Henry, b. 1858, m. Lizzie Chadwick by whom there were: Lt. Com. W. H. Stiles, Jr., John C. of St. Louis, Hugh G. of Savannah, Dorothy m. W. T. White, Elmer m. G. Lee Cook (dec.) of Louisville, Robert m. Susie McGowan, Joe, and Phillip. (b) Gulielma, d. May 11, 1930 and is buried in the family cemetery. (c) William Gordon lives in Texas. (d) Mary C. (dec.) m. E. J. Swann of Canada. (e) Alfred, Ellen, Ethel, and Robert M. all died when young. (f) George m. Penelope Crumbliss and lives in Rome, Ga. (3) Robert Macky, 1836-1874, lived on the adjoining estate, "Malbone"; m. Margaret Couper of Hopeton by whom there were: Robert M. (dec.); Caroline C. m. W. S. Lovell, lives in Birmingham and is the author of "The Golden Isles", 1932; Hamilton C. lived in Bartow all his life until his death on March 15, 1923; John C. lives in Brunswick; Eilzabeth M. m. Franklin B. Screven of Savannah; Margaret C. lives in Savannah; Katherine m. R. L. Mercer of Savannah; Isabel C. m. H. S. Marshall of New York City.

TRIPPE, Turner Hunt: b. Feb. 28, 1801, near Sparta, Ga., moved with his family to Eatonton while yet a child. Graduated from Franklin college in class of 1822 with first honor. Admitted to the bar at Eatonton in 1823; in 1824 he married Mary Ann Gatewood, of Putnam county, making their home in Clarkesville, Ga., until 1826; elected solicitor general of the Western circuit in 1828, serving for a number of years. When elected judge of the superior court in the Cherokee circuit in 1839, he moved his family to Cassville that year. In 1856 he retired from public life to his country home, "Linden". He did not love the practice of law; the contention and strife of the court room were distasteful to him; the majesty of the theory of law, he loved, but not its practical application. He was a Whig, a Methodist. At the beginning of the war, he, with Gen. W. T. Wofford and Col. Hawkins F. Price, was elected as Union delegates to Georgia's Secession Convention from this county. They did not yield their convictions of right, but finding a majority of the convention determined to secede, voted that the action of Georgia might be practically unanimous. Too old for Confederate service, he was a lieutenant of the Bartow Home Guards in 1863; having given his double-barreled gun to the service, he rode his own pony along the guarded roads, equipped with a single-barreled bird gun. In April, 1866, he was elected judge of the county court and was incumbent of the office when he died in 1867. Children identified with the county were: (1) Mary m. Dr. Weston Hardy, b. in Anderson district S. C., a graduate of the Charleston Medical College in 1839, one of the pioneer doctors until after 1881. (2) Frances, b. June 1832, m. Abda Johnson in 1852. (3) Anna R. m. John E. Glenn of S. C. (4) Martha m. Col. Tom Hooper, son of Judge J. W. Hooper, was law partner of J. C. Branson. (5) Sarah m. James Vincent (both dec.). (6) Julia C. m. Hez Best, Jr., in 1868. (7) Robert Barron, b. 1846, practiced law in Cartersville and was a judge of county court, removed to Atlanta and died there in 1890.

TRIMBLE, Augustus Crawford: b. Dec. 11, 1818, in what is now Newton county, Ga., a son of William Trimble and Harriett, who was a daughter of Amos Wellborn. William Trimble was killed by lightning and his widow married Dr. Adams Q. Simmons who together with Amos Wellborn and Dr. Elijah H. George worked out the formula for Simmons Liver Regulator, once a popular household remedy. About 1836 Amos Wellborn, b. in 1776 at Heard's Fort, Wilkes county, accompanied by his grandson Augustus Trimble, removed to Cass county, settling at old Adairsville and opened a tavern there, but in a few years he removed to Walker county where he died in the 50's. Augustus Trimble, only 18 years of age, remained and entered the mercantile business in partnership with Hodge and Bailey and this store was located on the east side of the road north of Adairsville. Merchandise then was shipped from Augusta to a Ga. r.r. terminus below Union Point and from there wagoned to old Adairsville. Augustus turned to farming and bought land north of the town. On June 20, 1839 he married Louisa A., daughter of Wiley Brogdon who came from Jackson to Gwinnett county to Cass at the same time as did Amos Wellborn and was a neighbor of the Trimbles and acquired land and property. Augustus Trimble was one of the founders of the old Oothcalooga Baptist and Poplar Springs Methodist churches; a clerk of the superior court; physically incapacitated, he served in the Home Guards during the Civil War. He was a Freemason, a Methodist. By his first wife, b. April 13, 1824, d. Jan. 19, 1847, he had: (1) Josephine M., b. June 6, 1840, m. 1st Charles Stone, 2nd J. L. Camp, lived in Rome, Ga., died Aug. 15, 1902. (2) William Wiley, b. May 8, 1843, educated in Adairsville schools, served in the 1st Georgia Regiment, then in Co. I, 1st Ga. Regt.; farmer on old homestead; m. Lucinda, daughter of Col. John W. Gray, by whom there were ten children; those living in the county are Clara, Minnie m. T. J. Noland of Adairsville, Ella and Layton. (3) Virginia R., b. April 14, 1845, on October 3, 1866 m. William L. LeConte, a grandson of Louis LeConte who was the father of Drs. John and Joseph LeConte, the founders of the Univ. of Calif. Wm. LeConte saw hard service as a private first three years of Civil War and before Battle of Chickamauga he was appointed adjutant of 66th Ga. with rank of 1st lieut., and served as such until wounded in 2nd day's battle of Atlanta; he was returning to his command on foot when he learned of the surrender. After his marriage he became a resident of Adairsville and then spent his married life there with the exception of eight years. He represented the county in the legislature in 1890-91 and died at the home of his son in Atlanta, Aug. 7, 1920. Their children were William L., d. in 1870; James Augustus, b. July 19, 1870, m. Emma Kinman, lives in Atlanta; Joseph N., b. Sept. 27, 1873, grew up in Bartow, practiced medicine in Atlanta, d. 1911. Mr. A. C. Trimble married the 2nd time, Loany A. Fain who died leaving two daughters, Harriett and Helen who both married the Rev. Eli Smith. Mr. Trimble married the 3rd time in the early 70's Miss Mary Thompson of Augusta. He died May 15, 1894 and is buried in Poplar Springs cemetery.

TUMLIN, Lewis: son of William, b. Jan. 6, 1775, d. Oct. 8, 1856, and Rebecca Tumlin, d. Oct. 16, 1846; was born in Gwinnett county, May 9, 1809. He came to Cass county as a young cattle driver and earned his first money as a guard employed by the government to protect the settlers from the depredations of the Indians. Without education and much of this world's goods, endowed with tireless energy and a strong character, he soon became a large property and slave owner and trader and leader in politics. A "dyed-in-the-wool" Democrat, he took part in local and national politics. Col. Tumlin served as sheriff of the county in 1834-36-38-40; as senator in 1842-43-51-52; for many years he was a formidable aspirant for Congress from the 7th district, and in 1853 missed election by 257 votes. He was presidential elector for his district on the Breckenridge and Lane ticket in 1860. Lewis Tumlin was one of the 38 men who aided Mark A. Cooper in saving the Iron Works in the panic of 1857 and has his name on the monument. Hospitality was with him a principle and he dispensed it with a lavish hand. The latter part of his life was spent in overseeing his large plantations in north and south Georgia. He died June 2, 1875, at his plantation on the Etowah river and is buried in the Cartersville cemetery after removal from the family lot on Cassville road. Col. Tumlin was married in 1835 to Miss Jane Scott who died Feb. 15, 1849, aged 34 years, by whom there were: (1) Josephine L., b. Aug. 24, 1836, m. Sanford Erwin, d. Sept. 9, 1859. (2) Ada m. Captain Rice of Nashville (dec.). (3) Samuel S., d. Dec. 6, 1863. (4) Napoleon lived and died at Acworth. His 2nd marriage was on May 25, 1852, to Lucie Elizabeth Goldsmith, b. Jan.

1, 1832, d. Mar. 1, 1859, a daughter of Maj. Turner Goldsmith of S. C., and this county, and their children were: (1) Lula m. Thomas J. Lyon who lived in this county until his removal to Atlanta, both died in 1913; their children were Cora m. C. P. Bird, Thomas J. and Henry W., all of Atlanta. (2) Cora m. Frank Gray of Adairsville by whom there were four children; the 2nd time to W. W. Austell (both dec.). (3) Henry m. Georgia Roberts and lived at one of the Tumlin farms, southwest of Cartersville, all his life. Their children were: Lucie m. Dr. H. M. Martin (dec.); Augusta m. C. C. Chamberlain of Atlanta; Lillian m. Dr. T. E. Lindsey of Rome; Lewis m. Alluwee Brown and with his family lives with Mrs. Georgia Tumlin. On Dec. 24, 1865, Col. Tumlin married Mrs. Mary L. Lee of Stone Mountain, Ga., by whom there was one child, Elizabeth. At an early date William and Rebecca Tumlin moved their family from near Abbeville, S. C., and settled in Gwinnett county, Ga., later moving to Cass. There were four sons and five daughters: Imri who died and is buried on Cassville road; Lewis the subject of the previous sketch; the Rev. George W.; William; Rebecca who married William Wade and later Dr. Humphrey; Nancy who married James Lockridge, Jr.; Polly who married a Martin; Elizabeth (d. Nov. 9, 1868) married a Mr. Humphries; Ann married William Ginn whose son, W. W. Ginn, one of the county tax receivers, was the father of Mrs. Sam Verner and Mrs. J. W. Johnston of Cartersville. Most of these deceased children are buried in the Tumlin cemetery on Cassville road. At the age of 19, George W. Tumlin married Rachel Wade of S. C. by whom there were: N. J. Tumlin of Carrollton; Capt. William M. Tumlin of Cuthbert, captain of a Bartow county company; Henry I. Tumlin of Anniston, Ala.; Virgil M. Tumlin of Atlanta; James Tumlin of Carrollton; C. L. Tumlin of Cuthbert; Mary Tumlin (G. W.) Muir of Lexington, Ky.; and Martha Tumlin (John Winn) Gess of Fayette county, Ky. His second marriage was to Laura Terhune of Cass county by whom there was Rev. G. S. Tumlin. George W. Tumlin was ordained to the Baptist ministry in 1848 and served churches in this county in that early period. A successful and a beloved pastor, he was able by his great energy and excellent business capacity to establish and finance early churches. He accumulated estates in Cass county and Southwest Georgia. Being attracted to Bowdon in Carroll county, about 1860 he made his home and established a church there. He died at Bowdon July 17, 1867*. Geo. Samuel Tumlin, a minister of the Baptist denomination, was born Dec. 16, 1852, on his father's plantation, near the Etowah river, in Cass county. He was the son of Rev. George W. Tumlin and Laura Terhune, daughter of Cornelius Terhune, originally of New Jersey. He attended school in Bowdon, Ga., graduating there in 1870; the next summer and fall he took a business course in Baltimore; graduated in law from Athens, Ga. in 1871, was

---

*Information from Mary Belle Gess McDonald of Atlanta.

Rev. George W. Tumlin (donated by Mary Belle Gess McDonald).

judge of county court of Bartow from 1883 to 1885. On June 10, 1874 married Alice Gilreath of Cartersville. To them were born ten children, all but one of whom are living. In 1877, he entered the ministry, being ordained by Rev. Robert Headden. In 1885 he was pastor of the church at Marietta; in 1891, he accepted a call to the church at LaGrange, where he remained until taking his family to Texas in 1895. The next six years he ministered to the Broadway Baptist church at Fort Worth, later serving churches at Rockdale, Sulphur Springs and Amarillo. In 1914 he returned to Georgia and again ministered to the church at Marietta. All of his children are now living in Texas. In 1918, when the Cole Ave. church of Dallas called him to its pulpit, he accepted, serving there until 1921. He died suddenly June 6, 1925 at the home of his daughter, Mrs. C. B. Carswell in Dallas. When the beautiful new church at Amarillo, Tex., was erected, the interior decorations and a bronze tablet were given as a memorial to his work at that church by Mr. and Mrs. R. B. Masterson (Laura Tumlin). He rests in Grove Hill cemetery, Dallas, his grave marked by a slab of Georgia marble.

UPSHAW, James: with his wife, Lucindie Upshaw, formerly of Va., came to Cass from Elbert county, Ga., about 1836 and settled in the Pine Log district. The Upshaws were farmers and reared large families. Of the children of James and Lucindie Upshaw these married and reared families in the county: (1) Polly m. a Mr. Lott and left no descendants in the county. (2) Matilda m. Levi Pierce and lived at Pine Log. (3) Juliann m. Martin Maxwell. (See Maxwell sketch.) (4) Sara, b. 1818, m. Joseph L. Dysart, b. Nov. 13, 1817. Their daughter, Lizzie, 89 years old, is yet living with a grandson of J. L. and a son of John Dysart, J. Milton Dysart who lives south of Cartersville and was tax collector in 1895-96. Granddaughters, Lena and Flora Dysart, daughters of Jim and Georgia Pierce (a daughter of Levi Pierce) Dysart, live near Pine Log. (5) Martha Gatewood m. Ausley A. Vincent (see Vincent sketch). (6) Clara P., Patrick, Caroline and Mildred (Parker), lived in Dooly county. (7) Thomas S., b. 1825, d. July 1, 1895, a farmer in the Pine Log district, Methodist; m. Mary Lowe, daughter of Isaac Lowe, by whom there were: (a) Elbert M., m. Elizabeth Adair by whom there were: Linton, Dr. Bell of Atlanta, Paul (dec.), Elbert and Corinne of Atlanta, Thomas m. Lois Pittard (dec.) of Cartersville, and Lamar m. Lillian Goode. (b) Ella m. in 1876 Dr. William B. Vaughan, b. Nov. 7, 1855 at Cassville, died at White, Nov. 10, 1931, where he practiced medicine. In 1891 he graduated from Southern Medical College and Emory conferred an honorary degree in June, 1925; a Methodist and a Mason, the first mayor of White. Their children were: Ora m. E. C. Goode, Bessie Cheney (dec.), Lucile m. L. G. Hughes and lives in Cartersville. (c) Madison L., b. March 16, 1864, m. Irene Maxwell (dec.) by whom there were Leo (dec.), m. Bob Collins, Murray and Troy. (8) Jeanett, b. Aug. 31,

1831, m. in 1848, Dr. J. Martin Lott who practiced medicine at Pine Log and Cassville in the 50's. (9) Emily m. James Gibson and lived in La.

VEACH, James Madison: b. in Frederick county, Va., of Welch descent, Aug. 14, 1823. He was educated in Virginia but soon left home to earn his living. Worked in New York; later seeking a milder climate he came to Georgia, finally settled at Adairsville where he erected in 1858 a flour and grist mill that grew into the J. M. Veach Milling Company. Mr. Veach also conducted a large store in the town of Adairsville and was one of the men to build up the town. In 1859 he married Julia A. Echols of Chattooga county. During the Civil War he was a purchasing agent for the Confederate army. In 1892 he was elected without his knowledge as representative in the general assembly and in 1893, while serving, prepared a bill providing for a system of state banks; a Mason, Methodist, died in Adairsville Feb. 8, 1897. Of seven children these survived him: (1) George Albert, b. April 14, 1862, educated at Dahlonega, Ga.; when 17 years of age entered father's milling business, farmer, county commissioner for two years. Mason, on Oct. 14, 1885, married Mattie Dobbins (d. May 13, 1924), daughter of Miles G. Dobbins, by whom there were: Everett D. (dec.) m. Lillian Bradley, Julia m. John Stewart, J. M. m. Marguerite Dyer. lives in Adairsville, Susie m. Milton P. Gaines, lives in Adairsville, Mary m. Richard N. Milner, Grady A. m. Serena Riser, lives in Adairsville. (2) Anna L. m. Noah H. Grady of Chattanooga, Tenn. (3) Henry Madison, b. Oct. 30, 1867, educated in schools of Adairsville, graduate of Eastman Business College at Poughkeepsie, N. Y.; at father's death the business was incorporated by the two brothers and the mill, in his day, had a daily capacity of 350 to 400 barrels; one of the organizers of the Adairsville bank and a director of the Bankers' Trust Company of Atlanta; active citizen of the town, Mason, K. of P.; died Oct. 8, 1919.

VINCENT, Susan Edwards: daughter of Wm. Edwards, a Revolutionary soldier and widow of Pleasant Hart Vincent of French descent, came to Cass county from DeKalb with her children in 1835 and settled in the Pine Log district. Mrs. Vincent lived until after the Civil War. She died in 1877. A Federal soldier died in her home and she buried him in her own family lot. Of her eight children, these reared families in the county: (1) Mary, b. 1809, m. Chesley Bostick by whom there is one child in the county, Mrs. Oliver Richards. (2) Aulsey Ayres, b. March 7, 1811, in Madison county, was a trader with the Indians, bought land in 1838 and in 1846 purchased 160 acres on Pine Log creek, active in public affairs, was county commissioner six years, a Whig and then Democrat; m. the 1st time Martha G. Upshaw by whom there were 13 children: Aulsey E. m. Agnes Adair and now lives in Plains, Ga. James U. m. Sarah Trippe and Louella Styles, died in Texas. Lucinda m. G. W. Hughes and both died in Tyler, Tex.

Chesley B. m. Ida Stephens (dec.) by whom there is one daughter in the county, Lorena Barton. Malvina m. W. T. Bradford, who died in 1932, by whom there were Dela May, Clyde and Mattie (Harris). Lucius m. Sallie Mahan, daughter of David, and their daughter, Orie m. B. B. Branson of Kingston. Lula lives in Pine Log. Lorena m. L. G. Darnell (dec.), lives in Cartersville. His second wife was Mrs. Jane E. Bell, formerly Jane Lowe, by whom there were Stella, m. J. P. Adair, and Eddie, who died in Tex. His 3rd wife was Margaret McEver. (3) S. Margaret, b. 1829 in DeKalb county, m. in 1846 William Jackson Hicks, of English descent, a son of Jefferson Wyatt Hicks and Malinda Phelps, who came to this country in 1836, drew 1000 acres for service in War of 1812, fought in the Battle of New Orleans, died in 1841 and is buried in the Baker cemetery. W. J. Hicks was a bookkeeper for Etowah Iron Company several years, went to Calif. in 1850, in 1860 enlisted in Phillip's Legion. A son of Margaret and W. J. Hicks, James John W., b. 1848, m. in 1869 Sarah C. White, at Hartwell, Ga.; served in Co. "I", 1st Ga. Cav. C. M. S., died in 1898; Lucy H. Rucker, a daughter, lives at Elberton. Eppe W. (dec.), a son, m. Mattie Ward and have children in Cartersville.

VIRGINIA COLONY: "Little Virginia" was settled on the Cherokee and Cass county lines by families who came directly from Virginia about 1850. They came at the insistence of David Mahan who had come early and had seen the possibilities for the tobacco grower in this section while there was an over-production in Virginia. These Virginians grew tobacco successfully along the Salacoa creek and erected four factories and packing houses until the revenue tax became so high there was no profit and operations ceased. Mr. Taylor was the teacher for the children and the colony had one of the first traveling libraries. The colony consisted of the following families that settled across the Cherokee line: Col. Prichett; Thos. Hutcherson; the Richardson's; George W. Jefferson, Mrs. Edna Tate of Fairmount is a granddaughter; D. W. Ferguson; the Templetons; David, Calvin, and Joseph Mahan, sons of William Mahan who came after his sons did. David died June 7, 1906, and is buried in Cassville cemetery. The following settled in Cass: Solomon Fuller; Obadiah Taylor, Jr., and his wife, Jane Riddle, whose daughter, Elizabeth, married Joseph Mahan and Mrs. R. E. Adair, J. B. Mahan, Mrs. Rebecca Upshaw, and Mrs. Ella Wooten of this county are children; James and Vadin Riddle; Augustus Hubbard; Capt. John Patton; Dr. Uren who practiced in Pine Log, and Dr. Young who practiced around Salacoa.

WIKLE, Jesse Richardson: b. April 13, 1823, near Waynesville, N. C.; in 1843 moved to Dahlonega, and in 1850 became editor of The Dahlonega Watchman; was admitted to the bar, but did not practice regularly; in 1845, he was married to Mary Hooper, daughter of Matthew Hooper of Franklin county and a descendant of the Hoopers who were conspicuous during the Revolution; in 1849, while a resident of Cherokee county, he was elected a delegate to the convention on the admission of California as a state, representing the Union ticket; came to Cartersville in 1851, where he engaged in mercantile business, served as postmaster, and from 1854 was agent of the W. & A. railroad until in 1860, he moved to Cassville and became the editor of The Cassville Standard and was a supporter of Douglas and Johnson. In June, 1861, at the beginning of the Civil War, he entered the Confederate army as a member of the 18th Ga. Regt., with the rank of captain; after the close of the war, he moved to his farm near Cartersville, and was elected judge of the inferior court; in 1865, he was elected to the convention to revise the constitution of the State and was made chairman of one of the committees; he was postmaster at Cartersville from 1870 to 1885, when he resigned; when the First National Bank was established, he was its first president, and continued in that capacity until a short time before his death on Nov. 14, 1908, at his home on Erwin street; buried in the city cemetery. The children of Jesse R. and Mary Wikle were: (1) John Henry, b. July 24, 1847, in Dahlonega, d. May 10, 1930, attended Cherokee Baptist College at Cassville; at the age of 16 appointed enrollment officer, then enlisted in 1864, Co. I, Ga. Cav.; in 1865, read law and was admitted to the bar in September 1866, and became a law partner of Gen. W. T. Wofford, and was associated with him as receiver of the Alabama Great Southern railroad; he was for a while editor of The Cartersville Standard; county commissioner for 10 years, mayor of Cartersville for three successive terms; author of city charter of 1906; wrote a number of charters for the city; was president of the Building and Loan Association, a K. of P., Methodist; in 1869 married Virginia Shepherd, daughter of John W. Shepherd, by whom he had two daughters: Mary Lou and Jessie. Mary Lou married Chas. M. Milam, and died in 1908, leaving one son, John W. Milam. (2) Ignatius Few, lived for a time in Cartersville, was for many years in the U. S. railway mail service (dec.). (3) William Hooper, merchant in Cartersville (dec.). (4) Jesse Lane, physician and a prominent citizen of Anniston, Ala. (5) Charles Adams, druggist in Atlanta and Marietta (dec.). (6) Douglas, lawyer and practiced in Nashville, Tenn., for several terms a member of the house and senate of Tennessee, and for ten years judge of the 17th judicial circuit of Tenn., Methodist. (7) Mary, prominent in home and foreign missions (dec.). John L., brother of Jesse R., merchant and farmer, served several terms as magistrate (dec.). W. S. D. Wikle, brother of Jesse R., assisted him in his newspaper work, and was afterwards engaged in the manufacture of printer's rollers in Atlanta (dec.).

WOFFORD: Two brothers came from the county of Cumberland in England and settled in Pennsylvania near the Maryland line*. One

---

*From the genealogy of the Wofford family of South Carolina.

of these brothers, Absolom, was the father of five brothers who settled in Spartanburg district, S. C., before the Revolution in which each one served. Col. William Wofford, b. Oct. 25, 1728, one of the five sons, founded the iron works in the Spartanburg district and was the progenitor of the Woffords in that state and Georgia. He later came to Habersham county. His son, Nathaniel Wofford, along with some relatives, came to Cass county from Habersham in 1833 and settled in the 5th district where they had drawn lots for their father's Revolutionary service, settling at what is yet known as Wofford's Cross Roads. Nathaniel Wofford was justice of the inferior court of Cass in 1833-34. He married Lydia Hopper and their children identified with the county were: (1) John, b. Oct. 23, 1808, d. Apr. 13, 1895, was a veteran of the Seminole War in which he was commissioned to ride with important dispatches to Washington on horseback, receiving for this service $500 in gold; served in the Mexican and Civil Wars; buried in Florida; married Rebecca Cochran by whom the following children are identified with this county: (a) John, m. Texanna Burge, daughter of W. T. Burge of this county and their children are identified with Miami, Fla. (b) James C., b. Mar. 10, 1840, d. Dec. 30, 1913, served as depot agent 45 years in Cartersville, served as mayor of the city several terms and on board of education. He served duration of the Civil War, surrendering in Kingston in 1865, seeing active service in the maneuvers from Missionary Ridge to Atlanta. He was known as "Chuck"; married Henrietta Satterfield, daughter of John and Mary Satterfield, by whom there were: Marilu m. Paul Gilreath; Beck m. Robert Donahoo of this county and are now living in Miami, Fla.; James H. m. Florence Stephens by whom there are J. H. Jr., Sadie (Powell) and Keith; Eva (dec.) m. W. T. McLeod by whom there was a daughter; Annie; Bruce; Lois (dec.) m. F. A. Shouse; Nora. All of Cartersville. The other children of John and Rebecca Cochran are identified with Florida. (2) James m. the 2nd time Camilla Miller. He was sheriff of the county in 1836, in the house of representatives from Cass in 1843-43, clerk of the superior court, 1856-58. One son, James, was killed in Confederate service. (3) Thomas J., b. June 6, 1812, d. 1904, m. Martha Wofford, b. Nov. 25, 1812, d. Sept. 25, 1884, sister of Gen. Wofford, represented Cass in 1859-60. His family is identified with Gadsden, Ala. (4) William B., speaker of the house of representatives is identified with Habersham county history. His sons in this county were: Ab P. Wofford, practiced law in Cartersville, m. Lula, daughter of Judge Parrott and their six children are identified with Texas; Ben m. Sally Furr, a sister of Mrs. Thomas Leake, and lived in this county; John W., was admitted to the Cartersville bar in March, 1866, represented the county in the senate in 1874-5, later became judge of the criminal court of Kansas City, where he is identified; Mary m. Jim Wofford, son of Thomas; Lottie m. Jim Wofford, son of James who was killed in the battle of Kennesaw. (5) Sallie, b. May 2, 1800, d.

May 2, 1882, m. Jack Grant of Ryo, Ga., who served in Mexican War; a son of Jack Grant, 91 years of age, lives at Ryo. (6) Lottie m. James W. Rich who came with the Woffords from Habersham; a son, William W. Rich, served in the Mexican and Civil Wars, becoming a colonel in the latter service. He entered the service as a captain of the Cherokee Cavalry. He served several offices in the county, and is buried in Cartersville. A daughter, Savannah, m. John Trotter, and their daughter, Clara (Mrs. John Starnes), lives in Cartersville. Col. Rich and his father both farmed in the county. Ike Baker, a grandson of James W. Rich, lives on the old Young place.

WORD, Mrs. Joyce A. Jones: widow of Col. Robert Word of the War of 1812, after her husband's death in 1830 came to Cass county where her daughter, Mrs. J. W. Hooper was living. Judge Hooper was the executor of the wills of his wife's father and his own father and many children involved came to Cassville to be near him. The children of Col. and Mrs. Robert Word were: (1) Eliza J. m. Charles Murphy a lawyer in the county. (2) Sarah A. m. Judge J. W. Hooper. (3) Elizabeth m. William Latimer who ran the hotel by that name in Cassville, which was destroyed during the Civil War. Their descendants live in Athens. (4) John J., as a lawyer became noted for his political sagacity, represented Cass county in the legislature of 1843 and was elected clerk of the house of representatives in 1845, served as solicitor general of the Cherokee circuit from Nov. 15, 1848 to 1856, died at Montavale Springs in July, 1857. (4) Jane B. m. Charles J. Hooper, brother of John W. Hooper, and later married James Word. (5) Mary was the 3rd wife of Col. Lindsay Johnson of this county. (6) Thomas A., b. Jan. 4, 1818, in Laurens district, S. C., from 1850 to 1853 held the office of clerk of the inferior court at Cassville until he was then elected ordinary and held the position for four years. In 1853 he married Cathrine J. Sylar of this county by whom there were: Julia, Marcellus who lived in Cartersville and had a drug store and whose widow still lives here, and Thomas. In Jan. 1860 he was elected clerk of the superior court, which office he held continuously until his death in Jan. 1880. He married twice. (7) William T. (8) Robert C., b. in 1825, practiced medicine in this county until the Civil War, m. Adelia E. Patton, daughter of Robert Patton, another settler of Cassville. In 1862 he bought from Dr. Francis R. Goulding and sold in 1865 what is now known as the Beck place, south of Kingston*. Dr. Word practiced with his cousin, Dr. Jeff Word, in Rome, and afterwards removed to Decatur where he lived and died on July 21, 1890. A daughter, Ida W. Ramspeck, is the mother of Congressman Robert C. Word Ramspeck of Georgia.

WOOLLEY, Andrew Feaster: b. Nov. 29, 1801 in Fairfield district, S. C.; came to this county in 1836 and bought tracts of land

---

*The earliest abstract of title on the Beck place is in 1836.

in the 16th district on the Etowah river north of Kingston; he married Mary Anne Moore, b. 1802, Abbeville district, S. C., and d. in 1873. Mr. Woolley was a major of a militia company in his district and called Maj. Woolley the rest of his life. He was a member of the house of representatives in 1839. His home was a stage stop on the route from Cassville to Rome. Horses were changed and meals were served; the coachman would blow his horn as many times as he had passengers to give warning. Maj. Woolley died on Dec. 12, 1865, broken hearted over the destruction of the Civil War and is buried in the family cemetery. The children of A. F. and M. A. Woolley were: (1) Sarah m. Joel C. Roper who became a captain of one of the county companies in the Confederate service. J. C. Roper, a son, lives in Columbus. Mary Roper (Hardin) lives in Atlanta. (2) Mattie m. Capt. Julius Peek of Cedartown. (3) Mary, m. Peter Coffee Harris, identified with Cedartown, Ga. (5) Feaster, a twin, married, lived and died at the old home place. He served as captain in the Confederacy; married Augusta Jordon by whom he had eight children. Two hundred acres of the original plantation were bought in 1931 by a great-grandson, Will H. Hardin of Atlanta.

WRIGHT, Augustus R.: b. June 16, 1813 in Crawfordville, Ga.; educated at Franklin College; studied law at Litchfield, Conn.; read law in Augusta; in 1834 admitted to the bar in Crawfordville; in 1835 moved to Cassville where he formed partnership with Warren Akin, making his home there and became a prominent jurist; performed many wedding ceremonies while at Cassville; judge of Cherokee circuit, 1843-49; a Whig, then ardent Democrat; represented 5th district in Confederate Congress; a brilliant orator and statesman; member of Constitutional Convention of 1877; organized and elected colonel of Wright's Legion during war. After 1854, Col. Wright is connected with Floyd county history; died March 31, 1891 and is buried in Rome. His sons, Seaborn and Moses, became noted lawyers and orators.

WYLY*: "the Wylys" are mentioned in White's "Statistics" as being original settlers. William Clark Wyly, b. Jan. 18, 1804, bought land in the county in 1837 in the 5th district, justice of peace in 1853. His brother, Augustine Clayton, b. 1829, lived in the county, married Josephine, daughter of Dr. Thomas Hamilton, who was living in the county at that time—1855. Augustine C. M. was justice of peace in 1858, and lived at "Vineland" until about 1866.

YOUNG, (Colonel) James C.: b. Sept. 16, 1822, d. Sept. 20, 1880; came from Laurens district, S. C., in 1851 to Cass along with other families who came at the same time. Before the war he was a prominent and prosperous farmer, introducing much fine stock in the county. He built the first section of what is now known as the Granger-Smith home. He married Sarah Watts of S. C., by whom he had 11 children.

---

*Information from Miss Madeleine J. S. Wyly, of Rome.

Those identified with Cartersville are: (1) Marylu (Tune), taught a private school here, married and now lives in Laurens, S. C. (2) Fannie m. J. P. Rogan by whom there is one daughter, Sarah. (3) William W., b., Dec. 6, 1863, m. Jessie Smith, daughter of C. H. Smith, by whom there were Caroline, Marilu (Munford), Charles, Octavia (Harvey); a member of Young Bros. Drug Co., established in 1889. (4) G. W. ("Mank"), b. 1866, married Lucy Heyward, by whom there were: Heyward, Hugh, Sarah (Hebble); member of Young Bros. Drug Co. (5) Susie m. Walter Akerman, by whom there were: Hugh, Joe, Martha, and Billy, who now live in Orlando, Fla.

YOUNG, Robert Maxwell: b. June 5, 1888 in Greenville district, S. C., was a son of Capt. William Young of Revolutionary service under Gates, Morgan, Moultrie and Col. Washington. He was educated in the best schools in S. C. and graduated with distinction in 1812 from Jefferson College in Philadelphia and afterwards settled in Spartanburg, S. C., and practiced there for 15 years. In 1839 he purchased a farm of 600 acres on the Etowah river, south of Cartersville, building a brick home made from native clay and on land formally owned by an Indian. He moved his family there in 1841. "Walnut Grove" is one of the few remaining southern homes and was noted for its hospitality. Dr. Young began his medical practice in this county when he came and continued a popular practice until in 1856 he devoted himself to rural pursuits. He was a staunch Democrat, a Baptist, and died at his home on Jan. 13, 1880. While at Spartanburg, he married in 1827 Elizabeth Caroline Jones, b. Nov. 28, 1808, d. May 26, 1884, a daughter of a wealthy South Carolinian planter, George Jones. There were four children: (1) George William, died in 1861 while acting as assistant surgeon in the 14th Ga. Regt., at his post at Cheat Mt., Va. A grandson, Roland Lyon, lives in Atlanta. (2) Robert B., was killed in 1864 while colonel of the 10th Texas Inf., at the battle of Franklin, Tenn. (3) Louisa J. m. Dr. Thomas F. Jones, b. April 3, 1832, who was a son of Gen. Thomas F. Jones of Laurens, S. C.; he first married a Miss Reynolds, a sister of Mrs. S. W. Leland, in Greenwood, S. C., but he came to Cass county in 1857 and during the Civil War was captain of Co. A, 16th Batt. of Partisan-Rangers and after the war settled at Kingston, where he was a prominent physician; he died Nov. 13, 1899, leaving the following children: Tom m. Pearl Landrum, Louise (dec.) m. J. C. Milner, by whom there are Louise and Ella Milner; Carrie, Emily, and Mamie live at the old home of Dr. Young. (4) Pierce Manning Butler: a sketch is found elsewhere.

CHAPTER VI

MILITIA

The militia dates back to colonial days. It was primarily for protection against the Indians and after their removal much of its effectiveness was lost.

Each county in the State was divided into militia districts, and these districts were laid off into captain's districts and the said captain enrolled persons subject to militia duty in each district. The captains were elected by the popular vote of the members of the militia.

The State was divided into divisions, brigades, and then districts. The Cherokee territory was placed in the 1st Brigade and 7th Division, and when Cass county was created this was not changed*.

General musters were held twice a year, and as the governor of the State could not review, personally, these musters, aid-de-camps were appointed with the rank of colonel. They wore cockade hats with red plumes, epaulets, brass swords and spurs, and carried pistols—an enviable position. These colonels held their rank while the governor who appointed them remained in office, but they held the title of colonel for life! Muster grounds were near Cass Station and Kingston. Other ranks were voted for in elections.

From records in the State Department of Archives are the following commissioned military officers of Cass county:

On July 9th, 1834, the "Cassville Rangers" were attached to the 82nd Regt. G. M., and Posey Mattox was commissioned captain, Lathona Rankin, 1st Lt., R. B. Hall, 2nd Lt., John Leverton, ensign.

July 1837, 819th district, James J. Teat, captain.

April 1842, 849th district, James Jackson, captain.

---
*Acts of 1831, p. 34.

April 1842, 849th district, Thomas F. Phillips, 1st lieut.

Oct. 15, 1844, 952nd district, Thompson M. Henson, captain.

Oct. 15, 1844, 828th district, Thomas G. Dunlap, captain.

Sept. 1844, Achilles D. Shackelford, colonel, 101st Regt., G. M.

Sept. 1844, James Gaston, colonel, 82nd Regt.

Nov. 1844, Alfred M. Linn, major, 329th Battalion.

Nov. 1844, 849th district, Elisha Wright, 2nd lieut.

Feb. 1845, 874th district, Robert N. White, captain.

Feb. 1845, 874th district, John H. Love, 1st lieut.

Feb. 1845, 874th district, Howard M. Findley, 2nd lieut.

Feb. 1845, 874th district, John M. Smith, ensign.

May 1846, 973rd district, Joseph P. Terrell, captain.

May 1846, 973rd district, Wm. McBrayer, 1st lieut.

May 1846, 973rd district, A. R. Wigginton, 2nd lieut.

Sept. 1850, 1041st district, W. W. Rich, captain, "Burke Guards," Batt. 157th.

Feb. 1851, 851st district, Mark A. Hardin, captain.

Feb. 1851, 851st district, Thomas T. Prater, 1st lieut.

Feb. 1851, 851st district, Henry Jolley, 2nd lieut.

Feb. 1851, 851st district, M. D. L. Dosier, ensign.

July 1851, 828th district, Edward Smith, captain.

Published in The Cassville Standard was the following notice:

"Headquarters, 12th Div. G. M.
Cassville, Ga., Aug. 26, 1852.

The Commandments of the 1st and 2nd Brigades, 12th Division G. M., will pay strict attention to the proper officering of the Regiments in their respective brigades, and the appointment and equipment of their staff officers—particularly the brigade inspectors—preparatory to the approaching Annual Review and Inspection of the militia of the State. The want of interest manifested by the superior officers in the proper organization of their command their almost entire neglect of their duties—has, in effect, repealed our militia laws. Officers of every grade will be held accountable for any failure to perform their duties by a rigid enforcement of the militia laws of the State. By order of Maj. Gen'l John H. Rice, Com. 12th Div. G. M.; Abda Johnson, Aid-de-camp."

PATROL COMMISSIONERS FOR 1859

Cassville District—John A. Terrell, J. P.; A. M. Linn, J. H. Walker.

Cartersville District—J. L. Wikle, J. P.; P. L. Moon, John Greenwood.

Allatoona District—A. P. Dodgen, J. P.; E. Moore, D. R. Thomas.

17th District—T. R. Milam, J. P.; F. C. Bailey, George Tumlin.

Kingston District—T. R. Couch, J .P.; E. V. Johnson, F. A. Huson.

Adairsville District—S. M. Nowell, J. P.; J. R Loveless, J. M. Veach.

6th District—M. T. Hays, J. P.; J. W. Henderson, J. Carson.

Pine Log District—W. H. King, J. P.; W. Johnson, J. Adair.

Wolf Pen District—S. Bell, J. P.; F. M. Ford, B. Pool.

Iron Works, or Stamp Creek—W. D. Smith, J. P.; M. A. Cooper, T. H. Hicks.

The boundary lines of the militia districts of this county are not authentically on record. There is a general understanding of where they lie. These lines have been conveniently used in times of elections.

CHAPTER VII

JUDICIARY

The superior and inferior courts were created at the time of the organization of the county in 1832, as was the Cherokee circuit.

The superior courts settled the cases of arrest and prosecution of the Cherokee Indians under criminal laws of the State. Five justices of the inferior courts were elected among the most prominent men of the section and had a great deal to do with the affairs of the county.

Lawyers and judges rode their circuits in buggies or on horseback in those days and made travel an interesting exchange of anecdotes and humor as they stopped at homes or taverns when night came.

Cassville as the seat of justice became the home of the circuit judges and prominent lawyers.

Court was first held in the home of Chester Hawks, now the home of W. D. Pittard, first clerk of the superior court in Cassville.

Much of the civil litigation and criminal business of Cherokee Georgia arose out of injunctions brought in relation to the holdings of the Indians before and while in the act of their removal*. Persons were appointed to value and pay for all improvements on property the Cherokees owned and abandoned in their removal by virtue of the treaty of 1828. These improvements and possessions had to be sold by public outcry at the court house to citizens of Georgia.

Judge John W. Hooper, appointed Dec. 8, 1832, was the first judge of the Cherokee circuit, selected because of his legal acumen at the time when there were such complicated questions concerning the federal, state and Indian laws. He received a quarterly salary of $525.00. He was a law partner of Judge Underwood

---

*Grice's Georgia Bench and Bar, p. 169.

in Cassville and they were friendly with the Ross party. Judge Hooper tried to protect the Indians oppressed by the land speculators and subjected himself to the criticism of Governor Lumpkin and the Indian agents in Cass. After legislative investigation of Judge Hooper's official conduct, ordered by Governor Lumpkin, Judge Hooper came out with "flying colors." The Cherokees were proud to find a Georgia judge who possessed sufficient virtue and honesty to stay the hand of unprovoked injustice at such a time.

In 1835, Elias Boudinott, editor of The Cherokee Phoenix, was the Indian interpreter in the criminal cases in the Cherokee circuit and lived at the time near Cassville. He received $2.50 a day for his services. Chief John Ridge and his son appeared in court at Cassville in 1835 and were entertained by Colonel Hardin.

Among the lawyers who lived and practiced at Cassville were: Zachariah B. Hargrove, who owned and sold property in Cassville, and was one of the founders of Rome; William Hardin, C. D. Terhune, who lived in Cassville at the time and has descendants now in Rome; Henry Lightfoot Sims and Robert Mitchell, employed as attorneys by the Cherokee authorities; T. G. Barron, David Irwin, Warren Akin, Turner H. Trippe, A. R. Wright, James Milner, Julius M. Patton; Telemon Cuyler, John H. Lumpkin, J. W. H. Underwood, W. H. Underwood, Andrew J. Hansell, J. H. Underwood—all of the latter group were later identified with Floyd county.

The supreme court of Georgia was organized in 1846 and as it was a perambulating court, the March term and third session was held at Cassville. The judges at this session were Lumpkin, Warner and Nisbet, and the following lawyers of this county were admitted: A. D. Shackelford, James Milner, Warren Akin, D. R. Mitchell, Julius M. Patton, John J. Word, William T. Wofford, Turner H. Trippe, Wm. B. Terhune.

The first session was held at Talbotton in January, 1846; the first case was M. C. Moore vs. Vincent Ferrell, appearing for the plaintiff, Underwood & Trippe of Cassville, for the defendant, Warren Akin.

JUDGES OF THE CHEROKEE CIRCUIT
(Created Dec. 3, 1832-date)

*John W. Hooper—1832-35; 1849-50.
Owen H. Kenan—1835-38.
　*Turner H. Trippe, sol.-gen.—1835.
*Turner H. Trippe—1838-42; 1853-59.
George D. Anderson—1842-43.
John A. Jones—1843.
*Augustus R. Wright—1843-49.
*John H. Lumpkin—1850-53.
　John J. Word, appointed sol.-gen. Nov. 8, 1851.
Leander W. Crook—1859-60.
Dawson Walker—1860-65.
*James Milner—1865-68.
*Josiah R. Parrott—1868-72.
Cicero D. McCutcheon—1872-1880.
Joel C. Fain—1880-88.
　*J. W. Harris, Jr., solicitor general, 1881.
Samuel P. Maddox—1888.
　*A. W. Fite, solicitor general, 1888-92.
*Thomas W. Milner—1888-97.
*Augustus Fite—1897-1916.
　*Thomas C. Milner, solicitor general, 1910-12.
M. C. Tarver—1916-27.
　*Claude C. Pittman, solicitor general, 1925-27.
*Claude C. Pittman—1927- ——.

Claude Cleveland Pittman: son of Robert McGrady and Leila (Thomas) Pittman; was born February 20, 1885 in Gordon county; graduate of Reinhardt, 1909, Emory, Ph. B. degree, 1912, University of Ga., LL.B. degree, 1915; began practice of law in Cartersville, June 1915; Methodist; Lion; Mason; Shriner; member of Junior Order; senator, 42nd district, 1919-20; solicitor-general, Cherokee circuit, Jan. 1, 1925-Feb. 28, 1927;

---
*Denotes those who lived at the time in this county.

judge, Cherokee circuit, Feb. 28, 1927-date; married Feb. 20, 1918, Emily Daves, daughter of W. W. and Annie (Hopkins) Daves of Cartersville, by whom there are Walter, Emily Ann and Mary.

The first minutes of the county court were destroyed by the Federal army. The earliest list of grand jurors were taken from The Cassville Standard of 1852:

Grand jurors of the Cass superior court for the September term of 1852 were: Thomas Hamilton, foreman; David Quarles, Leonard Morgan, Owen Lynch, Zachariah Edwards, Arthur Haire, Wm. Solomon, James M. Veach, Henry Williams, Thos. W. Brandon, Robert C. Word, Joseph Willingham, Hawkins F. Price, Wm. Blalock, Harvey S. Crawford, David Lewis, Thomas G. Barron, Joel T. Rowland, Robert H. Patton.

Their presentments found that the "grog" dealer was the source of nine-tenths of crime and the representatives were requested in the next legislature to promote the passage of an act submitting to a vote of the people the question "whether or not it be their will to have a law enacted suppressing the retail of spirituous liquors in this State"!

The grand jurors for the inferior court in Sept. 1852, were W. C. Wyley, foreman, John Smith, D. B. Cunyus, Jos. H. Jones, Weston Hardy, Jonathan McDow, Larkin Towers, Jas. McGinnis, Joseph Bogle, Robert M. Linn, John S. Rowland, Wm. Davis, Solomon R. Lowry, W. H. Felton, Joel Foster, Christopher Dodd, Thos. J. Wofford, James Douthit, Jos. Spounts, W. S. Sorrels, A. W. Buford, Leonard C. Huff, Lewis Munford, H. W. Cobb, clerk.

The first Cass inferior court record is on May 28, of the May term, 1855. Arthur Haire, Nathan Howard, Alfred M. Linn and John W. Henderson were the justices, and the following were jurors: H. F. Price, A. C. Day, R. T. Hill, Richard Gaines, John A. Barron, Jarrett Addington, W. B. Bishop, Ebenezar Loveless, J. R. Stevenson, Jacob Pew, Daniel R. Thomas, W. W. Wheeler,

John F. Milhollin, clerk.

In 1857 the question of the removal of the court house and jail was causing strife and holding back the actions for improvements in the town of Cassville. An act of the legislature in 1857 was submitted so that the people would not be taxed to pay for the removal, and that property owners in Cassville would be paid damages, provided that an election was held before 1860.

In May, 1858, at a meeting it was decided to leave the question to the qualified voters, and in June the result of the election was 5 to 595 in favor of "no removal" from Cassville.

Then war.

"Whereas, the court house and other buildings, both public and private, at the county site, in Bartow county, have all been destroyed during the war, and that there is no house at the county site in which the Ordinary of said county can store the records, or the court be held with comfort or convenience.

Sec. 1. . . . That the Ordinary of Bartow county be, and is hereby empowered to hold the court of Ordinary for said county, and transact all other business pertaining to the same, at his own residence, or another convenient place, in said county, until a court house shall be provided in said county.

Sec. II. . . . That the superior and inferior courts of said county shall be held at the town of Cartersville, in said county, until the justices of the inferior court shall have made proper and suitable provisions for holding said courts at the county seat; and all writs, processes, subpoenas, and summons issued by the clerks of said courts shall be made to conform to this act. Approved Dec. 15, 1865."*

Owing to the unsettled state of the county, at the February term of court in 1865, it was decided to allow time for drawing and summoning juries; the first Bartow superior court held after the war was in March, 1865. The sessions were held in the Baptist church at Cassville

---
*Acts of 1865, p. 61.

and Dawson A. Walker presided as judge. The grand jurors for that term were: Thomas G. Barron, foreman; Hawkins F. Rice, Archibald G. Johnson, William Headden, Travis Cotton, Phillips J. Guyton, Joshua Gore, William Lowe, Jos. L. Dysart, James A. Stone, William Stedham, Wm. F. Weems, Robert Nelson, Ausley A. Vincent, Levi Pierce, Robert H. Guyton, William H. King, Riley Milam, William O. Bowler, Hillery P. Gilreath, Lewis M. Munford, William Sylar. The petit jurors were: F. A. Boston, Lewis McDonald, J. B. England, J. B. Neville, Wm. Purser, C. Drake, Jeremiah Purser, John Shuler, Jacob Mosteller, A. Fountain, J. D. Layton, James Elkins.

The first presentments after the war are from the minutes of Cass superior court, bk. A, pp. 25-28. Cass or Bartow superior court, Sept. term, 1865:

"We, the grand jurors, selected and sworn for the first week, September term, 1865, Cass superior court, beg leave to make the following general presentments:

"Owing to the loss and absence of a portion of the county records, it was not practicable for our body to give them the usual examination. We have, through a committee, examined the walls of the jail building, who report that the walls are apparently sound. We therefore recommend the inferior court to have said building so repaired that it may be made available for the safe keeping of prisoners; provided they find it practicable after they shall have had it examined by competent workmen. We deem it highly important that our county have some safe place for the keeping of prisoners, as it will be a great inconvenience to the sheriff to carry prisoners to other counties for safe keeping, and a heavy burden to the county. Owing to the condition of our county for the past few years, the working of the roads has been neglected, but we are informed that District Commissioners have been appointed. We recommend that the roads be put in passible order before winter sets in. The past season has been one of unusual drought, consequently the grain crops are remarkably light. There being but a small portion of the open land in the county cultivated, we fear that unless the grain produced in the county is used exclusively for the ordinary subsistence for man and beast, that there will be great scarcity and want in our county during the ensuing year.

"We would therefore appeal to and urge the citizens of this county, to abstain from the distillation of grain of any kind, that can be converted into breadstuffs, and would urge all good citizens to used their influence against the conversion of the grain of the county into ardent spirits.

"We hope every citizen of the county will let his benevolence preponderate over his self-interest in this matter when they consider the destitute conditions of our county. We would suggest that the next legislature of our State, adopt such legislation as will effectually prevent the evil for the next year. Our observation and experience has suggested to our minds, the expediency and propriety of a change in our judiciary system so far as to separate the trial of criminal cases from common law and equity cases, by establishing courts of exclusively criminal jurisdiction and holding the sessions quarterly.

"The circuits of the superior courts as now arranged, are small, and we believe the judges would have ample time to attend those courts, as the terms would probably be short. We believe the organizations of such courts, would lessen instead of increase the expenses of the counties, as criminals and prisoners would be much more promptly disposed of, and the expense of keeping prisoners materially lessened. It is the speed and certainty of punishment that deters evil disposed persons from committing crimes, and we are convinced that a more speedy execution of our criminal law, would have a salutary effect in preventing the commission of crimes. We therefore respectfully suggest that the delegates who may be sent from this county to the approaching convention, bring this (as we deem it) important question before that body and ask it to embody these views in the constitution which may be adopted. There having been no cases disposed of at this term of our court, owing principally to the absence of parties and witnesses, and some doubts entertained as to the present status of all our laws, we would suggest to His Honor Judge Walker, the propriety of holding an adjourned term of the court for this county, after the convention shall have met and acts of the courts during the existence of the late war.

"We respectfully recommend to our next members of the legislature to urge the passage of a bill authorizing the inferior courts of the several counties to fix the license fee for retailing spirituous or malt liquors at such sum as they deem proper, not less than fifty dollars per year.

"In taking leave of His Honor Judge Walker we take pleasure in bearing testimony to the able, courteous and dignified manner in which he presides, and for his uniform courtesy to this body.

"We also return our thanks to our able and energetic solicitor general, Col. J. R. Parrott, for his faithful discharge of official duty and for his courtesy and attention to this body.

"We respectfully request that these presentments be published in the Atlanta Intelligencer.

Jurors of Cass (or Bartow) Superior Court, Sept. term, 1865.

1. Joseph Bogle, foreman.
2. George H. Gilreath.
3. Charles W. Howard
4. John R. Adair
5. John W. Shepherd
6. Alred M. Linn
7. Benajah Sheats
8. Duncan Murchison
9. William P. Elliott
10. James M. Carson
11. Brice C. McEver
12. Jesse R. Wikle
13. Thomas H. Kennedy
14. William C. Gillam
15. John Smith
16. James W. Lewis
17. Henderson W. Fite
18. Ausley A. Vincent
19. Travis Cotton
20. Henry W. Waldroup
21. David W. K. Peacock
22. Joshua W. Thompson
23. Christopher Dodd

Dawson W. Walker, Judge Supr. Court, C. C."

After the court house, its records, and the county jail were destroyed, the agitated question of the county site had to come before the people again. Citizens in Cassville were financially unable to rebuild, and the site was preferable on the railroad.

By an act of the legislature* and approved in November, 1866 the question of the location was provided for:

"Whereas, the county site of Bartow county was entirely destroyed by the Federal army; and whereas, the former citizens of said town have declined an attempt to rebuild it; and whereas, the people of said county are desirous of locating the site at some point on the Western & Atlantic"; the election was to be held at Cartersville on the first Monday in January, 1867 and each voter endorsed on his ticket the place he desired the county site. After the consolidation, the justices of the inferior court had to procure the necessary land and means to build at the point receiving the highest number of votes. In Section 7 of the act it was provided, "That should the county site be located at Cass Station, on the Western & Atlantic railroad, then, and in that event, J. J. Howard, Abda Johnson, W. T. Wofford, Nathan Land, Elisha King, Christopher Dodd and G. W. Hill be, and they are hereby appointed, commissioners; and

---
*Acts of 1866, p. 36.

they are ... authorized to act in conjunction with the justice of the inferior court of said county of Bartow, in laying off the town and erecting public buildings of said county."

In December, 1866, the undersigned members of the inferior court informed the voters that citizens of Cartersville had given ample means to build a court house, "superior in every respect to the old court house at Cassville," provided that the location would be in Cartersville. It was signed by W. T. Burge, John L. Wikle, David Vaughan and John Kennedy.

The result of the animated election in January, 1867 was:

	Cartersville	Cass Station
Manassas (Cassville)	000	143
Cartersville	680	32
17th District	135	107
Kingston	9	223
Adairsville	1	224
6th District	6	69
Pine Log	64	84
Wolf Pen	40	28
Stamp Creek	83	00
Allatoona	67	9
	1085	919

It was not unmixed with bitterness on the part of some, but the election was noticed as the largest vote polled since the Civil War.

During this time court was held in the second story of a building on the corner of Main street and East Public Square in Cartersville.

A brick court house*, at a cost of $20,000, was finished in 1873 and was located on the W. & A. railroad. The jail was erected behind it at a cost of $15,000. As early as 1868 a poor house was recommended by the superior court and in 1871 property consisting of 328 acres in the 5th district was bought for the pauper farm

---
*Now used by the J. M. Veach Co.

from W. W. Rich. Modern buildings were erected in 1930 under the administration of A. V. Neal.

Strange to relate, the noise of the trains compelled the action for a new location, and construction of the present court house began in October, 1901, and was completed and dedicated in January, 1903. The first court session was held in it the second Monday in January of that year. The jail remained at the old site and was remodeled in 1930.

COUNTY COURTS

By an act of the legislature* on December 15, 1866, amending the Code, the inferior courts were denominated county courts, and further provided, "That all proceedings to set apart property exempt under the insolvent laws of this State shall hereafter be had in the county court instead of the inferior court, as heretofore practiced."

At the election held in May, 1866, Judge Turner H. Trippe was elected judge over Jesse R. Wikle and John Jolly, and William J. Conyers was appointed solicitor over Andrew Rice and Robert C. Saxon. After Mr. Conyers' death in 1866, the solicitor was Andrew H. Rice, pro tem, until Thos. W. Dodd was elected. At the death of Judge Trippe on Jan. 20, 1867, John L. Wikle acted as judge pro tem, until April, 1867, Jesse R. Wikle was elected judge.

The Constitution of March, 1868 abolished the then existing county courts and provided that unfinished business be completed by the superior courts. This court raised taxes, so was thought to be unnecessary.

As an amendment in the 6th section and 3rd article of the Constitution of Georgia, passed Feb. 22, 1850, re-passed Dec. 5, 1851†, enacted "The powers of a Court of Ordinary or Register of Probates, shall be vested in an ordinary for each county, from whose decisions there may be an appeal to the superior court, under such re-

---
*Acts of 1866, pp. 22, 52.
†p. 50.

strictions and regulations as may be, or may have been prescribed by law." The ordinary is ex-officio of said court, and is elected every four years and commissioned by the governor.

The board of commissioners of roads and revenues, "to consist of 5 persons", was established by an act of the general assembly in 1874*.

The county court of Bartow was created by an act of the legislature in February, 1874†. John C. Branson of Kingston was the first judge, R. W. Murphy, solicitor. Both appointments were made by the governor for a term of 2 years. The first court session was held in April, 1874 and it adjourned sine die in the November term of 1875. The purpose of the court was to relieve the superior courts of the trial of misdemeanor cases with less time and expense.

In February, 1877‡, a criminal court for the county of Bartow was organized; the judge was appointed by the governor for a term of 2 years. Hon. James W. Harris was the judge, G. S. Tumlin the solicitor until the October term of 1877. Robert B. Trippe served as judge and J. B. Conyers as solicitor until October 1879.

By another act of the legislature in 1879§, the county criminal court was abolished and all business was transferred to the superior court.

G. S. Tumlin was judge and J. J. Conner was solicitor of the Bartow county court from October 1883 until the court adjourned sine die in the October term of 1885.

By an act of legislature in October, 1885‖, the county court of Bartow was abolished and an act was passed creating the city court of Bartow with jurisdiction over the whole county. A judge was appointed for a term of 4 years to hold quarterly sessions. The solicitor general of the Cherokee circuit acted as ex-officio in the

---
*Acts of 1874, p. 334.
†Acts of 1874, p. 48.
‡Acts of 1877, p. 71.
§Acts of 1878-9, p. 368.
‖Acts of 1884-5, pp. 486-7.

court until by an act in August, 1904 the solicitor general of the city court was appointed by the governor of the State and chosen from among the lawyers in the county for a term of 4 years.

PERSONAL SKETCHES OF THE CITY COURT JUDGES

1885-1889

JAMES MONROE NEEL: b. Jan. 22, 1850, in Gordon county; was reared in Bartow county at Adairsville. He attended the common schools and later the University of Kentucky. On his return from college he taught school 2 years, in the meantime pursuing the study of law with his uncle, David W. Neel of Gordon county, and was admitted to the bar on Feb. 1, 1874. He began practice as junior partner to Col. W. R. Rankin at Calhoun. In 1875 he opened an office in Adairsville and later removed to Cartersville and became associated with Gen. W. T. Wofford. At the end of 2 years he became partner with Judge Robert B. Trippe. In 1881 he became head of Neel, (J. J.) Conner, & (W. J.) Neel. For a time later he was senior member of Neel & (O. T.) Peeples. In 1907 he became associated with his son, J. M. Neel, Jr. Mr. Neel was recognized as one of the most profound and able lawyers in this section. He was appointed the first judge of the city court. He represented the county in the legislature of 1892-93 and in 1893 he introduced the Neel Pleading Act which was an act regulating pleading in civil actions in the courts of the State (Acts of 1893-, p. 56).) A retiring and modest man outwardly, he was forceful and a master of pleading in the court room. He was forearmed in a case on trial. His counsel was sought by all. He was in possession of a fine law library. Among his clients were the N. C. & St. L., S. A. L. and L. & N. railroads. Judge Neel was a member and deacon of the Baptist church. He was a member of the Cartersville bar until his death on Nov. 30, 1930. He first married Anna Anderson of Adairsville by whom there were Ella; Joseph F., lives in Wauchula, Fla.; Oliver A., lives in Charlotte, N. C. His second wife was Julia Anderson, a sister of Anna, and to them were born Laura m. Gratton Hammond, lives in Orlando, Fla.; Juliet m. M. R. McClatchey of Atlanta; J. M. Neel, Jr., m. Sara Holmes of Cedartown, continues his father's practice in Cartersville; Robert W. of Atlanta; Isa m. R. O. Jackson, lives in Rockmart, Ga.; Fred D. Neel m. Vance Nelson, and is a member of Cartersville bar and at present is serving his second term as solicitor general of the city court.

1889-1894

SHELBY KENNARD ATTAWAY: b. Jan. 2, 1860, Batesville, Ark., was a son of William S. and Jane Henderson Attaway, natives of Georgia. They removed to Cartersville when he was a child. He received an education in the Cartersville schools and North Georgia College at Dahlonega. He taught school a short time in Alabama, in the meantime studied law and was admitted to the Cartersville bar in 1884. Appointed judge of the city court in 1889. In December 1892 he married Lutie Whitehead by whom there was one son, Wallace, of Atlanta. Judge Attaway died October, 1894 while in office, and is buried in Cartersville.

1894-1909

JOHN W. AKIN: Sketch is found elsewhere.

1909-1914

AUGUSTUS M. FOUTE: b. Nov. 16, 1838 in Roane county, Tenn., a son of William L. and Martha L. George Foute. Reared on his father's farm, he attended the common schools and graduated from Ewing-Jefferson College. Began in the mercantile business but entered the army on July 4, 1861 and from a private was promoted to the adjutancy of the 26th Tennessee Regiment. Mr. Foute lost his right arm in the battle at Kennesaw mountain in June, 1864. At close of the war, he taught school while preparing for the bar and was admitted in April, 1868, in Fulton superior court. He began practice in Cartersville immediately where he made his home. In 1886 he was elected one of the representatives from this county and as a legislator had an eye single to the welfare of his people. A Democrat; Baptist; a vice president of the Baptist convention; judge of the city court August 1909-May 1914. In 1875 he married Laura, daughter of O. D. Anderson, by whom there were: Anna; Julia (dec.) m. Fred Lambert of Ashburn; Mary m. Paul Jones of Canton; A. M. Foute, Jr., Houston, Texas. Judge Foute died May 19, 1914 and is buried in Cartersville.

1914-17

JOSEPH MORRIS MOON: b. June 24, 1852, at Allatoona, a son of Pleasant L. and Sarah Morris Moon, natives of South Carolina; came to Cass county in 1856 from Cobb county. "Joe" was educated in the Cartersville schools, Emory and Henry College, Va., and was a graduate of the University of Georgia. He was admitted to the Cartersville bar in 1875; was mayor of Cartersville in 1882 and in 1908-09; clerk of the city in 1889; was judge of the city court, May 22, 1914-Feb. 1917; was member of the city school board; a Democrat; Methodist. On Jan. 29, 1891 he married Emma Lola, daughter of Capt. Wm. M. and Mary Puckett, by whom there were 2 daughters; LaNelle m. Dr. Sam Bradford of Pine Log; Ina Collins m. Lester N. Webb. "Little Joe" Moon was a beloved character in the town. He was a lover of books and possessed a large personal library. He died Feb. 26, 1917, and is buried in Cartersville.

1921-25

WILLIAM THOMAS TOWNSEND: b. April 27, 1879, in Pickens County, Ga., a son of Kimsey H. and Mary Townsend. Mr. Townsend spent his early life on his father's farm, attended the common schools near him and taught in various country schools in his native county from 1897 until he entered the North Georgia Agricultural College at Dahlonega in 1899. In 1903 he left college to accept an appointment for 4 years' service as a supervisor of schools in the Philippine Islands. Returning to Georgia in 1908, the college at Dahlonega conferred the B. Ph. degree upon him, and in 1910 he received his B. L. from the University of Georgia. He was admitted to the Cartersville bar in 1910, where Mr. Townsend has been a successful and prominent member; a Democrat, member and deacon of the Baptist church; Mason; K. of P.; Pi K. A.; chairman and member of local draft board during World War; judge of the city court, Oct. 21, 1921-Oct., 1925; Lion. On Sept. 1, 1911, he married Bessie B., daughter of James B. and Eliza Newton Conyers, to whom were born *Carter, Mary Eliza, Thomas and Bessie.

*BRig. Gen. ELiAs CARTeR TowNseND
M. ZeLLe WADe oF CoLo. SPRINGS

1917-21; 1925-

GEORGE HARGRAVES AUBREY: b. Oct. 22, 1851 in Columbus, Ga., a son of William and Rosa Meigs Forsyth Aubrey. William Aubrey was born in Cowbridge, Wales, G. B., and when 16 years of age came to America and settled at Mobile, Ala. He soon succeeded in the mercantile business; became a colonel in the Texas war for independence under Gen. Sam Houston; he amassed a second fortune in Baltimore, Md., which was confiscated during the Civil War; in 1873 he came to Bartow and farmed 8 miles north of Cartersville and died in 1880 and is buried at his home near Aubrey. Rosa Forsyth was a daughter of the distinguished governor of Georgia, John Forsyth, and Clara Meigs of Boston. Besides George H. there were William L., Harry and Katherine. Judge Aubrey was educated in the grammar schools of Columbus and Baltimore, Pen Lucy and Loyola colleges; in 1864-5 he served as a private in the Home Guard; came to Bartow in 1872 and began the practice of law in Cartersville in 1888; chairman and member of the draft board for the county in the World War; judge of the city court; member of the house of representatives, 1923-23-Ex.-24; Democrat; "the representative citizen" of Cartersville. In 1881 he married Harriet H. Smith, daughter of Maj. Charles H. Smith by whom there were: Rosa m. H. E. Gooding of Columbia, S. C.; Octavia A. m. Bradley Howard (dec.) of Cartersville; Marion G. m. Sherman Granger of Cartersville and Montreal, Canada; Katherine (dec.) m. R. S. Munford of Cartersville; William H. m. Louise Friedley of Pennsylvania.

CHAPTER VIII

EARLY CHURCHES

BAPTIST CHURCHES

"The brethren and sister members of the Baptist church whose names will be herein inserted residing in the vicinity of Raccoon creek, Cass county, have met together on the 20th day of May in 1837 for the purpose of becoming constituted into a church at that place, have received the Presbyters, John Crawford and Allen Dykes. They then agree to adopt the faith of the Coosa Baptist Association as the faith upon which they agree to become constituted." Thus read the first, well-preserved minutes* of this old church. After the brothers and sisters were found orthodox, the presbytery extended the right hand of fellowship and pronounced them a church in order. The members present at this meeting were Isack Brock, Sarah Brock, William Shaw, Rebecca Shaw, Reuben Underwood, Sophia Underwood, James Rush, Bertha Rush, Nathaniel Burge, Nancy Burge, Martin Stedham, Hanah Stedham, John Pinkerton.

The first building was of logs on an acre Robert Henderson gave on the west side of the creek. In 1840 Nathaniel Burge deeded 2 acres of land on the east side of the creek upon which a church was built. The Negroes used the church building for their services after the Civil War until 1876. After necessary improvements in the course of years, in 1917 the old building was torn down and the present church was constructed.

The church at first observed foot washing and was non-missionary. Until 1872 they "stood aloof" from the Georgia Baptist Convention. Some points in Order of Conference, which was held on Saturday before preaching on Sunday, and in the Decorum were: "3. Roll call

---
*Possession of Roy Taff, Stilesboro.

1. Original Raccoon Creek Baptist church (courtesy of Mrs. J. W. L. Brown). 2. Stilesboro Academy. 3. Sam Jones Memorial church. 4. Pine Log Methodist church, showing camp ground in rear. 5. Peeples Valley school. 6. Smithville school.

of male members. 5. All matters of dealing shall be brought before the church in gospel order and any member acting otherwise shall be liable to the censure of the church. 6. Call for acknowledgements. 11. No person shall be allowed to speak but three times on the same subject, without leave from the moderator. 13. No male member shall absent himself from the conference without leave from the moderator, and any male member failing to fill his seat on communion season shall be accountable to the church for his conduct if not present. 14. We will not receive any excuse for voluntary drunkenness, and no member shall be allowed to distill or traffic with ardent spirits in any way for the sake of gain. 15. No member shall be held in fellowship with this church who will take the benefit of any law to avoid the payment of any just debt. 16. No member of this church shall be allowed to participate in the gidy dance or skating rink, or circus shows, or other things of like character, or encourage the same by their presence and approval. 17. Any male member failing to fill his seat for three successive conference meetings, it shall be the duty of the said brother to give full satisfaction to the church for such absences or he will be subject to dealing for his conduct, for we believe it to be the duty of all male members to attend their conference meetings."

"Satisfactory acknowledgements" on record were made by brothers "for dancing", "for taking the benefit of the homestead law", "for going into a circus show", "for patronizing wheels of fortune", and for these the members were "cited to the church"; otherwise, fellowship from the church was withdrawn for: dancing, attending circuses, for avoiding the payment of a just debt, female members for fornication and adultery, for violation of the rules of the church, for profane swearing, for "walking disorderly in having joined" any other church.

Only one reference is made of the Civil War and there is only a skip in the minutes from March, 1864 to June, 1865. A motion was adopted to assess a tax on the male members to cover the church expenses but from the reports on record this was not practical. The pastor was paid per annum, $120 in 1872, $350 in 1875, $300 in 1877, $325 in 1882. Pastors have been: Allen Dykes, 1839-52; John W. Lewis; H. F. Buckhanan, 1855-59; John W. Crawford, 1859-64; James G. Ryals, 1864-66; Andrew J. Rippie, 1866-67; James G. Ryals, 1867-83; James McBride, 1883-89; E. B. Bassett, 1890-95; J. J. Bennett, 1896; L. E. Roberts, 1896-1903; M. L. Keith, 1904; Ben H. Hunt, 1905-06; J. E. Hudson, 1907-; J. G. Hunt, 1910-; J. A. Edge, 1913-15; J. G. Hunt, 1915-25; T. J. Tribble; W. R. Callaway, 1931-32.

The Pettit's Creek Baptist church, by a deed of conveyance, dated March 2, 1839, is on record from Greenville Pullin, Armstead Dodson and James Magee, of one part, and A. Dodson, James Jones and Z. Edwards on the other part as trustees of the church. This church was situated between Nancy creek and the old Cassville and Burnt Hickory road, west of Cartersville. In May, 1844 Greenville Pullin granted 3 acres for the church to the deacons, Pendleton Isbell and Andrew M. Hamilton. In 1846 the church was reported the largest and strongest in the Coosa Association. It was moved to Cartersville in 1856 into a brick building on Market street, west, with a Sunday school room and a gallery for colored members in the rear. There was a cemetery on the hill behind the chuch. During the Civil War the interior and brick walls were demolished by the Federal soldiers and used in erecting quarters for the officers. The members joined the Methodist and Presbyterians in worship and helped them rebuild their churches. The Baptist, a poorer congregation, later rebuilt on the same church lot. In 1889 the U. S. government gave $5,000 in part compensation for vandalism of war and this was the nucleus for the present Baptist church which was erected in 1904-05. The present membership is 521.

Pastors have been: Jas. G. Ryals, 1863-70; R. B. Headden, 1871-83; F. M. Daniel, 1883-85; Wm. H. Cooper, 1885-90; C. E. W. Dobbs, 1891-93; W. R. Brisco,

1894-94; W. H. Patterson, 1895-98; A. W. Bealer, 1899-1902; J. E. Barnard, 1903-08; S. C. Dean, 1908-11; J. M. Long, 1911-13; Aquila Chamlee, 1913-14; C. L. McGinty, 1915-19; L. E. Dutton, 1919-23; I. A. White, 1924-29; J. C. Jackson, 1929, supply; G. N. Atkinson, 1929-.

The Connesena Baptist, above Kingston, was deeded in 1838 by Thompson M. Henson. The hardshell and missionary Baptist dissolved in this old church. The building has been remodeled and has remained on the same location.

The members of the Baptist church in Oothcalooga valley left the first old log church and built a church on the west side of the road. It was destroyed by the Federals in 1864, and after the war they held their meetings in an old school house in front of the present Adairsville Baptist church in the town. Later the present Oothcalooga church was erected on the same site as the Oothcalooga cemetery on the Dixie highway.

The Cassville Baptist church is on record as having James Phillips, John Russell and John Crawford as trustees in 1838. The old church was called "Beulah" and from 1839 Rev. John Crawford served as pastor for 21 consecutive years. The first location was on the highway north of the town on the Chunn property. Before the Civil War a wooden structure was erected south of the town and was not destroyed when the town was burned. In 1910 the present brick church was erected on the same site.

In July, 1849 a site was deeded by Thomas J. Wofford for the Baptist church at Wofford's cross roads to James Lockridge, David Lewis and Alfred W. Buford, trustees of the church. It is on the same site today.

New Hope Missionary Baptist church on the Canton road, east of Allatoona, is one of the oldest churches in the county. It is, also, a cemetery site.

The Macedonia Baptist church was erected on land belonging to Col. Morris in the 17th district before 1860.. It was in this church that in 1861 a company of older men in this district organized themselves into the "Macedonia Silver Greys". In the first church a balcony provided a place for the colored members and it was situated on the lower elevation of land below where it stood when it was demolished by the cyclone of March 21, 1932. A beautiful brick church was rebuilt in 1932 by the Owens brothers, long residents of the community and members of the church, J. B. Owens, T. Benton Owens, A. D. Owens, R. J. Owens and C. A. Owens, sons of John S. and Sallie Jones Owens. The church was formally dedicated Nov. 6, 1932, with the dedicatory sermon delivered by the Rev. Clifford A. Owens, a son of the late Rev. Thomas A. Owens, former residents of the community.

The Euharlee Baptist church was incorporated by an act of legislature in 1852. E. B. Presley, A. H. Spencer, A. Yarbry, Vinson Reynolds and Allen Dykes were named trustees.

The church at Kingston was constituted Nov. 19, 1852, with the Presbytery composed of John Crawford, George W. Tumlin, William L. Tweedle and James W. Givens. The members were William E. Smith, John C. Elliott, John B. Tippins, David Montgomery, Elijah Elliott, Precila Smith, Jane Foster and Matilda Burroughs. A church was built in 1853 near the cemetery, and membership grew so that in 1854 and again in 1858 the building was enlarged. It became a member of the Middle Cherokee Association in August, 1853 and in 1859 a Sunday school was added. The church membership was 160. The church was burned during Federal occupation and was not reorganized until July, 1866 when all the congregations were meeting in the Methodist church. A building was erected in 1873 at the foot of Johnson mountain. In 1899 the present church was erected in the town of Kingston facing the park. Pastors have been: James W. Givens, W. A. Williams, G. W. Tumlin, A. W. Buford, John C. Elliot, Joel Goodwin, Thos. Rambaut, J. M. McBryde, C. W. Stillwell, W. A. Clemmons, J. M. Brittain, John A. McMurray, Chas. E.

Wright, Geo. D. Harris, D. K. Moreland, D. E. Espy, W. W. Goldwire, A. J. Buford, B. M. Pack, E. D. Barrett, S. G. Tumlin, W. M. Dyer, E. M. Dyer, W. L. Head, A. J. Morgan, J. E. Hudson, J. M. Barnett, G. S. Bond, W. S. Adams, J. G. Hunt, G. M, Crow, A. B. Cash.

The old Salem Primitive Baptist church, which was on the present A. F. Jackson place near Taylorsville, was organized about 1850. In 1870 it was removed on the Rockmart road in Polk county and is now the Buncombe Primitive church. The graveyard on the lot with the church is almost entirely gone.

The Baptist church at Crow Springs was built in 1868 on land given by J. L. Luther. It was originally on a hill, but later removed nearer the spring.

The Oak Grove church was organized the Saturday before the second Sabbath in September, 1871. The first minutes were destroyed by fire in March, 1884, in the Roger's depot, and from the new book a record is found that A. H. Rice was pastor and W. H. Lumpkin was clerk. Rev. W. W. Goldwire was the first pastor, succeeded by M. B. V. Lankford, A. S. Tatum, P. E. Hawkins. A. J. Buford became pastor in 1892 and served until A. H. Rice became the pastor again in 1893. In 1902 J. E. Hudson was called as pastor and served until October 1907, Rev. C. H. Yearly was called. Rev. J. P. McGraw served from October, 1902 to June, 1913 when J. M. Barnett became pastor. From 1924 H. E. Cowart served until the present pastor, Rev. Hart. W. H. Lumpkin and his son, W. H. Lumpkin, Jr., served as clerks until the former's death and the latter's service in the World War when E. R. Williams served in his place. In 1925 Mrs. T. Q. Richardson served until succeeded by H. B. Moor. Some of the charter members were: Mr. and Mrs. R. L. Rogers, Mr. and Mrs. H. M. Rogers, Mr. and Mrs. W. H. Lumpkin, Mr. and Mrs. R. Chapman, Mr. and Mrs. James Lockridge, Mr. and Mrs. G. W. Lockridge, Mrs. Mary Loveless, Mr. and Mrs. T. F. Bridges, Mrs. Josephine Kennett, Mrs Cornelia Hargis, Mr. and Mrs. Louis Young.

Footwashing churches are the Zion Hill and Pine Grove churches, the Olive Vine church, Pleasant Valley Association, on the Tennessee road, and the Primitive Baptist Church of Christ, Marietta Association, above the Etowah river at Macedonia. The latter was built before the Civil War. The footwashing or communion season is observed the 1st Sunday in May and September. Rev. Bard L. Abernathy, who had 13 brothers and 3 sisters who lived to be grown and married in this section, preached 46 consecutive years at this church, reared a large family in this county, died about 1912 and is buried at Macedonia. His nephew, J. T. Abernathy, preached here until his death in 1929. Rev. Willis Hembree is the present pastor.

METHODIST CHURCHES

In his new home in the 17th district, Thomas W. Brandon began a Sunday school class, and in 1836 he, with the help of neighbors, erected and organized on his own land the first Methodist church in his district. It was on the site of the family burial ground above the present river bridge at Euharlee. Built of hewn logs, with a large fireplace at one end, it was used as the first school house as well as church. Mr. Brandon taught the Sunday school classes, and one important feature of the exercises were the writing lessons. They had no literature, only a few Testaments from which a chapter was read and questions propounded. The old united Methodist churches were called societies, and this new church was named "Brandon's Society" in honor of its founder. In an old class roll book of 1840 are the following members of a class: Thomas W. Brandon, teacher, Francis L. Brandon, Leroy J. Brandon, Moses A. Brandon, Vincent Brown, Wilson Saxon, Samuel Smith, Vincent Simmons; wives of the members, and the Brandon, Henderson, Burge and Cothran slaves. In 1840 John W. Glenn was the presiding elder or circuit rider, Joseph T. Turner, senior pastor, and John M. Milner, junior pastor. Later a new frame church was built on the west side of the present railroad, nearer the town of Stilesboro. Mr. Brandon was instrumental in the building of this church, and it was known as Brandon's Chapel. The church was destroyed by a cyclone in 1898. The present building was completed in 1899 in Stilesboro and in the course of years has had a large membership.

The Methodist church in Cassville faced the court house square and was not destroyed during the Civil War. No records of its early history have been found. It was a quaint frame building with a balcony for colored members, and a porch supported by large pillows ran across the entire front. It had green blinds and the interior had a mellow light. When it was remodeled in more recent years, all traces of the old church were demolished. The present church is on the original site.

A log church was built in Oothcalooga valley in 1838 by the settlers in that community, Augustus C. Trimble, Wiley Brogdon, and Wiley Kinman. Isaac Rutherford was the pastor. It was formerly an Indian mission, and later the Baptist and Presbyterians used it until they could build. The "old school" Presbyterians became weak and disbanded, but the Methodist wanted a church of their own, so they built and organized the Poplar Springs church which is yet located on the Fairmount road, east of Adairsville.

The Connesena Methodist church was organized in 1845, and was built by Maj. Feaster Woolley and B. F. Reynolds, west of Kingston. It was an excellent building for those days, with a gallery for Negroes. The church was removed to town, rebuilt in 1856, and was dedicated in 1858 by Bishop Lovic Pierce. Later it was rebuilt at the present location, overlooking the Kingston park. Hon. J. P. King of Augusta, presented the church with a bell at its completion in the late 50's.

When Cartersville was a hamlet, the nearest Methodist church was "Ebenezar", which was on the west side of the city cemetery. As the town began to grow the need for a church was recognized. Property on what is now the corner of Church and Erwin streets was deeded by Lewis Tumlin, T. R. Huson, Ker Boyce, Farish Carter and Stephen H. Long to John Leake, E. D. Puckett, W. Reckett, William H. Felton, Joseph T. Hamilton and Milton Loveless, trustees and their successors. Bids were made for the building of this church in 1848. The wooden building then erected proved unsatisfactory and it was torn down and a new one built with two entrances, one for the men and one for the women. After the Civil War the Baptist and Presbyterians helped to repair the damage inflicted by war, and in 1871 a brick church was built at the cost of $8,000 on the same site, whi'e the old building was rolled on the lot back of the church and was used for a school. During 1904-07 the present building was erected and was named the "Sam Jones Memorial".

Dr. Felton was one of the early pastors, but after the war those who have served have been: W. C. Dunlap, 1865-; Gen. C. A. Evans, 1866-68; Jos. L. Pierce, 1869-72; Geo. R. Kramer, 1872-; Lewis J. Davis, 1873-; A. J. Jarrell, 1875-; J. H. Timmons, 1877-; Jos. H. Baxter, 1878-; P. M. Ryburn, 1879-; A. J. Jarrell, 1881-; F. G. Hughes, 1883-; John B. Robins, 1884; W. A. Dodge, 1886-; B. E. L. Timmons, 1887-; H. J. Adams, 1888-; Henry J. Ellis, 1890-; S. P. Richardson, 1891-; J. H. Mashborn, 1892-; W. F. Quillian, 1894-; A. J. Jarrell, 1896-; B. P. Allen, 1897-; W. R. Branham, 1900-; G. W. Yarbrough, 1901-; T. J. Christian, 1903-; G. W. Duvall, 1905-; H. B. Mays, 1909-; Wm. Dunbar, 1911-; W. T. Hunnicut, 1912-; J. G. Logan, 1916-; S. A. Harris, 1918-; L. M. Twiggs, 1922-; T. R. Kendall, 1923-; W. H. Clark, 1924-; W. S. Robison, 1928-1932.

The Pine Log church and camp ground were built approximately before 1858. The Pine Log camp ground was incorporated in November, 1858. The church is built with hand-dressed lumber and is in good condition today. Annual camp meetings are held here every year in August. It is on the Tennessee road and L. & N. railroad.

Miller's Chapel was founded and built by B. S.

Miller on the old Canton road before the Civil War, but was not completed until after Mr. Miller's death in 1860. It is said that during a revival in this church, cannons were heard in the battles below Cartersville.

Sometime in the 50's "Stegall's Chapel" was erected by Emsley Stegall on lot No. 905 in the town of Emerson. "Stegall's Church" was deeded* in January, 1873 by Emsley Stegall to Emsley Stegall, Wm. H. Felton, B. H. Childers, Henry Holland and J. H. Hyer, trustees of the church. Dr. W. H. Felton, Rev. Robt. H. Jones and Sam Smith were regular pastors during this time. At a later date, Col. C. M. Jones gave a lot on the hill back of the town upon which a frame building was erected, and this was burned. In 1923 a brick building was erected on the same lot.

"Felton's Chapel" was first built by Dr. and Mrs. W. H. Felton to use as a school room when they taught in 1866, just after the war. On the same site Capt. John Felton had previously erected a bush arbor for religious services and there Dr. Felton had preached many sermons. The first frame building was cut in half when it was later used as a school house. It was situated on lot No. 199 in the 5th district, 3rd section, on the Tennessee road. In February, 1908, the lot was deeded by Mrs. Felton to John W. Jones, J. A. Monfort, Mrs. Laura McElwain Jones, Mrs. Rebecca A. Felton and Mrs. Annie Jones Pyron, trustees of the "Robert W. Jones Memorial Church", and on the lot was erected a brick church in memory of Robert W. Jones who had just died. The chapel was then removed to East Cartersville. No services are held in the Robert Jones church.

"Best's Chapel" at Crow Springs was built in 1869 with hand-dressed lumber, on land given by Mr. George H. Gilreath. The church was remodeled about 1889. The land is now owned by J. C. McTier of Cassville. It was named for Rev. Hezekiah Best who preached independently in a log school house until the church was built—he being largely instrumental in the first

---
*Book R, p. 537.

building. Many young preachers have felt the call to preach from this little chapel.

The Taylorsville Methodist worshipped in Stilesboro or in Polk county until 1906 a church was organized in the school house by J. M. Dorsey, W. E. Puckett, C. J. Porter, Dr. R. E. Adair, Sam T. Burns, Lee Jolly and Sam Allison. The Woman's Aid Society, composed of seven women, helped build and furnish the present church, which was completed in February 1907.

The Oak Grove Methodist church has served that community of the same name since the early 80's. The church was totally destroyed in the cyclone of March 1932. It was replaced by a stone building in 1932.

PRESBYTERIAN CHURCHES

On a Sabbath morning, Feb. 26, 1843, a congregation composed of Arnold Milner and his wife, Lucy Neit Milner, Mrs. Woods, Henry and Richard A. Milner, met to dedicate a new building erected by Arnold Milner to the worship of God. It was located near his home on the Etowah river, southeast of the town of Cartersville. A Presbyterian church was organized on the above date by Rev. Charles Wallace Howard, and named "Friendship". Richard A. Milner, a son of Arnold, was then a licentiate and served the church as the first pastor until his death. Colored members were admitted to the church and those at that time were slaves of Mr. Milner. During 1844 the church was taken under the care of the Cherokee Presbytery. In October, 1853, Friendship church was removed to a new church building in Cartersville on Main street, keeping the name until in April, 1887 it was changed to the First Presbyterian. Ruling elders in the 50's were Rev. R. A. Milner, Dr. William Anderson, A. Milner, James C. Sproull, Dr. N. Hart, George Agnew and Henry Milner. In July, 1855 Rev. R. A. Milner was called to become joint pastor of the Friendship and Euharlee churches at a salary of $700 a year. He had just accepted the nomination from the prohibition party in this county to run on their ticket for the legislature.

A committee asked that he withdraw from the canvass that he might accept the call which he did in October, 1855. He died on Nov. 13, 1855. In 1890 the wooden steeple and the balcony for colored members were removed and the present front of the church constructed. Pastors of the church have been: R. A. Milner, 1843-55; W. B. Telford, 1856-60; J. M. M. Caldwell, 1860-63; T. E. Smith, 1863-64; A. G. Johnson, 1866-68; T. E. Smith, 1868-84, and to his son, John W. Akin erected a tablet inscribed on a wall of the church: "Rev. Theodore M. Smith, a Presbyterian minister sent forth from this church, who while pastor in Jacksonville, Fla., during the yellow fever scourge in 1888 laid down his life rather than desert his post of duty; Scholar, Gentleman, Mason Christian; steadfast in life, hopeful in death; confident of immortality, whose self-sacrifice for others merits the Master's commendation, 'Greater love hath no man than this, that a man lay down his life for his friends', is erected this tablet by the friend of his youth."; G. J. Griffith, 1885-supply; J. S. Hillhouse, 1886-93; E. D. McDougall, 1893-96; W. F. Hollingsworth, 1897-98; E. M. Craig, 1898-1907; H. C. White, 1903-04; W. A. Cleveland, 1904-09; L. G. Hames, 1910-20; L. C. Vass, 1920-23; Clyde Johnson, d. 1924; Richard C. Wilson, 1924-31; Russell F. Johnson, 1932-.

In 1895, under the pastorate of Rev. E. D. McDougall and the interest of Mrs. John Postell, a mission chapel that was primarily a Sunday school was started and a building erected on Tennessee street. This property was used by the Presbyterians for 15 years, and the property was deeded by the Fords for church purposes. About 1910 George F. Brown, a young Baptist preacher, became interested in starting a Baptist church on the east side of town and on the 26th of March, 1911, Mr. and Mrs. J. G. Smith, Mr. and Mrs. C. E. Smith, Gertie and Lona Smith, Buford Smith, Mr. and Mrs. Lonnie Smith, Mr. G. O. Smith, Mr. and Mrs. W. L. Blaire, Rebecca Blaire, Mr. Luther Ingram and Mrs. Sara Holland with Rev. George Brown, organized the "East Side Baptist Church", using the old Presbyterian church mission building. By March, 1911 the lot and the building were purchased and from time to time additions improved as members increased. Pastors since Rev. Brown have been Arthur Smith, A. F. Smith, Gordon Ezell, John E. Barnard, G. W. Hulme. During Rev. Hulme's pastorate the lot on which the Tabernacle now stands was purchased, and on Oct, 1, 1924 George V. Crow was called as pastor and the church was changed to the name of the Tabernacle Baptist church. The membership has grown to 1045 members, largely through the preaching of the "beloved George Crow".

There were Presbyterian churches in Cassville and Kingston before the Civil War, but they were never rebuilt nor reorganized.

The Euharlee Presbyterian church was organized on Dec. 17, 1853, with 16 members, made up of Scotch-Irish Presbyterians who had moved here from South Carolina. Ruling elders were Charles Sproull, William Templeton, Riley Milam, Dr. W. L. Kirkpatrick, and the deacons were Turner R. Milam and Robert Templeton. Rev. Richard A. Milner served this church while he served the Friendship church as pastor and this custom is carried on today. Slaves of the members were admitted to communion, and after the war their names were written as "freedman" and "freedwoman". In 1896 the Euharlee Presbyterian Institute was sponsored by this church. The site of the church has remained the same.

The Cumberland Presbyterian church was organized at Dickson, Tenn., in 1810. The "Bartow" Cumberland congregation was organized in 1869, and it is situated on the Pine Log-Adairsville road. About 1883 the name was changed to "Smith's Chapel", but after 20 years it was changed to the original name of "Bartow". The church is a member of the Chattanooga Presbyterian East Tennessee Synod and the pastors come from Tennessee. Rev. H. A. Daniel, a Bartow countian and a graduate of Bethel College, is the present pastor.

The 18th Division Convention of Georgia Odd Fellows, about 1906, with the Sam Jones Tabernacle in the background.

EPISCOPAL CHURCHES

The Episcopal church of Cartersville had its beginning in a chapel near the home of the Stiles. In 1872 a lot was purchased for a church in Cartersville on Market street. It was finished by 1879 and called the "Church of the Ascension". Rev. H. R. Reese was the rector. The present rector is Rev. William S. Turner.

The Episcopal churches at Kingston and Cassville were never rebuilt after the Civil War.

SAM JONES TABERNACLE

A proposition was made in 1886 by Rev. Sam P. Jones to erect a tabernacle for the purpose of holding annual revivals in the city of Cartersville, provided the citizens of Bartow county would purchase 10 acres of land upon which to build it. The committee appointed to raise the sum was R. H. Jones, chairman, A. M. Foute, R. M. Patillo, W. H. Howard, J. T. Owen, T. W. Akin, S. L. Vandivere and E. D Graham. The business of the tabernacle was negotiated by the Union Tabernacle Association. The first sermon and dedication service was on the 3rd of September, 1886, and was preached by Rev. J. B. Hawthorne. There was room for the pitching of tents on the grounds. During Sam Jones' life-time people came from everywhere. The railroads ran special trains and made cheap rates to and from Cartersville. The most celebrated preachers of all denominations have been in revivals at the tabernacle here and up until about 1925 the revivals were annual events. Among the prominent evangelists have been Gypsy Smith, Sr., Bishop Arthur Moore, Gypsy Smith, Jr., Sam Small, Dr. Biederwolf, Bob Jones, John Brown, Frank Wright, Walt Holcomb, Bishop W. A. Candler, Bishop Galloway, George R. Stuart, L. P. Brown, J. A. Bowen, French Oliver and Luther Bridges.

CEMETERIES

Cartersville (city).
Benham (fam.) Grassdale road.
Tumlin (fam.) Cassville road.
Underwood (fam.)

Hargis (fam.) Burnt Hickory road.
Brown (fam.) Cassville.
Cassville (city and Confederate).
Adairsville (city).
Poplar Springs (church) Fairmount road.
Slaughter (fam.) Fairmount road.
Bowdoin (fam.).
Oothcalooga (church) Dixie highway.
Mt. Carmel (church).
Barnsley (church).
Cement (fam.).
Spring Bank (fam.).
Connesena (church).
Woolley (fam.).
Reynolds (fam.).
Terhune (fam.) almost demol.
Kingston (city and Confederate)
Mt. Pisgah (church) Rome highway.
Mt. Tabor (near Floyd county line).
Euharlee (church).
Arnold (fam.).
Burge (fam.) Etowah river.
Brandon (fam.) Etowah river.
Stiles (fam.).
Stilesboro (city and church).
Burge (fam.) s. of Stilesboro.
Rowland (fam.) on Leake place.
Shelman (fam.)
Leake (fam.) Stilesboro road.
Hawkins and McCormick (fam.)
Old Salem (nearly demolished).
Taylorsville (city).
Dickerson (fam.).
Salem (old church site).
Sproull (fam.)
Mt. Zion.
McDaniel (fam.)
Thurmond (fam.).
Raccoon (church).
Douthit (fam.) Dallas road.
Dobbs (fam.) on Field's place.
Key (fam.) Dixie Highway.
Emerson (city).
New Hope (church) Canton road
Macedonia (old church site).
Lower Furnace (on Cooper place).
Cooper (fam.) near home site.
Upper Furnace (Goodson fam.).
Stamp Creek (ch. and school).
Corbin (fam.).
Miller (church).
Wofford and Rich (fam.).
Chitwood (fam.).
Aubrey (fam.).
Wofford's Cross Roads (church)
Upshaw (fam.).
Possum Trot or Olive Vine (church and school.)
Pine Log (church).
Vaughan (fam.).
McEver (fam.) Milner place.
Baker (fam.).
Friendship (Milner fam.) Dixie highway s. of Cartersville.
Lewis (fam.).
Mt. Zion (abandoned church site).
Shinall (fam.) s. of White .

1. The remains of the Mark Cooper flour mill. 2. The Friendship monument. 3. Confederate monument in Cassville cemetery. 4. Confederate monument in Kingston cemetery. 5. The Sam Jones monument. 6. The tomb of Mrs. W. H. Felton.

CHAPTER IX

SCHOOLS

This historian will not detail all provisions of the State for education. The want of educational advantages in 1832 and in 1932 differ in degree only. The Cassville Academy had been incorporated by an act of the legislature in 1833 and not until 1838 was a report given of 60 students. The State appropriated $58 to the academy and $99.25 to the poor school fund in the county in the late 30's. With the exception of the college history, this will be a record of the private schools and teachers.

In the early 40's, Rev. Nathan Smith taught a school in the first Raccoon creek Baptist church. Dr. Pearly Ford taught in his residence near Stilesboro, north of the present Taylorsville road.

In 1840 a two-story brick school house with a large auditorium was erected by Col. Simpson Fouche on the present Rowland Springs road, which had before and since the Civil War been used as a residence. Here Col. Fouche taught the Lewis, Rowland and Howard sons.

Between 1845 and 1858, Rev. James Hardin George* educated at Franklin College and Yale, taught and lived in a house north of Kingston. It was a small select school for boys preparing for college, but a few girls attended. Several children were born to Rev. and Mrs. Martha Taylor George while living there. After he left he became an Episcopalian minister in Georgia. He is buried at Griffin. Mr. "Jimmie", as he was called, taught Mark A. Hardin, Richard Hargis and Lt.-Col. Waring.

A female school was taught by Mrs. Vernon at Kingston in the 50's.

In the summer of 1852, Rev. Charles Wallace Howand, giving up his pastorate of the Huguenot church in

---
*Mrs. John S. Candler, a daughter, is the only living survivor of this large family.

Charleston, S. C., brought his family and ten sons of his congregation to his property in Cass county and opened a school at "Spring Bank", north of Kingston. As there was only a log house on the property, the boys lived in tents until provision was made for them. Mrs. Howard with eight small children of her own supervised these students and teachers. Music, French, and mathematic teachers assisted and the Swedish system of gymnastics was used. The school was discontinued during the Civil War, but afterwards was opened as a school for girls. Mr. Howard was aided by his daughters who were then educated. Many of the daughters of Cherokee Georgia went to this "Seminary", among them Miss Martha Berry, founder of the Berry schools, her sisters and cousins, Mrs. Kate Strong, Frances Trippe (Johnson), Louisa Young (Jones), and a granddaughter of Judge J. W. Hooper. This school was continued years after Mr. Howard's death in 1876.

In 1852 William P. Fain, who died in September of the same year, advertised "Two Run Academy", 4 miles from Cassville, in The Cassville Standard, and this was the commencement write-up: "Classes were examined in spelling, reading, composition, arithmetic, grammar, natural philosophy, and Latin. The Misses Dillard, Trippe, Fain, Gilreath and Jones gave lie to the insinuation that females were unworthy of a good education." Among the male students were John and Henry Clardy, Patrick and A. Gilreath, Enoch Gaines, John Cicero, Ansel Fain, Lemuel and John Dillard, Asbury Weems, Wm. Puckett and Frank Norwood. Col. James Milner delivered an impromptu address.

This same year there was in Cassville a female institute under Mrs. S. S. Bradley and a male school under R. F. Neely, a scholar of the University of Dublin; Mrs. Neely conducted the female school in connection with Mr. Neely. During 1853 there was a male and female school in Cartersville, "teaching done entirely by analysis", by Mr. and Mrs. J. S. Lassiter. Parents were referred to Rev. G. W. Tumlin, Lewis A. Tumlin,

James T. Livingston, trustees.

The Mount Paron Academy in Euharlee announced in February, 1853 that Mr. and Mrs. R. F. Neely were to have charge of this school. "Mount Paron Academy is located in a healthy region of the county, eight miles west of the Cartersville depot, and in the midst of a population where the temptations to vicious and immoral conduct are few. The scholastic year will be divided into two sessions of five months each. The rates of tuition are as follows:

"Orthography, reading ,writing, arithmetic, per session _____$ 6.00
English, grammar, geography, with the above _____ 8.00
Mathematical, natural, moral and intellectual science _____ 10.00
Latin and Greek _____ 15.00
Embroidery, drawing and French _____ 8.00

"Trustees: T. W. Brandon, D. Garrison, E. B. Pressly, W. H. Dykes, T. H. Ligon."

The tuition was about the same in all the schools at this period.

After the death of his wife in July, 1853, Dr. Francis F. Goulding began a very select school for boys in his home south of Kingston. As the property was deeded in February, 1854 and advertised for sale in 1859, one can only surmise the years of actual teaching.

CASSVILLE FEMALE COLLEGE

In January, 1853, the citizens of Cass county took steps to erect a female institute with Rev. C. A. Crowell in charge of the subscription list. He had raised $5,000 since 1852 and in January, 1854, the Cassville Female college was incorporated* with power to confer degrees and the following were appointed trustees: Rev. Crowell, Rev. A. R. Wright, Julius M. Patton, T. H. Trippe, Geo. H. Gilreath, H. F. Price, Levi Branson, Joel Foster, John W. Burke, William Hardin. The college was to be under the Georgia conference of the Methodist Episcopal Church South.

*Acts of 1854, p. 117.

On a cornerstone in the yard of the Chunn's in Cassville today is this inscription: "Cassville Female College, laid by the Free Masons, May 10, 1853." Nathan Land gave the land for the college on the hill west of Cassville and the building was of brick. Rev. Churchwell A. Crowell was the first president. In the summer of 1855, Sarah Joyce Hooper, daughter of Judge Hooper, was the first graduate of the college. Her music teacher, Schwarzenski, a Pole, wrote in his broken English, a poem, "Lines to Miss Sarah Joyce Hooper", a copy of which is now in the possession of Mrs. Hallie Rounsaville of Rome, Ga.

Not until 1857 is a record found, when the fourth annual session announced its faculty in February, with:

"Rev. Wm. A. Rogers, president, professor of natural science and mathematics.

Rev. A. G. Johnson, professor of English and Latin literature.

S. G. Smith, professor of vocal and instrumental music.

Mrs. E. Louisa Smith, principal preparatory department and ornamental department. Tuition:

Primary Department, per an'm	$16.00
Preparatory Department	24.00
College Department	50.00
Music Department	50.00
Ornamental Department	20.00
Incidental Expenses	2.00
Board, lodging, washing	10.00"

Commencement exercises of the colleges were gala occasions and usually occupied a week of activity. Many visitors came from far and near, and a designated committee of visitors saw and heard the public or oral examinations of the different classes. Dr. Lovic Pierce preached the opening sermon and the address to the Mnemosynean society by Rev. W. J. Scott of Marietta was on the "Education of Women". There were 50 or more students, but those giving graduating compositions on the program in August were: Misses Helen A. J. Underwood, Rome, salutatory; A. Watters, Floyd county; Judith A. Fain, Cass county; J. R. Latimer, Cassville;

A. Field, Gordon county; Josephine M. Trimble, Cass county; Martha W. Trippe, Cassville, valedictorian to audience, faculty and class; and L. O. Day, Cassville, valedictorian to board of visitors, trustees and president. A plan was originated at this commencement by Warren Akin to raise an endowment of $20,000 and Mr. Akin headed the list with $1,000. The girl students were requested to dress simply. Most of them boarded with the Lands and Chunns.

In 1858 the only changes in the faculty were in the music department, Mr. and Mrs. E. M. Edwardy having charge, and Mrs. Anna Davies, principal, in the preparatory department.

At the commencement in July, the junior class compositions were given by Margaret A. Branson, Elizabeth A. Headden, Louanna A. Carpenter, Temperance E. Land, Cassville; Martha A. Hodge, Cass county; Julia S. Simmons, Dalton. Josephine Hardin was a member of this class.

The graduating compositions were by Lila M. Land, salutatory, Cassville; Julia A. Gill, Cave Spring; Lucy E. Carpenter, Cassville; Sarah E. Erwin; Ella E. Robert, Marietta; J. Florence Candler, Villa Rica; Fannie M. Rush, Floyd county; Orianna L. deVerdery, Cedartown; Georgia R. Kelsey, Cassville, valedictory to board of visitors, faculty and class; Caroline B. Thomason, Cass county, valedictorian to audience, trustees and president. Charles Wallace Howard delivered the annual address before the Mnemosynean society.

The faculty for 1859:

"Rev. Daniel Kelsey, A. M., president, professor of mathematics and natural science.
Rev. A. G. Johnson, A. M., professor of English, Latin literature.
Miss Amelia M. Tompkins, moral science, belle lettres, painting and drawing.
J. W. Kinabrew, M. D., professor of physiology and hygiene.
R. H. Guyn, professor of vocal and instrumental music.
Mrs. R.H. Guyn, assistant, music department.
Mrs. E. A. Kelsey, wax and needle work."

In the write-up of this year's commencement, no names were mentioned, but five girls received degrees. Rev. W. R. Branham preached, and the address was given by Dr. W. H. Felton. The visiting committee included: H. Best, president; W. T. Wofford, Thomas Compton, J. W. McGehee, R. C. Saxon, J. W. Yarbrough, Wm. Cunyus, sec.; J. A. Crawford, T. G. Barron, J. A. Terrell, J. N. Simmons, B. F. Bennett, Thos. A. Word.

After the resignation of Rev. Kelsey, Rev. B. Arbogast, former president of Wesleyan Female Institute of Stanton, Va., was elected president in 1860 and continued in that office until the college was destroyed by Sherman's army in 1864. Arthur Haire as secretary of the board of trustees advertised it in 1860: "We offer advantages which cannot be secured further South. Six years of successful operation."

Graduates in 1860 were: Misses Sallie E. Buford, Lidie A. Field, Lou A. Brown, Sarah E. Cobb, Julia F. Bevill. Others who attended this college were Anna Brown, Betty Fain, Keziah Lynn, Elizabeth Reynolds and Frances Wright.

CHEROKEE BAPTIST COLLEGE

In January, 1854*, the Cherokee Baptist college was incorporated in Cassville with John Crawford, John H. Rice, Humphrey W. Cobb, A. W. Buford, A. R. Wright, Thomas J. Wofford, Lewis Tumlin, Z. Edwards, W. T. Wofford, R. M. Young, D. B. Cunyus, Geo. W. Tumlin, W. C. Wyly, Elisha King, Mark A. Cooper, John W. Lewis, Thomas G. Barron, James Milner, Joseph Bogle, Ira R. Foster, Farish Carter, E. M. Galt, Edwin Dyer, George W. Selvedge, Leander W. Crook, William Martin, S. S. Bailey, William Peck, "and their successors", as trustees, to be under control of the Middle Cherokee Baptist Association. This was looked upon as special work of the Baptist north of the Chattahoochee river. A regular ten months' college course of four years was provided; also, an academic department for an English

---
*Acts of 1854, p. 117.

and classical education. Rates for tuition were:

"Collegiate department, per month ---------------------------------$34.00
Academic department --- 28.00
Incidental Expenses -- 2.00
Board and washing, per month--------------------------------- 10.00"

The faculty for 1856:

"Rev. Thomas Rambaut, president, professor of ancient languages, mental and moral philosophy.
Rev. W. H. Robert, professor of mathematics and natural science.
John B. S. Davis, professor of Belle Lettres.
W. H. Sullivan, Tutor.
      John H. Rice, Sec'ty, B. of T."

The college was completely destroyed by fire on the 4th of February, 1856, but as soon as possible a brick edifice of three stories was erected with two wings, 40 by 36 feet, two stories high. It had a well-arranged chapel that seated 800 people, two large halls, seven recitation rooms, a library, two apparatus rooms, and two halls for literary societies. There were 98 students enrolled in 1857. It was located on Chapman hill, on the road between Cassville and Kingston.

Wylie M. Dyer, of LaFayette was the first graduate of the college in July, 1857. Orators from the freshman class at the commencement of that year were: J. C. Branson, J. E. Carswell, W. L. Goldsmith, R. B. Headden, 2nd prize; J. C. Robert, J. W. Jewell, Oglethorpe county; W. D. Lawrence, Putnam county; J. B. Tippen, Cherokee county; Samuel Tumlin, 1st prize; T. G. Wilkes, of Atlanta. Speakers from the sophomore class were: James H. Anderson of Ringgold, Albert G. McMurry, R. C. Latimer, Wm. A. Chunn, Preston B. Word. An endowment of $50,000 was planned by the trustees and 100 persons were asked to obligate themselves to execute their bonds for the sum of $500 each, but in a report on education the endowment amounted to $22,000 and the property was valued at $25,000. Rev. Joseph Walker, editor of the Christian Index, preached the commencement sermon. Dr. H. V. M. Miller delivered an address before the Alpha Pi Delta society on, "The

Errors in the Present System of Teaching in Colleges". The winners of declamation in the preparatory department, first prize to James Goldsmith, Cartersville, and second to William Clayton, Kingston.

The faculty in 1858 included:

"Rev. Rambaut, president.

J. D. Collins, A. M., natural science, English literature and rhetoric.

W. H. Sullivan, A. M., ancient languages and literature.

Wiley M. Dyer, A. M., mathematics.

Wm. A. Mercer, principal of academic department and secretary of board of trustees."

At the commencement in July, the freshman declaimers were: W. D. Bird, Floyd county; J. H. Cobb, J. M. Dillard, W. E. Henderson, W. B. Patton, J. H. Mercer, W. J. Mercer, C. F. Mercer, G. S. Cobb, B. F. Jessup, Twiggs county; R M. Tarver. Whitfield county; J. F. Key and J. N. Ware, Floyd county. From the sophomore class were: J. C. Branson, J. E. Carswell, W. L. Goldsmith, R. B. Headden, Cass county; S. M. Dyer, LaFayette; J. B. Tippin, Cherokee county; T. G. Wilkes, Atlanta. From the junior: James H. Anderson, Ringgold; Albert G. McMurry, William A. Chunn, Ezekial S. Candler, Carroll county; F. M. Henderson, Wilkes county; John H. Reece, Rome. Col. W. H. Stiles delivered the address to the Alpha Pi Delta society.

Trustees in 1858 were: John Crawford, E. Dyer, J. W. Lewis, T. U. Wilkes, J. M. Wood, A. Webb, A. W. Buford, S. G. Hillyer, G. W. Selvidge, J. S. Rowland, M. A. Cooper, Lewis Tumlin, W. T. Wofford, Ira R. Foster, J. J. Howard, C. W. Sparks, L. Dillard, Turner Goldsmith, J. H. Rice, J. W. Kinabrew W. A. Mercer, Madison McMurry, T. M. Compton, R. L. Rogers, T. A. Sullivan, J. H. McClung, Thos. J. Wofford, R. M. Young.

During 1859-60 Rev. Rambaut continued as president with J. D. Collins professor of natural science and agriculture, English literature and history. New professors were S. H. DeVore, A. M., mathematics and astronomy, and T. A. Seals, A. M., ancient languages and literature.

At commencement in July, 1859, President Rambaut preached the commencement sermon, and the literary address to the Alpha Pi Delta and H. H. H. societies was given by Judge E. R. Harden of Dalton. Degrees of B.Ph., A.B., and A.M., were conferred. Speakers from the graduating class were: A. G. McMurry, valedictory address on "Independence of the Intellect"; Jas. H. Anderson, "A Character Is a Completely Fashioned Will"; William A. Chunn, "Happy Consequences of the American Revolution"; E. G. Candler, "Peace Hath Her Victories, No Less Renowned Than War". Sophomore prizes were won by W. J. Mercer and R. M. Tarver.

In November, 1859, the trustees and faculty petitioned the senate and house of representatives the use of twenty-five thousand dollars for the permanent endowment of the school of natural sciences in the Cherokee Baptist College.

The last writeup of the college: "On the regular commencement day, addresses were delivered by Messrs. Headden, Tippin, Carswell, Saffold and Tarver. The three first mentioned received diplomas as graduates." Rev. C. W. Howard delivered the literary address.

In 1863 an act*, approved April 14, provided that the trustees of the said colleges "shall have until the expiration of three years after the ratification of a treaty of peace between the U. S. and the Confederate States of America, in which to resume the exercises in said colleges, without forfeiture of their charters, or the reverting of said college buildings, grounds, and property to those who contributed to them."

These colleges were the first attempted in Cherokee Georgia, and though the Federal army wantonly destroyed them, their record is a crowning accomplishment of the patriotic and devoted men who made the attempt.

Many families had tutors or a governess for their children. Before a school was built a few children in the Stilesboro community were allowed to attend classes in the Shelman home where a governess was employed.

*Acts of 1863, p. 192.

Seeing a need from the steady growth of a school in Stilesboro, a new building was erected in 1859 on the present site. The land was given by Russell H. Cannon, the architect was William Cunyus, and the house was built by public contributions. It was not incorporated until 1892 with nine trustees. Over the door is painted, "Deo ac Patrae MDCCCLIX". This school house is one of the landmarks of the county. It served the "enemy" in time of war and is in service today, due to the preservation of the Stilesboro Village Improvement club. Some of the early principals were Rev. William Cunyus from 1859 until 1866, in 1867 James G. Ryals, in 1869 J. D. Collins, in 1871 I. G. Hudson, in 1874 H. J. McCormick, in 1879 W. R. Thigpen.

Sherwood's Gazetteer of 1860 reported Oakland Institute in the eastern part of the county.

The following is a report of the public schools in 1860, found in the State Department of Archives:

No. of free white children between 6 and 18—3987.

No. who have been taught elementary branches of an English education—males, 860; females, 604.

No. who have been taught higher branches—males, 173; females, 130.

Average rate of tuition in the elementary branches per year, $14.25.

Average rate of tuition in the higher branches—$20.07.

Grand jury assessment, 20 per cent—$1200.

No. of children under 6 attended present year—males, 19; females, 10.

No. of children over 16—males, 97; females, 19.

Total number of males and females—1912.

No. of school houses in county: 18 proper; 1 institute and 2 colleges—male and female.

No. of schools taught in this year—30.

No. of teachers—males, 12; females, 7.

No county academy.

Nathan Land, Ordinary.

The public school fund provided instruction only in the elementary branches for an English education.

Dr. and Mrs. Felton, beginning in 1866, conducted a

mixed school for about two years as a means of livelihood in their home. Friends' and neighbors' children made up a list of about 80 pupils.

In January, 1866, John H. Fitten started and was principal of the Annianna Institute, one mile north of Adairsville, which continued until about 1881. This was a private boarding school for boys, though a few girls atttended. "For sons of parents who desire a place for their sons where temptations could not be as corrupting as the city public schools", was an advertising slogan. "Hops" were featured at commencement in 1875. The school was in the house erected by Charlie Hamilton and the school auditorium is still in evidence in the attic of the house today.

Ronald Johnston, educated at the University of Edinburgh, began teaching in the county in 1868 and from a private tutor became principal in the schools in Cartersville, Cass Station and Euharlee. He taught in the county for more than 25 years. Other teachers for many years were: J. Walter Pritchett, Revs. F. P. Brown, O. L. Smith, Theo E. Smith, S. G. Hillyer, Jr., Mr. and Mrs. L. B. Millican, and J. M. Attaway.

The schools at this period were called academies, high schools, institutes and seminaries, with the boys and girls in separate departments. Sometimes there was one for boys and girls. There were schools for children and a colored school under the African M. E. conference in Cartersville .

At the Euharlee Male and Female school in 1867 the trustees were T. W. Brandon, Thos. Tumlin, Eli Barrett, A. G. Johnston. Rev. A. G. Johnston and Ronald Johnston were principals. In 1868 there was an orphan school at Cassville under the direction of Mrs. McMurry.

In 1869 the Pine Log Masonic Institute was opened on the Tennessee road with A. A. Vincent, chairman, A. J. Weems, Wm. Allen, J. M. Brittain, W. H. King, Levi Pierce, D. Mahan, J. R. Adair, James Carson as trustees in the early 70s. Rev. J. M. Brittain* was prin-

*Father of M. L. Brittain, president of Georgia Tech.

cipal in 1870-71. A. W. Fite was principal for one year in 1876. This remained an institute until in 1894 it was called the Pine Log High school.

Mrs. C. N. Mayson taught a private school in Kingston after the Civil War. R. G. Johnson and Rev. J. T. Lin taught in Kingston. The first school in the Taylorsville district was Oak Bower, across the line in Polk county. When the town of Taylorsville was established a school house was built. The present school is a modern brick building.

On July 3, 1871, the Cartersville Female High school was opened by Miss Lottie Moon of Albermarle county, Va., and Miss Anna C. Safford of Greensboro, Ga. The school was back of the First Presbyterian church. Latin, Greek and Latin languages were taught in the advanced course and the tuition was $2.40 for primary, $3.00 for intermediate, $3.60 for advanced courses. The trustees were: J. R. Parrot, W. H. Gilbert, Abda Johnson, P. L. Moon and John W. Wofford. In June of 1873 Miss Moon and Miss Safford felt the foreign mission call and went to China where Miss Moon, under the Southern Baptist convention, spent 39 years of her life in service. Miss Safford went under the auspices of the Presbyterians.

Mrs. Sarah Frances Brame, graduate and a teacher of the Mary Sharp and Judson colleges, taught here a few years after the Civil War as Miss Beall. This cultured and accomplished woman opened a private school in 1871 on Main street where primary, preparatory, and academic courses were offered, with Hebrew added to the other languages. After Misses Moon and Safford left many of those pupils attended Mrs. Brame's Female School, then back of the First Presbyterian church. The trustees were J. J. Howard, C. G. Trammel, P. L. Moon, A. Johnson and John A. Erwin. The kindergarten system of teaching was begun in 1885 by Mlle. V. Goulong as a feature of Mrs. Brame's school. Mrs. Brame later taught in the Terrace house on Main street.

In 1873 Gen. W. T. Wofford set aside a parcel of land for an academy, and for church and Sabbath school purposes, at the cross roads, just east of Cass Station. In 1875 it was called Wofford's Academy, in honor of the general, and the building was erected by voluntary contributions. The original trustees were W. T. Wofford, W. H. Wood, John McKelvey, J. A. Matthias, A. W. Archer and J. H. Walker. By 1889 all of the original trustees had died but one, and the following were elected: F. R. Walker, C. M. Quillian, M. M. Rogers, W. T. Gaines, B. F. Posey, A. M. Strain and J. H. Gilreath. Professor Matthew Marshall was principal from 1875 to 1880. This location has been a strategic point for education. It later became the Massachusetts-Georgia Model School and at present is a county school.

Out of courtesy to Mrs. A. O. Granger, the Massachusetts Federation of Women's clubs aided the Georgia Federation with a thousand dollars when the third model school in the State was located, Feb. 17, 1903, on the old Wofford's Academy site. The Georgia Federation continued its support until the Tallulah Falls schools became their interest. The Cherokee Woman's Club assisted afterwards. Mrs. M .L. Johnson was manager of the school and during her splendid administration was able to continue after the building was destroyed by fire in 1905. Mrs. Lilla Clarke and Miss Tommie Dozier were the first teachers. Miss Ruth Walker, a student, and daughter of Mr. and Mrs. J. H. Walker, was given the U. D. C. Vassar scholarship in 1914.

Miss C. V. Hendricks taught at Stegall's Station in 1874. She was only teacher found in old county papers.

Teachers in Adairsville in the late 70's were: Miss Emma Jackson, principal of the Adairsville Academy, which was called the academy until 1889; F. M. Durham; a Mr. McCall, T. M. Fulton and Wiley Dyer were other principals. In 1881 L. C. Dickey was principal of the Bartow Institute for males and females. In 1884 this was called the Bartow Classical and Scientific Institute, and Col. Henry D. Capers was president and principal at this time.

In 1882 Miss Lucy Carpenter taught a private school

in Cartersville, with Mrs. J. W. Harris, Sr., as assistant. In 1886 this became the West End Institute with Mrs. Florence Candler Harris (Mrs. J. W. Harris, Sr.) as principal. It was chartered under this name in June, 1891. Mrs. Harris and Mrs. Brame were rival teachers until in the early 90's they taught together. Mrs. Brame was an aunt of Mrs. Harris. Mrs. Harris taught the West End Institute* on Main street until 1900. After the public schools were in effect, many families continued sending their daughters to private schools.

In October, 1886 in a mass meeting Sam Jones, pledging $1,000 himself, canvassed $8,000 for a much needed college in Cartersville. It was deeded under the name of the "Sam Jones Female College" by the Union Tabernacle Trustees and incorporated for a period of 20 years. The capital stock was $10,000 and there were 129 shareholders. The cornerstone was laid in Sept., 1887. In 1889 a petition was signed by certain stockholders alleging that the corporation was never legally organized, a receiver was appointed and the property was sold to the city for $2500 and converted into a school building.

During 1879 there was an attempt to establish free schools and in 1886 a mass meeting was held to adopt a system, but not until December, 1888 was there an act of the legislature† establishing a system of schools in Cartersville, to be supported by a tax of one-fourth per cent on taxable property. The board was composed of John W. Akin, W. H. Howard, W. C. Baker, Martin Collins, J. K. Rowan, T. W. Milner, W. L. Kirkpatrick, S. Roberts, J. H. Wikle, J. M. Neel, J. A. Crawford, A. W. Fite, J. C. Wofford, A. M. Foute, A. Collins, Charles H. Smith. John W. Akin was president of the board.

In September, 1889, two white public schools were opened which became known as the West Side and East Side schools.

---

*Present home of Emory Vaughan.
†Acts of 1888, p. 323.

The West Side, with nine grades, used the Sam Jones Female College building, and L. B. Robeson, now a resident of Marietta, was principal with Misses Alice Hodnett, Mamie Ware and Leila Hall as assistants. There were 158 pupils.

The East Side school used the site of the East Cartersville Institute on Gilmer and Carter streets which began in the 80's. S. D. Lee was principal with Misses Ida Lee, Lena Ford and Jennie Thomas as assistants. There were 96 pupils.

The Negro public school, on Summer Hill, was in the building formerly used as a male high school by Ronald Johnson. A. C. Demry was principal, Nora Jackson, assistant.

In 1891, W. W. Daves, who was superintendent of the East Cartersville Institute in 1887, became superintendent of the two schools and continued so for 15 years. From 1906 Henry L. Sewell served 13 years, and was succeeded by L. C. Evans in 1920. H. B. Robertson has served since June, 1923, with the exception of one and a half terms by W. E. Dendy.

In 1930 new buildings were erected on the two former school sites and the high school was remodeled from the old college building. The Negro school on Summer Hill was made into a modern, well-equipped school by the aid of the Rosenwald fund in 1922.

In January, 1901, the Cherokee Baptist High school was incorporated in Adairsville under the Middle Cherokee Association with J. J. Connor, W. H. Lumpkin, J. P. Lewis, W. M. King, B. O. Crawford, R. L. Rogers of Bartow; J. W. Swain, W. L. Hines, R. L. McWhorter of Gordon as trustees. These buildings were later used for the present public schools; J. C. Tribble of Cassville is principal.

THE COUNTY SCHOOLS

In July, 1896, a charter was granted to the Euharlee Presbyterian Institute, in the town of Euharlee, to be under the control of the Cherokee Presbytery. George

T. Goetchuis, Rome; Enoch Faw, Cobb; J. E. Hansell, Polk; J. E. Jones, Chattooga; W. S. Hamiter,, E. D. McDougall, J. F. McGowan, H. H. Milam, W. P. Whitesides, of Bartow, were trustees. By an amendment in August, 1910 the elders of the Euharlee Presbyterian church were to serve as trustees of this school. On this same property and in the same buildings, the Bartow County Rural High school operated about three years. In August, 1917, it was deeded back to the owners in the Euharlee community. At present it is one of the county system.

In 1910 Armaretta Brooks (Mrs. J. W. Matthews) started the first school in the State for illiterate parents at the Macedonia school house, in the 21st district. All in all, she taught them about six months but it was the first time that the grown-ups of a community went to school after the children had left the school house.

In 1871 records show that the county board of education was appointed by the governor. In later years it was commissioned by the governor after being recommended by the grand jury.

The first record of a county superintendent was of Col. R. C. Saxon, 1881-1896, who organized the first teachers' institute in 1886; R. A. Clayton, 1896-1907; Henry H. Milam, 1907-1916; Jesse W. Jackson, 1916-1925; G. C. Nelson, 1925-1929; S. E. Hamrick, 1929-1932; P. W. Bernard 1933-.

County demonstration agents have worked successfully at intervals but proper provision for a permanent one has not been made.

Since 1926 the idea of consolidated schools has grown and consolidations have been made at Smithville Peeples Valley, Cassville, Kingston, Pine Log and Emerson. There are 40 white and 14 colored schools in the present county system. Cartersville and Adairsville have the only independent systems.

In the last years there have been additional enactments of the legislature to provide funds for educational purposes and this county receives such benefit.

CHAPTER X

NEWSPAPERS

In the State treasurer's printing fund report in 1835 there is a statement of $12.00 paid John B. Hood & Son for printing done for the public in The Cassville Gazette —the first newspaper in Cassville.

The Cassville Pioneer, edited by Donald M. Hood was last published in January, 1849. Mr. Hood removed to Rome.

In February, 1849 at the urgent suggestion of W. T. Wofford, John W. Burke*, the publisher of The Athens Banner, came to Cassville to establish a weekly Democratic paper. The first number of The Cassville Standard was published on March 15, 1849.

Mr. Burke plunged into politics. He moved back to Athens in September, 1850 selling out the paper to Benjamin F. Bennett. In January, 1852 Mr. Burke returned to The Cassville Standard at the insistence of friends and for the sake of the party, and because of his personal interests in Cassville he bought back the paper. As a delegate to the State Union convention in 1852, though not promising to support the Southern Rights party, he had agreed not to run an opposition ticket in his paper. Wofford brought out the "Tugaloo Ticket", so to keep friendship and his word to his party, Burke sold The Standard to W. T. Wofford in February, 1852. John A. Reynolds became publisher with Wofford in November. Mr. Burke then formed a partnership with J. D. Carpenter in a dry goods store and represented the Southern Mutual Insurance Company. Mr. Burke preached his first sermon in Cassville and on October 11, 1853, he and Warren Akin became licensed Methodist preachers. Mr. Burke was an itinerant preacher in Cherokee Georgia

---

*From the diary of J. W. Burge, in possession of his grandson, E. W. Burke, Jr., Macon.

until 1856. Later he established The J. W. Burke Co. in Macon, Ga., and was editor of The Wesleyan Methodist.

Sometime between 1852 and 1857 Samuel H. Smith became editor and proprietor of The Standard, with B. F. Bennett, publisher. The Standard was "devoted to the markets, foreign and domestic news."

On February 26, 1857, Mr. Smith sold to John H. Rice, who came to Cassville in 1845 and was an active citizen there, and Milton A. Candler. Mr. Rice established The Franklin Printing House and Book Bindery in Atlanta that year, and while he was away B. F. Bennett was publisher with Mr. Candler. While living at Cassville Mr. Candler married Miss Eliza C. Murphy, daughter of Charles Murphy in Decatur, on June 9, 1857. Mr. Candler left The Standard in July, and John H. Rice* became editor and proprietor. In 1856 Mr. Rice was elected major general of the State militia for the northern district of Georgia. On account of a physical breakdown, Mr. Rice sold The Standard in March, 1858 to B. H. Leeke and B. F. Bennett. Politics were so "warm" over the election of Joseph E. Brown and Dr. J. W. Lewis, Mr. Leeke sold out to Mr. Bennett and E. M. Keith, who came to assist Mr. Bennett in April, 1859.

In the meantime, Samuel H. Smith established The Cartersville Express in 1858 and was co-editor with Dr. W. T. Goldsmith, and at the end of the year the two papers were being printed in co-partnership. In 1859 the stockholders of The Standard were Joseph Chapman, Thos. M. Compton, Wm. Lattimer, Wm. Headden and M. McMurray. Jesse R. Wikle came from The Dahlonega Watchman and bought an interest in the papers.

The two papers dissolved by mutual consent, and from February, 1860 Jesse R. Wikle was the proprietor of The Cassville Standard with the motto, "The Constitution must be maintained inviolate in all its parts." The

---

*Mr. Rice moved out west in 1867 and became renowned in the newspaper circles of Kansas and Miss. He married in 1847 Nancy, daughter of John Russell who came to Cassville in 1834 from Laurens district, S. C., and died at Cassville, Dec. 22, 1857. Mr. Rice died at Fort Scott in 1904.

Cassville papers had always been Democratic until the rupture of the party over the presidential candidates of 1860. S. H. Smith and Dr. Goldsmith were advocates of Breckenridge and Lane.

When Cassville was burned in 1864, The Standard office was destroyed and an illustrious newspaper, recognized in the State as being one of the leaders, closed its career under that name. The old issues on record are perfectly preserved. A typographical error was a rarity and the editor showed erudition in local and world affairs.

In January, 1865 The Cartersville Express, with S. H. Smith, editor, and Robert P. Milam, proprietor, began publication as a weekly. A semi-weekly Express was published for a short time, but it went back to a weekly publication in 1867 and continued as such until again in 1870, The Cartersville Weekly Express was published semi-weekly. C. C. Morgan assisted Mr. Smith in 1868. Mr. Smith was editorially assisted by Col. J. J. Howard in 1870, and the paper was $3 a year. In 1871 James Watt Harris was co-editor until in August, P. H. Brewster purchased an interest in the Semi-Weekly Express and became co-editor. The Cartersville Standard, under the joint proprietorship of Wikle and Word, entered the field, July 14, 1870.

Back in 1867 The Daily Opinion was published in Atlanta and called itself the official paper for Bartow and other counties. In 1868 The Georgia Weekly Opinion, still in Atlanta, was published for the same counties.

In 1871 The Cartersville Express and The Cartersville Standard consolidated under the name of The Standard and Express, and was published weekly and semi-weekly under the firm name of Smith, Wikle & Co. By 1872 this paper had nine columns and had such writers as P. H. Brewster, local editor; J. W. Harris, political editor; S. H. Smith, news and local editor; W. S. D. Wikle, publisher. In August of this year, W. D. Trammel bought the interest of Mr. Wikle and The Standard and Express was published and edited by S. H. Smith & Co.

In December, 1875 C. H. C. Willingham came from The Rome Courier to edit The Cartersville Express, and to break up the "cotton rings" in the city. He paid $2,500 for the equipment. During the time of Dr. Felton's hot race for Congress, The Express was suppressed to stop Mr. Willingham's advocacy of "this independent business". The politicians put him out of business only temporarily as it was only a question of insufficient means to meet an emergency. As a competitor to The Express, in November, 1875, W. A. and A. Marschalk edited The Planters Advocate.

In July, 1878 Frank P. Gray of Adairsville and T. E. Hanbury became the editors of The Express. Mr. Gray was not a Felton man. In January, 1879 Mr. Gray left and S. A. Cunningham of The Chattanooga Times became his successor.

In October, 1873 W. A. Marschalk and Col. J. W. Harris bought out the interest of Mr. Smith and Mr. Brewster on account of Mr. Smith's health. He died in Cartersville in November, 1873. He was a local Methodist preacher and served many churches in the county while he was editor. He was a chaplain in the 60th Ga. Regt. He was known as "genial fat Sam". In 1874 John H. Wikle purchased The Express. Mr. Brewster established for a short time The Sentinel in Cartersville.

Late in 1878, Mr. Willingham began The Free Press, an "independent democratic journal". On Dec. 30, 1884, Mr. Willingham died at his home near Cartersville, leaving 5 sons. Alex M., a son, became editor of The Free Press in 1885. Alex and Jesse B. Willingham had assisted their father while he was editor.

In May, 1879 Cartersville entertained the Georgia Press Association and again in 1889.

In 1880 John W. Akin became associate editor with S. A. Cunningham on The Cartersville Express.

The Cartersville American was established in 1882 by Douglas Wikle who was editor and proprietor. Articles in the issues of 1884 would be a credit to any paper today, especially those written by W. J. Neel under the title, "The Tatler Talks".

The Cartersville Courant started January 29, 1885 and was published and edited by Dr. and Mrs. W. H. Felton and D. W. Curry. After a spirited legal fight between Mrs. Felton and the Willingham sons, The Courant used the press and further equipment of The Free Press. On March 4, 1886, Dr. and Mrs. Felton gave up their editorial management on account of the tax on the editress' strength, but not before Mrs. Felton made a name for herself. Her facile pen flashed in the editorial columns and won recognition from all over the State.

The Courant Publishing Company under Frank J. Taylor and A. M. Willingham edited the paper until Mr. Taylor sold his interest to the latter.

On Jan. 13, 1887, the papers consolidated under the name of The Courant-American, Mr. Willingham and Douglas Wikle, editors and proprietors. In 1889 they sold it to Elam Christian and D. B. Freeman of Cedartown, and in November, 1889 Mr. Willingham bought Mr. Christian's interest. In January, 1891 Mr. Willingham sold his interest to D. B. Freeman and Company. H. A. Chapman from Americus became editor with Mr. Freeman* and he and Mr. Freeman published The Courant-American until 1904.

The News Publishing Company was incorporated in 1896 by Robert L. Willingham. In 1904 The Cartersville News and Courant were published by Freeman and Chapman continuously until their consolidation. In October W. J. Neel became co-editor and served until March, 1906.

The Tribune Publishing Company, which started The Bartow Tribune, was incorporated March, 1910 by P. F. Callahan and C. A. Perry. In 1914 they sold their interest to Mr. O. T. Peeples who merged it with The Cartersville News in 1917.

On January 1, 1918 M. L. Fleetwood of Thomasville, Ga., became general manager of The Tribune-News. O. T. Peeples was president of the publishing company.

---

*See sketch in Knight's "Georgia and Georgians", p-2186.

In April, 1920 M. L. Fleetwood became sole owner of The Tribune-News. D. Aug 20, 1966.

The Adairsville Banner was established in 1895; J. E. Scott, editor. The paper was discontinued about 1905. In January, 1932, it was reestablished by Ed Burch.

The Bartow Herald was established in April, 1929, by W. L. Harris of Marietta, and in June, W. R. Frier, Jr. of Douglas, Ga., became editor. In March, 1931 Mr. Frier purchased Mr. Harris' interest. D. Jan 15, 1969

CITY OFFICIALS, 1933: Front row, Mayor T. W. Tinsley, Alderman N. A. Bradley, Alderman R. E. Miller, Jr., Alderman C. H. Wheeler, Alderman E. R. Mines, City Manager J. W. Dent. Back row: Fire Chief Ben Mills, Chief of Police L. V. Payne, City Recorder R. V. Jones, Assistant City Clerk H. M. Crane, City Attorney Colquitt Finley, City Clerk T. A. Upshaw.

CHAPTER XI

POLITICS

Cass county in the early elections for county officers became naturally politically minded. Because of its prominent citizens the county was active in the issues of the day.

The earliest record of a political address was in 1844 when Alexander H. Stephens came to a barbecue given by the Whigs at Russell Springs near Cassville. He was introduced by Hon. Bartley Terhune* who had the reputation of being the ugliest man in north Georgia. The issue was Henry Clay vs. James K. Polk for president. A feature of the occasion was a wagon drawn by 6 horses covered with clay, and another team driven around covered with poke stalks and berries.

In the Twenty-eighth Congress†, William H. Stiles of Cass served as a representative and Mark A. Cooper resigned his seat as a representative in 1843 to be succeeded by A. H. Stephens.

Local politics became "hot" in 1852 when the Democrats divided into the Southern Rights and Union parties. Know-nothingism arose and became a gubernatorial issue, while the Whigs found refuge for a time in the American party.

In the Union Democratic convention at Milledgeville in April, 1852 Col. Lindsay Johnson was appointed vice-president and the delegates to the Baltimore convention from Cass were Lewis Tumlin and John S. Rowland. Delegates from this county to the Constitutional Union convention in Milledgeville in July, 1852 were John J. Word and John A. Crawford. In September, 1852 Warren Akin declined nomination as an elector for the 5th Congressional district on the ticket for Webster and

---
*Brother of Cornelius D. Terhune, lived and died in Rome.
†March, 1843-March, 1845.

Jenkins.

The county was politically divided over the presidential candidates. The Union ticket for Franklin Pierce had as its elector from this, the 5th Congressional, district John J. Word; on the Disunion or Southern Rights ticket for Pierce was Joseph E. Brown; on the Whig ticket for Winfield Scott was Turner H. Trippe. In the final result for the county the Southern Rights ticket was beaten by the Union ticket over 100 votes.

In 1857 the county was even more actively interested. W. H. Stiles, among 4 others, was mentioned for governor, as was John W. Lewis later. Joseph E. Brown was elected by compromise. Delegates to the State Democratic convention in June, 1857 from Cass were: Dr. J. W. Lewis, W. W. Clayton, J. G. Ryals, J. R. Wilkes, and E. V. Johnson. The county voted officially for J. E. Brown for governor; A. R. Wright for Congress; Hawkins F. Price, senator; Joseph L. Neel, representative. John W. Hooper, Sr., announced his candidacy as an independent Democrat for Congress. Hon. Brown addressed the citizens of Cass on July 13, and Benjamin Hill at Cartersville on August 31, 1857. The district convention was at Calhoun in July.

In August, 1859 Warren Akin was nominated by the Opposition party in Atlanta as a candidate for governor to run against Gov. Brown. Mr. Akin, an old-time Whig, made a brave and conscientious canvass, but Gov. Brown won, carrying this county by a majority of 184 votes. Mark Johnston was elected to the senate; Thomas J. Wofford and Mark A. Hardin, representatives.

The year 1860 will be remembered as the year of conventions. The split over the platform and principles was on account of the interference with slavery in the states and territories.

The 5th district elector on the National Democratic ticket for Stephen A. Douglas and Herschel V. Johnson was James W. Harris; the elector for the Bell and Everett ticket was J. R. Parrott; the elector for Breckinridge and Lane, who were elected by the Seceder's convention, was Lewis Tumlin. An editorial said, "All avowed disunionists support Breckinridge. They know he can't be elected, but think he can carry off enough democratic votes to secure the election of Lincoln, when they believe the time will have arrived for them to precipitate the cotton states into a revolution."

During the heated campaigns, Stephen A. Douglas spoke in Kingston, Judge Linton Stephens addressed the citizens in Cassville, and in August Robert Toombs spoke in Cartersville and was introduced by W. H. Stiles. Jefferson Davis* spoke in Cartersville while on a tour of the states.

The county's delegates to the Secession convention in January, 1861 were William T. Wofford, Turner H. Trippe and Hawkins F. Price. Mr. Trippe was one of the 17 on a committee to report on an ordinance of secession. In the process of voting all three voted "nay", but when they saw the honor of their State at stake, they came home and immediately volunteered their services. Cass as a whole was against secession from the Union.

In the important Constitutional convention in 1865, among its delegates was J. R. Parrott of this county, and at this time Gen. Wm. T. Wofford was chosen one of the representatives from Georgia to the Federal Congress.

After the Civil War, the Democratic and Republican parties showed a more bitter division of feeling and sentiment. Democratic clubs were organized in each militia district of Bartow in 1868. Dr. S. W. Leland was president of the 822nd, and Capt. J. L. Neel of the 856th.

At the Reconstruction convention of 1868, J. R. Parrott, a Republican from Bartow, was elected president of the convention. Other prominent Republicans at this time were Henry P. Farrow and James Milner of Bartow.

On March 31, 1868, Gen. P. M. B. Young was elected to represent the 7th Congressional district in conventions held in Cartersville and Kingston in October. He was not qualified under the Republican regime to take

---

*Avery's History of Georgia, p-183.

his seat until Jan. 16, 1871.

At the State Democratic convention in July, 1868 Gen. William T. Wofford was alternate delegate at large. In August, 1868 he announced his candidacy for Congress from this district, but because he and Gen. Young were both loved and respected, it was urged that no contest be between them.

In 1870 H. P. Farrow, familiarly known as "Potash Farrow", was appointed attorney-general by Governor Bullock. During Bullock's disgraceful regime Bartow became involved because of the illegal bonds of the Cartersville & Van Wert railroad, which will be discussed in another chapter. J. R. Parrott was appointed judge of the Cherokee circuit by Bullock.

Gen. P. M. B. Young was re-elected from this district as a representative to Congress in 1871. He was the hope of his party in the fight against radicalism and the disorganization of the Republican regime, and was thought to be the man for the crisis. He was the youngest member and the only member from the "reconstructed south".

The independent party of Georgia had its origin in this district when Dr. William H. Felton opened his campaign in the 7th Congressional district in June, 1874 as an independent candidate for Congress. His opponent was Col. W. H. Dabney of Floyd county, and after a heated campaign Dr. Felton won by a majority of 82 votes in the November election*.

Again, in 1876, Col. Dabney was Dr. Felton's opponent and Dr. Felton won by a majority of 2,500 votes in his county.

In the Constitutional convention of 1877, members from the 42nd Congressional district were Gen. W. T. Wofford, Hawkins F. Price, Col. Abda Johnson, John Fitten, A. R. Wright and D. B. Hamilton.

The campaign in 1878 was the hottest after the Civil War. Judge George N. Lester of Cobb county, and judge of the superior court, was Dr. Felton's oppon-

---

*See Mrs. Felton's "Memoirs of Georgia Politics", pp. 143-159.

ent. Dr. Felton won by a majority in this district of 1,350 votes.

Barbecues continued to be given by the candidates during this time. Dr. Felton made his canvass in a buggy or on horseback. Campaign literature was handled by the county papers and the latest news was obtained from the railroad station telegraph operator.

These campaigns made life-long friends or enemies of the Feltons in the county and the influence is felt to this day.

In July, 1880, Mark A. Cooper declined candidacy for the legislature on account of his age and his wife's health. John C. Branson of Kingston and Col. T. W. Milner of Cartersville ran. In 1880 Gen. P. M. B. Young and Capt. T. J. Lyon were elected to the National Democratic convention in Cincinnati.

In 1880 the Democrats put a new man in the race, Judson C. Clements of Walker county. Dr. Felton was defeated possibly because of the over-confidence of his friends. His defeat restored party regularity in the "bloody 7th". He was defeated again by Clements in 1882 and 1884.

Never have politics been so hot, nor so interesting, as in the days of Dr. Felton's races. In 1884 Dr. Felton was chosen to represent his county in the State legislature where he served 6 useful years.

An editorial in the county papers of 1884 stated that, "whiskey or no whiskey would be the issue before the people of Bartow in the fall elections". Such men as J. M. Veach, R. M. Patillo, A. C. Trimble, Dr. W. I. Benham, Col. Montgomery, J. J. Howard, M. G. Dobbins, R. D. Combs, B. F. Bibbs, W. C. Edwards, R. H. Jones, T. E. Smith, R. G. Mays, J. W. Gray, A. Y. Sheats, J. M. Davidson, J. P. Lewis, Col. M. R. Stansell and others were willing to vote and work for prohibition. The Rev. Sam P. Jones was largely instrumental in abolishing the liquor traffic in the county and subsequently became one of the most powerful advocates of prohibition in the State.

After the election on the 3rd Wednesday in December, 1884 it became unlawful for a person to sell liquor in Bartow county.

In 1886 there was a split in Bartow over Gordon and Clements in the gubernatorial race.

The last gubernatorial aspirant from this county was John W. Akin in 1903.

The contest between J. M. Brown and Hoke Smith in 1907-09 disturbed county politics. The county has been Democratic to date.

The most recent issue that covers and rides county politics is the Cartersville city franchise.

CHAPTER XII

RAILROADS

Because of the fact that the W. & A. has played an important part in the history of this county, the following data from the "Western and Atlantic Railroad", by J. H. Johnston, will introduce this chapter.

Actual survey of the Western and Atlantic railroad from the Chattahoochee river to Allatoona heights began in July, 1837 and in December, 1837 an act was approved providing for the building of the road as surveyed, and work began in March, 1838.*

"The legislature having passed the Act (of 1841) approved December 4, 1841, to suspend all work from a point two miles northwest of the Etowah River (Cartersville) and to disband the corps of engineers, very little was accomplished in constructing the road for sometime."†

The United States Military railroad operated the W. & A. from Sept. 1, 1864, to Sept. 25, 1865, and there are no records in the State. During the Civil War the depots at Etowah and Cartersville were destroyed and the railroad bridges‡ were destroyed and rebuilt many times. (One railroad bridge over the Etowah was built in 1879.) In the annual report of the W. & A., 1866-67, in the possession of H. H. Green of Cartersville, is the statement that the depot at Cartersville had been completed. It was also reported that the depots at Adairsville, Kingston and Cass had been repaired and new platforms built. New water stations were erected at Allatoona, Rogers and a new one was needed at Harris.

To clear up the Cassville railroad project, after the act of the legislature was approved in January, the

---
*p-20.
†p-27.
‡Tradition has it that the first train to go over the railroad bridge at Oothcalooga creek fell through.

editorials in The Cassville Standard read as follows:

On February 26, 1852: "Mr. Wadley is emphatically a business man in every sense of the word—and has done much already to improve the condition of the State road. He is constantly on the road looking into, and correcting errors, making improvements, etc. We predict that he will make not only the best, but the most popular superintendent we have ever had."

"As our readers may feel anxious to know what progress is being made in our railroad movements, we will observe that subscriptions are still coming in handsomely and there is every probability of getting as much or more than is necessary for the work. Geo. G. Hull, Esq., resident engineer, rode over the contemplated route on Tuesday last, and expresses the opinion that there is nothing at all impracticable or unfavorable in it. We are also glad to learn from him, that he will be up again in a few days, to make the survey authorized by the legislature. This being done, we are ready to go ahead with the work. Mr. Hull, though quite young, has proved himself an excellent civil engineer, and we doubt not he will make our survey promptly and upon the most favorable route."

In the issue of The Standard on April 1, 1852: "Messrs. Hull, Stovall, and Clam, are now engaged in surveying the proposed change in the W. & A. road, to bring it through Cassville. Judging from the skill and energy thus far displayed by the corps, we can promise our friends here a speedy completion of the work. The result of their labors will be made known in our next issue."

From the issue of April 8, 1852: "The survey of the railroad detour by this place has been completed, and we are gratified to state that the route proved to be practicable under the act, and at a cost not far surpassing that which was anticipated. Some arrangements remain to be made before we can enter upon the work."

From The Standard on May 13, 1852: "It will be gratifying, no doubt, to the friends of this project to learn that Mr. Geo. G. Hull, resident engineer of the State road, is expected up next week to locate the track of the proposed change; and that immediately thereafter proposals will be received for grading. We trust that in a few months now, the old hills around Cassville will re-echo the sound of the steam whistle, as the engine takes a view of our village."

A practical reason for the route remaining as it is today were the difficult, gravelly ridges between Cassville and Adairsville.

The Standard in May reprints a table prepared for Hunt's Merchant's Magazine, by David M. Balfour of Mass., in which it appears that on the 1st of January, 1852, of the number of railroads in each State, that in Georgia there were 11 railroads, covering 804 miles. "Georgia up to 1837 had only one road, seven miles long, and now she is the fifth State in the Union in respect of her railroads."

On May 27, 1852 the editor, John W. Burke, wrote: "We took a short trip to the Northwest last week, and having enjoyed ourselves vastly, we desire to make a few notes for the benefit of our readers. We will say first that we went per W. & A. railroad to Ringgold, thence to LaFayette and Chattanooga, etc. . . . Railroad—We got on the cars at Cass Station, and were speedily transported over the State road, at the rate of 20 miles per hour, in comfortable cars; and we can testify to the improved condition of this great State work. There is one feature in this road now which deserves special notice—that of having good conductors. We had the pleasure of going up with Elisha King, Esq., of this county, who is acknowledged to be the best conductor in the Union. Dinner.—We stopped at the new and flourishing town of Calhoun where passengers on the up trains take dinner."

Stops are mentioned at Ringgold, and LaFayette and at Chattanooga—"a few minutes travel brought us to this embryo city, which is doing wonders in the way of improvements, and bids fair to be quite an important point."

In Sept. 20, 1852 issue: "The down passenger train on the State road ran over a cow on Friday last, throwing the engine off the track, near Chickamauga creek, and killing two firemen and crippling the engineer. The passengers escaped safely. One of the killed was Littleberry James, formerly of this place. He was an upright, clever man, and we regret his untimely death."

Passenger trains began to run on Sunday, "same as other days", in July, 1852.

THE CARTERSVILLE AND VAN WERT RAILROAD COMPANY*

The Cartersville and Van Wert Railroad Company was incorporated in Georgia by an act of the legislature, approved Dec. 13, 1866†, to construct and operate a railroad from Van Wert (near Rockmart) to Cartersville, to extend indefinitely in either direction and to connect with the Western & Atlantic railroad at Cartersville. The employment of State convicts, without cost other than for sustenance, was granted. (The corporators of the company met in Cartersville on Wednesday, Jan. 16, 1867, at the law office of Col. J. R. Parrot for the organization. Dr. S. F. Stephens was elected president, J. R. Wikle secretary, A. E. Marshall of Monroe county, agent of the company; the corporators included the above and J. J. Howard, Lewis Tumlin, John L. Rowland, J. W. Curry, Wm. T. Wofford, Wm. T. Burge, all of Cartersville; J. F. Dever and Seaborn Jones of Polk.) The principal office of the com-

---

*From information compiled by W. L. Stanley, Chief Public Relation Officer of the Seaboard Air Line Railway.
†Acts of 1866, p. 121.

pany was at Cartersville.

A special act of the legislature, approved March 12, 1869*, provided for endorsement of 7 per cent bonds by the governor on behalf of the State to the amount of $12,500 per mile of completed road. By joint resolution of the legislature, March 12, 1869 the State endorsement of bonds was limited to that portion of the line between Van Wert and Cartersville.

By joint resolution of the legislature, Oct. 5, 1870†, the restriction of State guaranteed bonds to the portion of the line between Van Wert and Cartersville was rescinded. (Bonds were not to be sold until a certain mileage had been completed.) The directors in 1869 were Mark A. Cooper, president, Dr. S. F. Stephens, R. H. Cannon, Abda Johnson, Thomas Stokely, J. G. Stocks, D. W. K. Peacock, Wm. H. Gilbert of Cartersville, and Col. E. Hulbert, superintendent of the State Road, Seaborn Jones and J. F. Dever of Van Wert.

Construction on the road began January 4, 1870, and was completed Sept. 12, 1870, from Cartersville to Taylorsville, 14 miles. The line was constructed with a five-foot guage and laid with 54 pound rail. The contract for construction was made Nov. 4, 1869, with William W. Lamon, L. S. Baum and S. E. Robbins. On Jan. 25, 1870, the contract was assigned to Lamon, Conant and Co., by whom the work was done. From Taylorsville to Rockmart the line was graded for a three-foot guage railroad, but no track was laid.

By a special act of the legislature of Georgia, approved Oct. 25, 1870‡, the name of the company was changed to The Cherokee Railroad Company§. (From a newspaper account in April, 1871, the capital stock was increased to $3,000,000 and H. I. Kimball was elected president with O. A. Lochrane, George Cook, John Harris and Abda Johnson, directors. Maj. Cooper declined to be a director.)

The line from Cartersville to Taylorsville was operated by the company under its own management from Oct. 25, 1870, to March 19, 1872, when on that date, in an action brought by Henry Clews & Company in the U. S. Circuit court, D. W. K. Peacock was appointed receiver and operated the road until Nov. 1st, 1876, when S. L. Stephens was appointed receiver in an action in the State court and took possession.

By an amendment of the Constitution of the State of Georgia, approved by the legislature Feb. 25, 1875, the State guarantee of bonds was declared void in the Cherokee Railroad Company.‖

On Nov. 5, 1878, the railroad was sold at public auction to Jesse R. Wilke for $29,500, who failed to make payment and the sale was annulled, and on March 4, 1879, the property and franchise were

---

*Acts of 1869, pp. 152-200.
†Acts of 1870, p. 500.
‡Acts of 1870, p. 310.
§See Mrs. Felton's "Memoirs of Georgia Politics", pp. 241-245.
‖Acts of 1875, p. 27.

sold at public auction to the Cherokee Iron Company for $22,500, which company was incorporated in 1873, and approved on Feb. 18*, to manufacture pig iron. The office was changed to Cedartown. The line was to extend to the Alabama line. In 1881 the guage of the line between Cartersville and Taylorsville was changed from five feet to three feet.

A special act of the legislature, approved Aug. 27, 1879†, amended the original charter of the Cartersville and Van Wert Railroad company, permitting suits to be instituted and tried at other points in Georgia than Cartersville.

On Nov. 13, 1882, the Cherokee Iron Company leased this property for 99 years to the East and West Railroad Company of Alabama which was organized on Feb. 24, 1882, under the laws of Alabama. Thus a line from Cartersville to Esom, 46 miles, was in operation and leased.

In July, 1887, the East and West Railroad of Alabama moved its local office from Cedartown to Cartersville and Capt. J. J. Calhoun of Cedartown was in charge.

For failure to pay bond interest, an action was brought in the U. S. Circuit Court for the Southern Division of the Northern District of Alabama and on March 16, 1888, John Postell of Cartersville was appointed receiver, serving until November 2, when he was replaced by Charles B. Ball.

Under the Alabama Railroad Incorporation Act, Code of 1886‡ a certificate of incorporation was issued by the Secretary of State Jan. 11, 1894, incorporating the East and West Railroad Company to operate the property formerly owned by the East and West Railroad Company of Alabama, and to succeed to all of the franchise rights of the latter company. Under the Georgia General Railroad Incorporation Act of 1892 a charter was issued Jan. 15, 1896, incorporating the East and West Railroad Company in Georgia as successor to the franchises and rights of predecessor corporations.

The E. & W. of Georgia was organized on Jan. 8, 1894, and operated the line from Cartersville to Pell City, Ala. and later acquired branch lines.

On April 23, 1902 the entire capital stock of the East and West Railroad Company was bought by a syndicate for the benefit of the Seaboard Air Line Railway.§

On May 20, 1903, the East and West Railroad Company was consolidated with the Chattahochee Terminal Railway to form the Atlanta and Birmingham Air Line Railway, which organization was effected on April 22, 1903, and which operated among other lines, the

---
*Acts of 1873, p. 171.
†Acts of 1879, p. 223.
‡Civil Code of Ala., 1886, p. 384, Law Library G. C.
§By an agreement, dated Mar. 23, 1903, the L. & N. Railroad company was granted trackage rights between Wellington, Ala. and Cartersville.

line between Cartersville and Pell City, Ala.

On Sept. 30, 1909, the property and franchises of the Atlanta and Birmingham Air Line Railway were sold to the Seaboard Air Line Railway which operates this small but important branch line.

About Jan. 1, 1920, the old frame depot building of the Seaboard on the State's property at Cartersville was removed.

"Under a tenant-at-will lease contract with the N. C. & St. L. Railway, the Seaboard uses a track on the right of way between Cartersville and Junta, paying a monthly rental for such use."*

OTHER RAILROADS

Cartersville and Cartersville men have been interested and connected with railroads from an early date.

As early as July, 1857 a railroad meeting was held in Cartersville in contemplation of a railroad from Jacksonville, Ala., to this city.

In 1871 the discussion of the Atlanta and Blue Ridge railroad was before the county, and Maj. Mark A. Cooper, J. H. Wikle, and Gen. Wofford were actively interested. It was thought to be a good extension or connection with the Cartersville and Van Wert railroad.

The Cartersville and Gainesville Airline railroad, approved by a legislative act Dec. 26, 1886, was changed in September, 1891 to the Cartersville, Gainesville and Port Royal Railroad company, and in October of the same year to the Cartersville, Gainesville, Augusta and Charleston Railroad company. The railroad was to be constructed from Cartersville to, "At, above or below the city of Augusta." This enterprise was conceived and fostered by citizens of Cartersville: John T. Norris, D. W. K. Peacock, John Postell (former assistant engineer of the W. & A.), Clark Baker, T. W. Milner, J. Watt Harris, G. H. Aubrey, and others. Valuable contributions from property owners along the proposed line, such as rights of way, timber and mineral rights, and options upon realty, were secured, but the necessary funds for actual construction could not be found, and like so many other schemes, intrinsically meritorious for Southern development, this one failed.

Under the name of the Atlanta, Knoxville and Northern Railway company, a new line entering the State in

*Johnston's "Western and Atlantic Railroad", p. 166.

Murray county made a connection with the Western and Atlantic railroad at Junta, one mile north of Cartersville, and by contract acquired trackage over the W. & A. from Junta to Atlanta. On Feb. 11, 1905, the Atlanta, Knoxville and Northern Railway company sold to the Louisville and Nashville Railroad company all its railroad properties in the State, together with its trackage rights.

CHAPTER XIII

THE TOPOGRAPHY OF THE COUNTY

WATER COURSES

About four-fifths of the county is drained by the Etowah river and its tributaries. There is a dispute about the origin of the name "Etowah". The Handbook of American Indians, Bureau of Ethnology Report, Bulletin 30, 1907, gives, "Etowah (properly I'tawa'), of unknown meaning." It was "vulgarly called the Hightower River" as reported in Silliman's Journal in 1818, and Hightower is a corruption of I'tawa. One traditional Indian meaning of the word Etowah is "council". It may be of Creek origin as it dates back further than Cherokee history.

The extreme northern part of the county is drained by the Oothcalooga*, Cedar, Little Pine Log, Pine Log, and Sallacoa creeks. The complete list of creeks is: Ashpole, Allatoona, Ballard, Barnsley, Bolong (Bolton on a 1832 map), Boston, Big Spring branch, Carter branch, Cedar, Clark, Clear, Connesena, Drummond swamp, Dry, Euharlee, Floyd, Fox, Fitten branch, Gudder, Hill, Jones branch, Little Pine Log, Macedonia slough, Manning, Tom, McDow (Stoner), McKaskay, Mud, Nancy, Oothcalooga, Pyle, Pumpkinvine, Pettit (this was first called Mill creek), Pine Log, Raccoon, Richland, Rocky branch, Salacoa, Stamp, Stiles, Two Run, Tanyard, Trimble branch, Ward.

The Etowah has considerable potential water power, as yet undeveloped. It has been spanned in many places by ferries, fords, bridges and dams. In pioneer days there were the Murchison, Island, Shellman, Douthit and Sally Hughes fords. The latter was named for an Indian woman who lived at and kept the ford. The ferries were Hardin's, Lyon's, Milam's, Douthit's, Row-

---
*The traditional spelling is with double o.

land's, Puckett's, Reynolds', Webster's.

In modern times the Etowah has received the refuse from the mines near its banks, and its depth is not what it was in 1875 when a meeting was held to open the Etowah from Canton to Rome for navigation.

By legislative acts authority was granted:

In 1835 to "Elias Pitner to establish a ferry across Hightower river in the county of Cass on his own land." Also to "Lewis Tumlin to establish a ferry across the Hightower river on lot 536, 4th district, 3rd section."

In 1837, "That Stephen Mays, of the county of Cass, be, and he is, hereby authorized to erect a bridge across the River Etowah, on his own land, at or near the site of his present ferry, in said county, and he, and his heirs and assigns, shall be entitled to demand and collect toll at the same, at the following rates to-wit: for each road wagon, team and driver, the sum of fifty cents; for each four-wheel pleasure carriage, fifty cents; for each Jersey, and other light wagon, twenty-five cents; for each horse, or ox cart, twenty-five cents; for each horse and rider, twelve and a half cents; for each footman, six and a quarter cents; for each led or loose horse, six and a quarter cents; for each head of meat cattle, three cents; for each head of hogs, sheep, or goats, one cent."

In 1839, "That . . . Arnold Milner, of the county of Cass, be . . . empowered to establish a ferry across the Etowah river, on his own land . . . at or near where he resides, and shall charge and receive the following rates of toll, viz: all road wagons, loaded, $37\frac{1}{2}$ cents; unloaded, 25 cents; all four-wheeled pleasure carriages, 25 cents; all two-wheeled carriages, ox carts, horse carts or light wagons, $12\frac{1}{2}$ cents; man and horse, $6\frac{1}{4}$ cents; stock of all kinds, 3 cents per head." Also Thomas R. Huson was authorized to erect a mill dam across the Etowah, in the 4th district and 3rd section, upon his own land, provided it did not obstruct the 'free passage of fish therein".

In 1840 Thomas R. Huson was authorized to erect a bridge across the Etowah, near the place where the

W. & A. railroad crossed the river on his own land, and was entitled to collect the same rate of toll as was granted to Stephen Mays in December, 1837.

In 1841 John W. Lewis was "entitled to construct and keep a mill-dam across the Etowah river, on his own land, in the 21st district of the 2nd section . . . . Provided, the said Lewis construct a slope or slopes for the free passage of fish." Also Joseph Wilson was authorized to erect a mill-dam on the Coosawattee, which section was then a part of this county.

In 1849 John S. Rowland was authorized to establish a ferry or build a bridge across the river on his own land and to take toll.

In 1850 C. D. Terhune was empowered to build a dam across the Etowah on his own land.

In 1858 free bridges were built by citizens of Cartersville, Stilesboro, and other sections by subscriptions, over the Etowah at Brown's ford and Hardin's old ferry. The inferior court appropriated $3,000 to the building of them.

Bridges at Douthit's ferry and Milam's ferry over the Etowah were built by public subscription in 1859. On May 21, 1864, Milam's bridge was destroyed with fire by Federal soldiers. County commissioners have since that time spanned the Etowah with bridges known as: the Leake bridge, the Euharlee bridge, the Hardin bridge, and the McReynolds bridge.

The old wooden bridge over the Etowah river, south of Cartersville, was built in 1883 at a cost of $3,477.20 by a Negro contractor, W. W. King. Judge J. H. Wikle was a county commissioner at the time. The old bridge is now replaced by a concrete bridge on the Dixie Highway—further up the stream. On July 4, 1928, it was dedicated to the World War veterans of Bartow.

"Lest We Forget

In honor of the young men of Bartow county
Who served their country in the World War, 1917-18
'To those who fought and died
To those who fought and survived'."

MOUNTAINS*

Bartow county lies in parts of three physiographic divisions of the eastern part of the United States. About 75 per cent of it is in the Coosa valley section of the Great Appalachian valley; about 15 per cent is in the Appalachian mountain region; and about 10 per cent is in the northwestern edge of the Piedmont plateau.

The Coosa, or western part, consists of a rolling plateau in a late stage of topographic development. A few low, isolated hills have the following elevations: Walker mountain, 1,050 feet; Sproull mountain, 1,200; Quary mountain, 1,050; and Mullinax mountain, 1,100 feet above sea level.

The Appalachian mountain part lies east and southeast of the plateau. The mountains enter the county at the northeast corner and extend in an irregular south-southwesterly direction across it. The highest elevation, 2,000 feet, is on Pine Log mountain at the eastern county line. Elevations gradually decrease toward the south, the highest point on Little Pine Log mountain being 1,620 feet, on Brushy Knob, 1,527; on Pine mountain, 1,552 feet, and on Signal mountain 1,300 feet.

The Piedmont plateau section begins about midway of the eastern county line and includes a roughly semicircular area in the southeast corner. It is characterized by narrow valleys between steep hills which reach elevations of 1100 feet, until the elevations become somewhat lower toward the southeast.

CLIMATE

The climate is characterized by long summers and short winters. The winters are usually mild, but occasionally a little snow falls. Before the Civil War, many people came from south Georgia because of the higher and healthier climate in this county.

SOILS

The soils of the county are varied and mixed in their occurrence and may be grouped according to the color

---
*Compiled from Soil Survey of Bartow county, U. S. Department of Agriculture, No. 11, 1926 Series.

of the subsoils as follows: red, brown, yellow and gray. The chemists group the soils in 26 soil series, represented by 44 soil types and 16 phases of types, besides 3 miscellaneous classes of material.

The most productive soils are derived from dolomite, limestone, and shale, and are adapted to all crops incident to the temperate zone. The bottom lands of all creeks and rivers are especially productive and fertile; the valleys along the creeks are the most favorable for agriculture, the river valleys being the choice. In the past the county and the lands cultivated have been known for the superior quality of cotton grown thereupon.

Much of the original growth in the virgin forests was longleaf pine, but at present only scattered second-growth trees occur. Shortleaf pine, loblolly pine, blackjack, black, Spanish, and post oak, white hickory, and scattered hardwoods of other varieties also occur.

MINERAL SPRINGS*

Bartow Spring: about one mile east of Emerson, a chalybeate spring once had a reputation, but remains unimproved. In the Survey of 1913, the flow was said to be two gallons per minute.

Rowland Springs: purchased in 1843 by John S. Rowland, and prior to the Civil War this was one of the most important summer resorts in the State. White in his "Statistics of Georgia", 1849, wrote that they were "situated about 6 miles from Cartersville, too well known to need a particular description. They are becoming every season the centre of fashion. Multitudes from every part of the State resort here to partake of the excellent water, as well as the liberal fare of the worthy proprietor." The hotel accommodated 600. It boasted of 4 state governors as guests one season. At one time Gov. and Mrs. J. E. Brown were frequent guests. The tract of land contained 2,100 acres and in the 50's was used as a stock farm. This resort lost its former popularity, and the property lost some value in the exchange of

---
*See Bulletin No. 20.

owners. It has long since been a place for picnics, and under the ownership of Mr. and Mrs. Bob Donahoo tried to regain its reputation for the entertainment of summer visitors, but the Florida "boom" enticed the Donahoos away. It is said to have an altitude of 900 to 1000 feet. There are two main springs, located in a pasture, shaded by oaks and within a few hundred yards of each other. In an analysis the following elements are found in the water: soda, potash, lime, magnesia, alumina, ferric oxide, manganous oxide.

Satterfield Springs: just a name now. They are on the roadside about two and one-half miles northeast of Cartersville on the road to Rowland Springs.

Gillam Springs: near Kingston, are on the property that belonged to the Gillam family and were once a popular place for summer picnics.

Crow Springs: in the 5th district, were first settled by William Crow of South Carolina before the Civil War. A son, Linton C. Crow and his family, lives at one of the springs. Best's chapel and a Baptist church are located near the other spring. Zimri Jackson operated a saw mill at the springs at one time.

SALT PETRE CAVE

Here the Indians are said to have been in the habit of meeting for the purpose of dancing and to indulge in other pastimes and festivities. Inside the cave the air is damp and unpleasantly cold. The descent into it is steep and abrupt. The sections of rooms are of different sizes, shapes and levels. Some have free access, others the visitor must gain on his hands and knees. The continual drippings of water on the lime stone have in many of the rooms formed beautiful columns, strange figures, and interesting formations. Salt petre was mined here during the Civil War, but there is no data concerning the activities. The cave has never been fully discovered and it is believed to have an outlet in the Etowah river. It is four miles southwest of Kingston.

Another unexplored cave exists on Little Pine Log creek.

CHAPTER XIV

AGRICULTURE

When the history student considers that this section was inhabited at the time of De Soto's explorations in 1540, he can make an estimate of how long this farming section has been in cultivation.

The Indians had cleared land for their corn patches and the agricultural value of these lands, especially in the Etowah river valley, was early recognized.

Early agriculture was similar to that of any other remote inland pioneer settlement. Cash crops became important following the Civil War. Large estates were not so common as in many other Georgia counties. The earliest advertized record of a farm was in The Cassville Standard, 1852:

"Cherokee Plantation for Sale: For sale 500 acres of land, lying on the W. & A. adjoining the town of Cassville, with 150 acres of cleared land, and $3500 worth of improvements on it, consisting of a new framed gin house, and cast gearing and packing screw, good framed Negro houses, dwelling, 400 acres of good level valley land. It can be bought for $4,500. Augustus R. Wright."

Some of the farms have been abandoned on account of erosion and others on account of their inaccessibility, rough surface and low productivity. In 1880 a census shows 1,850 farms; in 1925, 2,644. The census of 1920 reported an average value of all farm property as $3,659 a farm. In 1925 and values in the Etowah river valley ranged from $75 to more than $100 an acre.

Corn and wheat were the most important yields of the early settlers, but cotton has always occupied a larger area than any other crop. In 1879 21,969 acres were grown, producing 10,111 bales. The area devoted to this crop increased uniformly and rapidly until 1920, when 55,357 acres were planted, producing 25,717 bales, but by 1925 the area had decreased to 35,624 acres, yielding 13,947 bales.

The yield of cotton averages between ½ and ¾

bales to the acre, but yields of 1½ bales have been obtained on some land.

Corn occupies nearly as large an area as cotton but the acreage remains fairly uniform. Corn yields between 40 to 50 bushels to the acre, and as much as 75 bushels has been obtained.

Other products planted on a small scale are wheat, oats, rye, hay, vegetables of nearly all varieties, watermelons, sweet potatoes, peanuts, apples and peaches.

Peaches are being rapidly planted for the market. In Adairsville, Halls Station and Emerson orchards have been successfully cultivated and peaches placed on a ready market. Robert Boyd, A. Abramson and M. Fugazzi & Co. have been successful in the peach markets. The Elberta is the most profitable market variety, but several other varieties are grown.

Because of the damage done to the cotton crops by the boll weevil, the farmers were forced to seek other cash crops. Some of the farmers are learning crop rotation.

As farming was the main source of living in the county from the very beginning, agriculture and the farmers themselves played an important part in the progress of the county. It has been said that if a wall such as the great wall of China were built around the borders, Bartow could produce without access to the outside world every necessity within her boundary to make life comfortable and happy.

Such men as Charles Wallace Howard and Mark A. Cooper made it possible for this county to have the best and latest authority on farming. Mr. Howard wrote extensively in the late 60's on agricultural subjects, and many articles on the conditions and resources of Georgia. He published in Atlanta in 1858 The Southern Homestead for the southern planters and their families. Mark Cooper was not only a miner, but a farmer. In 1868 he was on the executive committee of the State Agricultural society.

Agricultural associations became important in the

county at an early date. In 1852 "The Floyd County Agricultural Association" was changed to "The Etowah Agricultural and Mechanical Association" in a meeting at Judge Eve's, in Floyd county, and the fair ground was permanently located at Waleska. The fair that year was held in October. Messrs. Woolley, Pepper, Hardin, Akin and Eve took prominent parts. Floyd, Cass and adjoining counties were in the association.

The Cass County Agricultural society was organized in 1857 with Thomas G. Barron, J. C. Young, G. H. Gilreath as the executive committee and S. H. Smith, secretary. The first annual fair was held on the 1st and 2nd of October, 1857 near the Cass Station depot.

This society was incorporated in 1858,* James W. Watts, B. W. Lewis, A. J. Weems, J. S. Sproull and Abda Johnson, incorporators.

The annual fair was held in September, 1860 but during the Civil War it evidently was discontinued because in September, 1867, an effort was made to resurrect the society. H. F. Price was elected president, Nathan Land, vice-president, and W.A. Chunn, secretary. It was then called the Bartow County Agricultural association. By October, 1870 the fair ground was erected on the Cartersville & Van Wert railroad, opposite the present city cemetery. Col. Abda Johnson was president of the association, Capt. D. W. K. Peacock, secretary and treasurer, Dr. S. W. Leland, J. J. Howard and W. H. Stiles were the executive committee.

About 30 acres were used for the buildings, amphitheatre, race track and stock yards that extended to Pettit creek. A brilliant feature of the fair was the tournament of the knights, in replica of the days of knighthood. The winning knight was crowned by a queen, carrying out every detail of the days of chivalry. The committee for the tournament that year was composed of W. H. Stiles, Thomas Tumlin, J. G. Lowry, J. E. Roberts and John W. Wofford. Gen. P. M. B. Young acted as commandant for the knights, and those winning

---
*Acts of 1858, p. 172.

were Frank Aycock, Henry Stiles and W. G. Dodson. This attractive custom continued for several years.

The name of the association was changed in 1871 to the "Central Cherokee Georgia Agricultural Association."

In October, 1870 the Agricultural club of the 828th district was organized in Cassville; B. F. Wade was secretary.

On the first Saturday in May, 1859, farmers from Cartersville, Euharlee, Taylorsville, Rockmart and Cedartown came together for the first time and started the custom of meeting at Stilesboro for a picnic, which on that special day was in celebration of the completion of the new school building. Up to 1932 this custom has been an annual event, except the year 1865. Most of the picnics are held on the grounds of the historic old school house.

Bartow has an unusual record of organized farmers' clubs.

In March, 1883 the Euharlee Farmers' club was organized for "the mutual improvement of its members in matters pertaining to agriculture." It has the distinction of being the oldest in the United States by virtue of its continuous operation. It is composed of 12 members and three elected honorary members; a new member is taken in only at the death or resignation of an active member of the club. Every member is obligated to attend the monthly meeting held at the home of a member. Reports of farming operations and any experiment are given for the benefit of the club. Beneficial programs are arranged and "religious and political subjects are debarred from the program of a regular meeting". This club secured the first county agent for Bartow. Some of the presidents have been: G. A. Fink, W. H. Baker (1893), G. A. Fink (again in 1898), D. S. Stephens (1900), and H .H. Milam, Sr. H. H. Milam, Jr., served as secretary until he was elected president in 1920, succeeding his father, which office he has continued holding. The original members were G. A. Fink, H. H. Milam,

Sr., Dr. F. R. Calhoun, T. R. Hammonds, Daniel Sullivan (b. 1818-d. 1893), Joe C. Dodd, J. P. Bradley, N. N. Adams, D. S. Stephens, J. H. Cole (resigned 1888); later there were J. T. Jolly, Lester Stevenson, T. W. Tinsley. Present members are H. H. Milam, president, Robert M. Stiles, sec., J. W. L. Brown (died Aug. 1931), Charles H. Cox, Fritz W. Dent, W. H. Felton, J. H. Gilreath, John K. Headden, R. W. Jackson, R. S. Munford, V. E. Nelson, G. H. Uren; honorary members are M. L. Fleetwood, W. R. Frier and J. W. Vaughan. Recent members are Speer Nelson and Charlie McCormick*.

The Bartow County Agricultural club, No. 3, or the Stilesboro club, was organized on Dec. 3, 1883 at the home of Charles S. McCormick with "improvement in agriculture" its aim and object. Monthly meetings were held at the home of members; each member was required to conduct some agricultural experiment of general interest and a report made in writing. A subject for an essay was given each meeting and a fine imposed if it was not ready. An inspection committee was appointed to inspect plantations. A fine of 25 cents was imposed on unexcused absences and tardiness. In 1887 a purchasing agent was elected to buy the club's needs for experiments. Wives of the members were honorary members. The charter members were H. J. McCormick who served as first president 11 years, C. P. Sewell, J. F. Mason, H. T. Culpepper, N. B. Cannon, J. W. Cunyus, L. F. Shaw, T. S. Hawkins, J. R. Jolly, Dr. J. S. Beazley, J. T. Conyers, C. S. McCormick. Others later to join were Arthur Davis, J. L. Colbert, Dr. W. H. Baker, J. J. Conner, D. M. Taff, S. M. Roberts, Thos. W. Leake, V. B. McGinnis, C. T. Shelman, Starling Roberts, J. W. Burge, R. R. Beazley, and others. The last meeting was held about 1911.†

The Pettit Creek Farmers' club was organized in 1884 and J. G. Lowry was the first president. Other

---
*Minutes in possession of H. H. Milam.
†Minutes in possession of T. S. Hawkins.

members were Dr. W. H. Felton, Thomas Lumpkin, W. H. Lumpkin, J. H. Gilreath, Zimri Jackson, W. A. Jackson, George Headden, F. R. Walker, Dr. Howard Felton, W. W. Ginn, M. L. Johnson, R. L. Rogers, Sims Munford, J. S. Leake, T. W. Tinsley, Levi Shaw, A. B. Cunyus. The club was carried on in much the same manner as the other clubs. Members visited other clubs and discussions and ideas were passed from one to another. This club discontinued about 1917.

A farmers' club was organized in Adairsville in January, 1914. The first meeting was held with W. W. Dodd who served as president as long as the club existed.

Captain William Browne, formerly of Tennessee, was a Jersey stock breeder in the 70's and 80's at Cassville. Horse and stock breeding was carried on at Kingston on the Withers place and at Adairsville by Capt. Charlie Hamilton.

While it is not agricultural history, it is interesting to the sporting world to know that "Joe Cummings", a bird dog owned by Col. J. W. Renfroe of Atlanta, about 27 years ago, was loaned for a number of years to R. H. Renfroe of Cartersville. The dog was later sold to a man of New York to whom the dog netted thousands of dollars in prizes. The dog had a national reputation.

The last fair grounds were erected south of Cartersville in 1914 by the Bartow County Fair association, which was incorporated in June, 1913. Agricultural buildings were erected for exhibits of the county farmers and an attraction was the horse racing on a well-rated track; most of the horses were trotters.

Since 1920 the grounds have become a municipal park and in 1925 a golf course was laid out.

A man that has done much in the interest of agriculture in this century was Col. James J. Conner. Born Nov. 26, 1847 in Montgomery county, Ga., when 20 years of age he moved to Dublin where he read law under Col. Jonathan Rivers, and was admitted to the bar in 1871. He practiced in Dublin 10 years, served as mayor two years and was solicitor general in the circuit during that time.

On Nov. 9, 1875 he married Lucy C., daughter of Rev. and Mrs. J. G. Ryals of Bartow county, and in 1881 they came to this county to live. He practiced in Cartersville as a partner of J. M. Neel for 5 years, and settled on a farm on the old Alabama road on the south side of the Etowah river. He represented this county in the Georgia legislature, 1902-6, and during his term of service saw the governor sign his bill providing for the establishment of the Georgia State College of Agriculture at Athens, and served as chairman of the board of trustees until his death. "Conner Hall" on the University of Georgia campus was named for Col. Conner. In 1926 the University conferred the honorary degree of doctor of laws upon him.

Recognizing his work for agriculture, in 1912 Col. Conner was appointed commissioner of agriculture by the State and he served one term. From 1906 to 1911 he served as president of the Georgia Agricultural society. He was a member of the Stilesboro Agricultural club when it existed; a Democrat; Baptist; Master Mason.

The children of J. J. and Lucy R. Conner (dec.) are: Thomas B. of New York; J. Ryals, who was a brilliant pianist, died while a professor of mathematics at Bryn-Mawr College; Mary of Cartersville; Robert E., Civil Service; Lucile m. Dr. I. M. Lucas of Albany; Annabel m. H. H. Whelchel of Moultrie; Harry of Cartersville.

Col. Conner died July 31, 1930 and is buried in Cartersville. His funeral was attended by State officials and prominent agriculturists of the State.

CHAPTER XV

MINERALS

For years the district around Cartersville has been an important producer of metallic and nonmetallic minerals.

Three railroads serve the district; the Louisville & Nashville, the Nashville, Chattanooga & St. Louis, and a branch of the Seaboard Airline. Hydroelectric power is available from the transmission lines of the Georgia Power Company, and plenty of water for all purposes is available from the Etowah river.

Many plants are not built for permanence, for want of capital for extensive development, and because equipment is sometimes moved to a less costly experiment, or scrapped.

Actual operations are executed by lease or option on the property owned by individuals and companies. The deposits are largely "placer" in character, without any true vein matter.

The geology of the district has been fully described in a number of bulletins and reports by the U. S. Geological Survey, and by the Georgia Geological Survey. The reader is referred to these for the geology and genesis of the ores.

BARYTES*

This heavy mineral, white or blue white in color, as a product was overshadowed by iron, manganese, and ochre until the World War cut off German importation. In 1915-17 the Cartersville district began to take first rank in the State's production. With the possible exception of a county in Missouri, this county is the largest producer of any county in the United States.

Its chief uses are in the manufacture of paint and rubber and in barium chemicals.

---
*Bulletin No. 36, W. J. Weinman.

Mining is done altogether by open pit work, the barytes is mined in mass by steam shovel and loaded on tram cars to the log washer where it is prepared for shipping.

In 1887 the U. S. Geological Survey Mineral Sources mentioned barytes as a useful mineral at Cartersville and Emerson. It is said that the Pyrolusite Manganese Mining company mined at the "Big Tom" mine in the 80's, grinding at a flour mill near the old Tennessee house in Cartersville. The Nulsen mine in the Emerson gap is the oldest barytes mine in the State; small deposits were mined in 1905.

On the Etowah river the Thompson-Weinman company, since 1917, has operated the largest grinding plant and it is the only plant in the county. They produce two grades of barytes, and in addition 3 grades of marble and 2 grades of talc, obtaining the latter from their mine in Cherokee county. This company is the most important in the State, and controls and operates mines not only in Georgia but in Tennessee and Pennsylvania.

Besides Cartersville and Emerson, small deposits have been found near Grassdale, Stilesboro and Kingston.

Other companies that have produced are: Nulsen Corporation; New Jersey Zinc; Krebs Pigment & Chemical; Big Tom Barytes, J. E. & W. C. Satterfield; Bertha Mineral; New Riverside Ochre; Du Pont de Nemours & Co.; Paga Mining; Peebles & Sloan; P. R. Renfroe and others.

At the present writing, barytes is imported from Germany as a ship ballast and offers serious competition to local producers.

BAUXITE[*]

Bauxite, varying in color from pale gray, buff, and brown to deep red, depending on the iron content, may be defined as an ore rather than a mineral, being a hydrate of alumina.

Its most important use is in the production of metallic aluminum. It is used in the manufacture of aluminum

---
[*]Bulletin No. 31, 1917; B. C. Sloan.

salts, of bauxite brick, of alundum for use in an abrasive, of calcium aluminate to give a quick set to plaster compositions.

The deposits lie in lenses of various shapes and sizes containing from a few hundred tons to many thousands. In the county the deposits are found between Adairsville, Kingston and Barnsley.

Mining is done by means of open cuts, or pits and shafts; the overburden being trammed to the dumps by hand or mule power. Both ore and overburden are so soft that blasting is rarely necessary.

The principal companies operating from 1916-1926 were the Republic Mining and Manufacturing, sursidiary to the Aluminum Company of America, Porter Warner, and Merrimac.

Very little mining has been done since 1926. An enormous deposit in Arkansas is a large competitor.

CEMENT*

Natural cement rock was found north of Kingston before 1850 by Charles Wallace Howard. After the Civil War he founded the Howard Hydraulic Cement company, north of Kingston on the W. & A. railroad, and operated six kilns of the dome type, 24 feet in length, with a daily capacity of 40 barrels each. In the 80's it was successfully operated by G. H. Waring†. This plant has not produced since 1912 and is now in ruins.

GOLD‡

The Dahlonega gold belt passes through a small

---
*Bulletin No. 27.
†In 1867 George Houston Waring gave up his home in Savannah and moved to north Georgia to go into the lime business with Rev. C. W. Howard at Spring Bank. Later Mr. Waring bought out Mr. Howard's interest and the Howard Hydraulic Cement plant ran successfully at Cement, Ga. He built a large home across the railroad from the Howard's, which he called "Annandale", and lived there until he died. He and his wife, Ella Susan Howard, a daughter of Rev. C. W. Howard, were buried near the home. In 1926 their bodies were moved to Myrtle Hill, Rome, Ga., as the cement works and the home had been previously sold. The children of Mr. and Mrs. Waring grew up at Cement and at present Mr. and Mrs. G. H. Waring II, and Miss Mary Johnstone Waring live in Grand Rapids, Mich., and their sister, Nell, Mrs. Roger Noble Burnham, wife of the sculptor, lives in Los Angeles, Calif.
‡Bulletin No. 19, J. W. Tudor.

area of the southeast corner of Bartow. Allatoona in the late 50's, as a centre in vein and placer mining, caused almost a "boom". A branch, known as Gold branch, which enters the Allatoona creek has old placer works along its course. The Cherokee Indians panned gold in this section before their removal. The history of these mines is only by hear-say. Men who did the actual mining went to California or elsewhere, and the State kept no records. The Allatoona vein, east of the town, was prospected before the Civil War, and at the present writing is being prospected again by a group of men in partnership. The "Allatoona Gold Mining Company" petitioned a charter in July, 1932*. Gold is alleged to be buried on the C. M. Jones' farm on Pumpkinvine creek. As late as 1932 Indians are coming back in search of buried treasure. David Quarles was the only white man said to have seen the mines, and he was blind-folded on the way to the place where the Indians led him.

IRON

"Without it a nation is imbecile, powerless, defenseless, degraded and barbarous".—M. A. Cooper.

The iron age has come, flourished and gone, evidenced by the cessation of the manufacture of the huge axles and wheels that mark the spot where Mark A. Cooper and other enterprising Georgians melted the ores from the hills of this county, and made the railroad bars which bound the Tennessee river and the Atlantic ocean, as well as the ovens and skillets in which the mountaineers of Georgia cooked their meat and baked their corn cakes.

About the time of the removal of the Cherokee Indians, Moses and Aaron Stroup, Germans, came to this county and began the manufacture, in 1837, of iron with the old style trip hammer. A bloomery forge was built on Stamp creek which made only hollow ware and castings. Another furnace was erected on Allatoona creek by the Stroups which operated until 1861.

The Cass County Iron Manufacturing company was

---
*J. W. Tudor, H. B. Brown, and J. S. Morgan.

incorporated in 1839*, with James Averit, Charles Knapp, Jesse Clark, William Cox, D. C. Ambler, John M. Dew and John Ambler as directors, "for the purpose of manufacturing iron and other metals from the ore oi raw material, and to manufacture such articles for market as they may find to their interest. . ." The capital stock was not to exceed four hundred thousand dollars.

In 1842, retiring from politics, Mark A. Cooper came to Cass county and bought a half interest in Moses and Jacob Stroup's† furnace on Stamp creek. Passing through here during his campaign days as a candidate for Congress he had spent a night with Stroup and became fascinated with the possibilities of the locality.

Cooper and Stroup built another furnace and operated for some time, on pig iron alone, without profit. There was no market in Georgia with the New York market paying $20.00 per ton. To overcome this difficulty the town of Etowah began under the guidance of the Etowah Manufacturing and Mining company which was organized in 1845 and constructed‡: (1) A rolling mill, at the cost of $30,000, for the manufacture of merchant iron; a nail factory, with 10 machines; one machine for railroad spikes; shops, warehouses, operative houses, hotel and store. (2) A blast furnace and foundry producing hollow ware, heavy machinery and pig metal, with shop, office rooms and operative houses. (3) A merchant flour mill, five stories high, the first good one south of Richmond, with a capacity of 2 to 3 hundred barrels per day, and built at cost of $50,000. (4) Two corn mills. (5) Two saw mills.

The machinery was operated by power developed from the Etowah river, upon the banks of which the plant was located.

---
*Acts of 1839, p. 121.
†Jacob Stroup was born in 1771 and died Nov. 8, 1846. His wife was named Sarah. They are buried in the Goodson and Tidwell cemetery above Cooper's iron works.
‡On lot No. 434 were the flour mills and corn mill; on lot No. 428 was the Etowah rolling mill (near forks of road); on lot No. 429 were the stables and houses; on lot No. 438 were carpenter shops; on lot No. 298 was the blast furnace. All in the 21st district.

The company owned 1,000 acres of timber and mineral lands in Dade county from whence Mr. Cooper hauled coal with difficulty to Etowah. This town grew to a population of about 2,000 people. Employment was given to 5 or 6 hundred people, 100 being Negroes. A church, bank and academy were, also, built.

The flour made here was "fit for a queen". Two or three barrels were shipped to Queen Victoria of England, hoping to build up export trade, and Mr. Cooper received a letter of thanks and appreciation of the bread she was eating. Iron from this foundry being sent to Sheffield, England, converted into steel there, was manufactured into razors and articles of cutlery. Samples were sent to Colt and by them made into pistols and other tools that were approved by the War Department. Pig iron from Cooper's furnished foundries in Atlanta, Macon and Augusta. In later years, more for family entertainment than for commercialism, Mark Cooper made excellent arrows of steel for archery contests. The bows and arrows of home manufacture excited the warmest praises.

In a letter of Mark Cooper's, "The Mineral Resources of Georgia", written to the editor of The National American in 1859 is stated:

"With no little opportunity to observe, we have ventured the assertion, that the resources of northern and western Georgia, in iron ore, are superior to any portion of the Union. . . . This iron district lies northeast and southwest, coming down from North and South Carolina. . . . the best and most convenient locality for it being in Cass county.

This county alone, it is believed, has concentrated in its limits as much iron ore as all Pennsylvania together, and is of superior quality. Here are found the chief operations in iron of the State of Georgia. This iron and gold region of Georgia (they lie contiguous) is traversed by the Etowah river, from its source to its junction with the Oostanaula at Rome. That part of it which lies in Cass county has been partially explored by geologists who are familiar with all the remarkable localities in the Union. . . . we cannot do better than to give the published opinion of such men, taken from a book of highest authority recently published, 'The Iron Master's Guide', speaking of the ore of Cass county, says: 'Of the wonderful profusion of these ores, and of their richness, I can, unhesitatingly, speak in the highest terms; and the best varieties and largest quantities I saw were among these, within two or three miles of the Etowah river, where it is crossed by the railroad. I have visited almost all the great iron ore deposits of the United States; I have explored the beds of the Iron Mountain of Missouri, but have never been so impressed by any exhibition of ore as by the mines of the Etowah district. They pass along within from one to five miles of the great limestone formation of Cass county, so that this essential material for flux, in the making of iron, will everywhere be conveniently supplied. They are near a rich agricultural district, where provisions can be offered at the cheapest rates, and yet they extend into the heart of the Allatoona chain of hills, where the air, in the heat of summer is most salubrious, and the climate like that of the table lands of Mexico. Where the Etowah river has broken through these hills, the high ledges of rock still resist its progress, and a succession of falls over them furnish abundant water power for the most extensive works. A large portion of this region is covered with a heavy growth of good hard-wood timber—the original unbroken forest...'."

In another letter Mr. Cooper writes, in 1859:

"Who, in Europe or America, that considers these subjects, has not heard of the 'Pilot Knob' and 'Iron Mountain' of Missouri, so famous for iron ore? And we have greater than these in Cass county. ... and yet it creates no sensation in Cherokee Georgia ... is not known, or cared for by our legislators and statesmen at Milledgeville. They are not even prompted to appoint a competent man to examine and report the facts!

The main progress has been made within fifteen years past. Prior to that, one or two small blast furnaces, and these of recent origin, with many primitive forges, now abandoned, was the limit of iron operations in Georgia. During these 15 years, there have been erected six charcoal furnaces ... all blown by water power and using charcoal as fuel."

*Name	Location	Date of Erection	Owner or Manager	Amount Produced
Allatoona (hot blast)	Allatoona Cr.	1844	T.F.&D.R. Moore	375½ T. in 22 wks. in 1858
Etowah (cold blast)	Stamp Cr. 2 mi. n.e. of Etowah R. Mill	1844	Etowah Mfg. & M. Co.	779½ T. in 44 wks. in 1856
Lewis' (cold blast)	Stamp Cr. 1 mi. from Union	1847	Dr. J. W. Lewis	400 T. in 30 wks. in 1856
Milner (cold blast)	Pettit's Cr. 6 mi. s. of Cassville	1852	Heirs of A. & H. Milner	400 T. in 17 wks. in 1856
Ford, or Fire Eater (cold blast)	Stp. Cr. 2 mi. n.w. of Pool's	1852	D.S.&F.M. Ford	536 T. in 23½ wks. in 1856
Poole (cold blast)	Stamp Cr. 8 mi. n. of Etow. R.	1855	Benj. Pool & J.W.Lewis	316 T. in 15 wks. in 1856

*From "Iron Manufacturers' Guide", published in N. Y., 1859.

Cooper states these furnaces as:

"Lewis' Furnace; the Fire Eater, or Ford's Furnace; Pool's Furnace; Milner's Furnace; Allatoona Furnace; and the Etowah Furnace and River Furnace, owned by the Etowah Manufacturing and Mining Company. All are blown by water power and use charcoal as fuel. The five first produce annually an aggregate of about 2500 tons of Pig Metal. The two last are making at the rate of about 3,000 tons per annum. Pig metal here sells at about $25 per ton. All of these furnaces produce more or less of castings... There is, however, but one foundry with a cupalo. This is Etowah Furnace, habitually producing cast machinery and hollow ware."

Brown and red hemetite ores were used then in all these furnaces and the tons of supply were of a superior quality.

The iron works being so far from the State railroad, and because of the inadequacy of wagon transportation, Mr. Cooper's Etowah Railroad company was incorporated in 1847*. "For the purpose of opening a communication from the crossing of the State railroad at Etowah river, or its vicinity, up and along the Etowah valley, by Etowah Mills and Iron Works, to Canton, or beyond that point." Mark A. Cooper, Moses Stroup, Leroy M. Wiley, John W. Lewis, D. H. Bird, Jabez Galt and George S. Hoyle, incorporators. Although he gave to the State road as much freight as it received from any of the stations between Atlanta and Chattanooga, the last session of the legislature in 1857 refused to aid him in the building of it. The company built the road to the rolling mill at the cost of $50,000 and Mark Cooper built the section up the remainder of the property. By October, 1858 the railroad was finished and was celebrated by the firing of a salute from ordnance made and cast at the Etowah foundry. M. L. Kendrick was contractor and Eugene LeHardy was chief engineer of the road.

When Stroup could not pay his share in the improvements of Etowah, Mr. Cooper bought his interest in the company. Leroy M. Wiley, a native Georgian in business in New York, became Cooper's partner. Later Cooper bought his interest and became sole proprietor.

---
*Acts of 1847, p. 185.

When the panic of 1857 came the concern owed Wiley $100,000 for purchases and the property had to be sold to pay the debt. It was put in judgment in the Federal court at Marietta and there being no purchaser, at Mr. Wiley's insistence, Cooper bought it. The debt was to be paid with the property in 3 years at $200,000. In buying Mr. Cooper had the endorsement of the leading business men of Georgia who were his friends. He made a net profit of $20,000 the first year and by 1860 he returned the notes to his friends and erected the Friendship monument.

THE FRIENDSHIP MONUMENT

The monument erected by Mark Cooper, about 1860, as a tribute to the thirty-eight Georgians who aided him in a financial crisis, is said to be the only one in the world—a record of a debtor so honoring his creditors.

Engraved on the four sides—front, south side—

"This monument is erected by
Mark A. Cooper
Proprietor at Etowah
as a grateful tribute to the
friendship and liberality of
those whose names are
hereon inscribed, which
prompted them
to aid him in
the prosecution
and developments of
the interests at
Etowah."

On the west side are the friends: Wade S. Cothran, John Banks, William L. Mitchell, J. E. Hurt, Pleasant Stovall, John M. Flournoy, James R. Jones, H. S. Smith, Wareham Cromwell, Hon. M. J. Wellborn, John W. Lewis, Lewis Tumlin, Joseph Banks. On the north side*: Matt Whitfield, Reuben Jordan, W. Maxey, Michael Dennis, Gen. Robert Bledsoe, Samuel Pearson, D. R. Adams, Elisha Perryman, W. B. Carter, J. H. Gatewood, Andrew Reed, Alfred Shorter. On the east side: Dr. Wm.

---
*All of Putnam county.

C. Daniel, Thomas Stocks, Thomas P. Saffold, N. G. Foster, T. B. Baldwin, Thomas J. Burney, Dr. H. J. Oglesby, Wiley & Zimmerman, S. R. Camey, Charles A. Hamilton, M. M. Anderson, Dr. Richard Banks, Thomas P. Stovall.

Although Sherman destroyed everything else at Etowah, he left this monument. The river road has always been a popular drive and many a party stopped at the monument. Vandals began to deface its surface, so under the direction of the Cartersville chapter of the United Daughters of the Confederacy, Mrs. L. J. Bradley, chairman, on April 26, 1927, it was unveiled with proper ceremonies after removal to the city park. Many of the descendants of Mark Cooper were present.

On July 19, 1862, Cooper sold the property to Quimby & Robinson of Memphis, Tenn., for $400,000, who in turn sold to the Etowah Mining and Manufacturing company, composed of Gen. Gustavus W. Smith, pres., W. T. Quimby, v-pres., Joseph S. Cleghorn, W. A. Robinson, William Battersby, John L. Villalonger, J. W. Lathrope, John Richardson, John Cunningham, A. W. McConnell, cashier and secretary. This company conveyed the property to the Confederate States of America in August, 1863, as a security for the advance of $500,000 on a million dollar contract to furnish munitions of war. Ordnance and a few cannon were made for the government before Etowah was totally destroyed. Wilbur G. Kurtz in an article, "From the Iron Works on the Etowah", in The Atlanta Constitution of May 18, 1930, states:

"A mighty army of nearly 100,000 men traversed the W. & A. railroad. They swarmed all over Bartow county, and one particular unit, the 23rd corps, commanded by Gen. Schofield, entered Cartersville, driving the Confederates toward the river. The Confederates burned the Etowah railroad bridge after retreating on May 20, 1864. Reilly's Brigade of Cox's division of this corps, went into camp at Cartersville on the same day. On the 21st (of May) the 104th Ohio infantry marched to Etowah and burned the depot. On the 22nd the 100th Ohio, the 16th Kentucky, and the 8th Tennessee marched to the big stone flour mills and burned them, together with the adjacent buildings, destroyed large quantities of corn and flour. On the same day

Col. J. S. Casement, of the 103rd Ohio took the second brigade, consisting of that regiment and the 24th Kentucky, and proceeding to the Iron Works, totally burned and destroyed the office, the rolling mill, the nail mill and all other adjacent buildings—the mill village as well. These Federal troops were all from Cox's division of the 23rd corps. Brigadier General Jacob D. Cox was afterwards governor of Ohio."

Mr. Cooper had paid all his debts with the sale of the property and had $200,000 left, which sum he held for the Confederacy. He would not speculate when he was offered property in Atlanta and other places, nor would he buy cotton at 15 cents when in less than 90 days it sold for 50 cents. In 1887 the Cooper property was bought during a temporary "boom" by an Atlanta syndicate under the name of Etowah Iron & Manganese company; composed of J. W. Rankin, L. J. Hill, Aaron Haas and A. W. Hill, but none of the extensive plans materialized. Capt. D. W. K. Peacock was active in promoting Bartow minerals at this time.

Another old furnace was the Bartow Iron, located at Bartow station on the W. & A. railroad. Before the Civil War it was promoted by I. O. McDaniel, father of Governor Henry McDaniel and was last operated in the 80's by H. M. Neal.

The rock house*, south of Allatoona, was built in the early 70's by Ira O. McDaniel, father of ex-Gov. Henry D. McDaniel, who had mineral interests and farms near Allatoona. He moved to this home after the war had depleted a prosperous business fortune. Ira O. McDaniel was born Jan. 19, 1807, in Pendleton district, S. C.; in 1832 he was one of the preceptors at old Penfield Institute; in 1847 he established a business in Atlanta where he became a prominent citizen until his retirement to Allatoona. For him was built the first brick house in Atlanta where Keely Company is now. He died in Allatoona in August, 1887. In 1863 Mr. McDaniel's wife, Rebecca Walker of Walton county, died leaving 4 sons, and he later paid a visit to his old home in Pendleton district. He met a boyhood friend, the widow of Col. Sam W. Wilkes, who was killed at Manas-

*Information from Col. Sam W. Wilkes.

ses, and married her. They, with a son, Sam Wilkes, b. Aug. 31, 1854, came to Allatoona in 1869. Sam Wilkes at an early age became the station agent at Allatoona and at the age of 21 was appointed justice of peace of the 819th militia district. He returned to Atlanta in 1879 where he has been a prominent citizen and for a third of a century served as freight agent of the Georgia railroad*. Ira O. McDaniel, Jr., lived at the rock house until he committed suicide. The house has passed into other hands but will be always a spot of interest because of its unusual structure. It was made of native rock and sand from Allatoona creek.

Men to develop the iron industry after the war were ex-Governor Joseph E. Brown, L. S. Munford, John W. Akin, and Rev. Sam P. Jones.

Governor Brown, Robert L. Rogers and Martin H. Dooly operated a furnace at Rogers Station until 1877. A short distance down from Rogers, on Nancy creek, a furnace was operated from 1870 to 1880 by Lewis Tumlin, T. J. Lyon and a Mr. Curtin.

Governor Brown proposed a railroad in 1880 from Cartersville to the ore banks in the northeast section of the county. In 1883 a standard gauge road was built from Rogers Station (now discarded) to the Guyton ore bank to haul ore and was built by those interested in the county and Governor Brown's Dade Coal company. In 1897 the Iron Belt Railroad Mining company was incorporated, composed of John W. Akin, L. S. Munford, S. P. Jones and T. W. Baxter. The railroad was extended to Sugar Hill, a distance of about 14 miles and was said to be the longest privately owned railroad in Georgia at that time.

There were two bloomeries in the early iron industry, both on Allatoona creek: One was located near its mouth and operated by Dr. Menimler; the other was located opposite the Allatoona station. It was owned and operated by T. C. Moore & Company until after 1881.

Since 1900 Bartow has produced a considerable

---
*See "Georgia and Georgians", p 2220-4.

1. Ochre Bull Pen, New Riverside Ochre Co. 2. Ochre Mine, New Riverside Ochre Co. 3. The Washing Plant of the Paga Mining Co., subsidiary of the Thompson-Weinman Co. 4. Lime quarry at Ladd's. 5. Partial view of Ladd Lime and Stone Company plant.

tonnage of limonite ores. The largest operations were at Sugar Hill by the Georgia Iron and Coal company about 1902.

Other companies working iron ores have been Southern Leasing, Etowah Development, Southern Steel, LaFollette Coal and Iron, and others.

LIMESTONE*

The history of this industry dates back to the early settlers when they made their first brick homes and used the crude lime for agricultural purposes.

The oldest quarry that has been in constant activity in the county is now owned by the Ladd Lime and Stone company. It is two miles from Cartersville and situated near the Seaboard railroad, which handles the shipping. At the close of the Civil War a Mr. Ladd—thought crazy because he sat around looking at the possibilities for so long—began actual work. He worked the quarry until a Mr. Roushe bought it, then in 1904 Mr. W. A. Jackson and J. W. Knight bought from him; later still, Mr. Jackson bought Mr. Knight's interest. Mr. Jackson after 5 or 6 months sold it to Mr. Henry Harvey who sold his interest in 1909 to the present company. This company at the time made ordinary lime, and ran a small stone crusher until 1913. During that year they erected a modern crushed stone and pulverizing limestone plant, and in 1920 erected a modern hydrated lime plant, which is the most modern in the South and the only lime plant† in Georgia.

The ground limestone is used for agricultural purposes, asphalt filler and by fertilizer manufacturers. The crushed stone is used principally in road construction, concrete work and fluxing stone in furnaces. One variety of stone is used by the Coca-Cola Company—being retreated, it is manufactured into carbonic acid gas. From the residue is manufactured epsom salts.

On this property has been constructed the Etowah

---
*Bulletin No. 27, 1912; W. A. Jackson, J. H. Wofford.
†Operates 8 kilns.

Cole-Mix company which crushes rock for road construction.

MANGANESE*

This heavy ore, running from dark blue to black in color, is absolutely essential in the manufacture of steel —there being no substitute.

Its uses may be grouped into three classes. 1. Metallurgical, in which the largest tonnage is used in the manufacture of alloys of iron and steel. 2. Chemical, used as oxidizing agents and coloring materials for calico printing, paints, etc., and making dry batteries. 3. Minor uses, as a mordant in dyeing and compounds for medical, chemical and manufacturing purposes. Hon. Frederick H. Payne, Assistant Secretary of War, states that, "Of the raw materials necessary to us in war, none is more important than manganese".†

The "Cartersville district" is a belt along the "Cartersville fault", extending from Sugar Hill to south of Emerson. It has yielded nine-tenths of the ore mined in the State.

Methods of mining depend on the location of deposit and depth below the surface. Different methods are used: open cut, underground, hydraulic and with steam shovel.

Manganese, manganiferous and iron development are connected and most producers in this section mine all these ores. Iron and manganiferous industry obscured manganese until the early 60's in this county. A lot in the 4th district was first mined in 1859, and work was resumed after the Civil War. The Dobbins mine, bought by Miles G. Dobbins, Sr., in 1867, was mined from 1866 by the Pyrolusite Mining company, E. H. Woodward of New York, president, and is considered the oldest in the State. The Pyrolusite Manganese company was sold in December, 1883 to the Dodge estate. It was leased in 1891 to the Etowah Iron company.

In 1874 Willard P. Ward, using local ore at the

---
*Bulletin No. 35, B. S. Sloan, Frank Smith.
†In an address to American Manganese Producers Association in 1930.

Diamond furnace on Stamp creek, 4 miles southeast of White, made the first ferro-manganese in the South and held patents for some time.*

The largest deposit in present activity is at Aubrey† on the Tennessee road. This mine, containing iron also, was first worked by the Pyrolusite company; in 1885 by the Dade Coal company; then by the Southern Mining company with L. S. Munford, Sam P. Jones, J. W. Akin and T. W. Baxter as directors. In 1889 the company was bought by Joel Hurt of Atlanta who reorganized it and became president of it under the name of the Georgia Iron and Coal company. It has changed names until in January, 1931 it became the Manganese Corporation of America, Mr. Hurt still at the head. The company owns over 12,000 acres in Bartow and properties in other counties. It operates the only section that remains of the old Iron Belt railroad.

Some other companies operating in the past and present are: The Bartow Mining and Manufacturing, incorporated in 1884 with Miles G. Dobbins, Sr. and Jr., D. C. Dobbins, E. E. Freeman and John D. Cunningham, directors. Ex-Governor Joseph E. Brown owned property in the county and did much to develop this industry. The Etowah Iron company, formed in July, 1890 by A. O. Granger‡ of Philadelphia, and Senator Gazzam, operated the Dobbins mine in 1891 and during that year erected a 4-mile railroad from that point to the Etowah river where Mr. Granger built the first large manganese washing plant in this section. The Etowah Iron company

---

*Bulletin No. 35, p. 116.
†Named for William Aubrey, father of Judge G. H. Aubrey.
‡Arthur Otis Granger, b. 1846, Providence, R. I., enlisted in 1862 in Penna., was confidential clerk of the Military Division of the Miss.-Atlanta campaign, and military secretary to Gen. Sherman, 1865-6. He was president of the Granger Water Gas Co., other electrical companies and the Chataugua Lake Railroad Co., and the American Gold Dredging Co. He was a member of Franklin Institute, Royal Geographical Soc. of Eng., Republican, Presbyterian, writer and miner. Upon his removal to this county in 1889 he added to the Young home in Cartersville where he erected the second largest observatory in the South. His wife was Caroline Dickson by whom there were Henry (dec.), William Rowan, Nathaniel Nelson (dec.), Sarah Granger (Hansell), Rene, and Sherman.

changed to the Blue Ridge Mining company in 1900. Southern Leasing, under B. C. Sloan, has operated here for many years. The Tennessee Coal, Iron and Railroad company, subsidiary to U. S. Steel, owns over a thousand acres in the county where iron and manganese have been mined, principally by Southern Leasing. The Etowah Development, incorporated September, 1904 owns the property made famous by Mark A. Cooper and through which the Etowah river flows. E. J. Lavino & Company, of Philadelphia, one of the largest producers of ferromanganese in the U. S., have tested and own property adjoining the Manganese Corporation of America.

This district supplied a good portion of manganese used during the World War.

The mining of this mineral has always been precarious on account of the uncertainty of the market. At present the dumping of Soviet ores has paralyzed the American industry. Comparisons show that domestic manganese is more favorable than foreign, but Russian and other foreign competition leave the American producer without protection.

OCHRE*

In this county this mineral is yellow in color. It is used by linoleum and oilcloth manufacturers, and in some paint and colored cardboard products.

Important markets are in England, Scotland, Canada, Pennsylvania, New Jersey and Michigan. Deposits occur in a belt 6 to 8 miles long lying in a north and south direction east of Cartersville.

The process of manufacture by filtration and drying is simple. The ochre after being washed from the crude material is passed to vats, dried by steam and packed in barrels or sacks.

The first ochre mined in the county was in 1877, though it had been discovered before that date, on property near Cartersville by E. H. Woodward. He was mining manganese on the Dobbins property.

Property, near the old wooden bridge which has

---
*Bulletin No. 13, Ray Dellinger, R. C. May, L. B. Womelsdorf.

been replaced, on the Etowah river, has been worked since 1878 by A. P. Silva, Maltby and Jones, and the Georgia Peruvian company, organized in 1890, which sent the first American ochre from this mine to Europe that same year. The shipment consisted of a consignment of 50 tons to England.

Systematic mining and use of modern machinery were introduced in 1891 by E. P. Earle of New York and J. C. Oram of Vermont, who became interested in the company and firmly established ochre industry in the county. In 1893 W. B. Shaffer established the Standard Peruvian company adjoining the Georgia Peruvian, and in 1896 it consolidated with the Georgia Peruvian which is still owned by E. P. Earle.

Other companies are: The Cherokee Ochre and Barytes, organized in 1898 by T. R. Jones, J. W. Akin, Tom Baxter and William Bird, later to become the Cherokee Ochre, owned and operated by J. T. Norris (dec.)—now owned by Mrs. L. C. Hall; the Blue Ridge Ochre, organized in 1899 by John Postell, Joseph Hull and Robert H. Cooper; the American Ochre, 1902, owned by a company in Warrior's Mark, Penna.; the Riverside Ochre, 3 miles east of Cartersville, incorporated in 1905 by W. C. Satterfield and A. E. Tucker, which became the New Riverside Ochre in 1912.

There are many privately owned properties which have been mined in the past. At present, the Cherokee Ochre and New Riverside Ochre are the only ones in operation.

SHALES AND BRICK CLAYS*

Shale is laminated clayey rock, and clay is soft plastic earth.

Shales and clay deposits extend from the Gordon county line through Adairsville to Kingston, and there are deposits at Barnsley.

Brick burning is said to have been done on the old Hawks place at Cassville before the Civil War. The court house that was burned by Sherman's army was

*Bulletin No. 45, 1931.

made of native brick and some of the brick are still in use in the remnant of a sidewalk in front of a store. The Female College was built of this native brick clay, also.

A brick plant was built at Adairsville about 1906-07 by the Adairsville Brick company which manufactured common and face brick from a deposit of shale found there. It was later operated by the Georgia Brick and Tile company*, until sold to the B. Mifflin Hood company in 1924. This company changed the product to roofing tile, manufactured from a deposit of alluvial clay adjoining their shale deposit.

SILVER

Silver is mysteriously alleged to exist near streams that flow into Raccoon creek. Cherokee Indians have come back in the course of years, since their removal, and have been known to work secretly. A silver mine was reported found in 1879, one and one-half miles south of Allatoona, in what was called the old "Betty Crow cut".

SLATE†

Slate is a rock which has more or less perfect cleavage and thus adapted to various commercial uses. Its natural color in this county is green.

The belt of deposit extends in the northeastern half of the county.

Bartow county slate contains a high potash content which can be extracted profitably as a by-product in the manufacture of Portland cement. It has been so worked on a small scale.

While the Louisville and Nashville railroad was under construction, the slate deposits were noticed and after the completion of it, prospecting was done and the Georgia Green Slate company operated one and one-half miles northeast of Bolivar.

The Richardson Company, Lockland, Ohio, purchased property in 1920 at Flexatile, the trade name of the company which was given to the community around

---

*Georgia Brick and Tile company was composed of H. M. Veach, R. L. McCollum, B. Mifflin Hood, George A. Veach, J. P. Bowdoin, C. L. Kroger, J. J. Neer, W. W. Trimble, G. W. Keeling.
†Bulletin 34, 1918; J. W. Schweizer, R. E. Palmer.

the plant. The slate crushed into granules was used as the surfacing for roofing. They also sold slabs of slate for architectural purposes, and as a by-product sold slate dust for a mineral filler in fertilizer. While operating the quarry the company experimented with coloring slate and developed a line other than the natural colors. Colored roofing had its origin in this county. Slabs of slate were quarried, sawed into proper sizes and marketed as slate shingles on this property before the Richardson Company owned it.

In 1927 the Funkhouser Company, Hagerstown, Maryland, purchased the plant from the Richardson Company and makes the green colored surfacing for composition roofing only. This is the only plant of this nature south of Virginia.

CHAPTER XVI

THE ETOWAH GROUP OF MOUNDS*

One of the most famous places in the county is located upon the Tumlin plantation three miles southwest of Cartersville. This group of Indian mounds takes its name from the Etowah river upon the north bank of which they are located.

The largest of these is 71 feet high and over 400 feet in diameter at the base. It is known in the old records as Mound "A", and undoubtedly upon it stood the public or chief's house, "on the north side of the public square around which the houses of the principal men were assembled." This is the only one left that has not been fully excavated.

The Temple Mound, "C", stood at the west side of the square facing the east. In 1925-27 the thorough exploration for Phillips Academy, by Dr. Moorehead, uncovered about 100 burials, most of which were in stone tombs. (Mr. John P. Rogan of Tennessee acting for the Smithsonian Institution in 1882 excavated mound "C" and found burials from which he saved only the heads which are now in the Army Medical Museum at Washington, D. C., and other specimens are in the National Museum.)

Mound "B", on the east side of the square, slightly higher than "C", from a description by Cornelius in 1818 of breastworks on this mound, is supposed to have supported the stockade into which the women and children of the Cherokees were gathered in time of war. Dr. Moorehead did not encounter burials when he tested it. Both "B" and "C" were smaller than "A".

Originally, a deep moat with fishing facilities enclosed these mounds on three sides. Floods and cultivation of the land surrounding them have obliterated

*From information furnished by Dr. Warren King Moorehead.

the moat and smaller mounds.

The exploration of the Etowah site by Dr. Moorehead resulted in the discovery of many interesting facts; chief among these was the development in primitive art. Upon copper plates and shells were engraved figures showing officials or rulers of the Etowans in full costume. They were clad in bird feathers and garments made from wild or native cotton. Idol heads of clay were discovered, effigies of human figures, and long swords of flint, and many pottery vessels. The skeletons discovered were of rather small persons, buried so long that very few of the skulls could be preserved. The village had been occupied for a great length of time and in places fire pits, or village refuse, extended down into the ground as much as six feet.

Although the best Etowan art is inferior to that of early Mexico, Mrs. Zelia Nuttall of Mexico found many striking resemblances between the two. Modern archaeologists do not believe there was a connection between the higher culture of Mexico and Etowah.

The earliest knowledge of these Indians is principally derived from the various narratives of De Soto's expedition in 1540. Mr. C. C. Willoughby of Harvard, after careful examination of both French and Spanish records, is of the opinion that the early European travelers, or traders, did not visit Etowah during its occupation. While he does not assign the origin of the Etowah group of mounds to any specific branch of the Muskhogean people, who occupied most of the gulf region east of the Mississippi river to South Carolina and to the Cherokee territory in Northern Georgia, he states "that the builders of this group were members of the Muskhogean family." Many of the early historians believe that Etowah was a populated village and was visited by De Soto's explorers. "In brief, original Etowah is strictly prehistoric, although Cherokees were upon the site in historic times."*

The earliest description in modern times are by

*From "Etowah Papers."

the Rev. Elias Cornelius in Silliman's American Journal of Science and Art in 1818; in C. C. Jones' Antiquities of Southern Indians in 1873; in Charles Whittlesey's report, in 1881, for Smithsonian; Cyrus Thomas' report of a partial exploration for Smithsonian in 1887; the 12th Annual Report of the Bureau of Ethnology.

A volume has just been published, 1932, entitled "Etowah Papers" which includes complete records of the exploration of Dr. Moorehead on these mounds, with maps, pictures, and contributions on Etowah art and history.

After the last exploration, collections were sent to Oglethorpe and Emory Universities, Georgia; the State capitol, and Phillips Academy Museum, Andover, Mass. There are private and personal collections.

CHAPTER XVII

CIVIL WAR*

In 1860 the county, along with the State, was agitated over the question of secession. Cass was the arena of a fierce political contest the summer of 1860 over the presidential candidates.

Cass went overwhelmingly against disunion at the State convention on January 16, 1861. The three representatives, Turner H. Trippe, H. F. Price, and W. T. Wofford, from this county voted "nay" on every vote cast, but as loyal Georgians they accepted the situation and at once volunteered for Confederate service. It was the irony of fate that Cass should suffer more than any other county in north Georgia during the years of '64-'65.

The county as a whole had reached its heighth of prosperity by 1860. Southern mansions were scattered around, log cabins were remodeled; there were better educational facilities; Negro slaves were the delight or despair of their masters—and bringing a good price, as was cotton. Many families were in a financial and social position that gave them the inalienable right to boast, after they had lost everything, of "the days before the war". This spirit deterred progress for years afterward.

There were so many South Carolinians living in the county that when that state seceded many wanted to enlist at once, and not wait until Georgia seceded.† Volunteer companies were organized before the necessary equipment could be made, as the uniforms were made by hand, or before the State was ready to issue arms. The words of Lieutenant John F. Milhollin to

---
*Authorities: Sherman's "Memoirs"; Johnston's "Narratives"; Hood's "Advance and Retreat"; French's "Two Wars"; Polk's "Biography" of Leonidas Polk; Rebellion Records; Howard's "Autobiography".
†Georgia seceded on Jan. 19, 1861.

Colonel H. H. Waters, in a report on Jan. 26, 1861, "May the gods take care of those true hearted men who saved the honor of Georgia in convention by cutting loose from the prince Lincoln.", seemed to express the general sentiment of all.

Among the first companies organized, "unofficially" were the following which were taken from the talley sheets for the election of officers on record* in the State Archives:

The "Cherokee Cavalry" was organized at the Cassville Armory on Jan. 26, 1861, with Capt. W. W. Rich, 1st Lt. John Mathias, 2d Lt. Emory Best, 3d Lt. Thomas Dodd, as officers. They were voted for by members of the infantry company: R. T. White, E. V. McConnell, A. B. Thompson, E. L. Brown, E. F. Best, Wm. C. Sherrald, J. H. Homis, James Kinney, Rico Hargis, T. J. Dodd, Saml. Levy, Martin Walker, John Mathias, E. J. Bobo, Ransom Griffin, W. C. Gaines, Wm. H. Hargis, John C. Williams, G. P. McKelvey, S. J. Bishop, Jonas Bobo, J. C. Williams, P. G. Collins, H. H. Rodgers, R. C. Saxon, Charles McElreath, John Phillips, N. M. Rogers, T. J. Stone, T. W. Bridges, R. Chapman, J. J. Phillips, Nathan Thompson, J. F. Goldsmith, John Crow, L. S. Stepp, Saml. Smith, A. Haire, Robt. Melson, James Vaughan, W. B. Bohannon, M. McMurray, J. C. Wofford, D. H. Roberts, C. J. Waldroup, Daniel Bruce, William Griffin, John Carroll, Southern Dorias, A. G. McMurray, Joseph Day, R. P. Jones, A. H. Rice, P. R. Brooks, Isaac Johnson, J. C. Smith. This was witnessed and sealed by Wm. Sylar, J. P., Richard Gaines and Wm. Chunn, F'rs. A list of voters from this same company on May 29, 1861, were: W. S. Day, R. P. White, J. G. McReynolds, Thos. Carpenter, Marion Dykes, Wm. L. Aycock, J. L. Fullilove, Jas. W. Reagan, Wm. B. Patton, J. S. Sleigh, John H. Cobb, J. A. Long, E. V. H. McConnell, R. N. Best, John C. Branson, Jas. Kenney, Geo. T. Lattimer, Benj. F. Godfrey, H. W. Carswell, R. C. Latimer, T. G. Wilkes,

---

*Errors in spelling may occur as these names are copied from an original list in longhand.

C. L. Goodwin, Lt. J. F. Milhollin, G. S. Cobb, Benj. F. Barron, John F. Crow, A. M. Franklin, Wm. Sylar, J. P., John Loudermilk, F., Harvey Russell, F. All members on the latter list later became members of Co. B, Phillip's Legion, and 7 of the former list.

The following are letters copied from the originals in the State Archives:

"Cartersville, Cass County, Jan. 23, 1861.

"To His Excellency, Joseph E. Brown: . . . You are aware that I have been active in organizing, at this place, a Volunteer Corps, known as the 'Etowah Infantry'. This company now numbers fifty-five (55) bona fide members; besides there are now ten applicants for membership, who will be admitted at our next meeting. By the first Saturday in February next . . . I can increase our present number to eighty—making a full company of good and efficient men—soldiers of the right material and stamp. It is my desire to have this number immediately placed upon Marching Order, i. e., furnished with uniforms and fatigue dress, tents, knap-sacks, rubber cloths, canteens, etc. This will require funds. Many of our members are poor men and cannot undergo even the expense of uniforming themselves properly. You know, Governor, that we have many wealthy citizens around Cartersville—some are willing to assist us now—others, being slow to appreciate the necessity of preparation, tell us publicly and privately that when the 'Etowah Infantry' is ordered out, then, they will see that it is properly uniformed, equipped, and put in complete marching order. . . . A simple notification from you to prepare my company for active service would, indeed, enable me to have upwards of 80 good and efficient men put in complete Marching Order, in a few days, ready to repair to any point at which they might be needed, without delay. And this would be done without any expense to the State, save for the additional arms required. A line to that effect would be gratefully received by every member of our corps. Hoping you will pardon this obtrusion, I am, Sir, With the highest regards, your obedient servant,

P. H. Larey."

"Republic of Georgia, Cartersville, Ga., Jan. 31, 1861.

"Gov. J. E. Brown: I understand you wish to enlist a number of men for the Georgia Service and being somewhat desirous of trying my luck in the wars, I write you to know if I can get a commission believing that you would as soon do a small favor for an old pupil of yours as any one else. I wish to know on what terms you give commissions and how long does a man have to enlist for. I am a commissioned lieutenant in our company, 'The Etowah Infantry', and would like very much to remain if there was any likelihood of us having to march. Our company has a strong influence working against it but I am proud to say has survived it all so far and have more men in ranks than we have arms for. I think we could raise one hundred men at least for the Georgia Service. Hoping to hear from you soon and anxiously expecting a commission, I am very respectfully yours,

Geo. W. Maddox."

Members on the original muster roll of the "Etowah Infantry" as organized by Captain Peter H. Larey were: Peter H. Larey, George W. Warwick, Peter March, William A. Deweese, Samuel P. Larey, James Hudgins (his mark), Washington L. Johnson, Thomas J. Stone, William E. Henderson, Williamson M. Goodwin, David A. Rice, Joseph M. Hardin, Vann. B. McGinnis, Theodore F. Gouldsmith, John C. Sims, James M. Fulghum, Francis M. Johnson, Wade H. Redden, Robert S. Pritchard, George J. Howard, Seervin Price, M. D., H. Hertzberg, William C. Drake, Theodoscius F. Stephens, Andrew J. Mosteller, Jefferson Murphey, Miller J. McElreath, John S. Edwards, Alfred Henderson (his mark), Hugh Henderson (his mark), James Reid (his mark), Richard R. D. Sproull, John Henry Landers, John R. Hawkins, Henry J. McCormick, William F. Brown, Thomas K. Sproull, James M. Goldsmith, Abel Miles, Augustus R. Churchill, James M. Smith, Marcus P. Maxwell, Jacob Jones, Andrew J. Atwood, William R. Mountcastle Jr., James F. Maddox, William H. Howard Jr., William L. Dale (his mark), Henry T. Jones, Hiram W. Howell (his mark), George W. Pinion, Russell J. Bean, Samuel Smith (his mark), George W. Maddox, James M. Byers, Franklin Phillips, John A. Kingsy, William E. Hilton, Richard H. Chapman, Adolphus D. Hardin.

On March 27, 1861, Capt. Larey wrote again to Governor Brown that, "We are now ready and anxious to be ordered to whatever point you may see proper." Other records of this infantry are:

"State of Georgia, Cass County.

"This is to certify that we the undersigned who were officers of the Etowah Infantry at the time of its organization and as such signed the bond given to His Excellency, Joseph E. Brown, Governor, or his successor in office, for the arms and accoutrements furnished to said company, are thereby willing to continue accountable for the same until relieved by another set of bondsmen. Given at Cartersville, Ga., on the 9th day of April, 1861. Signed by,

John J. Jones, 1st Lieut., Wm. T. Goldsmith, 3rd Lieut., Geo. W. Maddox, 4th Lieut.

I sign the above with the condition that a new bond be executed within sixty days, and the one having my name attached by, delivered up within that time—sixty days—otherwise to be of no effect.
Wm. T. Goldsmith."

A newspaper article in 1907 states that this company was organized in the spring of 1859 to insure the protection of Capt. Peter Larey from arrest on account of a previous visit to Kansas. Gov. Brown called a meeting of the boys in the depot as it was State property, and as Larey and his company would be in military service of the State, he would refuse any requisition by the U. S. authorities who might carry him back to Kansas.

The company left Cartersville in April and became Co. E of the 7th Battalion Georgia Vols., seeing service at Pensacola. At the end of their ten months service, many re-enlisted in other commands.

Measures were taken in the May term of the Cass county inferior court*, 1861 to provide for these companies.

"Ordered by the court that the clerk of this court and the county treasurer prepare as early as convenient the bonds of the County of Cass to the amount of twenty thousand dollars in such amounts as may be found convenient not less than fifty dollars each; said bonds to bear interest at the rate of eight per centum per annum and to be signed by the clerk of this court and county treasurer to which shall be attached the Seal of this court; and that the said treasurer shall negotiate said bonds at par; and the money raising from said bonds shall be disposed of as follows: This said treasurer shall pay to the captain of each company called into the service of the State or the Confederate States from this county the sum of twelve dollars for each man in his company taking his receipt therefor and the obligation of said captain to see to it that said money be expended in the proper equipment of his company; and for the further purpose of supporting the families of those volunteers who are or shall be called into the service of this State or of the Confederate States which last shall be expended under the direction of this court. It is further ordered that the provisions of the foregoing

*Book C, p. 226.

order be applicable to the company of Capt. W. H. Howard, Jr., now at Pensacola. It is further ordered that the collector of taxes of this county be required to receive said bonds in the payments of county taxes or any other debt due the county.

Ordered by the court that the following named individuals be appointed to look after the families of those who have gone and of those who shall go into service of this State or of the Confederate States, from their respective districts and report what relief they may need to this court from time to time, and that they be requested to relieve their immediate wants of any family in their bounds, to-wit:

Pine Log, Lindsay Johnson; Etowah, Thomas F. Stokes; Allatoona, Luke W. Ginn; Wolf Pen, James Wofford; Cartersville, Bennett H. Conyers; 17th District, Thomas W. Brandon; Kingston, Andrew F. Woolley; Adairsville, Hazle Loveless; 6th District, John W. Henderson; Cassville, Samuel Levy."

Another "unofficial" company was the "Kingston Home Guards", organized May 8, 1861, at Kingston, when the following were elected officers: W. B. Telford, captain; Samuel Sheats, 1st lieutenant; A. A. Terhune, 2nd lieutenant; Ronald Ramsey, 3rd lieutenant. Noncommissioned officers were: T. R. Couch, 1st sergeant; D. Murcherson, 2nd sergeant; Wm. B. McElroy, 3rd sergeant; J. B. H. Lumpkin, 4th sergeant; B. F. McMakin, 1st corporal; Wm. C. Ragins, 2nd corporal; Wm. J. Vaughan, 3rd corporal; Nelson Gilreath, 4th corporal; J. Dunlap, secretary and treasurer.

Names of the members were: O. H. Pruice, W. C. Gillam, Benjamin Johnson, A. H. Collister, W. P. Elliott, Joel Goodwin, Allen Martin, N. H. Eddy, C. W. Howard, J. B. Cox, H. S. Crawford, Herman Pettit, B. Burchfield, H. Pilynin, J. Morrison, A. F .Woolley, A. J. Dutton, Jas. Morrison, J. H. Gadimir, Lafayett Fricks, Reuben Hall, Sam E. Self, John Underwood, W. S. Fountain, C. W. Presley, H. C. Miller, Aron Fountain, L. M. Fountain, T. V. Hargis, H. F. Perser, J. R. Carnes, Benjamin Kitchen, William Allen, Chester Bagwell, J. W. Devino, Robt. Carr, Elihu Raney, Joseph E. Elliott, Cary Wermitt, J. D. Vaughan. In a letter later to Governor Brown, written on May 16, 1861, Capt. Telford reported that there was a prospect of having 60 men in this company.

The necessity for such a company was explained in

the following letter:

"Kingston, Ga., May 10, 1861.

His Excellency,
Governor J. E. Brown,
Milledgeville, Ga.

Sir: The undersigned have been appointed a committee to address Your Excellency to solicit arms for the company, the details of which organization are given within. The object of this company of which we are members, is to guard the public interests at home. The necessity of such an organization is now urgently apparent. Yesterday a Negro was hung up by direction of a vigilant committee, and at this moment a white man is in charge of the same committee —he is accused both of treason and insurrection. Our community is fearfully excited. It is absolutely necessary that there should be an armed body of discreet persons, not only to scare suspicious characters, but to protect those unjustly suspected. The Kingston Home Guards is composed of persons over age, on which position renders it difficult for them to leave home. The captain, Mr. Telford, is a Presbyterian clergyman. The organization is a respectable and effective one. We shall need at least sixty weapons. As the company will sometimes act as mounted men and at other times on foot, we should prefer the short carbine if that can be procured. We have the honor to be your obedient servants, C. W. Howard, O. H. Pruice, A. A. Terhune, committee."

Men in the 851st G. M. district organized themselves into a home guard company, called the "Macedonia Silver Greys", at the Macedonia Baptist church, on May 18, 1861, with Thos. J. Pyles elected captain, John A. Beck, 1st lieutenant, R. B. Couch, 2nd lieutenant, John Brooks, 3rd lieutenant. Captain Pyles wrote the following letter to Adjutant General Wayne on the same date:

"Euharlee, Cass County, Ga.

"Dear Sir: The citizens of the vicinity of Macedonia church having organized themselves into a company for home defense (being men mostly not subject to duty) and wishing arms of some sort (through me, their commander) most respectfully solicit you to send them swords and pistols for mounted men if you can. If not expedient to do so, send guns of some sort for about 80 men."

Later he wrote, "If you cannot furnish us with swords and pistols, we are very desirous to be supplied with some sort of arms for which (of course) we expect and are willing to give bond for the forthcoming. . . . I will inform you that we all have accepted our commissions and have taken and subscribed to the oath as required. Very respectfully your obedient servant, Thos. J. Pyles, captain of the Macedonia Silver Greys."

The names on the list of voters for this company were: Thos. Gore, W. T. Adams, John Dawson, P. J. Drummonds, R. M. Arnold, J. L. Leak, C. W. Demsey, Butler Kenady, Hillery Meeks, John Brooks, W. P. Demsey, Wm. Stone, David Lowry, G. (or T.) M. Young, John S. Statchen, Joshua Gibson, R. Melton, J. T. Dawson, John O. Baker, W. Lumpkin, R. B. Couch, R. W. Kay, I. W. Kay, J. M. Lumpkin, Matthew Campbell, Wm. Ligon, W. S. Meeks, John Beck, C. Dodd, J. S. Henderson, Joel Stone, J. M. Loveless, T. D. Hackett, B. T. Leek, Lewis J. Ramsey, H. I. Randal, Wm. S. Voingo, W. H. Boyd, W. H. Thompson, John Robertson, Obediah Owens, W. T. Hilliams, W. E. Foster, Wm. Cooper, W. G. Stone, J. Adams, F. Whitaker, Jasper Hitt, Elijah Lumpkin, C. H. White, Ewell Henderson, J. M. Arnold, J. T. Henderson, John S. Owens, T. A. Owens, Marc W. Hiliams, W. S. Voingo, S. H. Drummonds, Joel Stone Quinn, A. J. Lumpkin, Wm. Gore.

Kingston has preserved her war history through the pen of Mrs. A. E. Johnson*, and her reminiscences reveal the early activity of the women in organizing the Soldiers' Aid society in the Presbyterian church, with Mrs. Anne Woolley, president; Mrs. Josephine Beck, Mrs. W. B. Telford and Mrs. E. V. Johnson, vice presidents; Jane Howard, secretary; Mattie Woolley, treasurer. They made uniforms, underwear, socks and sent supplies at once to the army. In the fall of '61 so many soldiers were passing through Kingston sick and wounded, and having to remain over there for train connections, the women from necessity and kindness of heart fixed up temporary quarters in the town, using churches and the vacant stores. Mr. Doc Tippin met the trains late at night, after the depot was closed, to look after the incoming soldiers and died from exposure. Dr. R. C. Word and Dr. C. N. Mayson gave their services as long as they could.

In Kingston was said to be the first "Wayside Home", which became one of a system from Georgia to Virginia. It was located on the lot adjoining the Irby Sheats home. It was discontinued when Kingston contained two Federal hospitals in 1864. These hospitals were near the Word-Beck place and Mrs. Beck kept a record of the Federals who died at one of these hospitals. The women

---

*Mother of Wade Johnson.

served heroically until many had to refugee, and the town was used in the summer of '64 by the Union forces for their own purposes.

Near Kingston were the salt petre mines from which gun powder was made for the Confederate States Nitre and Mining Bureau. Henry P. Farrow was superintendent until it was captured. Mark Hardin worked it, with his slaves, at one time during the war.

THE ANDREWS RAILROAD RAID
With particular reference to that portion of it in Bartow county. From data written and given by Wilbur G. Kurtz.

The attempt to destroy the Western and Atlantic Railroad in Georgia, by disguised soldiers from the Federal army in Tennessee, as a military measure to isolate Chattanooga from Atlanta, is one of the most picturesque and exciting episodes that happened in this section up to 1862. Gen. O. M. Mitchell, commanding a division of Buell's army, in April, 1862, authorized James J. Andrews, a civilian, spy and contraband merchant, to conduct a party of men from three Ohio regiments to some point on the W. & A. railroad, where they could seize a locomotive, and while running northward, wreck the railroad in their rear by destroying the track and burning the bridges.

Andrews, because of rain and delays, postponed his attempt to seize the locomotive and wreck the railroad, until the 12th—a fatal mistake for him. The raiding party reached Marietta on the night of the 11th, and 20 of them, including Andrews, boarded Capt. William A. Fuller's passenger train, the "General", northbound, about 5:20 o'clock on the morning of the 12th. There was a stop of 20 minutes for breakfast at Big Shanty and there the raiders got possession of the train and three box cars.

The distance covered by the raiders was 87 miles; 35 of them fell within this county. Captain Fuller, Anthony Murphy and Jeff Cain had started the pursuit on foot, when at Moon's station they acquired a small push car which they, with the aid of section hands, kicked and pushed down the grade toward the Etowah river. A little north of Allatoona they encountered a missing rail but jumped in time. Arighting the push car, around McQuire's curve they sped until they came upon the engine, "Yonah", which was just about to make a return trip to the Iron Works. The "Yonah", the namesake of the mountain peak in northeast Georgia, was a locomotive manufactured by Rogers, Ketchum & Grosvenor, and had been in the State Road service since April, 1849. It was in Maj. Mark A. Cooper's service at that time, and had been seen by the Andrews raiders when they passed Etowah station this same rainy morning.

Captain Fuller hurriedly explained the situation and the "Yonah", with Frank Gober or Dick Pinion engineer, was whirled about on the turn-table at the Etowah Station; a flat car was coupled up, loaded with rails and tools, and with the engine crew and Captain Fuller's men, the train steamed northward. Only two piles of crossties slowed the "Yonah" down, and at Rogers Station the tank-tender gave the pursuers the first information about the fugitive engine which had stopped there for wood and water.

At Kingston on this morning, Oliver Wiley Harbin, engineer of the passenger train that ran between Kingston and Rome, was using the "William R. Smith", and had backed down a siding on the southwest side of the depot. Harbin, in his account, recalled that he had gone to the depot platform and was standing just outside the door of the agent's office, when the "General" pulled up from the east, and stopped a little above the depot. Andrews walked to the depot and explained to Harbin, as he had done at Rogers, that he was an ordnance agent with three cars of powder, en route to Gen. Beauregard at Corinth, Miss., and that he was using the regular morning train to forward the shipment. He then asked for the switch key, so as to take a siding and await the coming of the down train. Harbin referred him to the agent, Uriah Stephens, and Mr. Stephens handed the keys to Andrews, who then backed to a siding south of the main track.

The down freight, the "New York", came in and halted on the main track. There is some question as to the length of time the "General" waited at Kingston, and different versions of extra trains and the verbal altercation between the yard switchman and Andrews about the irregularity of the proceeding. The "General" left Kingston just before the arrival of the "Yonah".

Harbin recalled that he was oiling his engine when Captain Fuller ran up from where the "Yonah" had halted below the "New York". Fuller hastily explained what had happened and that the Rome engine must take up the pursuit. Meanwhile, Murphy, deciding that the "New York" was a more efficient engine was arranging for its passage, with the "Yonah's" flat car coupled to it, when he discovered that the "Smith" was pulling out and by hard running he caught up with it.

The "William R. Smith" crowded with excited men from Kingston, Murphy and Cain in the cab, Harbin at the throttle, Captain Fuller on the pilot, Kernodle as fireman, rushed out of Kingston. Two miles north they ran into a pile of crossties placed on a curve, and one-half or three-quarters of a mile farther along, the engine was slowed down to brush aside another pile of ties. Another two miles and the "Smith" was brought to a full stop. Two rails had been removed on the east side of the track.

Waiting on a siding at Adairsville was a through freight, the "Texas", south bound. Andrews had passed it, and had explained himself to Peter Bracken, the engineer. Andrews was lucky enough not to encounter other extra trains and to have a clear track in front of him to Calhoun.

From where the "Smith" was detained three miles from Adairsville, Fuller and Murphy started afoot to meet the "Texas", which they knew was due. When met, Bracken stopped at their signals and acceding to their request, the train was backed to the Adairsville siding, freed of its cars, and still in reverse, took up the pursuit.

To this well-known story, suffice to say that the "Smith" ran over an improvised section of rails and ran to the end of the chase above Ringgold. It had reached Adairsville in time to see the "Texas" pull out and closely followed it. The "Smith" was followed by the "Catoosa", the locomotive of a passenger train on a siding at Calhoun when the raiders passed northward.

NORTHERN INVASION

Bartow county was a battle front from May '64 to November '64. The operations inside the county lines show the military genius of the two opposing generals.

The Union Army under the command of Gen. W. T. Sherman was composed of the Army of the Cumberland under Gen. George H. Thomas, which consisted of the 4th Corps under Maj. Gen. O. O. Howard, the 14th Corps under Maj. Gen. J. M. Palmer and the 20th Corps under Gen. Joseph Hooker; the Army of the Ohio, or 23rd Corps, under Maj. Gen. J. M. Schofield; and the Army of the Tennessee under Gen. J. B. McPherson which was composed of the 15th and 16th Corps while in this county.

The Confederate Army under the command of Gen. Joseph E. Johnston was composed of Gen. W. J. Hardee's Corps, Lt. Gen. John B. Hood's Corps, Lt. Gen. Leonidas Polk's Corps, or Army of Mississippi.*

From headquarters in Chattanooga in March, Sherman had been ordered to go as far as possible into the enemy's territory, and Gen. Johnston was ordered to break up the Union supplies, recruit more men and his own intentions were to make an "offensive defensive". Both armies sought control of the W. & A. railroad. On May 5th, Gen. Sherman began his movement upon Gen. Johnston at Dalton. Gen. Sherman's army numbering 98,797 men and 254 guns, and Gen. Johnston's about 45,000.

The data concerning the "Cassville affair" has been

---

*French's Division of Polk's Corps did not join this army until Cassville was reached.

written and compiled by Wilbur G. Kurtz, artist and historian, and from here he takes up the narrative.

Shortly after midnight, Monday, May 16th, the Confederate army under the command of General Johnston abandoned its position at Resaca in Gordon county, where it had held Gen. Sherman's force at bay for two days, and crossing the Oostanaula river immediately to the south of the town retreated by different routes toward Adairsville.

Early on the 17th the army marched to Adairsville, Johnston's headquarters' escort reaching there a little before dawn and in advance of the retreating army. Polk's and Hood's corps were routed by the Spring Place road, and Hardee's on the main highway. During the afternoon Gen. Hardee engaged in a rear guard action three miles north of Adairsville, Cheatham's division of that corps, assisted by Wheeler's cavalry, being participants. They were re-enforced by Brig. Gen. W. H. Jackson's cavalry which had just joined Johnston's forces.

The Federal works were placed between the old Bowdoin church and the Stewart house, across Oothcaloga creek and the railroad. In the Rebellion Records, Vol. 38*, Brig. Gen. Wood of the Federal army reported that, "At Adairsville, the enemy was met in heavy force; (near an octagon-shaped gravel house built by R. C. Saxon just over the Bartow county line) indeed it was subsequently learned that his (Johnson's) entire army was assembled there. My division had advanced on the west side of Oothcaloga creek, and in the vicinity of Adairsville met a heavy force of the enemy strongly and advantageously posted, while the remainder of the corps which had advanced on the other side of the creek, had earlier met a still heavier force and been checked. A stiff skirmish at once occurred along the entire front of the division, which was kept up until night." In the "Autobiography of Gen. O. O. Howard", Vol. 1, he writes of the retreat from Adairsville, that after a severe skirmish, "On the 18th we were busy

*Part I, p. 376.

destroying the Georgia State Arsenal at Adairsville."

Johnston stated that when he abandoned Calhoun, he expected to make a defensive stand just north of Adairsville, but when the position was reached during the forenoon of the 17th, he saw that the breadth of the valley greatly exceeded the front of the army, so the project was abandoned. The army remained 18 hours at Adairsville. General Johnston stated that he "determined to fall back slowly until circumstances should put the chances of battle in our favor, keeping so near the U. S. army as to prevent it sending re-enforcements to Grant, and hoping by taking advantage of positions and opportunities to reduce the odds against us by partial engagements." Sherman never had any intention of sending troops to the Virginia front. Two months later, the failure to make a more stubborn resistance at Adairsville was cited by his critics as one of the many instances where Johnston failed to do all that he might have done. Cassville was cited as another instance.

At 6 p.m., May 17th, at the Adairsville headquarters, Johnston and his chief of staff, Brig. Gen. W. W. Mackall, together with the three corps commanders held a conference. A map of the country between Adairsville and Cassville was under discussion. Johnston inquired how long it would take the army to go the 9 or 10 miles to Cassville over one road. Hood said it couldn't be done. Hardee said that ensuing delay of such a march would mean a fight. Lt. T. B. Mackall wrote in his diary that, "Hood has been anxious to get from this place south of the Etowah", and this was two days before the conference near Cassville.

Johnston pointed out that whatever his own army did, the Federal army would march from Adairsville to Cassville by at least two roads—one column on the direct road and the other by Kingston, furthermore, when the one was near Cassville, the other, due to the divergence of the roads, would be 5 miles away, and then would be the time to attack the Cassville column and defeat it before the Kingston column could come up. Gen. Hood was present at this conference.

At 1 o'clock a.m., May 18th, the Confederate army left Adairsville. Hardee, marching by the Kingston road reached "Spring Bank", the residence of Rev. C. W. Howard, at 4 o'clock a.m., which event forms the opening chapter of Miss Frances Howard's book, "In and Out of the Lines". Reaching Kingston, Hardee marched toward Cass Station and went into camp on the ridge west of the station. Ector's and Sear's brigades of French's division arrived from Rome and took positions somewhat in reserve with Polk's corps.

Hood, who followed Polk on the direct road from Adairsville, reached Cassville at noon. Polk's troops were formed in a double line across the Adairsville road, one mile north of Cassville. Hood's corps was to the right of Polk, also in a double line, astride the Spring Place road, which runs southward from Mosteller's mill to Cassville. These were the Confederate positions on the Cassville front at 2 p.m.

During the day, the Federals had marched southward in close pursuit, participating in a hot exchange of skirmish fire. The 4th corps under Gen. Howard and two divisions of the 14th corps under Maj. Gen. Palmer, moved by the direct road from Adairsville to Kingston which parallels the railroad. During the afternoon, Gen. Howard paused at "Spring Bank" and both the general and Miss Howard record the spirited interview that insued.

It was from "Spring Bank" that forenoon that the Confederate cavalry advanced to the Barnsley home ("Woodland") where they engaged the Federal 15th corps. It was during a skirmish here that Col. Earle was killed. In the book, "Army Life of an Illinois Soldier", by Charles Wright Wills, 103rd Illinois infantry, he wrote: "May 18, 1864. Our cavalry had a sharp fight here this p.m., and on one of the gravel walks in the beautiful garden lies a Rebel colonel, shot in 5 places. He must have been a noble-looking man; looks 50 years old, and has on fine form and features. Think his name is Irwin. I think there must be a 100 varieties of the rose in bloom here and the most splendid specimens of cactus." Accounts prove that the colonel was shot near the house by the mounted infantry of Wilder's brigade. His body was not allowed to be moved by the Federals, but finally Mr. Barnsley had the body buried under a few feet of ground and on a small headstone in the yard near the house is this insecure inscription:

Col. R. G. Earle
2d Regt. Ala. C. S. A.
Killed near this spot by U. S. Forces
May 18, 1864.

Gen. Hooker's 20th corps, moving by Field's mill on the Coosawattee, by the Richard Peters farm near Calhoun, and by Adairsville, approached Cassville on the main highway therefrom. The present Dixie Highway, between the two towns, is not identical at all points with the old road.

The Army of the Ohio, or 23rd corps, commanded by Maj. Gen. Schofield, moved by the Spring Place road from Field's mill to Mosteller's mill, and on toward Cassville. Thus there were 3 Federal columns from the north.

All of McPherson's troops marched by "Hermitage", west of the railroad and Barnsley's, and though they were not concerned in the affair, when they reached Kingston, they were in a position to outflank Gen. Johnston's forces at Cassville.

At Gen. Johnston's headquaters, at 9:30 a.m. on the 18th, Generals Hood, Hardee and Polk came to discuss plans for the day. Johnston was in excellent spirits at this meeting. A telegram had been received from the Virginia front telling of the losses in Grant's army. Johnson declared that the Confederacy was as fixed an institution as England or France. Another event happened in this day of conferences. At 5 p.m. Lt. Gen. Polk, who was the Episcopal Bishop of Louisiana at the outbreak of the war, was notified that Gen. Johnston desired baptism in accordance with the following request of Mrs. Johnston:

"Atlanta, Ga., May 16.

"My Dear General Polk: You are never too much occupied, I

well know, to pause to perform a good deed, and will, I am sure, even whilst leading your soldiers on to victory, lead my soldier nearer to God. General Johnston has never been baptized. It is the dearest wish of my heart that he should be, and that you should perform the ceremony would be a great gratification to me. I have written to him on the subject, and am sure he only waits your leisure. I rejoice that you are near him in these trying times. May God crown all your efforts with success, and spare your life for your country and friends. With high esteem, I remain, very truly yours,

L. McLane Johnston."*

That night after the usual conference, Gen. Johnston was baptized. Kneeling in his tent with but four present, the Bishop General administered the rite, Generals Hardee and Hood being the witnesses.

At 7 a.m., May 19th, Gen. Johnston issued the following proclamation which was received with exultation:

"General Orders,   Headquarters Army of Tennessee,
No. ——   Cassville, Ga., May 19, 1864

"Soldiers of the Army of Tennessee, you have displayed the highest quality of the soldier—firmness in combat, patience under toil. By your courage and skill you have repulsed every assault of the enemy. By marches by day and marches by night you have defeated every attempt upon your communications. Your communications are secured. You will now turn and march to meet his advancing columns. Fully confiding in the conduct of the officers, the courage of the soldiers, I lead you to battle. We may confidently trust that the Almighty Father will still reward the patriots' toils and bless the patriots' banners. Cheered by the success of our brothers in Virginia and beyond the Mississippi, our efforts will equal theirs. Strengthened by His support, those efforts will be crowned with the like glories.

J. E. Johnston, General."

Pursuant to battle plans, Hood's corps was ordered northward on the Spring Place road, Polk's troops advanced on the Adairsville road, French held in reserve north of Cassville. Johnston's plan was for Polk to meet the advancing columns on the Adairsville road, and when the battle was joined, Hood, from his road, would fall upon the Federal left flank, and between the two of them, Hooker's troops would be worsted before Howard could come from the railroad below.

Hood, after marching 2 or 3 miles, discovered that Federal troops were approaching in rear of the right

*From "Leonidas Polk, Bishop and General," by W. M. Polk.

of the position from which he had just marched and they appeared to be on the Canton or Fairmount road. This has been a moot question ever since, for there has been as much official denial that Federals were on these roads at that time, as official affirmation that Federals were there. Instead of notifying Johnston, he halted his entire corps and fell back to a position covering the Fairmount and Canton roads, facing his men to the right and rear. Johnston did not hear of this until he sent his chief of staff with a message to Hood directing him not to move too far to the right, for Hardee's corps, on the left was being pressed by a Federal column moving from Kingston—but if the enemy advanced from the north (on Adairsville road) he was to strike promptly and hard! With Hood's change in alignment much time was lost and Johnston states that he "heard of this erratic movement after it has caused such a loss of time as to make the attack intended, impracticable; for its success depended on accuracy in timing it. The intention was therefore abandoned."

In after years, this part of the "battle of Cassville" was carried on in wordy disputes between Gen. Johnston and Gen. Hood. Both officers convince themselves that their motives and actions have been impugned, but as for anything being settled, that is still a matter of unfinished business. Hood in his book, "Advance and Retreat," tried to clear himself and denied all other reports of his actions.

A picture of the forenoon's actions are from Lt. T. B. Mackall's diary:

"Thursday, May 19—Moved out to attack enemy, but column reported advancing on Cartersville road (this could mean the road from Canton to Cartersville, via Cassville). An order was written about 7 or 8 a.m., thanking troops for patience and telling them they would be led against enemy. Gen. Johnston rode over to Gen. Hood's and then passing by general headquarters road out Spring Place road, north of creek, with Hood and Polk and Hardee, to show former where he was to form his lines for attack. Gen. Mackall rode from headquarters east of town to join him; found Generals Johnston, Polk and Hardee returning. Sear's Mississippi brigade formed across road (part of French's division of Polk's corps—in reserve). Riding back, all passed Cockrell's Missouri brigade resting on road (another brigade of French's division, in reserve), and in town met Hindman's column, advance of Hood's corps, moving to take position on Polk's right. After a few moments in town, rode rapidly back out Spring Place road; general (Johnston) saw Hood and returned to campground and dismounted; Hood's corps passing, Polk's troops shifting. About this time, 10:20 a.m., a few discharges of artillery on Adairsville and Cassville road, and in ten minutes reports of artillery in easterly direction (somebody seems to have been on Canton road). General Mackall, who had ridden out to Hood with directions to make quick work, sent word back by courier, who reported to me that 'enemy in heavy force close to Hood on Canton road.' I tell general, who says it can't be. Armstrong on that road reported none. Called for map; said if that's so, Gen. Hood will have to fall back at once. Presently Gen. Mackall rode up at a rapid rate, spoke with general (Johnston) who sent him back in haste, riding one of his horses. Mason went off on another; still firing had ceased; confusion in passing backward and forward of Hood's and Polk's troops. At this time could be heard officers all around reading orders to regiments and cheers of troops. Some regiments in field where headquarters were. Polk detains two of Hood's brigades, as Hardee on his left had not closed up gap. . . .. On 20th, asked Gen. Mackall who reported force of enemy on Canton road on 19th when we were at Cassville. He said Gen. Hood said they had a line close to him. Gen. Mackall could see nothing and didn't believe it. . . ."

Whatever Hood did with his corps north of Cassville, he did not cooperate in any attack as proposed by Gen. Johnston's proclamation.

In the meantime, the Federals were pushing down upon them in three columns. The central column—the 20th corps—had that morning detoured from the Adairsville road above Two Run creek, and drove a column (Geary's division) southward as far as the railroad to connect with Howard. Butterfield's division, of the 20th corps, took position at the Col. Hawkins F. Price home —the house is yet standing and is now the home of John Law. Williams' division of the 20th corps was on Butterfield's left, and covered the broken ground of the gravelly plateau between the Adairsville and Spring Place roads. Gen. Hooker's headquarters were at the Hawkins F. Price house on the 19th. Butterfield and Geary, pressing toward Cassville, drove the Confederates across Two Run creek to the ridge where stood the Cassville Female and the Cherokee Baptist colleges. Butterfield's infantry and artillery, moved from the Price house by a field road, now practically obliterated, and finally reached the Female College from which position a Confederate line of infantry and artillery had been driven. Taking position just to the south of the college, battery C, 1st Ohio light artillery fired at a retreating column of Confederates withdrawing from Cassville, and at a battery posted on the ridge east of the town. This was in the afternoon.

At noon General Johnston had decided that he would either have to act defensively or retreat. At 4 p.m. he ordered his line to fall back to the ridge east of the town and this was executed under fire. From T. B. Mackall's diary:

"Instructions to change line. Generals Johnston and Mackall and Polk ride on high hill overlooking town and back from original line. New line marked out, and troops rapidly formed on it and along a ridge. Late in afternoon considerably skirmishing and artillery, enemy's skirmishers occupied town. At one time confusion; wagons, artillery and cavalry hasten back; noise, dust and heat. Disorder checked; wagons made to halt. Consternation of citizens; many flee, leaving all; some take away few effects; some remain between hostile fires."

This new position was the ridge east of Cassville, the general direction of which is north and south. The intrenched line, cast up that afternoon began at the Posey house, now the George Gaddis place on the Canton road, just where the roads fork. Somewhat southwest of the Posey place the line skirted the eastern edge of the cemetery, then dropped southward on the ridge, passing to the west of the Gen. W. T. Wofford house site. At that time the direct road between Cass Station and Cassville was to the east of the present paved highway, a ridge intervening. The line crossed this road and continued on the said intervening ridge to the present paved highway above Cass Station. Ridge and line parallel what is now the paved highway, southward to a point about one-half mile northwest of Cass Station, where the line crossed highway and railroad, again mounting a ridge south of the railroad and immediately west of the Cass Station depot. The southern extremity of this line was at the Foster house, three quarters of a mile southwest of the depot. The intrenched line of works were approximately three and one-half miles long. Most of this intrenched line is still visible, and is there to confute the many erroneous statements that have been made regarding its locations.

Hardee's corps was on the left—astride the railroad. His extreme left was not happily situated but he made the best of it by heavy field works; his right was at the Kingston highway. His position was threatened by Gen. Howard. Polk's corps was in the center, his right extending above the old highway between the station and village, and ending at a small ravine. His position was threatened by Gen. Hooker. Hood's corps held the rest of the line, his right at the Posey house. His position was threatened by Gen. Schofield. This line was not quite long enough to accommodate all the infantry and artillery. French's troops were the last to retreat; when he reached his position on Polk's right, he placed Hoskin's battery to the left of the ravine with one-half of Ector's brigade. Cockrell's Missourians were in line on the left of Cantey's division; this left Sear's brigade and the other half of Ector's to be placed in reserve.

Meanwhile, the Federals pressed forward—their artillery near the Female college keeping up a hot fire on the new line, the shells shrieking across the town. Off to the Federal left in front of Hood's right, other batteries opened up, some of the fire, directed toward Hoskin's battery near the ravine, enfiladed French's line for a short distance where it ran forward to include the battery. The possibility of this had been noticed by Brig.-Gen. Shoup, chief of artillery, before the line was shifted; he reported it to Johnston who gave orders that traverses be built to protect the exposed point. Shoup's report was made in the presence of Gen. Polk.

Details of French's position are given because of

what followed. Gen. French, who kept a diary, stated that Hood's line was not a prolongation of Polk's line at the ravine, but fell back at about 25 degrees. A study of the terrain does not bear out French's statement. Hood's line changed direction—but forward, not backward. Instead of Hoskin's battery being on a salient, it was at a re-entrant angle, which, however, did not obviate any enfilading fire.

Some years after the war, October, 1894, an anonymous article appeared in The New Orleans Picayune charging that the failure to fight after Johnson's retreat to the line east of Cassville was due to objections made by Generals French and Hood. According to the article, French sent a message to Gen. Polk that his position was enfiladed and that he could not hold it. Polk sent his inspector-general, Col. Sevier, to examine the position; Sevier reported to Polk that French's line was badly placed with respect to enemy lines. Polk then sent Sevier to Johnston; Johnston had heard something of this from Gen. Shoup and had recommended traverses, the same recommendation was repeated, and Sevier was requested to inform French accordingly. The latter is said to have "persisted in his inability to hold his position", and Sevier so reported to Polk. Polk, also, sent Maj. Douglas West to inspect French's line and he declined to form an opinion but reported that French was "highly wrought up about the exposure of his division." French was living at this time at Winter Park, Fla., and his reply clears himself of the blame and he denied making any such statements, or that he influenced his corps commander, Polk, to join Hood in a protest to Johnston against any attempt to hold the line—a position which Johnston later described as the best he saw occupied during the war.

About 4 p.m. Walter G. Morris, Polk's chief engineer, reached headquarters and received instructions to make a report on the various positions and the feasibility of making a defensive stand. His report indicated that Polk's line, where French's troops were posted, was greatly exposed for the defensive, and that the Federal batteries would make any advance extremely hazardous. He had only a skeleton map of the environs and only two hours of daylight to make such a report; darkness prevented him from making a personal inspection of Hood's line, and the character of the approach to the Federal guns on Hood's right. The map he made appears in the Official Records Atlas, Hood's "Advance and Retreat", and in French's "Two Wars". A more erroneous map would be difficult to discover, considering that Cassville, the intrenched ridge, the cemetery, and the Canton road are where they are. The Morris map shows Federal lines in the narrow space between Cassville and Polk's line—an impossible circumstance with Polk's battery immediately over it. The Federals never claimed to have a line there other than a regiment or two of skirmishers in the village that night—concealed in or by the houses; their artillery and infantry lines were on the ridge west and north of Cassville.

Gen. Polk's headquarters at 4 p.m., May 19th, were at the McKelvey place, now the home of M. L. Johnston, on the old Cassville road. Polk's entourage was encamped near the spring, but the general occupied the log cabin that is yet in existence nearby. Gen. Johnston's headquarters were not far away on the banks of a muddy brook.

After a meagre luncheon, Gen. French met Gen. Hood and staff moving southward and Hood asked French to ride with him to Polk's headquarters to eat supper. French's presence at Polk's headquarters, without an invitation from the latter, was made the basis for the charge that Hood brought French along to influence Polk in joining with him in a recommendation to Johnston to abandon the line. Johnston was already there.

In headquarters this night, the two corps commanders called an informal council of war to discuss the situation.

General Hood, who began the discussion stated his

position: "After our lines had been enfiladed for one or two hours before sunset, as Gen. Shoup had preadmonished Gen. Johnston, Polk and I decided, upon consultation; to see the commanding general and apprise him of our real condition; to state also that, whilst our position was as good as we could desire to move forward from and engage the enemy in pitched battle, the line we held was unsuited for defense; and if he did not intend to assume the offensive the next morning, we would advise him

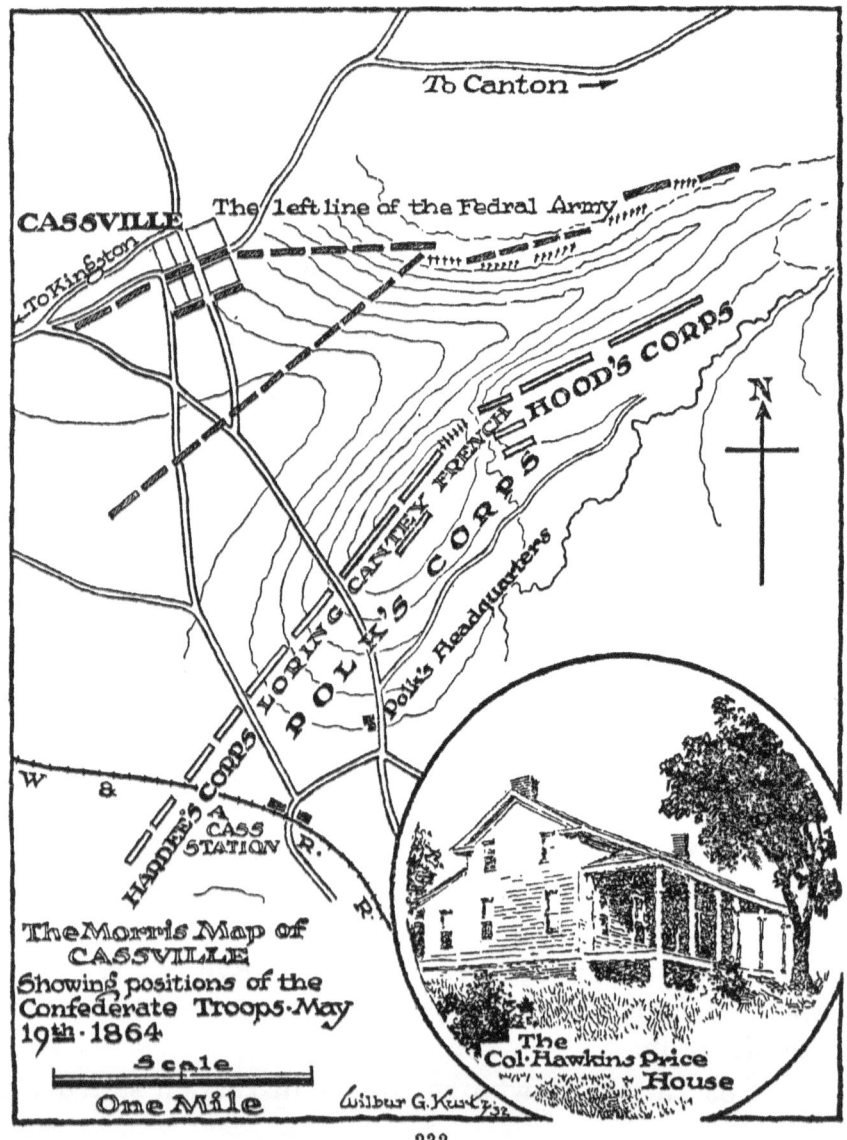

The Morris Map of CASSVILLE Showing positions of the Confederate Troops May 19th 1864

to change his position. This is the sum and substance of our suggestion . . . to viz: that if he did not intend to fight a pitched battle, we would advise him to change our position for one better suited for defense."

Polk never made a statement about the affair as he was killed 26 days later, but Morris in his reports, stated, "Lieut. Gen. Polk expressed himself convinced that he

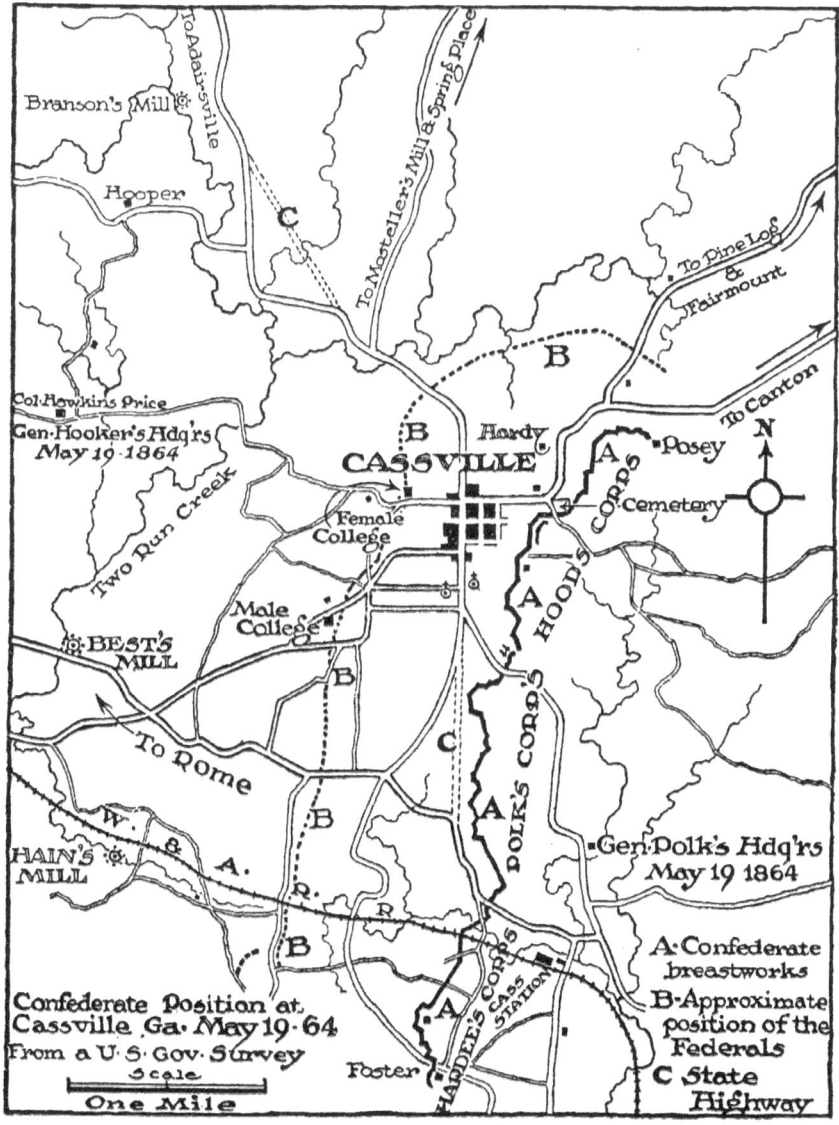

*Map drawn by Wilbur G. Kurtz. For History of Bartow Co.

could not hold his line against attack, and that Maj. Gen. French, who occupied that part of his line in question, was of the same opinion as was his engineer officer (myself), who had examined the position and reported that traverses would be of no avail. Gen. Hood stated that he was also convinced that neither he nor Gen. Polk could hold their lines for an hour against such an attack as they might certainly expect in the morning.... In reference to this proposed forward movement, Gen. Johnston's attention was particularly called to the advantages of taking possession of the positions occupied by the batteries of the enemy on the extreme left, either by a special flank movement, or by prompt action at a time when the Confederate lines would be advanced. Lt. Gen. Polk expressed himself entirely willing and ready to co-operate with Gen. Hood to accomplish this object. After some moments of silence, Gen. Johnston decided to withdraw the armies to the south of the Etowah."

That night at one a.m. the Confederate army abandoned the ridge east of Cassville, and by afternoon of the 20th, all had passed through Cartersville and were south of the Etowah, with the bridges burned behind them. In after years, Johnston declared that he always regretted the retreat from Cassville. Johnston's "Narratives" stated that Hardee remonstrated the decision and was confident he could have held his position.

Johnston established headquarters near the Bartow Iron Works at Stegall's Station (now Emerson) on the railroad. Hardee's headquarters were at the Moore Tavern, an old hostelry that stood near the old railroad underpass. Polk's headquarters were at Allatoona near the No. 41 railroad crossing. Hood's troops, as rear guard, were posted between Stegall's and the river; while Jackson's and Wheeler's cavalry to left and right, closely watched the next Federal movements.

Thus Sherman was left master of all the country north of the Etowah.

It was hoped that Sherman would follow them to

the Allatoona range, but that officer had seen the country before and he knew that Johnston could give him infinite trouble there. The Federals moved by way of Euharlee and Stilesboro to the Dallas road; Thomas crossed the Etowah on his own pontoons south of Kingston, Hooker crossed Milam's bridge, McPherson laid his bridges so as to take the Van Wert road.

The Confederates had only one victory at this time. On the 24th Maj.-Gen. Wheeler saw that the Federal army was moving westward from Cassville, as if to cross the Etowah near Kingston, and on the road between Cassville and Kingston encountered Federal troops guarding a large supply train of wagons. A sharp battle ensued which resulted in Wheeler carrying off 70 loaded wagons, with their teams, 300 equipped horses and mules, 182 prisoners, and burned a greater number of wagons than were brought away. Mr. J. L. Milhollin of Cassville remembers seeing this capture.

On the 23rd, Johnston sent Hardee's corps toward Dallas to meet Sherman, Polk moved in the same direction on the left, and the next day Hood followed Hardee. The Cobb county historian will recount what took place after the troops left Bartow county.

After the retreat of Johnston from Cassville, Sherman ordered a 3 days' rest at Cassville, in the meantime getting ready with light equipment for their advance by Dallas. From the "Autobiography of Gen. O. O. Howard" are recounted several interesting incidents.

"In the fearful skirmish which took place on May 19th in the rough woodland between Kingston and Cassville, Kingston served as a field hospital."*

"The 2nd day after Johnston's departure from Cassville and Cartersville, Ga., (May 22, 1864) was Sunday. Sherman had his headquarters, for railroad convenience and to be accessible to all his commanders, at the village of Kingston. Gen. Corse was at the time his chief of staff. Sherman and he occupied a small cottage (now the Hargis home) on the south side of the main street. While Sherman sat at the window, apparently in a deep study, he was interrupted by the sudden and the continual ringing of the church bell. Thinking that some fun-loving soldier, or some of the already enterprising

---
*p. 534.

'bummers', were pranking with the bell, perhaps with a view to his annoyance, he told Corse to send over a patrol and arrest the bell ringers. My friend, Rev. E. P. Smith, representing the Christian Commission had gone to the church and prepared it for service, not being able just then to get anyone to help him, he was obliged to climb up to ring the bell, the rope having disappeared. As he dropped down he caught the bottom of his trousers and slit them to his waist. Just then a corporal with a file of men opened the church door and said to him, 'Fall in'! My friend said, 'What for?' The corporal answered, 'To take you over there to Gen. Sherman's headquarters.' Smith pleaded, 'Can't go in this plight; take me where I can fix up.' The corporal answered, 'Them's not the orders, fall in'. Corse standing by the back door, received him and said, 'You were ringing that bell?' 'Yes, it is Sunday and I was ringing it for service.' Corse dismissed the guard and as he stood in the doorway, he reported the case to Sherman who stopped his work for an instant, looked up at Corse's face and glanced over to Mr. Smith as Corse said, 'It is Sunday and he was ringing the bell for service.' Sherman answered, 'Sunday! Sunday! Didn't know it was Sunday; let him go.'

Howard continues:

"A number of officers were having a chat in groups about the bivouac at Cassville on the morning of May 21st, when it being about refreshment time, some officer proposed that the whole party go over to his tent and have a drink all around. Gen. Thomas John Wood, one of my division commanders, undertook to rally me on my oddities and exclusiveness. He wound up by saying, "What's the use, Howard, of your being so singular? Come along and have a good time with the rest of us. Why not?" Sherman interposed with some severity, saying, "Wood, let Howard alone! I want one officer who don't drink!"

In the fighting on May 19th, Mercer's brigade was thrown out in Walker's front, and the 63rd Ga. under Maj. J. V. H. Allen was put in advance of the brigade to support the skirmish line. When orders came to retire the brigade to the line of battle, the 63rd was nearly surrounded by the enemy. Among the killed in the brisk skirmish was Legare Hill, son of Joshua Hill of Madison, Ga. Two of his comrades took up the lifeless body, conveyed it to a little cottage, pinned his name on his jacket and left him there. Although this was done in full view of the Federal skirmishers, not a shot was fired at the two men until they had joined their comrades. The Federals later took the body of young Hill, buried it, and marked the grave by a headboard.* In Sherman's Memoirs† is the account of Mr. Hill, with a former member of Congress, going to Sherman at the Neal house in Atlanta to get a permit for Hill to go back to Cassville to obtain the body of his son killed there. Sherman gave the permit with a note to the commanding officer, Gen. John E. Smith at Cartersville, to furnish escort and ambulance. While at dinner negotiating for this permit Sherman gave Mr. Hill a message to Gov. Brown, promising him protection if Gov. Brown would come to Atlanta to advise the steps to withdraw the State troops from the armies of the Confederacy. From history we know the troops were not withdrawn.

In "An Artilleryman's Diary", by Jenkins Lloyd Jones, private in the 6th Wisconsin battery, are some interesting accounts of the Federals after the retreat of Johnston.

He wrote: "July 12, 1864. Passed through Cassville at 10 a.m. A very pretty country town hid away among the hills. A large college used as general hospital by the rebs here. Ascended to the observatory, had a splendid view. A large library filled with books going to waste. Marched through Cartersville 3 p.m. A place of some pretentions in time of peace, occupied by the cavalrymen relieved at Kingston." From July 13th until Nov. 10th, he was stationed in a fort on the steep cliff commanding the railroad bridge over the Etowah river, which was erected by Sherman's construction corps. He wrote daily about events and of foraging for blackberries, peaches, and green corn up and down the river. He spoke of the vicinity of Stilesboro as a "guerrilla hole". He wrote after the battle of Allatoona, "I don't think there has been more desperate fighting done this year than yesterday at Allatoona."

During July, the 10th Ohio cavalry camped in Cartersville about 6 weeks. Gen. Judson Kilpatrick made his headquarters in the E. M. Field home, and the regi-

---
*From Confederate Military History, Vol. VI.
†Vol. II, p. 137.

ment occupied the site of the old Methodist church and the blocks around it.

The Battalion of Cadets from the Georgia Military Institute at Marietta reported for field duty in May, 1864. Clayton H. Marsh of Bartow was mortally wounded on November 22, at Oconee river where they were gallantly fighting with the 14th Kentucky cavalry. On the train to Savannah, Gen. Hardee spoke of the wounded boy as having the "brow of a conqueror". He died on the 26th. He was a son of Peter Marsh and he has a sister, Mrs. B. R. Padgett, nee Carrie Marsh, living in Atlanta. Other cadets who served with these gallant youths were: Thomas W. Miller, color corporal, Paul Goldsmith, George Pattillo, George A. Fitten (d. 1895), and family records show that Robert H. Rowland served. Col. J. S. Rowland furnished his company with uniforms when they were in Savannah.

BATTLE OF ALLATOONA

After the battle of Atlanta and continuous skirmishes around there, Allatoona, in October 1864, became the scene of one of the most sanguinary battles of the Atlanta campaign.

Gen. Hood, then commanding the Confederate forces, directed Gen. A. P. Stewart to have French's division fill in the cut at Allatoona with logs, brush, rails, etc., and to destroy the railroad bridge over the Etowah river.

Gen. Stewart's corps had begun at Big Shanty, on the evening of Oct. 3rd, destroying the railroad from there up to the Acworth station in their effort to work their way back toward Tennessee.

As it was known that the Allatoona pass was fortified with 4 pieces of artillery, and garrisoned with three and a half regiments of infantry, though Hood did not know that a million rations of bread was stored there for the Federal army, it was considered of the utmost importance to capture the forts.

There were small redoubts overlooking the storehouses on the railroad on the east and west side of the cut, which were built the previous June. The redoubts were connected by a foot-bridge over the cut. On the west side remains of the little fort are visible today. From the heights on the east side, a pine tree served as a signal tower. After the war this tree was cut down by order of ex-Governor J. M. Brown and Sam W. Wilkes to be made into souvenir boxes and gavels. These souvenirs were sent to Gen. Corse, Gen. Johnston, Gen. J. B. Hood, the Y. M. C. A. of Boston, the Smithsonian, Sam W. Wilkes and others.

Gen. Sherman learning of the Confederate movement in his rear, sent a message over the heads of the Confederates from Vinings to Kennesaw, and from Kennesaw Mountain to Allatoona, for Gen. John M. Corse to come from Rome to assist Col. Tourtellotte hold the garrison at Allatoona.*

From Acworth, where the Confederates were, the enemy could be seen communicating messages from Allatoona to the signal station on Kennesaw. About daylight on the 5th of October, Sherman received the message that "Corse is here" and he watched the battle from the mountain during the day. During the engagements among the signal messages were such as, "Hold fort, we are coming"; "Sherman says hold fort, we are coming"; in an answer from Corse, he signaled; "Where is Sherman?" "Tell Allatoona hold in. Sherman says he is working hard for you." These messages and the circumstances were the inspiration for the gospel song, "Hold the Fort for I Am Coming", by P. P. Bliss years afterwards.

The Confederates marched during the night of October 4th. Crossing the Allatoona creek bridge, Col. Adaire, with the 4th Regiment Mississippi volunteers, was left near the block-house with instructions to capture it and destroy the railroad bridge over the creek. About 3 p.m. they came in sight of Allatoona and Gen. French placed the artillery on the hills south and east of the railroad. The 39th North Carolina regiment, under Col.

---

*See "The Confederate Soldier in Civil War", p. 242-244.

Coleman, and the 32nd Texas, under Col. J. A. Andrews, were a supporting force. Not knowing the roads in the darkness, they found themselves in front of the Federals and not on the main ridge of the numerous chain of hills in this section. Resting until dawn of October 5th, they were about six hundred yards west of the fortifications and then were seen the Federal fortifications—west and east of the railroad cut.

Gen. Sear's brigade of French's division (Stewart's corps) was sent to the north or rear of the Federal works, Cockrell's Missouri brigade to the center of the ridge, while Gen. W. H. Young, who was later captured prisoner, with the 4th Texas regiment formed in the rear of Gen. Cockrell. Maj. Myrick was to open on the Federal works with his artillery and was ordered to continue until the attacking force interferred. Gen. Sears and Gen. Young were to carry on a flank attack with movements down the ridge.

"About 6 a.m. the Federal troops* were in the following position: the 7th Illinois infantry and the 39th Iowa infantry in line of battle facing west, on a spur that covered the redoubt immediately on the hill over the cut; one battalion of the 93rd Illinois in reserve, the other in line of skirmishes, moving along the ridge in a westerly direction, feeling of the enemy, who was endeavoring to push a force around our right flank; the 4th Minnesota, 50th, (57th) and 12th Illinois infantry were in the works on the hill east of the railroad cut; the balance of the command were out on skirmish. . . . Under brisk cannonade, kept up for near two hours, with sharp skirmish on our south front and on our west flank, the enemy pushed a brigade of infantry around north of us, cut the railroad and telegraph wires, severing our communication with Cartersville and Rome. Cannonading had not ceased when at 8:30 I received by flag of truce which came from the north on the Cartersville road, the

---

*From Gen. Corse's report in Rebellion Records, Vol. 39, Series I, pp. 761-766.

following summons to surrender.

"Around Allatoona, Oct. 5, 1864.
Commanding Officer, U. S. Forces, Allatoona.

Sir: I have placed the forces under my command in such position that you are surrounded, and to avoid a needless effusion of blood, I call on you to surrender your forces at once and unconditionally. Five minutes will be allowed for you to decide. Should you accede to this, you will be treated in the most honorable manner as prisoner of war. I have the honor to be, very respectfully yours,
S. G. French,
Maj.-Gen. Commanding C. S. Forces."

French did not even know that Gen. Corse had come to the aid of Col. Tourtellotte in holding the garrison and as a reply was not waited upon, not until after the war was the following reply known:

"Headquarters, 4th Division, 50th Army Corps,
Allatoona, Ga., Oct. 5, 1864, 8:30 a.m.
Maj. Gen. S. G. French,
C. S. Army, etc.:

Your communication demanding surrender of my command I acknowledge receipt of, and would respectfully reply that we are prepared for the 'needless effusion of blood' whenever it is agreeable to you. I am very respectfully, your obedient servant,
John M. Corse,
Brig.-Gen. Commanding U. S. Forces."*

The Confederates fought until the Federals were confined to the fort on the west side of the cut. Those on the east side had to cross the cut over a steady and deadly fire from the Confederates below. Rapid fire and extraordinary fighting continued all day of the 5th until about 4 p.m.

Word was received that Sherman's forces were moving up from Kennesaw and unless French could move to New Hope church by the block-house at Allatoona creek and thence to the Sandtown road, he would be closed in by Sherman's steady and on-coming movement. French decided to withdraw because he deemed it more important not to permit the enemy to cut his division off from the army than to carry out the last assault. The wounded that were able to be moved to the ambulances were treated at the springs near the

*Ibid.

ridges. The others were left in charge of surgeons detailed to remain with them. A hospital was manned in the house yet standing in Allatoona. In Col. Tourtellotte's report he wrote that the Confederates left in confusion, leaving their dead and wounded and that they withdrew "as individuals, not as an organization". Praises were given to officers and privates of the opposing forces that day. Even after Gen. Corse was minus a cheekbone he issued commands when he thought he heard an order to cease firing. In a reply to Sherman at Kennesaw, he signaled, "I am short a cheek-bone and one ear, but am able to whip all hell yet"! When ammunition gave out, one soldier volunteered to cross the cut which was under fire of the Confederates.

In official reports the Federals lost 706 and the Confederates 799. Many officers were among the number killed.

Gen. Sherman, in his "Memoirs", wrote: "I esteemed this defense of Allatoona so handsome and important that I made it the subject of a general order, No. 86, of October 7th, 1864, viz:

"'The general commanding avails himself of the opportunity, in the handsome defense made at Allatoona, to illustrate the most important principles of war, that fortified posts should be defended to the last, regardless of the relative numbers of the attacking and attacked.... The thanks of this army are due and are hereby accorded to General Corse, Colonel Tourtellotte, Colonel Rowett, officers and men, for their determined and gallant defense of Allatoona, and it is made an example to illustrate the importance of preparing in time, and meeting the danger, when present, boldly, manfully, and well.

"'Commanders and garrisons of the posts along our railroad are hereby instructed that they must hold their posts to the last minute, sure that the time gained is valuable and necessary to their comrades at the front. By order of

Major-General W. T. Sherman.
L. M. Dayton, Aide-de-camp.'"

A memorial of this bloody struggle is the grave of an unknown soldier on the edge of the railroad track in Allatoona pass. It is marked and kept up by the workmen of the W. & A. railroad. Many poems and songs have been written to this unknown hero who "died for the cause he thought was right".

On their retreat from Allatoona, the Confederates came to the block-house which the Federals had built at the railroad bridge over Allatoona creek. Gen. French summoned the garrison to surrender. They refused, and he then opened a hot musketry fire upon them, and also turned his cannon against the position. These soon forced the raising of the white flag. There is no complete record of the block-houses built during the war to protect the railroad bridges over the streams of the county. One at the Pettit creek bridge was destroyed long ago.

Again, Federal headquarters were north of the Etowah river. Brig.-Gen. Green B. Raum, commanding the 3rd division had his headquarters in Cartersville. Gen. Sherman reached Cartersville by the 10th of October and occupied what is now the Granger-Smith place.

Sherman was still in doubt as to Hood's intentions, but, "I moved the Army of the Tennessee (consisting of the 15th, 17th, 14th and 20th corps) . . . to Kingston, whither I repaired in person on the 2nd of November. From that point I directed all surplus artillery, all baggage not needed for my contemplated march, all the sick and wounded, refugees, etc., to be sent back to Chattanooga; and the four corps above mentioned, with Kilpatrick's cavalry, were put in the most efficient condition possible for a long and difficult march. This operation consumed the time until the 11th of November. On the 12th of November my army stood detached and cut off from all communication with the rear. . . . The whole force moved rapidly and grouped about Atlanta on the 14th of November . . ."*

From Kingston began Sherman's famous "march to the sea". While there he received what might be called the permission from Gen. Grant to carry out the plan.

The brick house on the Branson place was used as the Federal hospital at this time, and the up-stairs walls are yet defaced with the writings and drawings of the Federal soldiers.

---

*From "Gen. Sherman's official account of his great march through Georgia and the Carolinas", p. 70-71, to Maj. Gen. H. W. Halleck, chief of staff. (New York, Bunce E. Huntington, 1865.)

No official record can be found of a precise order for the burning of Cassville. Miss Howard's account places it on the 5th of November, and committed by the 5th Ohio cavalry. In the "Army Life of An Illinois Soldier", by Charles W. Wills, is this account:

"Oct. 12, 1864. Last night while our train was passing through Cassville, a town four miles south of Kingston, an ambulance gave out and the driver unhitched and concluded to stay all night. That was some 3 miles from where we stayed. Nine stragglers also laid down beside the ambulance for the night. The 17th corps came through there today and found the driver dead, with a bayonet thrust through him, and the traps of 9 men laying around. The horses and the 9 men are missing. I heard tonight that the bodies of the 9 men had been found altogether. Our men burned the town. I expect we will lie here tomorrow, and if Hood's army is in this vicinity, go for it next day. Nobody thinks he will dare to fight us. We have parts of 5 corps here."

During these distressing times, many families remained in their home, without protection of husband or brother. Miss Frances Howard's book, "In and Out of the Lines", gives a vivid account of how the women faced the enemy. The following letter from Mrs. C. W. Howard was found in the State Department of Archives and History:

"Kingston, Spring Bank, May 25, 1864.
His Excellency, Gov. Brown,

Dear Sir: I send you by express today a box containing the Colonial documents of Georgia. Through your kindness they were sent to Mr. Howard several years since, and as they are of such value, I did not think it prudent or safe to keep them at this time, when this section of the country is in a measure exposed to Yankee invasion. As Mr. Howard is in the army, I have acted in his place, and had them carefully packed and shipped. Trusting they will reach safely their proper destiny,

Susan J. Howard."

This active family lived on the railroad north of Kingston and after the Federals came to Kingston, they were watched and finally ordered to leave or face arrest. They went to Mr. Barnsley's for refuge. While there it was thought that "Sally" Howard, a typical feminine rebel, acted for the Confederate scouts and the following letters tell of her activities:

"Spring Bank, Bartow Co., Ga.
April 18th, 1865.

To whom it may concern:

During the month of August 1864, my family consisting of my wife and four daughters were required by General Sherman's orders to leave their home which is directly upon the railroad. By permission of Col. Dean, commanding post at Kingston, they removed to the residence of Mr. Barnsley. While there one of my daughters, now in another part of the State, saw one or perhaps more of the Confederate scouts. This she did without Mr. Barnsley's knowledge, on property not on his land. I am sure he would have prevented it, if it had been in his power. Should it be thought proper to make retaliation for this act of my daughter, it would be unjust to involve Mr. Barnsley in it. I ask of an honorable enemy to let my family and property bear the consequences.

C. W. Howard, Capt. Co. I, 63rd Ga. Regt."

"Spring Bank, July 29th, 1865.

"Mr. Barnsley,

Dear Sir: While away from home my father sent me two notes from you, the contents of which surprised me greatly. I answered them by return mail, giving a full account of my interview with the scouts. On reaching home, I learned my letter had not been received.

Your informant states what is not so, but a direct falsehood. I informed you of every meeting I had with the scouts before I left. I never heard of the so-called Confederate Lodge, until I saw it in your note. The house was burned when Mrs. Matthews and myself met the scouts there, which was but once. I told you of it the night my brother came. Twice Rachel Mathews and myself saw scouts at Mr. Newman's, and once Miss Hood and myself met some on our way to the carding mill, each time I told you of the meetings. I also explained to you all about the young man who came to your yard for the saddle. I did not denounce any family to the scouts, and am wholly in the dark as to the family you refer to. I did speak to the scouts about Mr.———— only, but not until they were in pursuit of him. This is a full statement of every interview I had with the scouts. I am deeply grieved that I should have for an instant caused you pain, nothing was farther from my intentions. I can never think but with gratitude of your great kindness to myself and family. I hope this explanation will erase all unpleasant impressions.

Very respt.,
Sallie W. Howard."

This letter was entirely satisfactory with Mr. Barnsley and Miss Sally in September wrote to Julia Barnsley that, "We have all taken the oath. I can't say it makes any difference in my feelings."!*

Many families refugeed to north Georgia from other states, only to find themselves caught in the midst of battle.

The George R. Gibbons (died Nov. 11, 1907, at his home in Grassdale) family from Bridgewater, Virginia, refugeed in October, 1863, to what is now Grassdale and bought several plantations as an investment. Their home in Virginia had been in the midst of battle and had at one time served as headquarters for Stonewall Jackson. One of his daughters served romantically as a Confederate spy or scout. In the possession of Miss Hattie Gibsons of Cartersville is this original permit:

"Office of Provost Marshall
Kingston, Ga., Sept. 2, 1864.
Guards: Pass two ladies through the lines. By order of
Col. B. D. Dean, Comdg. Post,
E. J. Kuhn, Capt. Provost Marshall."

The two ladies were Miss Bettie Gibbons and Polly Brady, a country girl who was her companion in their disguise.

Dr. Alexander N. Harris, driven by the bushwackers out of east Tennessee, came on horseback to Kingston in 1865 and rented a house and farm near Pine Log from the Gibbons. His son, Nat E. Harris, came with the rest of the family on Nov. 3, 1865. Dr. Harris died on November 6th at the home of his nephews, James and McDonald Harris, who had refugeed from Virginia and settled above Kingston on what is now the Holcomb place. He is buried in the Connesena cemetery. The Harris family were on the Gibbons farm about 3 years and while living there "Nat" borrowed enough money from Alexander Stephens to enter the University of Georgia. In the meantime he studied under Dr. Felton, riding down twice a week from Pine Log for lessons. He entered the University in the fall of 1867. He became governor of Georgia in 1915.†

*These letters are in possession of Mrs. Addie B. Saylor.
†Information from his son, Walter A. Harris of Macon.

Gen. Peter Charles Harris, brother of the late senator of Georgia, William J. Harris, was born in Kingston at the Branson place while his parents lived there a year after the war. His father was persuaded to come there to practice medicine by his brother, Peter Coffee Harris. Gen. Harris graduated from West Point in 1888, and was brevetted by President McKinley for gallantry in the Spanish-American War; was major general in the Philippines, and adjutant general during the World War for four years and then retired.*

RECONSTRUCTION

On a visit home, Gen. W. T. Wofford, seeing the condition of this section, begged authorities to allow him to bring his brigade here but at first was refused. On Jan. 23, 1865, by request of his own people, Gov. Brown, and by his own desires, Gen. Wofford was appointed department commander for north Georgia.

Col. Isaac W. Avery, in his "History of Georgia", gives an eye-witness account of the devastations left by Sherman in this once favored section.

"Left for months outside the protecting aegis of both governments, the hiding place of guerillas in both armies, the theater of that worst of all strifes that exist between hostile local factions, it realized in all its dread malignancy what is meant by a state of anarchy . . . Strolling bands of deserters and robbers, herded in the mountain caves, made predatory excursions from their fastnesses and in their inhuman collisions and murderous orgies kept up a reign of terror. . . . It was a labor of love for General Wofford, and he entered upon his difficult duty with zeal. He called in and organized 7,000 men, large numbers of them deserters and stragglers. He exhibited decided executive ability in his work. . . . He obtained corn, which he distributed among the starving people. His cool and resolute tact was the very quality needed for handling the turbulent lawlessness of his section. He sent a flag of truce to Gen. Judah, the Federal commander in north Georgia, and obtained a personal conference in which he induced General Judah to do the noble act of distributing corn to the starving people whose names were furnished by General Wofford."

Gen. Wofford's headquarters were at Kingston and

---
*Information from Sen. Harris before he died.

this station served as the distributing point. He asked for 30,000 bushels of corn, and permission to use government stock scattered over the country. General Judah granted all this.

On the 12th of May, 1865, Gen. Wofford made the last surrender this side of the Mississippi river.

A veteran of this surrender wrote to Mrs. Felton in July, 1906:

> "As to that Kingston surrender, I know considerable about that. When we had surrendered in North Carolina a large number of my regiment, myself included, did not wait to get paroled. We pushed home. After we had been at home a few days we were told that we would be carried off to northern prisons if we were not regularly paroled. So we made our way to Kingston and received our paroles. There was at that time a large number of soldiers at home, sick and wounded, besides a large number of others who had deserted and had been hiding out in the mountains. Some lived and slept in caves. Then there were a large number who claimed to be scouts, but they pillaged more than they scouted. The day of the parole, I saw the motliest crew I have ever seen before or since. These so-called scouts were strutting around with broad-brimmed hats, long hair and jingling spurs. You could see the old "moss back" who had crept out of his cave. You would find groups of sad-looking men who had followed Lee, Jackson, Johnston, and Wheeler through the war. Some of them carried the mud and dust of 5 or 6 states on their old clothes. From all over north Georgia and north Alabama they gathered at Kingston."*

The name—"Wofford Scouts"—must be a misnomer. There are no records of those who were recruited those last few months. The men who were called "scouts" pillaged and caused fear and suffering when the people wanted peace. The feuds between the "hog backs" and the true Confederate was a long time dying out.

Mr. John McGuire of Kingston remembers names of bands of these so-called scouts. Colquitt's scouts, made up of the stragglers from the 11th Texas, were located along the Etowah river. The Tate and Aycock scouts were around Cassville. Baker's scouts were around Pine Log. Matt Moore's scouts were around Euharlee.

Colquitt killed Baker over the ownership of a mare and the two bands were bitter enemies after that. People

---

*From one of Mrs. Felton's scrapbooks.

who remember say they were more afraid of the scouts than they were of the Yankees.

It has been said that there were eighteen thousand men paroled at Kingston.

For one year the Freedman's Bureau was to continue after the declaration of peace. W. H. Pritchett was the agent at Cartersville, in 1866, and as he had lived in Cartersville and was well-known, many indignities were escaped.

Oaths of allegience to Andrew Johnson were required of all citizens who had fought on the Confederate side. Emancipation of slaves stripped many owners of their entire fortunes, and their freedom was required without renumeration.

In March, 1867, a meeting was held in Cartersville to discuss the military occupation of the ten rebellious states. Capt. C. W. Howard, Gen. W. T. Wofford, Col. J. R. Parrott, Col. Abda Johnson, J. C. Jones, Col. W. Akin, Dr. S. T. Stephens, and J. R. Wikle were the committee. It was, "Resolved by citizens of Bartow, that in view of the recent action of the 39th Congress, in the passage of the Military Bill, and the amendments thereto, that the citizens of Bartow county, hereby express their readiness to comply with the requirements of said Bill and its amendments in the formation of a new Constitution and in the adoption of the constitutional amendment."

An editorial in the county paper in 1869 stated: "We do not have midnight marauding Ku Kluxes here. We boast of a better state of society that frowns down on such doings."

The county, although literally stripped of everything, began to resume the appearance of former days—due to the energy and spirit of an earnest working people. This section was traversed by land speculators; occasionally they bought and settled. The population consisted of frugal, industrious and persevering people —made up of merchants and farmers.

"Bill Arp" gave a fair insight of the southerner's

sentiments in these days of reconstruction in his report of being called "Before the Rekonstruktion Committee".*

SHERMAN'S ROMANCE WITH CECILIA STOVALL

When one considers the sterness of the military career of Gen. W. T. Sherman, his romance with Cecilia Stovall comes as a refreshing breath from the horrors of war.

Cecilia Stovall of Augusta, Ga., was a great belle and beauty in her day and her superior personal charms rendered her a queen in the social and military affairs of her time. In her veins coursed the bluest blood of several generations of Southern aristocracy.

On a visit to her brother at West Point, she met one young cadet, among others, who up to that time had remained impervious to "woman's smiles and woman's wiles". He gave her a love which was in keeping with the violence of his after-enterprises when he was known to the world as Gen. William Tecumseh Sherman. He lost no time in his wooing, but when he offered her his heart and hand, she shook her pretty head and said, "Your eyes are so cold and cruel. How you would crush an enemy! I pity the man who ever becomes your foe." To this he answered, "I would ever shield and protect you."

She returned to her Augusta home and gave her heart to a young West Point graduate, Dick Garnett, in charge of the arsenal there, but parental objections forbade a marriage. While on a visit to South Carolina Cecilia met Charles Shelman of Cherokee Georgia and was wooed and won by him. He built for her the magnificent home, "Etowah Heights", on the Etowah river and she brought with her many priceless portraits of generations back and objects from travel abroad. She witnessed the crowning of Queen Victoria. The floors of the home were hardwood and the woodwork of mahogany; framed in the walls of the grand old parlors were French plate mirrors and the rooms were furnished in elegant antiques. Rare and valuable books filled the library. In the home Mrs. Shelman reigned as a queen; gracefully and charmingly, she was the embodiment of the "grande dame" until the end of her days.

In 1864, when Gen. Sherman was leaving this county with the 23rd corps, via Stilesboro to Dallas, an officer called the attention of smoke rising from a house that looked like the home of a Confederate grandee. The Shelman home was not on the main highway, but in sight of their march. With one accord they galloped to the house and saw their soldiers greedily possessing themselves of valuables before applying the torch.

Gen. Sherman was impressed by the beautiful surroundings and asked an old Negro man who had stood at the gate who lived there. Tremblingly but with pride he answered, "Dis sah, is de home of

---

*See "Bill Arp's Peace Papers".

Mrs. Cecilia Stovall Shelman."

"Was she Miss Cecilia Stovall of Augusta?"

"Yas sah, yas sah, de very same."

"Great God!" exclaimed Sherman, "Can it be possible?"

For a moment his head bowed low and his face softened as memories of the past flashed through his mind.

"Where is your mistress?" he asked the old Negro.

"Bless de Lawd, sah, when misses hear tell dat de Yankees wuz comin' an' de Marster gone to war an' dat dey gwine kill an' burn, she called ter me an' say, 'Joe, we is all gwine 'way to be safe from de enemy. Pray to de soldiers to spare our home an' God bless you, Joe', she went with de chil'lun 'round her, Lawd only know whar, sah."

Instantly a command was given for every soldier to leave the house and premises untouched, and for those who had taken valuables to replace them. Guards were placed to see that these orders were carried out.

Before leaving the grounds Gen. Sherman said to old Joe, "Say to your Mistress for me that she might have remained in her house in safety; that she and her property would have been protected. Hand her this when you see her", and he placed in his hand a card on which was written:

"My Dear Madam: You once said that you pitied the man who ever became my foe. My answer was that I would ever shield and protect you. That I have done. Forgive all else; I am but a soldier.   W. T. Sherman."

This faithful old slave, Joe, many years after the war and after the death of Gen. Sherman, made a trip to Washington to a G. A. R. convention hoping to see Gen. Sherman to tell him that his mistress thanked him for saving her home.

CHAPTER XVIII

ORGANIZATIONS

MASONIC

The following are copied from newspaper notices:
The Cassville Lodge, No. 136. A. Y. M. had the following men elected in 1853: James Milner, W. M.; Abda Johnson, S. W.; Arthur Haire, J. W.; J. D. Carpenter, Treas.; John A. Erwin, S. D.; John H. Rice, J. D.; Robert Melson, Tyler.

The Oothcaloga Lodge, No. 154, A. Y. M., elected in 1853 Robert Butler Young, W. M.; Jonathan D. Phillips, S. W.; George W. Ransome, J. W.; Alex Stroup, S. D.; Thos. M. Evans, J. D.; Thos. M. Compton, Sec.; Robert T. W. Braswell, Treas.

"A. Y. M." must have been intended "F. & A. M.", or some other branch of Masonry. There is a conflict with the county Masonic data.

The same year the F. & A. M. at Cassville had T. A. Word, W. M.; A. C. Day, S. W.; J. H. Rice, J. W.; S. Levy, S.; G. L. Upshaw, T.; W. A. Rogers, S. D.; A. H. Rice, J. D.; R. Melson, T.

On October 28, 1859, the Ornan Lodge, No. 233 at Kingston was chartered with A. Terhune, W. M.; A. Y. Sheats, S. W.; T. R. Couch, J. W.; E. R. Cheshire, S. D.; J. R. Towers, J. D.; M. A. Hardin, Treas.; J. H. Carter, Sec.; J. A. Boyce, T. The other members were S. Sheats, S. T. Parker, N. H. Eddy, C. Dodd, J .C. Roper, A. R. Hudgins, Burris Johnson, Wm. Tumlin, W. B. McElroy, H. A. Clemons, W. W. Clayton, E. V. Johnson, S. B. Sea, C. Y. Mayson, R. S. Phillips, B. F. McMakin.

The Cartersville Lodge, No. 63, F. & A. M., was organized before the Civil War but records were destroyed by fire. It was re-organized in 1887 and Judge A. W. Fite was elected Worshipful Master; other Masters have been A. M. Pucket, John W. Akin, Martin Collins,

W. H. Lumpkin, J. W. Harris, George S. Crouch, Paul F. Akin, J. S. Calhoun, E. Mathews, W. C. Walton, H. C. Nelson, Wm. T. Townsend, N. N. Granger, W. J. Taylor, J. B. Harwell, Elbert G. Shaw, H. G. Davis, Holland W. Smith, C. G. Alexander, Frank Layton, Hugh B. Pettit, Rex Waters, C. A. Edwards, J. A. Osment, Elbert Shaw, C. A. Edwards.

The hall and records were destroyed by fire in 1932.

Names and dates of Masonic organizations in the country are as follows:

Cartersville No. 63—Chartered Oct. 27, 1887. A. W. Fite, W. M.; A. M. Puckett, S. W.; J. A. Crawford, J. W.

Pine Log No. 136—Chartered Oct. 30, 1850. James Milner, W. M.; John W. Burke, S. W.; Warren Akin, J. W.

Adairsville No. 168—Chartered Oct. 27, 1852. Richard A. Milner, W. M.; Robert Patton, S. W.; Jonathan Dew, J. W.

Stilesboro No. 260—Chartered Nov. 2, 1866. James A. Cowan, W. M.; R. H. Cannon, S. W.; Thos. K. Sproull, J. W.

Cedar Creek No. 275, Folsom—Chartered Oct. 30, 1890. W. A. F. Stephens, W. M.; A. D. Adcock, S. W.; L. R. Greene, J. W.

Cassville No. 295—Chartered Oct. 29, 1874. F. M. Walker, W. M.; R. I. Battle, S. W.; W. J. Hix, J. W. (Charter of this lodge was surrendered Jan. 23, 1930.)

Kingston No. 394—Chartered Nov. 1, 1894. S. L. Bayless, W. M.; A. Y. Sheats, S. W.; L. P. Gaines, J. W.

Euharlee No. 457—Chartered Oct. 29, 1903. J. F. McGowan, W. M.; T. H. Taylor, S. W.; W. G. Kennedy, J. W.

Jno. W. Akin No. 537, Taylorsville—Chartered Oct. 28, 1908—J. M. Dorsey, W. M.; J. S. Edwards, S. W.; W. A. Dodd, J. W.

White No. 660—Chartered Oct. 26, 1915. R. E. Wilson, W. M.; L. G. Hughes, S. W.; M. A. Bolding, J. W.

JUNIOR ORDER UNITED AMERICAN MECHANICS

The Cartersville Council, No. 27, Junior Order United American Mechanics was formally organized Oct. 18, 1904, with a total of 52 charter members. The following were installed as officers: Howard E. Felton, Past Councilor: John R. Trippe, Councilor; Jas. W. Stanford, Vice Councilor; James B. Smith, Recording Secretary; G. W. Hendricks, Jr., Financial Secretary; S. P. Satterfield, Treasurer; T. P. Tedder, Chaplain; J. V. Bishop, Warden; Lindsey Collins, Conductor.

During the first few months of the council very few new members were initiated. The public apparently misunderstood the meaning of the word Mechanic and erroneously believed the lodge to be some kind of a labor organization. Due to this all but 29 of the charter members dropped out for non-payment of dues.

On the second Tuesday night in December 1905, seven of the 29 members held the usual meeting and immediately afterwards, in the early part of 1906, three men joined the lodge and rendered valuable assistance in bringing the real purpose of the council before the public. These three men were Judge A. W. Fite, Col. Thos. C. Milner and Paul Gilreath. A steady and gradual growth began and in 1918 the roll book numbered 200. Approximately 50 members served in the World War.

Since 1918 the council has shown a more rapid growth, until today, it numbers approximately 600 and is recognized as a valuable asset to the city of Cartersville and to Bartow county.

The financial affairs of the Cartersville Council are in splendid condition, the assets totaling more than $4,000. In the past ten years the lodge has donated $3,000 in cash as Christmas gifts to widows and orphans of deceased members. In the 28 years of existence the council has lost 68 members by death and has paid to their heirs the sum of $62,000. Ninety-nine Bibles have been placed in the schools of Bartow county and American flags and flagpoles have been presented to the consolidated schools of the county.

The councilors have been: J. E. Barron, J. V. Bishop

H. V. Bishop, L. O. Bishop, L. A. Bishop, H. E. Black, W. H. Branton, E. C. Chitwod, H. J. Collins, W. W. Daniel, C. G. Darnell, Gordon Ezzell, H. E. Felton, H. H. Green, T. J. Glawson, Cap Garrison, Paul Gilreath, John C. Haney, R. E. Jenkins, A. L. Johnsey, T. E. Johnsey, Rufus V. Jones, J. D. Keever, J. H. Law, E. R. Mines, C. S. Mayes, O. R. McElroy, J. D. McEver, J. A. Osment, E. G. Shaw, J. R. Shellhorse, Bill M. Smith, Jule A. Smith, J. W. Stanford, Sr., J. R. Trippe, J. B. Waldrup, W. C. Walton, G. L. Williamson, Loyd Williamson, R. J. Waters, C. A. Edwards and R. G. Norris.*

KNIGHTS OF PYTHIAS

Cartersville Lodge, No. 42, Knights of Pythias, was instituted April 14, 1890. The lodge now owns its lodge room, five office rooms and one store room. It has given more entertainments and entertained larger crowds than any other organization in the county. Its equipment is not surpassed by any lodge in the South. It is possibly the wealthiest lodge per capita in Georgia. Its members have been prominent in the religious, educational, political and financial affairs in this county, and have been recognized by the State organizations, by the Supreme Lodge and other supreme organizations.†

MEMORIAL

The Ladies' Memorial Association was organized in 1867 by Mrs. Jane Kinabrew, president, Mrs. E. W. Chunn, Mrs. Mary Bogle, Miss Lizzie Gaines (Quillian) and Miss Ellen Bogle. They patiently but slowly erected the monument in the Cassville cemetery, at a cost of $550, to honor the Confederate soldiers buried there. In 1872 the Georgia Legislature donated $300 to the association. The monument is of brick with a marble tablet on each of the four sides, in the shape of shields with these epitaphs: on the north side, "Rest in Peace our Southern Braves. You loved Liberty more than Life"; on the south, "Is it Death to fall for Freedom's Cause?";

---

*From data compiled by L. O. and J. V. Bishop.
†C. M. Milam is the devoted leader of the lodge.

on the east, "It is better to have fought and lost than not to have fought at all"; on the west, "Dedicated to the memory of southern heroes by the Ladies' Memorial Association of Cassville, A. D. 1878."

In September, 1866 men and women met at the Methodist church to organize the Ladies' Aid society for the purpose of aiding and assisting the destitute widows and orphans of the county after the Civil War. On motion Mrs. Rebecca A. Felton was elected president, Mrs. J. J. Howard, vice-president; Mrs. M. A. Kennedy, secretary; Mrs. William Davis, treasurer. The executive committee was composed of Mesdames J. A. Erwin, J. R. Parrot, Lou Milner, W. H. Gilbert, Thomas Stokely, J. W. Shepherd, James Milner, S. A. Peacock, W. W. Leake, Nancy Jones and W. H. Pritchett. The work was divided into 4 districts and each district had a visiting committee.

The Bartow Chapter, United Daughters of the Confederacy, No. 127, was organized Aug. 19, 1897, through the efforts of Miss Sally May Akin. It was named for Gen. Francis Bartow and Miss Mamie Wikle was the first president. The charter members were Mary F. Mountcastle, Annie Hopkins Daves, Laura A. Graham, Kate Graham Akerman, Laura Graham, Mary Cobb Satterfield, Jessie Ione Cobb, Lillian Andrews Greene, Kate Hudson Postell, Nannie A. Allday, Frances Johnson Akin, Sally May Akin, Mary de Verdery Akin, Annie Harris Milner, Mary Sayre Calhoun, Marion C. Smith, Mamie Wikle, Melissa Edwards, Eugenia Bass Norris, Virginia Mountcastle, Annie Turpin Calhoun, Lily Johnson Bradley, Mary Octavia Smith, Mrs. M. L. M. Anderson, Mrs. A. L. Murchison.

The Confederate monument on the court house lawn was unveiled Dec. 8, 1908 and was erected under the committee composed of Mrs. Lila Calhoun Morgan, president, Mrs. Lily Johnson Bradley, treasurer, Mrs. Mary C. Satterfield (Backus), Mrs. Robert Gilreath, Mrs. Burton C. Ferguson, Miss Eula Whitehead, Miss Marion Smith, and Miss Jessie Cobb (Mrs. Dixon).

The Cassville Chapter, United Daughters of the Confederacy was organized in May, 1898, as an auxiliary of the Bartow chapter in Cartersville, but in a short time received a separate charter. Mrs. Julia Trippe Johnson was the founder and its most meritorious work was the placing of marble headstones at each of the Confederate graves in the Cassville cemetery and other graves outside. Members of the chapter in 1900 were: Mrs. Julia Trippe Johnson, Mrs. Kate Maxwell Searcy, Miss Lena B. Teat, Miss Berta Smith, Miss Lilly Dodgen, Miss Manie Saxon, Mrs. Rebecca Fariss Crow, Mrs. Aileen Best Battle, Mrs. Sue Crawford Fariss, Miss Carrie L. Smith, Mrs. Cammie J. Herring, Mrs. Georgiana Vernon, Miss Ida E. Vernon, Miss Mona L. Chunn, Miss Emma Price, Mrs. Frances J. Akin, Mrs. Clara Johnson Best, Miss Hattie M. Gibbons, Miss Hattie Ione Price, Mrs. Laura Lewis, Miss Gertie Chunn, Miss Lydie Saxon.

The organization of the Etowah Chapter of the Daughters of the American Revolution* took place at "The Oaks", the home of the late Mrs. L. S. Munford on April 20, 1909, the organizing regent, Mrs. Louis Munford Peeples, presiding. In August, 1909 the chapter in Cartersville was named "Etowah" on account of its euphony, its origin and its local significance.

One real daughter, Mrs. Mary Proctor, daughter of Wiley Traywick, was born 1799, in North Carolina, died in Bartow county, July 29, 1911. The graves of the following Revolutionary soldiers have been located and reported: Maj. John Lewis is marked and buried in Adairsville; Charles Baker, Pete Crow, William Cheeke, William Edwards, John White. In the 1840 Census pension list from Washington, which this chapter made possible for this volume, are listed: John Lewis, aged 83, living with Baylis W. Lewis; Rubin Edwards, aged 82, living with Reuben Edwards; Hugh Bruster, aged 80, living with William Brewster; Benjamin Haris, aged 81, living with John Stokes; Charles Baker, aged 79, living with Charles Baker.

---
*This data of the D. A. R. was compiled by Mrs. S. E. Hamrick.

| Members* | Rev. Ancestors |

Frances Adair — John Ball
Mrs. R. E. Adair (Lula Mahan), Regt. 1930-31 — John Ball
Mrs. L. M. Anderson (Malinda S. Tarplee) — Wm. Tarplee
Mrs. G. H. Aubrey (Hattie Hutchins Smith), Regt. 1914-17
    Drury Hutchins, Jonathan Reid
Mrs. L. J. Backus (Mary Cobb Satterfield) — James Barnett
Mrs. L. J. Bahin (Helen McDorman) — Thomas Cobb
Mrs. Madison Bell (Marie Gilreath Cole),
    C. M., Regt. 1912-14 — William Pearson
Mrs. C. R. Brown (Martha Peek) — John Peek, Henry Peek
Mrs. Louie Buford (Ida Vernon Greene) — John Patton
Mrs. A. T. Calhoun (Emma Thornton) C. M. — Alexander Douglas
Mrs. Julian Calhoun (Julia Gilbert Jones), C. M.
Mrs. Sam Candler (Kate Hammond), Regt. 1931- — Wm. Cheeke
Mrs. W. A. Cleveland (Lee Sypert), C. M.
Mrs. J. T. Daves (Mary Peeples)
    Jacob Strickland, Wm. Pearson, Wm. Gilbert
Mrs. Malcolm Dewey (May Belle Jones), C. M. — Wm. Gilbert
Mrs. Clifford Dodgen (Jim Vernon) — James Patton
Mrs. Colquitt Finley (Cora Walton), Regt. 1923-26 — Jacob Crow
Maria Finley — Jacob Crow
Mrs. A. W. Fite (Flora Conyers), C. M. — Thos. Word
Mrs. W. C. Fite (Margaret "Rosebud" Johnson), C. M. — Thos. Word
Mrs. Lindsay Forrester (Agnes Smith) — Wm. Boyd
Serena Dillard Gilreath, C. M. — Wm. Pearson
Mrs. Geo. H. Gilreath (Serena Munford), C. M. — Wm. Pearson
Mrs. J. Hugh Gilreath (A. Nora Rowan), C. M. — Thomas Cantrelle
Mrs. Robert Gilreath (Lizzie Bell Cobb) — James Barnett
Lillian Andrews Greene, C. M. — James Buford
Mrs. Clark Griffin (Orie Best) — Lewis Saxon
Mrs. S. E. Hamrick (Gladys Bray Massengale), Regt. 1926-28
    James Davenport, Robt. Love, Robt. Henry, Wm. Deaver
Mrs. J. J. Hill (Frances Lewis), C. M., Regt. 1919-22
    John Lewis, John Earle, Richard Gaines, Wm. Halbert
Mrs. Bradley Howard (Octavia Aubrey), Regt. 1922-23 — Robt. Forsyth
Aileen Jackson — Michael Dickson
Mrs. F. T. Jackson, (Guill Monfort) — Abraham Parham Jones
Elinor R. Jones, C. M. — Wm. Gilbert
Mrs. Fred Knight (Cathrine Satterfield) — Andrew Bryan
Mrs. L. M. Larrimore (Lucinda F. Stephens) — Cornelius Keith
Evelyn Lewis
    John Earle, Richard Gaines, Wm. Halbert, Maj. John Lewis
Mrs. L. P. Lewis (Sallie Maude Jackson) — Michael Dickson

---

*C. M. denotes charter member.

Members	Rev. Ancestor
Roslyn Lumpkin	Joseph Irby, Sr.
Mrs. R. C. May (Mildred Lewis), C. M.	
	John Earle, Richard Gaines, Wm. Halbert, Maj. John Lewis
Mrs. Marvin McClatchey (Juliet Neel)	Richard Gaines
Mrs. R. H. McGinnis (Roberta Duke)	Henry Duke
Rosannah Milam	Bartlett Milam
Mrs. Ab Monfort (Leila Merrill)	Abraham Parham Jones
Mrs. O. T. Peeples (Louis Munford), C. M., Regt. 1909-12, 1928-30	
	Jacob Strickland, Wm. Pearson, Wm. Gilbert
Mrs. R. L. Uilling (Mabel Lewis), C. M.	Capt. Nathaniel Harris
Mrs. C. C. Pittman (Emily Daves)	David Caldwell
Mrs. R. H. Renfroe (Sallie May Battle)	Elisha Battle
Mrs. S. Q. Roberts (Emogene Munford)	Wm. Pearson
Florence Rowan, C. M.	Thos. Cantrelle
Mrs. G. G. Rucker (Lucy Herndon Hicks)	
	Edward Herndon, Wm. Cheeke, Wm. Edwards, James Gaines, David Hicks, John McMillian, Jno. White, Wm. Ayres, Isaac Vincent.
Mrs. C. L. Rudicil (Lydie Rowland), C. M.	
Mrs. Tom Simpson (Cyrena Buford)	James Buford
Mrs. Ralph Smith (Wilma McGinnis)	James McGinnis
Mary Stephenson	John Thompson
Mrs. Ed Strickland, Jr. (Loulie Lumpkin), Regt. 1917-19, Joseph Irby, Sr.	
Mrs. Evans Strickland (Zeta White)	Hugh McCormick
Mrs. P. M. Tate (Edna Ferguson)	John Dent
Sarah Tate	Thos. Byrd, Sr.
Mrs. J. W. Vaughan (Frances Williams), C. M.	Charles Word
Mrs. A. G. White, Sr. (Mallie McGinnis)	James Watts
Mrs. A. G. White, Jr. (Elizabeth Vaughan)	Charles Word

In Memoriam: Mrs. Rebecca Latimer Felton (W. H.), Flora Conyers Fite, C. M.; Mrs. Callie Goodwyne Freeman (D. B.), C. M.; Mrs. Marion Buford Greene (J. G.), C. M.; Mrs. Mary Cleghorn Hills (W. S.), Mrs. Mary Barton Howard (W. H. Jr.), C. M., Mrs. Sallie Fannie Griffin Jones, (T. R.), Mrs. Emma Jones Munford (L. S.), C. M., Mrs. Kathrine Aubrey Munford (R. S.).

The Oothcalooga Chapter, D. A. R.*, in Adairsville, was organized on June 6, 1924, Mrs. G. M. Boyd, Sr., organizing regent.

Members	Rev. Ancestor
Mrs. (N. C.) Verda Wray Anderson, C. M.	Levi Phillips, Va.
Mrs. (G. C.) Maecliff Chamlee Boaz	Elisha Dyar, Md.
Miss Margaret Frances Bonner, C. M.	Elisha Dyar, Md.
Mrs. (G. M. Sr.) Julia Humphreys Boyd, C. M.	
	Humphreys Boyd, S. C., John Moore, S. C.

---

*Compiled by Mrs. W. P. Whitworth.

Members	Rev. Ancestor
Mrs. (G. M. Jr.) Josephine Knapp Boyd, C. M.	John Rice, Mass.
Mrs. (A. E.) Ella Dyar Brogdon, C. M.	Elisha Dyar, Md.
Mrs. (J. P.) Addie Richards Dell	John Nicholson, N. C.
Miss Alice Mae Dyar, C. M.	Elisha Dyar, Md.
Mrs. (C. B.) Ethel Richards Dyar	John Nicholson, N. C.
Mrs. (F. L.) Emma Benson Dyar	Richard Gaines, Va.
Mrs. (Paul, Jr.) Rachel McEntire Dyar	
Mrs. (M. P.) Susie Veach Gaines, C. M.	John Butler, Va.
Mrs. (Paul, Jr.) Mary F. Chamlee Gilreath, C. M.	Elisha Dyar, Md.
Mrs. ((C. R.) Pauline Boyd Goodhart, C. M.	John Moore, S. C.
Mrs. (O. W.) Janie Richards Hendricks	John Nicholson, N. C.
Mrs. Alice Butler Howard, C. M.	Jacob Strickland, N. C.
Mrs. (C. R.) Wilma M. Hutchinson	Richard Scruggs, Va.
Mrs. Julia Veach Stewart, C. M.	John Butler, Va.
Mrs. (T. W.) Mattie Richards Whitfield	John Nicholson, N. C.
Mrs. (W. P.) Ellen Reed Whitworth, C. M.	Jacob Strickland, N. C.
Mrs. Minnie Dyar Woodson, C. M.	

The Carl Boyd Post, No. 42, of the American Legion was established in Cartersville Oct. 9, 1919. The charter members were W. E. Strickland, J. B. Conyers, R. W. Knight, F. W. Knight, W. H. Lumpkin, Joe Nelson, R. L. Collins, Rupert C. Cox, L. F. Fincher, Lee Scheuer, Earl Scheuer, W. A. Galt, J. B. Uren, J .H. Shaw, Foster F. Smith.

The post was named in honor of Col. Carl Boyd, of Adairsville, aide to Gen. Pershing during the World War. The post won a cup in 1924 for compiling the first complete list in Georgia of its veterans.

The Cartersville Auxiliary to the Carl Boyd Post was organized Dec. 5, 1926.

TEMPERANCE

"According to a previous notice, the Cassville Temperance Society met in September, 1852. The president being absent, Maj. John W. Burke, 1st vice president, was called to the chair. T. C. Shropshire, Esq., was then called on and responded to a very eloquent address, setting forth the evils of intemperance, and claiming that moral suasion could not avail anything as a remedy. His remedy was the law, when a majority of the people wished it. Col. Warren Akin being present was invited to speak but declined. He, however, afterwards enlivened the audience with a few thrilling remarks, when an animated discussion arose, in which Col. Akin, Capt. Wofford, M. A. Higgs, Gen. J. H. Rice and the chairman participated. The attendance was large and attentive, and we hope some good was effected. On motion it was resolved, That at our next meeting we invite opposition to resolutions passed at a previous meeting, declaring our belief that a law of prohibition ought to be passed, and asking for a law giving the decision to the people".

The Sons of Temperance reported in 1860 a division organized at Cartersville, Cassville, Euharlee, Stamp creek, Ford's furnace and Pine Log.

A Temperance club was organized in Cartersville on Feb. 20, 1866 with the following officers: J. J. Howard, president; Dr. W. W. Leak, vice-president; S. H. Smith, secretary; J. H. Gilreath, assistant; Dr. I. A. Thomas, treasurer. The pledge of the club was, "We, whose names are herewith annexed, do solemnly obligate ourselves, in a pledge of honor, that we will not drink any alcoholic liquors as a beverage during the year 1866."

The Cartersville Woman's Christian Temperance Union was organized in 1892 with Mrs. Mary Dobbins Freeman the first president. Successive presidents have been Mrs. A. O. Granger, Mrs. George H. Aubrey, Mrs. Sam P. Jones, Mrs. W. J. Neel, Mrs. Nannie Allday, Mrs. A. B. Cunyus. Vice presidents are elected from the denominational churches. Mrs. Annie Laurie (A. B.) Cunyus, a niece of Sam P. Jones, began singing in revivals with her uncle and father, Joe Jones, and has continued singing in evangelistic meetings. She has been musical director of the Georgia W. C. T. U. for the past 25 years.

CIVIC AND OTHER ORGANIZATIONS

In 1875 a few public spirited men met and organized "The Cartersville Library Association". Col. J. J. Howard, president, Capt. D. W. K. Peacock, vice-president, G. S. Tumlin, secretary, J. L. Moon, librarian, and J. W. Harris, Jr., treasurer.

The nucleus of the present library was started when the Woman's club was over the Young Brothers' Drug store. Later the club room was moved to the Bank of Cartersville on Bank Block, the library growing slowly.

In 1903, a two-story brick building was erected by members of the Cherokee club at the corner of Church street and Public Square. The first floor was the library and reading room. Miss Mary Munford was library chairman at that time and upon her death a few weeks later, the club honored her memory by naming it "The Mary Munford Memorial Library of the Cherokee Club". Mrs. L. S. Munford, the mother of Mary Munford, served as chairman for 13 years, during which time she maintained a librarian and supported a book fund. At her death she was succeeded by her daughter, Mrs. O. T. (Louis Munford) Peeples. The library now has 3536 volumes; a splendid reading room of reference books and magazines; a genealogical department supported by the Etowah Chapter D. A. R.; and a membership of 450 readers and borrowers. In September, 1932, this was made a public library. Mrs. John P. Adair is librarian.

The Cherokee Woman's Club was organized in October, 1895, at the home of Mrs. Mary Johnson (Harris) Best, upon the invitation of Mrs. Best, Mrs. Frances Johnson (John W.) Akin, and Miss Louis Munford (now Mrs. Peeples), the founders. The first president was Mrs. Charles Wallace. The club house, built in 1903, was the first club house in Georgia to be built and owned by a woman's club. It had the honor of having as one of its presidents, a past State president, Mrs. A. O. Granger.

The club joined the State Federation in 1896, and the General Federation in 1899.

A federation composed of every woman's organization in Bartow county was formed at the Cherokee Club house in October, 1922. The church societies, patriotic and charitable organizations, and the women's clubs were all represented. The presidents have been: Mrs. O. T. Peeples, Mrs. Irby Sheats, Mrs. E. O. Davis, Mrs.

Francis Vaughan.

Young Men's Christian Associations have been organized here as early as 1875, but they have never been permanent.

A local fire company was organized in 1867. The Cartersville Hook and Ladder club was organized in 1875. This became a social club and the firemen were the beaux of the town. The sponsors were selected from the most popular girls.

Other social clubs are too numerous to mention.

The San Souci club in Adairsville was organized in March, 1914, by Mrs. R. L. Franklin with thirty members. It two years' time the members erected their own club house in which a library of 2,500 volumes was later opened. After the completion of the club house, the club joined the Federation of Women's Clubs.

The first Parent-Teacher Association organized in Bartow county was in the Douglas Street school in Cartersville in 1920. The first woman's club, known as the Civic School Improvement club in Taylorsville grew into a Parent-Teacher Association.

The Feltonian Woman's Club in Taylorsville was organized in 1925 at the home of Mrs. Walter B. Jolly who became the first president. It joined the Federation the same year and was named in honor of Mrs. W. H. Felton.

The Cartersville Rotary club was organized April 30, 1924, with 18 charter members.

The Cartersville Garden club was organized in the home of Mrs. W. E. Wofford in October, 1928, by Mrs. Mary Jones Turner. Mrs. Francis Vaughan was the first president. Since that time Adairsville organized a Garden club. The women of Stilesboro organized the Stilesboro Improvement club and hold an annual chrysanthemum show in the old school house, an event years before garden clubs were established.

The Lions club was organized in Cartersville in April, 1929, with 27 business men as charter members. The charter was received on the 16th.

CHAPTER XIX

MANUFACTURIES

Many of the pioneers' activities and enterprises came from the urgent demand for the necessities of life. Among these enterprises were the tan yards in which were made shoes.

The tan yards were established by a Mr. Kilpatrick a mile or two south of Rowland Springs; by John Kennedy on the Tennessee road; by Judge Joseph Bogle in Cassville; by Turner Conoway south of Adairsville; by Rev. Samuel G. Jones on Pumpkinvine creek.

A cotton factory under the name of the "Oothcalooga Cotton Mills", erected by Col. J. W. Gray in 1872 and 1873, was operated in Adairsville for ten or twelve years. With 18 cards, 56 looms, and 2,000 spindles, employing 70 operators, consuming 18 bales of cotton per day, it manufactured 3,500 yards of goods per day.

The Cartersville Car Factory and Building Association was established in April, 1872, with a capital of $5,000. Charles B. Wallace was president until about 1880. All traces of this old factory, which was in front of the old Akerman place, have been destroyed.

There were grist mills scattered around on nearly all the water courses where there were settled neighborhoods.

The Mosteller mills have been in operation since the 18th day of October, 1859. Berryman F. Mosteller, born in 1825, in Greenville county, S. C., in 1836 moved with his father, a native of Germany, to Georgia and bought from William C. Blalock, in 1838, the property on which the mills are located. The Mostellers came to Georgia in two prairie schooners which were made by them in North and South Carolina and the wagon beds are in possession of the family today.

Berryman Mosteller erected an old-fashioned, sash-saw mill, which was rebuilt and modernized by his son,

A. J. Mosteller, in 1910, and since that time it has operated under the trade name of Cedar Spring Manufacturing company, general contracts and builders. A wool carder was erected in 1866 and continued in operation until 1905, when the women of the country could get clothing so cheap their hand work ceased to be profitable.

The mills have operated with the same wooden gearing since the beginning. The cogs were hand-made from old hickory and seasoned under water. The third water wheel now running was designed by A. J. Mosteller, built by Hanover Foundery and Machine company, at Hanover, Penn., and was set up in 1908. The mills were rebuilt to the roller plan sifter system by Mosteller brothers in 1901.

A. J. Mosteller spends part of the time in Orlando, Fla. His great uncle, George Mosteller, made the first commercial paper that was made in the U. S. at his paper mill on the Catawba river in Lincoln county, N. C., and another great uncle, David Mosteller, built the first traveling threshers in the Carolinas and Georgia.

Besides the saw mills, there is a corn and wheat mill, built in 1856-58. The spring is a popular place for picnics and furnishes the source of the water supply for the mills. Adairsville is the mailing and shipping center.*

As early as 1866 a number of citizens proposed to erect a cotton or woolen manufactory somewhere on the Etowah river; a committee composed of Dr. W. W. Leak, J. J. Howard, James Milner, William Davis and W. J. McClatchey were appointed. This dream was not realized until 1903.

A Cartersville citizen, Mr. Paul Gilreath, answered a "blind ad" in The Atlanta Constitution, inserted by the E. L. McClain Manufacturing company of Greenfield, Ohio. After two years of correspondence with Mr. Gilreath, and searching in different sections in the South, the site was selected on Judge Akin's farm between Pettit and Nancy creeks, and northwest of Cartersville. Ground was broken in June, 1903 for what was to

---
*Information from A. J. Mosteller.

be the modern cotton mill and village of the South, and the first unit was completed in 1904.

The mill operated under the name of the American Textile company, and at the time, it was the only cotton mill in America built and operated by one man, E. L. McClain. William M. McCafferty, brother-in-law of Mr. McClain, was the general manager; J. W. Brown, father of C. R. Brown, formerly of Dalton, was superintendent.

Atco, derived from the company's initials, was the name given to the town.

All kinds of drills and sheeting of cotton were manufactured. In 1927 the mill was increased to double its original size, and the number of spindles was raised to approximately 50,000.

On July 1st, 1929, the American Textile company sold their entire interests to the Goodyear Tire and Rubber company of Akron, Ohio. This plant is one of a chain of plants in the South and the plant at Atco makes cotton cords for the manufacture of automobile tires. Goodyear Clearwater Mills No. 3 maintains the standard of beauty and activities started by the American Textile company.

The local branch of the Southern Cotton Oil company in Cartersville was built in 1902 and is located on 10 acres on south Erwin street with private sidings on the W. & A. and L. & N. railroads. The oil mill, ginnery and fertilizer plants are on the same location. From the raw cotton seed oil is taken from which is manufactured Snowdrift lard, and Wesson Oil by plants of the Southern Cotton Oil company in other locations. The crushed seed is used as cotton seed meal and fertilizers; the hulls are used as feed. Another product, which are linters, are used for manufacturing mattresses and rayon. The average product per ton of cotton seed are 310 lbs. of oil, 950 lbs. of cotton seed meal, 540 lbs. of hulls, 110 lbs. of linters. Sam McGowan is the present local manager. The concern is a member of the Inter-State Cotton Seed Crushers Association.

The Cartersville Mills was organized in May, 1920,

with Joseph S. Calhoun as president. In 1924 the Gate City Cotton Mills, Atlanta, purchased controlling interest. Knit underwear has been the main product. The plant employs 250, and has a capacity of 3,500 dozen suits of children's union suits per week. At present, The Fleitman Textile Corporation of New York owns controlling interest, but 40 per cent of the stock is owned locally. Present officers are Elroy Curtis of New York, president; John Fletcher Fowler of Cartersville, vice president; J. E. Fullager of New York, secretary and treasurer; R. C. Gordon of Cartersville, assistant.

Two old firms are Scheuer Brothers and Knight Mercantile company:

Scheuer Brothers was founded by the senior partner, Moses Scheuer, who came to Cartersville from Germany in 1874. He was first employed as a clerk in the New York store; then he clerked for S. & M. Leibman for one year. In 1878 he bought out John D. Head and commenced business for himself. At the end of the year he was joined by a brother, Albert, who had been in business in Washington city. The firm then took the name of Scheuer Brothers. In 1880, Isadore, another brother, came from Germany, and in 1881 Julius Scheuer came from Washington city where he had been several years. The last brother, Max, came to join the firm from Germany in 1884. Heidelsheim, in the Grand Duchy of Baden, was the ancestral home of these brothers. Their father was Leopold Scheuer who taught in this place for 50 years. The family of Mr. Moses Scheuer, who married Fanny Baer (dec.) of Brucksal Baden, Germany, possess a loving cup, dated 1840-1890, which was given to Leopold Scheuer as a token of love and devotion from his scholars at the close of his scholastic career. The Scheuers are mentioned in the Jewish Encyclopaedia as having come to the city of Frankfort in the 17th century. Noted as educators and rabbis. Isadore Scheuer is now living in Cincinnati. Max Scheuer with Earl and Lee, sons of Moses Scheuer, maintain this merchandise store in Cartersville.

The Knight Mercantile company was established in 1865 by Aaron Knight who was born Feb. 1, 1838 and died in November, 1893. His first store was on his home lot, then he removed to a small wooden building on east Main street. Later, J. W. Knight, a son, was taken into the firm and it became Knight & Son*. In 1899 the company erected the present building which it has since occupied. Upon the death of J. W. Knight in 1921, three of his sons became owners. At present it is the Knight Mercantile company under Robert W. Knight and Jack A. Knight. Besides the store, the company operates on the Seaboard tracks, north of Cartersville, a planing mill and lumber yard. R. W. Knight was appointed aide de camp by Gov. Richard B. Russell, Jr., in 1932.

---

*J. W. Knight m. Lalla Collins, daughter of Martin Collins who came to Cartersville from Pickens county after the war and reared a family here. He died in 1922.

CHAPTER XX

BANKS

Before banks were established in the county, certain men acted as agents. In 1834 Zachariah B. Hargrove was receiver in Cassville for the Bank of Macon. E. M. Compton was agent in Cassville for the State Bank of South Carolina in 1859.

The first bank in the county was the Planter's and Farmer's Bank in Cartersville. With a special charter from the State, it was organized on July 1st, 1872 with a capital of $100,000, of which $50,000 was paid up. Miles G. Dobbins was first president, D. W. K. Peacock, cashier. In 1874 John J. Howard was elected president. The board of directors were M. G. Dobbins, J. J. Howard, Lewis Tumlin, V. R. Tommey, president of Georgia Banking and Trust company of Atlanta; B. J. Wilson, capitalist of Atlanta.

The First National Bank was established in May, 1889 with J. R. Wikle, president; J. A. Stover, vice-president; J. H. Vivian, cashier; and with a capital of $50,000. The directors were the above officers and W. C. Baker, J. C. Wofford, L. S. Munford and Hiram Blaisdell (who erected the first gas plant in Cartersville on Cook street). It was first located in what is now the rear of Scheuer Brothers' store; later it was located on the west Public Square. In 1905 the bank occupied a new home on the corner of Main and Erwin streets. Much of the success of this bank was due to a past president, Joseph S. Calhoun who died in September, 1927. He was recognized as a leading banker in the State. At the time of his death he was vice-president of the Georgia Bankers' Association and acted on the executive committee of the American Bankers' Association. On July 1, 1929 the First National and the Cartersville National banks consolidated into what is now the First National Bank with a capital of $200,000 and into a remodeled building. Present officers are: Charles M. Milam, president; Bob H. McGinnis, vice-president; R. A. Shaw, cashier; Wm. M. Dorsey and Paul C. Franklin, assistant cashiers; J. J. Hill, chairman of board of directors; F. W. Knight, H. W. Leake, R. S. Munford, W. J. Weinman, R. W. Landers, H. Carl Nelson, J. A. Monfort, J. M. Smith, directors.

The Cartersville National Bank was organized Sept. 11, 1895 with a capital of $25,000. The directors were W. S. Witham, president; E. Strickland, vice-president; H. E. Cary, cashier; R. A. Clayton, bookkeeper; J. E. Field, J. W. Knight, J. S. Leake, W. H. Lumpkin, C. P. Ball. At the time of its consolidation with the First National, J. J. Hill was president, P. C. Flemister, vice-president, C .M. Milam, vice-president and cashier, P. C. Franklin, assistant cashier, L. P. Lewis, assistant cashier.

The Home Savings Bank and the Farmers and Merchants' Bank were both organized in 1906 and merged with the Bank of Cartersville in 1908.

John J. Howard and Son were private bankers from about 1877 to 1894.

The Bank of Adairsville was organized March 24, 1899. The directors were W. S. Witham, president; H. M. Veach, vice-president; N. D. Pinkston, cashier; D. W. Loudermilk, N. C. Anderson, R. L. McCollum, J. E. Scott. It has closed only from July 16 to Sept. 13, 1926, since its organization.

The Farmers' Bank was organized in Adairsville Aug. 12, 1911 with R. L. Franklin, president; C. W. Satterfield, vice-president; L. O. Benton, W. A. McCutchen, S. Davis, J. H. Gunn, J. T. Bray, W. W. Trimble and J. T. Terrell, directors. On Dec. 4, 1918 the bank merged with the Bank of Adairsville. The present directors are M. P. Gaines, president; C. W. Satterfield, vice-president; O. B. Bishop, cashier, O. Y. Yarbrough, J. M. Veach, J. E. Scott, J. T. Terrell, J. C. Hambright, G. F. Newton, C. C. Bennett, A. Abramson.

The Bank of Taylorsville was organized and chartered in June, 1905, with a capital stock of $25,000. The directors were: A. O. H. Davis, L. W. Jolly, B. J. Davis, W. A. Dodd, A. G. White, N. B. Anderson, W. D. Trippe, vice-president, W. E. Puckett, R. T. Eberhardt, cashier, W. S. Witham, president. The present officers are: J. I. Harris, president, J. P. Davis, vice-President, M. A. Perry, cashier.

A bank in Kingston was organized in 1904 with L. P. Gaines, president, and R. C. Bachellor, cashier. It is closed at present.

CHAPTER XXI

NEGROES

This county had a comparatively large percentage of slave owners before the Civil War.

Plantation life was a little world within itself. Each black servant had his or her own work to do. As each daughter of a white family married and began housekeeping, she had specially trained servants given her as part of her dowry. Though she did not do manual labor, she superintended the work of the Negroes and the household. Cotton was planted, raised, spun and woven, all by hand, and enough was made to supply the demands of the ordinary plantation—the slaves doing most of the work.

Negro servants often had the care of the small children. Mrs. Josephine Hardin Beck wrote, in her recollections of the early days, that her mother with her small children made trips to Randolph county with her Negro driver, "Uncle Ben", as her only protector. One was needed in the days of Indians and "Pony clubs".

The evidence of the hiring of slaves is shown by a copy of promissory notes that Mrs. Bessie Conyers Townsend holds: "On or before the 25th day of December next I promise to pay Bennett H. Conyers, or bearer, agent for Mrs. Patsey McKoy, one hundred and fifty dollars for the hire of Patrick, Jenny and child, and promise to furnish said Negroes the necessary clothing, etc., and pay their taxes for the year 1857, and return said Negroes to said Bennett H. Conyers, the last of the present year, the 1st day of January 1857. (Signed) Charles Rodohan." Another such promissory note was written as the above in 1863, as B. H. Conyers continued as agent for Patsey McKoy for the hire of a Negro woman named "Lucy".

In the appraisement of large estates the price of

slaves will give an idea of their value.

In the estate of Lindsay Johnson (dec.), in 1863-4, the following difference in value is shown:

"Negro man Jack, 65 years old, $100, Negro woman Ibby, 48 years old, $1000—$1100.

Negro girl Harriett, 9 years old, $2000, Negro man Willis, 40 years old, $2500—$4500.

Negro boy Marshall, 3 years old, $800, Negro child, 10 months old, $300—$1100.

Negro man Talt, 20 years old, $3500, Negro man Henry, 21 years old, $3500—$7000. Etc. . . ."

These Negroes were distributed among the children of Lindsay Johnson and read as follows: "Received of Abda Johnson, administrator of the estate of Lindsay Johnson, deceased, the following named Negroes, viz: Elijah, Lucinda, Sol, Jim, Peggy, Jack, Ibby, Harriett, Si and Bi, said Negroes being assigned to me by the freeholders appointed to distribute the Negroes of said estate and valued by them at sixteen thousand, three hundred dollars. John A. Johnson (Signed), Dec. 1863."

Mariah Johnson, an ex-slave of Col. L. Johnson's family, is yet living near Rydal. In the appraisement of the Johnson estate, "Maria" with eight other slaves were valued at $16,800 and assigned to the William Johnsons in 1864.

In the appraisement of the estate of John L. Rowland in 1864, his slaves were valued anywhere from $1400 to $200 each, and in the total number of 125 named slaves, not counting the babes, they were valued at $82,000, "specie value", and at $246,500, "Confederate value".

Major Rowland and Col. Lewis Tumlin were considered the largest slave owners around Cartersville. Asbury Kemp, an ex-slave of Col. Tumlin is still living and says that Col. Tumlin refused $1600 for him at the age of 20. His weight was 200 pounds.

In the minutes of the inferior court of Cass county, May term of 1863, appear a number of petitions as this:

"To the Inferior court of said county: The petition of Martha

Knowles, a free person of color residing in the county and state aforesaid respectfully sheweth that she is twenty six years of age and of dark complexion and that she has come to the conclusion that it will be best for her interest and happiness in sickness and in health, to sell herself into perpetual servitude and slavery to a good kind master, whose duty and interest it will be to protect me, feed and clothe me properly and which will save me all expense, care and taxation; and being well acquainted with Thomas F. Stocks, a citizen of said county, she desires, for the reasons aforesaid to sell herself into perpetual servitude and slavery to the said Thomas F. Stocks, his heirs and assigns forever. Your petitioner therefore prays that the justices of this honorable court will privately examine your petitioner to satisfy yourselves of her free and voluntary consent to the sale of herself into slavery to the said Thomas F. Stocks and that the said sale may be openly made in this honorable court this regular term thereof."

This was duly recorded in the minutes of the court and granted.

Some of the outstanding Negroes in Cartersville have been*:

J. T. GASSETT, b. in Tennessee, received his education at Maryville College, Maryville, Tenn. He came to Cartersville sixty years ago, taught an independent school for several years and later opened a first-class grocery store, receiving the patronage from both races. He was a good business man and gained the respect of all. He reared a large family in Cartersville. He died about 1922.

HAYNES MILNER was born in South Carolina and came to Cartersville about 65 years ago and opened the first colored blacksmith's shop. He carried on a good busniess on Main street until his health broke down and Haynes died in 1928. Haynes was a heavy drinker in his younger days, but after being converted in the parlor of the Rev. Sam Jones home, he lived a changed life.

GREEN AND WADE ROBISON were born slaves at Eufaula, Ala., and were owned by Mr. Eaves. After the Civil War they came to Cartersville and bought 200 acres of land in a settlement that is yet known as "the Mission", just off the old Burnt Hickory road. Green Robison gave an acre of land for a school site. He and his brother were among the prosperous farmers of that community. Both deceased.

MOSES KISER, Jr., son of Moses and Savannah Kiser, was born in this county. He finished the public school in Cartersville and later attended Morris Brown College in Atlanta, and Columbia University, where he received his A. B. and M. A. degrees. He is now a professor at Wilberforce University, Wilberforce, Ohio.

*These short biographies were compiled by Annie M. Jackson Anderson, a teacher in the public school.

WAYMAN ROBERSON, was born in Cartersville, a grandson of Abraham Roberson who was a slave of the Leakes; finished the city school here and graduated from Morris Brown College and the Meharry Medical College, Nashville, Tenn. He is one of the leading colored doctors in Rome, Ga.

ANGELINA PEACOCK: was a business woman, owning property on Main street and running a restaurant where the McEver store now is. She died December, 1902.

Servants who worked for the Rev. Sam P. Jones family were: Angeline Jones, born in this county, worked for Rev. and Mrs. Jones 10 or 15 years. Levi Choice, employed as a yard man and butler, worked for them 12 years or more. Katie Martin, a native of this county, was with the family 35 years as a house maid, died in 1926. Mattie McCoy, born in this county, was the cook for the Jones family 36 years. "Matt" was almost famous in her "white folks'" kitchen; she reared a large family, yet she could be found working up until her death in April, 1927. One of her daughters, Annie McCoy Young, is a gifted cateress.

ED BELL, came to this county from Canton, Ga., right after the Civil War. He remembers Cartersville as no one else does in its early struggles. Ed remembers when: the freedman's bureau was where the Sewell drug store now is and rations were given out to the Negroes every Friday; the post office was opened twice a week and was located on the corner of Market and Gilmer; a Negro by the name of Milner taught his race before the war, and after the surrender the colored school was located on McEwen hill; the religious services were held in the white churches. A certain section of Main street in Cartersville has been humorously called "Bull Neck" since the early days. Ed relates that Negro quarters were in this section near a pond where excess water accumulated. Smallpox broke out among refugees that were housed in this quarter and they were quarantined. One person may have come out and some one called, "There goes old bull neck"! Before the E. & W. railroad was built Mechanicsville was called "Lickskillet". Ed Bell is a paper hanger and Baptist preacher.

There are two colored Baptist, two Methodist, one Northern Methodist churches in Cartersville. Many colored churches are scattered in other communities.

Kingston has many Negroes who farm and work on the railroads. There are two colored churches in Kingston.

Only three lynchings can be remembered: Will Jackson for insulting a white woman; John McCorker, about 1915, for insulting a white woman; John Willie Clark, 1930, for the murder of Joe Ben Jenkins, chief of police.

During the evacuation of the Negroes soon after the World War, the county did not lose a large quota. Many bought property and had to stay north, while others returned here to a milder climate.

The Negroes show a distinct and promising desire to acquire an education, and their attendance has been noticeable in the proportion of children who take advantage of the public schools. The State has been equitable in the distribution of public funds to give the Negro population of this county the facilities for acquiring an education on a par with that given to the white. The city of Cartersville has one of the best school buildings in the State, the construction of which was contributed by the Rosenwald Foundation.

It seems to be a reasonable deduction from the education which they have received, that the percentage of Negro criminals, as shown by the records of the county, is much less than it was a generation ago, and makes an exceedingly favorable showing as compared with that of the whites. In proportion with the population of the county, the criminal record is remarkably good and an excellent commentary of the Negro population.

Although the "old time darkey" has gone and slavery is no more, the Negro presents himself a useful and friendly neighbor, and many retain and demonstrate the kindly qualities of other days.

CHAPTER XXII
BARTOW'S DISTINGUISHED CHARACTERS
AMOS TAPPAN AKERMAN

Col. Akerman, born Feb. 23, 1821, in Portsmouth, N. H., was the son of Benjamin and Olive Akerman. His paternal grandfather was Joseph Akerman, and his maternal grandfather was a soldier of the American Revolution.

He graduated in 1842 from Dartsmouth College and soon afterwards came to Georgia, teaching and studying law with John McPherson Berrien in Savannah. He located at Elberton, practiced law there, and married Martha Rebecca Galloway of Athens in May 1864.

Col. Akerman enlisted in the Confederate army and served as captain three years in one of Gen. Jos. E. Johnston's divisions. He was a member from Georgia in the Reconstruction Convention in 1867. He was a Grant elector in 1868 and while at Elberton was appointed United States district attorney for Georgia and in 1870 was appointed by President Grant United States Attorney-General, serving until Jan. 10, 1872. Grant was fortunate in having a Southern Republican so honored and respected, but Col. Akerman had to resign this position when he ruled the illegality of the government granting land to the Pacific railroads.*

Col. Akerman came to Cartersville to establish his permanent residence when he accepted his appointment in 1871. After he left Washington he practiced his profession here, was a beloved character in the town and a prominent member of the Presbyterian church. The Akerman home south of town, on the present Dixie highway, was destroyed by fire. At the time of his death, Dec. 21, 1880, he had been appointed judge of the U. S. Federal Circuit Court of Appeals, and would have accepted if he had lived.

Col. and Mrs. Akerman had seven sons, the three eldest were born in Elberton, the others in Cartersville. Mrs. Akerman died in 1912 in Athens.

(1) Benjamin, b. in 1866, was a mining engineer, most of the time in Mexico; married Kate Graham; died in 1927 in Wash. Oregon. (2) Walter, b. in 1868, was postmaster in Cartersville 22 years; a teacher in the city, Chatsworth and Menlo schools; in Y. M. C. A. Overseas service in World War; U. S. marshall four years; married Susie Young by whom he had six children born in Cartersville; at present Special Agent Public Relations for Seaboard Air Line. Resident of Cartersville. His children live in Florida. (3) Alexander†, b. in 1869,

---
*See Mrs. Felton's "My Memoirs of Georgia Politics", p. 93-4.
†In Who's Who in America.

Judge Alexander Akerman was U.S. District Judge in Orlando, Fla. From 1929 until his death in Aug. 1948, retiring in 1940.

married Minnie Edwards, daughter of W. H. Edwards, began law practice in Cartersville; asst. U. S. attorney, South Dist. 1910-12, lawyer in Orlando, Fla.; appointed U. S. district judge with headquarters in Tampa, Fla., in 1929. One son, Walter, was born in Cartersville. (4) Joseph, b. in 1873, is a surgeon in Augusta, Ga. (5) Charles, b. in 1876, lawyer in Macon, is chief counselor for the Macon, Dublin, Savannah railroad. *d. Nov. 1937 x Macey* (6) Alfred, b. in 1877, was state forester for State of Massachusetts, professor of forestry, University of Georgia, and at present professor of forestry at University of Virginia. (7) Clement, b. in 1880, was on Pershing's staff at Chaumont after the Armistice; at present professor of economics in Reed College, Portland, Ore.

COLONEL CARL BOYD*

Carl Boyd was born Jan. 24, 1879, in Adairsville and grew to manhood there. He was the son of Gideon M. and Julia Humphreys Boyd. The grandfather of Gideon M. Boyd, John Moody Boyd, born in Virginia, served in the War of 1812 and died in Mississippi in 1862; his father, James Boyd, served as 1st lieutenant in the Seminole War and died in 1852. Gideon M. Boyd, the son of James and Martha Stocks Boyd, at the age of seventeen entered Co. E, 14th Ga. Regt., C. S. A., and surrendered with Gen. Lee's army at Appomattox, April 9, 1865. In 1876 he married Mary Julia Humphreys, who is an ex-regent of the D. A. R. and a Gold Star Mother. Mr. Boyd engaged in the flour mill business soon after the Civil War in Adairsville, and before his death on May 3, 1923, had become a prominent fruit grower and farmer; he had served as the first mayor of Adairsville and from 1917 to 1921 had served as chairman of the Bartow county board of commissioners. He was one of the founders of the Adairsville Methodist church, where he was an active member.

The boyhood of Carl Boyd was chiefly characterized by a spirit of friendliness that endeared him to everyone that knew him and a faculty of getting things done without unnecessary friction. He went to school in Adairsville and graduated from the United States Academy on June 11, 1903. He was appointed 2nd lieutenant and assigned to the 3rd cavalry at Fort Yellowstone, Wyoming.

In September, 1905 he was assigned to Camp Stolsenburg, P. I.; in September, 1907 to Fort Clark, Texas; later, to Fort Sam Houston, to the Riding School at Fort Riley, Kan., and back to the 3rd cavalry at Fort Sam Houston, where he was appointed 1st lieutenant March 11, 1911. He represented the United States in the International Horse Show at Madison Square Garden that year. Later, he served in a mountain howitzer battery on the Mexican border, and in this hard service became personally acquainted with John J. Pershing.

His special training for the great work of his life began when, in the summer of 1912, he was sent to France to review his French preparatory to being assigned as instructor in that language at the Academy. In 1913 he was sent back to France as an exchange mili-

*Excerpts from an article written by J. A. LeConte.

tary observer and attached to the 7th Regiment of Dragoons. When the World War began he was placed under the American ambassador at Paris and acted as military observer and military attache at that embassy.

On July 1, 1916 he was appointed captain, and on August 5, 1917, major. When the United States entered the war he asked for active service; and, on his arrival in France, General John J. Pershing placed him on his personal staff. On Oct. 12, 1917, he was appointed as aide-de-camp with the rank of colonel, and was appointed lieutenant-colonel July 30, 1918.

From the first he made himself the buffer which absorbed the thousand and one petty jars and annoyances to which his Chief was subjected. The sightseer, the seeker of personal privileges, and civil officials demanding special attention for troops from their districts had first to see Col. Boyd, and only he whose mission was of sufficient importance was allowed to take up the General's time. When some new matter came up Gen. Pershing's first words were: "Where is Boyd?" He accompanied the general on his important conferences with high officials of the allied nations.

The value of his services was recognized by the French Government in the award to him of the title of Chevalier of the Legion of Honor. King Albert, in March, 1918 decorated him with the Belgian War Cross and conferred upon him the Order of Leopold. From General Pershing he received the Distinguished Service Medal.

Carl Boyd married in September, 1903 Miss Annie Peebles by whom there was one daughter, Anne. Mrs. Boyd is now Mrs. John R. Edie of Paris, France.

In February he was taken with influenza and died on the 12th of February, 1919. He is buried in the American cemetery at Suresnes, France. In a cable to his mother Gen. Pershing said, "In the death of your son Carl, of pneumonia at Paris today, the government loses a gallant officer who has given throughout the war the most loyal and distinguished service. We at General Headquarters lose a tried and trusted companion, and I lose a faithful aide, counselor, and friend."

Col. Boyd was the brother of Willis M. Boyd, of Adairsville, G. M. Boyd, Jr., of New Mexico, Mrs. Pauline B. Goodheart of Kansas City, Mo., and Robert Boyd of Adairsville.

MARK ANTHONY 'COOPER

Among the pioneers in the development of the mineral, agricultural, and manufacturing resources of the South, Mark A. Cooper occupies a position which many who have distinguished themselves in the walks of literature and statesmanship might envy.

Mark Anthony Cooper was a son of Thomas Cooper who was a son of Captain Thomas Cooper and Sally Anthony—a descendant of Mark Anthony. Mark Anthony's father was a native of Genoa, Italy, and he went to Holland to escape religious persecution, his people being Protestants. From Holland the father sent his son to Italy to school. The boy was harshly treated and, with a classmate, ran away to sea. On the Mediterranean their ship was captured by Algerian pirates and they were put in chains and set to cutting wood in the forests under a brutal overseer. Having knocked him in the head, they made their way by night to a British vessel in the harbor and the captain, taking pity on them, concealed them until the ship sailed for the West Indies. There they were transferred to a ship which went to Virginia. They worked three years in New Kent county, Va., to pay for their passage. Mark Anthony prospered and built a mill and trading post on the head of the James river. About 15 Georgia families are descended from him, including the Coopers, Candlers, Terrells, Clarkes, Jordans, Branhams, Harveys, Stovalls, Carters, Boykins, and Nisbets.

Mark A. Cooper was born on April 20, 1800, two and one-half miles west of Powelton, Ga., and was one of six children He was schooled in Hancock county; his primary teachers were John Denton, Dr. David Cooper, and Mark Andrews. His academic course was at Mt. Zion under Nathan S. S. Beeman and Benjamin Gildersleeves; then at Powelton Academy under Ira Ingraham. He attended Franklin and Columbia, S. C., colleges and was graduated from the latter in 1819 with third honor.

He studied law in Eatonton in the office of Judge Strong, and in 1821 was admitted to the bar in Augusta. He opened an office at Eatonton with James Clark as a partner.

On Aug. 23, 1821, he married Evaline Flournoy of Eatonton; she having died, he lived alone, giving himself to his profession, until on Jan. 21, 1826, he married Sophronia A. R. Randle, b. June 28, 1801-d. Feb. 6, 1881, a daughter of John and Susan Coffee Randle of Hancock county. There were ten children by this marriage: Thomas L., b. Oct. 8, 1831, served as a colonel of the 8th Ga. Regt. and was killed instantly when thrown from a horse while in Confederate service in Virginia on Dec. 23, 1861; John Frederick, b. July 27, 1834- d. Sept. 5, 1861 from wounds received in the first Battle of Manassas; m. Harriet Smith, sister of Maj. C. H. Smith by whom there were Paul, Walter of Atlanta, and Fred. Paul m. Alice Allgood, by whom there were Mark, Andrew and Frederick, all of Rome, Ga. Mark Eugene, b. November, 1842, was a Confederate veteran and died in December, 1907, never married; Volumnia A. married Thomas Pleasant Stovall of Augusta and Cartersville; Camilla E.; Sophronia; Antonia; Susanna, married William A. Pope of Wilkes county; Rosa L. died at the age of 68 and had lived with her father all her life.

Mr. Cooper was a successful lawyer and attended every term of his circuit whether he had a case or not. He prepared a book of these cases for his own use. He served one term as solicitor-general of the Ocmulgee circuit in 1828.

In 1831 he, with Charles P. Gordon, called the first railroad meeting in Georgia at Eatonton and obtained a charter for the railroad from Eatonton to Augusta which in later years became extended to Ross' Landing, now Chattanooga. As a member of the legislature from Putnam county in 1833, he was privileged to have this railroad charter extended to Athens and Madison.

In 1833 he organized a company with a capital of $50,000 to build the first cotton factory in the State on Little river, near Eatonton.

Up to this time he had farmed, and in 1835 he engaged in banking in Columbus, Ga., organizing a loan company with a cash capital of $200,000 which paid an annual dividend of 16 per cent. He managed this company successfully, even through the panic of 1837. After several years the stockholders divided, and Mr. Cooper left Columbus and cultivated a small farm in Murray county.

He was elected major of a battalion, organized in Macon, when the Federal Government made a call for troops against the depredations of the Seminole Indians in Florida in 1836. General Scott's report to the War Department stated that, "Maj. Cooper's command was the only command that sallied outside of their breastworks to attack and drive the enemy". Mark Cooper had previously served as paymaster in an expedition against the Seminoles under Governor Troup.*

Maj. Cooper was a Jeffersonian Republican and was one of the leaders in the organization of the States Rights party. He went to the U. S. Congress in March, 1839-41 as a States Rights Democrat from Columbus. As a member of the Ways and Means committee, he, with Colquitt and Black, held the balance of power between the Whigs and Democrats and brought about the election to the speakership of R. M. T. Hunter of Virginia. Mr. Cooper resigned a full term in Congress in 1843 to run for governor against George W. Crawford and was defeated by 200 votes, mainly by the influence of Howell Cobb. Mr. Cooper said, "Crawford beat me on the liquor question." This ended his political career as far as participation was concerned; he was always vitally interested in politics, and in July 1880, he declined candidacy for the legislature from this county on account of his age and his wife's health.

Maj. Cooper had seen this section of the county when he was campaigning for Congress in 1838, and saw its possibilities. His prominence as the "Iron King of Georgia" is fully discussed in the chapter on minerals found elsewhere in this book. He was among the first, if not the first, men in America who had iron converted into steel. As an authority on minerals he wrote many current articles on iron ores. He was an agriculturist as well, and was the first president of the Georgia Agricultural Society, having been elected at its first meeting on August 1, 1846, at Stone Mountain.

He was instrumental in the passage by the Georgia Legislature

---

*Militia Records, Ga. Dept. of Archives and History.

in 1836 of the bill creating the W. & A. railroad and years later acted as superintendent of the road. He made the cannon from which were fired seven salutes, celebrating the completion of the tunnel at Tunnel Hill in 1849, and incidentally saved the life of Hon. John P. King, president of the Georgia Railroad, by a timely warning that the gun might burst near him.*

Maj. Cooper was against disunion, but he became an ardent supporter of the Confederacy and a warm friend of Jefferson Davis. He wrote Mr. Davis a plan of attack against Gen. Scott which proved a victory for the Confederates at Manassas. Having fought under Gen. Scott, Maj. Cooper knew Gen. Scott's tactics. When he had an opportunity he would not speculate on the misfortunes of the Confederacy, but instead bought Confederate money and lost a fortune.

He was a prominent Baptist; was baptized by Jesse Mercer at Eatonton and was one of the founders of Mercer University, serving as a trustee from 1838 to 1845. He served as trustee of the University of Georgia for 40 years and was a trustee of the Cherokee Baptist College at Cassville during its existence. He was a moderator of the Middle Cherokee Baptist Association in 1854-55. He was always a respected and admired figure in conventions and associations, which he regularly attended.

Maj. Cooper erected a beautiful home on a knoll among the hills near the iron works and this home suffered destruction twice. It burned in March, 1857 at a loss of $10,000, was rebuilt, but again in 1884 was completely destroyed.

After the Civil War he spent the rest of his days quietly at his home, Glen Holly, until his death on April 17, 1885. He and his wife and members of his family are buried in the cemetery not far from the old home place.

Major Cooper was a man of tremendous energy and yet he had poise and calm which inspired confidence and gave him power to lead men. A man who could conquer and survive three financial panics had qualities of unusual strength. During an epidemic of smallpox that broke out at the iron works during the Civil War, he sent his family away, personally attended the sick, and cured the majority on a diet of buttermilk.

A writer from Griffin wrote a word picture of Maj. Cooper in his latter life. "Maj. Cooper showed that he had lost none of the energy and fire of his earlier years. He is one of God's grand specimens of the genus homo and though the suns of nearly 75 summers have bronzed his noble face and bleached his hair to snowy whiteness, he is still young in vigor, resolutions and enterprise. Glorious old man! Who is able or worthy to walk in his footsteps when his lease of life expires?" Maj. Cooper left a glorious heritage to his children and children's children.

---

*See Johnston's "Western and Atlantic Railroad", pp. 39-42.

Mrs. Rebecca Latimer Felton, Dr. William Harrell Felton (donated by W. H. Felton and Mrs. Annie F. Ogram).

DR. AND MRS. WILLIAM HARRELL FELTON

Two lives closely entwined in importance and service are those of William H. and Rebecca Latimer Felton. This illustrious son and famous daughter have created imperishable chapters in the records of achievement in Bartow county and in the South.

William H. Felton, the only child of John Felton, who served as a captain in the War of 1812 under Gen. Floyd, and Mary D. Felton, was born in Oglethorpe county, June 19, 1823. His ancestors came from New England and Pennsylvania to North Carolina and were of Scotch-Irish extraction. William H. Felton was educated in the old "field schools" and at twelve years of age he entered a grammar school under Ebenezer Newton. He entered Franklin College in 1838 and graduated in 1842. He began the study of medicine with Dr. Richard D. Moore of Athens and in 1844 graduated from the Medical College of Georgia in Augusta.

Dr. Felton married Ann Carlton, daughter of J. R. Carlton of Athens, in 1845. She died in 1851 leaving one daughter, Annie A. who married in November, 1874 Mr. John R. Gibbons, scion of a prominent Virginia family.

In 1847 Dr. and Mrs. Felton moved with his father to Cass county where John Felton farmed on the Tennessee road until his death in August, 1870. Dr. Felton had an active practice in the county until the strain proved too severe for his physical strength and he had to give up a strenuous profession.

In 1848, licensed by the Methodist church, he became a favorite and powerful preacher in the county, and was instrumental in building many churches. He helped found the Methodist church in the town of Cartersville and preached the first sermon in it. He never received one cent of salary during all the years he preached and he performed many marriage ceremonies. He was made a deacon in the Methodist church by Bishop Andrew and an elder by Bishop George F. Pierce.

Dr. Felton became a Whig early in life. He made his first political speech in Watkinsville, Ga. He represented Cass county in the Georgia Legislature in 1851-52.

At the commencement of the Madison Female College in 1852, Dr. Felton delivered the literary address and fell in love with the youngest graduate, Rebecca A. Latimer, who read an essay on, "Poetry—Its Practical Nature and Moral Tendency". After months of wooing they were married on Oct. 11, 1853, by Rev. J. H. Echols of Madison Female College.

Rebecca Latimer was born in DeKalb county, near Decatur, on June 10, 1835, the daughter of Maj. Charles Latimer, who was born in Maryland, and Elinor Swift Latimer. Rebecca Latimer was well-educated and was talented in music and art.

After their marriage they came to Dr. Felton's home in Cass county near Cartersville and farmed until the Civil War found them refugeeing to Macon where he served in the Ocmulgee hospital. Mrs.

Felton under the name of "Femina" wrote of these days.

In 1874 Dr. Felton entered the race for U. S. Congress as an independent candidate from the seventh district. The virulent campaign of six months gave to this district the cognomen, "the bloody seventh", but he won with a majority of 82 votes. At this time their home was the old Capt. Felton's place on the Tennessee road.

His most outstanding achievements during the six years of Congressional service were: his introduction of a bill to remonetize the silver dollar; a bill* appropriating money for the improvements of the navigation of the Oostanaula and Coosawattie rivers and another bill to improve connections between the Etowah and Coosa rivers—because of the latter he was dubbed "Etowah Bill" and a boat on the Coosa was named for him; his bill† to repeal the third section of the act entitled, "An Act of the Resumption of Specie Payments", gave him an opportunity to display his oratory in what was ever afterwards called the "wrecker speech"; the bill making national quarantine effective; and a revision of the tariff which admitted quinine into the U. S. on the free list of imports.

This "country doctor" electrified the houses when he launched one of his eloquent thunderbolts with statistical data that seemed to be at his finger tips. Possessing fine natural ability—improved by careful study and mature reflection—he was a man of unflinching courage and firmness, fearless independence, and scrupulous honesty; despising the petty tricks of politicians and demagogues, he acted according to his own convictions.

During his political campaigns and the years in Washington, Mrs. Felton was his private secretary and general counselor. Her pen was as ready and as active as her brain. His super-excellence as an orator and debator was largely due to the fact that every speech passed first through her hands. She gave inspiring sympathy and enthusiastic loyalty. She was considered the best politically informed woman of the South in Washington and was a fore-runner of what the future woman could accomplish in national politics. While in Washington they were frequently remarked upon for their striking appearance.

Dr. Felton was defeated for Congress in 1880. He wrote in 1884 that "Independentism, with me, is perhaps a more cherished creed than to many other people. My efforts to restore to this part of the country the purity of the ballot box and to relieve our people from the tyranny of the caucus as understood and enforced by the "machine" in Georgia, was to me a patriotic work. What I have done, was always considered my duty—and what I have failed to do has not been a failure of the heart, but of the judgment perhaps." Dr. Felton was always for the people and had a heart in sympathy with the laboring classes.

*H. R. No. 2270.
†H. R. No. 805.

In 1884 he was elected representative from Bartow to the Georgia Legislature in which he served three terms. His outstanding achievements while serving were: the advocacy of the local option law; author of the bill leasing the State Road 29 years at $35,000 per month, and later prevented the sale of the W. & A. railroad; author of two bills establishing reformatories for juvenile convicts; reformation in the convict system of Georgia; and promotion of the measure which culminated in the Normal Industrial School for girls.

He died on Sept. 24, 1909 and the monument erected on the court house square in Cartersville by his wife bears this inscription, "A fearless patriot, A spotless record" and "A model citizen of Bartow county for 62 years."

Dr. and Mrs. Felton lost four children in infancy. One son, Howard Erwin Felton, who graduated from the Atlanta Medical College in 1893, practiced medicine in Rome and in Cartersville. He married Retha Grimm of Rome, who is deceased, by whom there were William H. m. Lillian White, and Annie m. Alfred Ogram. Dr. Howard E. Felton died in December, 1925.

Mrs. Felton was one of Georgia's pioneer leaders in the cause of woman's suffrage. She was a member of the board of lady managers of the Chicago Exposition in 1893 and served as temporary president until Mrs. Potter Palmer was elected. She was chairman of the executive board of the Atlanta Exposition in 1894 and served as a juror at the St. Louis Exposition in 1904; she was a trustee of the Georgia Training School for Girls. Mrs. Felton was active in the fight for temperance until her latter years. She was a delegate and state chairman of the woman's auxiliary of the Progressive National convention, called the "Bull Moose", at Chicago in 1912. Dr. Howard E. Felton was one of the two Bull Moose electors at large for the State of Georgia. She was the only woman to be called into conference when the late Warren G. Harding was made President of the United States.

On Oct. 3, 1922, Mrs. Felton was appointed to the Sixty-seventh Congress by Governor Hardwick to fill the vacancy caused by the death of Senator Watson, and she took her seat Nov. 21, 1922 until Senator Walter F. George was seated on November 22. Mrs. Felton took the oath of office in the court house in Cartersville—the first woman senator of the United States. In 1922 the University of Georgia conferred the degree of doctor of letters.

Mrs. Felton wrote her own "Memoirs of Georgia Politics", published in 1911, and "Country Life in Georgia in the Days of My Youth" in 1919. She wrote articles for the newspapers until her death and addressed many women's clubs all over the South. For ten years she wrote on timely topics under "The Country Home" for The Atlanta Journal.

Mrs. Felton died on the 25th of January, 1930, and with her husband is buried in a mausoleum in the Cartersville cemetery, erected by her before her death.

DR. AND MRS. FRANCIS ROBERT GOULDING

The fact that Mrs. Goulding is buried in Kingston and that Dr. Goulding lived and taught there, makes Bartow claim them as distinguished citizens.

Dr. Francis R. Goulding, born Sept. 28, 1810, near Midway, Ga., is too well-known as the author of "The Young Marooners" and other books for children and as the inventor of the first sewing machine to require a biographical sketch here. His father founded the Columbia Theological Seminary, and he himself had the missionary spirit.

In 1833 he married Mary Wallace Howard of Savannah, born in 1808, a sister of the Rev. Charles Wallace Howard. At the age of sixteen she was considered a most beautiful girl, and poets and artists raved over her. Percival of Boston, among the earliest of American writers, wrote to her an "Ode to a Southern Beauty". At her request Dr. Lowell Mason, then a bank clerk in Savannah, composed the music to Bishop Heber's missionary hymn, "From Greenland's Icy Mountains"; it was dedicated by Mason to Mary Howard, and first sung by her in the Independent church in Savannah in 1824. She aided in founding in China one of the first Chinese missions supported by a Georgian.

When Mrs. Goulding's health failed, Dr. Goulding brought her to Kingston, but she died in 1853 and was the first to be interred in the Kingston cemetery. Carved on her grave is,

"Mary Howard
beloved wife of
Rev. F. R. Goulding
died July 14, 1853.
She made home happy."

Dr. Goulding then in February, 1854 bought from Nathan Land the lot on the W. & A. railroad south of Kingston, now known as the Beck place, and conducted a boys' boarding school and wrote while there a book on the "Instincts of Birds and Beasts".

Dr. Goulding advertised his home for sale in 1859 as he had left and remarried, and in 1862 Dr. Robert C. Word bought the place. Dr. Goulding died Aug. 21, 1881 and is buried at Rossville. Of six children by Mary Howard, there is one living son, Capt. B. L. Goulding of Chattanooga. He was "Frank" in the "Young Marooners" and is an old commander of the U. S. V. in Tennessee, having served in Co. A, 1st Ga. "Republican Blues" from Savannah.

CORRA HARRIS

By her residence in the county since 1913, Mrs. Corra Harris is claimed as the county's most distinguished citizen. It is an appreciated fact that the facility of her pen and the brilliancy of her mind have made her the medium to express what the men and women about her feel but are unable to express.

Corra May White was born March 17, 1869, on a plantation, "Farm Hill" in Elbert county, six miles from Ruckersville, Ga. She was the eldest daughter of Tinsley Rucker White, who was a Confederate veteran, and of Mary Elizabeth Mathews White. She had only 36 months of actual schooling, but she became a voracious reader in the family library, an accumulation of three generations, and was under the directorship of her cultured mother. She received a first grade license to teach school at the age of sixteen, and taught a six weeks' summer school.

On February 8, 1887, she married Lundy Howard Harris, a young graduate, and later professor of Greek, of Emory College, who died Sept. 18, 1910, in Bartow county. In November before their marriage he was licensed to preach by the North Georgia Methodist conference. His first charge was in the Redwine circuit and here began the experiences which made Mrs. Harris famous when depicted in "The Circuit Rider's Wife."

It was in 1899 that Mrs. Harris attracted the attention of one of the editors of The Independent by an article she wrote in defense of the South's attitude toward the Negro problem at the time of the Sam Hose lynching. From that year she became a contributor to the magazine and a staunch friend of Hamilton Holt, the editor. While living in Nashville Mrs. Harris wrote her first book, "The Jessica Letters."

Mrs. Harris bought her home, "In the Valley", in 1913 and it includes 300 acres. The house was originally an Indian chief's log cabin. Incidentally, Col. Tom Bowman, a young lieutenant of one of the companies who drove out the Cherokees from this very section in May, 1838, married Mrs. Harris' grandmother's sister, Miss Blackwell. Her home is noted for its hospitality and a long list of distinguished people and "every-day" folk have been guesst and visitors. She is interested in agriculture, religion, and road building, but has never been an active force in her home community near Rydal.

Mrs. Harris was sent to Europe by the Saturday Evening Post in 1911, and again in 1914 as the first woman war correspondent.

The degree of doctor of literature was given her by Oglethorpe University in 1921. In 1927 Rollins College gave the degree of humane letters, and the University of Georgia that of doctor of literature. In 1931 she was awarded the George Ford Milton medal, by the University of Tennessee, for the most outstanding work of a Southern writer.

In 1930 Mrs. Harris was offered the "Chair of Evil" in Rollins College, Fla. She contends that evil is the oldest classic of human nature and should be taught as the mediaeval history of men by the best people rather than vice is by the worst people. The publicity attending this suggestion was world wide—including favorable editorials in The London Times, New York Post and other leading papers. But the comments of the sensational press were offensive, and after delivering one course of lectures Mrs. Harris declined to occupy the "Chair of Evil" in Rollins College.

She is a constant writer and when her health permitted wrote as many as 16 hours a day. Once Mrs. Harris has written a thought or an article, she never looks at it again. A studio was built a few hundred yards from the main house and six of her books have been written there.

Of 24 books, 19 are in book form: The Jessica Letters, 1904; A Circuit Rider's Wife, 1910; Eve's Second Husband, 1910; The Recording Angel, 1912; In Search of a Husband, 1913; The Co-Citizens, 1915; Justice, 1915; A Circuit Rider's Widow, 1916; Making Her His Wife, 1918; From Sunup to Sundown, 1919, in which she was co-author with her daughter, Faith Harris Leech who died the same year; Happily Married, 1920; My Son, 1921; The Eyes of Love, 1922; A Daughter of Adam, 1923; The House of Helen, 1923; My Book and Heart, 1924, which is her own biography; As a Woman Thinks, 1925; Flapper Anne, 1926; The Happy Pilgrimage, 1927. Mrs. Harris contributes to most of the popular magazines of today.

Mrs. Harris began a Candlelit Column in The Atlanta Journal on November 15, 1931; contributing in every Sunday, Wednesday and Friday edition—a column in which she tells "what life has taught her" as well as comments on local and current events. Col John T. Boifeuillet said of her at the time, "Her individuality will imprint itself upon the journalism of the day even as it is so distinctly and delightfully impressed upon the literature of the age."

CHARLES WALLACE HOWARD

Charles Wallace Howard stands preeminently as a scholar, clergyman, and writer. He was born Oct. 11, 1811 in Savannah, Ga., a son of Charles and Jane Wallace Howard who were of English descent. He was a brother of Mary Howard, the first wife of Dr. Francis R. Goulding.

He was a graduate of Franklin College and the Theological Seminary at Princeton, N. J. When twenty-one he was ordained for the Presbyterian ministry at Athens and accepted a pastorate at Milledgeville. He was instrumental in the erection of Oglethorpe University and when it was completed filled the chair of belle-lettres.* In April, 1835 he married Susan Jett Thomas of New Orleans, daughter of Gen. Jett Thomas of the War of 1812.

In 1838* Rev. Howard was sent to London by the legislature of Georgia to procure copies of the colonial records relating to the history and settlement of this State. Clerks employed in transcribing the documents came upon something very painful in connection with King George II. This gave great offense, and though the Rev. Howard was in no way to blame, he was abruptly told that the work must

---

*From "Memoirs of Georgia", Vol. I, p. 296.
*House Journal, 1838, pp. 18, 68.

stop. By urgent pleading, and the fact that Georgia had gone to heavy expense, he was finally allowed to finish. He and his wife witnessed the crowning of Queen Victoria.

The Rev. Howard was not strong in health and sometime in the late 30's he bought property in a higher climate, north of Kingston, and called it "Spring Bank". A picture of the house may be seen in White's "Historical Collections of Georgia".

In 1845 he was called to Charleston, S. C., to reorganize the famous old Huguenot church, and served as rector until in 1850 he was sent abroad for a year to regain failing health. Inscribed in the church records after his death is this: "This page in the records of the French Protestant Church, is dedicated to the memory of the Rev. Charles Wallace Howard, first pastor of the church on its reorganization in 1845. . . . A theologian, his was the power to make plain the dealings of God with man. A Christian, his was the power to illustrate the adaptedness of Christianity to the necessities of our nature. A Christian teacher and orator, his argument convinced the reason, his wise, persuasive words subdued the heart and brought it into harmony with the intellect. His ministry in this church will be remembered with a loving veneration as long as there is a survivor who worshipped under its blessed influence.*

In 1852 he with his family came to their home at Spring Bank and opened a select school. Representative families from all over Cherokee Georgia sent their children and daughters to Rev. Howard's school.

At the beginning of the Civil War he immediately entered the Confederate service and served as captain of Co. I, 63rd Ga. Regt., in which he was lovingly called the "Old Captain". At the time he went into service he was working on a history of Georgia, but war interrupted his labor. After his parole in May, 1865, he turned the school over to his daughters and devoted himself to writing and research. Traveling on horseback, he made examinations of the mineral, coal, agricultural, and stock raising possibilities in this section and wrote many valuable articles on this subject. He wrote and published a manual of Grass and Forage Plants. In the county paper of 1867 appear his articles on "The Condition and the Resources of Georgia". He had one of the first mills on Connesena creek, and was founder of the Howard Hydraulic Cement plant above Kingston.

The Rev. Howard died Dec. 25, 1876, at a home, "Ellerslie", he had on Lookout Mountain. He and his family are buried in the family cemetery at Spring Bank.

At the time of his death, Gen. J. E. Johnston wrote to members of the family that, "His loss is a great one to Georgia. For his capacity, patriotism and virtue made him more truly useful, since the war, than any other Georgian. I valued his friendship as highly as any that I could claim, and I shall regret his death and cherish his memory during

---

*From "The Mothers of Some Distinguished Georgians", p. 70.

the remainder of my life."; and from the Georgia State Agricultural Society, of which he was a life-long and active member, came this tribute: "Whereas, this convention desires to give a suitable expression to its high appreciation of the long continued and distinguished service of Charles Wallace Howard to the cause of Southern agriculture, and of his earnest co-operation in the work of this society: And whereas, his fine natural powers and high culture, his large attainments in agricultural knowledge, and his gifts as a writer and speaker, eminently fitted him for usefulness in the sphere of public service, and they were all devoted to it with an interest and zeal such as is common only in subserving private interest; And whereas, he had in an eminent degree the power of acquiring knowledge and of diffusing it among others, in a manner not only lucid but attractive—and was largely instrumental in educating the people of the State in agricultural topics, and in elevating and stimulating their tastes; Be it therefore resolved, that a page of the printed minutes of this society be printed with the inscription:

'To the Memory of Charles Wallace Howard'."

There were thirteen children, all of whom are deceased. The oldest son, Jett Thomas Howard was in the Confederate service, and he married Mary Guerard by whom there is one son yet living in Savannah, Charles Wallace Howard; a granddaughter, Miss Emily Ravenel, lives in Savannah and Spring Bank remains in their possession. Jane Wallace m. Henry Bryan and their daughter, Ella Bryan, wrote under the cognomen of "Clinton Dangerfield". Ella Susan m. George H. Waring and lived at Cement. Frances Thomas, b. April 10, 1843-d. Mar. 6, 1907, wrote the family's and neighbors' war experiences in, "In and Out of the Lines". Sarah W. Howard lived at Spring Bank until a few years before her death in 1929.

SAMUEL PORTER JONES

Samuel Porter Jones was born in Oak Bowery, Chambers county, Ala., Oct. 16, 1847. He was a son of John J. Jones, who was a lawyer in Cartersville and a captain in the Confederate army, and Queenie Porter Jones who died in 1856 and is buried at Oak Bowery. His brothers and sisters were: J. Josephus*, b. April 22, 1846, who became an evangelist after his brother, but did not acquire quite the fame of Sam, and died on Dec. 4, 1902 at the home of his brother; Annie E., married John T. Stocks of Atlanta and died in 1922; Charles T. lived in Bartow county until just a few months before his death in December, 1931. He married Laura Fickle by whom there are Sam, Robert, Charles, Henry Grady, Queenie (Shepherd), William C., Annie L. (Moore), Rhea, and Frances (Jones).

When Sam Jones was nine years of age his mother died, and his father came to Cass county in 1855. On January 19, 1858, he married Jane Skinner, daughter of Julius and Lucinda Houston Skinner, who came to Cartersville in 1851, and by whom there were two

*See Benham sketch.

1. C. H. Smith, "Bill Arp" (donated by G. H. Aubrey).
2. Sam P. Jones.

children, Louella, and Cornelia.

Samuel Gamble Jones, the grandfather of Sam Jones, was born Aug. 16, 1805 and died Feb. 20, 1895 at his home in Cartersville. He was a beloved local Methodist preacher in this county after the Civil War, and until 1925 his birthday was celebrated by his descendants in Cartersville or Rome. His wife, Elizabeth Anne Edwards, born July 10, 1810-died May 19, 1877, was the daughter of Rev. Robert L. Edwards, called the "Holy Ghost Preacher" in pioneer Methodism. Of their eleven children, four were Methodist preachers: Robert H. Jones of Cartersville, William E. Jones of Atlanta, A. Parks Jones of LaGrange, and Dr. James H. Jones of Alabama. Rev. Samuel G. Jones and his wife were born and married in South Carolina, and lived there until four children were born to them. They removed to Chambers county, Ala., and he was ordained to preach there in 1848. 1839.

The schooling of Sam Jones was under Prof. Slaton in Alabama, and Dr. and Mrs. Felton and Prof. Ronald Johnston in this county. Mrs. Felton in one of her books wrote of Sam Jones as being a "bright, devilish pupil".

While his father was away in Confederate service and separated from his step-mother when she refugeed, Sam Jones learned to love drink and quickly ruined his physical being. At his father's insistence, he studied law and was admitted to the Cartersville bar on September 21, 1868. In November, 1869 he married Laura McElwain of Henry county, Ky., whom he had met on a previous visit to Kentucky after the Civil War.

Friends, relatives, and he himself, have told of the distress of his days of dissipation—making his conversion all the more powerful when that time came. At his father's deathbed in August, 1872, he promised to reform and kept the promise.

His real conversion was under his grandfather's preaching at Felton's Chapel soon after his father's death. One week after his conversion, because of the absence of the preacher in charge, and his grandfather's hoarseness, at New Hope church, Sam Jones preached his first sermon. After reading his text, "I am not ashamed of the gospel of Christ, for it is the power of God unto salvation to every one that believeth, to the Jew first, and also to the Greek", he closed his Bible and before people that had known him all his reckless life, he adopted the preacher's plan, who said, "Brethren, I can't preach the text, but I can tell my experience in spite of the devil."

He was licensed to preach by the North Georgia conference in October, 1872, and his first charge was the Van Wert circuit in Polk county, where he served three years. In 1875 he served the DeSoto circuit in Floyd county for two years. It was his presiding elder, Rev. Simon Peter Richardson, who influenced and strengthened his growing character, and taught him "that the pulpit was not a prison but a throne". In 1878 he served the Newborn circuit in Newton county two years, and it was here that he began his first evangelistic work. His last pastoral charge was Monticello in Jasper county, where he served one year. In 1881 he was appointed agent of the North Georgia Orphans' Home, saving it from financial ruin by his evangelistic messages and personal magnetism.

His first recognition from the newspapers was during a revival meeting in Memphis, Tenn., in January, 1883, which laid the foundation for his fame as a pulpit orator. His most remarkable revival was in Nashville, Tenn., where the Ryman auditorium was erected to accommodate the crowds who came to hear him. It was built by Capt. Ryman, a convert of his preaching. Two converts who deserve mention here were Rev. Sam Small—lawyer, journalist and preacher, and Tom Dunham—reformed gambler and loyal family friend.

Sam Jones' lectures and revivals covered the United States and parts of Canada. He won fame that no other evangelist has attained, though many have tried to imitate him. His influence has been admitted by the most distinguished clergymen in the United States. He still is the most quoted preacher by the masses who has ever lived in America, and is recognized as the most unique public speaker. His originality, his splendid flow of English and style of sweeping human emotions at will were peculiarly his own; stinging sentences and tongue lashings from him were accepted as a matter of fact.

Several times he had chances to make his home elsewhere, but through the love that the home people manifested, he made his home in Cartersville where he was active in all civic affairs. He was instrumental in advancing the mineral interests in the county; becoming a large property owner, he invested in the town and county. It was largely through his hatred of liquor that others were able to later abolish the sale of it in the county by State law, and in his day and by him, the saloons in Bartow county were closed.

Sam Jones—and he loved to be called just plain "Sam Jones"—died Oct. 15, 1906, on a train when on the way home from Oklahoma to celebrate his birthday with a big party. His body was brought to Cartersville on a special train and taken to Atlanta to lie in state at the Capitol after the funeral service in Cartersville which was held at the Tabernacle. It was interred in the Cartersville cemetery and a monument was erected near the railroad so that his railroad friends might be reminded of his life and works as they passed to and fro upon the line.

Mrs. Laura McElwain Jones, born June 30, 1850, died in an Atlanta hospital January 18, 1926, and is buried in the family lot. She lived at her home, "Roselawn", on Market street until her death and was renowned as a gracious hostess and benefactor, and a devoted church worker. The children of Sam and Laura Jones were:

Mary, b. Sept. 1871; m. the first time, J. Evans Mays (dec.) by whom there were Laura, and Eva (Caldwell) (dec.), and m. 2nd time, W. R. Turner (dec.) of Marietta.

Annie C., b. May 11, 1873, d. May 24, 1924; m. first W. M.

Graham and 2nd, to Ruohs Pyron, live stock breeder in Ga. and N. C. Endowed with many of her father's gifts, she was a philanthropist in her own inimitable way until her death in Cartersville. She and Mr. Pyron lived at the "Bill Arp" home on the Tennessee road.

S. Paul, b. May 31, 1875; m. twice and died in Atlanta, Dec. 16, 1925, leaving five children. He was a reporter for The Atlanta Constitution. Buried in Atlanta.

Robert Wilkerson, b. Dec. 24, 1877, d. Jan. 26, 1907; m. Lillie Baker by whom there was one son, Sam; died while a young ordained preacher. Buried in Cartersville.

Laura, b. October 1881; m. B, C. Sloan, by whom there is one son, died in 1931 in New Orleans and is buried in Cartersville.

Julia B., b. April 1885; m. Rev. Walt Holcomb who was a co-worker with Rev. Jones at the time of his death and is now a member of the Tennessee conference. There are two children, John and Louise, both born in Cartersville.

Books about Sam Jones are: Sam Jones' Sermons and Sayings, 1885; Sam Jones' Own Book with Autobiography, 1886; Life and Sayings of Sam P. Jones, 1907, which was compiled by Mrs. Jones and Rev. Holcomb; Thunderbolts by Sam P. Jones. He contributed weekly letters to The Atlanta Journal until his death.

MR. AND MRS. WILLIAM JESSE NEEL

William Jesse Neel, a son of Captain Joseph L. and Mary Swain Neel, was born in Adairsville, February 15, 1861. He attended the common schools, Col. Fitten's school in Adairsville, and the North Georgia Agricultural College at Dahlonega.

In 1884 he read law with his brother, J. M. Neel, in Cartersville and wrote for the county paper clever articles under the nom de plume, "The Tattler Talks".

In 1885 when Cleveland became president of the United States, William J. Neel received a departmental appointment in Washington While in this service he entered the Georgetown University Law School from which he graduated with first honor in 1888. His efficiency in the public service was such that he rapidly won promotion until he became chief of the Indian Division in the Treasury Department in 1887, serving until July, 1889, when he resigned his office and returned to Georgia. He was a law partner with McHenry and Nunnally in Rome until 1894.

He identified himself with the affairs of the town and county and in 1892-3 represented Floyd county in the general assembly. He was a member of the city council; served as mayor pro tem and with Hon. Seaborn Wright helped purge Rome of saloons.

He was an active force in the Baptist church while living in Rome, and in Cartersville served as a deacon and superintendent of the Sunday school for years. He was a trustee of Hearn Institute and Mercer University.

William J. Neel was especially gifted as an orator and writer.

Journalism and literature lost when he gave his splendid talents to the law. At the time he left Rome and came to Cartersville to live, an editorial from The Rome Tribune wrote, "The world needs you, Will Neel—needs your white soul, high purpose, gentle ways and Christian example".

He and his wife settled in Cartersville, in 1905, where he continued his practice and despite ill health was urged to run for the legislature. While in the house of representatives from Bartow county, he, with Covington and Hardman, introduced a State-wide prohibition bill* which he felt was the crowning joy of his life. He died at his home in Cartersville, March 24, 1907 and is buried in the city cemetery.†

In June, 1892 W. J. Neel married Isa Williams, a daughter of Alfred C. and Harriett Elizabeth Beall Williams. Mr. Williams, who died in 1891, came with his family from Villa Rica in 1858 to Cartersville where he established a lucrative mercantile business and lived in east Cartersville. Mrs. Williams was born in May, 1835 in Campbell county, Ga. She died in Cartersville on July 19, 1925, leaving three daughters of her ten children. Harriett E. (Lillie) married Henry J. Porter who started business in 1889 with J. W. Vaughan in Cartersville and later became a prominent merchant in Birmingham, Ala. and New Orleans, La., and died in December, 1931. "Fannie" married J. W. Vaughan, by whom there are James, Francis, Charles W., Elizabeth (White), Ruth (Williford, dec.), and Irma.

Isa Williams (Neel) graduated from Mary Sharpe College in 1882 and assisted her aunt, Mrs. Brame, with her private school in Cartersville. Later she studied languages at Berlitz College in Germany. In 1911 she became president of the Georgia Baptist Woman's Missionary Union and has served twenty consecutive years as president of this body of women. She has served as vice-president of the Southern B. W. M. U., and was chosen as the Union's representative to the Latin-American Congresses in Panama and Havana and to the Baptist World Alliances in Stockholm and Toronto. In November, 1931 she was elected vice president of the Georgia Baptist Convention. Mentally and culturally equipped, Mrs. Neel has been prominent in civic, literary, and religious activities of the State, but her greatest efforts have been expended in service through the Baptist denomination.

In 1931 she was honored by Mercer University by having conferred upon her the degree of doctor of laws—the first woman to have received a degree from this institution. In September, 1932 she accepted the chair of sociology at Bessie Tift College in Forsyth, Ga.

MAJOR CHARLES H. SMITH
("Bill Arp")

The Georgia philosopher, Charles Henry Smith, was born at

---

*Acts of 1907, p. 81.
†See "Men of Mark in Georgia".

Lawrenceville, Ga., June 15, 1826. His father, Asahel Reid Smith, was born in Vermont of Scotch-Irish descent, and came, in 1817, to Gwinnett county where he first taught school and became a prominent merchant. His mother, Caroline Maguire, was a daughter of an Irish refugee, James Maguire, and was born in Charleston, S. C. The tragic story of Caroline Maguire and her brother is told in Maj. Smith's, "From the Uncivil War to Date".

Charles H. Smith grew up as a "town boy" and attended the old field schools, and later Franklin College. In 1849 he married Mary Octavia Hutchins, daughter of Judge N. L. Hutchins of the Oconee circuit, and after his marriage he began the study of law. In 1851 they moved to Rome, Ga., where his brother was practicing medicine, and in 1852 he became a law partner of Judge John W. H. Underwood, an unusual partnership which continued for thirteen years.

In the spring of 1861 after the proclamation of President Lincoln "to disperse in twenty days", Mr. Smith wrote a "decently sarcastic" answer which he read to a group of friends on a street in Rome. Among them were Dr. Miller, Judge Underwood and a countryman, William Earp. After hearing the article, Bill Earp* of Kingston was standing near and asked Mr. Smith if he was going to publish the article. When Mr. Smith told him that he might, Bill Earp asked him what name he was going to sign to it and when he said he didn't know, Bill Earp said, "Well, Squire, I wish you would put mine, for them's my sentiments"; and thus was the nom de plume of Mr. Smith adopted and made famous.

Mr. Smith went to Virginia where the Confederates were fighting and served as major on the staff of General Bartow. After Gen. Bartows' death in the battle of Manassas, Maj. Smith was transferred to Gen. G. T. Anderson's staff where he served for 18 months. He was appointed in 1863 by President Davis to assist Judge Nisbet in trying treason cases and he was judge advocate general of the military court at Macon, where his knowledge of law served his country more than his gun. He was among those who accompanied Mr. Davis on his humiliating flight from Millen to Macon. At the approach of Wilson's raid on Macon, he left for Lawrenceville where his wife had refugeed in '64. At Yellow river, hearing of Stoneman's raiders ahead, rather than have the enemy obtain them, Maj. Smith tied the records of the treason court in a carpet bag to a rock and dropped them in the river.

During the war, while connected with George Adair and E. Y.

---

*The original Bill Arp spelled his name Earp. In a re-printed article from The Fort Worth (Texas) Daily Democrat in 1877, was this notice, "Bill Earp, late of Georgia, the man who furnished the witticism and odd sayings which Charles H. Smith prepared and published some years ago, was accidentally killed near his place, Decatur, Tex., last Monday, March 5. He fell from a wagon loaded with corn, the wheels passing over his neck killed him instantly. He was a remarkable man; perfectly illiterate, but replete with original ideas and witty sayings." He lived near the Branson place at Kingston.

Clark in editing The Southern Confederacy in Atlanta, he began to write letters under the title of "The Roman Runagee" and continued them until after the war. With his native courage and wit he wrote these letters of the refugee period during the desolations of war and the unspeakable indignities of reconstruction at a propitious time for the Southern heart, and demonstrated Maj. Smith's theorem of the livableness of life. This "subloomnary world" was a favorite expression and it was expertly depicted by "Bill Arp".

In January, 1865 Maj. Smith returned with his family to Rome and he with a little salvage of his pre-war property, started a store. Later he practiced law with Judge Joel Branham. While living in Rome Maj. Smith served in the senate from Floyd county in 1865-66, and as mayor of the city in 1868. Maj. Smith's sisters and brothers married into the Wade Cochran and J. C. Sproull families of Rome.

In 1877 Maj. Smith with his family came to Bartow and bought the old Fontaine farm (now the Pyron farm) on the Tennessee road, where he engaged in farming and writing. During the 80's when his lectures took him away from home a great deal of the time, they moved to Cartersville where their home, called "The Shadows",* was on Erwin street. Here Maj. and Mrs. Smith often entertained, and many noted men of Georgia were guests. He was a beloved character; a kindly, sweet-natured man devoted to his family and friends.

The children of Charles H. and Octavia Hutchins Smith were: Hines Maguire of Chattanooga, Tenn.; Royal Randolph of Atlanta; Harriett Hutchins married G. H. Aubrey of Cartersville; Frank Clifton of Los Angeles, Calif.; Victor (dec.); Marian Caroline, who has just written and published, "I Remember"; Stella Octavia married Robert Brumby (dec.); Ralph E., born in Rome, graduated from the Atlanta Medical College in 1891, practiced medicine and surgery and lived in Jacksonville, Fla., for 35 years until his death in September, 1932; Carl Holt of Mexico City; Jessie married W. W. Young of Cartersville.

Mark Twain stated to "Personal Intelligence" in The New York Herald that Bill Arp was one of the few real American humorists. He often wrote in the style of Josh Billings, that of an illiterate person, humorously misspelling, but always to the point of the subject at hand. Maj. Smith had no set plan for his work as a writer. He undertook a task when the notion seized him and could write as well with children playing about his knees, or persons talking in his room, as when alone in his library. He was a constant reader and his lecture trips over the South produced a source of fresh facts.

For twenty-five years before his death he wrote a letter every Sunday for The Atlanta Constitution. His other publications in book form are: Fireside Sketches; From the Uncivil War to Date; Peace

---
*Location is now the home of Mrs. H. R. Maxwell.

Papers; Bill Arp's Scrap Book; and his first book, Bill Arp, so-called, A Side Show of the Southern Side of the War, published by The Metropolitan Record Office in New York, 1866.

Major Smith died on Aug. 24, 1903, and is buried in Cartersville. After his death an editorial writer said of him, "We cannot say that he was the best man in the South, but we do say that he was one of the best loved men".

GEN. WILLIAM TATUM WOFFORD

William Tatum Wofford was born in Habersham county, Ga., on June 28, 1824. His grandfather, Benjamin J. Wofford, came to Cass county with his relatives and died on March 2, 1836, aged 68, and is buried on Stamp creek. His father, William Hollingsworth Wofford was born in Habersham and died young. His mother was Nancy M. Tatum Wofford, 1791-1867.

William T. Wofford attended the common schools in Habersham and a school in Lawrenceville until he entered Franklin College from which he graduated about 1840. He began the study of law in Athens and was admitted to the bar there in 1854. He immediately located at Cassville where he attained eminence as a lawyer, and after the Civil War he was a member of the Cartersville bar.

In 1847 he raised a company of cavalry and went to Mexico to join in the war between the United States and that country. He distinguished himself and for his conduct was complimented by a public resolution of the Georgia General Assembly in 1850: "Also to Capt. Wm. T. Wofford, of Georgia, Mounted Battalion of volunteers, for service rendered in a battle with a very superior number of guerillas at Matesordera".*

He returned to his home near Cass Station, and in 1849 was elected to the house of representatives from Cass and served two terms. He did not aspire to a seat in the next house, but was elected clerk for the 1853/1854 term. Governor Towns, in recognition of his qualities for leadership, appointed him a delegate to the Southern Commercial Congress at Montgomery, Ala.

On Aug. 16, 1859, he married Julia A. Dwight, daughter of Dr. Samuel B. and M. A. Dwight of Murray county, by whom there were three little daughters who died in infancy. One daughter (dec.), Lena, grew to womanhood in the county and married W. I. Harley of Sparta, Ga. There are two sons, Wofford and William. Mrs. W. T. Wofford died Sept. 9, 1878 and is buried beside her husband.

Captain Wofford was elected a delegate to the National Democratic convention at Charleston, S. C., in April, 1860, and carried his county against disunion as a delegate to the Secession convention in Milledgeville in 1861.

He entered the war as a captain, but at the organization of the 18th Georgia regiment at Camp Brown in April, 1861, he was elected colonel. On Jan. 17, 1863, he was commissioned brigadier-general

---
*Acts of 1850, p. 415.

and his brigade was composed of the 16th, 18th, 24th Georgia regiments, Cobb's Legion, Phillip's Legion.

In the battle of Chancellorsville, on the 5th of May, 1863, and in the second battle of Fredericksburg, he did conspicuous service. In the first battle his brigade was on the right of Lee's army. He saw the Federal troops moving back when Jackson struck them, and begged to be permitted to charge the enemy's flank.

At the fateful heights of Gettysburg he added to his growing military reputation. On the third day of this fight, Gen. Longstreet sent for Gen. Wofford and carried him to Gen. Lee, who questioned him closely as to the progress of the charge he had made the day before. Gen. Wofford said he believed he could have taken the heights if supported. Gen. Longstreet asked him if he believed he could do it then. Wofford with deep reluctance said he did not think they could be carried at all, strengthened as they must have been during the night.

Gen. Longstreet, in his recommendation for a promotion said, "Gen. Wofford was distinguished by the energy and rapidity of his attack, and the skill and gallantry with which he handled his brigade." Lt. Gen. Anderson endorsed, "Gen. Wofford has constantly exhibited superior head courage and ability." Gen. Lee said Gen. Wofford had "always acted with boldness and judgment, displaying great zeal and promptness." Gen. Wofford was twice wounded—in the battle of the Wilderness and in the battle of Spottsylvania.

In 1865 Gen. Wofford was elected to the Federal Congress from the Seventh district, but Georgia was considered out of the Union and he was not allowed his seat. Later a younger hero was chosen instead of this older one. After the war he lived on what is known as the M. L. Johnson place.

He was a delegate from his senatorial district to the Constitutional convention in 1877. He was mentioned for governor after Bullock.

On Oct. 2, 1880, he married Margaret Langdon of Atlanta.

Gen. Wofford was gentle by nature and popular with his people. He was tactful and charitable. He died at his home near Cass Station on the 22nd of May, 1884, and was buried with a simple ceremony at his request in the Cassville cemetery.

PIERCE MANNING BUTLER YOUNG

Pierce Manning Butler Young, a son of Dr. Robert M. and Caroline Jones Young, was born Nov. 15, 1836, at Spartanburg, S. C., and came with his family to Cass county in 1840. He was a descendant of a patriotic family of South Carolina.

Up to his fourteenth year he was in delicate health, but he entered the Georgia Military Institute at Marietta, then under the superintendency of Col. Brumby, and in five years graduated with honor. In 1857, John H. Lumpkin, congressman from the Seventh district, procured his appointment to the United States Military

1. William Jesse Neel. 2. Isa Williams Neel (donated by Mrs. W. J. Neel). 3. Mark A. Cooper at the age of 70. 4. Gen. P. M. B. Young. 6. Col. Carl Boyd (donated by Mrs. G. M. Boyd, Sr.).

Academy at West Point, and while there he made lasting friendships with men who, in less than four years, were distinguished officers upon a field of battle. Among them were Gen. Custer and Gen. Kelly.

In the graduating class of 1861, in March, after his native State and Georgia had seceded, Cadet Young resigned to enter Confederate service. He first reported for duty at Charleston where he took part in the attack upon Fort Sumter. His patriotic ardor drove him to Montgomery where he offered his services to President Davis. While on a fifteen days' leave of absence at home he received orders to report to Gen. Bragg, then commanding at Pensacola, Fla., and was made Apr. 1, 1861, a second lieutenant in the artillery corps. Artillery service did not have enough dash to suit him and immediately after the battle of Manassas he went to Richmond where he entered into the thick of battle. On Aug. 15, he was appointed adjutant in Gen. Cobb's Legion, destined to become a famous body of soldiery.

He remained in Richmond until in October, 1861, he was elected lieutenant-colonel of Benning's regiment, but at the solicitation of Col. T. R. R. Cobb, he accepted the position of major, commanding cavalry and was ordered to Yorktown. In October he with his command checked McClellan's advance on Richmond.

On Nov. 15, 1862, he was appointed lieutenant-colonel in Cobb's Legion and was active in campaigns in northern Virginia and in Maryland.

On Sept. 13, 1862 at Burkeville, just before the battle of Fredericksburg while leading a brilliant charge with violent fury and heedless of danger, Col. Young was struck in the leg and his horse was killed under him. As he was lying in the path of the charge, he waved his hat, held up his wounded leg—the horse lying on his good one—and shouted, "Give 'em hell, boys, give 'em hell"!

In January, 1863*, he was appointed colonel† of Cobb's Legion and followed Gen. Lee to Gettysburg and highly distinguished himself on that bloody and memorable field. On the return of the army he was again seriously wounded in the breast, while in command of a cavalry brigade, at the conflict near Brandy Station in August§. On Sept. 28, 1863, he was made brigadier-general of cavalry and assigned to Gen. J. E. B. Stuart's corps.

He always fought in the front ranks with a charged sabre and with Napoleonic strategy. On the battle field he looked like a mounted oriflamme, a banner for his own troops and a target for the enemy. His military bearing won for him the immortal titles of "dashing" and "gallant". He was generous in appreciation of a fellow officer in arms. There is a story of a charge he made down a railroad cut to capture a strongly-posted Federal battery. As he swept

---
*Date from his scrap book.
†The date of appointment on his monument is Nov. 1, 1862.
§His official report of this battle is in Rebellion Records, Vol. XXVII, p. 732.

along at the head of a thousand troopers, one of his aides said, "This is not war; it is suicide; do you realize what you are doing?" "I do", was the light response, "I'll be a major general or in ———— in half an hour."

In October, 1863, he saved the commissary and quartermaster train of the Army of Northern Virginia by a bluff. He covered the hills with dismounted men and one piece of artillery, making enough noise to make the enemy think there was a corps instead of just a few hundred men.

In the battle at Ashland, Va., June 1st, 1864, Gen. Young was again severely wounded. On Nov. 15, 1864, he was promoted to the rank of major-general.

One of his most daring exploits was the capture and raid of a corral of cattle which Gen. Grant had brought together as a base of supplies on the Chickahominy in 1864. Together with Gen. Hampton, they were able to capture the cattle for their own supplies.

When Gen. Sherman had almost invested Savannah in 1864, Gen. Young by daring strategy saved 13,000 Confederates from being captured, by leading the Confederates out of the city before their way of escape was closed. At the close of the war he was fighting near Augusta two days after the official surrender.

Gen. Young was the youngest major-general in either the Southern or Northern armies and was mentioned seven times in general orders for gallant conduct in the face of the enemy. He has been called "Georgia's Henry of Navarre" and was considered one of the "beaux sabreur" of the Confederacy. His only reproach as a soldier was a love of display.

After the war he came to his home in Bartow. In October, 1868 Gen. Young was elected to the Fortieth Congress from the Seventh Georgia district and was re-elected successively to the Forty-first, Forty-second and Forty-third. While at Washington he added much dash to Washington society where he was always popular. He made a colorful congressman and served his constituents to the best of his ability. It was not an easy time for a democratic representative. He was placed on the military committee of the lower house of Congress and was made one of the board of visitors ordered by Congress to West Point—an honor given to no other Southern man after the Civil War up to that time. Gen. Young was not only the youngest congressman but the best looking!

Summoned from private life, in 1878 he was appointed one of the United States Commissioners to the Paris Exposition by President Hayes. He was a delegate to the National Democratic Conventions of 1868, 1876 and 1880.

In July, 1885 President Cleveland appointed him consul-general to St. Petersburg, Russia, but while in Washington, D. C., on leave of absence in December, 1886, Gen. Young resigned his position at St. Petersburg on account of the effect the severe climate had upon his health.

On Nov. 25, 1892 he was commissioned by Gen. J. B. Gordon major-general commanding the Georgia division of the United Confederate veterans, to be in effect until his successor was elected. The local camp of Confederate veterans was named in his honor.

In March, 1893 Gen. Young was appointed American minister to Guatemala and Honduras, Central America, and on April 12, 1893, he was formally installed. Trade and friendly relations were encouraged by appointing a man of Gen. Young's attributes.

Gen. Young, though popular with the ladies, never married and when his appointment from "cold" Russia to "hot" Guatemala came, someone wrote:

"All hail, the gallant Georgian
Who goes to Guatemala,
To bear aloft our country's flag
And eat the hot tamale!—
The nation's int'rests will be safe
With such a pink of duty,
But how will fare it with the heart
Of some Honduran beauty?"

Gen. Young at one time was engaged to Miss Mattie Ould of Richmond, Va., a famous beauty and noted for her repartee. One evening while in her father's library, her head resting on her lover's shoulder, the father entered unexpectedly. Shocked and indignant, he approached Gen. Young when with her ready wit she said, "Oh, father dear, it's nothing. It is not the first time an Ould head has been put on Young shoulders"!

A soldier who loved battle and the opportunity it offers to bravery and skill died of a slow disease. He returned to New York from Central America, broken in health and died July 6, 1896 in the Presbyterian hospital in New York City. He was buried in Oak Hill cemetery at Cartersville with the greatest pomp and ceremony ever seen in Cartersville. The funeral was held in the Sam Jones tabernacle and the Confederate veterans and Masons had charge. Talks were made by Gen. C. A. Evans, Col. C. D. Phillips and Judge J. W. Akin. An imposing monument marks the last bivouac of a brave soldier and patriotic citizen of Bartow county.

ASA G. CANDLER, JACOB ELSAS, GEO. T. WOFFORD

Men who have lived here a short time to achieve success and wealth elsewhere were the late Asa G. Candler, the late Jacob Elsas and George T. Wofford.

Asa Griggs Candler apprenticed himself to Sayre & Kirkpatrick, druggists in Cartersville from July 1, 1870 to January, 1873. He worked all day, read and studied at night, and slept on a cot in the drug store. After serving his apprenticeship here he went to Atlanta where in the course of years he had a drug store of his own and by 1892 the Coca-Cola Company was organized with Mr. Candler as president. He is further identified with Atlanta history.

Jacob Elsas, a native of Germany, began his business career in a log store in Cartersville, later building a brick store that was destroyed during the Civil War. In the seventies he removed to Atlanta where he became one of the city's industrial pioneers and founder of the Fulton Bag and Cotton Mills. At the time of his death on March 6, 1932, he was considered one of the most prominent men of Atlanta.

George T. Wofford, although born in Forsyth county on Dec. 15, 1868, came to Bartow with his parents when just a month old. A son of Eliphaz and Pacific Wofford, members of old Raccoon Baptist church and farmers in the county, he was educated in the county under Prof. Ryals. At the age of 21 he entered the Sullivan & Crampton Business College in Atlanta and after graduation filled several bookkeeping positions. He was transferred as head bookkeeper of the Standard Oil Company to Birmingham on Jan. 1, 1898, where he became chief clerk and assistant manager. In 1902 he started his own company under the name of the Wofford Oil Company on a small scale. In 1918, after experimenting with the surplus benzol that had been manufactured in Birmingham during the World War, he developed the fact that benzol could be used as a motor fuel by blending it properly with gasoline. In March, 1918, Woco-Pep was born and introduced to the motoring public by the Wofford Oil Company of Alabama. The name WO-CO is derived from the company name. Mr. Wofford owns and is president of the Wofford Bond & Mortgage Company in Birmingham. Mr. Wofford is related to the Wofford family in this county and in South Carolina. He is prominently identified wtih Birmingham, Ala.

COUNTY OFFICERS, 1933—Front row, left to right: Tax Receiver Smith Mansfield, Sheriff George W. Gaddis, Tax Collector John C. Haney, Ordinary R. M. Gaines. Back row: Commissioner A. V. Neal, Clerk of Superior Court W. B. Moss, Chairman of Board of Eductaion John K. Headden, Coroner G. W. Hendricks, School Superintendent P. W. Bernard.

CHAPTER XXIII

REGISTERS

JUSTICES OF THE INFERIOR COURT
Created Dec. 3, 1832

Samuel Mayes, 1833-34
James A. Thompson, 1833-34
Isaac L. Parker, 1833-33
James Orr, 1833-34
Nathaniel Wofford, 1833-34
Elias Pitner, 1834-36
John Murcheson, 1834-35
Malachi Jones, 1834-35
Elias Pitner, 1834-36
David Hargis, 1834-35
R. J. Loyless, 1834-37
S. P. Burnett, 1835-37
K. W. Hargrove, 1835-37
Samuel L. Chunn, 1835-37
John M. McTier, 1836-37
Cornelius D. Terhune, 1837-37
Ezekiel Milsaps, 1837-38
Samuel Smith, 1837-38
James Phillips, 1837-37
K. W. Hargrove, 1837-38
William L. Morgan, 1837-38
Andrew B. Cunningham, 1837-38
David Irwin, 1837-38
James Phillips, 1838-41
Cornelius D. Terhune, 1838-41
Reese McGregor, 1838-39
John Russel, 1838-41
Joseph Jones, 1839-
Henry Loyless, 1839-
David Lowry, 1840-41
Chester Hawks, 1841-42
Cornelius D. Terhune, 1841-42
Robert Hamilton, 1841-42
John S. Rowland, 1841-42
Samuel McDow, 1841-43
Charles M. Griffin, 1842-43
Garrison Linn, 1842-44 (resigned)
James Milner, 1842-45
William W. Clark, 1842-45

John Dobbs, 1843-45
Bryan Allen, 1843-45
Nathaniel Nicholson, 1844-45
Joseph Bogle, 1845-49
Nathaniel Nicholson, 1845-49
Joshua Bowdoin, 1845-49
James S. Elliott, 1845-48
Philip J. Guyton, 1845-49
Telamon Cuyler, 1848-49
William Hardin, 1849-53
Nathan Land, 1849-52
Wade S. Cothran, 1849-50 (resigned)
J. W. B. Summers, 1849-53
Donald M. Hood, 1849-52
Charles M. Griffin, 1850-53
John R. Towers, 1852-53
Thomas G. Barron, 1852 (declined)
Joel Foster, 1852-53
William Hardin, 1853-54
Joseph Bogle, 1853-54
William C. Wyly, 1853-57
Alfred M. Linn, 1853-57
George H. Gilreath, 1853-54
Nathan Howard, 1854-57
John W. Burke, 1854-55
John W. Henderson, 1854-57
Arthur Haire, 1855-57
Madison McMurry, 1857-61
Robert F. Wyly, 1857-58
William P. Rogers, 1857-60
James A. Maddox, 1857-61
Thompson Colbert, 1857-59
Augustine C. Wyly, 1858-59
E. V. Johnson, 1859-60
James C. Jones, 1859-61
William S. Thomas, 1860-61
Levi Branson, 1860-61

James C. Jones, 1861-61
John A. Terrell, 1861-61
Jesse R. Wikle, 1861-61

John Kennedy, Jr., 1861-61
B. O. Crawford, 1861-61
Robert C. Saxon, 1861-61

After change of name to Bartow county:

John A. Terrell, 1861-65
Jesse R. Wikle, 1861-62
John Kennedy, Jr., 1861-65
B. O. Crawford, 1861-65
Robt. C. Saxon, 1861 (declined)
Madison McMurry, 1862-65
Joseph L. Neel, 1862-65
J. L. Wikle, 1865-68

William T. Burge, 1865-66
John Kennedy, Jr., 1865-67
David A. Vaughan, 1865
B. O. Crawford, 1865-66
William J. Conyers, 1866-66
Thomas Tumlin, 1866-68
Jesse R. Wikle, 1867-68

CLERKS OF SUPERIOR COURT

(County officers with date of commissions. All created by Act of Dec. 3, 1832.)

Chester Hawks*, Mar., 1833-
Wm. M. Jones, Jan., 1840-
Arthur Haire, Jan., 1846-
Augustus C. Trimble, Jan, 1848-
Humphrey W. Cobb, Jan., 1850-
James Wofford, Jan., 1856-

Thomas A. Word, Jan., 1860-
F. M. Durham, July, 1880-
W. W. Roberts, Jan., 1895-
L. W. Reeves, Jr., Nov., 1900†-
W. C. Walton‡, 1902-
W. B. Moss, 1933-

CLERKS OF INFERIOR COURT

Leathern Rankin, March, 1833-
Wm. C. H. Smith, May, 1834-
Geo. B. Russell, Jan., 1836-
Arthur Haire, Jan., 1842-
Zachariah Aycock, Jan., 1846-
Elihu C.B. Christian, Aug., 1848-
Jonathan D. Phillips, Jan., 1850-

Wm. Thrailkill, Jan., 1852-(refused to qualify.
Jonathan D. Phillips, Apr., 1852-
David C. Ayers, Jan., 1854-
John F. Milhollin, Jan., 1855-
B. F. Godfrey, Jan., 1862-
Joseph S. Day, Jan., 1866-

ORDINARIES

(Created by constitutional amendment of Dec. 5, 1851; term of office four years. Acts 1851/52, p. 49)

Jonathan D. Phillips, Jan., 1851-
Thomas A. Word, Jan., 1852-
James W. Watts, Jan., 1856-
Nathan Land, Jan., 1861-

Jere A. Howard, Feb., 1864-
G. W. Hendricks, Jan., 1889-
Effie Hendricks, Jan., 1928-
R M. Gaines, Dec., 1928-

---

*Chester Hawks came to Cassville from Gwinnett county with his mother, who was formerly from Greenville district, S. C. He died in 1856, leaving his children: Peter, Mary m. Dr. Boyd of Rome, and Julius.

†After this date officers went into office beginning of calendar year.

‡William Clairborne Walton, b. April 6, 1871, is a son of Rev. Robert Hall Walton, graduate of Union Theological Seminary of Virginia and chaplain in Confederate army, died in Kingston in 1876, and Ann Thomas Lewis Walton of Virginia. There were six children. Besides W. C. there are Miss Minnie and Frank Walton at Cass Station, and Rev. Fletcher Walton. Mr. Walton married Persis Hall by whom there are six children.

SHERIFFS
(Created by Act of Dec. 3, 1832, p. 58)

Benjamin F. Adair, Mar., 1833-
Lewis Tumlin, Jan., 1834-
James Wofford, Jan., 1836-
Lewis Tumlin, Jan., 1838-
Joseph Bogle, Jan., 1840-
Zachariah Aycock, Apr., 1842-
Robert M. Linn, Jan., 1844-
Jacob O. Dyer, Jan., 1846-
Alfred M. Linn, March, 1848-
Thomas Booker, Jan., 1850-
John F. Brown, Jan., 1852-
Edward A. Brown, Jan., 1854-
Joseph Bogle, Jan., 1856-
John C. Aycock, Jan., 1858-
A. M. Franklin*, Jan., 1861-
Wm. L. Aycock, Jan., 1862-
A. M. Franklin, Feb., 1864-
Wm. L. Aycock, Jan., 1866-
W. W. Rich, May, 1868-
Christopher B. Conyers, Jan., 1873-resigned June, 1873.
James Kennedy,, July, 1873-
A. M. Franklin, Jan., 1875-
James Kennedy†, Jan., 1879-
A. M. Franklin, March, 1880-
J. A. Gladden, Jan., 1883-
W. W. Roberts, Jan., 1885-
A. M. Franklin, Jan., 1887-
W. W. Roberts, Jan., 1889-
A. M. Franklin, Jan., 1891-
Leroy Burrough, Jan., 1893-
H. R. Maxwell, Oct., 1898-
R. L. Griffin, Dec., 1890
H. R. Maxwell, Oct., 1902-
T. W. Tinsley, Nov., 1906-
C. N. Smith, Nov., 1908-
W. W. Calloway, Nov., 1914-
W. E. Puckett, Dec., 1920-
G. W. Gaddis‡, June, 1922

TAX COLLECTORS

James R. Kinney, Apr., 1834-
Ezekiel Millsaps, Jan., 1835-
Mansfield Simmons, Jan., 1837-
Benj. Laughhedge, Jan., 1844-
Robert Russell, Jan., 1845-
Andrew Adams, Jan. 1847-
Moses M. Dillard, Jan., 1850-
Dempsey F. Bishop, Apr., 1851-
Silas Bell§, Jan., 1852-
William P. Rodgers, Jan., 1853-
John S. Owens, Jan., 1854-
John C. Aycock, Jan., 1856-
William G. Smith, Jan., 1857-
Riley Milam, Jan., 1860-
G. W. Brown, Jan., 1861-
G. W. Brown, Mar., 1862-
Daniel S. Ford, Aug., 1866-
Edward Harling, Oct., 1868-
Z. A. McReynolds, Feb., 1871-
J S. Owens, Jan., 1873-
William F. Corbin, Jan., 1875-
J. F. Sproull, Jan., 1877-

---

*Felix Drayton Franklin, 1792-1885, formerly of Md., came to Cass in 1835 from Warren Co. with his wife, Nancy, and children: Caroline m. W. W. Hannon and Lucius and W. F. Hannon are grandchildren; Augustus Montgomery, b. Apr. 19, 1820, m. Elizabeth Williams and their children were Alice (Morris, J. H.), Ada (Goodwin, H. B.), F. H., Carrie (Ginn, Luke).

†James Kennedy, b. in 1833 in Laurens district, S. C., came to Cass with his father, John Kennedy when three years of age; served in Confederate army; in 1866 married Fannie Dobbs, by whom there were six children. He died Feb. 21, 1886.

‡Born Aug. 29, 1883, in Cassville.

§Silas Bell, 1809-1883, was a prominent citizen in Wolf Pen district all his life; m. twice; by Susan Allen (d. 1932) there was W. T. Bell (d. 1932) who m. Gertrude Wischmeyer. Their children are Frederick and Irma Bell. A grandson, Silas Stinnett, lives at Sugar Hill.

W. W. Rich, Jan., 1879-
Bailey A. Barton, Jan., 1881-
J. F. Linn*, Jan., 1887-
W. W. Ginn, Jan., 1891-
J. M. Dysart, Jan., 1895-
J. M. Bohanan, Oct., 1896-
F. D. Smith, —— 1890-

Joseph Shaw, Oct., 1902-
F. V. Smith, Oct., 1904-
Joseph Shaw, Nov. 1906-'12, died
Chas. M. Shaw, May, 1915-
Nat Donahoo, Dec., 1916-
J. D. Pittard, Dec., 1920-
John C. Haney, Dec., 1928-

TAX RECEIVERS

Roney B. Hall, Jan., 1835-
Richard Baker, Jan., 1837-
Simeon Bogle, Jan., 1839-
Henry Williams, Jan., 1841-
William D. Walker, Jan., 1842-
Alex Stroup, Jan., 1847-
Humphrey Cobb, Jan., 1849-
Zachariah G. Turner, Jan., 1850-
Andrew M. Floyd, Jan., 1852-
William H. Puckett, Jan., 1854-
David H. Teat, Jan., 1857-
Calvin Allen, Jan., 1859-
A. F. Morrison, Jan., 1860-
D. F. Bishop, Feb., 1862-
Francis M. Durham, Mar., 1866-
Z. M. McReynolds, Aug., 1868-
W. T. Gordon, Feb. 6, 1871-
J. S. Bailey, Jan. 11, 1873-
A. M. Foute, Jan., 1875-

J. H. Walker, Jan., 1877-
W. W. Ginn, Jan., 1879-
Nathaniel Donahoo, Jan., 1887-
Albert Smith, Jan., 1891-
J. T. Bennett, Jan., 1893-
J. M. Anderson, Jan., 1895-
J. T. Bennett, Oct., 1896-
W. T. Pittard, Dec., 1890-
J. F. Bennett, Oct., 1902-
J. W. Adams, May, 1908-(unexpired term).
F. M. Willis, Nov., 1908-
T. A. Hughes, Nov., 1910-
W. T. Pittard, Oct., 1912-
John C. Haney, Nov., 1914-
J. A. Ingram, Dec., 1920-
Smith Mansfield, Dec., 1928-
John C. Haney, Mar., 1932-

SURVEYORS

Nealy Goodwin, Mar., 1833-
Samuel Flournoy, Jan., 1838-
George W. Hill†, Jan., 1840-
Reuben H. Pierce, Jan., 1842- commission returned.
Joushley Jones, Jan., 1844-
A. L. Sylar, Jan., 1846-
William Latimer, Jan., 1850- commission returned-
David House, Jan., 1854-

Edwin R. Hawkins, Jan., 1856-
David House, Jan., 1858-
B. H. Leeke, ——, 1860-
R. H. Cannon, Feb., 1864-
George W. Hill, Jan., 1866-
Henry J. McCormick, Jan., 1873-
George W. Hill, Jan., 1877-
D. W. K. Peacock, Jan., 1881-
Henry J. McCormick, Jan., 1887-
C. W. Jones, Jan., 1893-

---

*Died July 13, 1889. His sons, F. L., J. H. and R. L. Linn live in Folsom district. Their mother was a daughter of Tarleton Lewis, who is buried at Flexatile.

†Born Dec. 17, 1810 in Rutherford county, N. C.; m. in 1832, Sarah Adaline Hill who died and is buried in this county. He first came to this county in 1838 as a school teacher. In 1868 he married Rebecca F. Hancock of this county. They later removed to McLennan county, Tex., where he died in 1888.

H. J. McCormick, Jan., 1895-
Hill J. Jolly, Oct., 1896-
R. R. Smith, Oct., 1898-

W. W. Phillips, Nov., 1906-
W. W. Daniel, Oct., 1912-
W. W. Phillips, Nov., 1914-

CORONERS

John Pack, March, 1833-
Joseph Gladden, May, 1834-
Joseph Hargis, Jan., 1836-
John G. Guerineau, Jan., 1838-
Joshua Gibson, Jan., 1840-
John G. Guerineau, Jan., 1842-
Barney Mitchell, March, 1843-
Joshua Gibson, Jan., 1844-
Richard Gaines, Jan., 1850-commission returned-
Richard Gaines, Jan., 1852-
N. G. Hilburn, Feb., 1862-
J. M. Lackey, Aug., 1868-
William E. Earp, Feb., 1871-

James H. Harrison, Jan., 1874-
D. B. Mull, Jan., 1875-
C. M. Gladden, Jan., 1879-
D. B. Mull, Jan., 1881-
A. M. Willingham, Jan., 1883-
J. B. Rowland, Jan., 1885-
J. Frank Patterson, Jan., 1887-
W. C. Walton, Jan., 1895-
J. F. Patterson, Oct., 1898-
W. J. Ingram, Dec., 1890-
J. H. Harrison, Oct., 1902-
W. J. Ingram, Nov., 1910-
G. W. Hendricks, Dec., 1928-

CHAIRMAN OF THE COUNTY COMMISSIONERS

G. M. Boyd,, 1917-18
G. M. Boyd, 1919-20,
Hamilton C. Stiles, 1921-,
M. L. Upshaw, 1923-
B. B. Branson, 1925-
A. V. Neal, 1927-

G. H. Gilreath, clerk.
J. J. Calhoun, clerk
W. W. Calloway, clerk
R. W. Dent, clerk
R. G. Gilreath, clerk
A. C. Jolly, clerk

TREASURERS
(Abolished after Dec. 31, 1916)

John C. Maddox, Aug., 1867-
J. H. Cobb, Aug., 1868-
A. M. Foute, Feb., 1871-
B. F. Godfrey, Jan., 1873-
H. W. Cobb, Jan., 1875-
J. M. Smith, Jan., 1891-
H. W. Cobb, Jan., 1893-

John H. Cobb, June, 1894, appointed by Ordinary-
B. F. Godfrey, Jan., 1895-
John H. Cobb, Oct., 1898-
W. H. Milner, Oct., 1902-
John H. Cobb, Oct., 1904-
Martin Collins, Nov., 1910-
George H. Gilreath, Nov., 1914-

By an act* the office of treasurer was abolished, making the clerk of the board of county commissioners act as ex-officio treasurer. By an act in 1924† the county board of commissioners was abolished and after Jan. 1, 1927, a single commissioner of roads and revenues was provided for and to be elected by popular vote, to hold office for a term of four years.

---

*Act of 1915, p. 151.
†Acts of 1924, p. 276.

Arthur V. Neal: b. Sept. 9, 1871 in Bartow county; farmer; worked for seventeen years with Knight Mercantile Company in Cartersville, Ga.; named deputy sheriff; elected county commissioner on Jan. 1, 1927; member and steward of the Methodist church; Mason, member of Junior Order; m. in 1911 Lillie Warlick by whom there are Mary Sue, A. V. Neal, Jr., Katherine and Virginia (twins), and Bobby Neal.

OFFICERS IN THE MUSTER ROLLS OF THE CONFEDERATE STATES ARMY IN BARTOW COUNTY*

1st Regiment Georgia Volunteer Infantry, 1st Co. E, "Etowah Infantry".† Mar. 18, 1861. One of the four companies to form the 1st Georgia Independent Battalion; Peter H. Larey, Capt., Maj., Apr. 1861; William H. Howard, Jr.‡, 1st Lt., Capt. 60th Regt., Co. K; Geo. J. Howard, 2nd Lt., 1st Lt.; Thomas R. Sproull, Jr. 2nd Lt.; George W. Warwick, 1st Sergt,. Jr. 2nd Lt.; Theodoscius F. Stephens, 2nd Sergt.; James M. Goldsmith, 3rd Sergt., 2nd Lt., 1st Lt. 60th, Co. K; Jacob Jonas, 4th Sergt, 2nd Sergt.; Richard H. Chapman, 1st Corp.; Samuel C. P. Larey, 2nd Corp., Jr. 2nd Lt.; Henry T. Jones, 3rd Corp., 4th Sergt.; Augustus R. Churchill, 4th Corp; John C. Sims, surgeon.

1st Regiment Georgia, Volunteer Infantry, 2nd Co. E, May 1, 1862: Thomas J. Massey, Capt.; Thomas B. Cox, 1st Lt.; Wyatt E. Sanders, 2nd Lt.; Andrew E. Small, Jr. 2nd Lt.; James Postell McKay (or McCay), 1st Sergt.; L. D. Horne, 2nd Sergt.; O. Hambright, 3rd Sergt.; William M. Goodwin, 4th Sergt.; William L. Braswell, 5th Sergt.; Felix G. Smith, 1st Corp.; Daniel F. Griffin, 2nd Corp.; William Foster, 3rd Corp.; William S. Sullivan, 4th Corp.; Thomas P. Bennett, musician; Gustavus A. Hornaday, musician.

14th Regiment Georgia Volunteer Infantry, Co. K, July 9, 1861: Thomas F. Jones, Capt.; John P. Burge, 1st Lt.; E. Franklin Field, 2nd Lt.; Washington L. Goldsmith, Jr. 2nd Lt., 1st Lt., Capt., 1861, Maj. 1863, Lt.-Col. 1864; G. Washington Chapman, 1st Sergt., 1st Lt., 1863; John C. Allen, 2nd Sergt.; Augustus Y. Chapman, 3rd Sergt., 1st Sergt.; James M. Dobbs, 4th Sergt.; R. Augustus Holt, 1st Corp., Capt., 1863; J. Samuel Jones, 2nd Corp.; Robert P. Milam, 3rd Corp.; James M. Fields, 4th Corp.; Andrew J. Goldsmith, pvt., 3rd Sergt., 1st Lt., 1864; Thomas Carter Moore, Pvt., Jr. 2nd Lt., Capt. and A. C. S., 1862, Adj., Asst. A. C. S., P. A. C. S., 1865.

18th Regiment Georgia Volunteer Infantry, Co. F, June 13, 1861, "Davis Guards": Joel Cole Roper, Capt.; W. B. Centre, 1st Lt.; Andrew F. Wooley, 2nd Lt., 1st Lt., Aide-de-camp to Gen. Wofford, Capt. and Adj.-Gen., May 23, 1863; John Forsyth Hardin, Jr. 2nd Lt.,

---
*From war records in Georgia Soldier Roster Commission, State Capitol. The local U. D. C. is interested in having these officers in the history until the complete compilation is finished by Miss Lillian Henderson.
†See pp. 211-13.
‡A brother of Geo. J. Howard and his widow married Gen. Evans.

2nd Lt., 1st Lt., Capt., 1863; John Roland, 1st Sergt.; J. W. Forrest, 2nd Sergt.; A. J. Earp, 3rd Sergt.; John C. Reynolds, 4th Sergt, 2nd Lt., 1st Lt., 1863; James A. Cantrell, 5th Sergt.; William J. Brandon, 1st Corp., 2nd Lt.; Thomas W. Dodd, 2nd Corp.; Thomas Galphin, 3rd Corp., 2nd Sergt.; John D. Murchison, 4th Corp.; Jefferson R. Brandon, Pvt., Jr. 2nd Lt., 2nd Lt., Nov. 1863; Benjamin F. Reynolds, Pvt., Jr. 2nd Lt.

18th Regiment Georgia Volunteer Infantry, Co. G,, "Lewis Volunteers", May 1 ,1861: John C. Maddox, Capt.; Farish Carter Tate, 1st Lt.; George Washington Maddox, 2nd Lt., 1st Lt., Capt., Sept. 5, 1862; Jesse M. Powers, Jr. 3rd Lt. and A. Q. M. in Nov., 1862; William Jones, 1st Sergt.; James B. Buice, 2nd Sergt.; James Fielding Maddox, 3rd Sergt.; Thomas E. Ripley, 4th Sergt.; Z. M. Harris, 5th Sergt., Jr. 2nd Lt., 1st Lt.; H. M. Brawner, 1st Corp.; J. W. Dykes, 2nd Corp.; A. M. D. Kelley, 3rd Corp.; J. G. Turner, 4th Corp.; Buck Harwell, fifer; D. M. Stradley, drummer; Peter C. Lyons, Pvt., Corp., 2nd Lt., 1st Lt., 1863; J. J. Marsh, surgeon.

18th Regiment Georgia Volunteer Infantry, Co. H, "Rowland Highlanders", June 13, 1861: Frank M. Ford, Capt., Lt.-Col., 1864, joined Gen. Wofford, 1865; William L. Wofford, 1st Lt., Aide-de-camp, 1863, reported to Gen. Wofford, 1865; John Grant, 2nd Lt., 1st Lt., Capt., March, 1864; W. D. Smith, Jr. 2nd Lt., 2nd Lt.; W. W. Cotton, 1st Sergt.; Jasper Vaughn, 2nd Sergt; J .V. Ford, 3rd Sergt; John T. Wofford, 4th Sergt., Q. M. Sergt.; Sanford R. Hampton, 5th Sergt.; H. K. Miller, 1st Corp.; W. H. Windsor, 2nd Corp.; Amos T. White, 3rd Corp.; F. M. Holden, 4th Corp.; J. W. Smith, color guard; G. W. Lawless, musician; James R. Rich, musician; George R. Smith, Pvt., Jr. 2nd Lt., 2nd Lt., 1st Lt., March, 1864.

18th Regiment Georgia Volunteer Infantry, Co. K, "Rowland Infantry", Mar. 1, 1861: John A. Crawford, Capt., assigned to commandant conscripts, 1864; W. G. Smith, 1st Lt.; Thomas Douthit, 2nd Lt.; Nat T. Wofford, Jr. 2nd Lt., 2nd Lt., 1st Lt., 1862; T. C. Underwood, 1st Sergt., Jr. 2nd Lt., 2nd Lt.; A. J. McMurray, 2nd Sergt., 2nd Lt., ordnance officer, 1st Lt., 1864; E. P. Price, 3rd Sergt., 2nd Lt., and enrolling officer; M. A. Smith, 4th Sergt. William Brown, 5th Sergt., 2nd Lt., 1st Lt., Capt., 1864; Baylus M. Langley, 1st Corp.; J. V. Smith, 2nd Corp.; John B. Scott, 3rd Corp.; J .P. Smith, 4th Corp.; John W. Box, musician; D. R. Floyd, musician; John Loudermilk, Pvt., Sergt.-Maj., 1861.

18th Regiment Georgia Volunteer Infantry, Co. K, "Kingston Vcls.", June 11, 1861, (Original muster roll) Camp McDonald: John W. Hooper, Jr., Capt., Maj., 1863; Joseph Dunlap, 1st Lt.; William M. Tumlin, 2nd Lt.; David L. Brownfield, Jr. 2nd Lt., 1st Lt., 1862; William C. Gaines, 1st Sergt., Jr. 2nd Lt.; Virgil M. Tumlin, 2nd Sergt.; James H. Dodd, 3rd Sergt.; James Reed, 4th Sergt.; William D. Adams, 5th Sergt..; Andrew J. Payne, 1st Corp.; James K. P. Dunlap, 2nd Corp.; George V. Vise, 3rd Corp.; Francis M. Martin, 4th Corp.; John L. Camper, 5th Corp.; Isaac A. Roe (Row), Pvt. 2nd

Lt., 1st Lt., Capt., Jan. 1863.

22nd Regiment Georgia Volunteer Infantry, Co. G, "Fireside Defenders", Bartow and Floyd counties, Aug. 30, 1861: J. J. Jones, Capt., Asst. Q. M., 1862; I. D. Ford, 1st Lt.; George W. Kinney (Kenney), 2nd Lt.; N. B. Ford, Jr. 2nd Lt.; W. F. Jones, 1st Sergt., 2nd Lt., 1st Lt., Capt., July, 1862; Stephen G. Rudy (Rhudy), 2nd Sergt.; S. B. Treadway, 3rd Sergt., 1st Lt., July, 1862; George W. Thomas, 4th Sergt., 2nd Lt., 1st Lt., Capt., Oct., 1862; T. L. Ellis, 1st Corp.; Franklin Bishop, 2nd Corp.; S. F. Woodruff, 3rd Corp.; 1st Sergt., Sergt.-Maj., 1862; William T. Sharpe, 4th Corp.; John H. Johnson, Pvt., 2nd Sergt., 1st Lt., Nov., 1862, commandant of conscripts, Ga. and Va., 1864; J. Joseph Jones, Jr., Pvt., Co. H, 4th Regt., Jr. 2nd Lt., 1st Lt., ordnance officer, 1864.

23rd Regiment Georgia Infantry, Co. A, Aug. 31, 1861: Benjamin C. Pool, Capt.; Clayton F. Irwin, 1st Lt.; William J. Boston, 2nd Lt., Capt., April, 1862, Maj., 1864, surrendered April, 1865; Tyre B. Davis, Jr. 2nd Lt., 2nd Lt., 1st Lt., 1864, Capt., Jan., 1865; W. F. Covington, 1st Sergt; Joseph L. Alexander, 2nd Sergt.; Thomas P. Costner, 3rd Sergt.; S. S. Goodwin, 4th Sergt.; Lumpkin Bruce, 1st Corp.; Joseph Logan, 2nd Corp.; D. J. Guyton, 3rd Corp.; George W. Hunt, 4th Corp.; John M. Brown, Pvt., Maj. 8th Regt. State Troops, Dec., 1861.

26th Regiment Georgia Volunteer Infantry, Co. G, "Bartow Light Infantry", Sept. 21, 1861. (Became Co. H, May 8, 1862): Benjamin F. Moseley, Capt.; C. H. M. Howell, 1st Lt., Capt., May 1862; Josiah H. Tillman, 2nd Lt.; Joseph A. Ousley, Jr. 2nd Lt.; A. J. Liles, 1st Sergt., Sergt.-Maj., Adj., 1862; G. S. Watts, 2nd Sergt.; L .C. Creech, 3rd Sergt.; William S. Abbott, 4th Sergt.; Alonzo M. Rushin, 1st Corp., 2nd Lt., 1st Lt., 1862; Daniel O. Zeigler, 2nd Corp., Jr. 2nd Lt., 2nd Lt..; John Aaron Carter, 3rd Corp.; Joseph W. Howell 4th Corp.; Perryman Carter, Pvt., 1st Lt., 1861; Henry H. Smith, Pvt., 1st Lt., 1862. Capt., Dec. 1862. "This company was organized Sept. 21, 1861 and went into camp, Liberty county, Ga., Sept. 24, 1861. Was ordered to Savannah Ga., Oct. 5, 1861. Ordered from Savannah to St. Simons Island, Ga. Feb. 17, 1862, but before reaching that point was ordered to Brunswick, Ga., arriving there Feb. 22, 1862."

36th Regiment Georgia Volunteer Infantry, Army of Tenn., Co. D, March 11, 1862; John Loudermilk, Capt., Maj., April 1864; Joseph Davis, 1st Lt.; Willis Martin, 2nd Lt., 1st Lt.; Henry Young, Jr. 2nd Lt.; D. W. Loudermilk, 1st Sergt. ,2nd Lt., 1863; William A. Deweese, 2nd Sergt., Jr. 2nd Lt.; Jesse Brown, 3rd Sergt.; T. M. Loudermilk, 4th Sergt.; Allen Henson, 5th Sergt.; James Morris, 1st Corp.; William W. Tracey, 2nd Corp.; William M. (W. T.) Mitchell, 3rd Corp.; Geo. W. Wheeler, 4th Corp., 1st Corp.

40th Regiment Georgia Volunteer Infantry, Co. B, Army of Tenn., "Howard Guards", Mar. 4, 1862: John M .Dobbs, Capt., surrendered as Capt. Co. A, April, 1865; Arnold J. Milner, 1st Lt.; Edward B. (or Edmund) Ford, 2nd Lt., 1st Lt., Oct., 1863; George W.

Satterfield, Jr. 2nd Lt., 2nd Lt., 1863; James P. Johnson, 1st Sergt.; Jason N. McElreath, 2nd Sergt.; Robert D. Moon, 3rd Sergt.; Robert G. Mays, 4th Sergt. Capt., and A. C. S., May, 1862; James P. Corban (Corbin), 5th Sergt., 1st Sergt., Mar., 1863; Augustus A. Skinner, 1st Corp., Q. M. Sergt.; David Heyman, 2nd Corp.; John Keys, 3rd Corp.; Solomon Herzberg, 4th Corp. "Between March 31, and April 17, 1865, the 40th, 41st and 43rd Regts., Ga. Vol. Inf., were consolidated to form the 40th Batt. Ga. Vol. Inf., and surrendered at Greensboro, N. C., April 26, 1865." War Record.

40th Regiment Georgia Volunteer Infantry, Co. H, Army of Tenn., Mar. 4, 1862: Joseph L. Neel, Capt., paroled Charlotte, N. C., May 6, 1865; Ebenezer Loveless, 1st Lt.; Z. B. Aycock, 2nd Lt.; W. I. (or W. J.) Swain, Jr. 2nd Lt., 1st Lt.. 1862; Richard W. Venable, 1st Sergt.; John H. King, 2nd Sergt.; T. F. Lynch, 3rd Sergt., Jr. 2nd Lt., 2nd Lt., 1865; G. W. T. Goldsmith, 4th Sergt.; William Nabors, 5th Sergt.; W. A. Williams, 1st Corp.; John L. Mosteller, 2nd Corp., 2nd Lt.; Jeremiah G. Mosteller, 3rd Corp.; F. M. Long, 4th Corp.

40th Regiment Georgia Volunteer Infantry, Co. I, Army of Tenn., March 4, 1862: Abda Johnson, Capt., Col., March, 1862, surrendered April 26, 1865; Erastus V. Johnson, 1st Lt.; James W. Wofford, 2nd Lt., 1st Lt., 1862; Thomas J. Dodd, Jr. 2nd Lt.; Joseph G. Lowry, 1st Sergt.; James C. Wofford, Pvt., 2nd Sergt., 1862; E. G. Hardy, 3rd Sergt.; Henry J. Wade, 4th Sergt.; John M. Grogan, 5th Sergt.; John W. Hardy, 1st Corp.; Richard L. Green, 2nd Corp.; James T. Casey, 3rd Corp.; John W. P. Best, Pvt., regimental surgeon, 1862; William A. Chunn, Pvt., 2nd Lt., 1st Lt. State Troops, Oct., 1861, Co. I; James Henry Carter, Pvt., Regm. Capt., and A. Q. M., May, 1862; Richard C. Carter, Pvt., Jr. 2nd Lt.; Thomas W. Dodd, Pvt., Capt.; Marion J. Dudley, Pvt., Asst. surg.; Henderson W. Fite, Pvt., Asst. Surg., Regm. Surg., Dec., 1863.

60th Regiment Georgia Volunteer Infantry, Army of Northern Va., Co. H, April 25, 1862: Moses Asbury Leake, Capt.; James C. Milam, 1st Lt.; Samuel H. Smith, 2nd Lt., Chaplain; R. Stiles Phillips, Jr. 2nd Lt., 2nd Lt., 1st Lt., Capt.; William H. Stiles, Jr., 2nd Lt., 1st Lt., Capt., Aug., 1863, A. Q. M., 1863; Thomas A. Owens, Jr. 2nd Lt. ,2nd Lt., 1st Lt., 1863; R. H. Couper, Jr. 2nd Lt., Lt. of Frazier's Battery, 1863; A. H. Rice, Jr. 2nd Lt., 2nd Lt.; Robert Milam, 1st Sergt., Aug.,1862; John H. Mayfield, 2nd Sergt; M.H. Snow, 3rd Sergt.; A. J. Jones, 4th Sergt.; H. N. Bailey, 5th Sergt.; Jesse J. Pritchett, 1st Corp. (W. R.); S. A. Bailey, 2nd Corp.; J. F. Cramer, 3rd Corp.; Joseph S. Humphreys, 1st Sergt.

60th Regiment Georgia Volunteer Infantry, Co. K, Army of Northern Va., May 10, 1862: William H. Howard, Jr., Capt.; James M. Goldsmith, 1st Lt.; H. N. Hagin, 2nd Lt.; J. C. Rhodes, Jr. 2nd Lt.; 2nd Lt.; G. W. Northcutt, 1st Sergt.; James J. Hagin, 2nd Sergt., 2nd Lt., Dec. 1862; W. H. Crew, 3rd Sergt.; W. R. Patterson, 4th

Sergt.; John White, 5th Sergt.; M. J. McElreath, 1st Corp.; Jackson Griffin, 2nd Corp.; William Griffin, 3rd Corp.; Joseph R. Green, 4th Corp.; W. B. Bishop, Pvt., 1st Sergt., 1863; O. F. Brintle, Pvt., 3rd Lt., 1862.

63rd Regiment Georgia Volunteer Infantry, Co. I, Army of Tenn., Bartow and Gordon counties, Dec. 23, 1863: Charles Wallace Howard, Capt.; William M. Bray, 1st Lieut.; W. B. C. Coker, 2nd Lt.; J. T. Howard, Jr. 2nd Lt.; J. T. Coker, Jr. 2nd Lt; W M. Carter, 1st Sergt.; J. M. Coker, 2nd Sergt.; D. W. Humphries, 3rd Sergt.; J. M. Hanson, 4th Sergt.; D. R. Conley, 5th Sergt.; L .S. Northcutt, 1st Corp.; D. G. Coker, 2nd Corp.; J. McClellan, 3rd Corp.; J. M. Thompson, 4th Corp.; H. C. Durham, Pvt., 4th Sergt., 1863, detailed M. D.; J. F. Henson, Pvt., 4th Corp.

8th Battalion, Georgia Volunteer Infantry, Co. A, Army of Tenn., Bartow and Floyd counties, July 15, 1861 (incomplete): Isaac Davis, Capt.; R. T. Fouche, Capt., 1864; Henry M. Lumpkin, 1st Lt., Capt., 1862; Sanford Venable, 2nd Lt., 1st Lt.; James M. Shaw, Jr. 2nd Lt.; R. B. Salmon, Jr. 2nd Lt.; W. B. Bell, 2nd Lt.; W. B. Baker, 1st Sergt.; W. Bell, 2nd Sergt.; J. W. Bridges, 3rd Sergt.; J. W. Allen, 4th Sergt.; J. L. Taylor, 1st Corp.; J. A. Reid, 2nd Corp.; C. Taylor, 3rd Corp.; J. W. Stubbs, 4th Corp.

1st Regiment Georgia State Troops, Co. F, Feb. 7, 1863: Elihu G. Nelson, Capt.; Thomas E. Dickerson, 1st Lt.; Isham Alley, 2nd Lt.; John D. Deaton, Jr. 2nd Lt.; A. M. Puckett, 1st Sergt., 2nd Lt., 1863; E. D. Puckett, 2nd Sergt.; James M. Smith, 3rd Sergt., 1st Sergt, 1863; J. M. Hardin, 3rd Sergt.; William S. (M) Sullens, 4th Sergt., 3rd Sergt.; James McMahan, 5th Sergt.; John F. Lindsey, 1st Corp.; M. A. Keith, Jr., 2nd Corp.; Elijah Deaton, 3rd Corp.; James D. Terrell, 4th Corp.; L. S. Smith, color guard; S. D. Smith, drummer; William A. Suggs, fifer; J. W. Evans, drummer. (John W. Bogle, Pvt., detailed in Tanyard by Gov. Brown, 1864; J. R. M. Burge, Pvt., Jan., 1864. On detail duty with W. & A. R. R., 1864.)

4th Regiment Georgia Reserves Infantry, Co. H, May 10, 1864: Robert C. Saxon, Capt.; W. N. Strange, 1st Lt., Acting Asst. Q. M.; J. Joseph Jones, 2nd Lt.; William A. Milner, 3rd Lt.; Samuel F. Milam, 1st Sergt.; Peter Marsh, 2nd Sergt.; W. A. Davis, 3rd Sergt.; Turner Jones, 4th Sergt.; Frank A. Pritchett, 5th Sergt.; David J. Weems, 1st Corp.; ——— King, 2nd Corp. "This company was organized at Cartersville, Ga., April 1864. The regiment was formed at Atlanta, Ga., April, 1864 (at a big spring where Grant Park now is), and sent to Camp Sumter at Andersonville, Ga., to guard Federal prisoners. The major part of this company was paroled at Montgomery, Ala., May 1865, the remainder at Andersonville, Ga. The roster of this company is on record in the ordinary's office of Bartow county, Ga. (Signed) Samuel F. Milam."

1st Regiment Georgia State Troops, Co. I, 1st Brigade, Oct. 5, 1861: A. M. Linn, Capt.; J. F. Leeke, 1st Lt.; William A. Chunn, 2nd

Lt.; J. H. Gilreath, Jr. 2nd Lt.; S. E. Puett, 1st Sergt.; Lewis D. Henderson, 2nd Sergt.; M. B. Erwin, 3rd Sergt.; Samuel E. Smith, 4th Sergt.; John L. Munford, 5th Sergt.; W. E. Edwards, 1st Corp.; James M. Thomas, 2nd Corp.; Robert Chapman, 3rd Corp.; John G. Linn, 4th Corp.; M. C. Allen, Q. M.-Sergt.; Ronald Johnston, Pvt., Com.-Sergt.

4th Regiment Georgia State Troops, Co. E, 2nd Brigade, Oct. 31, 1861: Robert H. Rowland, Capt.; Thos. K. Sproull, 1st Lt.; John Y. (A) Alexander, 2nd Lt.; Wm. O. Watson, Jr. 2nd Lt.; Theophilus G. Bowie, 1st Sergt.; Jas. W. Jolly, 2nd Sergt.;' Richard M. Lyon, 3rd Sergt.; Jacob B. Barber, 4th Sergt.; Peter D. Whelan, 5th Sergt.; Chas. W Bowie, 1st Corp.; John B. Murray, 2nd Corp.; Benj. F. Stidham, 3rd Corp.; Wm. P. Rutledge, 4th Corp.

Original muster roll of Captain Thomas F. Jones, Co. A, 16th Georgia Battalion of Partisan-Rangers, Army of the Confederate States of America. (Lt.-Col. Sam J. Winn, from the 1st of July, 1863 when last mustered, to the 31st day of December, 1863.): Thomas F. Jones, Capt., May 10, 1862; Benjamin F. Reynolds, 1st Lt., May 14, 1862, Euharlee; William I. Benham, 2nd Lt., May 14, 1862, Euharlee; Richard H. Chapman, Jr. 2nd Lt., May 14, 1862, Euharlee; Henry T. Jones, 1st Sergt.; Isaiah Cox, 2nd Sergt.; John H. Howell, 3rd Sergt.; Sidney I. Johnson, 4th Sergt.; Joel L. Hulsey, 1st Corp.; Alfred H. Stokes, 2nd Corp.; Bennett Reynolds, 3rd Corp.

1st Georgia Cavalry, Co. H, Army of Tennessee (incomplete): William M. Tumlin, Capt.; April, 1862; V. M. Tumlin, Lt.; Thomps Little, Lt., resigned, 1862; Nood Robertson, Lt.; Isaac Bently, Lt.; J. M. Jackson, Sergt., Lt.; Robert Hambrick, Sergt.; James Carroll, Sergt.; A. J. Fonely, Sergt.; Ray R. Lavender, Sergt.; B. W. Dodd, Ordly. Sergt.; Robert Bently, Corp.; Marion Windon, Corp.

8th Regiment Georgia State Troops, Co. E, 3rd Brigade, Nov. 7, 1861: Jacob W. Pearcy, Capt.; Benton F. Chastain, 1st Lt.; Francis M. Kitchens, 2nd Lt.; John P. Cole, Jr. 2nd Lt.; Robert L. Smith, 1st Sergt., Sergt.-Maj., 1862; Jonathan F. M. West, 2nd Sergt.; Lorenzo D. Rodgers, 3rd Sergt.; Decator Teague, 4th Sergt.; Benj. R. Frady, 5th Sergt.; William A. Kell, 1st Corp.; J. C. Goble, 2nd Corp.; Joshua C. Petit, 3rd Corp.; Francis M. Walker, 4th Corp.; Charles W. Clark, Pvt., 2nd Corp.; William T. Day, Pvt., Adj.; James M. Henderson, Pvt., 4th Sergt.; William Jones, Pvt., Adj., Sergt.-Maj.

Phillips' Legion Georgia Cavalry, Co. B, 4th Brigade, "Johnson's Rangers", June 11, 1861: Wm. W. Rich, Capt., Lt.-Col.; Augustus M. Franklin, 1st Lt.; John F. Milhollin, 2nd Lt.; Thos. G. Wilkes, Jr. 2nd Lt.; John L. Fullilove, 1st Sergt.; Wm. B. Patton, 2nd Sergt.; Robt. N. Best, 3rd Sergt.; Robt. C. Latimer, 4th Sergt.; Jas. R. Kenny, 5th Sergt.; Eli V. H. McConnell, 1st Corp.; John H. Cobb, 2nd Corp.; John F. Crow, 3rd Corp.; John G. Reynolds, 4th Corp.; John C. Branson, Pvt., Adj.; H. W. Carswell, Pvt., 3rd Corp.

Phillips' Legion Georgia Volunteer Infantry, Co. O, May 6, 1862,

Cobb and Bartow, "Marietta Guards": Thomas K. Sproull, Capt. (until Apr., 1863); William O. Watson, 2nd Lt., 1st Lt.; Henry J. McCormick, 2nd Lt., Capt.; Theophilus G. Bowie, 3rd Lt., 2nd Lt., 1st Lt.; A. H. Summers, 1st Sergt.; J. B. Harris, 2nd Sergt., 2nd Lt.; Benjamin F. Guess, 3rd Sergt.; James M. Smith, 4th Sergt., 2nd Lt., 1st Lt., 1864; William J. Eubanks, 5th Sergt.; F. Callaway Scott, 1st Corp.; J. H. Drake, 2nd Corp.; Benjamin F. Stidham, 3rd Corp.; William P. Rutledge, 4th Corp. This company mustered into service at Camp Prichard, May 6, 1862."

1st Georgia Cavalry Regiment, Co. I, Wheeler's Corps, Army of Tenn.: J. F. Leak, Capt.; J. H. Gilreath, 1st Lt.; A. J. Fuller, 2nd Lt.; W. C. Edwards, 3rd Lt.; O. U. Glasgow, 3rd Lt.; M. B. Erwin, 1st Sergt.; S. E. Smith, 2nd Sergt.; R. L. Griffin, 3rd Sergt.; H. A. Loveless, 4th Sergt.; R. L. Chapman, 5th Sergt.; T. J. Bridges, 1st Corp. O. P. Hargis, a member of this company wrote his experiences of three months in the rear of Sherman in a little booklet, in possession of Harry Hargis, Gainesville, Ga.

In the Georgia Soldier Roster Commission can be found complete enrollments of the names, ages, and occupations of the men and boys in each district. Each roll is a "true enrollment of the (present) Militia Company districts as required by the Act of 14th of December, 1863, for reorganizing the Militia of the State of Georgia." All the rolls were signed by Hawkins F. Price, aide-de-camp. In the

42nd Senatorial District Georgia Militia were: 819th, Daniel R. Thomas, E. O.*; 822nd, J. R. Wikle, E. O.; 827th, W. H. King, E. O.; 828th, Joseph S. Day, E. O.; 856th, James M. Veach, E. O.; 851st, T. K. Sproull, E. O.; 952nd, James M. Stephens, E. O.; 963rd, Joseph Davis, E. O.; 1041st, Silas Bell, E. O.

In the muster rolls of the 101st Militia District is a list of names subject to military duty belonging to the 101st Regiment Ga. Militia, numbering in all 770 men. March 5, 1862.

822nd District: Charles T. Shellman, Capt.; John L. Rowland, 1st Lt.; Thomas K. Denson, 2nd Lt.; David Heyman, 3rd Lt.; Samuel R. Kramer, 1st Sergt.; Milton Loveless, 2nd Lt.; Felix Sheats, 3rd Sergt.; E. G. Smith, 4th Sergt.; W. Cleghorn, 1st Corp.; Singleton McGuire, 2nd Corp.; Marion J. Guyton, 3rd Corp.; J. N. McElreath, 4th Corp.

828th District: E. J. Bobo, Capt.; 851st District: R. E. Phillips, Capt.; Thomas Tumlin, 1st Lt.; S. M. Franks, Lt.; D. P. Brandon, Lt.; P. H. Dodd, Sergt.; B. T. Luke, Sergt.; A. J. Rodgers, Corp.; A. McDonald, Corp.; H. Yarbrough, Corp. (These records are incomplete.)

In 1932 there are eight living pensioners and twenty-seven widows.

AN INCOMPLETE LIST OF SPANISH-AMERICAN WAR VETERANS include: A. Abramson, served as clerk of Commissary

---
*Enrolling officer.

Department; Capt. Frank Crenshaw, Lucius Hannon, J. B. Hendrix, Jim Hilburn, Sam H. Jones, Arthur Milner, Tom H. Milner, Madison Milam, Sam Milam, Jr., Harrison Porter, Ben Purse, Eugene C. Rowan, Frank Satterfield, George W. Woodrow, Col. Oscar J. Brown.

WORLD WAR VETERANS

(Compiled by Mrs. Claude Irby and Officers of the American Legion)

George A. Abernathy, Bart E. Abernathy, Lenford (or Leonard) Abernathy, Fred C. Abston (M.), E. E. Adair, Chas. Adams, Jesse Adams, J. H. Adams, Edgar Clifford Adcock, Willie E. Addington, Andrew Adkerson, Marion F. Adkins, Joseph Alexander Akerman (N.), James Hugh Akerman (Capt.), Leroy C. Alexander, Joseph Alexander, Posey Thomas Alford, George J. Alford, James Edward Alford, Percy Alford, W. L. Alford, Arthur E. Allison, Farris Almond, Chas. E. Alred, Julius W. Andrews, S. A. Andrews, Ernest F. Arnold, Pat Euell Arnold, William E. Arnold, Will Arwood, John R. Atwood, Sam A. (R.) Atwood, Frank C. Atwood.

Wm. M. Baggett, C. D. Bagwell, Tom M. Bagwell, Claude Bailey, Homer Bailey, Alonzo Baker, James E. Baker, John Oscar Baker (Corp.), Alfred W. Ballard (Corp.), Lee Ballard (Corp.), Cliff Banks, Neel Banks, Howard N. Barnes, Edward Barrett (Corp.), Forrest Barrett, Hubert Lawrence Barron (N.), Walter F. Baxter, Hugh G. Beason, Ernest J. Beavers, (d. June 1932), William C. Beavers, Homer Clinton Bell (N.), Warren D. Bell, (Corp.), John Wesley Biles (N.Ens.), Howard Bing, Howard V. Bishop, John A. Bishop, Lucius O. Bishop, Clyde Dennis Black, Joe H. Black, Horace H. Blalock, Bob Bohannon, Frances Marion Bohler, Norman F. Boswell, Joe P. Bowdoin (Maj.), Max N. Bowdoin, Robt. Boyd, Vester Boyd, Willis M. Boyd (1st Lt.), A. L. Bozeman, Homer A. Bozeman, Jim P. Bozeman, Sam J. Bozeman, Howard Bradford, Dr. Harry Bradford, Crisp Lewis Bradley (N.), William N. Bradley (Corp.), Willis Lee Bradley, Wm. B. Bradshaw, (Corp.) Edward Bramlett (N.), Wiley Harlin Bramlett, (N.), Arthur S. Branton (Corp.), Bethel G. Brawner, Luther Bray, Robert Cecil Brazelton, Wiley W. Brewer, James Brock, John B. Brock (Corp.), Roy S. Brock (Corp.), William T. Brock, Walton Milton Brooks, Dr. John Brown (N.), James R. Brown, John B. Brown, James A. Broxton, Jr., Jack Bruce, Andrew William Buford (N.),Madison Bunch, James M. Burdette, Felix Burdict, Sam D. Burns, Robert A. Burns, Turner Cicero Burton (N,). James W. Butler.

Jesse Cabe, J. Taylor Cagle, Thomas P. Caldwell, Carl Van Buren Calloway (N.), James W. Carlisle, Sam E. Calloway (Corp.), Daniel Lorenzo Campbell (2nd Lt.), Bill Carden, Carl C. Chamlee, Tom J. Champion, Oscar T. Chastain Stewart King Chilton (N.), Gus Chitwood, Raymond M. Chitwood, Thomas Edgar Chitwood, William Howard Christian (N.), William Amos Chumler (N.), Leonard W.

Clark, Henry G. Cleveland, William L. Cline, Sam Collett (Corp.), Murphy Colett, Albert Jesse Collum, Charles Joseph Collins, John F. Collins, Robert Lee Collins, Grover C. Colston, Christopher Thorwell Conyers (N.), James Bennett Conyers (Capt.), John L. Conyers (2nd Lt.), William Newton Conyers (2nd Lt.), Milton M. Cook, Homer Cook (Maj), Oscar Lee Cornwell, James Glynn Cowart (Slight Wound), Jess P. Cowart, John L. Cowart, Andrew J. Conway, Andy Cox, Robert L. Cox, Rupert D. W. Cox (Sgt.), Bill Craig, Thomas W. Croft, George Sanford Crouch (N.), William B. Crouch, Leslie W. Crow, John R. Culberson.

Milton L. Dabbs, Stephen Darden, Moses N. Darden, Quillian Manson Darnell, Joel Thomas Daves, Joe B. Davis, Levi King Davis, William R. Davis, Caney J. Day, Herman Day, Dock N. Denny, James W. Dewberry, Arthur A. Dickson, George C. Dobbs, Glover Frank Dodd, (2nd Lt.), Harold A. Dodd, Hubert N. Dodd, Howard G. Dodd, Jerry Dodd (Corp.), John Dodd, Paul H. C. Dodd, Warren Stanley Dodd (N.), John C. Doss, Vernon Loyd Doss (N), Boyd V. Dover, Charles C. Dover, Homer Dover, John F. Dover, Noah Dover, George Fay Durham, Chandler L. Dutton, Thos. B. Duckett, Samuel Dysart.

Thomas C. Earwood, Homer Earwood, William H. L. Edwards, Charles Lee Ellis (1st Lt.), Claude Howard Ellis, W. B. Ellis, Appleton Elkins, Calvin Elrod, Jerry C. Elrod, Robert Evans, Thomas E. Everett, William A. Edwards.

Oscar A. Fallis, Elvin C. Faqua, Willie Farris, Ernest Robt. David Danl. Faulkner, Walter M. Ferguson, J. L. Ferguson, Eugene S. Fields, James M. Field, Jr., (2nd Lt.), Roy O. Fields, Walter Max Field, Spencer Fields, Louie L. Fincher (Sgt.), Joel Albert Fite (N.), Joel A. Fite (2nd Lt.), William Conyers Fite (N. Capt.), J. P. Matthew Forsythe, Herman Foster; Ottis H. Fowler, William P. Fowler, Robert S. Franklin, Grover C. Freeman, John Freeman, Lewis R. Freeman.

Albert M. Gaines, Guy Gaines (Sgt.), Henry W. Gaines, Milton Pinckney Gaines (N.), William Andrew Galt (N.), Sidney Ralph Garwood (N.), William V. Gazaway, William B. Gibbs, William Gibson, Carl Griffin Gilbert (N.), Walter E. Gilbert (1st veteran to be buried in county), Howard C. Gilreath (Sgt.), J. H. Gilreath, Paul Gilreath, Jr., Wofford H. Gilreath (Corp.), Robert H. Goodnight, Joe Goodwin, Almond F. Gossett, Paul Warner Gould, Lee Graham, Graham Granger (2nd Lt.), Samuel H. Graveley, Roscoe Newton L. Green, Johnnie E. Green, H. H. Green, Lonzo B. Green, Roy S. Greenwood (Corp.), Hugh J. Griggs, Thomas F. Gullidge, Arthur Gunn (N.), Fred Gunn, Meridith Gunn, Emory M. Guyton, Roy Everett Guyton, Walter Hill Guyton.

Rex Wayne Haley (N.), Claude F. Hall, John Lelburn Hall (M.), Arthur Franklin Hanks, Robert Whitfield Hardy (N.), George Washington Harris, Howard Harris, John A. Harris, Luther Bonds Harris (N.), Peter Charles Harris (Adgt. Genl.), Romeo C. Harris, Chas. Debie Hart, Arthur Harvey (Severely Wounded), Robert Franklin Headden,

Allen Heath, Joseph H. Heath, Olin Heath, Vesta Heath, William Marion Heath, Joseph Carlton Hebble (N), Jerry Lee Heffner, H. Furd Heffner, Ernest E. Helms, James A. Henderson, John R. Henderson, Fred Hendricks, Olin C. Hendricks, Sam T. Hendricks (Severely wounded), James William Henson (N.), Roy Tilman Henson (N.), Dewey Herrod, Henry J. Hicks (2nd Lt.), Newton W. Hightower, Willie B. Hightower, Mike E. Hill, Abbie L. Hill, Thomas L. Hobgood, Horace C. Hogan, Daniel M. Hollaran, George Holcombe, Millard J. Holcombe, Perry Holcombe, Condie Mell Holland, Harlie W. Hood, Thomas W. Hooper, Frank H. Hornbuckle, Robert L. Hornbuckle, Service Houke, Jr., Newtie William House, (N.), Dr. Sam Howell, Oscar D. Howren, David L. Howard, William A. Hubbard, Henry L. Hufstetler, Alvey Roy Hughes, Grover Steveson Hughes (N.), Hardy Britton Hughes, Mack Loran Hughes, Leonard E. Hunt, William D. Hyde.

Raymond P. Ingram, James A. Irwin (Slightly Wounded, received French Croix de Guerre).

Frank Tourtelot Jackson, Harrison Burdine Jackson (N.), Lawson E. Jackson, Mose Jackson, Ralph O. Jackson, Stonewall Jackson, William M. Jackson, James Augustus Jarrett, John E. Jarrett, Rufus Jefferson, William Abner Jefferson (Severely Wounded), John Thomas Jenkins, Reuben Ellis Jenkins (1st Lt.), Homer Jimeron, Henry B. Johnson (Corp.), Albert H. Jolly (Corp.), Alfred C. Jolly, Frank Ramsey Jolly (N.), Henry B. Jolly, Hugh David Jolly (N.), Jos. B. Jolly, Oscar Kirkham Jolly, Thomas Bryan Jolly (N.), Walter B. Jolly, Ed. F. Jones, Edwin G. Jones, Harris Quillian Jones, James H. Jones, James R. Jones, Lon Jones, Taylor Rhea Jones, Thomas Catesby Jones (Capt.), William C. Jones.

Charles W. Kaylor, James Thomas Keever, Leon H. Keever (Slightly Wounded.), Hedley H. Keith, Arthur Saml. Kennedy (N.), George W. Kennedy (Sgt.), Henry Earl Kennedy (N.), Jolly H. Kennedy (Sgt.), William C. Kennedy, Alexander Kerr, Andrew J. Kerr, Wallace Keys, Will F. Keys, Robt. L. Kincannon, Herbert S. King, Richard King, G. C. Kirkley, William Virgil Kirkpatrick (N.), Harvey Kiser, George Kiser, Charles Elbert Kitchens (2nd Lt.), Fred W. Knight, Jackson A. Knight, Robert William Knight (Capt.), Joe Knight, Wesley Knight, Clee Knowles (Corp.).

Lee B. Lacy, Dewey C. Landers, Roy L. Langston, Lon Lanham, Homer Lanham, Andrew G. Lavasque, William L. Lavasque, Walter Cleveland Lawhon, John E. Lawhon, Jerome W. Layton, Joseph Lewis Layton (Sgt.), L. A. Layton, T. D. Layton, Earl Hudson Leach (Corp.), Carl C. Leachman, Erve Price Leak, Jesse Jones Leake, Herman Leake, Walter F. Lee, Howard Leonard, Eli Wallace Lewis, James Bradley Lewis (1st Lt.), Roy L. Lewis (Slt. Wound), Herschel H. Lipscomb, Robert L. Lipscomb, Robert Paul Littlefield (N.), Jim Marion Little Jr. (M.), William H. Lowary, Robert Lowry, Johnny Lowry, Claude Wilson Luke (N.) Wm. Henry Lumpkin (2nd Lt. Slightly Wounded.),

Benham Lumpkin (Capt.).

Jesse L. McCarson, Harry I. McCollum, Alvin J. McCoy, Esom McCall, Charles B. McCreary, Jesse L. McCreary, John D. McDaniel, Charles B. McDonald (Corp.), William McDonald, Charles Norris McEver (Corp.), Jim C. McEver, John Antone McEver (M.), Ernest L. McEntire, George P. McEntire (Sgt.), John McEwen (Capt.), Joe McEntire, Charles Matthew McEwen (2nd Lt.), Richard A. McGhee, Sam McGowan, Thomas D. McGowan.

Jas. Fred Madden, Paul Mansfield, Abbott Martin, Charles H. Martin, D. N. Martin, Melvin C. Martin, Will Martin, Jno. H. Marsengale, Fred Massey, Sidney Thomas Mathis, Joseph Milam, Edwin Postell Milam, Sam H. Millsaps, William O. Millsaps, Thomas Christian Milner (Corp, M.), Ben L. Mills, Willie Lee Mitchell, Charles S. Moffett, Merril Monfort, Chester P. Montgomery, Robert M. Moon, Walter Arnold Moore, William L. Moore, Jack W. Moore, Ralph Moran (N.), Fred C. Morris, Millard Moss, James T. Mote, Mitchell W. Mullinax, Emmett Russell Munford (N.), Robert A. Munford, William Harvey Murphy, William Charley Myers (Severely Wounded).

Fred Neel, E. C. Newhouse, Charles M. Newhouse, Henry Clanton Nelson (N.), Jesse Nelson, Joe C. Nelson, Mark Nelson, John E. Newborn, George Ernest Newman, Arthur Nicholson, Robert Northey.

Harold C. Oglesby, Horace Oliver, Frank Owens, Joe Owens, Ernest C. Owens.

John Palmore, Arthur Padgette, Jesse Lee Padgette, Sewell J. Padgette (Corp), John A. Parham, Thomas M. Parks, Wesley Parks, David R. Parker, Robert F. Patterson, William M. Patterson, Buck Patterson, Robert Thomas Pavlovsky (N.), Clint T. D. Payne, Jack M. Payne, Jas. Payne, Wallace Payne (M.), Lewis D. Peace,(N.),David Wm. Killin Peacock (Lt. Col.), E. L. Peacock, Jr. (1st Lt. Wounded), Hugh M. Peacock (Wounded), Barney R. Pearson, Ed C. Pearson, Robert A. Pearson, William Pearson, Horace Pelfrey, Charles Melvin Pendley, Henry A. Pendley, Amos Perkins (N.), Millard Arphax Perry (Sgt.), Hugh Boyd Pettit (N.), Roy S. Phillips, William Y. Phillips, Ambrose Butler Pickard (N.), Ulric Paul Pickard, Joseph F. Picklesimer, Winifred Picklesimer, Ralph W. Pinion, Paul D. Pittard, Sam M. Pittard, Jesse Q. Pittman (Sgt.), Homer Pope, Joe Frank Pope, Robert M. Posey, Curren M. Potts (Slightly Wounded), Charles A. Powell, Gordon Spencer Powell (N.), Robert R. Powell, Hugh Park Pruitt, Rube Pruitt, Henry Priest, Lewis E. Presley (Sgt.), Fred Prince, Henry G. Proctor, Hubert Mundy Pruitt, Luther E. Pruitt, Abe Puckett (Sgt.), Paul Puckett.

Homer E. Quila, Carl C. Quinn, Luther T. Quinn, John Aaron Quinton (N.).

Charles R. Rayford, Clarence M. Rayford, Tom Rainey, James C. Randolph (Corp.), Ernest Ray, Felix Ray, Homer Cleveland Ray, Lonzo C. Rayburn, Dole Reddick (Corp.), Samuel Perry Reece, Merith

Reed, Aaron Canada Reese, George W. Reeves (Corp.), Ralph E. Reeves (Corp.), Charlie Reynolds, Eugene S. Reynolds (Sgt.), Garland E. Rhyne, Joe L. Rice, Joseph P. Rice, Luther F. Richards, Arthur N. Roberson, Garnett L. Roberson, Dayton W. Roberts (Sgt.), Loyd B. Roberts, Robert H. Roberts, Sam Q. Roberts, Tom Roberts, Arthur Robertson, Joseph B. Robertson, James D. Rollins, John P. Rush, Sam L. Rush (Corp.), Mike Russell, Paul M. Rutland.

Fred A. Sanders, Julian Sanders, Will Sanford, Jesse H. Satcher, Bradley Smith Satterfield, Paul M. Satterfield, Walter M. Satterfield, Earl Baer Scheuer (2nd Lt.), Lee M. Scheuer (N. Ens.), Lawrence Self, Abner B. Sewell, Arthur Jesse Sexton (M.), James H. Shaw, Julius Clarence Shaw (N.), Prince F. Shaw, Silas Newton Shaw, Thomas Lee Shaw, Simon Shelly, Paul Llewlyn Sherman (Corp., slightly wounded), Arthur A. Shinall, Robert Shinall, Roy P. Shinall, Sam O. Shinall (severely wounded), Wallace L. Shinall, Emanuel M. Shook, William A. Sheelar, Ira Arnold Sisson, Wm. Norman Sisson, George W. Slaughter, Ira R. Slaughter, Joseph M. Sloan, Oscar Sloan, Buford W. Smith (Sgt.), Charles Smith, Clarence L. Smith, Clifford B. Smith, Conrad Smith (Corp.), Elbert D. Smith (severely wounded), Frederick Smith, Foster F. Smith, George F. Smith, Harold Edwin Smith (N.), Herman Albert Smith, Martin G. Smith, Oliver Eugene Smith (severely wounded), Richard C. Smith, Richard Dewey Smith, Ralph H. Smith, Robert A. Smith, Robert Henry Lee Smith (N.), Uit Smith, W. S. Smith, William Charles Smith, Lorenzo D. Spriggs, R. A. Spriggs, Emory L. Stegall, Horace A. Stephens, Reeves Stephens, Wylie Stephens, William H. Stevens (slightly wounded), Marion Stevens, Edward L. Stewart (wounded), Carl C. Stiles (severely wounded), Hugh G. Stiles (1st Lt.), John Chadwick Stiles (Capt.), W. Henry Stiles Jr. (Lt. Comd. N.), Robert M. Stiles (2nd. Lt.), John William Stokes (N.), Monroe Jefferson Stokes, Edward Strickland, Jr., Sidney B. Strickland, William Evans Strickland (2nd Lt.), Ernest Suddeth (Corp.), John L. Sullivan, General Lee Sutton, John W. Sutton, Will G. Sutton, William Sutton, Carlos T. Swanson, John H. Swanson.

John D. Taff, Roy Daniel Taff (N.), Marvin W. Tate, Alva Wofford Taylor, Arthur Taylor, Loyd R. Taylor, Noah M. Taylor, Thomas B. Teems, Mack D. Teague (Corp.), Ernest Willie Teague, Samuel C. Terrell, Claude Terry, John Thomas, William Franklin Thomas, Charles R. Thompson, Joel Thompson (slightly wounded), Robert E. Thompson, Earl D. Tierce, Roy R. Tierce, Columbus O. Tidwell, J. R. Tidwell, George Carey Tinsley (N.), Weston B. Tinsley (severely wounded), Oscar A. Tow, William A. Tolbert, William Franklin Tracy (N.), Charlie Tranham, Fred Tranham, Harold M. Tribble, William F. Tribble, John Henry Tucker (N.), Roy N. Tucker, James C. Tumlin, Joseph H. Turner, Seaborn E. Turner.

Charles Bell Upshaw (1st. Lt.) Elbert Madison Upshaw (1st. Lt.), William B. Uren, J. R. Uren (2nd. Lt.).

Herman C. Vandivere, Henry G. Vaughan, James Wilson Vaughan Jr., (2nd Lt.), Thomas Watson Vaughan (2nd Lt.), James M. Veach, James W. Venable, Toulmine Veal, Harrell Hicks Vincent (M.) Ralph Vincent.

Forrest Franklin Wade, Noah C. Waits, Willie Waits, Prior Washington Waldrup (N.), Thomas B. Walker (Sgt.), Lewis P. Warlick, Benjamin Arthur Ward, Samuel W. Ward (Severely Wounded), Adolph Waters, John W. Waters, Thad Waters, Ollie H. Watkins, John Wesley Webb (m. wounded), Martin Clayton Webb (2nd Lt.), Louis Clifton Weems (N.), Charlie H .Wehunt, Junius Gerome Welch, Samuel D. Welch, Solomon Jefferson Welch, J. Reuben Welchel, William Welchel, David A. Weaver (Corp.) Erwin Dyer Whittenberg, General W. Wheeler, John West, John Oscar Wheeler, Jesse J. White, Joel White, Willie (McCamy) White, Perry Whitley, Homer C. Wiley, Frank Williams, Henry McGinnis Williams (M.), Ollie Lee Williams (N.), Wesley A. Williams, Walter G. Williamson, Arthur Henry Willis, Chess Wilson, Willie Withrow (Severly Wounded), Dr. William Earl Wofford (Capt.), Arthur D. Woodrain, Edgar E. Worsham, Charlie O. Worthington, Foster Worthington, James R. Worthington, John Thomas Worthington, Roy L. Wood, Eugene McK. Woodall, Lewis F. Woodall, Luther R. Woodall, Arthur D. Woodran, Robert S. Woody, John L. Wooley, Earl F. Worley (slightly wounded), John L. Worley, Burton Thomas Wright, Marson Asbury Wright (N.), Reuben Wyatt.

Jack Yancey, William H. Yancey, Albert M. Yarbrough, Clark F. Yarbrough, Clifford J. Yarbrough, Homer Yearwood, Arthur N. York, Charles A. Young, Charles E. Young, David Young, Henry E. Young, James Heyward Young (2nd. Lt.), John W. Young, Roy O. Young, W. R. Young.

BARTOW WOMEN WHO SERVED IN WORLD WAR

Among the first southern women to go to France under the American Red Cross were Mrs. Verdery Akin McMichaels, now Mrs. Oliver Roosevelt of L. I. and N. Y., and Frances Akin, now Mrs. Harold Amberg of Chicago. They were daughters of the late Judge and Mrs. John W. Akin, formerly of Cartersville. They entered the service from Atlanta, and were among the thirty chosen from cities of the U. S. Mrs. McMichaels was the manager of a salvage warehouse in Paris. Miss Frances Akin was assistant of the department of requirements of the American Red Cross, and at one time served as an inspector of the Red Cross warehouse in Italy, then sent back to Washington as a special commissioner of the American Red Cross in Paris. She was also appointed chairman of the hospital beds endowed by the Georgia division of the U. D. C. while in France.

Miss Christine Lumpkin, now Mrs. Felix Jackson of Philadelphia and Sarasota, Mrs. Kate Graham Akerman, sister of Mrs. N. N. Granger of Atlanta, and Miss Myrtice Adair, now Mrs. Paul C. Boyd, served in overseas Y. M. C. A. Miss Jessie L. Crow served as nurse.

THOSE KILLED OR DIED IN SERVICE

Carl Boyd (Col.), Burton Paul Bradley (Capt.), Robert A. Burns, James W. Butler (killed in action), Ralph Raiford Davis (N.), Wm. E. Champion (Killed in Action), Cecil R. Cline, Tip Cox, Willie Cox, Lonnie C. Crow, Homer Easley, Thomas E. Everett, Samuel G. Harmon, Henry F. Hefner, Joseph F. Irwin, John Lowry, Homer Lanham, Isador Irving Machler (Killed in Action, M.), Victor H. Matthews, Delbert Lee Murphy (Killed in Action), Robert Henry Pharr (N.), Hoyt W. Smith (Died of Wounds), Joseph Sullins, Clyde Charlie Sorrells (N.). John C. Davis 1918 s.of Mr&Mrs William B. Davis Ralph Davis s.Mr-Mrs A.R. Davis Taylorsville

Colored: Albert Jackson, Tom Miller, Doc Pinkard, Willie Powell, Chester Scott.

NEGRO SERVICE MEN

Geo. Adcock, Julian N. Allen (Sgt.), Chas Andrews.

James Bailey, Joe Bailey, Roy Bailey, William J. Bailey, Gus Banks, Lee Roy Banks, Colonel Bates, Chas. Bell, Thos. Bell, Hubert Benahm, John Benham, Ellick Black, Early Branch, Orrie Branch, Howard Brooks, Arthur Brown, Edgar Brown, Elbert Brown, Jesse Brown, John Brown, Mark Brown, Melvin Brown, Theodore Brown, Willie Brown, Gordon Bursey, Jas. H. Bursey.

Benjamine Canty (Sgt. Maj.), Oscar Canty, Bradley Carson, Clive Carson, Eddie Carson, Wade Carson, Walter Carson, Ernest Carter, Oscar Carter, Henry Charter (Severely Wounded), Fletcher Childers, Jim Clark (Mess Sgt.), Joe S. Clemmons, Will E. Clifton, Alonzo L. Colman, John Collins, Oscar Collins, Andrew Conner, Charles William Cooley, Claude Craig, Antone Crawford, Fred Crawford, Prince Crawford, Richard Crawford, Willis Curry (Sgt.), Raymond Curtis.

Harry Green Daniel, Holly H. Davis, Jerry Davis, General L. Demry, Deson W. Dillard, George Dixon, Will Dorsey, Henry Dozier, Rudolph Dudley, Charlie S. Dukes.

Dennis Edwards, Fred Douglas Edwards, John Edwards, Rozzie Ellison (Corp.), John H. Evans (Severely Wounded).

Columbia Facin, John W. Fields, Julius Fields, Ernest Fletcher, Noah Fletcher, Wheeler D. Fowler, Mark Freeman.

Asbury Grimes, Ben Garnigan, Fred C. Gassett (Sgt.), Virgil George, Fred J. Gilliard (Corp.), Henry Godhigh, Erastus Godhigh, Pat Goode, Willie Goode, William H. Gordon, Harry Gore.

John Henry Hamilton, Walter Hamilton, James Hardy, Hershel Harris, Leonard Harris, Albert Haywood, Amos Henry, Ben Hester, Harvie Hill, Herbert Harris.

Kinett Ingram.

Curren Jackson, Willis Jewell, Ben Johnson, John T. Johnson (Corp.), John H. Johnson, Norris H. Johnson, Alvin G. Jones, Fred Jones, Gaines Jones, George Jones, Quill Jordan.

John W. Kelly, Moses L. Kiser (Corp.), Thomas P. Kiser, Carl Knight, Fredrick D. Knight (Sgt.).

Doc Lay, David Lee, George Lee, Oscar Lee, George Leonard

(severely wounded), James Edward Leonard, Richard L. Lewis, Thomas Lidsey, Mitchell Lott, Andrew Lumpkin (slightly wounded).

Jule McCoy, Barnes McCoy, Benjamin McClendon, Walter McDaniel, Frank McDaniel, Henry L. McGoogins.

Arthur Milner, Robert Milner, Zack Miller, James Mims, Brisco Moody, Jr., David Moore, William D. Moore, John Morgan, Jr., Alex Morris, Harvey Moore.

John W. Napier, Cornelius Neil (Corp.).

Chunk Parks, John Willie Patton, Will Patrick, James Patterson, Jim Peaks, Forrest Edgar Phinzy, Henry Pickins, Howard Pickett (Sgt.), Jesse Pitts, Shafter Porter, Andrew Powell, Murry Powell, Herman Pruitt (Corp.).

Jerry Reason, Thomas Reed, Essix Richards, Milton Richard, Charlie Richardson, Frank Richardson, Alfred Roberson, William Roe, Howard Rowe, John Robinson.

Eli Scrutchins, Clarence Scott, Willie Scott, William Seffus, John Shields, Silvester Shields, Cleveland Smith, Fred Smith, Joe Smith, John J. Smith, Oscar Spier, Robert L. Stafford, Arthur Stephens, Baney Stephens, Will Stephenson, Warren Stephenson, Howell Stockland, Tom Strickland.

Tonie Thompson, Percy Thurwood, Willie Graham Towns, Will Trippe, Robert W. Trimble.

Benjamin Upshaw.

James Wallace, Bud Weems, Frank Weems, James Calvin White, Leroy White, Mack Wilburn, James Wiley, Anderson Williams, Freeman Williams (Corp.), Horace Williams, Van Williams, Ellis P. Willis, Hayes Wilson, Anderson Wimberly, Alex Wise, Alfred Wise, Harry Wofford, Tom Wofford, Robert Wood, Robert Wright (Sgt.), Sam Wright.

Alex Young, Charlie Young, Eddie Young, Jr., Edgar Young, James Young, John H. Young, Lonzo Young, Mack Young (Sgt.).

DOCTORS AND LAWYERS

Some of the doctors before the Civil War not mentioned in family sketches were: Dr. William C. Anderson who came from Laurens, S. C., in the fifties and was a prominent citizen; Dr. Miles J. Murphy; Dr. S. E. Edgeworth; Dr. J. J. Mitchell, Dr. J. T. Groves; Dr. Daniel Hamiter, b. May 21, in Richland county, S. C., and died Dec. 15, 1889, was the father of Mrs. Nannie Allday of Cartersville and served as surgeon in the 22nd Ga. Regt.; Dr. S. F. Stephens, b. June 25, 1820, d. Nov. 25, 1889, came from Abbeyville, Dist., S. C., to Stilesboro in 1854 where he practiced until his death; the children were Ella (Dwelle), James E., John,*Charlotte (Anderson, Jno.), S. F. Jr., M. Grace (Milner).

In a physicians' meeting held in April, 1866, the following doctors signed a fee bill which included prices for their services as:

Visits in town (day)—$2

Night and inclement weather—$4
All visits within 3 miles—$2.50
Consultation—$10
Bleeding—$2
Cupping—$3
Prescriptions (ordinary)—$2
Prescriptions (special)—$5 to $20
Extracting—$1 to $2
Obstetrics, natural labor—$10 to $25
Complicated—$25 to $50

Dr. Charles H. Harris, Dr. Cramp Harris, Dr. W. H. Boyd, Dr. M. G. Williams, Dr. R. M. Young, Dr. J. Kinabrew, Dr. Weston Hardy, Dr. D. Hamiter, Dr. H. Ramsaur, Dr. W. W. Leak, Dr. W. L. Kirkpatrick, Dr. I. A. Thomas (m. Maggie Marsh), Dr. J. D. Sims, Dr. T. H. Baker, Dr. C. E. Sutton. Dr. Charles M. Griffin who was born in Ireland and practiced here until after 1881. This bill was criticized as being exorbitant by the women in the county and by some of the doctors.

Some doctors since the war who registered as medical practitioners in the county after 1881 were:

Dr. Robert I. Battle, b. in Davidson county, Tenn., a graduate of University of Nashville in 1861, surgeon and captain in the 20th Tenn., practiced at Grassdale and Cartersville until his death in 1920. Dr. Battle married Fanny Gibbons, a daughter of Mr. and Mrs. G. R. Gibbons, and their marriage was a thrilling war-time story. In Jan. 1864, he met her when he visited his cousin, Fanny Battle, a paroled spy who had been imprisoned at Camp Chase and was exiled from Tenn. to Ga. and was staying in the Maj. Winn home in Grassdale. In July he returned a captain of a scouting company near the Gibbons home, and as he had to work in concealment an early wedding was urged. Under cover of night—not even a Negro was called in to assist with the wedding preparations for fear of causing suspicion of their presence—the ceremony was performed at 11 o'clock the night of the 13th. A few days later Capt. Battle derailed a train of Yankee supplies. A reward was offered for him "dead or alive." His daughter Sallie May m. Robert H. Renfroe (dec.) of Cartersville. His son, **Dr. G. W. Battle**, a graduate of Atlanta Medical College in 1890, practiced in Cassville until his death in Nov. 1925. Dr. E. C. Jones, b. in Madison, Ga., graduate of Medical College of Ga. in 1849, practiced in **Taylorsville** until after 1882. **Dr. Richard J. Trippe**, b. 1861, Cherokee county, Ga., graduate of Atlanta Medical College in 1882, practiced in **Taylorsville, Stilesboro and Cartersville** until his death in 1909. **Dr. Richard S. Bradley**, b. in Gordon county, graduate of Southern Medical College in 1884, practiced in Adairsville. Dr. C. M. Chamlee practiced in Adairsville until his death in 1932. Dr. Franklin R. Calhoun, b. 1834, in Greenwood, S. C., d. 1909, a graduate of Medical State College of S. C., in 1877, practiced in Euharlee until his removal to Cartersville to live with his son, Dr. Alfred T. Calhoun, who was also born in Greenwood, S. C., was a graduate of the S. C. Medical College in 1890, and practiced in Cartersville from 1896 until his death in 1922. Dr. Fred V. Turk, b. in Cherokee county, graduated from Atlanta Medical College in 1892, practiced in Stilesboro until his death in September, 1917.

Dr. Samuel Wells Leland, a son of Rev. Aaron W. Leland, was born near Charleston, S. C., May 23, 1824. He moved to Bartow county with his wife (nee Reynolds) and daughter, Agnes, soon after the Civil War. A gifted physician, he soon obtained a large and lucrative practice, and the esteem and confidence of his friends and patients until his death on Aug. 11, 1884. He joined the Presbyterian church in 1877. Of a high and brilliant mentality, his conversational powers and eloquence of speech charmed his many hearers. He did not seek office, nor desired personal popularity; an independent thinker and outspoken upon all subjects, he was content to receive only the respect and esteem he deserved as an honorable gentleman and genuine patriot. His daughter married Alfred Gilbert, a son of W. H. Gilbert, a prominent citizen of Cartersville, and they afterwards lived in New Orleans where the only son, Samuel, now resides. Mrs. Alfred Gilbert died in 1932 and was buried in Cartersville.

The Bartow County Medical Society was organized sometime before 1906. The present members are: Dr. W. E. Wofford, president, Dr. W. C. Griffin, senior member, Dr. Sam M. Howell, Dr. R. E. Adair, Dr. Tanner Lowry, Dr. R. E. Wilson, Dr. J. P. Bowdoin, Dr. H. B. Bradford, Dr. A. L. Horton, Dr. H. S. McGowan, Dr. C. L. Ellis, Dr. Robert E. Burton, Dr. A. C. Shamblin, public health officer, secretary and treasurer, Dr. J. W. Stanford, and Dr. J. E. Griffith. Dr. Fain Hutchinson practices in Adairsville.

Present dentists are Dr. Joe N. Weems, Dr. H. P. McElreath, Dr. L. L. Lowry, Dr. Clark H. Griffin, Dr. Harold Choate.

Members of the bar in this county from the 1850's to date have been: Warren Akin, John A. Crawford, Alonzo C. Church, W. T. Wofford, J. D. Phillips, John E. Glenn, John H. Rice, A. H. Rice, F. C. Shropshire, B. H. Leake, E. D. Chilsolm, John J. Word, J. R. Parrott, Marcus A. Higgs, Abda Johnson, Julius M. Patton, W. A. Chunn, J. R. Wikle, Henry P. Farrow, J. G. Ryals, W. V. Webster, R. C. Saxon, John C. Branson, E. L. Brown, Jere A. Howard, Joseph Dunlap, E. M. Keith, Richard Maltbie, Thomas W. Milner, John J. Jones, P. H. Larey, John W. Wofford, Mark Johnston, J. W. Harris, Sr., W. J. Conyers, W. L. Pritchett, J. C. C. Blackburn, Thomas W. Dodd, A. M. Foute, John H. Wikle, John Coxe, A. P. Wofford, C. C. Parrott, J. A. Baker, Robert B. Trippe, J. B. Conyers, Sam P. Jones, James M. Neel, R. W. Murphy, W. D. Trammel, T. W. Hooper, M. R. Stansell, E. D. Graham, G. H. Aubrey, T. Warren Akin, A. W. Fite, John W. Akin, K. S. Anderson, J. W. Harris, Jr, W. J. Neel, T. J. Lyon, F. P. Gray, J. R. Gray, T. W. H. Harris, T. W. Milner, Albert S. Johnson, George S. Johnson, Douglas Wikle, W. M. Graham, Paul F. Akin, John T. Norris*, Watt H. Milner, Thomas H. Milner, Thomas C. Milner, Walter M. Ryals, John L. Moon, E. B. McDaniel, O. H. Milner, G. H. Bates, D. D. McConnell, Joe M. Moon, Sam H. Patillo, Theo M. Smith, D. Graham, J. H. Curry, J. J. Conner.

Present bar: Paul F. Akin, Judge G. H. Aubrey, Percy A. Bray, Colquit Finley, W. C. Henson, W. A. Ingram, Rufus V. Jones, J. M. Neel, Jr., Fred Neel, Judge C. C. Pittman, O. T. Peeples, Frank D. Smith, W. T. Townsend, Turley Warlick, J. R. Whitaker.

CONGRESSIONAL DISTRICTS

Fifth—Dec. 23, 1843-Mar. 23, 1861 (Acts of 1843, p. 54.).
Tenth—Mar. 23, 1861-Dec. 6, 1861 (Confederate Records, p. 146).
Fifth—Dec. 6, 1861-Oct. 26, 1865 (Acts of 1861, p. 101).
Seventh—Oct. 26, 1865-date. (Made up of 14 counties.)

SENATORIAL DISTRICTS

Fortieth—Dec. 23, 1845-1853 (Paulding and Cass; Polk added in 1851).
Forty-second—Dec. 6, 1861-date (Acts of 1861, p. 101). (Made up of Bartow, Floyd, and Chattooga.)
Cherokee Circuit—1832-1861-date (Acts of 1861, p. 101; Acts of 1832, p. 56). (Made up of Bartow, Catoosa, Dade, Gordon, Murray, and Whitfield counties. In 1874 a bill was proposed to change the Cherokee circuit to the Rome circuit, but Dr. T. A. Baker, representative, defeated the bill.)

CASS COUNTY SENATORS†

1833	David Irwin	1845	Rheese McGregor
1834	R. J. Loyless	1847	Francis Irwin
1835	William Hardin	1849/50	Edward D. Chisholm
1836	William L. Morgan	1851/52	Lewis Tumlin
1837	Stephen Mays	1853/54-1855/56	Russell H. Cannon
1838-9	Richmond Baker		
1840	Robert Hamilton	1857-58	Hawkins F. Price
1841	Thomas Hamilton	1859-60	Mark Johnston
1842-3	Lewis Tumlin		

BARTOW COUNTY SENATORS

1861-62-3 Ex. Daniel R. Mitchell
1863-4 Ex-64-65 Ex. Hawkins F. Price
1865/66-66 Chas. Henry Smith (Bill Arp)
1868 Ex.-69-70 Ex. 71-72-72 Adj.

John T. Burns
1874-5 John W. Wofford (res.)
1876 Mark A. Cooper
1877 James R. Gamble
1878-79 Adj. Samuel Hawkins
1880-81 Adj. R. T. Fouche

---

*Was b. in Cartersville, a son of Rev. J. T. and Ella R. de Jarnette who lived and died in Cartersville, brother of Mrs. Emy N. Hall of Milledgeville; in 1912 delegate to Natl. Dem. Conv.; prominent citizen until his death on Nov. 19, 1931.

†The dash (-) means biennial election and service for two calendar years; the slant (/) means annual election from same date within the year to same date within the next year. See Ga. O. & S. Registers.

1882-83 Ex.-83 Ann. Adj. Thos. H. Baker
1884-85 Adj. John W. Maddox
1886-87 Adj. Linton A. Dean
1888-89 Adj. Jas. W. Harris, Jr.
1890-91 Adj. W. T. Irvine
1892-93 Felix Corput
1894-5 W. H. Lumpkin
1896-7 Adj.-97 Wesley Shropshire
1898-99 Robert T. Fouche
1900-01 Thomas Baker
1902-03-04 John D. Taylor
1905-06 W. S. McHenry
1907 John W. Akin (d. Oct. 19, 1907.)
1908-08 Ex. Paul F. Akin
1909-10 R. Y. Rudicill
1911-12 Ex. W. H. Ennis
1913-14 John W. L. Brown*
1915-15 Ex.-16-17 Ex. W. M. Ransom (d. before 1917 Ex.)
1817-18 Richard Alden Denny.
1919-20 Claude C. Pittman
1921-22 James Morgan Bellah
1923-23 Ex.-24 John Camp Davis
1925-26 Ex.-26 Ex. Emried Dargan Cole
1927 Thos. Jefferson Anderson
1929-30 Seaborn Wright
1931-32 McConnell L. Johnson

REPRESENTATIVES

1833 John C. Miller
1834-5-6 Thomas Espy†
1837-8 D. P. Burnett
1839 Stephen Mays
Andrew Woolley
1840 Elnathan D. Hudgins‡
Coleman Pitts
1841 Robert H. Patton
Elnathan D. Hudgins
1842 David Morrow

1843 John J. Word
James Wofford
1845 Samuel Smith
James Wofford
1847 Samuel Smith
Henry McConnell
1849/50 Achilles D. Shackelford
William T. Wofford
1851/52 William T. Wofford
William Harrell Felton
1853/54 Alfred Linn
John A. Crawford
1855/56 W. Solomon
Abda Johnson
1857-58 J. R. Fulmore
Joseph L. Neel
1959-60 M. A. Hardin
Thomas J. Wofford
1861-62-63 Ex. Warren Akin
Samuel Sheats§

---

*A son of Judge and Mrs. James R. Brown of Cherokee county, was born in 1858, d. Aug. 17, 1931; a nephew of war governor J. E. Brown and first cousin of J. M. Brown; m. first Caroline Field (dec.) by whom there is a son, James, and second Pauline Newman by whom there are Pauline (Nunnally), Lewis and Julian Emerson. Mr. Brown was a progressive farmer; member of Raccoon Baptist church.
†Thomas Espy died in 1860 in his sixty-eighth year; b. in Lincoln county, N. C., moved to Cherokee, in 1848; justice of peace in 1834.
‡Elnathan D. Hudgins, b. 1812, d. Dec. 1891, buried at Calhoun; recruiting officer during Civil War at Griffin, Ga.; m. Margaret Chastain by whom there were fourteen children. Mary Hudgins, a granddaughter, m. H. B. Warlick, lives in Cartersville.
§Born in 1829; m. Martha Sheats who died Sept. 14, 1913, aged 80 years, and was a sister of Capt. A. Y. Sheats of Kingston. He was called "Little Sammy" Sheats. He died Mar. 18, 1878, and he and his wife are buried in Kingston cemetery.

1863-64-65	Ex. J. C. Roper	1882-83	Ex.-83 Ann. Adj. Augustus Warren Fite
	Jno. W. Hooper, Jr.		C. M. Jones*
1865/66-66	Nathan Howard	1884-85	Adj. William H. Felton
	J. C. Simms		Augustus W. Fite
1868	Ex.-69-70 Ex. F. M. Ford	1886-87	Adj-1888-89 Adj. Wm. H. Felton,
	M. J. Crawford (did not qualify in 1870;		Augustus M. Foute
1870	Ex. W.L. Goodwin, Jan. 28-	1890-91	Adj. William L. LeConte
1871-72-72	Adj. John W. Gray		William T. Burge
	John W. Wofford	1892-93	J. M. Veach,
1873-74	Thomas H. Baker		James Monroe Neel
	Thomas Tumlin	1894-95	J. H. Gilreath,
1875-76	Thomas H. Baker		G. A. Fink
	J. L. Neel	1896-97	Adj.-97 F. M. Durham
1877-	Thomas Tumlin		C. B. Vincent
	D. V. Stokely	1898-99	Kirby-S. Anderson†
1878-79	Adj. Thomas W. Milner		M. L. Johnson
	R. H. Cannon	1900-01	Kirby-S. Anderson
1880-81	Adj. Thomas W. Milner		M. L. Johnson
	John C. Branson		

*C. M. Jones: b. July 29, 1829 in DeKalb county; was a member and 1st Lt. of Co. F, 36th Ga. Regt., then colonel of 2nd Regt. Ga. Res. He bought 1000 acres along Pumpkinvine creek in 1873 and found rich deposits of minerals. At Emerson he built the first malleable iron plant in the State and was one of the founders of the town of Emerson. From there he built broad guage railroads to various mines on his property; he was a progressive farmer; was candidate for the populist party for State treasurer before 1895 and was a delegate to the National convention in 1892. In 1850 he married Sarah Carroll, b. June 9, 1831, d. Feb. 24, 1922, of Gwinnett county, by whom there were ten children and these lived in the county: Mary m. J. E. Morris of this county; Thomas H. has a son, Roy Jones, living at Atco; Charles W. m. Ella Cunyus; J. Melvin, b. May 17, 1869, m. Pearl DeWeese, died 1909, by whom there were Melvin and Robert; Lena, m. John Chambly of Canton. Col. Jones died June 25, 1910, and is buried at Emerson.

†Kirby-Smith Anderson, youngest son of John Marshall and Emily Anderson, was born in Kingston, Dec. 29, 1863. His parents came to Georgia from S. C. before the Civil War. His father served under Gen. E. Kirby Smith, and he numbered among his ancestors John Marshall, the McDaniels, and the Woodrows. His maternal ancestor, Richard Anderson, was an officer in the Revolution. Kirby Anderson taught school in north Georgia; began practice of law in Cartersville; in 1902 moved to Madison, Ga., where he became a partner with Emerson George; served as chairman of the board of county commissioners, served sixteen years as judge of county court, then city court; a Mason; during World War served as Co. chairman of Red Cross; teacher of a Sunday school class; a steward in the Methodist church until his death on Aug. 20, 1928. His wife was Miss Susie Butler of Jackson, Tenn., and his brother, Newton Anderson, now lives in Adairsville.

1902-03-04-05-06 John W. Akin
 Jas. J. Conner
1907-08-08 Ex. J. A. Price,
 W. J. Neel
1908-08-Ex. J. B. Crawford
1909-10 M. L. Johnson
 J. A. Price
1911-12 Ex.-12 M. L. Johnson
 Jno. J. Calhoun*
1913-14-15 Ex.-16-17 Ex. Emried Dargan Cole (d. May 27, 1928; buried in Cartersville.)
 W. A. Dodd
1917-18-19-20-21-22 Wm. Davis Trippe†,
 M. L. Johnson
1923-23 Ex.-24 Geo. H. Aubrey
 Wm. D. Trippe
1925 William H. Lumpkin (b. Aug. 2, 1892, in Bartow county)
 William D. Trippe
1827-28 Hadon Pierce McElreath (b. Oct. 5, 1880, Douglas county.)
 William D. Trippe
1929-30-31/32 Hadon P. McElreath
 William Shepherd Peebles (b. June 29, 1876, Nelson county, Va.)

WHERE EARLY RECORDS MAY BE FOUND

The oldest marriage records may be found in the Ordinary's office: Record Book "B", 1837-1843; "D", 1849-1853; "E", 1853-1868 up to date.

The oldest will record is Book "A", 1836-1885, up to date, Ordinary's office, county court house.

The Deed Records, A, B, D, E, F, J, K, L, M, N, and O were destroyed by the Federal army in 1864. The following may be found in the clerk of the Superior Court's office in the county court house:

C, Aug. 1837-Sept. 1838.
G, April, 1845-July, 1847.
H, July, 1847-May, 1848.
I, 1847-1850.
P, Sept. 1861-March 1867, up to date.

Minutes of the county court may be found in the same office from 1865 up to date.

Minutes of the Cass inferior court of the May term of 1855 to the May term of 1868 may be found in the office of the Ordinary.

Earliest tax digest, 1874-5-6-7, in office of Ordinary.

Minutes of court of ordinary, 1853-69; 1869-1880 up to date.

County newspapers on file 1857-58; 1866 up to date.

---

*John J. Calhoun: b. Feb. 13, 1838 at Calhoun Mills, S. C., d. Mar. 2, 1926 in Cartersville. Cousin of John C. Calhoun, and his wife was Elizabeth Sayre by whom there were Elizabeth, Louise (Vandeventer), Lila (Morgan), Sayre (dec.), Joseph (dec.), Estelle (Dobbins, dec.), and John.

†William Davis Trippe: b. Oct. 8, 1870, in Polk county. (See Ga. Official and Statistical Register, 1927.)

1840 CENSUS, CASS COUNTY†

Name of Head of Family	M.*	F.*	S.*	Name of Head of Family	M.	F.	S.
Elisha Lowery	2	1		Jeremiah Rich	1	1	
Francis Holden	3	1		Jas. M. C. Dawson	5	2	
Wm. Armstrem	1	2		James H. Russel	1	3	
Joseph Holden	4	2		Wm. Rich	6	4	2
John Harden	7	2	5	James Powell	1	7	
Blackston McKnabb	3	2		P. M. Tate	3	2	
Morris Quinn	4	2		Allen Powell	7	4	
Peter Quinn	2	1		Reider Boon	6	5	
Wm. A. Hooper	4	4	3	Hiram Runian	1		
Martin McBrier	6	6		Alixander Holady	3	5	
Eliza Hooper	1	1		Edmond Aldredg	3	1	
David Caley	5	4		Hezekiah D. McDonald	1	3	
James Wetherbee	4	2		E. D. Hudgeons	5	3	1
John Goodson	1	3		Harbert Hill	2	6	
Joseph Wilson	1	2	21	Zimery Grindle	1	2	
Henry H. Kirkham	1	3		Wm. Gassaway	5	5	
Robert Kirkham	3	4	8	A. S. Dorsey	1	2	
J. P. Bowen	3	3		J. J. Nix	1	1	
Daniel D. Roney	1	1		Russel Cannon	5	6	
John Love	3	5	2	Andrew Addams	3	3	
John Dillard	2	5		Joseph P. Gerrel	1		6
William Dillard	7	4		Charles H. Nelson	1	3	4
Moses McSpadden	2	3	6	Edmond Ellis	1	1	3
John H. Brack	3	5		Elisha Russell	4	3	
Samuel G. Surratt	1	5		Andrew Borders	5	1	4
Henry McConnal	4	2	1	Washington Drummand	2	3	1
Clemmons Lee	2	3		James R. Brock	3	1	
John Walravens	3	4		Elisha Lowery	1	1	
Wm. Walravens	4	1		Mary Turner	7	4	
Johnathan Walravens	5	2		Peter Traner	32	1	
Nathaniel N. Baxter	2			Samuel S. Crews	3	4	
Richard Couch	3	2		Ann Harvy		2	
Elijah Dillard	5	2		Silas Baker	3	2	
John Ellis	4	1		Luke W. Ginn	3	6	
Richard Kelly	1	2		David H. Teat	1	2	
George Pack	4	3		Henry Wingro	2	5	
George Sheels	5	4		Mary Hammond		3	
Alexander Strickland	2	2		Richmond Baker	4	3	
Sary Keith	2	3		Tilmon Driskel	3	6	
James M. Keith	5	3	1	John M. Baker	1	1	
Garrett Buckner	3	3		Gideon Trout	1	4	
Moses McSpadden	1	4		Stepen Slaton	7	4	
Richard Morris	6	3		George Hart	2	1	
Robert Benton	2	4		Sary Bachelder	1	3	
John Wimes	5	2		Moses Keys	6	5	
Richard Hudson	2	2		John Turner	3	4	
Wm. Gregory	2	2	6	Z. G. Turner	3	2	
Wm. Wooten	6	3		Gurtis Dempsey	1	3	
Chaney M. Linzey	2	2		Moses H. Gess	3	2	

†From Census Bureau, Washington, D. C. The Etowah D. A. R. made it possible to have this copied by B. D. Hill, Jr., as it includes the pensioners for Revolutionary service. It is the first to have any bearing on the county and the order of the taking gives a key to neighbors. This is a condensed form. The complete census is in the State Department of Archives and History.

*"M." and "F." are the number of white males and females under five years of age up to and over ninety years of age. "S." is the number of slaves in a family. No corrections in the spelling of proper names are ever made in copying a census.

Name				Name			
Martha Burnes	2	4		Romulous Pass	3	2	1
Thomas Burnes	1	1		Christopher Thomas	2	6	
J. M. Daniel	8		46	George F. Gulden	3	1	
John Dawson	6	2	9	William Addams	4	1	
Josep Sponce	2	4		James Packston	1	1	2
Ezekiel Putman	3	2	2	Azriah Bradley	4	6	
John J. Lackey	5	3		Decature Stephens	3	2	16
Samuel McMuken	5	2		Joseph Campbell	4	3	6
Olaman Dadgen	2	4		David B. Barrett	4	2	3
James J. Leat	3	2		George Stewart	6	2	1
Laxton Crow	5	1		James Henderson	4	6	
W. E. Foster	2	3		William D. Walker	4	6	
John Greenwood	2	4		John T. Miller	3	7	
Elisha Wright	3	2		Michael Pitner	2	1	
Johnathan Crow	4	5		Wiley Brogdon	2	6	13
Alphus H. Wilbour	4	1		Charles Adair	2	4	
John P. Campbell	1	3	6	Elisha H. Mathews	6	4	7
Daud Garrison	3	3		Issac Retherford	5	3	
Farrow Stegall	7	3	1	James R. Lunce	4	3	5
John M. Brown	7	2		Wm. McDonald	4	4	
John H. Sloan	6		3	Shadrick Harmer	1	1	
John Quirk	1	2		Jesse W. Morrow	4	4	
Martin Hurt	1	1		David S. Law	3	1	13
Rebecca Hunter	6	4		Azariah P. Baley	1	2	
P. W. Preast	9	2		Benjamin H. Baley	6	3	9
John K. Allen	3	1		James Dugger	1	4	
Wm. C. Burnett	3	5	5	Wm. Henderson	3	2	11
James Allen	7	3		Richard Henderson	4	3	5
Wm. N. Close	2	5	1	John Baley	4	5	
Joab Mosteller	6	4		Henry Braben	1	1	
James Gaines	4	6	5	Joshua Baley	4	6	5
Ezekiel Graham	5	3	7	Hilerey S. Gardner	2	1	
John Alin	5	4		Banister R. Bray	5	7	
Thomas Gaddis	1	2		Lewis Bray	2	7	
James Leek	5	1		David Sauls	2	4	
Wm. J. Wright	2	4		Joshua Bowden	7	2	4
Joseph Doss	4	5		Joseph Erwin	4	1	
Wm. Watts	5	5		Edward Mackin	1	4	
Wm. M. Penn	3	4		Joseph Bran	3	4	
Reuben Keep	3	1		James Macklereath	4	4	
John Keep	3	4		Johnathan Whitesides	7	4	3
N. B. Thomas	4	1		Benjamin W. Bell	7	2	1
D. M. Williames	2	5	4	John Mellwee	6	7	
Thos. W. Holsenback	3	2		Baylus W. Lewis	2	1	6
James Hammet	3	4		Benjamin Penn	4	1	5
Amos Wilbourn	3	6	1	John B. Lewis	1	3	
Duke H. Hodge	1	1		James Gray	6	4	
Benjamin Brown	5	4		Edward Boman	2	1	
James Day	10	2	4	Obediah Snow	7	3	
Isaiah Williams	3	1		David McMurrin	2	1	
Daniel Anderson	2	2		John Pickard	6	4	
David Morrow	3	3	1	Roubin Edwards	1	1	
John Mehand	2	1		Micajah Bryant	4	5	
Wesley Kinman	2	6		Andrew Ray	3	2	
David Sisk	1	1		John M. Dowdy	3	3	
Edward J. Maddox	6	3		Hiram Liles	3	5	
Wiley Beardin	5	6		Thomas Norwood	1	1	
John Beardin	4	4	8	John G. Bird	2	2	6
Mathew Quinn	2	3		Mathew Davis	5	4	
James Moris	5	6		John Lively	2	4	
John Black	5	4		James S. Erwin	3	5	1
Johnathan Black	3	5		Thomas Lively	3	2	
Nathaniel Black	6	5		William Kelly	6	6	
William Voight	3	1		S. R. Kelly	5	1	
Jesse Swain	5	7	6				

Name			
Thomas S. Hickman	5	3	
John M. Smith	5	4	
A. H. Warren	2	1	
Francis J. Andore	2		
J. W. Henajen	3	2	
William Johnson	1	2	
Turner Lard	1	1	
James Lard	4	1	
John Potts	1	6	
Warren Lard	2	2	
Benjamin Kirtland	6	3	
Jessey Liles, Jnr.	4	2	
Jessey Liles, Snr.	1	1	
Aaron Lard	1	1	
George W. Ballew	2	4	
Elizabeth Kelly	3	5	
Jain Castain	7	5	
William B. Grant	9	5	
John Peoples	4	3	
Jam. M. Erwin	4	3	19
S. S. Hand	4	1	
William Peopels	7	1	
Benjamin Balding	2	2	
Philip Ramsauer	4	4	8
William Stripling	4	4	
Samuel Norwood	9	6	
William Ponder	7	3	
Mary Countriman		5	
James Bruster	7	4	
Jain Ponder	1	1	1
Samuel Franklin	4	3	
Nathan Hutchens	2	1	
Moses Finley, Jnr.	5	1	
Moses Finley	1	1	
Allen Braseel	1	1	
John Ponder	3	4	
Silas Ponder	2	3	
John P. Ponder	3	1	
Leroy McWherter	6	5	
John C. Philips	3	3	
Thomas Philips	2	1	
William Thomas	3	2	
Jordan Gilly	8	2	
James Liles	4	4	
Mathew Robertson	5	7	3
R. M. Barnwell	2	4	19
Ephragm Davis	2	1	
Demcy Hathcock	3	3	
Daniel Kelly	3	3	
Felix H. Walker	3	7	
Martha Carns	2	1	
Russel Addams	2	1	
Nathaniel Addams	2	3	
Charles Horten	4	5	
John Johnson	4	3	
William Jarrett	5	3	
Dinah Rice	3	3	
Jesse Young	4	6	
John G. B. Addams	9	4	3
Jolly Atkins	5	3	
William Hopper	3	3	5
James Freeman	1		19
Warren Scroggan	2	3	
Zacheriah F. Wilson	1	1	
James Shelnut	1	1	3
Pleasant Watts	6	5	3
James Addams	7	2	
Mary Fulbright	5	3	
Edmond T. Penn	4	3	
Samuel Chambers	1	1	1
Hosea Butler	5	4	
Robert Chambers	1	3	
Absalem Butler	5	6	
William F. Passmore	1	5	
Elisha Trimble	5	4	4
Benjamin Ivy	3	3	
Elisha F. Ivy	1	2	
James M. Fields	3	1	5
Asbury Pinion	1	2	
Spencer Horten	6	1	
Thomas Bird	1	5	7
H. M. Finly	2	2	
Charles Riker	6	9	2
Elisha B. Finly	3	1	
William G. Dothit	1	1	
Robbert Henderson	2	1	11
John Goss (trangant)	1		
Joseph Jolley	5	5	
Archabald McDaniel	1		9
Vinson Brown	4	5	
James Brown	6	3	
Pendleton Isbel	7	4	1
Willis B. Bishop	1	1	
D. F. Bishop (Trangant)	1		
John S. Rowland	6	2	54
Joseph Michal	1	1	9
Moses Scott	2	5	11
James M. Hamilton	1	1	3
Lemul J. Hilbehesh	1	3	1
Nethaniel Bullet	2		9
Francis L. Brandom	6	4	
Geo. G. B. Addams	3	2	
John Manning	4	5	
James Reede	2	6	
James Jones	6	1	22
Wm. S. Sorrils	4	2	6
Samuel G. Hamilton	7	2	22
Abegal Hamilton	6	2	6
Arnold Milner	1	3	19
Mary Jackson (Trangant)		1	
Basley G. Coursesy	3	2	
Thomas Humphrey	3	3	
Francis Wisdom	1	2	
Charles Dodson	3	3	3
James S. Heath (Transant)	1		
A. M. Hamilton	3	1	3
Mary Hamilton	3	6	5
Wm. Gladdin	2	2	
Lemuel P. Butt	2	1	4
Samul Gladden	2	4	
Granvill Pullin	5	4	6
Joseph Gladden	3	5	1
Lee Hendrex	4	3	
Z. Edwards	5	8	2
James McGee	1	1	7
Robert Young	7	2	11

Name				Name			
Armstod Dodson	5	2	14	Pinkney Dedwily	1		
Menassee Cullens	3	7		Thomas Johnson	1		
Charles Coursey	4	5	3	Milton Loveless	1	1	
Mathew Carter	1	1		Jackson H. Wesmorland	3	4	
Ramon R. Ray	1	2	7	David Hubbard	3	2	
James Howerd	2	4		Soloman Thompson	2	3	
Elen Jackson	1	3		John Clayton	4	1	14
John McCarver	2	2		James Pattillo	3	3	
Miles Mallins	1	1		Buckner Harvill	3	4	
Francis R. Kilinsworth	1	1	5	Wm. Puckett	1	2	1
Wm. Bolt	1			Edmond D. Puckett	5	2	3
Larken Dodgins	3	5	1	Lewis Tumlin	3	2	14
Pleben Granagan	1			Henry Williams	4	2	1
Charles Morrissan	1	1		Felix Franklin	3	4	
Nancy Baty	1	5		John Kenady	5	5	4
Benjamin F. Williams	2	3		Terrel Corrender	3	4	
Robert Watson	3	2		Elizabeth Heath	1	1	
Thomas Breedelove	5	2		John McElroy	3	2	
Jesse Ball	4	5		B. S. Hardman	2	4	1
Clement Mullins	4	4		Uel Harper	2	3	3
Stafford G. Wallis	5	2		George Gladden	1	1	
Shadrack Strickland	1	2		Sothron Higg	3	1	9
John Chastain	2	6		Lewis Yarborough	3	3	
E. W. Ryley	2	4		Joseph Baker	1	4	
Wm. Neleigh	7	4	9	John Lother	10	1	1
Joseph Hicks	4	5		Wm. Lacourt	1	1	
Wood Vinson	2	1		Wm. Prigan	2	3	
John B. Hultensor	2	3		Henry Watson	3	8	
Mathew Kelly	9	1		Mary Baker	1	3	
R. P. Lacky	5	3		Benjamin P. Carlton	3	6	
John H. Bagwell	3	4		Mathew G. Kazy	2	3	
James Maben	15	2	17	N. R. Bramlett	1	3	
Rowland Bryant	6	5	1	James Williams	2	3	
Allin Pinsan	8	6	1	Wm. Martin	3	1	
Thomas J. Brown	2	3	13	Aron Underwood	4	7	6
Tomas Esby	4	2	6	Charles Martin	2	1	9
Jacob Reede	6	2		John Dobbs	5	6	11
John Hatch	3	3		James Gray	3	6	
Wm. Bridges	3	2		Alfred Manor	3	5	
Milton Hargis	3	3		Elijah Manor	4	6	
S. V. Smith	2	2	1	Wm. Lothredge	4	1	
Ebenezer Mitchell	4	3		Felix Arthur	3	6	2
George W. Winnett	1	1		John Leeroy	2	3	
Joseph Row	3	3		Irvin Martin	3	3	2
Wm. W. Carke	4	2	7	A. B. McFaddin	3	2	
George W. Tumlin	7	2	1	Sary Eaton	1	2	
Wm. M. Richards	3	3		Joseph Suthard	2	1	
Willey J. Norten	4	2	1	Joseph M. Suthard	1	1	
Wm. E. Mills	3	3		Pleasant Shaddix	2	2	
John Pitts	6	3	6	John Robertson	5	4	
Joseph F. Hamilton	2	3	3	David Qualls	1	1	
Elizabeth E. Smith				Jesse Stepp	1	3	9
John W. Lewis	4	2	40	Joseph Shaw	4	3	
Mary W. Lewis		1	7	James Dickenson	1	2	9
Jeremiah Milsaps	3	4		Wm. Dothit	5	4	7
Maryann E. Ford	1	3		Joashly James	2	4	
John Leak	6	3	20	Mark Williams	5	3	
Sary Carliles		1	5	Wm. Brewster	4	3	34
B. T. Harrisson	5	5		Benjamin F. Smith	1	1	
James Wesmorland	3	3		Archabald Ray	3	3	
Joseph Gladden	5	3		Anderson Massy	5	3	
James Parker	2	5		Andrew Countryman	2	3	
Mathew Holland	3	2		Wm. W. Shaw	6	5	
George Jewell	4	2	1	Mark Jackson	1	1	1

Name				Name			
Hiram Dunagan	7	4		James Blair	1	1	
Wm. Jackson	3	5		Samuel McDow	1	7	7
George Bell	5	4		Allen Cook	5	2	
Wm. Dunaway	4	4		Daniel Copelin	2	3	
C. C. Hickman	6	3		Reuben Norris	1	2	
John Demcy, Sr.	1	2		Hiram R. Prueitt	3	4	
John Demcy, Jnr.	1	2		Turner Conaway	1	2	
Martin Stedham	9	5	6	Joseph Henderson	3	2	
Ezekiel Henderson	1	1		Jacob B. Law	1	3	
John Walker	2	2		Joel Folkner	7	5	
Margret E. Sanford	2	4		James M. Owens	3	3	
Robert Hutchinson	4	5		Elisha Smith	4	1	
James Long	1	2		James Chernes	3	3	
David Burroughs	4	3	12	Wm. Eaton	2	2	
Robert Anderson	4	1		Wm. Smith	1	3	
Stephen Harris	4	3		James Benevill	2	3	1
Wm. Beck	6	3		Corneilus Burnes	1	1	
Ambrose Carson	5	2		Masourie Chernes	2	1	
Owen Reede	3	5		John A. Willis	5	1	
Joseph Henderson	3	5		Larrance Wood	2	3	
Shadrick Carson	1	1		Garvin Black	6	3	
I. H. Henson	2	5		Jesse M. Chambers	3	4	
Shem Cherns	2	3		James M. Townsen	4	3	
John Hood	1	2		Hugh Macklin	3	1	2
Jeorg Reede	3	5		Roger Murfey	1	1	6
Wm. Love	2	1		Lewis Ballard	7	2	
A. E. Sewell	1	1		L. D. Wood	1	8	1
Zachariah Dawson	4	4		Johenathan Tompson	1	2	
Martin Keey	6	4		Ludwell Williams	5	4	
Wm. Bassett	1	1		John Stokes	2	1	
Sinclare Self	4	6		Mairs Cochram	2	3	
Wm. M. Henson	1	2		John Wofford	3	3	
Wm. James	2	4	2	Rebecca Lankford		3	
Wm. G. Black	3	2		Mary P. King	1	1	5
John T. Ponder	3	1		Moses Pinson	1	1	
Leonard Morrow	2	3		Patiener Floyed	2	2	
Duncan Murceson	5	3		Elijah Pinson	4	5	1
Wm. Matthews	5	5		John Coley	4	4	
David Elmore	2	3		Charles Love	3	4	
Wm. Mathews	1	1		F. J. Griffith	4	2	
Andrew Miller	2	1	3	Robert W. Slawter	3	2	
Joseph Black	2	2		John Blalock	3	3	
Wm. Black	1	3		Robert Venable	2	1	
Andrew F. Wolley	5	3	12	Harriet J. Harmon	3	2	
Elias Godden	1	4		Cordy Drake	4	2	
Wm. Copelin	7	4		Edmond Drake	4	3	
Elizabeth Russell	5	2		Hartewell Drake	4	3	
Joshua Reeves	8	5		James L. Venable	4	2	
Wm. H. Wilson	4	3		Daniel Long	1	1	
James C. Gaines	2	1		Wm. Gray	1	2	
John Parker	3	1		Rebecca Franklin	2	5	
William Wilson	1	2		Benjamin Scott	4	6	
Mansfield Simmons	2	2		Daniel Beachom	6	3	
Daniel Mostiller	2	5		Wm. Blalock	5	4	3
King Chandalier	6	7		Robert N. McLin	4	1	2
Haily Shaw	7	6		Wm. Hays	3	4	
Harper Poore	1	3		Wm. C. Wyly	3	2	14
Zacheriah Aycock	7	5	4	Wm. Grass	3	4	
D. M. Penn	3	2		Henry McCrary	4	3	
Joseph McCutchens	7	4		George Stovall	1	1	
Zachariah Cox	5	4		Wilkins Stovall	4	3	
Joseph Mayhorn	3	7	3	James Stovall	2	7	
Larkin Towers	2	1	7	David Morgan	5	3	
Johnathan McDow	2	2	6	Joseph Morgan	1	1	
Reuben Gaines	1	1		Felix G. Denman	6	4	28

Name				Name			
Pleasan Potter	4	1	16	James Kirmham	4	2	1
Thomas Lownsen	4	5	9	John Still	1	3	
Jirrmiah Wilsun	5		1	Wm. Kinman	6	3	
Hugh Gaston	6	5		Stephen Mayes	2	6	18
Alixander Dickson	5	5		Michal Fincher	2	4	
Wm. F. Jones	2	2		S. P. Rowland	4	2	
James Waters	4	4		Vianna Ellis	4	4	
Johnathan Williams	1	3	2	H. C. Phillips	3	5	1
Joseph L. Disert	3	1	1	Williamson Daldy	4	4	
Prissilla Cherry		3		Wm. J. Tarvin	6	3	
Joseph Murdock	5	6		Rebecca Tarvin		1	
Jesse A. Beam	1	3		Meriah McKnabb	1	1	
Jackson Nichols	2	4		Dudley Airs	3		
Benjamin Keker	5	9		Martha Dunkin	5	3	
Madason M. Dugless	2	3		Joseph Dunkin	2	2	
Johnathan Tate	4	2		John Sutherland	2	1	
Albert Nichols	3	6		Joseph Howell	7	2	
Abraham Tate	2	1		James G. Langley	2	2	
Elizabeth Cannon				James Chrisman	2		
John Greswell	1	1		Clarasy Crawford	3	3	
John Willis	3	6		Joshua Stewart	1	5	
Thomas Hall	4	1		Asa Tate	4	5	
Philip McIntire	3	3	3	Miles A. Leatherwood	2	1	
John McIntire	3	2		John Black	4	6	
A. J. Carr	2	3	1	David A. Fraley	2	2	
E. P. Howell	4	2		A. W. McBrayer	3	5	
Thomas Evins	3	2		S. W. Wigley	1	2	
Francis Jordan	3	2		Overton Hitchcock	4		11
David Lyles	4	3		Joshua Philips	1	6	1
Martin Dowls	5	1		Wm. Copper	2	3	
Clark Turner	1	3		Nancy Candeler	3	2	1
Gibson Hix	2	2		John Harber	2	5	8
John E. Bowman	3	5		Robert Kirkham	2	4	
Joshua Dowsey	6	2		Nancy Burris	3	3	
Sherwood Boman	8	4		Demcy Finley	2	4	
Isaac Baker	3	7	4	Horace Smith	5	3	
Wm. Willinham	2	2	2	Abraham Chandlier	4	4	10
John Nichols	3	4		James Wills	1	1	
Gilbert Drake	2	2		John Worthy	4	5	
Samuel Pottes	4	3		Issac Randle	4	5	
Alfred Henrey	3	1		Green Rowland	5	3	
James M. Dicky	7	4		J. H. B. Clark	2	3	
Elijah Perkins	3	3		John Blalock	1	1	3
Ambros King	2	6		Hansford W. Blalock	2	2	
David Potts	3	4		John A. Cooper	3	2	
Edley L. Hamilton	1	1		Thos. G. Phillips	5	6	1
Anson Holcomb	1	1		E. W. Kinman	1	2	
George H. Crain	2	1		Wm. H. Kirkham	1	2	
Archabald Miller	9	6	1	Reube H. Jones	5	6	
Wm. Potts	2	4		Thos. Jordan	7	4	
Elijah Johnson	2	1		Roger Green	3	4	
Wily Matthews	3	1		Elias Lay	2	1	
Benson Nally	1	1		Wm. H. Langstan	1	1	
James Jordan	4	1		Charles Lay	5	1	1
G. F. Swagety	4	2	1	B. R. Mayes	1	1	1
Andrew Prater	1	2	2	Larkin Dunn	8	2	
Oliver Croyly	4	3	8	Johnathan Baugh	4	5	
Daud Young	2	3		John Baugh	1	3	
Wm. Stephens	7	3		Johnathan Baugh, Snr.	2	2	
Bazeley Goin	2	5		G. Higganbottom	3	3	1
Wm. Dawson	9	4	2	John Higganbottom	3	2	3
Robert Sego	3	2		Hiram Brooks	3	2	
John Jones	4	2		Joseph Trout	3	2	
Wm. R. McCrarey	5	4		Clark Jackson	3	5	
John Upton	2	5					

Name			
Richard Stratton	2	3	
Lewis Smith	5	3	
Thomas Conley Snr.	2	7	3
Alfred B. Wardsworth	1	2	
Thomas Conley, Snr.	2	7	3
Melington M. Blalock	4	5	2
Gabril Hight	5	3	2
Wm. Tate	3	4	
John Venable	5	3	
Volentine H. Cain	2	3	1
Samuel Hodge	3	5	
Robert Henry	1	1	
Tirey Jackson	3	2	
Joel Fain	5	3	2
Stephen Tolly	8	1	
David Miller	1	2	2
Obidiah Miller	6	4	
Wm. Jeffries	4	5	
Philip M. Bumgarner	1	2	
James Lay	1		
Alexander Cameran	4	5	4
John Lay	1	3	7
Benjamin P. Merciers	5	5	
Wm. J. Fuller	1	1	2
Jeremiah Robbins	5	5	5
Woodly A. Thomas	5	3	4
Jesse Godfrey	3	2	
Turner Philips	3	4	
Uriah Phillips	4	1	
Michiel Kirkham	7	2	2
Joseph Cooper	5	3	
Thomas Obrian	7	1	
John B. Rueker	2	3	
Thos. Norton	9	2	1
William Hardgroves	2		8
Samuel Adair	3	3	3
B. F. Adair	3	3	
Collens Monnald	4	1	2
Robert Saxon	2	2	
Amis Haitley	2	5	
Claborn Kinmon	4	4	
David Walis	5	5	
Edward Adair	5	2	
William Haward	4	2	9
Robert R. Or	3	3	3
Joseph Stokes	2	2	
Joseph Blackwood	2	2	1
William Curtis	2	3	
?	8	1	4
James P. Hubberd	1	2	
Jesse Leeroy	6	2	
Lemuel J. Hubberd	1	2	
James Kirkpatrick	7	4	1
Benson Cox	6	1	
John Rogers	3	2	
David Mackelwee	6	6	
George Mackaskee	3	3	7
Alixander Rogers	1	4	
Ephram Coleman	5	2	
Jacob Stroup	10	2	5
Allen Suggs	5	5	
John Davidson	4	4	
Thomas Carter	3	3	
Eli Latty	5	2	
Joseph Stroup	3	2	
Alixander Stroup	4	1	
Sanford Babb	1	2	
Joshua Knight	3	3	
Mary Yates		5	
Starke A. Brown	2	1	
Starkely M. Brown	1	3	
Seabourn Nally	5		
George Hinkle	4	3	
James Ritchie	5	7	
Daniel Chitwood	6	5	
Margret McCollum		2	
Samuel A. McCollum	1	1	
Thos. J. Wofford	4	1	8
Daniel Rice	3	3	
H. McCollum	1	1	
Richard B. Vinson	1	1	
Isaac M. Vinson	1	1	
George Alexander	1		17
David Masey	1	1	
John Guyton	2	2	9
John Smith	8	3	
Robert H. Guyton	4	2	
Nathaniel Guyton	5	3	
Patrek Moore	2	3	
James M. Drummond	3	3	
Susan Leeroy	1	2	
Thos. Cook	4	1	
Robbert Moore	2	3	3
Thos. Collins	2	1	
James McCollum	7	5	
Wm. Guyton	2	3	
Allen Walker	4	4	
Silas Bell	4	6	
Lucinda Fowler		1	
Jeremiah Wofford	2	2	5
James Wofford	4	3	
Archabald Ritchie	3	2	
John Branton	1	2	
Wm. Gains	1	2	
Linzey Hendrix	2	1	
Aley A. Vinson	1	2	1
Edward Buford	6	5	
Benjamin S. Miller	5	7	
Sary Ford	1	2	
Samuel Ward	3	3	
Nathaniel Griffin	3	4	
Charles Bostick	1	2	
Joseph Carter	3	3	
Susan Vinson	1	2	
Quinton A. Finly	3	4	
James Lovless	8	5	
Vardy Thomas	2	2	
Martha Allin	2	2	
John Gassaway	4	5	
Andrew Roe	3	2	
Tarlton Lewis	2	8	11
M. S. Edmonson	3	2	6
Wm. King	3	3	11
Joseph Willingham	5	3	1
Jesse Winsor	3	5	

Name				Name			
S. Davis	3	5		Joel Brawner	6	7	
Hirum Drum	3	3		John Swilliven	3	1	
Walter C. Dickson	4	6		John H. Wiginton	3	1	
Sinclair McMullin	2	8	10	John Milagan	3	7	
John Ponder	2	1		Rachel Thomas		2	
Hilrey Hendrix	8	5		George Worthy	2	1	
Evan Pearson	3	3	4	Tempy Williams		3	
Daniel Burton	3	2		Soloman Loovelady	2	6	
Jeremiah Trap	5	5		Mary White	1	2	
Joseph Pollard	3	3		Wright Hankins	4	7	
Brice C. McKever	4	5		Zacheriah Kitchens	1	4	
Ranson Foster	5	3		James Kitchens	3	3	4
J. N. Craven	4	3	5	Joel Fricks	4	1	
Silvanous Couch	2	3		John B. Fisher	1	2	
Stephen Boling	4	4		David Melton	1	6	
Jerehiah Green	5	4		Joseph B. Kenady	2	3	
Joel Reede	3	2		Henry D. Fricks	5	3	
William Burron	4	1		Ransom Bennett	4	5	
John Dykes	1	2		Milly Terry	2	4	
John Vaughn	6	3	1	Elizabeth McCoo	2	1	
James Upshaw	4	7	19	Charles Pitts	4	2	
Martin Maxwell	3	1	4	Humphrey W. Cobb	2	4	9
J. J. Upshaw	1	3	2	Robert Dickerson	2	2	
G. W. Stubbs		1	3	Wm. B. Seogans	1	2	
Levi Pierce	1	2		Benjamin Kitchens	8	5	
Wm. White	6	3		Calib Dickenson	3	3	
K. Gillis	5	5		Wm. Bell	2	4	
Elizabeth Trap	3	2		Joel Philips	2	6	
Issac Tate	5	2		Stephen Langford	2	4	
John Tate	1	1		Isaac Wigington	6	3	
Abegail Trap		5		Wm. Campbell	3	3	
James Trap	3	4		John Burk	4	2	
Charles Baker	6	4	13	Richard S. Hankins	1	1	
Samuel A. Bradley	4	4	5	James A. Hankins	1	1	
Robert Martin	3	6		James Hyatt	2	1	2
John L. Weaver	3	2		Basheba Fuller	2	1	
Joseph R. Terrell	3	5	16	Reuben Underwood	7	2	4
A. M. Nally	2	2		Wiley Roberts	1	2	
Aaron Nally	4	2		James Tallent	2	2	
Wm. F. Owens	1	6		Geo. W. Underwood	3	1	
John B. Habson	1	4		John Holder	3	4	
Mary Sea	3	4		Coalman Pitts	3	1	19
Solomon Dykes	4	3		Madock Moore	2	3	
Willis Smith	5	5		Thomas W. Brandom	3	4	1
John Huff	3	3		Thomas Barrett	3	3	
Mitchel Beasley	3	4		G. W. Hill	2	3	
Edward D. Baley	1	2		Silas Elliott	4	7	1
Linzy Oglesby	1		19	Isaih Morgan	5	4	
A. T. Fields	1	2		John Kitchens	5	4	
Vinson A. Barton	3	3		Drewry Wall	6	2	
Jesse Baker	3	6	1	David Holder	1	1	
Voluntine Smith	5	3	22	John Fuqua	3	1	
Wm. Rice	1	4		Jacob Williams	1	1	
Reuben H. Pierce	3	1		Robert Philips	5	3	
Stephen Ellis	5	5		Dalton Burge	1		1
Baley Kay	4	1		Nathaniel Burge	4	4	17
John N. Brown	3	3		James Graddy	5	2	
James Barton	3	2		T. W. Saxon	2	2	
Theodore M. Fuell	2	2	1	Aaron Burris	3	2	
Linzy Johnson	6	1	25	James M. Wade	4	1	
Wyett Hicks	5	3	1	Eldridge Wood	3	4	
A. J. Covington	3	2		Emanuel Lion	6	3	
B. B. Bradley	4	5		John Linch	6	1	
Wm. R. Ervin	2	1		C. W. Howard	2	5	14

Name				Name			
John Cobb	1	1		George H. Gilrath	5	4	
Elizabeth Hargis		4		Elijah Kirk	1	3	
Eli Hutto	1	1		John McElreath	5	2	
Benjamin B. Dugless	2	1		Tomas Booker	4	2	
John B. Dugless	2	2		Henry Waldrip	1	1	
Jesse M. Ogley	3	7		Richard Gaines	4	1	
Benjamin Kitchens	5	5	1	Asa Crow	1	4	
Moses Brandon	1	2		Sary Alixander	2	1	
Leroy J. Brandon	1	2		Joseph Jones	2	6	1
James Hays	5	4		Levi Hefner	2	3	
Mathew Turner	7	7		Plesent Frix	4	3	
Lewis McDonald	7	5		Abner England	2	2	
Abrahm Green	4	3		Abigail Williams	1	1	
John Pinkerton	4	1		Tilithy Richards	4	2	
Wm. Sorter	3	4		Wm. Crow	1	3	
Joseph Esman	4	2		Wm. Stovall	2	2	
Thomas G. Philips	3	1		Jeorge B. Reede	1	2	
Martin Forsythe	4	1		Johnathan England	4	6	
Rebecca Hilbourn	5	3		Sebastin Waters	1	5	
Susanna Parker	3	2		Joel Baker	4	3	7
Pleasant Baker	3	3		Green Lowery	1	1	
Samuel Smith	3	1		Joshua Gibson	6	3	
Moses Smith	1	1		Wiley Patterson	3	2	4
Isaac Roberts	5	2		N. N. Welch	2	2	1
O. E. Henderson	5	3		Fredrick S. Hunt	1	1	1
John Burk Snr.	2	2		E. Pinard	1	2	
Chapley Demcy	6	3		James Mason	4	3	1
Sharick Lowrey	6	3		Thomas Spencer	1	1	
Lowery Williams	1	2	14	John King	5	4	
Claracy Hefner	1	3		Jain Park	2	2	6
Travis Cotten	3	1	2	Henry Hately	3	3	1
Martin Keel	2	1		Jesse James	3	4	
Elijah Perkins	6	4		Josey J. Ward	2	1	5
John F. Carroll	4	5		Wm. Hadden	3	1	
Stephen Kirk	2	2		James Morrean	1	2	
James Campbell	2	2	1	Alfred C. Day	2	3	1
Clemmont Carroll	6	2		David B. Stewert	2	2	3
Lorenzo D. Jones	3	1		John C. Burnett	4	2	
Peter L. Barton	3	4		John Sprewel	4	4	
Martin Moody	4	2		Willington Blake	1	4	
Bery W. Gideon	3	6	1	J. H. George	2	1	3
Isaac Anderson	7	4	5	M'meriah Hassell	1	2	
Henry Boman	5	4		Sarah Branning	1	1	
Joseph Bogle	2		2	Benjamin B. Gains	5	2	4
Chany Blake	1	1		Thomas S. Leek	5	2	6
A. M. Russell	1	1	1	Dorcas Leek	8	2	7
Elizabeth Dillard	3	3	2	John Hall	5	6	
Samuel Simpson	1	2	5	Reuben Carter	3	2	
Elizabeth Bradford	2	1	2	Cooper L. Bennett	1	2	
Mark M. Johnson	4	4	1	John P. Atcheson	1	2	
John Stephens	7	7	8	Wm. Dodd	4	3	
Marthaann Finley	1	1	4	Aaron Godfrey	4	6	
Drewry W. Bowen	5	3	2	Levinah Hurt	1	4	
Anderson Owens	7	4		Christopher Dodd	2	3	
David Lewis	4	2		J. P. Thopson	3	1	
Richard Gaines	4	4		Emiriah Tumlin	7	1	2
Wm. S. Sewell	2	1		Daud Sisk	1	3	
L. W. Gaines	1	1		Wm. B. Lowery	1	1	
James L. Carpenter	1	1		D. W. Adrian	5	4	1
James Powers	3	2		Wm M. H. Adrian	2	4	1
Starlin Smith	1	5		A. K. Foster	7	1	2
Mathew Mullenix	2	1		Solomon R. Lowery	3	2	2
Thomas L. Carpenter	3	3	3	Charles Lowery	2	1	
F. W. Creamer	1	1		John Green	4	4	

Name				Name			
Alfred Grogan	5	3		Marshal Jackson	1		11
Daniel Sanders	3	3		Jesse P. Jones	3	2	
Sheneer King	5	2		George Calhoun	5	3	4
Thomas McAddames	1	2	11	Johnson Martin	2	3	
Jobe Rogers	2	2	14	Crawford B. Williams	2	4	
Mesheck Boose	6	2	1	John Williamson	2	1	3
Jonathan D. Buffington	3	4		John Crawford	5	2	5
James L. Stokes	5	5		Jeremiah Bassett	1	1	
Thomas G. Barron	2	1	7	Wm. Thompson	4	6	1
Nelson Kerr	1	3		Daniel McIntire	3	2	
James Furr	2	1		Wm. Lathimore	9	6	8
Nethaniel Fur	1	1		John G. Hill	3	1	3
John H. Campbell	2	2		Wm. Sayler	4	2	1
Jain Henderson	1	2		Jno. P. Spier	8	9	8
Isbell Teneer	3	2		James Miliner	1	1	4
Alfred Linn	3	2	13	James Philips	4	3	7
Henry P. Gaines	3	5	1	H. V. Miller	1	2	10
James Creamer	3	2		David Lowery	4	1	11
Elias Creamer	2	3		Stephenson Johnson	8	2	11
Garrisson Creamer	1	2		Milinda Hargroves	6	5	7
Robert Russell	5	5	2	A. Fricks	5	2	
Eli W. Dilday	4	1	1	S. D. Fricks	3	1	
John W. Ambrister	1	2		Robert H. Patton	10	5	18
Thomas G. Dunlap	2	2	1	George B. Russell	3	2	1
Henry F. McIntire	1	2	1	Reuben H. Pogue	7	3	
Sarah Ralls	3	3	6	John Russell	6	4	10
Joseph Chapman		2		John M. McTier	3	3	1
John B. Hood	5	2		James Madden	2	4	
W. D. Hassell	4	1		Wm. Fain	1	1	18
James L. Lancaster	5	5		Cornelus D. Terhune	4	2	5
Mary Luther	2	4		Allen Dyer	2	1	4
Augustas R. Wright	3	3	3	John H. Thompson	1	2	
Turner H. Tripp	3	5	8	Samuel Badget	2		3
John Brown	13	2	10	Samuel Morgan	3	2	1
Moses Strawhorn	4			Wm. J. Cantrill	2	1	2
Martha Kinney	2	2		John Gray	7	1	1
Eliza Gosa	1	2		Leander Goodwin	3	2	
Robert Nelson	3	2		Elias Baker	5	4	
Levinah Lawslis	4	2	4	Samuel Smith	6	5	5
John Watson	2	2		Wm. Turner	4	4	
Marey E. Long	1	4		Robert Hamilton	2	4	6
Gemima Luther	1	1		L. W. Runyan	3	2	
Tilman P. Retherford	2	1		Thomas Hamilton	5	5	49
Wm. G. Ervin	2	3		Michel Fricks	3	4	1
Clabourn P. Waldrip	4	2		J. B. Underwood	3	3	13
				Jacob Rinehardt	1	5	

Evan Peason, Assistant Marshal,

James Milner and John Russell, attested the Census,

James Phillips, J. I. C.

ERRATA

Footnote on p-63, the name should be Harry Hargis

P-71, Zim (dec.) m. Annie Tinsley, daughter of T. W. Tinsley

P-83, "Memoirs of Georgia", Vol. 1, p-865

P-98, Ann Tumlin m. Jesse Ginn

P-122, La Nelle Moon m. Dr. Harry Bradford

P-141, Francis R. Goulding.

P-196, S. R. McCamy; on monument Wiley is Willy

P-213, Co. E, 1st Battalion Ga. Vols.

P-259, Mrs. R. L. Pilling; Mary B. Howard (H. W.)

P-273, John S. Rowland

INDEX

Abromson, A. — 94-181
Adair, J. R. — 42
Adairsville — 22
Adairsville Farmer's Club — 185
Adair, Indians — 22
Akerman, A. T. — 277
Akin, J. W. — 43-152-158-166-198-201
Akin, Warren — 21-33-42-161
Allatoona, town — 28
American Legion — 260
American Textile Co. — 265
Anderson, K. S. — 327
Anderson, O. D. — 59
Andrews' R.R. Raid — 217
Attaway, S. K. — 121
Aubrey, G. H. — 123-172
Auchmutey, John — 93

Baker, Jesse — 43
Baptist Tabernacle — 136
Barnsley, G. — 18-44
Bartow, F. S. — 34
Bartow Herald — 160
Bartow C. & S. Inst. — 151
Bartow Medical Society — 324
Battle of Allatoona — 238
Battle, Cassville — 220
Bauxite — 188
Baxter, T. W. — 69-198
Barytes — 187
Beazley, Dr. J. S. — 48
Bell, Silas — 305
Benham, W. — 45
Best, H. — 47
Best's Chapel — 133
Bill Arp — 294
Black, Geo. S. — 20-52
Boston, F. A. — 49
Boudinott, Elias — 1-111
Bowdoin, J. — 49
Boyd, Carl — 260-278
Boyd, G. M. — 278
Bradford, S. W. — 76
Brainerd Mission — 1-2
Brame, Mrs. S. F. — 150
Brandon, T. W. — 25-47
Brandon's Chapel — 130
Branson, J. C. — 89-120
Brick clays — 203
Bridges, river — 176
Brogdon, Wiley — 84-96
Brown, J. E. — 24-198-201
Brown, J. W. L. — 326
Buford, A. W. — 51-144
Burke, J. W. — 20-141-155
Burge, N. — 49-124

Calhoun, F. R. — 25-328
Calhoun, J. J. — 328
Calico Valley — 76

Candler, A. G. — 301
Cannon, R. H. — 24-50
Carter, Farish — 23-132-144
Carpenter, J. D. — 19-20
Cartersville — 23
C'ville & G'ville R.R. — 172
Cartersville Mills — 266
C'ville & Van Wert R.R. — 169
Cassville — 19-21
Cass Co. Agri. Soc. — 182
Cassville Female College — 141
Cassville Standard — 155-7
Cement rock — 189
Cemeteries — 137
Census — 30-36-329
Change of name — 21-33
Cherokee Indains — 1-5-7
Cherokee Bapt. Col. — 144
Cherokee Baptist Hi School — 153
Cherokee Cavalry — 210
Cherokee Ochre Co. — 203
Cherokee Club — 262
Chunn, S. L. — 52
Churches — 124
City Court Judges — 121
Clayton, R. A. — 70-154
Clayton, H. M. — 70
Climate — 177
Cooper, M. A. — 144-146-161-181-279
Cobb, H. W. — 20-52
Company to remove Indians — 5
Congressional Districts — 325
Collins, Martin — 268
Conner, J. J. — 90-153-185
Consolidated Schools — 154
Conyers, B. H. — 52
Couche, T. R. — 26
County Courts — 119-120
Court House — 21-117-118
County Officers — 304
County Schools — 153
County Superintendents — 154
Crawford, Rev. Jno. — 19-53-124-127-144-146
Crawford, J. A. — 161
Creeks — 174
Crops — 180
Crow Springs — 129-179
Cunyus, D. B. — 50-144

D. A. R. — 257-259
Daves, W. W. — 153
Delegates — 32-162
Deweese, W. A. — 87
Dillard, Lemuel — 85-146
Dobbins, M. G. — 201
Doctors — 322
Dodd, Christopher — 54
Dodd, Wm. — 54
Douthit, J. — 55

341

Dykes, Allen	25--124
Dysart, J. L.	99
Early Settlers	19-42
East & West R.R.	171
Elsas, Jacob	301
Emerson	24
Errata	338
Erwin, J. A.	20-55-150
Etowah Infantry	212-13
Etowah Mounds	6-206
Etowah R.	6-174
Etowah R.R. Co.	194
Euharlee	25
Euharlee Farmer's Club	183
Fair Grounds	182-185
Farrow, H. P.	163-217
Felton, Rebecca L.	148-159-283
Felton, W. H.	164-132-159-283
Feltonian Club	263
Field, E. M.	56
Fite, A. W.	57-112-150-253-254
Fitten, Jno.	149-164
Fleetwood, M. L.	159
Flexatile	204
Ford, F. M.	57
Fouche, S.	58
Foute, A. M.	122
Franklin, A. M.	305
Friendship Church	134
Friendship Monument	195
Gaines, James	58
Garden Clubs	263
George, Rev. J. H.	139
Gibbons, G. R.	246-323
Gillam, L. M.	26-179
Gilreath, J. H.	60-85
Gilreath, G. H.	60-141-182
Gilreath, Nelson	60
Ginn, W. W.	98-37
Grand Jurors	113-115-117
Granger, A. O.	201
Gray, J. H.	61-158-264
Gold	189
Goldsmith, T.	60-146
Goldsmith, W. T.	60-156-213
Goodyear Tire & Rubber Co.	266
Goulding, Dr. F. R.	141-286
Goulding, Mary Howard	286
Hargis, M.	63
Hargove, Z. B.	111-269
Harling, E.	74
Hardin, J. F.	62
Hardin, M. A.	26-62
Hardin, William	3-61
Harris, Corra	286
Harris, Florence C.	143-152
Harris, J. W.	63-112-120-152-157-162
Harris, Rev. G. D.	76
Harris, Nat E.	246
Harris, Peter Charles	247
Harris, T. W. H.	64
Hay, W. P.	48
Hawkins, T. S.	93
Headden, Rev. R. B.	64
Headden, Wm.	64
Hendricks, G. W.	66
Henderson, W. B.	66
Henderson, O. E.	65
Hicks, Thomas	87
Hicks, W. J.	101
Hightower Mission	2
Howard, Rev. C. W.	134-139-181-215-245-288-249
Howard, Frances	223
Howard, J. A.	78
Howard, J. J.	69-146-150-182-270
Howard, G. J.	60
Hood, B. Mifflin Co.	204
Hooper, J. W.	9-67-110-112
Hurt, Joel	201
Huson, Francis	70
Iron	190
Iron Belt R.R.	198
Irwin, David	70
Jackson, L. E.	48-71
Jackson, Mark	70
Jackson, M. C.	71
Jackson, Z. W.	70
Johnson, Abda	72-170-249
Johnson, E. V.	71-162
Johnson, J. J.	71
Johnson, L.	72-161-273
Johnston, Mark	26-75
Johnston, R.	149-291
Jolly, Joseph	73
Jones, C. M.	327
Jones, J. Joe	46-290
Jones, S. P.	152-165-198-290
Jones, R. H.	74
Jones, Dr. T. F.	106
Judges, Cherokee Circuit	112
Justices, Inf. Ct.	303
Key, J. J.	75
Kinabrew, J. W.	75-143
King, W. H.	76
Kingston	25
Kingston Home Guards	214
Knight, Aaron	268
Knight Mercantile Co.	268
Knights of Pythias	255
Kurtz, W. G.	196-217-221
Ladies Aid Society	256
Ladies Mem. Assoc.	255
Larey, P. H.	88-211
Latimer, William	19-20-104
Lawyers	111-324
Leland, Dr. S. W.	182-324
Leake, Dr. W. W.	24-77
Leake, Jno.	77-132
Land, Nathan	21-76-142-148
Le Conte, W. L.	97
Lewis, B. W.	78
Lewis, Dr. J. W.	78-146-162
Lewis, H. D.	79

Lewis, N. D. ... 23
Library ... 262
Ligon, J. O. ... 66
Linn, A. M. ... 79-306
Lions Club ... 263
Limestone ... 199
L. & N. R.R. ... 173
Lockridge, J. ... 80
Lucas, W. H. ... 80
Lumpkin, W. H. ... 46-87
Loudermilk, John ... 92
Loveless, N. ... 63-92-132
Low, Juliette ... 95
Lowe, Isaac ... 80
Lyon, T. J. ... 98-165-198

Macedonia Silver Greys ... 215
Manganese ... 200
Mahan, D. ... 101
Masonic Organ. ... 252
May Day Picnics ... 183
Mayson, Dr. C. N. ... 26-81-150
Maxwell, M. ... 80
McCormick, H. J. ... 12-93
McGinnis, V. B. ... 93
McMurry, M. ... 26-146-149
McTier, H. F. ... 81
Milam, C. M. ... 82-255-270
Milam, Madison ... 82
Milam, S. F. ... 84
Milhollin, J. F. ... 82
Militia Districts ... 109
Militia ... 107
Miller, Dr. H. M. V. ... 83
Mineral Springs ... 178
Milner, Arnold ... 83-134
Milner, R. A. ... 84-136
Milner, T. W. ... 84-112
Morgan, Samuel ... 19
Model School ... 151
Moon, J. M. ... 122
Moon, Lottie ... 150
Mountains ... 177
Mosteller Mills ... 264
Munford, L. M. ... 14-84
Munford, L. S. ... 85-198
Murchison, Duncan ... 86

Neal, A. V. ... 308
Neel, J. L. ... 23-85
Neel, J. M. ... 121
Neel, Mrs. W. J. ... 293
Neel, W. J. ... 158-293
Nelson, E. G. ... 25
Norris, J. T. ... 203
Neville, J. B. ... 65-85
New Riverside Ochre ... 203

Ochre ... 202
Officers in C. S. A. ... 308
Oothcalooga Cotton Mills ... 264
Oothcalooga ... 2-6-22-131-174

Parrot, J. R. ... 86-112-162-164-169-249
Patton, Julius M. ... 20-141
Peacock, D. W. K. ... 170-197

Pettit Creek Farmers' Club ... 184
Pine Log ... 6-174
Pine Log Camp Ground ... 132
Pine Log Mas. Inst. ... 149
Pioneer Settlers ... 19-42
Pittard, Wm. ... 86
Pitts, Coleman ... 24
Pittman, C. C. ... 112
Poole, B. J. ... 58-193
Presentments ... 113-115
Presbyterian Mission ... 135
Price, H. F. ... 87-141-163-209
P.-T. A. ... 263
Public School System ... 152
Puckett, E. D. ... 87
Puckett, W. E. ... 48

Quarles, David ... 88-113

Records ... 328
Reed, Jas. ... 88
Removal, Court House ... 114-117
Representatives ... 326
Revolutionary Soldiers ... 257
Reynolds, Benj. ... 88
Rice, J. H. ... 144-156
Rich, W. W. ... 104-210
Rock House ... 197
Rogers, R. L. ... 87-198
Roads and Trails ... 18-38
Roper, J. C. ... 62-105
Rotary Club ... 263
Rowland, J. S. ... 89-161-273
Rowland Springs ... 6-178
Russell, Geo. B. ... 20-90
Ryals, Rev. J. G. ... 90

Sans Souci Club ... 263
Salt Petre Cave ... 6-179
Saxon, R. C. ... 90
Scheuer Brothers ... 267
Scott, J. E. ... 87-160
Senators ... 325
Secession Delegates ... 163
Senatorial Districts ... 325
Shale ... 203
Shaw, Wm. ... 74
Sheats, A. Y. ... 91
Sheats, Samuel ... 21-33-326
Shelman, C. T. ... 91-250
Sherman's Romance ... 250
Shepherd, J. W. ... 56
Slate ... 204
Smith, Samuel ... 92
Smith, G. H. ... 156
Smith, C. H. ... 294
Solicitors ... 112
Soldiers' Aid Society ... 216
Soils ... 177-8
Sou. Cotton Oil Co. ... 266
Spanish-American War Vets 314
Sproull, Charles ... 93
Sproull, J. T. ... 27
Stegall, Emsley ... 93
Stegall's Station ... 24

Stephens, Dr. S. F. ___27-170-322
Stilesboro _____ 27
Stilesboro Academy _____ 148
Stilesboro Farmer's Club___ 184
Stiles, W. H._____27-94-149-161
Stroup, Moses _____ 190
Sullivan, T. A._____20-146

Tabernacle, Sam Jones_____ 137
Taylor, Obadiah_____ 101
Taylorsville _____ 27
Tax Returns _____32-37
Templeton, W. A._____ 48
Terhune, C. D._____4-98
Tinsley, T. W._____ 82
Towers, T. F._____ 26
Townsend, W. T. _____ 123
Treaty of 1835_____ 4
Trimble, A .C._____22-23-96
Trippe, R. B._____96-120
Trippe, T. H._____95-141-163-209
Tumlin, Rev. G. S._____ 98
Tumlin, Rev. G. W.___98-128-144
Tumlin, Lewis__9-97-132-144-161
Tumlin, Thomas _____ 25

U. D. C._____256-7
Upshaw, James _____ 99
Upshaw, Geo. _____ 20

Walker, F. M._____ 63
Walton, W. C._____ 304
Wayside Home _____ 216

W. & A. R.R._____ 167
W. C. T. U._____ 261
Weems, A. J._____84-182
West End Institute_____ 152
White, town of_____ 28
Wikle, Douglas _____102-158
Wikle, J. H._____102-158-176
Wikle, J. R. ____101-119-156-170
Willingham, C. H. C._____ 158
Wofford's Academy _____ 151
Wofford's Cross Roads_____ 127
Wofford, J. C._____ 103
Wofford, Nathaniel _____ 103
Wofford, G. T._____ 302
Wofford Scouts _____ 248
Wofford, W. T._____155-
        , 209-247-249-297
Woolley, A. F._____ 104
Word, J. J._____104-112-161
Word, Dr. R. C._____104-216-286
Word, T. A._____ 104
World War Vets _____ 315
Wright, A. R._____105-112-141-144
Wyly, W. C._____ 105
Vaughan, J. W._____ 294
Vaughan, Dr. W. B._____28-99
Veach, J. M._____ 100
Vincent, A. A._____ 100
Virginia Colony _____ 101
Young Brothers _____ 106
Young, J. C._____ 105
Young, R. M. _____ 106
Young, P. M. B._____163-298

ADDENDA SECTION

The material to be found in this section is not to be considered as complete on any family or persons mentioned. The author of the book has tried to keep her records on Bartow County families as complete and updated as possible over the years but there are always many persons for whom data is incomplete. It should also be noted that there was no deliberate intention to gloss over any person(s) or families included but when the author began trying to contact members of various families for material to up-date their lines some were punctual in sending it in, while others were not. Due to trying to meet the printer's deadline for publication, we could not wait for those who were slow in sending their family data and had to go ahead without it.

Persons who may be interested in seeing more complete data and records on many of these Bartow County families are urged to see the Bartow County file kept at the Georgia State Department of Archives and History in Atlanta in which the author periodically places new materials she receives on people and events of this county.

The sequence of the material appearing in this addenda section follows: the sequence of page numbers in the original book. Any page in the original book which has up-dated material to supplement it is so indicated in the addenda section by reference to that same page number in the margin.

There will be found two brand new sections of material in the Addenda Section not previously contained in the original book, being: The Marriage Records and the Excerpts of letters from the late Wilbur Kurtz to Mrs. Mulcahy.

-- The Publisher - -

FARISH CARTER for whom Cartersville was named.
1780 - 1861
Courtesy of Vera Gaddis

THE REV. CHARLES WALLACE HOWARD

Photo presented by Eleanor Waring Burnham — (Mrs. Roger Noble Burnham) 3025 W. Fifth St., Los Angeles, California. Received February 28, 1940.

FROM WILBUR G KURTZ COLLECTION

THE REV. CHARLES WALLACE HOWARD
From
Wilbur G. Kurtz Collection
Atlanta Historical Society

MRS. CHARLES WALLACE HOWARD, *Circa 1886*
Courtesy of
Miss Emily Ravenel, Savannah

FRANCES THOMAS HOWARD, marked "For Emily Christmas 1890." Author of "In and Out of the Lines." Courtesy of *Miss Emily Ravenel, Savannah*

"THE LAST MEETING of LEE and JACKSON On the Eve of
The Battle of Chancellorsville"
by
Everett D.B. Fabrino Julio, 1843 - 1879
From the Col. Thomas Spencer Collection

Wilbur G. Kurtz, Mrs. Sproull Fouche, B.C. Yates
In living room of "Valley View," taken
by Thomas Spencer in March 1949
From
Wilbur G. Kurtz Collection
ATLANTA HISTORICAL SOCIETY

The Thomas Van Buren Hargis house, Kingston, Bartow County, Georgia. Sherman's Headquarters, May 19-23, 1864.

From the Wilbur G. Kurtz Collection
ATLANTA HISTORICAL SOCIETY

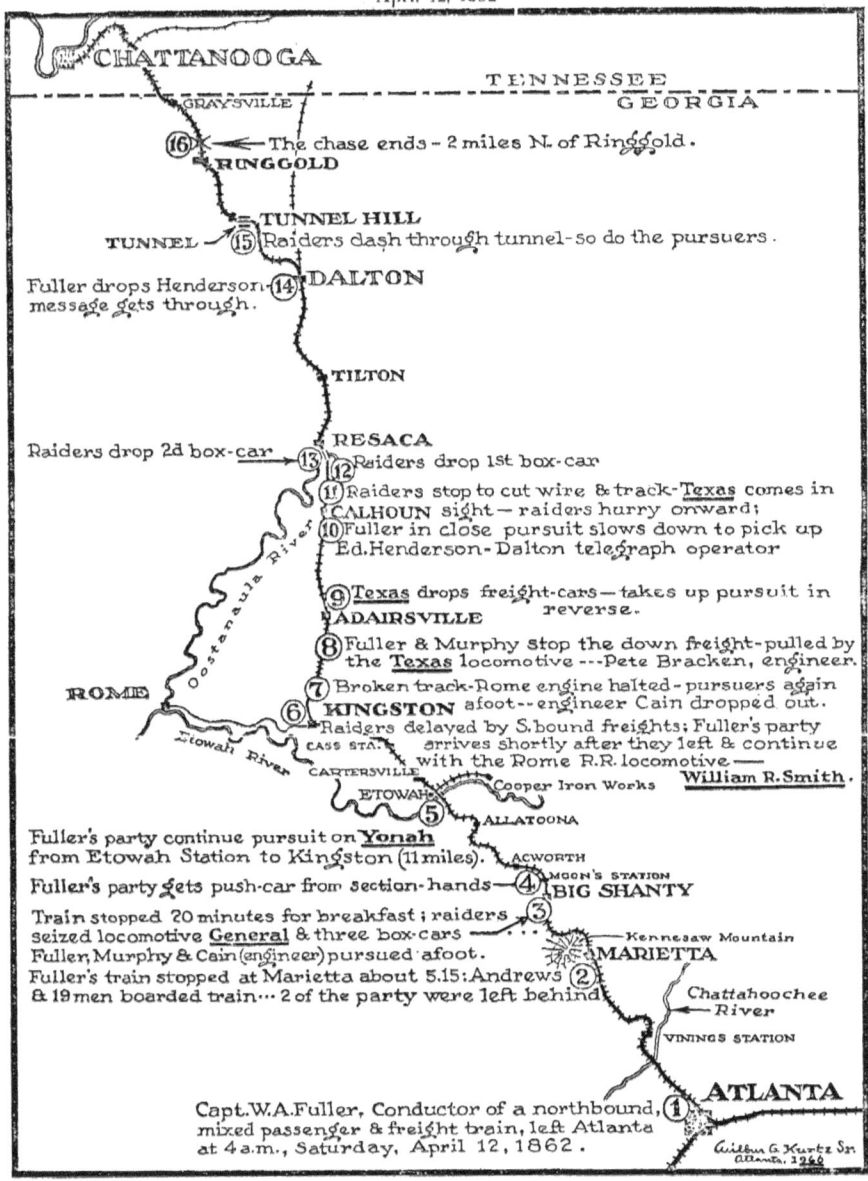

Page 1:   Robert Sparks Walker died September 26, 1960, from a heart attack he had on his beloved "Elise Chapin Wildlife Sanctuary," near Chattanooga, Tennessee, and is buried there.

Page 7:   Still uncertain about exact location of the Hightower Mission Station. See map of Georgia Circa 1825, Georgia Historical Commission. In 1975 found Hightower Mission Station to be on Etowah River, near south end of old 41 Highway Bridge--present Ga. 293 near Sally Hughs Ford.

Page 20:   Knight in Vol. 1, page 592, adds these names to Cassville settlers: B. D. Hamilton, S. L. Chunn, Dr. Underwood, William Headden, John Word, Chester Hawkins, Jesse P. Jones, Joseph Bogle, Dr. R. H. Patton, Thomas Dunlap, William Latimer, John H. Rice, J. M. Wilson, Hawkins Price, Nelson Gilreath, G. H. Gilreath, Richard Gaines, Abda Johnson, Mark Johnston, A. M. Franklin, H. W. Cobb, William Goldsmith.

From the Military Records, 1846-48 soldiers, in the State Archives: "Stockton, Alabama. September 20th, 1847. To His Excellency, G. W. Crawford: Sir, I had the honour this day of receiving yours of the 8th instant and hereby enclose to you at the opinion of Col. J. S. Calhoun the names of my privates also the name which will designate our company. We presume this will be sufficient without the designation of the officers under whom we were elected as the votes were unanimous. The company under my command is designated as the Cassville Draggons. Please send my commission and other commissioned officers to Mobile. List of my command: E. R. Forsyth, Elishu Drummonds, Toliver Owens, William Jolly, Nicholas Frost, J. T. Reagan, Silvanus Dedman, Mc Frost, J. H. Bailey, J. A. Bachelder, L. H. Ball, Benjamin Bowman, W. L. Bogan, J. C. Brown, William Blount, W. H. Caldwell, W. Childers, O. C. Cleveland, W. Cantrell, John Crawford."

Page 21: Wilbur G. Kurtz found the order for the burning of Cassville. The order is by Brig. Gen. John E. Smith, addressed to Col. Thomas T. Heath, 5th Ohio Cavalry and is dated Cartersville, October 30, 1864. The fire was November 5th. Heath's outfit was ordered to go over to Canton, burn that place, then "proceed to Cassville and make the same disposition as at Canton." The November 5th date is also given in Mrs. B. B. Quillian's article in "The Kennesaw Gazette," March 1, 1989. "She said that the male college and several residences has been burned October 12th, which was previously."

Page 22: Adairsville: Adairsville is no longer a "peach" center. Now textile mills, chenille rugs and spreads are the main industry. Alice B. Howard in a historical sketch wrote that "The Bowdoin House on the hill is constructed around the original Indian two-room cabin, the only known relic of the town's earliest days." Adairsville City Hall was built from a $30,000 grant from W. A. Graham, born in 1851, died in 1952, a millionaire at the age of 100, in Pryor, Oklahoma. In his written will was the clause toward the construction of the city hall. W. A. Graham, attended Col. Fitten's school in Adairsville, owned one-half interest in the Veach flour mills and after nine years sold his share for $15,000 and went to Oklahoma, starting a trading business which grew into millions. No children.

Adairsville Postmasters from 1832: Barnett S. Wardman, James Day, Augustus C. Trimble, David Morrow, Joshua Bowdoin, Mansfield Simmons, James Allen, Ephriam Porter, Isaac T. Teague, Donald M. Hood, Ebenezer Loveless, Oliver Anderson, Joseph L.

Cash, Cornelius Hibberts, Samuel Worrell, John M. Davidson, Joel H. Dyer, Jonathan Dyar, Elias B. Earle, Johnathan P. Dyer, Clifford Dyer (acting), Robert Franklin, Johnathan P. Dyer (acting), Charles Satterfield, Mrs. Jack (Cleo) Price, Mrs. Roy Broom, Mrs. Hazel Bradley--(Mrs. A. B. Howard).

Page 22: Horace Bradley was born in Adairsville, a son of James M. Bradley who was for many years a popular W&A RR Conductor. After his death in 1876, his brother, Horatio, succeeded him as conductor. Horace Bradley died July 22, 1896 in Denver, Colorado. He was chief of the Art Building at the Cotton States and International Exposition of 1895 in Atlanta and had 3 exhibits in it. Horace began to draw at an early age. His father moved to Atlanta and Horace graduated from Boys High in 1875. His first job was as a draughtsman with Capt. R. M. Clayton. He got out of this mechanical work and opened a studio in Atlanta where he painted and taught. His first success was in painting a portrait of Gen. Benjamin H. Hill. The State offered a $1000 prize for the best painting of the Senator and Horace won it. With the money he went to New York and opened a studio. Before going to New York he married Miss Fannie Sage of West End, daughter of B. Y. Sage. He was president of the New York Art League at the time of his death. A painting of his is in the Atlanta Historical Society. He was buried in Leonia, New Jersey.

Page 23: Cartersville: In the Addenda is a picture of Farish Carter, 1780-1861, courtesy of Vara Gaddis who is compiling the history of Cartersville for its centennial in 1972. In the copy of the Bartow History in the State Archives was found this penned note: "Correction: Farish Carter asked Nathan Owings Howard to name the town for him. Nathan Howard was a merchant and served Cass County in Legislature 1865-66." See page 327.

Visited Cartersville, Virginia in 1953, only other Cartersville so far found. Post mistress said she had had mail forwarded to Cartersville, Georgia. Another Civil War house in Cartersville, Sherman's officers spared and used during occupation, was the John Anderson house on S. Erwin Street.

Page 23-24: Cartersville: Walter Akerman was postmaster when the Cartersville post office was constructed on Erwin Street in 1914 at a cost of $42,574. Now it is used by the City School Board. A new Post Office was constructed in March 1965 on East Church Street. Larree Johnston (son of J. W. Johnston, died November 1963 & Kate Ginn) has been Post Master for 14 years. In 1915 there were 5 rural mail routes. On May 15, 1838, a post office bearing the name "Cherokee" was established in Cass County and the postmaster was Henderson Willingham. Post masters since have been: John Clayton, December 28, 1839; Wm. Milner, October 8, 1840; Aaron B. Puckett, May 28, 1846; Coleman Pitts, July 12, 1847; John F. Sproull, March 11, 1850; Sanford Erwin, July 5, 1851; Jesse R. Wikle, September 26, 1851; John L. Wikle, March 13, 1866; Thos. M. Compton, August 15, 1866; Charles E. Blacker, May 10, 1869; Jesse Wikle, September 8,1870; Wm. Milner, October 6, 1885; Walter Akerman, December 21, 1889; Martin Collins, December 21, 1893; Walter Akerman, January 10, 1898; Ab B. Harrison, November 1, 1910 (acting); Walter Akerman, November 29, 1910; H. J. Jolly, January 27, 1916; Walter Davis, September 5, 1919; Harry P. Womelsdorf, January 5, 1925 (1870-1954); Charles S. Mayes, March 21, 1933; Robert W. Knight, April 19, 1934; Joseph C. Nelson, December 10, 1939, died February 17,

1975; Larree Johnston, January 31, 1958.

Page 25-26: Kingston: Gen. William T. Sherman used the Thomas Van Buren Hargis home as headquarters May 19-23, 1864, and at other dates, in Kingston. He was the son of Milton Hargis of Cass Station. (Page 63 & 243). The house was destroyed by fire in mid 1950 - only a Georgia Historical marker shows its location, just west of the railroad station. "The Kingston House" in the Stone Mountain Plantation Manor complex is a misnomer. This house was moved in 1962-3 to Stone Mountain from its location, on the old Rome road, in Floyd County, less than a mile from the Bartow County line. It was six miles from Kingston, too far from the important railroad activities in the town of Kingston to have been used by anybody as army headquarters. This house was built by a man of unusual tastes in 1837, Bryan Allen, born November 30, 1805, died August 3, 1851, and his grave should be moved to Stone Mountain. It was a small Greek revival with palladian windows and fantail lights, but during the years it had changed owners and had vicarious renters, until it was sold to a committee by C. W. Kerce. Some of the material used to replace abused and deteriorated parts of the original house came from the 1837 pioneer home of Nathaniel Burge, near Euharlee. The idea was to recreate in a correct setting a gem-like architectural house of the South. Deed and district maps of the Allen house are in the Floyd County Courthouse. The Kingston Woman's History Club, organized in January 1900, erected a museum in 1970, in the park area, for their collection of Kingston history. They lead in the Memorial Day services held annually since 1865, during the month of April.

Page 27: Stilesboro: The community of Stilesboro along the railroad gradually disappeared. Now there is a new look less than a half-mile north. Georgia Power's Etowah Steam Plant on the Etowah River, 10 miles west of Cartersville, has completed two hyperbolic-shaped cooling towers and one 1,000 foot-high stack that can be seen for miles around. A third unit with a generating capacity of 850,000 kilowatts will go into service by 1975 or sooner. Coal burned at the plant will be shipped in special 100-ton capacity railroad cars. When completed, the plant will be the largest on the Georgia Power system and one of the largest in the Southeast.

Page 29: Atco is now incorporated with Cartersville. Goodyear Tire & Rubber Co., Mill #3, continue making tire fabric. Another product of Atco was Rudy York who started playing baseball in the Atco ball park and became a 13-year major league baseball player. From 1934 to 1937 he was with the Detroit Tigers and made 18 home runs in the month of August, 1937. He also played with the old Philadelphia Athletics, Boston Red Sox, and Chicago White Sox, hitting 277 home runs and compiling a .275 lifetime batting average. He played in three World Series and three All-Star games. Following his baseball career, culminating as a minor league manager and Boston Red Sox coach, at home he was a painter and forester, with baseball still his love. Rudolph (Rudy) Preston York was born August 17, 1913 at Ragland, Alabama, but spent most of his life in Atco and Cartersville. He died of lung cancer February 5, 1970, survived by his wife, Violet, two daughters, Mrs. Clayton Pruitt and Mrs. Fred Hines and a son, Rev. Joe York. The Atco ball park was named The Rudy York Memorial Field by the city of Cartersville in June, 1971 and Gov. Jimmy Carter proclaimed "Rudy York Day" in Georgia, August 21, 1971. He is buried in Sunset Memory Gardens.

Page 30: Ligon: Named for James Osgood Ligon. The Ligon Cabin was originally a Cherokee Indian log house on land drawn in the Lottery of 1832 by the Ligon family of Meriwether Co. and was added to in the 30's by "Phil" and Nan Ligon Phillips, adopted daughter and niece of Mrs. Ligon, and was used as a summer home until "Goulding House" and Barnsley's Gardens were acquired. It has been said that Sam Jones preached his second sermon after his conversion on the porch of the log cabin on account of high waters over the road to the church beyond Ligon.

Page 41: A 4-lane highway between Atlanta and Cartersville was out-dated by the late Fifties. Interstate 75 through Bartow County has been a political enigma and remains unfinished in 1971, from the Cobb County section to just below Adairsville. Division Office No. 6, State Highway Department is in Cartersville. Now I-75 is completed, by-passing Cartersville.

Additions to PIONEER SETTLERS.

Page 42: Akin: Paul F. Akin died May 6, 1959; Katherine Lovejoy Akin, July 19, 1881-October 29, 1959, both buried in Oak Hill Cemetery. Son, Warren Akin, prominent lawyer and citizen married Jean Goodheart; their sons are Warren Akin IV, Prof. and Wm. Morgan Akin, Atty. in Cartersville.

Page 43: Baker: Jesse Baker, born January 5, 1800, died February 15, 1870 in Bartow Co., son of Charles and Mary Goodwin Baker, married in 1825 Parthenia Moss, born March 16, 1809, died October 29, 1889. Children: 1. Ann Baker, born January 19, 1827 married September 12, 1853 John F. Stanford. 2. Nancy M. Baker born July 6, 1828, married J. M. Smith. 3. Elenor E. Baker, born May 22, 1830, married July 16, 1854 William K. Brawner, daughter Parthenia Victoria, born August 2, 1850, died 1939, married Henry Charles Garrison (1851-1886); children: Lola Virginia Garrison born November 27, 1877, died January 1958, married August 29, 1901 Joseph Buford Mahan, born March 9, 1878, died September 22, 1968, Rydal, Georgia. Children: Rubert S. Mahan, born July 15, 1902, died December 1964, married Emily Estelle Burtz; Ralph Alton Mahan, 1904-1939; Joseph Buford Mahan, Jr., born June 11, 1921 married Catherine Hines, Columbus, Georgia; Elizabeth Mahan, born June 4, 1911, married Ernest Garrison, Rydal, Georgia. Son: Joseph Claude Garrison of Atlanta. Charles Baker, 1762-April 26, 1848, father of Jesse, died in Cass County and a Revolutionary Marker was placed at his grave by the Mahan Family and the Etowah Chapter DAR of Cartersville in September 1945, just off Highway 411. Will recorded in Cass Co., 1847. (See Georgia Genealogical Society Quarterly, Vol. 7, No. 2, 1971, page 127.) Continued - Children of Jesse and Parthenia Baker: 4. James M. Baker, born September 11, 1832, killed at battle of the Wilderness. 5. Mary J. Baker, born November 8, 1834, died December 1885, married T. N. Stanford (see page 44). 6. Lucy Baker, born January 5, 1837, married a Mr. Stanford. 7. Dr. Thomas H. Baker died 1920 (see page 44). 8. John B. Baker, born July 15, 1841. 9. Frances Cordelia Baker, born July 8, 1843, died December 17, 1918, married John Rich. 10. Charles D. Baker, 1845-56. 11. William Clark Baker, born January 24, 1848, died July 23, 1904, married Carrie Gower (who had Baker Bible Record) lived in Tishomingo, Oklahoma. 12. Parthenia V. Baker, 1850-56. 13. Jesse A. Baker, born May 9, 1853, married Jennie Meriwether. 14. Augustus C. Baker, born July 11, 1866. The children of Joseph M. Mahan born February 5, 1833, died September 4, 1891, and Nancy Elizabeth Taylor, 1849-1909, were: 1. Rebecca J., 1868-1943, married 1st J. Lester Walker, 2nd M. L. Upshaw; 2. Sally Lula Mahan, 1870-deceased, married Dr. R. E.

Adair (page 42), daughter: Frances Elizabeth Adair. 3. Paul C. Mahan,1873-5; Maggi Beatrice, 1881-1965,married L. O. Wooten, Children: Mary Wooten Olbrych, Leon Wooten; Pearl Mahan, 1886-7; Joseph Buford Mahan married Lola Virginia Garrison.

Page 44-45: Godfrey Barnsley was born in Peak Forest, County Derby, England; Julia Scarborough was the second daughter of William Scarborough of Savannah (his home is planned for restoration) and Mr. Barnsley in a letter said his house in North Georgia was Italian, not English style. A daughter of Anna Barnsley Gilmour of London, Julia B. Gilmour married August 30, 1870 Francis Stanton Massy Dawson in St. Stephens Church, Paddington, London. A short time after the wedding Julia Massy-Dawson became Lady-in-Waiting to Queen Victoria. Julia B. Baltzelle married 2nd Charles A. Von Swartz. This marriage also ended in tragedy - his death due to tuberculosis. Addie Baltzelle, (a daughter) born June 31, 1864,died June 5, 1942,married A. Arrington Saylor. He died before his formula for synthetic silk made from wood pulp could be realized. Their children: Julia Saylor; Preston Saylor, a well-known prize fighter, shot his brother, Harry Saylor, the youngest son November 5, 1935. Preston has been free since 1943. (Later notes from the Saylor collection of Mrs. A. B. Howard). Much of the Barnsley wealth in silver, china and household goods was lost during the occupation of McPherson's and Garrard's soldiers in 1864. Through family reverses and depression, a few antique objects, furniture, decorative materials, linens were sold to individuals in private homes. Mrs. Saylor's possessions were sold at auction after her death. Between the years 1841 and 1851, Godfrey Barnsley acquired 21 160-acre Land Lots, a total of 3,360 in the name of Julia Henrietta Barnsley, his wife. Deed Book AA, Clerk's S.C. Office in Courthouse. (We forget that North Georgia was settled by participants in the 1832 Cherokee Land and Gold Lottery - see pages 12-16 on microfilm in the State Archives, D. 13, Box 76 - a United States Census of 1850 of Produce and Agriculture states Barnsley's cash value of farm - $15,000. One hundred and 70 acres of improved land and 1,810 acres of unimproved land.) The Barnsley family and unfinished home will never cease to be interesting. See Articles in July 10, 17 and August 7, 1969 in North Bartow News by Mrs. A. B. Howard. It is now owned by W. Earl McCleskey.

Page 45-6: Benham: Mrs. W. H. (Loulie) Lumpkin died June 15, 1950 in Dalton. Son: William Henry ("Pete") Lumpkin, born August 2, 1892, died December 16, 1958, married Margaretta Womelsdorf,daughter of Lee B. Womelsdorf (1873-1935) and Lyda Murray (1876-1942). Children: (1) W. H. Lumpkin III, born 1924 married Betty McCamy-Children: (Dr.) W. H. Lumpkin IV,born 1948; Anne E., born 1951, and Mary Julia Lumpkin,born 1955. (2) Dr. Murray Benham Lumpkin,born 1929,married Lillian Beall-Children: M. MacIntyre,born 1953; Lois Berrien, born 1954; Peter Benham, born 1957; Alice Elizabeth Lumpkin,born 1961, both sons live in Dalton. (3) Margaretta Lumpkin, born 1931,married J. Clarence ("Bud") Shaw,born 1929, son of J. Clarence (deceased) and Essie Shaw of Dalton. Children: Julius Clarence Shaw III,born 1953; Lyda Margaretta, born 1955; E. Lee Shaw, born 1957; Rebecca Lumpkin, born 1959. Mrs. Thomas (Lizzie) B. Lumpkin died April 6, 1943. Benham Lumpkin died December 10, 1963. Christine L. Jackson died April 7, 1966. Loulie L. Strickland-Billings died November 24, 1966. Annie Laurie Jones Cunyus, first born in home, "Fairview," built by Willis Benham for Frances Wright Jones in 1871, died 1958 (page 50). Lucy Jones Simpson died September 25, 1938, Evelyn Jones Sims died January 22, 1969. Sidney Benham

Strickland died April 1960. Roslyn Lumpkin died June 7, 1973. Of Thomas Jefferson style of architecture, the Benham home is now owned by the daughters of Sidney and Laura Strickland-June, Mrs. Arthur Brittingham of Floida, & Laurette, Mrs. David Smith of Burlington, Ontario, Canada, now living in the Benham Home. The Benham plantation has become a subdivision of new and modern homes.

Pages 47-48: Brandon: Dr. J. S. Beasley born August 12, 1832 died May 25, 1907, married Sarah E. Asbury (1853-1908). Children: (1) Jack S. Beazley, born July 4, 1867, died October 15, 1944, married 1st Lucy Saggus (died 1905); Son: Frank S. Beazley born January 6, 1897, married March 1971 Rena McCormick (page 93). J.S.B. married 2nd Jefferson Brandon, died February 1968. (2) Ned Beazley died 1939 married Hessie Baker, died 1948. Daughter: Margie (deceased) married Claude Brandon (deceased); Daughter Sarah married Howell L. Smith, Stilesboro. (3) Reuben Beazley married two Stockley sisters, 3rd Abigail Stanton (all deceased). Mary Brandon Skannal died April 4, 1951, Shreveport, La. (page 48). David P. Brandon died October 20, 1966, Texas. John Brandon died February 1967, Louisiana. Charles H. Brandon died June 1967, Shreveport. Mrs. Joseph (Matt Cole) Brandon died 1962. Son Joseph G. and Emily Brandon have built a home on the D. B. Cunyus homesite. The Brandon home sold to Georgia Power Company.

Page 49: Brandon: Henry Harrison Milam Jr. born January 14, 1880, died April 10, 1951, son of Henry Harrison Milam and Avarilla Brandon, married Romie Leake, daughter of Thomas W. Leake and Mary Ann Fur (page 77). Served 10 years as County School Superintendent, at one time president and member of the Euharlee Farmers Club, Presbyterian Church elder in Cartersville. Children: Mrs. R. F. Jolly; Louise Milam, retired teacher; Riley Milam; John L. Milam, Cartersville; Henry H. Jr., Ninety-Six, South Carolina; Herman W. Milam, Chatsworth; Robert Milam, Rochester, Minn. Louise Milam, sister of H.H.M. died in January 1968 in Cartersville. Another daughter of Thomas W. Leake and Mary Ann Furr (page 77), Elizabeth Leake Henderson died January 1970 in Atlanta, daughter Mary, now deceased, married Jack Scheuer, Atlanta. Son, Charles Henderson, Hollywood, Florida.

Page 50: Burge-Cunyus. (a) Dr. Henry D. Cunyus, 1848-1933 married 2nd Daisy Mathis. Children: Nannie, born 1895, married Rufus E. McCary: Children: Ralph, Frances E. Rhodes, Ruby Ayres, Taylorsville; Fannie, 1897-1965, married Robert Branton; Annie Daisy born 1902, married Alva W. Taylor, died 1963; daughter Dorothy T. Holstein, Taylorsville; 2 sons: Henry Daniel Cunyus, b.1907, d. 2-3-1983, m. Grace Stedham, d. 1965. Children: Barbara, Doris C. Earl: H.D. III; Gloria; Rome; Grace Vesta, b. 1911, m. R. B. Ford-daughter Marion. (e) John William Cunyus family all deceased except John W. d.1972.(g) Adolphus Burge Cunyus born July 17, 1862-April 4, 1937, married 1890 Annie Laurie Jones, born August 14, 1871, died December 5, 1958 (page 46). Children: Dorothy F. Cunyus, born December 18, 1896, married 1919 Rev. B. Frank Pim, May 1, 1892-March 14, 1951. Children: Dorothy Anne Pim married Clinton M. Roth, 3 children. Jean Pim married Walker Kinsman, Atlanta; Lt. Col. B. Frank Pim, Retired AAF; Lucy J. Cunyus born November 16, 1900, Bartow County Historian, married 1938, Edward Rice Mulcahy, New Haven and Atlanta. Children of Daniel Cunyus and Alice Hawkin living are: Walter Daniel Cunyus, Belleair Bluffs; Sue C. (Mrs. Vincent Meloy) and Corinne Cunyus, Tampa, Florida. Sarah Janes daughter of E. H. and Mittie Cunyus Janes, married Carlton McKinney of Atlanta. Sons: Carlton Jr., Minneapolis and Dr. Edward McKinney, Chattanooga. (b) Grandchildren of Nannie Cunyus Skannal: A. Cunyus

Skannal, Sligo; Mary S. Pons, Shreveport, Louisiana; Charles F. Skannal, Denver; Nannie S. Carter, Commerce,Ga.(c) Grandchildren of Frances Cunyus Conyers: John L. and Claude Conyers, Cartersville; Frances C. Holcomb, Atlanta; Eleanor C. Waldrip; Marcella C. Cartledge, Columbus (dec.); Joe J. Bennett, Los Angeles; Conyers Bennett, N.C., both dec.; Mary Drew and William B. Bennett, Atlanta. (Cunyus Genealogy by Walter D. Cunyus, State Archives).

Page 54-5: Children of Warren A. Dodd, 1858-1937 and Emma Harling Dodd, 1863-1959 (page 74): Mamie married W. M. Dorsey, now retired from Taylorsville to a home near son, William Matthew Dorsey, Albany; Hugh Dodd Dorsey, Charlotte, North Carolina; Josie married Walter A. Rhodes (died 1963). Sons: Warren (died July 1973) and Phillip Rhodes-Richards Paper Company, Ret. Atlanta. Stanley Dodd 1890-May 31, 1958, m. Caroline Knight,(dec.) lived in Miami; John Akin Dodd, 1896-1970 married Louise Efird, Atlanta; Clara Dodd (deceased) married James M. Smith (deceased). Children: James M. Smith, served as Mayor of Albany; Frank Dodd Smith married "Billie" Ham. Son: F. D. Jr., Cartersville; Miriam married R. Beverly Irwin of Atlanta; Children: R. B. Jr.; Clara married Warren Lee Travers; Louise married Lawrence (Larry) Chapman, Social Circle-son: Larry Chapman, Atlanta; Eva Dodd, retired teacher; Charles Dodd married Marian Bullock, Chattanooga. J. M. Smith married 2nd Lilybel Lavender-sons: Jack Madison Smith, Marietta; Fred L. Smith.

Page 56: Irene Walker Field is living in Monroe with children, Alice Field and Jerry Field. James Monroe Field, after many years as an oil prospector in Oklahoma and other western areas, retired to Cartersville with his wife, Mabel Kearns; farmed out "Meadowview," was active in organizing the AA's in Cartersville, died in October 1950. Margaret married J. B. White, died 1963. Sons: B. B. White and Jere F. White (attorney) and now Judge White, live in Cartersville. Son of Carolyn Field and Herbert M. Crane of LaGrange, Herbert M. Crane, Jr., lawyer, has just been named Judge of the Juvenile Court. Sara Tumlin Connor, deceased, - son: Clyde R. Connor, former Secretary and Treasurer of the Cartersville Federal Savings & Loan Association, retired, died January,1972, married Lizette Henderson, live in the old Tumlin home. Bernice and Clarence Tumlin, deceased.

Page 58: Mrs. Sproull (Edith Carver) Fouche died in January 1962 at "Valley View." (See picture in the addenda). Her nephew, Dr. Robert F. Norton, of Rome, now owns "Valley View" and it is more beautiful than ever. Edith Fouche wrote in a note: "Rebecca Caldwell married James Sproull in 1811. Several years after her son, James Sproull built "Valley View," Rebecca C. Sproull, a widow in 1825, left Abbeville District, South Carolina, was overseeing a large plantation, came to Cass and built "Rose Cottage" and made it one of the prettiest country houses in the county." (See Sproull, page 93). Sproull Fouche died in 1934.

Page 59: Gaines: Bessie Gaines Lang (Mrs. Joe M.) of Calhoun, died August 6, 1970. Kathryn Gaines Colley Korstian, Rome, Georgia has compiled the Gaines genealogy. Her branch of the Gaines family own the farm on which the Octagon House stood. This family too large for research now.

Page 60: J. Hugh Gilreath, born 1881, with Cliff Dodgens bought Lumpkin Hardware in 1925, and in 1929 became sole owner of J. Hugh Gilreath Hardware Company - now deceased.-

married 1st Nora Rowan (daughter of Robert C. Rowan). Children: (1) J. Hugh Gilreath, Jr. married Marian Nicholson. Children: Alice G. Duckett, Nancy G. Jackman, Louanne Gilreath. (2) Rowan Gilreath married "Dolly" Chumley. Children: Metta, Linda, Jim and Rowan Gilreath, all of Cartersville. (3) Elizabeth Gilreath married Max Schoener, Cincinnati. J. Hugh G. Sr. married 2nd Mrs. Kate Hammond Candler of Cartersville. Spartan A. Gilreath died in 1935. Ben C. Gilreath, druggist, established Gilreath-Champion Drug Stores (now owned by Tom J. Sr. and Tom J. Champion, Jr.) died December 25, 1960; wife, Estelle Strickland died July 25, 1971. Children of Grace Gilreath and A. W. Buford: (1) James A. Buford married Bessie French. Son: James W. Buford married Mollie Burton. (2) Mary Ann Buford married Harwell Hagewood. Son: Larry. Children of Paul Gilreath (page 265), Mayor, born November 25, 1872 died March 16, 1935, and Mary Lou Wofford born May 13, 1874 died January 27, 1956: (1) Paul Gilreath Jr. married Mary Frances Chamblee. Sons: Paul Gilreath III married Paula Jones. Children: Paul IV; Staley; Charlotte; David; Marietta; Charles Gilreath married Emily Thompson. Children: Charles Jr., Mary Wilda, Laura and Julia Ann, Cartersville. (2) James Wofford Gilreath married Elizabeth Newsome of LaGrange. Children: Sarah G. Thompson, Martha, Margaret Gilreath, Cartersville. (3) Susie married S.A.T. Newsome (deceased) of LaGrange. Children: Seth Jr., Mrs. Mary Estes, Martha Tatum, Newnam. Nelson Gilreath married Katherine Tanner. Children: Nelson, Charles T., James Paul, Deland, Florida. Pauline and Henrietta, Cartersville, (both deceased). Children of Lem and Mamie Burnham Gilreath: Reid, of Charlotte (deceased), Samuel (deceased), Robin, Eugene, Oregon; Rev. Morgan Gilreath, Green Sea, South Carolina, died March 1970, buried in Oak Hill, married Kate. Sons: Morgan Bennett Jr. married in 1969 Melissa Thornton of Atlanta; James Robinson Gilreath, South Carolina.

Page 63: John R. Banton married 1st Annie Stancil, 2nd Madeline Walker. Dixie Lee Hargis Richardson died in July 1964, 81 years old, in Smyrna. The sons of Harry Warren and Edna Sewell Hargis were Tom, Dick and Harry. Richard was head at Riverside in Gainesville. Richard Hargis died in August 1957 in Atlanta. Frank Neal Hargis, born March 3, 1885, died August 19, 1963, Kingston.

Page 64: Stephen Willis Harris died August 30, 1963 and Hamilton Harris died January 13, 1969, both identified with National NuGrape of Atlanta, with their step-father, W. R. Sullivan.

Page 64-5: More of the ten children of William Headden: Elizabeth Anne Headden born January 27, 1843; John Thomas Headden born April 6, 1845; Frances W. Headden born July 27, 1847; Walter Johnston Headden, born May 5, 1852, died March 3, 1928; Mary Virginia Headden born November 14, 1836; Edwin Aiken Headden born March 1, 1858; Charles Freeman Headden born May 12, 1860. Robert Franklin Headden, son of W.J. Headden, Cassville, d. 1961; Marie Headden Pittard died 1952; John K. Headden, born November 1, 1895, died August 20, 1969, Cassville.

Page 66-7: Paul C. Franklin born September 14, 1884, husband of Gabe Hendricks (born September 22, 1885), long identified with The First National Bank, died April 12, 1969. Children: Paul C. Jr. married Margaret Burke, Gaffney, South Carolina; Virginia Franklin married Cecil Hamby, Editor, Manchester, Georgia. Blanche Hendricks and Lucious Hannon both deceased. Bossie Hendricks born July 17, 1889 died August 19, 1971, married Dr.

H. P. McElreath died in 1970. Children: Mrs. O. E. Morgan, Woodstock; Mrs. J. D. Caldwell, Marietta; H. P. McElreath Jr., Atlanta; Robert McElreath, Sanford, North Carolina; Sam McElreath, Salt Lake City; James H. McElreath, Acworth. Lucy H. Layton, Charleston, South Carolina. Annie H. lived with Gabe Franklin; Robert A., Cartersville.

Page 70-1: Children of Sallie Maud Jackson, see page 78. Children of George M. Jackson and Florence Avis Dickerson (A. B. Cunyus sold his furniture and undertaker business to Mr. Jackson in December of 1899): Zim (deceased) married Annie Tinsley. Children: (1) Ann Jackson married Dr. Harold J. Choate. Children: 1. Dr. Hal J. Choate Jr. married Donna Pettit, daughter of Luke and Margaret Gaines Pettit; (2) Dr. Zim Choate married Martha Conner, daughter of Clyde and Lizette Henderson Conner. 2. G. Warren Jackson born 1908 (Jackson Furniture Co.) married Elizabeth Gemes (page 57) (74). Children: Hannah Jackson married Tom Alnutt Jr., Fairfax, Virginia; Harriett married Dr. John Lovejoy.

Robert D. Jackson married Gussie Trimble. Son, Robert D. Jackson, McDonough, Georgia. Lydia Jackson David died in 1966. Walter G. Jackson married Florrie Howard. Daughter: Ann J. Vandiver. Lawson Jackson died October 28, 1965 married Bettie Brandon (dec.) (page 47-48). Children: David Milton; Lawson Jr.; Virginia, married Charles Stern, Albany. Frank T. Jackson, Sandy Springs, son of Frank T. and Guill Monfort, Cartersville. Dickson Jackson, died 1969, married Loraine Farris, six children; had retired in Georgia from Michigan.

Page 72-3: In August visited for first time "Redlands," home of Harris Best and Mary Johnson, at Bass' ferry on the Etowah river, across the river is Murchison mountain. Home built about 1852 and in good condition. Owned now by Thompson-Weinman Company.

Rosebud Johnson died April 1967, m. Admiral William Conyers Fite (page 57), retired in Cartersville, died April 19, 1963. Rear Admiral of the Supply Corps, United States Navy. Son: William (Billie) Fite, Retired Army Colonel, Islamorado, Florida.

Page 73-4: A. C. Jolly, born April 17, 1890 wrote "Cartersville Chuckles" for 25 years in The Bartow Hearld, County Clerk, married Finch Verner. Daughter: Sidney Jolly.
New sketch:
William W. Shaw (1792-1873) and Rebecca Jackson Shaw (1797-1860), pioneers in Cass County. Son: J. Elbert Shaw, 1823-1882 married 2nd Nancy Jolly (not Maria), 1827-1872 (sister of Rachel Jolly, 1st wife). Son: Levi Franklin Shaw born December 16, 1858 died June 1, 1941, married in 1880 Clara E. Davis (1858 - 1941); granddaughter of Israel P. and Polly Smith Davis of Polk County. Children: 1. Elbert G. Shaw, born April 3, 1883-deceased, married Genevieve Vickery (1890-1954); Children: (1) David Franklin born 1910-deceased, married Doris Theus. (2) Henry Clayton Shaw born November 30, 1913 married in 1960 Virginia Dare Hamilton. (3) Elbert G. (Fritz) Shaw born, August 13, 1921, married Elizabeth Bowman; Children: John Clayton, David Shaw, Dalton. 2. Franklin H. Shaw born 1885-deceased, married Mary Harris born 1906-deceased. Sons: Lucius E. Shaw, born 1907, died 1948, married twice; James H. Shaw, born 1910, married 3 times; Children: Tommy Shaw and Jamie Shaw, California and Cartersville. 3. Clayton Davis Shaw, born 1889-deceased, married 1st Lena House; Children: (1)

Lena born 1908 married in 1925 Robert W. May; sons: Dr. Robert W. (Bob) May Jr.,born 1926,married Judy Moody; daughter, Terri Shaw. Dave May,born 1939, Cartersville. (2) Sarah,born 1910 married in 1931 Floyd E. Jenkins,married 2nd Joe Shear. (3) Frances Irene, 1912-1928. (4) William Levi, 1918-1928. (5) Clara Sue born 1915,married Billie R. McCormick (page 93). C. Davis Shaw married 2nd Bettie Young. 4. James Henry Shaw born 1891-deceased, married in 1920 Marie Carpenter; Children: Betty M. Shaw, born 1921, Atlanta; James H. Shaw Jr., born 1923 married in 1943 Hilda Henley; Children: Kathy, "Hank" and Randy Shaw; Charles C. Shaw,born 1928. 5. Julius Clarence Shaw,born December 31, 1893-deceased, married in 1926 Essie Evans, Dalton; Son: Julius Clarence Shaw Jr. born December 18, 1929, married Margaretta Lumpkin (page 45-6). 6. B. Irene Shaw born 1896, married in 1928 Robert W. Mitchell of Acworth; Children: Elizabeth I. Mitchell born 1922,married in 1945 J. T. Gardner; R. M. Jr., born 1926, married Johnnie Ruth Devane; Frances I. born 1930. 7. Norman Shaw born 1896-deceased. Robert A. Shaw Sr. died February 1975, Taylorsville, born June 18, 1898, son of James and Ellen Jefferson Shaw; Sons: Robert A. Shaw Jr., Cartersville; Thurmond E. Shaw, Annandale, Virginia. Sisters: Mrs. Roy Rhodes, Daisy Shaw, Mrs. Ralph Gaines.

Page 74: Col. Robert H. Jones was one of the eleven children of Rev. Samuel G. Jones. The Samuel Gamble Jones Genealogy is being compiled for the Georgia State Archives by Lucy Cunyus Mulcahy. Reunions now held yearly in August in "Roselawn."

Page 76: King Family: Samuel Walter Bradford died 1939 married Ella King, died 1943, daughter of W. H. King; Children: 1. Frank H. Bradford died 1963, married Martha Pepper, Pine Log. 2. Alma Bradford married H. R. Maxwell (page 80), both deceased, Cartersville. 3. Rosebud Bradford married 1st Charles Strickland (divorced); Children: Alma Strickland married W. Ryan Frier (page 160), died January 15, 1969; Rosebud Strickland married B. B. White, son of J. B. and Margaret Field White (page 56); Sarah Strickland; Crawford Strickland; Rosebud married 2nd Dr. Harry B. Bradford, Cartersville. 4. Virgil Bradford married Lillian Vincent, (both deceased). 5. Earl Bradford, deceased. 6. Oliver McConnel (Mac) Bradford born December 2, 1900 married Grace Goode, daughter of Hiram Carter and Myra Roberts Goode,who married 2nd Harley Goode (died 1967) by whom there is William C. Goode, with FAA in Fairbanks, Alaska, has retired in Rydal; son of "Mac" and Grace: James Oliver Bradford, Atlanta. 7. Talmadge A. Bradford married Lillian Boozer, Atlanta. 8. Lena Bradford Watts lives in Decatur.

Oliver C. Bradford, brother of Samuel Walter Bradford died 1925 married Minnie Bell (page 80); Children: (1) Dr. Harry B. Bradford married 1st LeNelle Moon (page 122), 2nd Rosebud B. Strickland. (2) Samuel R. Bradford married Jessie Roberts, had store at Pine Log; Children: S. Allen Bradford, died March 1965, married Avoleen Anderson; Willis Bradford married Lucile Mozley, kept the store at Pine Log; Hugh Bradford married Mary Donahoo, Cartersville; Roberts Bradford married Elizabeth Gaines; Hollis Bradford married Elizabeth Kelly, Ellijay; Elise Bradford married James L. Johnson, Ellijay. (3) Trammel Bradford married Eugenia Roper, lives on #411 Pine Log; son, Wendell T. Bradford married Louella Smith, lives in Old Bradford Home. 4. Lindsey Bradford married Lollie Gaines. 5. Lucy Bradford Fergerson, deceased. 6. Carl Bradford, deceased, Atlanta. 7. Bertie Bradford Dorrah, deceased.

Page 76: There is no marker for the graves of Judge and Mrs.
          Nathan Land in the Cassville cemetery. (5) James Henry
Land, born June 21, 1849, died July 5, 1922, buried in Jackson,
Georgia, married in October 1876 Mary Cowan Jones. Daughter,
Mary Land, born September 22, 1894, married Ernest L. McMillan of
Kerrville, Texas. (9) Delilah or Lila Land, 1840-1923, married
William Augustus Chunn, 1840-1921 (page 52). Gertrude Chunn
1867-1953. Eugene Latimer Chunn, 1870-1954, Cassville. Brother
Nathan Freeman Land died January 5, 1971 in Griffin, past 90
years of age.

Page 77: Another Leake Family from Laurens, South Carolina came
          to Cass County about 1847. Bryant Thomas Leake, 1828-
1908 married in 1847 Martha E. Cook, daughter of Abraham Cook
and Henrietta Irby. Of eleven children these reared families
in Bartow: (III) Louise Florence Leake born 1857, married in 1872
Alexander F. Dent, son of George Dent (1804-1872) and Frances,
buried in Kingston, had summer home on the Etowah River near
Hardin's bridge; Children: George Dent married Jennie Sproull;
Emma Dent married in 1905 Carey Dodd; Children: Bowdoin Dodd;
Mrs. Joe Barron, Rockmart; Frederick ("Fritz") W. Dent, died June
1934, married Pearl Dodd, died October 5, 1971; Children: (1)
John W. Dent born November 11, 1905, married Charlotte Flemister;
daughter: Sue, married Elliott Phillips. J. W. Dent is retired
President of Georgia Marble Company, Board Director, Mayor,
Cartersville. (2) Louise Dent married Charles Wheeler (of Carters-
ville), LaFayette. (3) Mildred married 1st Phillip Stiles, 2nd
Edward Clark, Columbia, South Carolina; Children: Judy C. Hair,
Rev. Erskine Clark. (4) Lucy married 1st H. Quigg Rucker (dec-
eased), 2nd Harry Patton, Carrollton, 2 daughters. (5) Frances
married Thomas Henderson (deceased), half-brother of Ratia Hen-
derson; daughter: True. (6) F. W. Dent, married, 3 children,
lives in Orlando. (7) Alex T. Dent married Marilyn Trippe of
Richmond, Indiana; Children: Dedde D. Burrus; Cathy married Mike
Harris; "Fritz" III Dent, Cartersville. (8) Margaret Dent married
Romulus H. Thompson, Atlanta; Sons: Dent & Mark Thompson. (9)
Charles C. Dent married Frances Kelly, Rome; sons: Fred & Jim
Dent. (10) (Lt. Col.) Joe Earl Dent married Louise Ryan, San
Antonio; son: Paul. (V) Walter William Leake, born 1854, married
Emma Milan.   (VIII) Villa Dean Leake, 1858-1924, married
Creed Cunyus, 1852-1917; daughter, Beulah died July 23, 1971,
Rome. (IX) Sara Mozell Leake, born 1863, married Dr. Henry Cunyus,
1848-1933; daughter Blanche died 1968; married 2nd Daisy Mathis,
Rome. (X) Joseph Burwell Leake, born 1863, married in 1890 Mary
Dent; 7 children, moved to Mississippi. (XI) Charles Thomas
Leake born 1865 married Mary Frances Lawson, moved to Cobb County
in 1910; children: Estelle Leake married William Ray Tapp; Ethel
L. Leake, died 1965, married Harry Miller; daughter Sarah Frances
lives in Powder Springs, Georgia, 5 other children. (Estelle
and Ethel Leake helped in the compilation of "The Ligon Family
and Connections," by Wm. D. Ligon.).

Page 78: Children of Prince Lewis and Sallie Maud Jackson (page
          71); Children: (1) Leon Lewis married Ann Sproull;
Children: Prince Lewis married 1st Helen Thaxton (deceased), 2nd
Paula Ponder; Jo Ann Lewis married Bob Ridgeway; John S. Lewis
married Melody Wilson, he is a lawyer in Cartersville. (2)
Cornelia Lewis married J. C. Bostwick (deceased), Thomaston.
(3) Earle Lewis married Evelyn Matthews; sons: Terry and Button
Lewis, Cartersville. J. J. Hill, born 1873 died 1964, married
Frances Lewis, 1880-1952. John B. Lewis died 1957; Mildred
Lewis May (Mrs. R. C.) died 1963. Evelyn Lewis died 1944.
Daughter of John B. and Pearl Lewis, Sarah, married Charles Smith.

Page 80: Mrs. Lucas was living and entertaining in "Clarendon"
          in 1889. The Alex F. Dent children lived here when
young. Mr. and Mrs. Walter Fountain live here at present. It
has been renovated and is maintained by Atlanta owners.

Page 82-3: James (not John) L. Milhollin, 1851-1943 married
            Carrie Elliott; daughter: Mary Lee Milhollin born
May 7, 1885 died September 28, 1971, married B. Luther Pettit
(deceased, brother of Hugh and Henry Pettit and Fannie P. Harris);
Children: Caroline Pettit married George Tinsley (deceased);
James Pettit married Frances E. McCormick; Children: Marilyn
married Arnold Baker; son David; Ida Lee Pettit married Billy
Joe Law; Sons: Dane and Cole; Dorothy Pettit married Lewis Hill
Shropshire; Children: Lewis Jr., William Benjamin, Dianne. The
Shropshires remodeled and live in the old John Clayton home used
as a Federal hospital and headquarters during Allatoona Battles
and Sherman did spend one night there. The house was built
prior to 1844 by John Clayton, born 1774 in Virginia and died in
the house November 6, 1864, partially from shock of the Yankee
invaders. He married Agnes Samuel. A sister of Agnes Clayton,
Elizabeth, married Jefferson Clark, nephew of Thomas Jefferson
and an early settler of Allatoona, and the Clark descendants, the
Thomases inherited the house after John Clayton's death. It
changed owners before the Shropshires rescued this historical
house at old Allatoona, just below the forts, not destroyed
by Allatoona Lake.

Mrs. Gertrude Milhollin Barge and Miss Willie Mae Milhollin still
live in Casville, 1971.

NEW SKETCH:
            Captain Elihu Gordon Nelson and his two first cousins,
            Melville Calhoun Nelson and Alvin L. Nelson, came from
Laurens, South Carolina and settled in and around Euharlee.
Elihu G. Nelson, born February 14, 1825 in Laurens, died March 5,
1871 in a drowning accident near the famous covered bridge at
Euharlee. He married in Laurens 1st Margaret McFurson (or Mc-
Pherson); Children: I. James M. Nelson, 1850-1871. II. William
A. Nelson born 1853 died in Texas. III. Hulsey Coley Nelson born
February 11, 1855 married Virginia Lee Fuller, South Carolina;
Children: 1. Mabel Claire Nelson married Dr. J. R. Nickles, South
Carolina. 2. Lillian Othello Nelson, Superintendent of Nurses,
Piedmont Hospital, Atlanta. 3. Conner Fuller Nelson married Lois
Seymour of Florida; Children: Marion Lee and Conner Fuller Nelson
Jr., Atlanta.
            Elihu G. Nelson married 2nd in 1858 Albina L. Bailey, 1840-
1891; Children: IV. Gillie Deborah Nelson born November 15, 1859
died 1923 married in 1881 L. Cicero Rainey. V. Emma A. Nelson
born October 4, 1861, died July 18, 1911, married in 1879 Sam M.
Kennedy. VI. Felix G. Nelson, born July 4, 1863, died May 11,
1898 married in 1885 Mollie Lowery. VII. Elizabeth Cochran
Nelson, born December 22, 1866, died January 3, 1957, married in
1886 John D. Johnson of Pontotoc, Mississippi. VIII. Frank
Elihu Nelson, born October 23, 1870, died November 11, 1948,
married in 1894 Elizabeth (Lizzie) Steed Williams, born November
14, 1875, died August 5, 1949; Children: 1. Jesse Elihu Nelson,
born January 20, 1895, retired farmer, married in 1917 Clarice
Goss of Euharlee; Children: Walter Elihu Nelson, born December 9,
1921, married in 1949 Louise Ledford of Cassville, no children;
Jesse William Nelson, born January 18, 1927, married in 1953 Marie
Jones of Atco; Children: Jan Dale Nelson born 1954, married
Michael Lanham; Sheena Marie Nelson, born 1956, married Edward
Haygood; Winfred Elihu born 1958; Jay Lynn Nelson, born 1963.

2. Henry Clanton Nelson born June 14, 1896, Tax Collector, 1932-50, retired, married in 1925 Ruth Payne of Adairsville, no children. 3. Annie Nelson, born August 6, 1898, d. Oct. 5, 1982. In 1955 named Teacher of the Year   4. Emmie Nelson, born September 6, 1900, on staff of National 4-H (Clubs) Service Committee, Chicago, as Associate, Program Services, listed in Who's Who of American Women, 1972-3 ed., retired 1969 to Nelson home near Euharlee. 5. Joe Frank Nelson, born August 8, 1902, died August 31, 1974, Engineer for Combustion Engineering, Inc., Chattanooga, 1929-67, retired, married in 1938 Mildred DeFur, died December 24, 1961; Children: Martha Elizabeth born June 19, 1940 married John Joseph Stokes: son: Frank Granville Stokes; Mary Frances, born July 18, 1943, married 1st Charles Ladd; daughters: Laura Ann and Donna; married 2nd in 1969 Charles Boyd Coleman, Jr., in 1970 legally adopted the two daughters. 6. Eva Sallie Nelson, born June 22, 1904, President, Rentz Banking Company, married in 1926 Olin Doan Barron of Rentz, Georgia, died August 17, 1964; daughters: Ellen Elizabeth Barron, born January 18, 1935, married in 1956 Gerald Adams of Dublin; son: Gerald Cordie Adams; Marie Lois Barron born February 17, 1938, married in 1961 Kennon Benjamin Gillis of Soperton; Children: Barron Nelson Gillis, Lee Ellen Gillis, Neil Lee Gillis. 7. Thelma Nelson, born April 17, 1907, married in 1938 Rufus Erwin Fields of Kingston; Children: Bettie Ann Fields, born September 15, 1938, married in 1970 Horace Bridges; R. E. Fields Jr. born May 4, 1940, married in 1965 Rhoda Kay Tatum; daughter Leigh Ann. 8. Jimmie Nelson born November 17, 1909, Soil Conversation Service, Alpharetta and Cartersville, married in 1946 Lois Eley of Scooba, Mississippi, born 1915; Children: (a) James Morris Nelson, born June 25, 1947, married in 1965 Judy Carolyn Tatum of Cartersville; sons: James Brent and Keith Tatum Nelson. (b) Cynthia Lois Nelson, born March 13, 1952. (c) Frank Eley Nelson born July 7, 1950. 9. William (Bill) Nelson, born January 8, 1911, married in 1933 Pauline Martin, born October 2, 1916, died April 6, 1961; Children: (1) Billy Frank Nelson born 1935, married 1955 Martha Dean Smith; son: Ronnie Nelson, born 1957. (2) Betty Nell Nelson, born 1944, married in 1962 Hollis Ezell of Cartersville; Children: Dena Beth Ezell and Bryan Hollis Ezell. 10. Edna Elizabeth Nelson, born March 21, 1914, married in 1938 Charles Glenn Morris of Mt. Berry, Georgia; Children: Charles Henry Morris, born in 1941, married in 1962 Linda Jo Henson of Marietta; Children: Charles David and Susanna Louise Morris. (2) Sara Louise Morris, born 1946, married in 1971 David Owen Yarbrough of Clarkesville, Tennessee, now doing mission work in Oregon. II. Herman Nelson born January 20, 1916, Assistant Superintendent of Schools, Spalding County, married in 1946 Grace Williams of Cartersville; daughter Teresa E. Nelson born 1948, married in 1969 Robert Mitchell Setzen. 12. Mary Ellen Nelson born September 19, 1918, married in 1934 Dave Carlton Taff of Stilesboro, died April 17, 1962; Son: Jimmy Carlton Taff born May 30, 1938, Soil Conversation Service, Hiawassee, married in 1963 Gail Fortenberry of Cartersville; daughters: Robin Renee Taff; Carrie Ellen Taff (born and died July 1970). E. G. Nelson and children are in the 1860 Cass County Census.

Page 85: Melville Calhoun Nelson, born January 16, 1850, Laurens, South Carolina, died February 17, 1927, Euharlee (son of Elihu and Charlotte Coleman Nelson, page 25) married in 1871 Alice Carey, 1856-1929 (daughter of George Wm. Cary and Othella M. Speer of Tennessee). Children all born in Euharlee: 1. Robert Speer Nelson, born July 8, 1873, died April 25, 1955 married 1910 Kate Gaines (died November 3, 1924); Children: Susan Elizabeth, born 1911, married 1935 W. A. Brooks; daughter: Betty Kate Brooks. 2. Thella May Nelson, 1875-1961, married 1902 John Bayless Mulinix

Jr. (died August 15, 1957); Children: Alice Carey Mulinix, John Nelson Mulinix. <u>3</u>. George Carey Nelson, born October 10, 1878, died December 12, 1963, married 1905 Jessie Broome (died September 28, 1963); Children: (1) Mary Alice Nelson, born 1906, married William V. Ebbitt. (2) George Cary Nelson, born 1914, married 1938 Malline Busby; Children: Elaine, born 1943, married 1966 C. Thomas Bonner; George Carey Nelson born 1948. <u>4</u>. Edward Vance Nelson born September 10, 1880 died February 6, 1955, married 1904 Laura Fink, died November 8, 1969; Children: (1) Myrtle Vance Nelson, born November 11, 1905, married 1925 Fred D. Neel died September 17, 1959; daughter: Julia Vance Neel, born 1934, married 1960 John Frew; daughter: Julie Neel Frew. (2) Laura May Nelson, born 1907, married 1934 Wilson Walker. (3) Margaret Helen Nelson, born 1909, married 1931 Marion Matthews McClelland; Children: (a) Marion Jr., born 1932, married Clara Estelle Adams; Children: Marion III, Charles, Mark, David, Stuart and Alison Adam McClellan. (b) Arthur Vance McClellan, born 1936, married Shirley Anne Jenkins; daughter Melanie Anne. (c) Helen France McClellan born 1938. (4) Joseph Calhoun Nelson, born 1912. (5) Adolph Fink Nelson born 1914, married 1941 Eunice Weems; Children: (a) Laura E. Nelson, married Terry Vann Jones; Children: Terry Vann Jr., Laura Elizabeth Jones. (b) Adolph F. Nelson Jr. married Mary Victoria Bozeman; daughter: Mary Victoria Nelson. (c) Martha Frances Nelson, born 1950, and Donna Vance Nelson, born 1955. (6) Glenn William Nelson, born 1916, married 1946 Willie Fay Sproull; Children: (a) Jimmy Ray Nelson married Jan Smith; Children: Mary L. and Susan Ashley Nelson. (b) Glenda Fay Nelson, born November 16, 1951. (c) Kathy Calhoun, born 1953; Steve Sproull Nelson born 1959. (7) Frances Lee Nelson, born 1919. (8) Warren Logan Nelson, born 1927. <u>5</u>. Henry Carl Nelson, born October 8, 1885, died October 26, 1976, Mayor twice, Director Cartersville Federal Savings and Loan Association married April 12, 1911 Nellie Lee Bradley, died April 15, 1957; Children: twins, Sarah Nell b. Aug. 5, 1922, d. Oct. 6, 1982, m. William Brown Nipper, Greensboro, Georgia; Children: Brenna Joyce, born 1946, married in 1968 Dr. Robert L. Brand Jr.; sons: Alexander Vaughan Brand; William Brown Nipper Jr., born 1949; Margaret Nell Nipper, born 1954. Elizabeth Anne Nelson, married in 1946 Joseph Albert Minish, Commerce; Children: Sarah Ellen Minish, born 1953, married in 1971 Roger Van Beauchamp; Elizabeth Ann Minish born 1955; Florence Lee Minish, born 1958. <u>6</u>. Warren Raymond Nelson, 1889-1963, Atlanta, married 1913 Virginia Lee Beale (deceased). <u>7</u>. Joseph Calhoun Nelson, born April 18, 1894 died February 17, 1975, married 1920 Frankie Patterson; son: Joseph C. Nelson Jr., born 1921, married Mary Elizabeth Smith; Children: Joseph III, born 1948, married Kay Byrd; Mary Elizabeth Nelson born 1952. <u>8</u>. Alvin Cliff Nelson, born December 20, 1898, married 1925 Josie Bibb Saggus; daughter Margaret Ann Nelson born 1926. married Floyd Grainger; daughter Josie Ann Grainger. Information from Betty Nelson Minish.

Page 86: Wm. T. Pittard died 1937, County Tax Receiver, married in 1844 Mary Hawkins, died October 25, 1948, daughter of Rev. Perry E. and Emily Pierce Hawkins. Lived in Grassdale and Cartersville until 1919. Children: Thomas Pittard, Harry Pittard, Pauline P. Lashley and Lucy P. Tyner.

Page 87: Pittard: Sam Pittard, 1892-1963, married Jo Sloan, teacher in Cassville School, lives in the old Pittard home in Cassville. Paul Pittard, 1896-1952, married Marie Headden, 1898-1952. Fannie Lumpkin, daughter of Elizabeth Pittard & Henry Lumpkin married Thomas Hicks. Children: (1) William Lumpkin Hicks, City mail carrier for years in Cartersville died 1970, married Daisy Murphy; daughters: Lois Ethel Mabry, Chattanooga; Frankie H. Gilpin, Newnan. (2) Richard Hicks, retired, Macon.

(3) Dell married Hiram Adams, Acworth. (4) Henry T. Hicks married Loie   , Valdosta. (5) Almon (J.A.) Hicks. (6) Frances Hicks, nurse (dec). (7) Charlotte married Ed Nichols, Acworth. (8) Tom Hicks, Decatur. (9) George Hicks, Engineer in the U.S. Navy. A reunion of these nine children was held in Acworth in 1962. Picture in Bartow Scrapbook.

Page 90: The James G. Ryals home has been beautifully renovated and is lived in by Judge and Mrs. J. L. Davis and daughter Grace. Judge J. L. Davis died December 15, 1981.

Page 91: Children of Samuel Irby Sheats, 1867-1950 and Emma Hill 1870-1945; Irby Hill Sheats, born 1900, Kingston, married Ruth Moore, Kingston; Louise Sheats Simmons born 1902, lives in Calhoun. A niece of Louisa Irby Watts Sheats, Catherine Henderson, 1848-1889, married James K. Rabb; daughter Grace Rabb, 1886-1945 married her cousin William Irby Henderson, 1880-1957. Children: Catherine H. Rollins b. 1910 (dec.); Helen Rabb Henderson b.1914 of Marietta; Dorothy Irby Henderson born 1921, retired teacher; all born in Kingston; daughter Nan Watt Rabb, born March 27, 1889, married Grover Cleveland Phillips. Leander Lee Irby, sister of Louisa Sheats married Sally Barber, son: Claude Irby, 1865-1937 married Virginia Baylis, born April 12, 1877, died January 1975, Dalton; daughter: Dorothy Irby, born 1900, married Crisp Bradley, 1895-1963, Dalton, Georgia; Children: Dr. Paul Bradley and Patricia Bradley (Husband, John Flynt, Ret. Georgia U.S. Representative.).

Page 22: Another early settler of Adairsville was Gilbert Gholston, born December 15, 1821 died February 22, 1904, son of Zachariah Gholston of DeKalb County, married Martha Ann Loveless, came to Adairsville during the construction of the W&A RR. Sisters of Gilbert Gholston: (1) Nancy J. Gholston married 1st Ebenezer Loveless, Post Master and Telegraph Operator in Adairsville; married 2nd George Reed; Children: 1. Ellen G. Reed, 1874-1939, married 1st Martin Henry Butler; daughter: Ruth Butler born April 25, 1892 married Joseph Bibb Bowdoin, son of Dr. J. B. Bowdoin; daughter: Alice Butler. married George Harold Howard; daughter: Patricia B. m. Harry Stevens, Atla., four children. Ellen Reed Butler married 2nd Warren P. Whitworth, died January 10, 1940. He served as Mayor, Councilman, WM of Masonic Lodge, Baptist deacon, President of Adairsville Bank and Director on school board. (2) Elizabeth Gholston married James Loveless; daughter: Genevieve married James Bond, Decatur. From "Families and Descendants in America of Golson, Gholson, Gholston" - James M. Black, Salt Lake City. Information from Alice B. Howard.

Page 93: The Sproull family has an annual reunion. Fifty-eight of the 90 living descendants of the late Fannie Sproul and William Ira Jackson had a reunion in August 1962 at the home of Hubert Harris near Taylorsville. J. Bob Jackson was "Chief of the Clan." William Kary Jackson died April 1964. Mrs. J. B. Sproull died March 1966. John Hunter McCormick (grandson of Malinda Sproull & Isaiah McCormick) died February 1, 1955, son of Captain Henry J. McCormick and Josephine Hawkins. Their son, John Hunter McCormick, in 1898, m. Ida V. Munford, b. Sept. 24, 1874, d. Jan. 20, 1945, reared these dhildren in "Rose Cottage": (1) Henry J. McCormick b. Jan. 5, 1899, m. Jeffie Rackley; son: Joel McCormick, b. 1940, m. Margaret McKinley, Tampa. (2) Rena, born January 10, 1902, married Frank S. Beazley (died 1971). (3) Clara Sue, born April 4, 1903, married Thomas P. Mann (dec.), Marietta daughter Barbara Mann married Forest L. Fowler; daughters:

Sheryl Sue, Virginia Claire, Mullie McCormick. (4) Dorris McCormick, b. September 20, 1904, ret. teacher, lives in "Rose Cottage." (5) Walter Gordon McCormick, b. 1911, m. Odie Wynn. (6) Billy Burge McCormick, b. Nov. 5, 1913, m. Sudie Shaw. (7) Munford McCormick d. at 18 or 19 years of age. (8) Frances E. McCormick, b. July 12, 1951, m. James Petitt (p. 83). Miss Campie Hawkins who lived in the old home place "Wildwood," Stilesboro, with niece, Catherine Jackson (Charles H.) Brock and family is now deceased.

Page 94-95: Children of (a) William Henry Stiles: W. H. (Harry) Stiles married Eleanor Williamson, lives in Bradenton, Florida; John C. Stiles died in 1934; Hugh (deceased); Elise Stiles lost at sea, end of WWI, nurse. Dorothy Stiles and husband W. T. White lived in Sebring, Florida. Elma Stiles Cook, died in July 1964 in St. Petersburg; Robert Mackay Stiles, born November 21, 1895, married Susie McGowan (dec.), maintained "Malbone"; dau. Margaret married Fred Knight Jr.; Children: Fred Knight, III, Susan and Margaret Stiles Knight, Cartersville. Robert M. Stiles organized the Farm Bureau in Georgia and was a Director in Cartersville, Production Credit Association, Cartersville Bank, and Coosa Valley A&P Commission, d. 2/21/1975. Joe Stiles & fam. live in Sebring. Philip Stiles mar. 2nd May Brockstad; Children: Wm. Henry (Bill) Stiles, Gulie Stiles. The original W. H. Stiles home was destroyed by fire in 1971 - had been empty for years. Dr. Joseph Franklin McGowan, half-brother of Dr. Hugh McGowan, came to Bartow from South Carolina in 1895,married Elizabeth Tinsley, sister of Thomas Warren Tinsley (1860-1942); Children: Marjorie married Wesley Roberts; Sons: W. M. Roberts, Wilmington, Delaware. Hugh Roberts, Albertville, Alabama. (2) Susie* (95) married Robert M. Stiles. (3) Sam McGowan (page 266),born October 10, 1896, Mayor, retired, found murdered on December 8, 1978, married Leah Dodds of Cedartown,died January 1965; daughter Susan,married J. O. Alexander, Atlanta; son: J. O. Jr. (4) John Reed McGowan, druggist, married Grace Tyler, Shannon, Georgia. (5) Vivian McGowan, musician,died January 6, 1964, Cartersville. (6) Homer Miller McGowan married Anna Elizabeth Hancock, daughter of Don and Wingfield Hudgins Hancock, Marietta.

Page 97-98: Eunice Ginn Adam (Mrs. Walter S.) died July 15, 1963 in Cartersville; daughter of William W. and Laura Ginn, was society editor and feature writer - "You Know What?" for The Tribune News, after their retirement from Baptist pastorates, until her death. Rev. W. S. Adams died January 1970,a native son also. Children of Lewis H. Tumlin (died March 1965) and Aluwee Brown Tumlin are: Georgia Tumlin married Paul Lucas, Atlanta; Henry Tumlin,born December 28, 1916 married Charlsie Crutchen, no children; he is manager and curator of The Etowah Mounds, past President of the Chamber of Commerce; Norton B. Tumlin married Doris Smith; Children: Terry Norton, Rebecca Aluwee, Lewis H. Tumlin III, Trudy Jane Tumlin; all live at the old Tumlin home; Scottie Tumlin married Jack McNair of Jonesboro.

Page 99: Thomas A. Upshaw, deceased; Children: Elizabeth Lois, m. W. P. (Red) Tuten, Hampton, South Carolina; Davis A. Upshaw, Cartersville; Thomas H. Upshaw, m. 2nd Adele Taylor (dec.) Ora V. Goode d. Feb.1951. Murray Upshaw,died July 10, 1960, married Betty Gaines, secretary and protegee of Mrs. Corra Harris; Children: 1. John Charles Upshaw married Glenda Scoggins - Children: Mary Johnna, Amy Laverne, Murray Bryan, Brent Weldon Upshaw. 2. George Thomas Upshaw married Janet Ransom; daughter: Elizabeth Anne. Troy Upshaw married 1st Rachel McEver (deceased), 2nd Elizabeth Guyton.

Page 100: Veach: George William Veach, son of Everett and
Lillian Bradley Veach, committed suicide in June 1964,
married Dorothy Gaines. Other children of Everett Veach: Helen
Veach Whatley and Esburn Veach, Atlanta; Sue Veach, dau. of George
W. and Dorothy Gaines, m. Peter Kouvenhoven, Fort Myers, Fla.
Milton P. d.Jan. 5, 1956. George V. Gaines, son of Milton P. and
Susie V. Gaines, m. Frances Carlton of Atlanta, d. Mar. 5, 1967.
Julia Veach Stewart d. Mar. 5, 1967. Mary V. Milner d. Oct. 7,
1970 in Atlanta. Susie V. Gaines d. Jan. 26, 1976 in Atlanta.

Page 104: Robert Word: Mrs. Robert Ramspeck died in June 1971,
buried in Decatur, was wife of Ex-Congressman. Robert
Word Ramspeck, grandson of Dr. Robert C. Word and Adelia E.
Patton. After his retirement from Congress in 1945, Robert
Ramspeck was chairman of the Civil Service Commission under
President Truman and later Vice-President of Eastern Air Lines.
They lived in Kensington, Maryland. He died September 10, 1972,
was buried in Decatur Cemetery with wife, Nobie Clay Ramspeck.
He was born in 1890 in Decatur.

Page 106: Colonel John Young, son of W. Hugh Young of Orlando
and grandson of G. M. and Lucy Heyward Young, lived
and went to school when a young boy in Cartersville. Graduate
of Ga. Tech, he was in the second group of NASA astronauts. He
was command Module pilot during Apollo 10 Moon Mission and on
the Gemini 3 and 4 earth-orbiting flights, and will command the
Appollo 16 Luna Landing Mission in March 1972. His brother,
Hugh Young and his wife are Baptist Missionaries in Japan at
present.

Page 112: Continuation of Cherokee Circuit Judges: Defeated in
1936 general election by James A. McFarland who died
before taking office in January 1937, William A. Ingram was
appointed by Governor E. Talmadge to fill unexpired term. Court
ruled that there was no vacancy and upheld Judge Claude C. Pittman so he served until 1938. Claude C. Pittman, 1927-1938, John
Chester Mitchell, 1938-43, Johnson Murphey Claggett, 1943-47,
Stafford R. Brooke, 1947, James Heddleston Paschall, 1947-57,
Harland Erwin Mitchell, 1957-58, Jefferson Lee Davis, 1958-
Jere F. White, Solicitor General.
Jefferson Lee Davis, present Judge of the Cherokee Circuit was
born August 28, 1912 in Cartersville, son of William Robert Davis
and Deborah Hobgood. He attended Georgia Tech, Atlanta Law, LLB
Degree, Baptist, Democrat, Attorney, member of the House of Representives 1947-8, 49-50, Senator 42nd District 1955-6. Married
April 1, 1942 Grace Eloine Green. Children: Ronald, by a previous marriage, now a lawyer in Cartersville; Jefferson Lee Jr.,
also a lawyer, and Sara Grace. They have restored in recent
years and live in the historic Ryals home, adding to the fast
diminishing ante-bellum homesites.

Page 121: Laura Neel Hammond died 1970; Juliet Neel McClatchey
died June 25, 1960; Marvin R. McClatchey died January
24, 1939. Children of Juliet and M. R. McClatchey: Marvin R.
McClatchey, Jr., married Sallie Bruce-Blackford, 8 children,
Atlanta. Julia A. McClatchey born January 4, 1913, married Russel
Jones Brooke, born April 1, 1910. Children: Russell Jones Brooke,
Jr., Marvin McC. Brooke, Julia Neel Brooke, Atlanta. James
Monroe Neel Jr. (page 85) died December 28, 1958. Children of
J. M. Neel Jr. and Sara Holmes: 1. Holmes Neel married Nell
Parish; Children: Sara Nell Neel, married 1971, J. R. DeBardalaben
Jr.; Robert Holmes Neel; Mary Parish Neel. 2. J. M. Neel Jr.
married Frances Maxwell of Atlanta; Children: Sarah Ann; J. M.

Neel ("Jay"); Joseph Lockhart Neel; David Anderson Neel, Cartersville. 3. William (Bill) Akers Neel married Marjorie Bozeman; Children: W. A. Neel Jr.; Susan, Elizabeth, Carolyn Neel, Andrew B. Neel, Cartersville. Ch'n of Isa Neel & Ralph O. Jackson,Rockmart (both dec.): Mary Ann married Tolbot F. Bennett; Ralph Jackson Jr.,married 2nd Elizabeth Marcum; Julia Neel Jackson married William Aldred. Fred D. Neel died 1959, see Nelson Family. Ella Neel, daughter of J. M. Sr. and Anna Anderson Neel died June 26, 1962. Information from Julia M. Brooke.

Page 123: William T. Townsend died May 1, 1938; Bessie Conyers Townsend died April 19, 1934. Elias Carter Townsend was Chief of Staff to General C. W. Abrams in Vietnam, now Retired Major General of the United States Army, 1970 married Zelle Wade of Colorado Springs, lived in San Francisco, died July 2, 1979. Mary Eliza married Clyde Shaw, daughter: Martha Eliza Shaw, Curator of Widener Memorial, Harvard University. Wm. Thomas Townsend Jr. (Dr.) married Julia Redmond, now headmaster of Providence Day School, Charlotte, North Carolina, died February 26, 1979.

Page 123: Judge George Hargraves Aubrey died July 9, 1934; Harriette H. Smith Aubrey died February 3, 1953. Octavia H. Aubrey (Bradley) Howard (page 69) died February 12, 1971 in Atlanta. Children: Jack and Willis Howard live in Jackson, Mississippi. Octavia H. Smith, Wilmington, North Carolina. Rosa Howard, Atlanta. Children of Katherine Aubrey (deceased) and Robert Sims Munford are: Sims Munford, married Virginia Townsend, Jackson, Mississippi; George Munford married Margaret Wilson, lived in Winston-Salem; Dillard Munford married Lillie Shepherd Davis, Atlanta, is founder of Munford-Do-It-Yourself Stores, Munford, Inc. Robert S. Munford (deceased) married 2nd Marilu Young, daughter of W. W. and Jessie Smith Young, famous Kindergarten teacher in Cartersville; one daughter: Faith Munford (Dr.), married Dr. Everett Charles Price, Houston, Texas.

Page 127: First Baptist Pastors: Guy N. Atkinson, 1929-1943; Marvin V. Stedham, 1944-1948; Joseph E. Abstance, 1948-1953; J. Howell Perry, 1954.

Page 132: Sam Jones Memorial United Methodist Ministers: Nathan Thompson, 1932-34; T. R. Kendall, Jr. 1934-35; Claude Hendricks, 1936-37; W. G. Crawley, 1938-39; B. W. Hancock, 1940-42; W. H. LaPrade, 1943-44; George King, 1944-48; W. M. Twiggs, 1949-54; A. B. Elizer, 1955-56, retired in Cartersville, died in December 1966; T. H. Wheelis, 1961-62; Zack Hayes, 1962-63; G. Robert Gary, 1964-71, resigned; Frank Jenkins, 1971-

Page 132: Pine Log Camp Meetings have been held continuously in August. During the Aug. 13-22, 1971,services held with Rev. Fred G. Shellnutt of Smyrna and Rev. Zack Hayes, retired United Methodist Ministers, doing the preaching, a Youth Recreation Building on the camp grounds was dedicated August 19, 1971, to memorialize Dr. Pierce Harris, a frequent guest minister during his life time. The Coosa Valley Area Planning and Development Commission started this building, with Jake Woods, Chairman. (The History of Morrison Camp Ground by Mrs. Della Blackstone Andrews can be found in the Northwest Georgia Historical & Geneology Quarterly, Vol. 3, July 1971, pages 14-18.).

Page 132: Rev. J. Hamby Barton preached his first sermon at the Pine Log campground in 1907 and served more than 60 years as a Methodist Minister, and celebrated a James Monroe

Barton Family reunion here in 1967. Children present were Carola Barton Garrison, Naomi Barton Hamilton, Lou Reeta Barton Northcutt, Rev. J. Hamby Barton, Rev. A. Eugene Barton (both retired) and Homer R. Barton.

Page 135: First Presbyterian Church pastors since 1933: Russell F. Johnson died in 1935; Jack Hand, 1936-39; J. Walton Stewart, 1939-41; B. Herman Dillard, 1941-46; L. B. Colquitt, 1947-54; J. Clyde Plexico, 1954-59; J. W. Stonebraker, 1959- ; Roger A. Martin, 1968-70; James R. Shroyer, 1970-71; Dr. A. W. Buchanan, 1971.

Page 136: Tabernacle Baptist: The "beloved George Crowe" retired, six years before he died in September 1956. Children of Rev. and Mrs. Crowe were Charles, J. M., Evelyn O. Jones, Sarah C. Goddard and Vara C. Gaddis, Cartersville. Pastors: Floyd J. Hendricks, 1944; E. E. Keen, October 1, 1946 resigned; George F. Brown, interim; S. R. Haman, 1953; Harry P. Wootan Jr., June 1962, resigned January 1, 1968; Melvin Wise, John Adkerson, Ebb Filpatrick, 1968; H. B. Merritt, January 1, 1969.

Page 137: Records now show that the Ascension Episcopal Church was formed on November 6, 1844 when interested persons met with Bishop Stephen Elliott in the Pettit Creek Baptist Meeting House. It was determined that a church, rectory and schoolhouse would be erected in the area that was on property of the late Mrs. Sproull Fouche. The buildings were erected and the church was constructed as Ascension Church by the Bishop Elliott on June 22, 1845, the Rev. Owen P. Thackera being the Deacon. In the course of time, Cartersville was growing into a town and it was determined to dispose of the original property and, with the proceeds and other funds, to erect a church in Cartersville. The present church located on the corner of Cherokee and Bartow Street was consecrated and the first service was on April 1, 1874, consecrated by the late Bishop Beckwith November 6, 1875. Due to lost records, a list of those serving is incomplete but the church has grown from Mission status to full Parish status with the addition of the Parish House in 1953 and a home for the Rector in 1960. Dr. Gordon was an early Rector. Rectors have been Dr. Albert K. Mathews (died 1954), Retired Colonel, United States Chaplain; The Rev. Douglas Winn, 11 years; the Rev. Louis A. Tonsmeire for the past seven.

Page 137: New Churches: Atco Baptist, Gilmer Street Baptist, Trinity Baptist, St. Francis Catholic, Church of God, Shepherd of the Hills Lutheran, First Congregational Methodist, Faith United Methodist, First Methodist now Sam Jones Memorial United Methodist, Bartow Cumberland Presbyterian, Cartersville Church of Christ, Evangelical Methodist, Douglas Street United Methodist, Elizabeth Street Church of God, Assembly of God and others.
Copied from the History of Methodism in Georgia and Florida by G. G. Smith, from 1795-1865, page 313: "The Cherokee District was still under the direction of Isaac Boring (1834-35). This year the Cassville Mission was established. Cass, now Bartow County, was then one of the largest and one of the most fertile of the counties in the Cherokee Country, and though the Indians were still in some parts of the county, it was being rapidly settled. Frederick Lowry was sent to it, and reported at the next conference 130 members."

Page 137: The Sam Jones Tabernacle has been torn down, but for the September 19, 1906 revival meeting "the undersigned merchants and business men of Cartersville hereby agree to close our stores and business during the hours of the future Tabernacle services, now being held in Cartersville: J. A. Monfort; Walter White: T. P. Tedder; Madison Milam; John W. Jones; Bennet Mercantile Co.; B. L. Vaughan, Clothing; Knight Hardware Co.; J. W. Vaughan and Co.; Strickland Brothers Co.; Lumpkin Bros.; Scheur Bros.; J. W. Grogan; F. Gresham; H. Wikle; H. T. Bradley Co.; J. T. Marr; D. F. Bradford; S. C. Smith & Son; Etowah Bottling Works; I. M. Hightower; D. R. Trippe; R. J. Donohoo; W. H. Wikle, Manager; A. Payne; Pettit Archer Hardware; J. Winlowsk(?); Calhoun Brothers; Abeomson(?) and Brothers; G. H. Gilreath; Stanford's; J. L. Smith; Adams & Co.; F. V. Eaves; J. J. Erwin; C. E. Venable; J. G. Gasset (Negro); Wholesale Mercantile Co. - From the Memorabilia of Sam P. Jones, the speakers for the September 15-22, 1907, meeting were the Rev. W. E. Biederwolf, the Rev. Walt Holcomb, the Rev. A. C. Dixon, the Rev. French E. Oliver, the Rev. Melvin Trotter, the Rev. J. A. Bowen, C.N. Crittenden and others. Music in charge of Messrs. Rhodeheaver and Smoot and Mrs. Annie Jones Pyron at the piano. This was after the death of Sam P. Jones in Oct. 1906.

Page 138: Tombstone recordings of the Kingston cemetery can be found in the Georgia Genealogical Society Quarterlies of June-July, September and December 1966, Vols. 2 and 3 by Mrs.R.H. Whitehead. The Cassville cemetery in Georgia Genealogical Society Quarterly of September 1967, Vol. 4, No. 1 by J. M. Edwards, Lucy Cunyus Mulcahy and Mrs. Jo Sloan Pitard; Racoon Creek Baptist Church cemetery compiled by Church of Jesus Christ of Latter-Day Saints in 1957. Copy in the State Archives.

Page 150: There is a biographical sketch of Lottie Moon in "The Lottie Moon Cook Book," compiled by Claude Rhea. (Word Books-Waco, Texas). Born December 12, 1840 in Albermarle County, Virginia, died enroute from China, December 24, 1912, anchored at Kobe, Japan. Japanese law decreed that the body be cremated. Her ashes were interred in Crewe, Virginia. A marble marker in memory of Miss Lottie Moon was placed by the Woman's Missionary Union of Georgia at the front of the First Baptist Church in Cartersville. No date. Miss Stafford died in Shanghai August 17, 1890 - a native Georgian.

Page 151: The trustees of the Bartow Classical and Scientific Institute on North Main Street in Adairsville, with headmaster L. C. Dickey, A. M., LL.G. were: J. H. Fitten, J. M. Veach, A. C. Trimble, B. W. Lewis, W. C. Allen, J. D. Bowdoin, J. G. Shaw, Gilbert Gholston, Dr. J. W. Bowdoin (page 49) (324), W. J. Hilburn, J. L. Chilton and J. W. Gray - Mrs. A. B. Howard, (no date).

Page 152: See Chapter IX about Florence Candler Harris in "Until Now" by Maybelle Jones Dewey.

Page 153: Cartersville School Superintendents continued: W. H. Tucker, 1933-34; S. E. Alverson, 1935-36; W. H. Brandon, 1936-54 (married Lois Daniel of Cartersville; children: Kathryn married Raymond F. Stainback Jr., Atlanta; Betty married Dr. Wm. A. Sims, Decatur, Alabama; W. H. Brandon Jr.); Jack Acree, 1955-61 (Executive Secretary of Georgia School Boards Association); E. C. Martin, 1962-65; Ray M. Hill, 1965 - (a native of Michigan, married Eudene Cook of Green County, Georgia.)

Page 154: County School Superintendents continued: P. W. Barnard, 1932-36; C. B. Perry, 1939-43 (married Eva Lou

McGowan, daughter of Dr. Hugh McGowan); John K. Headden, 1945-50; L. A. McArthur, Pine Log, 1951-52; John E. Bridges, 1953-56; Clinton J. Taylor, 1957-64, resigned July 2; Carl A. Merrill, 1964- .
Intergration in the city and county schools conformed without incident. The Freedom of Choice plan ended when in 1968-69 all schools were completely desegregated. Few new school buildings have been erected-First Grade building on Douglas Street. High school and auditorium on East Church Street (1951; Carl Nelson, Mayor; Francis Daves a native of Cartersville was the architect from Atlanta and Decatur), the high school stadium was named for William J. Weinman. Former Summerhill school is Junior High, 7-9. Cassville with Elementary No. 1 and 2, Cass High have Cass Elementary and Primary; Clover Leaf, Emerson, Pine Log, White have the largest enrollments in the county.
The Hickory Log Vocational School is owned and operated by the Bartow Association for Retarded Children. It is located near White, in the old county home property on the Tennessee Road, providing a 16-room dormitory and an apartment in one wing for staff members. This Association was organized in 1955 and began classes in the Cartersville First Baptist Church and for nine years operated there and in other buildings. In 1968 the Association opened the Chit Chat Training Center. Support comes from civic, church and business groups, individuals and United Givers. Mr. Garland Goodrum, former Presbyterian Industrial Missionary to the Congo is director of the school and resident. Al Munn and Sarah Hansell Munn of Cartersville have been leaders in the establishment of this needed facility.

Page 160: Newspapers: Milton L. Fleetwood died August 20, 1966. His son, John T. Fleetwood became President, Editor and Publisher of The Tribune News, married Jane Ackert and their children are Betty Jane, Lenna, John Jr., Jimmy, Billy, and Mary. They were named "Family of The Year" in 1961 in Cartersville. W. Ryan Frier died January 15, 1969, was Editor and owner of The Bartow Herald for forty years and operated the WBHF Radio Station, married Alma Strickland, two daughters, now Mrs. Richard Sjoblom and Mrs. Charles Sowell. John T. Fleetwood bought The Herald in May 1969 and the two papers became The Herald-Tribune with the June 5, 1969 issue. Other children of Milton L. and Beulah Fleetwood are Mrs. Argyle Crockett and Mrs. Alvin Barge, both of Atlanta. Charles F. Hurley is now editor.
The North Bartow News, published weekly, served Adairsville and surrounding communities with John T. Fleetwood Sr. as Publisher and Dorsey F. Martin, Editor.

Page 179: Saltpeter Cave, Kingston: New Historical Notes by Marion O. Smith, Atlanta, from the Georgia Speleological Survey Files, September 1971: This double-entranced cave, sometimes known as Hardin's Cave but more often referred to as Saltpeter Cave, is the largest in Bartow County and one of the most historical in Georgia. It is formed in the Knox Dolomite and has a length of approximately 2,000 feet. Several legends are associated with the cave. In 1923 Margaret Mitchell, then an Atlanta Journal reporter, visited the cave and wrote an article about her visit in which she mentioned the legend that a Cherokee tribe, hard pushed by the Creeks, retreated into the cave where they were "swallowed up."
It is not known exactly when white man first entered the cave. But William Brewer, surveyor for the 16th District wrote in his 1832 field notes that he had found some "ponds" where saltpeter had been manufactured by the Cherokees. White man must have found the cave within a few years because by 1854 it

was known widely enough to warrant a description in Rev. George White's Historical Collections of Georgia.

The cave was owned for many years by Mark Anthony Hardin. At the beginning of the Civil War he began, by use of an estimated 400 slaves, to mine the cave for saltpeter, then a necessary ingredient for the manufacture of gunpowder. Officials of the newly created Confederate Niter and Mining Bureau did not feel that the cave was being operated to its full capacity and on June 15, 1862, it was taken over by the Confederate Government. (Correction on page 62 - "until it was seized by the Federal Government." Hardin Sketch, page 62). Captain Henry Patillo Farrow, head of Niter District 14, served as superintendent of the mining operation, with his headquarters in Kingston. By the end of July, 1862, production reached 400 pounds per working day. The exact amount of saltpeter extracted from the cave is unknown but an October 1, 1864, report to the Secretary of War indicated that 29,913 pounds had been delivered from all of Niter District 14, the majority of which probably came from the cave.

Saltpeter Cave has been surveyed several times. In 1915 the Georgia Geological Survey made a sketch of it, applying names such as Ball Room, Bat Room and Jug Room. The most recent map was made in 1971 by members of the Georgia Geological Survey, using a tape and compass. Bartow County has a number of other caves. The largest of these is Anthony's Cave along Little Pinelog Creek with 545 feet of maze-like passage. Others include Jolley Cave on the bank of the Etowah River, Yarbrough Cave near Adairsville and Ladd's Lime Cave, which were the site of extensive paleontological diggings by Shorter College and Smithsonian Institute personnel in the 1960's.

Page 186: The Euharlee Farmers Club has continued through the years. Cotton crop now small, but soy beans grown more now. The farmers have the following organizations to aid them: The Agricultural Stabilization and Conservation Service (formerly the AAA); Bartow County Farm Bureau; Production Credit Association; Bartow Crop Improvement Association was active in 1945-55; the Soil Conservation District was organized in 1937. Bartow County was one of the first to be organized in Georgia; heading the Soil Conservation Service is Joe Myers, Cartersville. M. W. H. ("Alphabet") Collins died in 1971, came to Bartow as a County Agent in the 30's. In the 50's he organized and maintained the Georgia Institute of Genetics (seed breeding), north of Cartersville, until his retirement. The Bartow County Water Advisory Council started in 1969-70, which with a new plant and facilities will take water to many rural areas. The Bartow County Livestock Commission is inactive. Bartow County Forestry Unit and Forest Rangers, Cartersville.

Page 186: In Cartersville: The Agricultural Stabilization and Conservation Service, Wiley Vaughan, Chairman in 1964. Bartow County Farm Bureau, T. Ellis Richards, President Leon Lewis, Vice-President in 1964. Robert M. Stiles is a Commissioner (died February 21, 1975). Coosa Watershed Project, United States Department of Agricultural Research Service was once under Colonel Ellis G. Disker; Soil Conservation - Joe Myers, Sr.; New Airport Authority - Horace W. Howard, Jr. 1971; Bartow County Livestock Commission, Bartow County Forestry Unit.

Page 188: In July 1914, at Essex Falls, New Jersey, was formed an unusual partnership between Sam W. Thompson, Sam M. Evans and William J. Weinman of Nicholasville, Kentucky, that became incorporated as the Thompson-Weinman Company in 1921 in

Cartersville, Georgia. The character of these men was shown by "no debts" written in the contract, and when it was located on the old Brooks flour mill property, on the Etowah River, it was acquired by paying off the notes against the property. Money was never borrowed again. All that Thompson-Weinman & Company is today has grown from its own earnings, left after paying dividends (Contract written on a small bit of paper - laminated in the present office). Thompson-Weinman is still the largest producer of fine white limestone (now shipped in from marble quarries in Alabama) for industrial use in the country. The Paga Mining Company, whose product is barytes, had Barney (B.C.) Sloan, W. S. Peebles and W. J. Weinman in its origin, and in time Thompson-Weinman & Company bought their interests and also that of the original partner, Sam M. Evans. Willis Beavers, a native of Atlanta, is now Chief Executive Vice-President and has been with the company since 1936. Mr. William J. Weinman died in February 1966, Mrs. Weinman died in August 1971. Two children: Andrew (deceased); Frances Weinman married Horatio Luro - have lived at "Old Mill Farm" near the plant where Mr. Luro has trained and wintered race horses - one Kentucky Derby winner, "Northern Dancer." Two granddaughters, Mrs. Joseph Reagan, Miami Beach and Mrs. James Skakel, Los Angeles.

Page 201: The J. M. Neels now own and live on the Joel Hurt property at Aubrey. Mining manganese ceased in 1945 and iron ore was mined during the Korean conflict. No mining since then.

Page 203: The New Riverside Ochre Company has continued in operation with W. C. Satterfield's son-in-law, Ray Dellinger (married Evelyn Satterfield, page 52), (both deceased), manager; now the son, James (Jimmy) R. Dellinger (married Gay Pettit, daughter of Luke and Margaret Gaines Pettit) is General Manager. Nat Slaughter is Assistant Manager since 1967. John H. Cobb has been Supt. of New Riverside for 45 years, (Page 52-74).

Page 205: The Funkhouser plant has been in operation continously on #411. (No late research.)

Page 208: The Etowah Mounds are now in custody of the Georgia Historical Commission. A Museum was built in 1958. The present custodian and manager is Henry Tumlin, grandson of the first land owner, after the removal of the Cherokees - so right because he has lived with and known the Mounds all his life. See more about the Mounds in the Bartow Scrapbook and File in the State Archives. The Mounds draw many vistors as one of the features of "Stay and See Georgia."

Page 217-221: Wilbur G. Kurtz, born February 28, 1882, Oakland, Illinois. Lived and educated at Greencastle, Indiana, married June 14, 1911, Annie Laurie Fuller (died October 2, 1946), resident of Atlanta, Georgia, since 1911. Artist by profession, Historian by inclination. Creator of numerous paintings and murals pictorializing History of The War Between the States in Georgia--particular emphasis on Sherman's campaign of 1864. Historian for the Selznick film production of "Gone With The Wind" (1939). Children: Wilbur G. Kurtz, Jr. (1912); Nelle Louise (1914); Henry Harrison (1916); Annie Laurie (1920); Eugene Allen (1923). Grandchildren: Wilbur G. Kurtz, III, son of Wilbur Jr and Elma Smith Kurtz; Wm. and Nelle Fambrough, children of Mr. and Mrs. William Fambrough (Nelle Louise); Henry Harrison Kurtz, Jr. and Annie Laurie Kurtz, children of Mr. and Mrs. Henry

Harrison Kurtz. Wilbur Sr. m. (2nd) Annie Pye of Woodland, Ga., 2-9-1949. Wilbur G. Kurtz was tech'l adv. for the filming of "Gone With The Wind," Disney's "The Great Locomotive Chase," and "Song of the South." (In a letter to L.C.M. dated April 10, 1952: "Walt Disney announces he is going to do the Andrews Raid in live action - technicolor. Mr. Goff of the Disney Studios was in Atlanta in February and we had a long talk over the problems. He tells me I am to serve in an advisory capacity during the filming of this picture. He has his eye on the Tallulah Falls RR as a setting for the opus."). He assisted in the first restoration of the painting of The Battle of Atlanta in Grant Park's Cyclorama, and helped make Franklin Roosevelt's Little White House at Warm Springs an historical shrine, designing "The Walk of the States," laid from the Guest House - now museum, to the entrance of the Little White House, in 1949. He was considered an authority (yet he was so humanly humble in his unlimited knowledge) on the Atlanta Campaign and southern history, which is preserved in his many paintings, water colors and sketches in and around Atlanta and in private homes. His collections are in the Atlanta Historical Society. (Found one of his paintings in Clearwater, Florida.). He died February 18, 1967 in Atlanta. He was helping this author and Margaret Mitchell at the same time with our Civil War history.

Page 219: "Uncle Joe" Renard died May 1905 in Atlanta, Engineer on engine used by Captain W. A. Fuller who chased "The General." (From newspaper clipping.)

Page 223: Note by Wilbur G. Kurtz in 1964: Colonel R. G. Earle, killed at Barnsley's May 18, 1864, commanded the 2nd Alabama Calvary Regiment in Brig. Gen. Samuel W. Ferguson's Brigade of Brig. Gen. William H. Jackson's Division,of Maj. Gen. Stephen D. Lee's Cavalry Corp, which was in Polk's Miss. command as of Jan. 1864.Jackson's Division was shifted to Georgia when the Atlanta Campaign began-how it happened Col. Earle was in Ga. at the time of his death. O. R. 32-II-585.

Page 224: General Joseph E. Johnston's headquarters were in the William Neal McKelvy home on May 18th and 19th: "Most important conference of the Atlanta Campaign" - Colonel Thomas Spencer. (Tribune News, May 19, 1954). From other research by Spencer and Kurtz: The Samuel McDow house, 3 miles south of Adairsville was demolished in April 1947,soon after the pictures of it were taken by Wilbur Kurtz in February. Sherman and the 4th and 14th Army Corps passed the Samuel McDow house on their way to Kingston, but Mrs. McDow stayed in the house to preserve it. "Little Joe" Wheeler and his Confederate Calvary came to the home, staying long enough to wreck a Federal train on the W&A Railroad. The McDow house referred to in the Official Records as General Hooker's Headquarters indicate the Jonathan McDow house - a brick structure - that stood on Highway 41, south of Adairsville and was destroyed by fire in the 30's. It was also known as the Stoner-McDow house.

Page 232-3: These original drawings were done by Wilbur Kurtz for the Bartow County History in 1932. The Hawkins Price home burned in December 1956.

Page 247: Major General Peter Charles Harris, 85, died at Walter Reed, Washington, D.C. in March 1951. Major General Walter H. Harris, (retired, 82) son of Governor Nat Harris,died March 15, 1958 in Macon.

Page 250: L. L. Knight in Vol. 1, 31-33, tells of another

suitor for the hand of Cecelia Stovall-Dick Garnett. General Richard B. Garnett was killed in one of the Gettysburg Battles. In a letter from Wilbur Kurtz, 1949: "When Charles Shelman died in 1949, the furniture and other belongings were sent to Athens, among the effects was a photograph of "Etowah Heights." This photo shows a dozen or more people, in the yard - I imagine there was a family reunion and this is the same shot you used in The Bartow County History. I think it was in the 1880's for there are no leg-o-mutton or balloon sleeves - only tight sleeves and basques, the hall-mark of the 1880's."

Page 251: Bartow County Civil War Historical Markers, 008-1 through 50 are: Original Site: Adairsville 1830's, Mosteller's Mills, Pettit Creek, Campsite, Federal 23rd Corps, Emerson, Battles of Allatoona # 1 and #2, Railroad Block House, Historic Price House, Milam's Bridge, Gillem's Bridge, Woolley's Bridge, Old Macedonia Church, Cassville, Site Jonathan McDow House, Gravelly Plateau, Two Run Creek, Confederate Army of Tennessee at Cassville, Site: Cassville Female College; Site: Cherokee Baptist College, Confederate Line 5 P.M., May 19, 1864, The Army of the Cumberland at Stilesboro, Raccoon Creek, Mosteller's Plantation, Johnston's Army at Adairsville, Federal Armies at Adairsville, McPherson's Troops March to Barnsleys, Barnsley's 4th and 14th A.C. March to Kingston, "Spring Bank," The Federal Army at Kingston, The Andrews Raiders at Kingston, House of Thomas V. B. Hargis, Surrender of Confederate Troops, Hardee's Corps at Kingston, Confederate Memorial Day, General Leonidas Polk's Headquarters, Confederate Dead, Grave of General William Tatum Wofford, Battle of Allatoona, Bartow, Federal Fort, Etowah and the War, Mark Anthony, Cooper's Iron Works. Georgia Historical Commission, Atlanta, Georgia. There are two Unknown Confederate Soldiers buried in Adairsville that have been kept through the years. Identified,with ceremonies, buried in Eastview Cemetery, by Alice B. Howard, May 15, 1974.

Pages 252-263: New organizations (change of officers every year difficult to list): B & PW, B & PW Luncheon Club, Cartersville-Bartow County Chamber of Commerce, Cartersville Life Underwriters' Association, Cartersville Service League, new Cartersville Woman's Club, Civitan Club, Elks Lodge, Exchange Club, Golden Age Club, Jaycees, Kiwanis in Cartersville and White, Lions Club, & in Adairsville, Loyal Order of Moose, Magnolia Garden Club, Narcissus Garden Club, Optimist Club, Order of the Eastern Star, Pilot Club, Royal Arch Masons, Shrine Club, Veterans of Foreign War and Auxiliary, Legion Auxiliary, Cartersville Country Club. New Golf course named "Royal Oaks."

Page 252: The Mary Munford Library was moved (1962-3) to the remodeled former home of the W. S. Peebles on West Cherokee. Now a new Cartersville-Bartow Public Library on site of Sam Jones Tabernacle.

Page 263: The Stilesboro Improvement Club, organized March 25, 1910, still maintains the historic Stilesboro Academy Building as a meeting place and for their annual November Chrysanthemum Show. The first Saturday in May-Day Picnic continues meeting here.

Page 258: DAR. Maybelle Jones Dewey, daughter of Mr. and Mrs. T. Reno Jones of Cartersville died July 18, 1963 of cancer. Graduate of Wesleyan College, Editor of a Retail Business Journal until as wife of Professor Malcolm Dewey, 37 years Director of the Emory University Glee Club, she acted as official hostess at home and abroad until his retirement in 1957. He died in 1966 and both are buried in Oak Hill. She wrote "Push The Button," and "Until Now." Her sisters were Eleanor and Frances Jones. The T. R. Jones home is now Southernair Antiques.

Page 260: The American Legion Post 42 has had a staunch member in Victor H. Waldrop while and since retirement of his years with Goodyear - so much so that in April 1971 the Little League Field was named the "Victor H. Waldrop American Legion Little League Field." This active Legion takes part annually in the Memorial Day program at Kingston, Georgia, in April for the Confederate dead in the Kingston Cemetery.

Pages 252-263: Organizations - Cartersville, Georgia, 1971:
American Legion, Clifton Cox, Commander.
    Legion Auxiliary, Mrs. Conston Ross, President.
B & PW, Mrs. Mary Louise Lowry, President.
B & PW Luncheon Club, Mrs. Jerry A. Summey, President.
Beta Sima Phi Sorority:
    Alpha Mu Chapter, Mrs. Jackie Temples, President.
    Xi Alpha Alpha Chapter, Mrs. Laura Summey, President.
Cartersville-Bartow County Chamber of Commerce, Herschel Wisebram, President.
Cartersville Garden Club, Mrs. W. T. Slaughter, President.
Cartersville Life Underwriters' Association, C.J. Tibbetts, Pres.
Cartersville Service League, Mrs. John Cummings, Jr., President.
Cartersville Woman's Club, Mrs. B. E. Popham, President.
Civitan Club, N. J. Stewart Jr., President.
DAR Etowah Chapter, Mrs. Maria F. Harrison, Regent.
Elks Lodge, Jack E. Jolley, Exalted Ruler.
    Elks Aidmore Auxiliary, Mrs. Carol Caswell, President.
Exchange Club, Charles Crawford, President.
Golden Age Club, Mrs. C. H. Cox, President.
Jaycees, Jim Buford, President.
    Jaycettes, Mrs. Carolyn Knox, President.
Kiwanis Club, Archie Craven, President.
Lions Club, Joe A. Tilley, President.
Loyal Order of Moose, Jimmy Brown, Governor.
Magnolia Garden Club, Mrs. Frances Hawkins, President.
Masonic Lodge #63, J. A. Williams, Worshipful Master.
Narcissus Garden Club, Miss Mittie Taylor, President.
Optimist Club, Forrest Lovell, President.
Order of the Eastern Star, Mrs. Junior Graham, Worthy Matron.
Pilot Club, Dr. Cornelia (Chris) Johnson, President.
Rotary Club, William N. Shadden, Jr., President.
Royal Arch Masons, Chapter 144, William E. Cantrell, High Priest.
Shrine Club, George L. Smith, President.
VFW, Tommy Martin, Commander.
    VFW Auxiliary, Mrs. Louise Smith, President.
Welcome Wagon Newcomers Club, Mrs. Ann Sheffield, President.

Page 266: James Wofford ("Jettie") Gilreath (page 60) was Manager for three years. Harold Towslee Sr. was Plant Manager, Vice-President in charge of Manufacturing until he became Manager of the A. S. Haight & Co. (textile printers). John F. (Jack) Tyrrell became President and Treasurer in 1970. E-Z Mills was purchased by Cluett, Peabody and Co. in 1971, but had begun management in 1970. J. F. Tyrrell, President; R. A. Tyler, Plant Manager; Ed Gaines, Comptroller; Edna Harris, Employment Supervisor; Harold Towslee Jr., Knitting and Finishing. John Fletcher Fowler died in 1964 or 5.

Page 268: More on children of Martin Collins: (1) Lalla Collins married J. W. Knight (both deceased). Children: Fred died March 1951, married Catherine Satterfield; sons: Fred Jr. married Margaret Stiles, now head of Knight's; John Knight married Fay Bryson; Robert Knight, retired, never married, owns real estate; Caroline Knight married Stanley Dodd (deceased), lives in Miami; James Knight, married Jo Ginn, owns Marshall & Bell, Atla., Dec. (2) Annie Collins (died 1962) married T. E. Vaughan, daughter Sarah married Richard M. Holmes, Atlanta, one daughter. (3) Charles Lewis Collins (deceased) married Mittie Middlebrooks (deceased). Son, C. L. Collins, was County Ordinary until his death in 1962, which office his wife, Eva, now holds. Another son was Joe Collins (deceased) who was with Coca Cola in Atlanta. (4) Abner Collins married Hattie Masters (both deceased) reared large family in Cartersville, later moved to Florida. A son, Dr. Charles Collins of Orlando, Florida. (5) Maude Collins married Clinton Carnes, well-known in Baptist Home Mission Board circles in the twenties, two sons.

Page 267-8: Bartow County Industrial Roster, as prepared by the Cartersville-Bartow County Chamber of Commerce and from other sources. A large percentage of the industries listed have started since 1964.

Allatoona Dye Company
American Carpet Mills
Bartow Sportswear
Burgess Manufacturing Co.
Cannon Craft of Georgia
Cartersville Dyeing & Finishing
Cartersville Spinning Co.
Cartersville Undergarment Corp.
Chamblee Mills
Chemical Products Corp.
Click Southern Chemical Co.
Commander Carpet Mills, Inc.
Concord Mills
Custom Craft Carpets
Dan River Carpets
Delen Lingerie, Inc.
D & M Carpet Mfg. Co.
Diamond Carpets
Dura-Craft, Inc.
E-Z Mills, Inc.
Eagle Carpets
Esquire Carpet Mills, Inc.
Etowah Enterprise & Textiles
Fashionique Carpets, Inc.
Flamingo Carpets, Inc.
GAF Corporation
Geneva Metal Wheel Co.
Georgia Art Pottery, Cass Sta.
Georgia Pipe Company
Gold Kist Mills
Goodyear Tire & Rubber Co.
Harris Cement Products

Holly City Manufacturing Co.
Imperial Carpet Mills, Inc.
Jewel's Carpets, Inc.
John W. Hodge Co.
K.O.B. Carpet Mfg. Co.
Kerr-McGee Chemical Corp.
Kingston Concrete Pipe Co.
Lewis Carpet Mills
M.P. International Corp.
Majestic Carpets
Marquette Cement Mfg.
Nantucket Lingerie
New Riverside Ochre Co.
Paga Mining Co.
Pandel Chemical, Inc.
Philadelphia Carpet Co.
Porter Carpets
Pax Carpet Mills, Inc.
Promotional Services, Inc.
Pyro-Form, Inc.
Sabre Carpets
Southern Sample Service, Inc.
Southern Yarn Dyers, Inc.
Standard Textile Mills
Star Finishing Co.
Swan Carpets
Tahlequah, Inc.
Thompson-Weinman & Co.
Tuftwick Carpets
Twentieth Century Glove Co.
Union Carbide Corp. (Manager George C. Hooks murdered in October 1974).
William Davies Company

ADAIRSVILLE, GEORGIA INDUSTRIAL GUIDE

Cherokee Drapery, Inc.
Data Processing Center
Domestic Manufacturing Co.

Penfield Chenille
Research Coatings of Ga., Inc.
Tri-State Mfg. Co.

Industrial Rug Co.   Universal Ceramics Corp.
Kuhlman Chenille Co.   Kuhlman Mfg. Co.
C. M. Moore Mfg. Co.

Page 269: New Banks: The Cartersville Bank; Cartersville Federal Savings & Loan Association, December 1953, Carl Nelson, President; S. Luke Petit, Vice-President; L. E. Jackson, Vice-President; Clyde R. Conner, Secretary-Treasurer; Hassie Dalton Watkins, Assistant; Doug Hardin, Assistant; Board of Directors: T. J. Champion, C. R. Conner, H. H. Green, L. E. Jackson, H. Carl Nelson, S. Luke Pettit, Griffin Smith and F. J. Vaughan. Bartow County Savings & Loan Association, J. L. Davis, President, 1964.

Page 272: Blacks: Walter A. Johnson, at one time Principal of Bartow Elementary School, was a graduate of George Peabody College for Teachers (with degree), B.A. from Morehouse and Masters from Atlanta University, post graduate of University of Texas.
Professor and Mrs. J. S. Morgan were outstanding Negro educators even before integration. Mrs. Morgan, active in PTA and a faculty member in Summer Hill School died in August 1964. He is retired.
In the list of slaves of Major Willis Benham, made out in 1874, who were emancipated in 1866, is the name of a 6 year old girl, Parthenia. In 1958, she was living with the Clarence Benham family on Red Comb Drive. Thus the Benhams in Cartersville carry on the name of an early settler in Bartow from Connecticut. Many of these Benham men and boys have served in our Army and Navy and Air Force and future lists will carry their names.
Ned Wade, farmer, Baptist Deacon, lived and looked like an old patriarch, in that his children built and lived in homes around him, died in July 1959 at his home just off Cassville Road. His children were: Hugh, Arthur (deceased), Gartrell, both retired from Goodyear, and Ora Wade Wilmonte, 11 grandchildren, Robert, son of Arthur, served in Vietnam and is now a school teacher in the county. Dr. J. B. Harris born in Adairsville March 24, 1901, a member and former President of the Atlanta Medical Association and the Georgia State Medical Association, graduate of Morehouse College, Meharry Medical College, Lt. Col. in World War II, was named the National Medical Association's "Practitioner of the Year" in September 1969 the second Georgian to receive the national award. He has practiced in Atlanta for over 23 years.

Additions to Bartow's Distinguished Characters.
Page 277-8: Amos T. Akerman married Martha R. Galloway in May 1864. (1) Benjamin died in 1927 in Washington State. (Corrections by Alfred Akerman, University of Virginia.) (3) Judge Alexander Akerman, born in Cartersville, married Minnie Edwards in 1890, died 1952, daughter of William Clarke Edwards (her father's sister was the grandmother of Sam P. Jones), was United States Federal Judge in Orlando, Florida from 1929 until his retirement in 1940. He died at age 78 in August 1948. Children: Walter W., Emory, Alex Jr., and Mrs. Eugenia A. Carson, Orlando; Margaret (Albert) Menard of Mt. Vernon, New York, Amos T., of Boston. Robert H. Akerman, son of Emory and Sarah Howard Akerman is Associate Editor of the Atlanta Journal, since July 1973. Married Jean Eickelburg, live in Kennesaw, where he was in 1970 history professor at Kennesaw College. Three children.

Page 278: Willis Boyd born January 23, 1877, at 94 years of age, is the nation's oldest Scout Master; World War I

Veteran, teacher, has a long list of accomplishments. Veteran Hospital, Dublin, Georgia. Pauline (Mrs. Clarence R.) Goodhart died August 3, 1963, Clarence Goodhart died in 1970, both buried in Oak Hill; sons: Colonel Morgan Goodhart, Boyd Goodhart; daughter Jean, Mrs. Warren Akin, Cartersville. Daughter of Robert and Thelma S. (died 1966) Boyd: Betty married James H. Love; Dorothy married Henry B. Sinclair. Robert married 2nd Mary Duke Foster.

Page 279-80: Mark A. Cooper resigned January 26, 1843, before Congress assembled. "Glen Holly," home of Mark A. Cooper burned in July 1884, was his home for 30 years. Alexander Hamilton Stephens filled his vacancy. Most of the Cooper Iron Works community was lost when Allatoona Lake was formed by the damming of the Etowah river in that area in the late 40's. The Mark A. Cooper family burials were removed to Oak Hill. The Allatoona Dam was a project of the United States Army Corps of Engineers, under the Flood Control Act of 1941, for the development of the Alabama-Coosa basin. It was completed by 1950 and the Allatoona power plant is operated as a peaking plant to supply the additional power needed during periods of maximum demand. Lake Allatoona, in the Bartow County area, has Red Top Mountain, Wyatt Clark, Manager, and George W. Carver as State Parks, with facilities for homes, camping areas, marinas, and recreation areas. A museum room in the Reservoir Office of Allatoona Dam was opened in the summer of 1956, with colorful exhibits of the history of the area. Many Mark A. Cooper descendants live in Rome, Georgia. Mrs. Mark A. Cooper, Sr. has compiled Cooper genealogy.

Page 283: Dr. W. H. Felton in 44th Congress, March 1875-77, 45th Congress, 1877-78, and 48th Congress, 1879-1881. William Harrel Felton, born May 4, 1895, died January 31, 1948. Mrs. William H. (Lillian White) Felton, (dec.) lived in one of the Felton homes on the Tenn.Rd. in Cartersville and treasured much of Dr. and Mrs. Felton's memorabilia. Daughter, Ann, married John F. Collins, Jr., lived with her.

Page 286: Captain B. L. Goulding died in 1934 in Chattanooga - an old man when interviewed in 1932. Where Dr. Goulding lived is now known as "Goulding House," in Kingston, Georgia. Owned since 1941 and beautifully renovated by Grover Cleveland ("Phil") Phillips (died October 18, 1961) and his wife, Nan Ligon Phillips. Its early history was an Indian house of two rooms with room on back; two rooms were added later facing the railroad, and Dr. Goulding added 3 large, high-ceiling rooms and second floor by 1849-50. "Young Marooners" is claimed to have been written during his sojourn in Kingston. The house was used in 1864 as a Federal Hospital for the wounded, during the Kingston "occupation." (Dr. Goulding was buried in Roswell, Georgia, not Rosville - LCM). (See John Meban's excellent character sketch of Dr. Goulding.) Nan Phillips died July 17, 1977, deeded home and acreage to Berry College and they sold it.

Page 286: Mrs. Corra Harris died February 10, 1935. Mrs. Donald (Majorie) McClain was with her when she died in Emory Hospital in Atlanta. She is buried in the small stone chapel she had planned in front and across from the homesite. Mrs. Harris's office for writing remains with a few momentos, but the log-cabin house, so attractive in her day, was dismantled when visited in 1966. It is now owned by Trannie Raines and her husband, E. J. Smith.

Page 288-90: More on the children of Charles Wallace Howard and

Susan Jett Thomas of Athens. (Will not repeat dates on gravestone markers). 1. Jett Thomas Howard, 1836-1881, married 1st May 14, 1863 Mary V. Guerrard; Children: (1) Godin G. Howard married twice, 2nd wife Helen Walker; son: Barron Carter Howard married Gertrude Virginia Hammon, Richmond, Virginia. (2) Charles Wallace Howard, born March 20, 1866, died February 1940, Savannah; married 3 times. 1st Elizabeth G. Rieves; Children: (a) Charles Wallace Howard, 1892-1941; (b) Mary Guerard Howard, born May 16, 1894 married 1917, Valmore Walter Lebey, both deceased, no children; (c) Augusta Clyatt Howard, born January 25, 1897 married 1917 John Heyward Lynah, 1891-1935; Children: (a) John Heyward Lynah married 1941 Anna C. Hunter; Children: Nancy, Mary Savage, John Heyward; (b) Mary Howard Lynah, born 1923, married 1944 D. B. Higginbottom; Children: David Lynah, Sam, Nancy Lynah, (Mary Lynah is Secretary to the President of Armstrong College); (c) Savage Heyward Lynah married Ruth Artley Cain; Children: James, Thomas Ravenel; (d) Wallace Howard Lynah, twin to Savage Heyward. Charles W. Howard married 2nd, Elizabeth Aline Cain, 1886-1921; daughter: Aline Howard, born February 20, 1921, married Howell C. Henderson; Children: Jane Hamilton married Robert Lee Wilson, William Howell and James Pressly Henderson, Decatur; C. W. Howard married 3rd Bessie Garden of Savannah. (3) Emily M. Howard born November 18, 1867, died November 26, 1899, married Thomas Porcher Ravenel, 1850-1936; Children: Emily G. Ravenel born September 17, 1890; Elizabeth de St. Julien Ravenel, born January 22, 1893; Mary Wallace Ravenel, born July 18, 1898, married 1927 Thomas Heyward Gignilliat; Children: Margaret D. Gignilliat, married John D. Carswell; Mary Ravenel and Thomas Heyward Gignilliat all of Savannah. Jett Thomas Howard married 2nd Ellen Davenport. 2. Jane Wallace Howard, born October 16, 1837, died about 1926, buried on Lookout Mountain, married September 1, 1870 Henry Bryan (Janet in "In and Out of The Lines.") Children: Ella Howard Bryan, Howard Bryan. 3. Ella Susan Howard born April 21, 1839, killed in a horse-and-buggy accident, September 17, 1896 near Cement, Georgia, married June 2, 1858 George Houstoun Waring, born December 22, 1833, son of Dr. William R. Waring and Anne Moody Johnstone. (See footnote on page 189). When George H. Waring and family came to "Spring Bank" after the Civil War, they lived in an east-wing built on the Howard home. A newspaper account in 1884 tells of the success of the Howard Hydraulic Cement Works, "being the only one in the south," with "Maj. Waring and his son, Fred, reporting orders for the United States Government, Bridges over East River in New York, a bridge near Chattanooga, Union Depot in Chattanooga, post office and courthouse in Atlanta, pavements in cities. During prosperity George Waring built a brick home called "Annandale" north of the Works and on the same side of the railroad, which burned in 1923, after they had lived and died there. More about the children of George H. and Ella Howard Waring: (1) Frederick (Fred) Howard Waring. (2) Jean Howard Waring married in 1892, Raymond Robson (social affair described in a letter from Mrs. Virginia Baylis Irby), had two small daughters. (3) George Houstoun Waring II, married Evangeline Hendrix, daughter of Bishop Hendrix of Kansas City; Children: George Waring III married Irene - lives in Littleton, Colorado; Evangeline Warring; Nathan Scarrett Waring, Grand Rapids, Michigan; Eugene Hendrix Waring, Lansing, Michigan. (4) Eleanor Howard Waring (born about 1871) married in 1893 Bill Crump, divorced, married 2nd Roger Noble Burnham in Boston, later lived in Los Angeles where he was a sculptor; she wrote "Rome Then and Now." (5) Mair or Mary Johnstone Waring, had early interest in the Montessori method of teaching, received a medal from Queen Margherita of Italy, lived in Pittsburg in 1932-33 - data from her.

4. Eliza Lloyd Howard, 1840-1910, single, was "Lou" in "In and Out of the Lines." 5. Mary Savage Howard, 1841-1904, single was "Maria" in the book. 6. Frances Thomas Howard, 1843-1907, author was "Florence" in "In and Out of the Lines." She sold one-fourth of the 640 acres on which "Spring Bank" was located to publish it in 1905. See Deed Records MM, page 201, Deed Book JJ, page 323 in the Bartow Courthouse. 7. Sarah Wallace Howard, 1844-1929, single, "Sophy" in the book (see pages 244-5). These four sisters had the boarding school for girls at "Spring Bank" and Miss Fannie taught until about 1895. Martha Berry and her two sisters, the late Mrs. Bulow Campbell, Atlanta and Mrs. Alexander Bonneyman of Knoxville and the relatives from Savannah were among the pupils. 8. Charles Wallace Howard, 1846-50, Margaret, Caroline, John Wallace, twins Myrtis and Henrietta, born and died between 1847-1855.

The Southern Recorder, March 5, 1839, states "that Rev. Charles Wallace Howard has returned from England with some 20 volumes of documentary history." These Georgia Colonial Records survived the Civil War in Cass County-see page 244. The documents somehow reached the Governor, only to be destroyed by fire, all but three, when the home where a Professor Scomp was copying them burned in Oxford, Georgia in 1891. (See Preface of Colonial Records of Georgia, Volume 1, page 4-5). Rev. Howard brought a Scotch couple over (also Scotch cows) to help them with the experiments he was making on the farm land. The Scotchman built the stone walls around and the springhouse at "Spring Bank." In the old part of the Kingston cemetery is an old marker: To the Memory of Maria Bell, wife of Robert McLellan, born in Scotland, died November 9, 1852, aged 64 years.

ADDITIONAL DATA ON GEORGE H. WARING FAMILY:

George H. Waring I, died in 1902. George Houstoun Waring II, born April 18, 1871 at Cement, Georgia, died in March 1963, Grand Rapids, a Mechanical Engineer, graduate of Auburn in 1890. George Houstoun Waring III (called Houstoun) born October 5, 1901, Savannah, 45 years Editor of Littleton Independent and Arapahoe Herald in Littleton, Colorado; son: Dr. G.H.W.IV, Biology teacher, Southern Illinois University, has son G.H.W. V. Eleanor Waring Burnham died in 1960, Noble Burnham died in 1962, both in Los Angeles. Sculptor of General McArthur Memorial by Burnham, near Bullock Store, L.A. A daughter of Jean Waring Robson is living-Mrs. Jean Robson (Chas. W.) Rooney, Decatur; daughter Jean Waring (James E.) Routh writes for The Constitution under name of Jean Rooney. Atla. Info from Aline Howard Henderson, Decatur, and Geo. Houstoun Waring III, Littleton, Colo. Gravestone markers in the Charles Wallace Howard family cemetery near the homesite, fenced by Miss Emily Ravenel:
Sarah Wallace Howard, December 30, 1844-July 25, 1929.
Eliza Lloyd Howard, July 1, 1840-April 10, 1910.
E.B.D. Julio, died September 15, 1879 (the painter of "Last Meeting of Lee and Jackson.")
Frances Thomas Howard, April 10, 1843-March 6, 1907.
Jett Thomas Howard, January 28, 1836-March 25, 1882.
Mary Savage Howard, November 26, 1841-June 10, 1904.
Charles Wallace Howard, October 11, 1811-December 25, 1876.
Susan Jett Thomas Howard, December 7, 1815-November 11, 1896.
Charles Wallace Howard, June 29, 1846-February 22, 1850.
Mary Howard, infant daughter of Jett and Ellen Howard, died about 1877.

NOTE ON E. B. D. JULIO:
Through a little research in 1947 on the part of Colonel Thomas

Spencer of Atlanta, it was found that Everett B. C. Julio, who died September 15, 1879 at "Spring Bank" and buried in the Howard Family cemetery, was the artist who painted "The Last Meeting of Lee and Jackson at Chancellorsville." Letters from Eleanor Waring Burnham of Los Angeles to Wilbur G. Kurtz stated that Julio was the art teacher for the Waring children in the Charles Wallace Howard home and that Mrs. Waring nursed him through his last illness, also that the family had some of his pencil sketches. How he came to the Howard home is pure speculation. He had TB. Through my own research I found there were two of these paintings of Lee and Jackson. One was painted in 1869 in St. Louis but was shipped to New Orleans in 1870 where it still remains. It was on Exhibition in New Orleans as Mark Twain remarked about seeing it in his "Life on the Mississippi." (page 332) The second version, painted by Julio is in the David Boyd Hall, Chancellor's Office, on the campus of Louisiana State University in Baton Rouge, Louisiana - 10 feet by 7½ feet - too large for an Instamatic Photo. This plaque is by the painting:
"THE LAST MEETING OF LEE AND JACKSON on the eve of the Battle of Chancellorsville
by
Everett D. B. Fabrina Julio (1843-1879)"
Two oil paintings of this subject were done in New Orleans by the artist between 1869 and 1871. This painting is the second one. It was purchased by Louisiana State University President David French Boyd at a cost of $2000 and presented to the University in 1881. Julio was born on the Island of St. Helena. Before coming to America in 1860 he received a classical education in Paris. He continued his study in Boston and in 1867 moved to New Orleans, where he opened a studio."
In a brochure of the Anglo-American Art Museum on Louisiana State University campus is more about Julio and a lovely painting of his was on loan: No. 14 "Hay Wagon." "Julio was born of a Scottish mother and an Italian father on the Island of St. Helena, in 1843. Before coming to America in 1860, he received a classical education in Paris. He studied anatomy and composition in Boston with the noted Dr. William Rimmer at the Lowell Institute. For health reasons he moved first to St. Louis in 1864, but came further south to New Orleans in 1867 and opened a studio. Because it was more profitable, he specialized in portrait painting. His fame rests with the oversized double portrait "The Last Meeting of Lee and Jackson at Chancellorsville" which was probably completed by late 1869 and exhibited at Wagner and Mayer's Art Gallery in 1871 (or 1870 in New Orleans). Such was its popularity that steel engravings were made, patterned on Julio's oil, by a New York firm. (Printed under the steel engraving is as follows: "Entered according to the Act of Congress in the year 1873 by Everett B. D. Julio of Louisiana, in the Office of the Librarian of Congress at Washington, D.C."(another note by Thomas Spencer). Shortly thereafter, Julio painted a copy of the painting which was to have been subscribed for and given to Louisiana State University. The subscription failed and the then president of the University, Col. David French Boyd, paid $2,000 for it and presented it to the University in 1881. Julio was not satisfied with his own work and returned to Paris for study with Leon Bonnat. New Orleans friends planned a raffle of his paintings to finance the trip; however, before the raffle could take place, the Southern Club of New York bought the lot at Julio's price. As a result, there are probably more paintings by the artist in New York collections than in Louisiana today. Returning to New Orleans in 1874, Julio opened an art school and exhibition gallery. The artist suffered by tuberculosis

and, in 1879, went to Kingston, Georgia, seeking a better climate. It is possible that he died in Georgia, but according to an article in the October-January 1937 Louisiana Historical Quarterly, his death occurred in New Orleans on September 15, 1879. The curator, H. Parrott Bacot, now knows where Julio is buried.

Page 290: Memorabilia of Samuel Porter Jones is in the State Archives, Emory and Georgia University libraries.
The last child and youngest daughter of Sam P. Jones, Julia Baxter Jones (Mrs. Walt Holcomb), died May 6, 1967. Rev. Walt Holcomb, died February 19, 1965, both in Atlanta. Dau. Louise Holcomb 6-26-1917--1-25-1981 m. Wm. Albert Cade Jr.; Children: Deborah Julia, b. 1951, Wm. A. Cade III, b. 1953 in Calif., John Scott Cade, born 1955, lived in Atlanta. John Holcomb died October 3, 1961, married Frances Conyers. Children of Paul & Leila Jones, living in Atlanta are: Katherine Jones, Paul Jones & Howell M. Jones, both with the Atlanta Constitution, and Ann Jones Hawkins. (Eldest son, Porter, died in 1966 in New Orleans.) Last daughters of Rev. Joe Jones, Hattie Jones Henderson died August 1, 1982 and Helen J. Winslow, died December 13, 1971, both of N.C. Sons of Charles T. Jones missing in list of children: Henry Grady, William, and Rhea, all deceased. Charles T. Jones died December 21, 1831, wife died 1948. Their oldest son, Sam, had a son, Rev. Sam F. Jones, now a retired Methodist preacher in Texas. The Jones mill and house were bought and renovated by Phillip (deceased) and Lucy Rogers Word, and Clark Rogers in the 40's. Two daughters of C. T. Jones living: Annie Laura Neuner, Tampa; (Now dec). Frances Jones Jones, Atlanta. The Sam P. Jones home in Cartersville was made into a two-story house in 1895 by him "having the present structure raised and adding another beneath." Here Mrs. Jones "planted thousands of roses, bulbs and shrubs so that the place naturally acquired the name of "Rose Lawn." Owned by Marie Gilreath Cole (page 85)--Bell-Parmenter since 1927, the house and lot have deteriorated since her recent death. Home bought by Bartow Co. in 1975, now being renovated. Jones memorabilia in 3 museum upstairs rooms, shown week days. (On Nat'l Reg.)

Page 293: Mrs. W.J. Neel d. 9-6-1953, in Atla. at "Eventide," & is buried by her husband in Oak Hill. No dates on marker.

Page 294: Maj. "Bill Arp" Smith sold his farm to B. M. Dunn in 1889 (information from Charlie Dunn in Atlanta), "when cotton dropped to 4½ cents a pound" Mr. Dunn lost the property and sold it to Ab Baker, who sold it to Sam P. Jones for his daughter, Annie Jones Pyron. The Pyrons made it a "show place" in the county before they moved to Pinehurst, North Carolina in the early Twenties. (The R. M. Maxwells built a home on the "Bill Arp" site on north Erwin St.) After "Bill Arp" lived on the farm he wrote "For twenty-seven years we lived in Rome... then we retired to a beautiful little farm near Cartersville, where there were springs and branches, a meadow and a creek nearby, with a cane-brake border. There we raised Jersey cows and colts and sheep and chickens and peafowls, and lived well by day and feasted on music by night, for every member of the family is a musician. It was a lovely home, and all the younger children grew up there to manhood and womanhood." "Meadowbrook" was purchased in 1939 from 3rd wife, Kate, of Ruohs Pyron, by James M. Field, Jr. (page 56), died October 1950 in Cartersville, and Mable K. Field, who sold it recently to Rollins of Atlanta.

Page 297: A Revolutionary War Marker was placed in 1968 by James Puckett on the grave of Benjamin Wofford, 1768-1836, grandfather of General Wm. T. Wofford, on Highway #20, on line of the Kraft Paper Company and Allatoona Lake property.

Page 298: The Robert M. Young home, now called the P. M. B. Young Home, has been beautifully renovated and lived in by Gen. Young's great-niece, Ella Milner and John Cummings, her husband, and family. ("Walnut Grove Has Peacocks Again," Wylly Folk St. John, Atlanta Journal Magazine October 24, 1948). From Memoirs of P. M. B. Young, U. S. Publisher of Congressmen, Young said: "To hell or a Brigadier's spurs." - He got them.

Page 302: Charles A. Cowan was Mayor of Cartersville when the Allatoona Dam was completed in 1950; a new high school was built, the Sam Howell Memorial Hospital established, first carpet mill in 1959, a founder of the Cartersville Bank, elder in Presbyterian Church, prominent citizen and now rancher; he and his wife, Bernice, reared three fine sons, Charles Jr., Joel H. and Dr. John Cowan in Cartersville.

Page 302: The Atlantic Steel Mills were moved to Bartow County in 1975 under the influence of Mayor John Dent and there are other plants in this L&N Industrial Park.

Page 307: Clerks of the Superior Court--from the Georgia Official Register:
(L. W. Reeves, died September 1933)
W. B. Moss, 1933-36
W. C. Walton, 1936*
Wesley Smith, 1939-56-60
W. H. Bradley, 1961 to date

Ordinaries: R. M. Gaines, 1928-36
C. L. Collins, 1939 until his death May 2, 1962
Eva S. Collins, his wife, served until elected ordinary in 1964. Norma Tidwell succeeded her in the 70's.

Sheriffs: G.W. Gaddis, 1922-50; Frank Atwood, 1950-65; James T. Wheeler, 1965 to date.

Tax Collectors: John C. Haney, 1928-
Henry Nelson, 1932-50
Gordon Holt, 1950-56-60
Clk. Co. Com. acts as

Tax Receivers: John C. Haney, 1932*
Smith Mansfield 1936-43
Smith Mansfield 1961-4
1966, res. December 31, 1966
H. B. (Brad) Lipscomb, 1967-68

Surveyors: W. W. Phillips, 1932-
W. W. Daniel, 1936-50
Walter Burton, 1951-52
A. Lee Smith, 1967-68

Coroners: G. W. Hendricks, 1928-50, died 1950
W. C. Gaines, 1951-until death September 25, 1962
Arthur Shinall, 1962 to date.

County Commissioners: A. V. Neal, 1927-45-50, died April 3, 1960
Griffin Smith, 1945-50-68
Wayne Self, 1969-70-71
Olin Tatum, 1971-1980
Frank Moore, 1981-

Clerks: A. C. Jolly, 1927-39-43
J. B. Lewis, 1945-56
Paul Weldon, 1961-68
Jean Cowart, 1968-

Page 304: W.C. Walton d. July 9, 1953; Persis Hall Walton d. Feb.
         13, 1960; Children: John Walton, died 1963; Mary W.
Young, deceased; William C. Walton married Renee M. Sallenave, d.
1968, Carlsbad, New Mexico; Anne Walton, Atla.; Robert Walton m.
Lillian Cooper, son Roger, Sarasota, Florida; Harris Walton married
Jean Brand, College Park, Georgia.

Page 321: Two names to add to World War I Dead:
           John C. Davis, son of Mr. and Mrs. W. R. Davis.
Ralph Davis, son of Mr. and Mrs. A. R. Davis.

World War II Dead, compiled by Henry Tumlin in 1965: Department
of Veterans Service. Paul Able, Jewett Franklin Adams, Corris
M. Adcock, Vernon H. Alford, John L. Armstrong Jr., Ray E. Bailey,
George W. Baker, Freeman K. "Bill" Ballard, Homer R. Barton Jr.,
S. K. Bennett, Henry Bohannon, Lonnie C. Bradford, Ralph B. Bradshaw, James W. Brown, William W. Brown, Chris G. Carratt, Francis
Cole, John Henry Cornett, Paul Costlow, Thomas Davis, Adrian I.
Denning Jr., Harry N. Dorsey, Hoke B. Evans, Walton M. Ferguson,
William F. Fishback, Roy W. Frix, John J. Gaddis, Herman C.
Gulledge, Ralph Hamilton Jr., William Cecil Harris, Claude E.
Head, Billy Hicks, Carl H. "Buddy" Hill, Earnet Hill, James W.
Holt, Bryce Hopkins, Robert H. Hopkins, Wilburn L. Hornbuckle,
Robert Howren, Bill Hudspeth, Sanford D. Hufstetler, Daniel E.
Janvrin Jr., Joe Ben Jenkins, William H. Johnson, Fred W. Jolley,
Jefferson V. M. Jolley, Tom Kendricks, John A. Law, Howard A.
Leachman, Curtis E. Lewis, Howard G. Magouirk, Alley D. Massengill, James L. Massey, Oscar W. Matthews, Edwin D. Mattox,
Charles R. McClure, Quillian H. McMichen, John H. Mize, H. Richard Moon, John Henry Morgan, A. Q. Moss, Ernest W. Mulinix,
Thermon Pelfrey, Howard Phillips, Clinton Quarles, Collins T.
Randolph, Freeman Randolph, Bennie G. Reece, Frank W. Roberts,
John L. Roulhac, Archie N. Rutland, Paul H. Shinall, H. C. Smith,
Ralph Smith, Weldon Smith, H. A. Sneed, Raymond D. Stone, Bob
Tatum, Waymon E. Temple, Thomas C. Wade, Robertson V. B. Watts
Jr., Randolph A. Whiteside, Andrew J. Wills, Elbert Woods.
Korean Conflict: Hugh S. Chambers, Robert Ed. Cooper, Harald
Edwin Cox, Billy Henson, Warren Gunn Lewis, Oliver Hardy, McGuire,
James Lavon Scoggins, William Theodore Woodall, Melvin F. Hanson.

Vietnam Veterans Dead are being compiled by Pete Wheeler. News
of men in Vietnamese service published in The Bartow Herald are
in The Bartow File in the State Archives kept by the Bartow
County Historian, until 1969.

Page 324: Members of the bar since 1964: Warren Akin, P. A.
           Bray, Marion W. Corbitt, J. R. Cullens, W. C. Henson
(died May 1966), W. A. Ingram, H. A. Keever, Ben Lancaster, J. M.
Neel Jr., D. N. Vaughan Jr., Jere F. White, Herbert M. Crane Jr.
(Herbert M. Crane Jr. new Juvenile Court Judge for Bartow County
and Cartersville, September 1971. In April 1971, R. Earl Ingram,
son of R. L. & Lillian Ingram, was named Chief Investigator for
District Attorney David N. Vaughan to work in the Cherokee
Judicial Circuit.) A. D. Tull, David G. Archer, John V. Burch,
Charles Crawford, Jefferson L. Davis Jr., Ronald L. Davis, Sherman C. Fraser, Donald W. Gettie, James E. Greene, Wm. B. Greene,
John J. Jones, John S. Lewis, Frank Tony Smith, Hugh B. Pettit
Jr., Evelyn A. Whitesides.

Page 324: J. R. Whitaker in Bar of 1933: Robert F. Whitaker,
           son of J. R. and Eula Whitaker, born 1904 in Cartersville, died October 11, 1969 at Emory Hospital, where he had
been a member of Emory's administration since 1931 and had

served as assistant to the president since 1959. He was administrator of the Emory University Hospital from 1944 to 1953. In 1966 the Robert Fleming Whitaker Scholarship Fund of Emory University was established for "a man who has devoted most of his life to Emory." He began his service as secretary of the alumni association soon after his graduation with B. Ph. degree in 1926, and LLB degree in Law in 1927. Member of Glenn Methodist Church. Married Emily Tillman, one daughter-Mrs. Gail Nichols. Brothers--James L. Whitaker of Athens, J. S. Whitaker of Glen Ridge, New Jersey. Sisters--Mrs. William Young of Macon and Mrs. Charles Sewell of Cartersville.

Page 324: Dr. W. E. Wofford died by suicide December 15, 1959, Dr. Sam M. Howell, born March 10, 1890, died April 13, 1954. The Sam Howell Memorial Hospital was erected in 1962, William Baxter, Superintendant, with Dr. William Bethel Quillian Jr. and Dr. Harvey W. Howell in charge. Other doctors are Dr. H. B. Bradford, Dr. Lewis R. Whatley, Dr. William B. Dillard Jr., Dr. R. W. May Jr., Dr. Grover J. Brown Jr., Dr. Richard A. Griffin III, Dr. Donald C. Evans. (Dr. W. B. Quillian Jr. died January 30, 1975, son of W. B. Sr. and Mamie McNeely Quillian. Began practice in 1938. Lt. Col. in A. M. C. WWII, married "Dot" Howell. Sons: Howell Quillian, Boston; Park Quillian, Cedartown; Risa Quillian).
Optometrist: 1971-Drs. H.T. Cook, Norman A.Fox, B.F. Popham Jr. Chrop: Dr. R.J. Wright, Dr. Willard A. Gray, Mrs. Virginia Hamilton--Mrs. H. Clayton Shaw, is Pub. Health M.D. Dentists: Drs. H. J. Choate, Hal J. Choate Jr, Zim J. Choate, Reuel E. Hamilton, DMD, Harold J. Lowry, Jr., Harold J. Lowry Sr., Joe Rowland, Lester S. Smith. (Granddau. of Charlotte S. Anderson is Mrs. Carter Smith Sr. of Atlanta.) Dr. L. L. Lowry died in October 1966, Dr. Charles Bell Upshaw died May 10, 1967, Atlanta. Ailen Best Battle, wife of Dr. G. W. Battle died December 1968, Decatur. Dr. J. D. Sims who practiced in the Stilesboro community had daughter Maude, married J. G. B. Erwin of Calhoun, Georgia, died in 1960. Dr. R. B. Harris, dentist, died in Atlanta 1963, at age of 99. Lived with his daughter, Mrs. James M. Reeves, the former Lily Harris. Dr. Joe N. Weems, dentist, born December 24, 1875, died May 14, 1963. Dr. Joseph Patman Bowdoin, beloved and illustrious citizen and doctor of Adairsville (born 1866) died in May, 1942, buried in Eastview cemetery. 1975: Dr. Stephen Wohlgemuth. Cartersville.

Page 326-27-28: Continuation of Representatives:
112.	1933	McConnell Lindsay Johnson
		William Shepherd Peebles
113.	1935	William Harrell Felton
		William Shepherd Peebles
114.	1937-38 Ex	William Shepherd Peebles
		Rufus V. Jones
115.	1939	Percy Algiers Bray
		Ezekiel Jefferson Summerour
116.	1941	S. Luke Pettit
		William Paul Martin
117.	1943-43Ex 44Ex	S. Luke Pettit
		William Paul Martin
118.	1945-45Ex 46	S. Luke Pettit
		Claude C. Pittman (died October 23, 1969)
119.	1947-48Ex 48 2nd Ex	J. L. Davis
		Leroy N. Jenkins
120.	1949-49Ex 50	J. L. Davis
		Leroy N. Jenkins (died October 1967)
121.	1951-52	Rufus V. Jones
		Floyd S. Tumlin

122.	1953-54	Floyd S. Tumlin
		Troy Upshaw
123.	1955-56Ex 56	Troy Upshaw
		D. Vann Underwood
124.	1957-58	William B. Greene
		Woodrow H. Bradley
125.	1959-60	Henry Alexander Keever
		Woodrow H. Bradley
126.	1961-62Ex 62 2nd Ex	William B. Greene
		Charles V. Crowe Jr. (died Mrs.)
		Charles V. Crowe Jr.
127.	1963-64	William B. Greene
		J. R. Cullens
128.	1965-66	Joe Frank Harris
	1966 Dist. 14	Joe Frank Harris, Post I
		David N. Vaughan Jr., Post 2
129.	1967-68 Dist. 14	Joe Frank Harris, Post I
		David N. Vaughan Jr., Post 2

Page 326: Continuation of Bartow County Senators since 1932 (now 42nd District).

112.	1933	B. H. Edmondson
113.	1935	Joseph Samphford Crawford
114.	1937-38 Ex	McConnel L. Johnson
115.	1939	Moses Ebenezer Brinson
116.	1941	Hiles Hamilton
117.	1934-43 Ex. 44	Claude Cleveland Pitman
118.	1945-45 Ex 46	Thomas A. Cook
119.	1947-48 Ex 48 2nd Ex	Francis Lamar Baker Jr.
120.	1949-49 Ex 50	Claude Cleveland Pitman
121.	1951-52	Archibald A. Farrar
122.	1953-54	Tom Clemmons (deceased)
123.	1955-55 Ex 56	Jeff L. Davis
124.	1957-58	Bobby Lee Cook
125.	1959-60	Barry Wright, Jr.
126.	1961-62 Ex 62 2nd Ex	William A. Ingram
127.	1963-64	Jack Chambers Fincher Jr.
128.	1965-66	Jack Chambers Fincher Jr.
129.	1967-68	Jack Chambers Fincher Jr.
130.	1969-70	Jack Chambers Fincher Jr.

RECENT BOOKS ABOUT BARTOW'S FAMOUS CITIZENS:

"Corra Harris, Lady of Purpose." by John E. Talmadge, University of Georgia Press, 1969. (Grandfather, John A. Irwin, a pioneer of Bartow.)

"Rebecca Latimer Felton," by John E. Talmadge, University of Georgia Press, 1960.

"Pierce M. B. Young, Warwick of the South," by Dr. Linwood Holland, 1964.

"Letters of Warren Akin, Confederate Congressman." edited by Bell Irvin Wiley, 1959.

"Sam Jones," by Walt Holcomb, 1947. Other books by Walt Holcomb: "Best Loved Sermons of Sam Jones," 1950; "The Gospel of Grace," 1955; "Sam Jones-An Ambassador of the Almighty," "Popular Lectures of Sam Jones," "Sam Jones, Vol. IV of The Great Pulpit Masters Series."

In "White Columns of Georgia," by Medora Field Perkerson, 1952, devotes three Chapters to Bartow: "Sherman's Georgia Romance," "Mystery of the Murchison Sisters," "Murder at Ghost Castle." Pages 195-205-213, with descriptions and pictures of "Walnut Grove" "Valley View,", Benjamin Reynolds Home, "Goulding House" & "Springbank."

"Until Now," by May Belle Jones Dewey, 1947, writes of Florence Candler Harris, founder of School of Nursing of Emory University, Chapter IX.

ARTICLES ABOUT CARTERSVILLE PEOPLE:

"Georgia Notebook" Series for The Atlanta Journal by Bernice McCullar in 1967, "Dropout with Midas Touch was Carter Who Had Oats," Article on Robert E. Lee (April 1967) and love affair with Eliza Mackay, "Convict Leasing Furor Involved Three Governors" (April 19, 1967)--Dr. W. H. Felton mentioned, "Yanks Exacted High Price For Girls Disobedience," Rose and Julia Murchison, sisters imprisoned instead of the Howard sisters. "First Woman in U. S. Senate Got Assist From George," "General Angered State, Cass County Lost Its Name," October 5, 1966. "Only Friendship Monument in World Now at Allatoona," December 23, 1965.

"A Neighbors Recollection of Corra Harris," by William Tate, Georgia Review, 1951. "Her World of Fashion," by Genevieve Pou, The Atlanta Journal and Constitution Magazine, September 30, 1970, about Jessica Daves (Mrs. Robert A. Parker), Editor of Vogue Magazine from 1946 to her retirement, and author of fashion books, is daughter of W. W. Daves and Annie Hopkins (page 153) and brother of Francis M. Daves of Decatur, architect and researcher of Indian history.

"Atlantic Comes of Age," by William McClure, Atlanta Magazine, November 1964, about Dillard Munford, successful Atlanta industrialist, founder of Munford Do-It-Yourself, Munford Co., Inc., Division of Atlantic Co. Great-grandson of "Bill Arp" Smith and grandson of George H. Aubrey (pages 123,294). Dillard Munford was born May 13, 1918, in Cartersville, son of Robert S. Munford and Katherine Aubrey, escaped death when a baby, though his mother was killed, when a train struck their car on a dangerous town crossing.

"Cassville-The Courageous Georgia Town That Refused to Die," by Bernard Street, May 12, 1957, News-Tribune Staff writer, Rome, Georgia.

"Bill Arp's Humor in the Bleak South," by Joseph H. Baird, The Atlanta Journal and Constitution Magazine, October 18, 1970.

"History of the Stilesboro Improvement Club and Prologue," by Callie Jackson, March 1943. Callie Jackson, born 1886, died August 20, 1968 in Stilesboro; teacher and news writer for the Bartow Herald, "In and Around Stilesboro;" daughter of Mary S. McFadden and Levi Young Jackson, pioneers.

Series of Articles about the Barnsleys, "Castle of Dreams," "Woodlands," Barnsley letters by Mrs. A. B. Howard, July and August 1969, in the North Bartow News, also about the cement plant, built and operated by George H. Waring, north of Kingston --now only stone walls in evidence.

"Joe Jones Preached Too," by Lucy Cunyus Mulcahy, Tribune-News, 1967, The Georgia Genealogical Society Quarterly, September 1967, Volume 4.

"Cassville," by Georgia Magazine, December 1965-January 1964, page 22.

During 1945-46-47, Col. Thomas Spencer wrote many articles about the Civil War and other articles pertaining to Bartow County for the Tribune-News. On file in State Archives. Articles were written by Harris Dalton in 1963 in the Bartow Herald about Bartow history.

"Million Dollars Slipped Through His Fingers," by John Mebane in Journal and Constitution Magazine November 7, 1965. Dr. Francis Goulding died August 22, 1881 and is buried in Roswell, not Rossville. Page 286. Typographical error and Mr. Mebane wrote in his first draft about Dr. Goulding's sojourn in Kingston.

"Georgia's Forgotten," by Dr. Lynwood M. Holland, Atlanta Journal and Constitution Magazine, September 13, 1964.

"Cartersville," by Andrew Sparks, Atlanta Journal Magazine, April 10, 1949.

"Spring Water and Ingenuity Ran This Ante Bellum Farm" (Mostellers Mills), by Andrew Sparks, Atlanta Constitution Magazine, May 5, 1957.

"Why Do Little Towns Die?" (Euharlee), by Andrew Sparks, Atlanta Constitution Magazine, September 28, 1969.

The Northside News of April 29, 1971, Atlanta, carries the success story of Ira Collins, for 25 years head and founder of the Southeastern Meat Company of Atlanta. On his father's farm north of Cartersville, at 13 years, he was given a bull calf and from then on he was interested in meat, and this company became a realized dream. His brother, Bob Collins of Calhoun, another successful Bartow citizen, died with cancer in 1971.

From a newspaper clipping is the account of Charles W. Vaughan, son of J. W. and "Fanny" Williams Vaughan, retired as vice-president of the James O. Welch Co., in 1965 Cambridge, Mass. Now he is a consultant volunteer with the International Executive Service Corporation (U. S. Govt.), and makes many visits to South and Central America.

Page 266. Office personnel when Am. Tex. Co. was sold to Goodyear in 1929: J. A. Miller, Vice-President (deceased); Donald S. McClain, Treasurer, son of founder, later resident of Atlanta (deceased), m. Marjorie Miller, children: Helen Donehoo (deceased) and Donald Jr.; Lindsay J. Forrester, Secretary, moved to and died in Greenville, South Carolina in December 1959, married Agnes Smith; sons: Harrison S., Lindsay Jr., and Dr. James Forrester, Georgetown, South Carolina. Claude R. Brown Superintendent, deceased, married Martha Peek (deceased), daughter Martha Brown Miller of Portage, Indiana; A. B. Cunyus, Paymaster, (father of Lucy Cunyus, historian) d. Apr. 4, 1937; Earl Powell, Clerk, (Dec), m. Flora Griffin; children: Earl Jr., dec., and Flora, moved to Cedartown; Gordon Powell, Clerk, m. Mattie Belle Stanley, dec., one son: Stanley Powell. m. 2nd Sproull Kennedy. Retired in

Cartersville.
The Cartersville Mills became E-Z Mills, Inc. under the management of John Fletcher Fowler, making cotton knitwear. After his retirement, he died in August 1965 in Charlottesville, Virginia, Harold E. Townslee became head.

Excerpts from letters to Lucy Cunyus Mulcahy from Wilbur G. Kurtz, during 1939 and 1947-52, which exhibit his generous sharing of his interest in Bartow history and his inimitable humor:

"I spoke at the Kennesaw Seminar on "The Defense of the Octagon House." Illustrated it with plans and a perspective drawing of the house as I conceived it, and the narrative was perhaps the first attempt to organize the sparse data on what took place there late afternoon of May 17, 1964--when Cheatham's Division of Hardee's Corps seized the house in the nick of time and fought off Col. Francis T. Sherman's Brigade of Newton's Division--Federal Fourth Corps.-- and of the burning of the house next morning by the men of the 73rd Illinois. Your friend, Milton Fleetwood, was present; the subject being close to his habitat, he soon produced a well-sharpened pencil and I saw him jot down notes from time to time. He had never heard anything about the house or the affair there, and afterward when I told him that I first heard of it from Lucy Cunyus, his eyes lit up like two traffic lights and he exclaimed--"I'm glad you told me that; her book has stood the test of the passing years; never have I heard that anything in it has been questioned" (This "illustration"is in "Atlanta and the Old South," page 34.).

"I think you were the one who tipped me off about the Saxon house, or "Octagon House." In Life Magazine--November 24, 1947-- is an article with pictures on Carl Carmer's octagon house at Irvington, New York. The article states that a certain nut named Orson Fowler, who went overboard on phrenology, "discovered" that an octagon-shaped house came nearest to the ideal form of habitation--the sphere--since it eliminated dust-catching corners and admitted more sunlight...I'd like to learn if Robert C. Saxon got a look at Orson Fowler's book. This could have happened, for Saxon was bookish--had a fine library--was Bartow County school commissioner for 12 years. Saxon built his octagon 1856-7... to erect such a dwelling from consideration of fire hazard and central heating with eliminations of hall space and stair wells. Eight fire-places to one chimney looked like a bargain. My hunch that Saxon was influenced not by Fowler's specious knowledge of head-bumps, but by his advanced ideas in domestic architecture."

"I enclose two snapshots taken at Allatoona, Georgia...which you and I visited a year ago this month. Curiously enough, I have just sent in some data to the script dept. here at the Studio (Selznick Intl. Pictures, Inc., Culver City, California.) for their use in writing a montage of Sherman's March to the Sea. It was at Allatoona that Gen. Sherman wrote that letter to Grant, wherein he used the phrase: __ "I can make the march and make Georgia howl." The letter is dated October 9, 1864, just four days after the Allatoona battle." (Dated March 27, 1939, while he was acting consultant on the filming of "Gone With The Wind" - L. C. M.)

"That book review headed "Rome Then and Now" fooled me into reading the review; I thought it was Rome, Georgia, and bless Pat, it was an opus by none less than my old friend--Eleanor Waring Burnham (granddaughter of Rev. and Mrs. Charles Wallace

Howard). After all, I wasn't surprised that she would write the sort of book described in the review--for I recall her as a very energetic lady who let everybody know that she was alert to everything and had been around considerably. I attended one of her Salons one Sunday night in Los Angeles in 1939, and if the guests were not particularly distinguished, she, herself, made up for any of their shortcomings. As you say, those Howards were fascinating people--even if the Federal Gen. O. O. Howard twitted Frances about not being of the blood of all the Howards (She refused, if you recall, being related to any Northern Howard)."

"Col. Julian and I had an interesting trip on March 22. This time we explored the route from Calhoun to Barnsleys--as taken by the 15th Corps (in part) and Garrard's Cavalry--May 17-18, 1864. Just west of Oothcaloga Creek at the old Calhoun or Logan's mill site (site is right for the mill has been completely demolished) is a cross-roads. The one from the Oostenaula leaves the river at Lay's Ferry and crosses over to 41 highway about two miles south of Halls Station. The other is the Calhoun-Rome road, running S. W. from Calhoun. The federal report calls this crossing the Rome Cross Roads, and here a battle was fought on the 16th of May--a Confederate rear-guard consisting of part of Hardee's Corps held back the 16th Corps long enough for Johnston's wagon trains to get down towards Hall's. The next day, Garrard's Cavalry--having crossed at Lay's Ferry, took the Rome road and passing through McGuire's went as far as Hermitage, and then turned eastward to Barnsley's. Following Garrard, marched Logan's 15th Corps and Dodge's 16th Corps. These troops camped the night of the 17th at McGuire's-- the while, brushing aside a few Confederate cavalrymen that must have gotten back on this road after Garrard passed. On the 18th, the 15th and 16th Corps marched due east from McGuire's to Adairsville, and then dropped down to Barnsley's, reaching there --and camping on the domain--that evening. McPherson accompanied this column, and that's how he happened to be there to spend the nights--and that's where "Biddy" Flannagin saw him and gave as her considered opinion that "he's a gentleman, but wan that's in mighty low company." (From "In and Out of the Lines," page 27.)

"Garrard reached Barnsley's some hours ahead of Logan and McPherson and the Garrard troopers were the ones who got the worst of the running fight on that old back-bone road that runs directly from Barnsley's to Kingston--a fight that finished up at Barnsley's house--where Col. Earle was killed. Our problem was to find McGuire's Cross Road...the Atlas Plate and Dodge-Ruger map are wrong in that they show both Garrard and Logan going to Barnsley's via Hermitage. Its well we finally got around to this bit of exploring. The old Rome Road is practically gone. The new one ignores the old right-of-way in most haughty and imprudent manner. Where a curve is eliminated, or higher ground is selected, we could see (for the construction work is now in progress) that before long, a wide paved highway would supplement the old route as taken by the Federal forces... We stopped long enough to ask questions at McGuire's...we talked with a patriarch named Scott--he told us that he had heard his elders talk about the time the army came through there and that the old cross-roads were west of the present highway about 600 feet--indeed we were at the old cross-roads when we talked to him, for that's where his house stands. In 1864 the road ran through Hermitage, or so the map shows it...turning eastward we reached Hermitage....From Hermitage...we came to forks--one carried us to the summit of a high hill and a fire-warden's tower ...we got lost...finally we reached the Barnsley house...we did not enter...We did manage to see Barnsley's Chapel and on a large slab in the churchyard, reads

>Addie B. Saylor
>June 31, 1964-June 5, 1942

Harry's grave was not marked. I wanted to go to Conesena Baptist Church and we did get there. Wanted to see the Harris marker and I found it. How, I'll never know.

>Erected to the memory of
>Dr. Alexander Nelson Harris
>Born Jonesboro, Tenn.
>June 15, 1815
>Died November 6, 1865

Erected by his son, Gov. Nat E. Harris (See page 246).

"Since there were brothers: Samuel and John (or Jonathan) McDow and both owned land bisected by the railroad (south of Adairsville), and whereas John (Jonathan) owned 5 square miles east of same, and whereas Samuel's house on the west side--the one described is, so far as known to us, the only McDow house (then)...are we to infer then in 1864 both McDow houses were standing--both are referred to in the Official Records...Miss Alice Dyar says it is the Samuel McDow house...McGuire said the McDow house was still standing north of his (August 1932). John (or Jonathan) McDow's land was situated on the east side of the old Western and Atlantic Railroad (See MILLS on the Dodge Ruger Map No. II). When his land was cleared an apple orchard took the place of the virgin trees, a government still was built, a flour mill and saw mill also were erected. These stood where is now an artificial lake owned by J. M. Veach and named "Lake Marguerite" for his wife, the former Miss Marguerite Dyar."

"Cox (Brig. Gen. Jacob D. Cox's account) says (page 54) he was at McDows on May 18th...but he got here the 19th...He says he spent night of the 18th at Mosteller's Mill. Now Cox went to McDow's to confer with Gen. Hooker or Gen. Sherman...Gen. Joseph Hooker was at McDow's the night of the 18th and if Cox saw him it must have been on the 19th. Gen. Hooker was at the Hawkins Price place by 10 P. M. of the 19th."

"When the northern army came to Georgia, all the McDow buildings were destroyed by them except the two-story (wooden) home still standing near the road leading to Hall's Station. Mrs. McDow (mother of 17 children) refused to leave when her husband refugeed to south Georgia. With two slaves, a man and his wife, she remained and saved the home." The two-story brick Jonathan McDow House, Fed. Maj. Gen. Joseph Hooker's Headquarters, May 18, 1864, page 36, in ATLANTA and the OLD SOUTH, is a drawing from research by Wilbur Kurtz. Other paintings or drawing of Bartow County are the "Yonah" at Etowah Station as the "General" steams northward and the "William R. Smith" at Kingston, page 29. (Note from old newspaper: Died near Adairsville, November 21, 1875, Mrs. Mary McDow, wife of Mr. Samuel McDow, aged 72 years. She was born in Anderson, South Carolina in 1803. Jonathan McDow and Samuel McDow are in the Cass County Census of 1840--LCM.)

"Last Sat. Spencer, Yates and I called on Mrs. Fouche and spent over two hours at "Valley View.".... Mrs. Fouche was graciousness itself, and topped off the visit with coffee and coconut cake--before a log fire in the living room. Enroute to Milam's bridge we managed to get into an old cemetery back of somebody's house, and found the last resting place of the Cunyus and Burge ancestors (now completely vandalized). We had stopped at the Stiles places; tenants occupy the Henry Stiles place, "Etowah Cliffs." This reminds me that the Atlas Plate of that area shows a cross-roads settlement on the Cartersville-Milam's Bridge road, not far from the Fouche and Stiles home--called "Etowah Cliffs." My theory is that Henry Stiles or one of the family lifted that name from the cross-roads settlement and affixed it to the Henry Stiles home. Robert Stiles calls his place, as you know, "Malbone." And by the same street-car token, when Gen. Schofield dated a protest about Hooker usurping his pontoons at Milam's Bridge, "Etowah Cliffs"--he was at the cross-roads settlement enroute to the bridge and not over there off the road at the Henry Stiles house and family cemetery."

"We found "The Glen." Mr. Lamkin (of Athens)--in answer to my question, said this house was still standing--between the sites of "Etowah Heights" and "Waverly Oaks" (the latter the Chas. Shelman Jr. house) and Raccoon Creek. I'd seen the house before but it never occurred to me that this was the place where Charles and Cecilia (Shelman) had set up housekeeping and where all their children were born--for "Etowah Heights"----if your statement is correct, was not built until 1861. (One of the Dodge-Ruger maps marked its site "Unfinished"--and marking the site of "The Glen" with a curious and ironic typographical error SHERMAN. Yates, Spencer and I beat it up there to photograph it. Alack and alas--the house is there all right--what's left of it. A wing was lopped off- the hand hewn timbers destined for the forewood at the rear and the edifice restored all out of reason. Asbestos siding of a gleaming whiteness--composition shingles-- spic and span written all over it--the interior--which we didn't see, a perpetual astonishment to the neighbors, what with the tile baths, electric water heater, etc. The culprit in the piece is a certain Mr. Pickelsimer of Atlanta who took a fancy to the old house and did all these things to it. Page 250. (This was in 1947. House was later sold to "Jake" Cullens, LCM). There is a spring at the foot of a steep Raccoon Creek bank--a spring near a large tight cable--with a windlass atop the bank, across the road from the house--and here the water was drawn up for use at the house. This mechanized water lifter had vanished, but I saw one at work when I was an Indiana lad." (A painting of the Shelman House, "Etowah Heights" is on page 42 in' "ATLANTA and the OLD SOUTH," LCM).

"In October (1947) Spencer, Yates and I met Mr. and Mrs. G. C. Phillips at Kingston and we went to Barnsley's (which they owned at that time, LCM). Among the debris in that frame structure south of the brick part, I found Addie Saylor's autograph album---hitherto overlooked by all the collectors. The page that caught my eye read:

>To Addie,
>
>May you be as happy as I wish and you will be blessed indeed
>
>Cecilia S.
>Etowah Heights, August 12th/83

Mrs. Phillips placed this little book in her over-stuffed purse."

""Saturday Col. Spencer and I explored some of the area near Stilesboro. Our first stop was your grandfather's house, but 'twas a stop only. Things have happened to the old house; the second story has been removed and a gable roof has been

substituted, making it, or so it seemed, a story and a half
edifice, and from the appearance, it would seem that work had
stopped before completion. The Burge (W.T.) house--southward--
still presents its ancient aspect, though this was the first
time I ever saw it. '(The morning light prevented snap-shots.)
At the Little Berry Hawkins place we talked to Misses Bessie and
Campie Hawkins. They were real cordial and invited us in, for
a look at family relics and the family record. The three houses
are on the route of Gen. Geary's division of the 20th Corps,
marching to New Hope Church in Paulding County. The road peters
out at the Paulding County line. From there on, to Burnt Hickory
one might walk -- but no cars could get through. We
learned of a certain Dr. Sims of Stilesboro, who is alleged to
have had a conversation with Sherman at the old Academy, but
that's all we could find out about him. You mention Thaddeus
Sobeski Hawkins, and the daughters, Bessie and Campie, on page
93 of your history. L. B. H. was T. S.'s father. The former had
a penchant for naming his children for historic personages...the
maiden sisters said that their branch of the family was related
to Benjamin Hawkins, the celebrated Indian agent who is buried
on the banks of the Flint River near Roberta."

"Col. Julian and I went to Kingston, Rome and Cartersville.
We found the remains of Best's Mill, 2 miles west of 41 on the
road to Kingston. Howard's Fourth Corps camped here May 18th.
All that remains is a fragment of stone wall, near the highway
bridge over Two-Run Creek. In Kingston we talked with Dr. Ellis,
a charming gentleman. He referred us to John McKelvy whom we
found at his store on Kingston's main street. John must be 90
years of age. His father was William Neal McKelvy and he had a
brother (John's brother) Thomas Roderick McKelvy. John said he
was living at that little house now across the road from the M.
L. Johnson house--Cass Station--in May, 1864, when the Confederate army stopped there (May 18-19, 1864). John said he saw
Gen. Joseph E. Johnston there. The Gen. rode up on a horse and
told John's mother she must leave the house, because there was
going to be a battle. John and his mother left--added that there
were a lot of soldiers around--said he had heard that some of
the generals disagreed about fighting a battle there. Said there
was no house there, in 1864, where the M. L. Johnson house now
stands. Back at Kingston I photographed the Hargis house (now
gone 1971) and ran on to Rome to trace Maj. Gen. Jefferson C.
Davis' march...when he got to Rome he was still west of both the
Oostenaula and Coosa. However, he managed to get across and
just then, Rome's defender Gen. French, remembered he had a date
to join the rest of the boys at Cassville, so he lit out up the
road and reached Cassville in time to participate in that log
cabin council...McKelvy did not remember anything about the log
cabin...where Hood and Polk thought it advisable to retreat."

"One day last winter, I walked that intrenched line at Cassville from the cemetery southward to old 41. It was not a thrilling performance, but I think I found the vicinity of French
batteries. Later I photographed two old houses still standing
at Cassville--Day and Bogle, I have one of the Hardy house."

"Since the impounded waters of the Etowah will rise nearly
to track level at Allatoona, it has been decided to reroute the
N. C. and St. L. railroad in the Allatoona Range...There is a
big letter S in the line there, as the maps show. So while the
re-routing is being done, it was thought a good time to remove
the compound curves. Some fears are entertained that the hill

where Corse's Fort overlooks the big rock cut will be demolished for its dirt. (See water color on page 39 in "ATLANTA and the OLD SOUTH"). Yesterday's paper carried an article to the effect that the Government insists the unknown soldier's grave in the rock cut must be moved." (It was moved southward on the old town road)."

"At present (1952) I am engaged in writing the texts for castiron memorial tablets for the entire area of the Atlanta Campaign--13 counties in all--it just happens I've started with Bartow County..." (Wilbur Kurtz wrote the texts for at least 50 markers in Bartow County, and one for the Sam P. Jones Home that was not allowed to be placed, with the exception of the four written by Joe Mahan--Corra Harris Home, Felton Home, Sam Jones Tabernacle, "Bill Arp" Home. There are ancient markers of the Goulding House and the Wayside Home in Kingston, that need renovating." These markers are in GEORGIA HISTORICAL COMMISSION'S CIVIL WAR HISTORICAL MARKERS, listed 008.)

Wilbur Kurtz Autograph: "Lucy, you once said Sherman would never have marched through Georgia--at least the Bartow County part of it--without some fancied assistance you thought, came from me. My thought is that Sherman managed to get through very well in spite--not because of any help from me. Signed, sealed, and delivered in the Studio in this year of Grace, 1956, and on the 10th day of February thereof, Wilbur G. Kurtz."

The men mentioned in these letters from Wilbur Kurtz were: Col. Thomas Spencer, Ret. and historian; B. C. Yates, former Superintendant Kennesaw Mountain Park, Marietta; and Col. Allen Julian, Atlanta. Col. Thomas Spencer, died October 8, 1973, St. Petersburg, Florida. B. C. Yates died July 3, 1981; Col. Julian died January 17, 1979.

UP-TO-DATE:

Bartow now has the first political national figure since the Feltons in Joe Frank Harris-after 18 years in the Georgia House of Representatives, being elected Democratic Governor in the elections of 1982! A son of Mr. and Mrs. Frank Harris of Atco and Cartersville, he and his wife, Elizabeth, were inaugurated January 11,1983!

MARRIAGE BONDS, 1837-1843, BOOK "B"
OF CASS COUNTY, NOW BARTOW, IN ORDINARY'S OFFICE
BARTOW COUNTY COURTHOUSE, CARTERSVILLE, GA.

GEORGIA   )   To any Minister of the Gospel Judge of the Superior
)   Court Justice of the Peace. You are hereby auth-
CASS COUNTY) orized to join John Ambrester (or Ambuster) and
                  Elizabeth Phillips in lawful bonds of matrimony
                  agreeable to the Constitution and laws of this
                  State given under my hand and seal this 15th day
                  of May 1838. Signed: George B. Russell CCO (LS)

GEORGIA   )   I certify the foregoing was duly executed before
CASS COUNTY) me on this 15th day of May 1838. Signed: William
                  L. Morgan JIC.

Page 1

(As all marriage bonds are worded the same, only the names of the grooms-alphabetically listed brides, officials and dates will be copied. CCO=County Court of Ordinary, JP=Justice of the Peace, JIC=Judge of the Inferior Court, M.G.=Minister of the Gospel, (?) questionable spelling, Ex=executed by official and actual wedding date. Copied by Lucy Cunyus Mulcahy, Bartow County Historian, in 1971.)

A.

	Page
John Adair and Ann B. Graham 19th July 1838 Ex. 19th July 1838	13 George B. Russell CCO David Morrow JP
Asa T. Allen and Margaret Baker 13th September 1839 Ex. 10th October 1839	39 George B. Russell CCO David Garrison JP
William T. Adams and Emily Carnes 2nd November 1840 Ex. 5th November 1840	60 George B. Russell CCO T. M. Henson JP
William C. Allen and Mary Ann Watters 25th January 1841 Ex. 31st January 1841	64 George B. Russell CCO Isaac Rutherford, Min.
Osburn Adams and India Ann Jarrett 12th December 1840 Ex. 18th December 1840	65 George B. Russell CCO Rev. James Adams

B.

	Page
James C. Ballard and Sarah Denman 10th October 1837 Ex. 12th October 1837	6 George B. Russell CCO Thomas Townsend JP
Thomas Booker and Milly Owen 13th November 1837 Ex. 14th November 1837	7 George B. Russell CCO E. Milsaps JIC
Robert Black and Sarah Whitesides 25th November 1837 Ex. 30th November 1837	8 George B. Russell CCO Zachariah Aycock JP

James Madison Brown and Sarah Denman   6
29th May 1838   George B. Russell CCO
Ex. 31st May 1838   David Morrow JP

John H. Beazley and Ginny(?) Walker   16
17th September 1838   George B. Russell CCO
Ex. 20th September 1838   John Millican JP

William T. Bell and Eleanor B. Mays   17
11th October 1838   George B. Russell CCO
Ex. 11th October 1838   Zachariah Aycock JP

Azariah P. Bailey and Jane Gaston   17
24th October 1838   George B. Russell CCO
Ex. 24th October 1838   David Morrow JP

Edward E. (?) Bailey and Juliann Smith   19
18th November 1838   George B. Russell CCO
Ex. 2nd December 1838   J. T. Kirkham JP

William Bassett and Lucinda Smith   25
20th March 1839   George B. Russell CCO
Ex. 20th March 1839   John Russell JIC

E. J. (?) Baker and Sarah Baker   29
23rd May 1839   George B. Russell CCO
Ex. 23rd May 1839   Hiram Dunagan JP

Thomas H. Benton and Malvina M. Taylor   29
2nd July 1839   George B. Russell CCO
Ex. 2nd July 1839   J. H. George M.G.

John Bruige(?) and Sarah Bell   31
4th July 1839   George B. Russell CCO
Ex. 4th July 1839   David Morrow JP

Benjamin Bowman and Nancy Cochran   31
13th June 1839   George B. Russell CCO
Ex. 20th June 1839   David Morrow JP

Henry C. Bryom and Elizabeth Lay   33
3rd May 1839   George B. Russell CCO
Ex. 5th May 1839   J. T. Kirkham JP

Jesse A. Beam and Christina Waters   34
2nd September 1839   George B. Russell CCO
Ex. 5th September 1839   James Stovall JP

Philip M. Bumgarner (?) and Terresse Jeffres 37
16th October 1839   George B. Russell CCO
Ex. 17th October 1839   Joshua Bowdoin, M.G.

Sherod Bowman and Mary Ann Hogan   41
12th October 1839   George B. Russell CCO
Not executed

Bernhard Brickle and Srah Ann Concler(?)   44
26th December 1839   George B. Russell CCO
Ex. 26th December 1839   John Rhome (?) JP

John D. Brown and Elizabeth Owens   57
3rd September 1840   George B. Russell CCO
Ex. 5th September 1840   Joseph H. Jones JIC

L. R. (?) Bowman and Nancy Ann Baker   59
29th October 1840   George B. Russell CCO
Ex. 1st November 1840   J. H. Murdock JP

Joseph Blackwood and Mahala Douglass   65
14th August 1838   George B. Russell CCO
Ex. 16th August 1838   Wm. P. (?) Walker LD

Joseph Ballard and Margaret Countryman   65
30th January 1841   George B. Russell CCO
Ex. 2nd February 1841   Jehu (?) Pouler (?) JP

Samuel Badget and Lydia Ann Carpenter   66
22nd December 1840   George B. Russell CCO
Ex. 22nd December 1840   B. B. Gaines

Thomas W. Brown and Milla (?) Henderson   73
24th July 1841   George B. Russell CCO
Ex. 29th July 1841   Isaac Rutherford, M.G.

John Baker and Cynthia Pinson   78
17th August 1841   George B. Russell CCO
Ex. 26 August 1841   Z. (?) G. Turner JP

Thomas Brown and Elizabeth Madden   81
30th December 1841   George B. Russell CCO
Ex. 31st December 1841   Z. G. Turner JP

William K. Barron and Sarah Elizabeth Miller 82
22nd January 1842   George B. Russell CCO
Ex. 23rd January 1842   Stephen Ellis LD

William T. Blalock and Sarah H. Pruett   89
19th July 1841   George B. Russell CCO
Ex. 25th July 1841   Wm. D. Walker, M.G.

William H. Barnet (or Barrett) and Debyan Shaw 95
29th March 1842   George B. Russell CCO
Ex. 1st April 1842   Joshua Bowdoin, G.M.

William A. Brogs (Brays?) and Elizabeth Robbins 95
24th March 1842   Arthur Haire CCO
Ex. 24th March 1842   David Morrow JP

James H. Bailey and Manroura(?) Kinman   96
19th March 1842   Arthur Haire CCO
Ex. 20th March 1842   Banister R. Bray, M.G.

Ralph S. Barnett and Eliza E. Islen   97
27th September 1842   Arthur Haire CCO
Ex. 27th September 1842   J. H. George, M.G.

John C. Butler and Nancy Thompson   97
30th August 1842   Arthur Haire CCO
Ex. 1st September 1842   John Blalock JP

Henry Barron and Sarah Robertson   100
29th November 1842   Arthur Haire CCO
Ex. 1st December 1842   John Millican, JP

Abram P. Barron and Sarah Ward   100
26th December 1842   Arthur Haire CCO
Ex. 27th December 1842   Erwin Pearson, M.G.

James F. Butler and Floryan S. Watts   102
26th December 1842   Arthur Haire CCO
Ex. December 1842   John Millican JP

Michael O. Bryan and Barbary H. Kirkpatrick 104
23rd November 1842   Arthur Haire CCO
Ex. 24th November 1842   Irvin Martin JP

Davis Burroughs and Nancy Godfry   107
23rd March 1843   Arthur Haire CCO
Ex. 23rd March 1843   John Crawford, M.G.

William Burnett and Marendy Bradshaw   109
2nd August 1843   Arthur Haire CCO
Ex. 3rd August 1843   Silas Bell JP
Recorded August 28, 1843

William Bates (or Batey) and Talitha Keith 109
29th May 1843   Arthur Haire CCO
Ex. May 30th, 1843   Philip J. Guyton JP
Recorded June 17, 1843

C.   Page

Gamson Cramer and Nancy Gurganus (?)   3
11th August 1837   George B. Russell CCO
Ex. 11th August 1837   William Sylar JP

William D. Clark and Susan K. Seals   5
25th July 1837   George B. Russell CCO
Ex. 29th July 1837   LLC Franklin JIC

Edward Calahan and E. Clair Bennett   4
25th September 1837   George B. Russell CCO
Ex. 26th September 1837   William Sylar JP

William J. Cantrell and Mary Mays   8
12th December 1837   George B. Russell CCO
Ex. 12th December 1837   John Crawford, M.G.

Myers Cochran and Pheba Dickey   19
16th November 1838   George B. Russell CCO
Ex. 20th November 1838   Thomas Townsend JP

James Conner and Elizabeth Parks   22
9th January 1839   George B. Russell CCO
Ex. 9th January 1839   David Morrow JP

Elisha Crisman and Emily Bowdoin   37
26th October 1839   George B. Russell CCO
Ex. 31st October 1839   Allen Dykes, M.G.

William Contal(?) and Martha Cain   40·
5th November 1839   George B. Russell CCO
Ex. 6th November 1839   J. H. George, M.G.

Terry Creamer(?) and Gracy Gaines   41
7th November 1839   George B. Russell CCO
Not executed

Shadrack Carson and Elizabeth J. Faulkner   46
10th February 1840   George B. Russell CCO
Ex. 11th February 1840   William James JP

William Cooper and Nancy Caroline Faulkner   53
9th April 1840   George B. Russell CCO
Ex. 14th April 1840   Thompson M. Henson JP

Edmund Collins and Mary Turner   55
3rd July 1840   George B. Russell CCO
Ex. 6th July 1840   Z.(?) G. Turner JP

James F. Cooper and Sarah Frances R. Speir   56
18th August 1840   George B. Russell CCO
Ex. 20th August 1840   Turner H. Trippe J.S.C.

John C. Colehouse(?) and Elizabeth J. Ellis   59
3rd November 1840   George B. Russell CCO
Ex. 6th November 1840   Jas. R. Brock JP

George W. Cooper and Elizabeth Thomas   61
27th November 1840   George B. Russell CCO
Ex. 30th November 1840   David Morrow JP

Warren Clayton and Jane Watson   63
24th January 1841   George B. Russell CCO
Ex. 24th January 1841   Coleman Pitts JP

Samuel D. Chambers and Elizabeth Ann Barnett   72
16th June 1841   George B. Russell CCO
Ex. 17th June 1841   Joshua Bowdoin, M.G.

Josiah Creamer and Malinda Gaines   79
23rd December 1841   George B. Russell CCO
Ex. 23rd December 1841   I.(?) C. Sammons, M.G.

Francis Creed and Abalina(?) Hammonds   81
14th December 1841   George B. Russell CCO
Ex. 16th December 1841   Z. G. Turner JP

Turner Conaway (?) and Lavinia Bearden   94
2nd February 1842   George B. Russell CCO
Ex. 8th February 1842   Samuel McDow JIC

William Carter and Caroline Watts   102
24th January 1843   Arthur Haire CCO
Ex. 24th January 1843   John Chastain, M.G.

Andrew Countryman and Jane Hicks   107
18th April 1843   Arthur Haire CCO
Ex. 27th April 1843   Evan Pearson, M.G.
Recorded June 17th, 1843

Isaac F. Crow and Sarah Slaton(?)   110
4th August 1843   Arthur Haire CCO
Ex. 5th August 1843   Z. G. Turner JP
Recorded August 28, 1843

D.

Cornelius A. Dyer or Dywr and Sarah Foster   12
7th May 1838   George B. Russell CCO
Ex. 8th May 1838   Z. G. Turner JP

A. F. Dunagan and Emilia Minerva Dempsey   14
27 July 1838   George B. Russell CCO
Ex. 2nd August 1838   John Burns JP

Christopher Dodd and Sarah Ann Lowry   32
6th June 1839   George B. Russell CCO
Ex. 13th July 1839   B. R. Bray

Joseph Duncan and Sarah Sutherland   36
21st September 1839   George B. Russell CCO
Ex. 22nd September 1839   William Kinman JP

Joseph L. Dysart and Sarah E. Upshaw   37
27th September 1839   George B. Russell CCO
Ex. 3rd October 1839   Isaac N. Craven M.G.

Olleman Dodgen and Amelia King   53
3rd April 1840   George B. Russell CCO
Ex. 12th September 1840   Z. G. Turner JP

Wyley Dean and Selina Walker   56
18th July 1840   George B. Russell CCO
Ex. 18th July 1840   Silas Bell JP

Elisha Dodson and Kemily(?) Lay   80
6th January 1842   George B. Russell CCO
Ex. 6th January 1840   John Blalock JP

Hugh Davidson and June Foster   104
18th February 1843   Arthur Haire CCO
Ex. 19th February 1843   William Sylar JP

Joseph B. Drummond and Eleanor Melton   112
11th July 1843   Arthur Haire CCO
Ex. 18th July 1843   John B. Fisher JP

E.

Thomas Early and Jane Doster   12
22nd May 1838   George B. Russell CCO
Ex. 24th May 1838   David Garrison JP

Josiah B. England and Frances Minerva McCrary   46
4th February 1840   George B. Russell CCO
Ex. 6th February 1840   Joseph H. Jones JIC

William R. Erwin and Lucinda C. Upshaw   51
9th January 1840   George B. Russell CCO
Ex. 9th January 1840   Isaac N. Craven M.G.

Alfred Erwin and Mary Riche   71
12th May 1841   George B. Russell CCO
Ex. 20th May 1841   Silas Bell JP

William G. Erwin and Martha B. McCrary   88
8th February 1842   George B. Russell CCO
Ex. 19th February 1842   George R. Edward JP

F.

Ambrose B. Forsyth and Eliza Patten   18
15th November 1838   George B. Russell CCO
Ex. 18th November 1838   Thos. Townsend JP

Shadrach Farmer and Sarah Gilkeson(?)   21
19th January 1839   George B. Russell CCO
Ex. 29th January 1839   Evan Pearson M.G.

Nathaniel Furr and Mary Dixon   44
13th January 1840   George B. Russell CCO
Ex. 13th January 1840   William Sylar JP

Daniel Furr and Mary Dixon   58
22 October 1840   George B. Russell CCO
Ex. 22nd October 1840   John Millican JP

John Fuquay and Sally Huggins   68
21st March 1841   George B. Russell CCO
Ex. 24th March 1841   James Stovall JP

Middleton Faulkner and Mahala Branden(?)   92
17th September 1842   Arthur Haire
Ex. 22nd September 1842   David Morrow JP

Gabrial Forkner and Martha Bearden   94
9th March 1842   Arthur Haire CCO
Ex. 15th March 1842   Samuel McDow JIC

James F. Foster and Adaline Hatch   101
17th January 1843   Arthur Haire
Ex. 17th January 1843   William Sylar JP

Isaac Fricks and Nancy C. Jones   110
24th August 1843   Arthur Haire CCO
Ex. 24th August 1843   William Latimer JP

John Tabor(?) Fitts or Fritz and Elizabeth White 111
23rd June 1843   Arthur Haire CCO
Ex. 26th June 1843   Ransome Foster JP

William M. Faine and Catharine M. Anderson   113
24th August 1843   Arthur Haire CCO
Ex. 24th August 1843   John Crawford M.G.

G.

Richard M. Garrison and Caroline Baker   48
16th December 1839   George B. Russell CCO
Ex. 24th December 1839   David Garrison JP

L. W. Gaines and Metilda Creamier(?)   54
12th September 1839   George B. Russell CCO
Ex. 12th September 1839   B. B. Gaines M.G.

William Gooddin and Nancy Jane Dillard   58
21st July 1840   George B. Russell CCO
Ex. 21st July 1840   James R. Brock JP

Hugh Gaston and Martha Jane Yowell(?)   60
14th December 1840   George B. Russell CCO
Ex. 15th December 1840   Isaac N. Craven M.G.

Livingston Garrett and Ann England   68
15th May 1841   George B. Russell CCO
Ex. 23rd May 1841   James Stovall JP

Lewis V. Gannory(?) and Caroline Smith   69
16th March 1841   George B. Russell CCO
Ex. 16th March 1841   Irwin Martin JP

John Gault and Amanda M. Stroup   78
11th August 1841   George B. Russell
Ex. 16th August 1841   John W. Lewis M.G.

Elijah Gibson and Eliza Thompson   79
28th December 1841   George B. Russell
Ex. 28th December 1841   William Sylar JP

Thomas Gorham and Almedia J. Denson   82
13th January 1842   George B. Russell CCO
Ex. 13th January 1842   Z. G. Turner JP

William S. Gaston and Nancy M. Walker   83
9th February 1842   George B. Russell CCO
Ex. 9th February 1842   David Morrow JP

William Godard(?) and Jane W. Crow   91
5th July 1842   Arthur Haire CCO
Ex. 7th July 1842   Z. G. Turner JP

Jonathan Godwin and Eliza McCutchen   91
15th March 1841   George B. Russell CCO
Ex. 18th March 1841   Samuel McDow JIC

Nathaniel Grant and Margaret Vandaver(?)   99
6th December 1842   Arthur Haire
Ex. 6th December 1842   Nathl. Adams M.G.

George Gay and Harriett McRuskell(?)   105
4th March 1843   Arthur Haire CCO
Ex. March 1843   Silas Bell JP

H.

Joseph Hargiss and Elizabeth Moore   3
30th January 1837   George B. Russell CCO
Ex. 31st January 1837   John Crawford M.G.

Robert F. Hilburn and Louisa Bailey   10
16th December 1837   George B. Russell CCO
Ex. 21st December 1837   Bannister R. Bray Min.

Alfred Hightower and Huldah Julian(?)   14
8th May 1837   George B. Russell CCO
Ex. 11th May 1837   Nathan J. Adams M.G.

John Hood and Sarah G. Hood   17
16th October 1838   George B. Russell CCO
Ex. 18th October 1838   Thompson M. Henson JP

Amariah Hassell and Eliza H. Thompson   20
19th December 1838   George B. Russell CCO
Ex. 10th December 1838   J. H. George, Clerk

Joseph T. Hamilton and Mourner(?) R. Turner   26·
5th March 1839   George B. Russell CCO
Ex. 5th March 1839   J. M. Yarbrough M.G.

Luke H. Hodge and Eliza E. Crawford   45
15th January 1840   George B. Russell CCO
Ex. 15th January 1840   Evan Pearson M.G.

James Hawkins and Jurie(?) Kitchens   47
30th January 1840   George B. Russell CCO
Ex. 2nd February 1840   Thomas Brandon JP

Robert Henry and Louisa C. Hodge   48
5th November 1839   George B. Russell CCO
Ex. 5th November 1839   B. R. Bray M.G.

Raleigh Hall and Elizabeth Evans   54
3rd June 1840   George B. Russell CCO
Ex. 4th June 1840   J. H. Murdock JP

William D. Hassell and Catharine Lawson   60
26th November 1840   George B. Russell CCO
Ex. 26th November 1840   Evan Pearson M.G.

David Harris and Elizabeth Kirk   61
13th January 1841   George B. Russell CCO
Ex. 14th January 1841   William Sylar JP

Samuel Hensley and Charlotte Goodwin   64
14th January 1841   George B. Russell CCO
Ex. 17th January 1841   James R. Brock JP

John Hamilton and Sarah Ann Edwards   72
15th July 1841   George B. Russell CCO
Ex. 15th July 1841   J. C. Simmons M.G.

Walter W. Hannon and Caroline S. Franklin   76
22nd November 1841   George B. Russell CCO
Ex. 15th November 1841   Irwin Martin JP

Robert F. Henderson and Emelia Stidham(?)   77
16th November 1841   George B. Russell CCO
Ex. 19th November 1841   Barnabus Pace O.M.G.

J.L. Hancock and Mary Countryman   82
19th Januaty 1842   George B. Russell CCO
Ex. 19th January 1842   William Sylar JP

Jess Holland and Elizabeth Worly   86
5th April 1842   Arthur Haire
Ex. 7th April 1842   Lee Bates M.G.

Robert Hood and Dorcus B. Hood   92
14th November 1842   Arthur Haire CCO
Ex. 17th November 1842   J. H. George M.G.

Isaac M. Hubbard and Dicy Mullins   94
14th August 1842   Arthur Haire CCO
Ex. 18th August 1842   Z. G. Turner JP

Peter Hilton and Susan Waldroup   103
11th February 1843   Arthur Haire CCO
Ex. 11th February 1843   Philip J. Guyton JP

John J.(?) Haral(?) and Nancy C. Kitchens   108
12th October 1842   Arthur Haire CCO
Ex. 16th October 1842   John B. Fisher JP
Recorded June 10, 1843

Clark Holms(?) and Catharine Smith   109
6th March 1843   Arthur Haire CCO
Ex. 7th March 1843   Nathl. Adams M.G.

William Henderson and Morrison (?)   112
12th July 1843   Arthur Haire CCO
Ex. 13th July 1843   Wm. F. Bates M.G.

William Hendricks and Laury Hamitty Tate   93
21 December 1842   Arthur Haire CCO
Ex. 22 December 1842   Evan Pearson M.G.

I.

William G. Irwin and Louisa Goodwin   13
27th June 1838   George B. Russell CCO
Ex. 28th June 1838   A. B. Cunningham JIC

Elisha F. Ivil and Catharine A. Trimble   30
22nd June 1839   George B. Russell CCO
Ex. 23rd June 1839   F. H. Walker JP

J.

William Johnson and Ana Lord (?)   18
16th May 1838   George B. Russell CCO
Ex. 28th May 1838   John Ponder JP

Thomas F. Jamason and Mary Barr(?)   22
6th January 1838   George B. Russell CCO
Ex. 9th January 1838   Samuel Walker JP

Solenzo(?) D. Jones and Permelia S. Fricks   24
3rd March 1839   George B. Russell CCO
Ex. 3rd March 1839   Andrew A. Cobb M.G.

Elisha Johnson and Sarah Wilson   39
13th September 1839   George B. Russell CCO
Ex. 11th October 1839   William E. Wellhorn(?)

B.L. James and Dedenia Gladden   63
23rd January 1841   George B. Russell CCO
Ex. 24th January 1841   Coleman Pitts JP

Lindsay Johnson and Mary A. Powell   76
11th November 1841   George B. Russell CCO
Ex. 18th November 1841   John C. Simmons M.G.

Reuben T. Jones and Eliza C. Brewster   80
12th January 1842   George B. Russell CCO
Ex. 13th January 1842   John W. Lewis O.M.

William W. Jones and Elenor Wofford   84
1st May 1842   Arthur Haire CCO
Ex. 3rd March 1842   Silas Bell JP

Thomas Jourdin and Sarah Brown   99
17th November 1842   Arthur Haire CCO
Ex. 17th November 1842   Ransom Foster JP

William M. Jones and Louisa E. Upshaw   107
6th March 1843   Arthur Haire CCO
Ex. 6th March 1843   Evan Pearson JP

K.

Martin Keel and Sarah Stovall   1

7th January 1837
Ex. 8th January 1837
George B. Russell CCO
Lewis Ballard M.G.

James F. Kinman and Rosanno Wallace   62
14th November 1840
Ex. 15th November 1840
George B. Russell CCO
David Morrow JP

Andrew J. (?) Kunman and Sarah Ann Hately(?)   67
21st April 1841
Ex. 23rd April 1841
George B. Russell CCO
Joshua Bowdoin M.G.

Jesse Keith and Jane Winnett   73
13th July 1841
Ex. 18th July 1841
George B. Russell CCO
Isaac Rutherford M.G.

Alfred C. King and Reziah (?) Fitts   74
12th September 1841
Ex. 22nd September 1841
George B. Russell CCO
Stephen Ellis D.D.

William S. King and Rhoda Fitts   74
12th September 1841
Ex. 22nd September 1841
George B. Russell CCO
Stephen Ellis D.D.

Robert W. Kay and Elizabeth Jane Archey(?)   78
17th November 1841
Ex. 18th November 1841
George B. Russell CCO
William Gaines JP

George Kennedy and Elizabeth Wilson(?)   86
24th March 1842
Ex. 24th March 1842
Arthur Haire CCO
John B. Fisher JP

Athea(?) F. Kennedy and Jane Elliott   89
2nd July 1842
Ex. 10th July 1842
Arthur Haire CCO
Wm. Clardy JP

Benjamin Kiker and Lydia Hill   98
29th December 1842
Ex. 29th December 1842
Arthur Haire CCO
James Russell

David G. King and Susan Gaston   103
2nd February 1843
Ex. 2nd February 1843
Arthur Haire CCO
Evan Pearson M.G.

Ransom Kitchens and Sarah Hawkins   111
9th April 1843
Ex. 9th April 1843
Arthur Haire CCO
Silas Elliott JP

L.

Robert D. Long and Mary Brown   4
21st October 1837
Ex. 25th October 1837
George B. Russell CCO
Sam Walker JP

William Lanston and Elinda Gay   7
2nd December 1837
Ex. 3rd December 1837
George B. Russell CCO
M. M. Blalock JP

James F. Long and Catharine Hutchingson   18
27th October 1838
Ex. 28th October 1838
George B. Russell CCO
David Morrow JP

David Lish and Katharine Kinnard   28
31st May 1839
Ex. 2nd June 1839
George B. Russell CCO
Chaney M. Lindsay Min.

Aaron Lord and Mary Vanderford   40
26th November 1839   George B. Russell CCO
Ex. 27th November 1839   John Ponder JP

Turner Laird and Rebecca Powell   42
25th December 1839   George B. Russell CCO
Ex. 26th December 1839   C. M. Linsey M.G.

William B. Lowry and Angelina Dodd   45
22nd January 1840   George B. Russell CCO
Ex. 23rd January 1840   Wm. Sylar JP

Miles A. Leatherwood and Mary Ann Carlile   52
31st March 1840   George B. Russell CCO
Ex. 31st March 1840   Wm. Kinman JP

Daniel Lowry and Nancy Ann Dodd   66
30th January 1841   George B. Russell CCO
Ex. 31st January 1841   Wm. Sylar JP

Elisha Lowry and Salen Love   70
21st September 1839   George B. Russell CCO
Ex. 22nd September 1839   Thos. Byrd JP

Joseph Lewis and Frances Willeby   75
16th October 1841   George B. Russell CCO
Ex. 17th October 1841   Wm. Sylar JP

Alexander M. Lynch and Sarah Hutchison   87
24th March 1842   Arthur Haire CCO
Ex. 24th March 1842   Silas Elliott JP

William Lamb and Catharin Burt   85
12 April 1842   Arthur Haire CCO
Ex. 13th April 1842   W. D. Walker L.D.

M.

Henry Milner and Nancy Underwood   2
1 August 1837   George B. Russell CCO
Ex. 1 August 1837   R. J. Montgomery, Min.

Peter Mason and Eliza Ford   4
11 October 1837   George B. Russell CCO
Ex. 11 October 1837   E. Milsaps, JIC

Duncan Murchan(Murchison?) and Elizabeth Snow   14
7 April 1838   George B. Russell CCO
Ex. 8th April 1838   John Burris JP

Allen Mannings and Nancy Bishop   15
24 July 1838   George B. Russell CCO
Ex. 25 July 1838   David Garrison JP

William Miller and Elizabeth Dunn   22
8 December 1838   George B. Russell CCO
Ex. 13th December 1838   David Morrow JP

Norman J. Mays and Caroline Brewster   25
12 February 1839   George B. Russell CCO
Ex. 12 February 1839   E. Pearson M.G.

Thomas Meadows and Elizabeth Dodd   26
18 April 1839   George B. Russell CCO
Ex. 18 April 1839   William Sylar JP

James Milner and C. M. Gosa   28
10 June 1830   George B. Russell CCO
Ex. 11 June 1839   J. H. George M.G.

William Matthews and Susan Russell   47
16 January 1840   George B. Russell CCO
Ex. 16 January 1840   William James JP

B. R. Mays and Mary A. Harber   50
21 December 1839   George B. Russell CCO
Ex. 31 December 1839   William Kinman JP

John Midcalf and Sarah Norman   51
11 October 1838   George B. Russell CCO
Ex. 21 October 1838   J. T. Kirkham JP

Miles Mullins and Elizabeth Dodgings   53
13 February 1840   George B. Russell CCO
Ex. 13 February 1840   Z. G. Turner JP

Martin Monfort(Munford?) and Serena Dillard   54
12 September 1839   George B. Russell CCO
Ex. 12 September 1839   B. B. Gaines M.G.

Samuel Mathews(or Worthum?) and Isabella Lanier   67
20 February 1841   George B. Russell CCO
Ex. 21 February 1841   William Sylar JP

Lewis Morris and Esther N. Carroll   75
6 November 1841   George B. Russell CCO
Ex. 7 November 1841   Silas Bell JP

Charles Morrison and Rosanna Swiney   76
18 November 1841   George B. Russell CCO
Ex. 18 November 1841   William Sylar JP

William Morris and Elinor Perkins   80
15 January 1842   George B. Russell CCO
Ex. 16 January 1842   David Morrow JP

John R. Matthews and Margaret Black   81
28 December 1841   George B. Russell CCO
Ex. 2 January 1842   William James JP

Sanford Manor and Louisa Underwood   87
7 June 1842   Arthur Haire CCO
Ex. 19 June 1842   John B. Fisher JP

Samuel Moore and Emily Burris   92
29 October 1842   Arthur Haire CCO
Ex. 1 November 1842   Philip J. Guyton JP

Hezekiah Miller and Elizabeth I. Mercier   96
26 February 1842   Arthur Haire CCO
Ex. 27 February 1842   David Morrow JP

McC.

James McCracken and Charlotte Wofford   5

3 October 1837   George B. Russell CCO
Ex. 4 October 1837   Stark A. Brown JP

Andrew McDonald and Mary Dodd   13
3 June 1838   George B. Russell CCO
Ex. 3 June 1838   E. Milsaps JIC

A.M. McBrayer and Matilda New   27
19 April 1839   George B. Russell CCO
Ex. 25 April 1839   Thompson M. Henson JP

Herman McFalls and Caroline Williams   33
28 April 1839   George B. Russell CCO
Ex. 28 April 1839   Banistern R. Bray M.G.

Christopher McGinnis and Elizabeth Pursley   34
24 August 1839   George B. Russell CCO
Ex. 26 August 1839   William Sylar JP

Patrick McGuire and Marrinda Lackey   35
7 July 1839   George B. Russell CCO
Ex. 7 July 1839   William Sylar JP

James McGuire and Melinda Augusta   48
14 November 1839   George B. Russell CCO
Ex. 16 November 1839   David Garrison JP

David N. McCrary and Annias Kirtland   97
15 October 1842   Arthur Haire CCO
Ex. 26 October 1842   George R. Edwards JP

Ferdinando M. McReynolds and Ann Aycock   98
22 December 1842   Arthur Haire CCO
Ex. 22 December 1842   John Crawford M.G.

Fral McGovaron and Elizabeth McCaskel   106
15 February 1843   Arthur Haire CCO
Ex. 16 February 1843   Philip J. Guyton JP

N.

T.(?) A. Norwood and Elizabeth Hightower   45
21 January 1840   George B. Russell CCO
Ex. 26 January 1840   L(?)uroy McWhorter

Benson Nally and Christina Perkins   50
27 February 1840   George B. Russell CCO
Ex. 27 February 1840   James Stovall JP

Seaborn Nally and Varchies(?) D. Woodall   50
24 March 1840   George B. Russell CCO
Ex. 27 March 1840   Silas Bell JP

Jackson Nichols and Amand A. Dawson   94
22 June 1842   Arthur Haire CCO
Ex. 23 June 1842   Thos. Bird JP

O.

Robert Orr and Margaret Campbell   11
17 October 1837   George B. Russell CCO
Ex. 19 October 1837   M. N. Blalock JP

P.

Levi Pearce and Matilda Upshaw
7 December 1836
Ex. 8 December 1836
    1
George B. Russell CCO
Lewis Ballard M.G.

A.M. Penn and Sarah Aycock
10 January 1838
Ex. 11 January 1838
    9
George B. Russell CCO
Zachariah Aycock JP

Andrew Prater and Rachel Johnson
10 January 1838
12 December 1838
    20
George B. Russell CCO
Thos. Townsend JP

Henry H. Pitman and Nancy E. Barnwell
7 January 1839
Ex. 22 January 1839
    21
George B. Russell CCO
F. H. Walker JP

Thomas Philips and Malinda Butler
16 December 1838
Ex. 25 December 1838
    23
George B. Russell CCO
F. H. Walker JP

Fletcher Potter and Frances Harrie
11 December 1840
Ex. 17 December 1840
    61
George B. Russell CCO
James Stovall JP

Allen Pledger and Mary M. Gartman(?)
7 April 1841
Ex. 8 April 1841
    68
George B. Russell CCO
Green C. McSpadden JP

William Potter and Lucinda McDonald
22 February 1842
Ex. 27 February 1842
    84
Arthur Haire CCO
John B. Fisher JP

Elisha Pullin and Eleana M. Hatch
12 August 1842
Ex. 16 August 1842
    91
Arthur Haire CCO
William Sylar JP

Raglin Pricen(?) and Anny Hendrick
8 December 1842
Ex. 8 December 1842
    98
Arthur Haire
Wilkins Tate M.G.

Isaac Porter and Mary Rilly
17 December 1843
Ex. 18 December 1843
    105
Arthur Haire CCO
C. M. Lindsay M.G.

William P. Pearson and Mary Fricks
9 December 1842
Ex. 10 December 1842
    108
Arthur Haire CCO
Barnabus Pace LMG

Q.

David Quarles and Katharine Shaw
16 April 1839
Ex. 21 April 1839
    28
George B. Russell CCO
Allen Dykes, M.G.

George B. Quarles and Ann B. Smith
25 August 1840
Ex. 25 August 1840
    56
George B. Russell CCO
J. W. Yarbrough, Min.

Hughey Quinn and Sarah McBrayer
6 May 1842
Ex. 10 May 1842
    90
Arthur Haire CCO
James Stovall JP

R.

Daniel Rice and Elizabeth Speir   16
1 June 1838   George B. Russell CCO
Ex. 1 July 1838   F. H. Walker JP

Augustus M. Russell and Mary Eliza Speir 17
20 October 1838   George B. Russell CCO
Ex. 21 October 1838   William Sylar JP

Isaac Randall and Jane Fowler   32
27 April 1839   George B. Russell CCO
Ex. 27 April 1839   David Morrow JP

John Randall and Mary King   62
26 December 1840   George B. Russell CCO
Ex. 27 December 1840   John Stovall JP

Samuel Ray and Elmira Frances Jackson   62
4 January 1841   George B. Russell CCO
Ex. 5 January 1841   Hiram Dunagan JP

Hiram Runyun and Elizabeth Davis   106
17 March 1843   Arthur Haire CCO
Ex. 17 March 1843   William Sylar JP

S.

Willis Sims and Sarah Holcomb   2
9 July 1837   George B. Russell CCO
Ex. 9 July 1837   Cornelius D. Terhune JIC

William L. Sewell and Katharine Gaines   3
17 April 1837   George B. Russell CCO
Ex. 17 April 1837   John Crawford Min.

David B. Stewart and Virginia Phillips   6
8 November 1837   George B. Russell CCO
Ex. 8 November 1837   William Sylar JP

Anthony Stribling and Esther Ponder   10
5 April 1838   George B. Russell CCO
Ex. 8 April 1838   F. H. Walker JP

A.E. Sewell and Lucretia Reeves   30
29 June 1839   George B. Russell CCO
Ex. 30 June 1839   T. M. Henson JP

Moses D. Smith and Sarah Smith   35
27 August 1839   George B. Russell CCO
Ex. 29 August 1839   John Russell JIC

Stephen C. Smith and Matilda England   43
6 January 1840   George B. Russell CCO
Ex. 7 January 1840   Joseph H. Jones, JIC

Thomas Spencer and Ruth M. Lewis   43
24 December 1839   George B. Russell CCO
Ex. 24 December 1839   Evan Pearson M.G.

B. F. Smith and Mary B. Dickerson   49
9 March 1840   George B. Russell CCO
Ex. 10 March 1840   John W. Lewis O.M.

Horace Smith and Lauretta Reid(?)   57
2 April 1840   George B. Russell CCO
Ex. 2 April 1840   John Rhome JP

George W. Stubbs and Sarah Ann McMullin   58
19 August 1840   George B. Russell CCO
Ex. 20 August 1840   Isaac N. Crowell(?) M.G.

William Stokes and Margaret Harris   66
8 June 1839   George B. Russell CCO
Ex. 7 January 1841   James Stovall JP

James Suggs and Cose(no other name)   67
23 March 1841   George B. Russell CCO
Ex. 25 March 1841   Green C. McSpadden JP

John T. Stephenson and Maria Kirkpatrick   77
20 October 1841   George B. Russell CCO
Ex. 21 October 1841   Irwin Martin JP

Benjamin Stripling and Mary Kinsey   99
9 December 1842   Arthur Haire CCO
Ex. 11 December 1842   Stephen Elis L.D.

John G. Shaw and Catharine Shaw   101
20 January 1843   Arthur Haire CCO
Ex. 29 January 1843   William Latimer JP

Joseph P. Shaw and Mariann Shadix   102
25 July 1842   Arthur Haire CCO
Ex. 2 September 1842   Irwin Martin JP

Calvin (?) Shaw and Susan H. N. Barnett   113
11 August 1843   Arthur Haire CCO
Ex. 17 August 1843   Joshua Bowdoin M.G.

T.

James P. Thompson and Eliza Lowry   6
23 November 1837   George B. Russell CCO
Ex. 23 November 1837   William Sylar JP

Augustus C. Trimble and Louisa A. Brogdon   31
20 June 1839   George B. Russell CCO
Ex. 20 June 1839   David Morrow JP

Tuller (or Fuller) and Malinda Lay   39
22 November 1839   George B. Russell CCO
Ex. 24 November 1839   Jefferson A. Mims JP

Archibald B. Thomas and Mahla Holsenbach   55
30 July 1840   George B. Russell CCO
Ex. 30 July 1840   David Morrow JP

John W. Thompson and Eliza Venable   64
1 August 1839   George B. Russell CCO
Ex. 2 August 1839   Wm. D. Walker L.D.

Kinson M. Thomas and Elizabeth Long   69
10 June 1841   George B. Russell CCO
Ex. 10 June 1841   Isaac Rutherford M.G.

William Tatum and Rebecca Douglas   71

24 May 1841   George B. Russell CCO
Ex. 30 May 1841   James Stovall JP

Y.F.W. Tate and Elizabeth Copeland   74
1 July 1841   George B. Russell CCO
Ex. 11 July 1841   Jesse Miller JP

Staten Turner and Nancy Chastain   90
28 February 1842   Arthur Haire CCO
Ex. 3 March 1842   James J. Teat(?) JP

Alexander Todd and Martha M. McCelvey(?)   104
27 December 1843   Arthur Haire CCO
Ex. 12 January 1844   Irvin Martin JP

Nathaniel Tatum and Mary Butler   111
6 June 1843   Arthur Haire CCO
No executive date

                    U.

James B. Underwood and Sarah T. Hamilton   30
23 July 1839   George B. Russell CCO
Ex. 23 July 1839   J. H. George M.G.

John A. Upshaw and Mary E. McMullins   93
26 October 1842   Arthur Haire CCO
Ex. 17 October 1842   James Stovall JP

                    V.

William Vaught and Mary Warlick   2
20 June 1837   George B. Russell CCO
Ex. 22 June 1837   M. N. Blalock JP

Ausley Vincent and Martha G. Upshaw   8
2 January 1838   George B. Russell CCO
Ex. 4 January 1838   John Crawford Min.

William Vaught and Mary Budd   23
6 February 1839   George B. Russell CCO
Ex. 6 February 1839   David Morrow JP

Wood Vincent and Milly Myers   35
7 September 1839   George B. Russell CCO
Ex. 7 September 1839   Wm. M. Jones JP

James F. Venable and Martha Phillips   96
18 August 1843   Arthur Haire CCO
Ex. 18 August 1843   David Morrow JP

Levi Vandiver and Charlotte Grant   112
3 June 1843   Arthur Haire CCO
Ex. 4 June 1843   Nathaniel Grant JP

                    W.

James A. Watson and Malvina Wilson   1
25 February 1837   George B. Russell CCO
Ex. 26 February 1837   William Sylar JP

Zachariah Woodard and Rachel Copeland   21
8 November 1838   George B. Russell CCO

Ex. 8 November 1838   William James JP

Sidney White and Jane Morrison   23
18 December 1838   George B. Russell CCO
Ex. 18 December 1838   William James JP

Jacob Williams and Diana Smith   26
7 April 1839   Recorded by
Ex. 7 April 1839   John Russell JIC

Samuel Willson and Elizabeth T. Stedman   27
7 May 1839   George B. Russell CCO
Ex. 7 May 1839   P. Ramsour V.(?) D.M.

Nicholas N. Welch and Rebecca S. Walker   40
11 December 1839   George B. Russell CCO
Ex. 11 December 1839   J. H. George M.G.

George W. Wimette(?) and Elizabeth Mitchell   42
2 January 1840   George B. Russell CCO
Ex. 2 January 1840   Coleman Pitts JP

Andrew White and Eleanor Lynch   42
12 December 1839   George B. Russell CCO
Ex. 12 December 1839   Silas Elliott JP

James Watson and Elizabeth Lovelady   44
12 January 1840   George B. Russell CCO
Ex. 12 January 1840   Evan Pearson M.G.

Jonathan Wildman and Hannah B. Eastland   47
28 January 1840   George B. Russell CCO
Ex. 30 January 1840   Z. G. Turner JP

John Wilson and Evaline Babb   51
14 March 1840   George B. Russell CCO
Ex. 18 March 1840   Silas Bell JP

A.C. Wood and Elizabeth Lynch   55
4 July 1840   George B. Russell CCO
Ex. 26 July 1840   Thomas M. Brandon JP

William W. Wade and Rebecca Tumlin   59
7 November 1840   George B. Russell CCO
Ex. 8 November 1840   William Sylar JP

Anson B. Wigginton and Rachel Russell   70
18 January 1841   George B. Russell CCO
Ex. 21 January 1841   Chancey M. Lindsay M.G.

Charles Walker and Mary Ann Hayes   73
18 June 1841   George B. Russell CCO
Ex. 19 June 1841   Allen Dykes M.G.

Bennett H. Wilson and Sally Walravans(?)   75
19 August 1841   George B. Russell CCO
Ex. 22 September 1841   F. H. Walker JP

Luther Williams and Mill brory(?) Dudley   77
30 August 1841   George B. Russell CCO
Ex. 30 August 1841   Irwin Martin JP

Ausburn(?) White and Lucinda Green   89
11 March 1842   Arthur Haire CCO
Ex. 11 March 1842   Wm. James JP

Richard Williams and Mariah McKnabb   90
6 August 1842   Arthur Haire CCO
Ex. 7 August 1842   Thomas G. Phillips JP

Benjamin A. Whitzell and Lavina Hendricks   93
26 November 1842   Arthur Haire CCO
Ex. 27 November 1842   Joshua Bowdoin M.G.

William Winnett and Manervi(?) A. Hawkins   95
1 September 1842   Arthur Haire CCO
Ex. 8 September 1842   John B. Fisher JP

William C. Watts and Elizabeth Ivy   100
26 December 1842   Arthur Haire CCO
Ex. 28 December 1842   John Millican JP

Drury Wall and Elizabeth Hargis   106
11 March 1843   Arthur Haire CCO
Ex. 12 March 1843   W. Clardy JP

John W. Wilburn and Rebecca Waldroup   110
19 February 1843   Arthur Haire CCO
Ex. 26 February 1843   Z. G. Turner JP

Add to B.:

Ira Bryant and Jane Ponder   83
7 February 1842   George B. Russell CCO
Ex. 10 February 1842   Leeroy McWhorter

Jeremiah Bassett and Rachel Goddman   33
15 August 1839   George B. Russell CCO
Ex. 15 August 1839   William Sylar JP

www.ingramcontent.com/pod-product-compliance
Lightning Source LLC
Chambersburg PA
CBHW020054020526
44112CB00031B/109